Channel
"The Road Map
less traveled"

LSAT®
Lesson Book

Special thanks to those who made this book possible:

Matthew Belinkie, Kim Bowers, Jack Chase, Chris Cosci, Lola Disparte, John Fritschie, Bobby Gautam, Beth Gebeloff, Joseph Gordon, Joanna Graham, Rob Gray, Craig Harman, Ged Helm, Gar Hong, Rebecca Houck, Brandon Jones, Greg Mitchell, Joseph Moulden, Rachel Reina, Larry Rudman, Glen Stohr, Jay Thomas, Bob Verini, Walker Williams, Dan Wittich

TABLE OF CONTENTS

About Your Kaplan Resources

Welcome to your *LSAT Lesson Book*! Your Kaplan LSAT resources will be all you need to prepare for the LSAT, and this is the book that you'll use for all of the Core Sessions in your class. Before you start those Core Sessions though, let's start with some information on your resources.

YOUR LSAT RESOURCES

First—Get Acquainted with the LSAT

Start by reading the "About the LSAT" chapter in your *The LSAT Unlocked: Course Edition* book. There, you'll find details about the LSAT's structure and scoring, how to register for the test, and how best to study. For your convenience, the charts from that chapter are duplicated in the "Introduction to the LSAT" chapter of this book.

Second—Start Becoming an LSAT Expert

In this book, you'll work on the skills needed for LSAT success. We've broken down each of the skills into discrete **Learning Objectives**. Each section of the book will inform you of the Learning Objectives you're about to master, and you'll be provided with an opportunity to practice them thoroughly. This may involve full LSAT questions, or it may involve drills that help to hone your fundamental skills. Each of the full questions presented in this book is from a real LSAT. Historically, the LSAT was administered four times each year, and each year three of those exams were released by the Law School Admission Council for use as study material.

Each released exam contains four scored sections and is called a **PrepTest**. This book contains about 350 LSAT questions from PrepTests 47, 49, 51, 53, 54, 55, 57, 59, and 61. Beneath each LSAT-released question in this book you'll see a source ID (e.g., PrepTest47 Sec2 Q2, which means that question appeared originally as the second question of Section 2 of PrepTest 47). Every question with a source ID is licensed from the LSAC and comes from an official, scored LSAT.

Throughout this book, you'll see how LSAT experts—Kaplan teachers who have scored in the 99th percentile—analyze questions, games, and passages from released LSAT exams. Study these "worked examples" carefully; they provide a chance for you to think along with an LSAT expert as he or she attacks the LSAT efficiently and accurately. Expert analysis is always laid out with the test material in the left-hand column and the expert's thinking immediately to the right or beneath. Where the LSAT expert demonstrates a multistep method, we've included the steps to help you train to take the most effective route through the question.

Here are a few things to be aware of whenever you study expert analyses:

This column contains test material; always read it first, so you know what the expert is analyzing.

In this column, you'll see the LSAT expert's analysis of each part of the test question—here's your coach "thinking out loud" for your benefit.

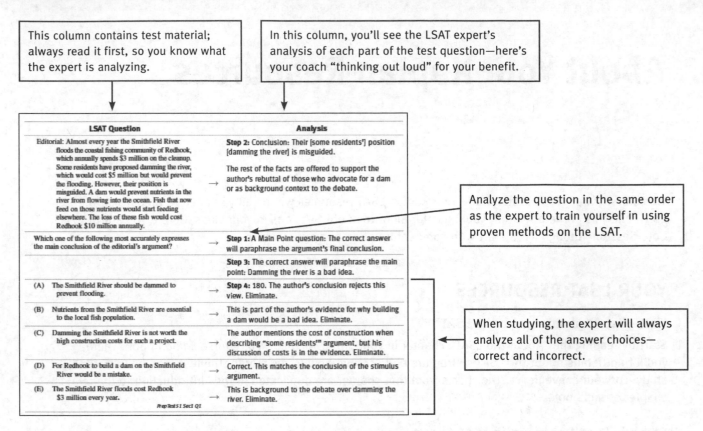

LSAT Question	Analysis
Editorial: Almost every year the Smithfield River floods the coastal fishing community of Redhook, which annually spends $3 million on the cleanup. Some residents have proposed damming the river, which would cost $5 million but would prevent the flooding. However, their position is misguided. A dam would prevent nutrients in the river from flowing into the ocean. Fish that now feed on those nutrients would start feeding elsewhere. The loss of these fish would cost Redhook $10 million annually.	**Step 2:** Conclusion: Their [some residents'] position [damming the river] is misguided. The rest of the facts are offered to support the author's rebuttal of those who advocate for a dam or as background context to the debate.
Which one of the following most accurately expresses the main conclusion of the editorial's argument?	**Step 1:** A Main Point question: The correct answer will paraphrase the argument's final conclusion.
	Step 3: The correct answer will paraphrase the main point: Damming the river is a bad idea.
(A) The Smithfield River should be dammed to prevent flooding.	**Step 4:** 180. The author's conclusion rejects this view. Eliminate.
(B) Nutrients from the Smithfield River are essential to the local fish population.	This is part of the author's evidence for why building a dam would be a bad idea. Eliminate.
(C) Damming the Smithfield River is not worth the high construction costs for such a project.	The author mentions the cost of construction when describing "some residents'" argument, but his discussion of costs is in the evidence. Eliminate.
(D) For Redhook to build a dam on the Smithfield River would be a mistake.	Correct. This matches the conclusion of the stimulus argument.
(E) The Smithfield River floods cost Redhook $3 million every year.	This is background to the debate over damming the river. Eliminate.

PrepTest51 Sec1 Q1

Analyze the question in the same order as the expert to train yourself in using proven methods on the LSAT.

When studying, the expert will always analyze all of the answer choices—correct and incorrect.

From time to time, you'll have practice exercises in which you'll have the chance to analyze a question. Use the spaces in the right-hand column to record your own analysis. On the following pages, we'll always provide expert analysis so that you can compare your thinking to that of an LSAT expert.

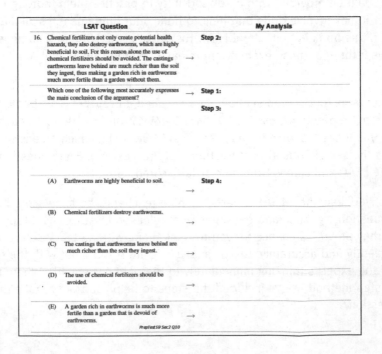

LSAT Question	My Analysis
16. Chemical fertilizers not only create potential health hazards, they also destroy earthworms, which are highly beneficial to soil. For this reason alone the use of chemical fertilizers should be avoided. The castings earthworms leave behind are much richer than the soil they ingest, thus making a garden rich in earthworms much more fertile than a garden without them.	Step 2:
Which one of the following most accurately expresses the main conclusion of the argument?	Step 1:
	Step 3:
(A) Earthworms are highly beneficial to soil.	Step 4:
(B) Chemical fertilizers destroy earthworms.	
(C) The castings that earthworms leave behind are much richer than the soil they ingest.	
(D) The use of chemical fertilizers should be avoided.	
(E) A garden rich in earthworms is much more fertile than a garden that is devoid of earthworms.	

PrepTest59 Sec2 Q10

The format of our expert analyses is the result of work by leading academics in learning science. Merely answering LSAT questions and checking to see whether you got the right answer can only take you so far. Studies indicate that studying expert thinking alongside actual test material produces better results and is a more effective (and faster) way to master LSAT skills. As you complete the questions, don't just check to see if you got them right or wrong; use each question as an opportunity to better understand the patterns of the test as well as your own strengths and weaknesses.

Third—Assess Your LSAT Skills

The tests you'll take as part of your course are the booklets you received labeled "Course Diagnostic," "Course Midpoint," and "Course Final." However, in your online resources you have access to every released LSAT. Your instructors will provide you guidance on which tests to take if you're looking for additional testing opportunities outside of class. If and when you do take any of these tests or sections, the answer key and scoring scale are contained at the back of each test, but we recommend entering your answers into Smart Reports® so that you can track your progress and receive personalized recommendations (see online resources info).

Using this Book in Conjunction with Kaplan's *The LSAT Unlocked: Course Edition* book

The other Kaplan book in your Home Study Kit is *The LSAT Unlocked: Course Edition* book. You'll see that the order of topics in the Table of Contents for both books is similar. However, all of the question content—exercises, LSAT questions, tests, etc.—is different in the *Lesson Book* than in *The LSAT Unlocked*, which features more in-depth discussion of the topics than this book. Your *LSAT Lesson Book* will be the book you use in all your Core Sessions. Your *The LSAT Unlocked* book will serve not only as your home study book, but will also be your treatise on all things LSAT. If you want to read ahead in *The LSAT Unlocked* about the concepts to be covered in a subsequent Core Session, you can do so. If you want to use *The LSAT Unlocked* as a review of what you learned in the Core Session, you can do that too. We would recommend you don't read ahead in your *LSAT Lesson Book* though, so that when you're approaching questions and exercises in your Core Sessions you're seeing them for the first time.

YOUR ONLINE RESOURCES

You can find information about how to access and navigate your Online Resources in the Preface of your *The LSAT Unlocked: Course Edition* book. There are lots of great assets available for your LSAT training in your online resources, so make sure you're familiar with their contents.

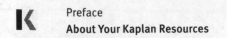
LOOKING FOR MORE?

At Kaplan, we're thrilled you've chosen us to help you on your journey to law school. Beyond this book, there's a wealth of additional resources that we invite you to check out to aid you with your LSAT preparation and your law school application.

- ((( ))) —The LSAT Channel—The next innovation in LSAT prep: Your course comes with live, online elective workshops from our highest-rated faculty. Access The LSAT Channel from your online resources and select workshops based on topic, difficulty, or teacher. You'll be able to interact and ask questions live during the lessons, or watch past programming you missed. It's hundreds of hours of additional live instruction available at your fingertips. Look for periodic special episodes featuring interviews with law school admissions officers on topics that will help you succeed in the application process and in law school.

- f 🐦 You Tube —Facebook, Twitter, YouTube—Kaplan is wherever you are. Like us. Follow us. Subscribe to us. Get regular tips all throughout the course of your study.

- Private Tutoring—After beginning their preparation, many students benefit from a little additional one-on-one instruction, guidance, and coaching. Our LSAT Prep PLUS courses are great values, supplementing our core In Person or Live Online experience with three hours of one-on-one time with an LSAT expert. You can also upgrade to a full private tutoring package of 15 hours or more, or add just a couple of hours as needed along the way. Tutoring hours can always be purchased a la carte. Simply speak with your instructor or call us at 1-800-KAP-TEST to discuss these options.

You have a lot to do. Ready to get started? Let's do this!

About the LSAT

WHY THE LSAT?

Each year, Kaplan surveys law school admissions officials, and consistently, over 60 percent say that the LSAT is their number-one consideration as they evaluate applications. Why do they put so much emphasis on this test? A breakdown of the components in the application offers the best explanation.

- **5** components of the standard law school application: LSAT score, undergraduate GPA, personal statement, letters of recommendation, and "resume factors," such as work experience, extra-curricular activities, and so on
- **2** quantitative measures: LSAT score and undergraduate GPA
- **1** quantitative measure comparable for all applicants: LSAT score

The LSAT doesn't care what you majored in or where you went to school. It's the one element of the law school application that measures all applicants on a level playing field.

WHAT THE LSAT TESTS

While the LSAT offers a standard, quantitative measure of all applicants, law school admissions officers would not value it so highly if the LSAT did not test skills relevant to—indeed, central to—an applicant's law school potential. Studies have consistently shown that LSAT score is more strongly correlated with law school performance, especially in a student's first year, than any other factor in the application.

THE FOUR CORE LSAT SKILLS

Reading Strategically—understanding the structure of a piece of text and the author's purpose for writing it

Analyzing Arguments—distinguishing an author's conclusion from her evidence and identifying the implicit assumptions the author has made

Understanding Formal Logic—determining what must, can, or cannot be true on the basis of conditional "If/then" statements

Making Deductions—determining what follows logically from a set of statements or rules

Law schools know that these skills are crucial to a student's success as a law student and in the practice of law later on. Because they are so fundamental to the test, these four core skills underlie all of the Learning Objectives found in this workbook.

STRUCTURE OF THE LSAT

The LSAT consists of five multiple-choice sections: two Logical Reasoning sections, one Logic Games section, one Reading Comprehension section, and one unscored "experimental" section that will look exactly like one of the other multiple-choice sections. These five multiple-choice sections can appear in any order on Test Day. A 15-minute break will come between the third and fourth sections of the test. The unscored, 35-minute Writing Sample essay section is always administered after the multiple-choice sections are concluded.

Aligning the four core LSAT skills to the sections of the test demonstrates why the LSAT is structured as it is.

FOUR CORE LSAT SKILLS BY SECTION

Core Skill	Primary Section Tested	Secondary Section Tested
Reading Strategically	Reading Comprehension	Logical Reasoning
Analyzing Arguments	Logical Reasoning	Reading Comprehension
Understanding Formal Logic	Logical Reasoning	Logic Games
Making Deductions	Logic Games	Logical Reasoning

Note that Logical Reasoning is the primary section for two of the core skills and the secondary section for the other two. Reading Comprehension and Logic Games are the primary section and secondary section one time each. This helps explain why the LSAT features two scored Logical Reasoning sections, one scored Reading Comprehension section, and one scored Logic Games section per test.

Section	Number of Questions	Minutes
Logical Reasoning	24–26	35
Logical Reasoning	24–26	35
Reading Comprehension	26–28	35
Logic Games	22–24	35
"Experimental"	22–28	35
Writing Sample	One essay	35

LSAT UPDATES

Beginning with the September 2019 LSAT, the LSAT will be offered exclusively in a digital format. The structure of the test sections and questions will remain the same, but all testing will be done in a digital interface on tablets. In July 2019, there will be a single transition testing date with both digital and paper-and-pencil formats. Additionally, as of June 2019, the Writing Sample will be completed at a separate time and place than the multiple choice portion of the test. For more information on these changes check out the LSAC website.

LSAT Scored Sections

Logic Games

One section with four games and 22–24 questions

Logic Games reward you for sequencing, matching, distributing, or selecting entities on the basis of rules that combine to limit the acceptable arrangements.

Logical Reasoning

Two sections with 24–26 questions each

Logical Reasoning rewards you for analyzing arguments to strengthen or weaken them or to identify their assumptions and flaws. Other LR questions require you to draw valid inferences from a set of facts.

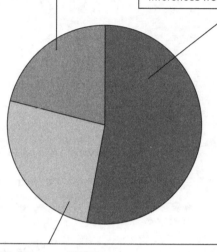

Reading Comprehension

One section with four passages and 26–28 questions

Reading Comp questions reward you for identifying the author's purpose and main idea, drawing valid inferences from the passage, and determining how and why the author uses certain details.

LSAT Unscored Sections

Experimental

The Experimental section is an additional, unscored section of Logical Reasoning, Reading Comprehension, or Logic Games. You will not know what type of section you will get, and it can show up anywhere, including after the break. You'll have to bring your A-game for the entire test, as there is no reliable way to determine which section is experimental while you're taking the test. The LSAT testmaker uses the unscored section to test questions for use as scored items on upcoming exams.

The Writing Sample

After you complete the five multiple-choice sections of the test, you'll write a short essay choosing between two possible courses of action. While unscored, your Writing Sample is submitted to all law schools to which you apply, and law schools use it as part of the evaluation process. As of June 2019, test takers will type their Writing Sample response during an online proctored experience. This will occur at a time and place apart from the other sections of the test.

HOW THE LSAT IS SCORED

Here's how the LSAT is scored. There are three different scoring scales: your raw score (# correct), your scaled score, and your percentile.

Percentile (Scaled score)	10th (139)	20th (143)	30th (146)	40th (149)	50th (151)	60th (154)	70th (156)	80th (160)	90th (164)	95th (167)	99th (172)
# Correct	37	43	48	53	57	63	67	75	83	88	94

*Source – PrepTest 81 (June 2017)

LSAT Score Breakdown

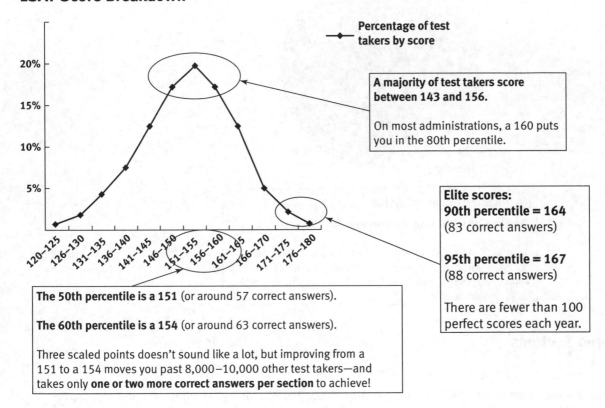

Percentage of test takers by score

A majority of test takers score between 143 and 156.

On most administrations, a 160 puts you in the 80th percentile.

Elite scores:
90th percentile = 164
(83 correct answers)

95th percentile = 167
(88 correct answers)

There are fewer than 100 perfect scores each year.

The 50th percentile is a 151 (or around 57 correct answers).

The 60th percentile is a 154 (or around 63 correct answers).

Three scaled points doesn't sound like a lot, but improving from a 151 to a 154 moves you past 8,000–10,000 other test takers—and takes only **one or two more correct answers per section** to achieve!

Raw score is simply the number of questions answered correctly.

Scaled score, the familiar 120–180 number, is a conversion of the raw score. Here, a raw score of 67—that is, 67 correct answers—converts to a scaled score of 156. A raw score of 57—meaning 57 correct answers—converts to a scaled score of 151. On a different test, a raw score of 57 might convert to a 150 or a 152. To account for differences in overall difficulty, each test has a slightly different raw score-to-scaled score conversion table.

Percentile score indicates how a test taker performed relative to other test takers over a three-year period. The conversion from scaled score to percentile score remains relatively stable, with only minor variations over the years. Test after test, a 151 scaled score is approximately a 50th percentile score.

The way in which the LSAT is scored has three important implications for your performance:

- First, only the number of *right* answers determines your score. There is no guessing penalty. Never leave a question blank on the LSAT.
- Second, every question is worth the same, regardless of how hard it is. Learn to spot difficult questions and leave them for the end of each section. Find the easy questions and rack up points. If you're going to run out of time or need to guess, you want to do so on the tough stuff.
- Third, every additional correct answer can leapfrog you ahead of hundreds—or even thousands—of other test takers, your competition. How's that for inspiration?

What's a Good LSAT Score?

What you consider a good LSAT score depends on your own expectations and goals, but here are a few interesting statistics:

Getting about half of all of the scored questions right (a raw score of roughly 50) will earn a scaled score of roughly 146 or 147, around the 30th percentile—not a great performance. However, getting only one additional question right every 10 minutes (of the scored sections) would produce a raw score of 64, or a scaled score of approximately 154, around the 60th percentile—a huge improvement.

So, you don't have to be perfect to do well. On a typical LSAT, you can still get 25 wrong and end up in the 160s, or about 20 wrong and get a 164, typically a 90th percentile score. Even a perfect score of 180 often allows for a question or two to be missed.

Here is a chart detailing some top law schools and the scores of their admitted students:

Rank*	School	25th–75th %ile LSAT* (Scaled)	25th–75th %ile UGPA*	25th–75th %ile LSAT** (Raw)
1	Yale University	170–175	3.79–3.97	90–96
6	New York University	166–171	3.65–3.89	84–92
10	Duke University	167–170	3.59–3.84	86–91
12	University of California–Berkeley	163–169	3.65–3.89	79–89
14	University of Texas–Austin	162–168	3.41–3.84	77–88
19	University of Southern California	162–166	3.56–3.85	77–85
26	Boston College	161–163	3.32–3.65	76–80
30	University of Wisconsin–Madison	156–163	3.30–3.72	66–80
41	University of Florida	156–161	3.33–3.77	66–76
51	Tulane University	155–160	3.22–3.62	64–75
65	Northeastern University	154–163	3.30–3.69	62–80
72	University of Cincinnati	153–158	3.24–3.76	61–71
86	University of Oregon	154–159	3.20–3.64	62–73

* *U.S. News & World Report*, 2018 Law School Rankings
** LSAT PrepTest 80, December 2016 Exam

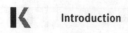

REGISTRATION FOR AND ADMINISTRATION OF THE LSAT

Historically the LSAT was administered by the Law School Admission Council (LSAC) four times each year. However, the LSAC has recently made changes to offer the LSAT more frequently.

LSAT FACTS

In 2019 the test will be offered seven times:

- Saturday, January 26
- Saturday, March 30
- Monday, June 3
- Monday, July 15

- Saturday, September 21
- Monday, October 28
- Monday, November 25

In 2020 there will also be an administration in February and April, resulting in nine test dates that year.

There are some exceptions. For example, Saturday Sabbath observers have the option to take the test on a specified weekday following a Saturday administration. Dates and times may also be different for tests administered outside the United States, Canada, and the Caribbean.

How do I register for the LSAT? Register for the LSAT online at www.lsac.org. Check the LSAC website for details on the procedures, deadlines, and fee schedules.

When should I register? Register as soon as you have chosen your test date. Test sites may fill up quickly. Registration is typically due about five weeks before Test Day. As of 2018 there is no longer a "Late Registration" period.

Can I change my test date or location? You can change your test dates or locations (subject to an additional "change" fee) via the LSAC website. Timely changes of test date are not reported to schools; "no shows" are reported, however.

What is the CAS? Upon signing up for the LSAT, you also need to register with the Credential Assembly Service (CAS) as part of the application process required by every ABA-approved law school. CAS receives your undergraduate transcripts and distributes a summary of your undergraduate performance, along with your letters of recommendation, evaluations, and LSAT score report to each of the law schools to which you apply. www.lsac.org lists the fees and sign-up details for CAS.

When are law schools' application deadlines? All law schools provide their application deadlines on their websites. Some schools require the LSAT be taken by December for admission the following fall; others will accept a later LSAT score. Because most schools use a "rolling admissions" process, taking the test earlier is preferable; also, taking the test earlier gives the test taker a chance to repeat the LSAT prior to most application deadlines.

Can I repeat the LSAT? Until 2017, there used to be a restriction that the LSAT could only be taken up to three times in a two-year period. That restriction has now been lifted.

How do law schools view multiple LSAT scores? This varies from school to school. Few schools now average multiple scores as was the policy in the past, but most consider *all scores from a five-year period* when evaluating applications. Applicants cannot choose which scores to report with their application.

Can I receive accommodations? The LSAC grants accommodation testing for physical, learning, and cognitive impairments, and there are a wide variety of accommodations available. A test taker must be registered for a test date before requesting accommodations. Full information about accommodated testing is available at

www.lsac.org/lsat/lsac-policy-accommodations-test-takers-disabilities.

LSAT STUDY SKILLS

The LSAT is a skills-based test. For this reason, improving your score is, in some ways, more like mastering a musical instrument or an athletic skill than it is like learning a subject in school. The LSAT is very practical, testing what you can do above what you know. As such, it is also practice-able and coachable. Expect Kaplan to show you the best ways to practice. Expect us to show you the patterns of the test and how to tackle every question type. Expect us to show you how to manage every section. Expect us to show you how, when, and why to use your resources. In return, you're going to need to work—hard. Reaching your full potential on the LSAT takes lots of practice. We will show you precisely what you need to do, but ultimately it's up to you to do it.

LSAT Strategy and the Three Levels of Practice

On Test Day, you'll be asked to deal with stringent testing policies and procedures, answer approximately 125 multiple-choice questions (of which typically 101 will count toward your score), and write a short essay. It's a grueling and intense four hours. Moreover, depending on how efficient your test proctors are, that four-hour process may end up lasting five hours or more.

A strategic approach to the LSAT means increasing your speed only to the extent you can do so without sacrificing accuracy. Your goal is not to attempt as many questions as possible; your goal is to get as many questions right as possible. If you had unlimited time to take this test, you'd likely perform quite well. But you don't. You have a strict 35 minutes to complete each section, and many students are not able to tackle every question in the time allotted. For you, this means three things:

- It's important that you learn not only how to answer the questions effectively, but also how to answer them efficiently.
- It's important to approach each section strategically, knowing which questions to attack first and which questions to save for last.
- It's important that you prepare for the rigors of 3½ hours of testing. You'll want to maintain your focus in the final section as well as you did in the first.

To achieve your goals, you'll want to incorporate three levels of practice: Mastery, Timing, and Endurance.

Mastery is about learning the patterns of the exam and how to identify them in new questions. Kaplan provides a proven method for the questions in each section of the test. You will gain command of the method and master efficient, effective strategies and tactics through repeated practice on skill-based drills and individual questions. You'll study the answers and explanations to learn how the testmaker builds questions and answer choices. You'll identify why right answers are right, why wrong answers are wrong, what traps you consistently fall into, and how to avoid them. That's what Mastery practice is for.

Once you've learned the skills, you'll try full-length section practice, or **Timing** practice. At 3½ hours, the LSAT can seem like a marathon, but it's really a series of sprints—five 35-minute tests. Learning section management—how to recognize and apply the patterns you've learned efficiently, maximizing the number of questions you get correct—is what Timing practice teaches you to do.

Finally, there's **Endurance** practice. Can you maintain your ability to identify and apply these patterns efficiently throughout the whole exam? Some test takers lose focus after two hours or so, and then struggle through the last two sections of the test. Others need warm-up time and underperform on the first section. Taking practice tests will help you build your stamina and focus. A word of warning, however: Repeated testing without practice and review can be counterproductive. Think about it like learning a musical instrument. If you're trying to learn the piano, do you schedule a recital every other day? No, of course not. It's piano *practice*—even the most routine parts, such as playing scales—that allows you to improve. While practice tests are important, they should be spaced out and taken only when you're sure you've made some improvement through your Mastery and Timing practice.

By approaching your practice in this way—starting with Mastery and then layering in first Timing and then Endurance—you'll be fully and properly prepared by Test Day.

LSAT Attitude

In the main chapters, you'll learn, practice, and master the methods, strategies, and tactics that lead to Test Day success. Nevertheless, two students with equal LSAT proficiency still might not produce the same score. Of those two "equal" test takers, the one with greater confidence and less stress will likely outperform the other. You can develop these positive psychological characteristics just as you can your LSAT skill set.

Stay Positive

Those who approach the LSAT as an obstacle and rail against the necessity of taking it generally don't fare as well as those who see the LSAT as an opportunity, a chance to show law schools one's proficiency with the four core skills. A great LSAT score will distinguish your application from those of your competition.

- Look at the LSAT as a challenge, but try not to obsess over it; you certainly don't want to psych yourself out of the game.
- Remember that the LSAT is important, but this one test will not single-handedly determine the outcome of your life.
- Try to have fun with the test. Learning how to unlock the patterns of the test and approach the content in the way the testmakers have crafted the exam can be very satisfying, and the skills you'll acquire will benefit you in law school and your career.

Confidence and Stress Management

Confidence in your ability leads to quick, sure answers and a sense of well-being that translates into more points. Confidence feeds on itself; unfortunately, so does self-doubt. If you lack confidence, you end up reading sentences and answer choices two, three, or four times, until you confuse yourself and get off-track. This leads to timing difficulties that perpetuate a downward spiral of anxiety, rushing, and poor performance. If you subscribe to the proper LSAT mind-set, however, you'll gear all of your practice toward taking control of the test. When you've achieved that goal—armed with the principles, techniques, strategies, and methods Kaplan has to offer—you'll be ready to face the LSAT with confidence. Your online resources have more good information, explanations, and other resources to help you minimize test anxiety, manage stress, and maximize your performance.

PART ONE

LSAT
Reasoning

CHAPTER 1

LSAT Reasoning

Welcome to your LSAT studies! By the time you reach the end of this book, you'll have practiced all of the skills and strategies necessary to master the LSAT. While it is common to divide the LSAT into sections and further divide those sections into question types, there are core thinking, reading, and reasoning skills rewarded throughout the test. In this chapter, you'll build important critical thinking and reasoning skills that lay the groundwork for all that is to come.

LEVELS OF TRUTH

Prepare

Every section of the LSAT rewards an ability to distinguish correct answers based on what must be true, what is possible (could be true or false), and what must be false.

LEARNING OBJECTIVES

In this section, you'll learn to:

· Characterize the levels of truth in statements (and thus of the correct and incorrect answers in various LSAT question stems)

The following chart shows how central this skill is to your LSAT performance.

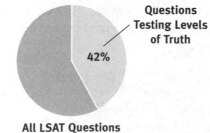

Questions
Testing Levels
of Truth

42%

All LSAT Questions
PrepTests 66–80; released 2012–2016

Characterizing Levels of Truth

Review how an LSAT expert characterizes the truth value of the correct and incorrect answers in two standard LSAT question stems.

Question Stem		Analysis
Which one of the following must be true?	→	Right answers: Must be true Wrong answers: Could be false or must be false
Each of the following must be false EXCEPT	→	Right answers: Could be true or must be true Wrong answers: Must be false

To understand how the expert characterized the answer choices, look at this chart.

Degree of Certainty	→	"Charge"
Must		True
Could		False

For all LSAT questions that ask for what *must be true, could be true, could be false*, or *must be false*, the correct answer combines one degree of certainty with one of the charges. The incorrect answers will combine the other degree of certainty to the other charge.

TEST DAY TIP

Any statement that must be true, could be true. Any statement that must be false, could be false. If the LSAT asks for a correct answer that *must be false*, you know the four wrong answers *could be true*, and thus, any answer that *must be true* is a wrong answer in that question.

Learning to characterize the correct and incorrect answer choices is the LSAT's most direct way of testing your ability to distinguish levels of truth, but the testmaker rewards this skill on statements made by the authors of Logical Reasoning arguments and Reading Comprehension passages as well.

LSAT STRATEGY

The LSAT always gives you exactly one right answer, so there's only ever one answer that falls into the level of truth targeted by the question stem.

Practice

For each of the following, make a note of which level or levels of truth the correct answer must display. Then make a note of which level or levels of truth the wrong answer choices will display.

Question Stem	My Analysis
[Example] Which of the following could be true? →	Correct answer: Could be true Wrong answers: Must be false
[Example] Each of the following could be true EXCEPT →	Correct answer: Must be false Wrong answers: Could be true
1. Which of the following could be false? →	
2. Manny must accept each of the following contract bids EXCEPT →	
3. Each of the following conflicts with the company guidelines EXCEPT →	
4. Which of the following pieces CANNOT be included in the performance? →	
5. If the statements above are true, each of the following could also be true EXCEPT →	
6. If the statements above are true, which of the following must also be true? →	
7. Each of the following could be false EXCEPT →	

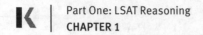

Expert Analysis

Here's how an LSAT expert would characterize those question stems.

Question Stem		Analysis
1. Which of the following could be false?	→	Correct answer: Could be false Wrong answers: Must be true
2. Manny must accept each of the following contract bids EXCEPT	→	Correct answer: A bid Manny could refuse Wrong answers: Bids Manny must accept
3. Each of the following conflicts with the company guidelines EXCEPT	→	Correct answer: An action that does not conflict with the company guidelines Wrong answers: Actions that conflict with the company guidelines
4. Which of the following pieces CANNOT be included in the performance?	→	Correct answer: A piece that cannot be included in the performance Wrong answers: Pieces that could be included in the performance
5. If the statements above are true, each of the following could also be true EXCEPT	→	Correct answer: Must be false Wrong answers: Could be true
6. If the statements above are true, which of the following must also be true?	→	Correct answer: Must be true Wrong answers: Could be false
7. Each of the following could be false EXCEPT	→	Correct answer: Must be true Wrong answers: Could be false

Perform

For each of the following, make a note of which level or levels of truth the correct answer must display. Then make a note of which level or levels of truth the wrong answer choices will display.

Question Stem	My Analysis
8. Rich could attend each of the following lectures EXCEPT →	
9. Which of the following must be the chairperson assigned to speak fourth? →	
10. Which of the following is an acceptable arrangement of the items, from left to right? →	
11. Which of the following entrees CANNOT be served at the dinner party? →	
12. Which of the following CANNOT be properly inferred from the statements above? →	
13. If Kate joins the study, each of the following must also join the study EXCEPT →	
14. If Nina does not go to the park, then which of the following could be false? →	
15. Each of the following must be false EXCEPT →	

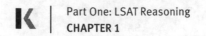
Expert Analysis

Here's how an LSAT expert would characterize those question stems.

Question Stem		Analysis
8. Rich could attend each of the following lectures EXCEPT	→	Correct answer: A lecture Rich cannot attend Wrong answers: Lectures Rich could attend
9. Which of the following must be the chairperson assigned to speak fourth?	→	Correct answer: The chairperson who must speak fourth Wrong answers: Chairpersons who could speak in a spot other than the fourth spot or chairpersons that don't speak at all
10. Which of the following is an acceptable arrangement of the items, from left to right?	→	Correct answer: An arrangement that could be true Wrong answers: Arrangements that must be false
11. Which of the following entrees CANNOT be served at the dinner party?	→	Correct answer: An entree that must not be served Wrong answers: Entrees that could be served
12. Which of the following CANNOT be properly inferred from the statements above?	→	Correct answer: Could be false Wrong answers: Must be true
13. If Kate joins the study, each of the following must also join the study EXCEPT	→	Correct answer: Someone who could decline to join the study Wrong answers: Individuals who must join the study
14. If Nina does not go to the park, then which of the following could be false?	→	Correct answer: Could be false Wrong answers: Must be true
15. Each of the following must be false EXCEPT	→	Correct answer: Could be true Wrong answers: Must be false

REFLECTION

Every time you practice LSAT problems in this book, pause afterward and look over your practice to learn more. Don't speed through this step. Carefully reviewing your practice can enrich your understanding of:

- Why is a right answer right? Maybe you got a question right for the wrong reasons, and you need to clarify your understanding.
- Why are the wrong answers wrong? Maybe your intuition told you an answer was wrong, but you couldn't explain why or replicate your thinking.
- Which of your LSAT skills are strong and which do you still need to work on?
- What patterns do the LSAT questions display? The best thing you can do on the LSAT is to spot its patterns; through frequent and thorough review you'll be able to do so.

For the exercises you just completed, look back at your work and think about these questions:

- Where was it easier to correctly identify the level of truth being asked for?
- Once the level of truth in the correct answer had been identified, did you always take a moment to think about and characterize the levels of truth that would be displayed by the wrong answers?
- What was challenging about this exercise?

TEST DAY TIP

On the LSAT, never confuse *true* and *false* statements with *right* and *wrong* answers. Always characterize what you're looking for before you evaluate the answer choices. You may even find it helpful to jot down what you're looking for. For example, in a "Must Be False" question you could jot down "1 MBF / 4 CBT" to signify there is one correct answer that must be false and four incorrect answers that could be true.

DETERMINING WHAT MUST BE TRUE, WHAT MUST BE FALSE, AND WHAT COULD BE TRUE OR FALSE FROM A SET OF STATEMENTS

Prepare

LEARNING OBJECTIVES

In this section, you'll learn to:

· Determine what must be true, what could be true or false, and what must be false given a set of statements

In all sections of the LSAT, you will be asked to deduce what must, could, and cannot be true based on statements or rules presented by the testmaker. Often, you will need to combine statements to make the relevant inferences. Take a look at a brief example.

Set of Premises	Analysis
(1) Ainsley owns at least two red shirts.	
(2) Ainsley has worn every shirt she owns.	
Determine the level of truth for each of the following statements: Must be true; could be true or false; or must be false	
Ainsley owns a blue shirt.	⟶ Could be true or false: No information has been given on blue shirts.
Ainsley has worn a red shirt.	⟶ Must be true: She owns red shirts and has worn every shirt she owns.
Ainsley owns four red shirts.	⟶ Could be true or false: The statement does not specify that she owns *exactly* two red shirts—she could own more.
Ainsley owns red shirts she has never worn.	⟶ Must be false: She has worn every shirt she owns.

LSAT STRATEGY

When two statements contain the same term(s), ask how the statements are related and how information in one defines or limits the information in the other.

Practice

In the following exercise, you are given a set of premises and a set of statements that may or may not be valid deductions given those premises. Note whether each would-be deduction must be true, must be false, or could be either true or false based on the premises.

Exercise 1

Premises and Possible Deductions	My Analysis
(1) Bob's fruit stand sells blueberries but not kiwis.	Cant buy K @ Bobs
(2) Every day I buy blueberries, I also buy kiwis. →	B, S, K
(3) Today, I bought blueberries and strawberries.	

Determine the level of truth for each of the following statements:
Must be true; could be true or false; or must be false

16. Today, I bought fruit from Bob's fruit stand.	→ could be
17. Today, I bought fruit from some place other than Bob's fruit stand.	→ must be true
18. Today, I bought kiwis.	→ must be true
19. Bob's fruit stand sells kiwis.	→ must be false
20. Bob's fruit stand sells strawberries.	→ could be true

Expert Analysis

Here's how an LSAT expert would have analyzed the premises and determined the levels of truth for the statements in the preceding exercise.

Premises and Possible Deductions	Analysis
(1) Duane's Toys carries purple beach balls and green beach balls.	Start with the most concrete information: Millie bought a purple beach ball today. That means she bought at least two beach balls (but she may have bought more), but it doesn't add any information about the color of the second beach ball. It may have been purple, red, green, or any other color. Because the department store does not carry purple beach balls, we know that Millie bought at least one beach ball elsewhere. We don't know whether Millie went to Duane's, as other stores may also carry beach balls.
(2) The department store downtown carries only red beach balls.	
(3) On any day Millie buys a beach ball, she always buys at least two, one for each of her nieces.	
(4) Today, Millie bought a purple beach ball.	

Determine the level of truth for each of the following statements:
Must be true; could be true or false; or must be false

21. Millie's purple beach ball was purchased at Duane's Toys.	Could be true or false. While Duane's Toys does carry purple beach balls, Millie might also have purchased her purple beach ball elsewhere.
22. Millie bought a green beach ball today.	Could be true or false. We know that Millie bought a purple beach ball today, which means that she must have purchased at least one more, but we don't know the color of the second one.
23. Today, Millie bought at least two beach balls.	Must be true. Millie bought one beach ball today, so according to the third premise, she must have bought at least a second one.
24. If Millie purchased a beach ball at the downtown department store, then that beach ball was green.	Must be false. The downtown department store only carries red beach balls.
25. If Millie purchased a red beach ball, then she bought it at the downtown department store.	Could be true or false. There might be other stores that sell red beach balls, and there is no premise preventing Millie from visiting other stores.
26. Millie's purple beach ball was purchased at the downtown department store.	Must be false. The downtown department store only carries red beach balls.

REFLECTION

In every section of the LSAT, the testmaker rewards you for being able to make valid deductions from the statements, assertions, or rules presented. As you review your practice throughout this course, consider the following questions:

- What level of truth was the correct answer calling for?
- Did you characterize the levels of truth in the one correct and four wrong answers before evaluating the answer choices? Were you distinguishing between what was true and what was correct?
- Which statements, assertions, or rules in the question, game, or passage were strong enough to lead to valid deductions?
- How did two or more statements, assertions, or rules combine to allow you to make valid deductions?

For the exercises you just completed, look back at your work and think about the following:

- In which cases was it easier or harder to make deductions from the given statements?
- In which questions could you make valid deductions from a single statement? Where did you have to combine statements to answer the question?
- Thinking back to your Diagnostic Test, can you remember cases in which the testmaker rewarded you for making valid deductions in each section: Logic Games, Logical Reasoning, and Reading Comprehension?

CHAPTER 2

Formal Logic

CONDITIONAL STATEMENTS

Frequently on the LSAT, the premises from which you are able to make deductions can be written as conditional statements. These statements always have two parts—a sufficient term and a necessary result or requirement—and can always be translated into an "If-then" format.

Conditional statements will appear in LSAT questions in all three sections of the test, but are most important in Logical Reasoning and Logic Games. The following chart shows the relative importance of Formal Logic on the LSAT.

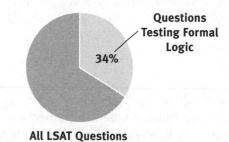

Questions Testing Formal Logic

34%

All LSAT Questions
PrepTests 66–80; released 2012–2016

LSAT STRATEGY

Although Formal Logic appears in a minority of LSAT questions, its importance is heightened by two considerations:

1. Most test takers have not refined the skill of understanding Formal Logic prior to preparing for the LSAT. Familiarity with Formal Logic will give you a competitive advantage.
2. Expertise in understanding and applying Formal Logic makes the correct answer to many LSAT questions unequivocal. There is little room for doubt or error if you have analyzed conditional statements correctly.

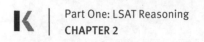

If my car runs, *then* it has fuel.

sufficient

necessary

Identify Conditional Statements

Prepare

> ### LEARNING OBJECTIVES
>
> In this section, you'll learn to:
>
> · Identify what is and is not a conditional statement (that is, understand what it means for a statement to be a conditional statement)

Before you can work with conditional statements to make valid deductions and inferences (and answer LSAT questions), you must be able to identify such statements.

> ### LSAT STRATEGY
>
> Every conditional statement has two parts:
>
> 1. A *sufficient term*, also known as the "trigger" or "if" term.
> 2. A *necessary term*, also known as the "result/requirement" or "then" term.

Consider this conditional statement:

> If you are in Australia, then you are south of the Equator.

Knowing that you are in Australia is *sufficient* to know that you are south of the Equator. Likewise, being south of the Equator is *necessary* to being in Australia. But be careful: Being in Australia is not necessary to being south of the Equator (after all, you might be in Madagascar or Argentina). Similarly, knowing that you are south of the Equator is not sufficient to know that you are in Australia.

Conditional relationships can be expressed in many ways other than the "If ... then" sentence structure. Take a look at how an LSAT expert identifies conditional statements.

Premises	Analysis
Is each of the following a conditional statement?	
The State of Pennsylvania requires a building permit for structures larger than 100 square feet. →	Yes. Because a building permit is a *requirement* for structures larger than 100 square feet, it's a necessary condition.
Whenever Bill eats cereal, he also drinks coffee. →	Yes. The word *whenever* indicates that Bill will drink coffee *every* time he eats cereal. Eating cereal is the trigger, or the sufficient condition.
Patty stopped to smell the flowers. →	No. This is just an action that Patty performed.
All of the jelly beans in this jar are either red or blue. →	Yes. Because this concerns *all* of the jelly beans in the jar, we know that each jelly bean in the jar *must* be either red or blue.

Practice

In the following exercise, read each statement and decide whether it expresses a conditional relationship. If it does, which term is *sufficient* and which is *necessary*?

Premises	My Analysis
1. Every person in this room is a doctor.	being in room → being doctor
2. The scientists should consider running another experiment.	no →
3. It's impossible to turn on this computer unless it's plugged in.	Not A unless B turning on sufficient plugged in necessary

If turned on, then plugged in →

| 4. I'm going to go to the family reunion only if my brother goes as well. | |

If I go, then my bro goes →

If A → B

A ~~only if~~ B

Expert Analysis

Here's how an LSAT expert would analyze those statements.

Premises	Analysis
5. To stay healthy, you need to exercise at least twice a week.	Yes. This could be written: *If you are to stay healthy, then you must exercise at least twice a week.* According to this statement, a person's staying healthy is *sufficient* to establish that she exercises at least twice per week, and her exercising at least twice per week is *necessary* to her continued health.
6. There are times when I think I'm going crazy.	No. This is an assertion of fact. There is neither a sufficient nor a necessary term in this statement.
7. Only competitors with a signed medical waiver are eligible for the event.	Yes. This could be written: *If a competitor is eligible for the event, then he has a signed medical waiver.* A competitor's eligibility is *sufficient* evidence that he has a signed medical waiver; a signed medical waiver is *necessary* for eligibility.
8. You can vote for chapter president only if your dues are paid.	Yes. This could be written: *If you can vote for chapter president, then your dues are paid.* Being able to vote is *sufficient* to know that your dues are paid. Having your dues paid is *necessary* to be able to vote.

This chapter continues on the next page ▶ ▶ ▶

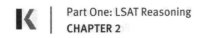
Expert Analysis

Here's how an LSAT expert would analyze the questions about each conditional statement in the exercise.

Conditional Statement		Analysis
If Patel or Beatrice presents on Day 3, then Darius will present on Day 4.		
9. What do we know if we are told that Patel presents on Day 2?	⟶	Nothing additional. Patel presenting on Day 2 triggers nothing.
10. What do we know if we are told that both Patel and Beatrice present on Day 3?	⟶	Darius must present on Day 4.
11. What do we know if we are told that Darius presents on Day 4?	⟶	Nothing additional. Though it's possible that Patel or Beatrice (or both) presents on Day 3, we don't know for sure.
If the lake contains bluegill, then it contains bass and walleye.		
12. What do we know if the lake contains bass and walleye?	⟶	Nothing additional. It might or might not also contain bluegill.
13. What do we know if the lake doesn't contain bluegill?	⟶	Nothing additional. The lake could still contain bass or walleye (or both).
14. What do we know if the lake doesn't contain bass?	⟶	If the lake doesn't contain bass, then there's no way it could also contain bluegill, since bluegill triggers bass being in the lake.

Perform

Check your understanding by analyzing the following conditional statements.

Conditional Statement	My Analysis
If Nancy and Bill are ranked in the top three, then Jim is ranked last (seventh).	
15. What do we know if Nancy is ranked third?	$\longrightarrow$
16. What do we know if Nancy and Bill are ranked first and second, respectively?	$\longrightarrow$
17. What do we know if Jim is ranked sixth?	$\longrightarrow$
If the store stocks red pants, then it also stocks green pants or blue pants.	
18. What do we know if the store stocks green pants and blue pants?	$\longrightarrow$
19. What do we know if the store stocks red pants?	$\longrightarrow$
20. What do we know if the store stocks yellow pants?	$\longrightarrow$

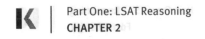
Expert Analysis

This is how an LSAT expert might abbreviate each of the statements from the exercise.

	Formal Logic Statement		Analysis		
21.	Viscachas are always soft.	→	If viscacha	→	soft
22.	Bob cuts the grass only when it's more than three inches tall.	→	If Bob cuts grass	→	over 3"
23.	I'll take a bike ride if it doesn't rain.	→	If NOT rain	→	bike ride
24.	No one involved in the crash sustained any injuries.	→	If in crash	→	NO injuries
25.	Every bag of chips in this case is smashed to smithereens.	→	If chips in case	→	smashed
26.	The only permissible form of identification is a driver's license.	→	If permissible ID	→	driver's license
27.	Johanna won't take karate unless Ellie and Michael agree to take it with her.	→	If Johanna karate	→	Ellie karate AND Michael karate
28.	My car will pass inspection if, but only if, I get a new muffler.	→	If car passes inspection → If get new muffler	→	get new muffler car passes inspection
29.	Whenever Melanie makes salsa, she includes freshly minced garlic and cilantro	→	If Melanie makes salsa →		includes garlic AND cilantro
30.	Unless the river has already crested, the town will definitely flood.	→	If river has NOT crested → or If town does NOT flood →		town will flood river has crested

Perform

Using the previous statements as reference, translate each of the following statements, each of which expresses a sufficient and necessary relationship, into simple shorthand.

Formal Logic Statement	My Analysis
31. Chloe refuses to move into a house without a second bathroom.	→
32. Carl won't get a good job unless he starts getting up before 11 AM.	→
33. All pets must be registered with the rental office.	→
34. Any student who masters Formal Logic will have an advantage on the LSAT.	→
35. All students registering for Crafting 201 must have completed either Basket Weaving 101 or Pottery 101.	→
36. If I'm not mistaken, this lo mein contains MSG.	→
37. Paul will be able to afford his dream car only if he gives up his weekly laser-tag matches.	→
38. Every plant that I've bought at Brown Thumb Nurseries has died.	→
39. Only applicants with flawless driving records and no convictions will be considered for the position.	→
40. No snack food can be considered nutritious unless it contains either whole grains or essential vitamins.	→

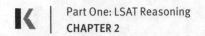
Expert Analysis

This is how an LSAT expert might abbreviate each of the statements from the exercise.

	Formal Logic Statement		Analysis
31.	Chloe refuses to move into a house without a second bathroom.	→ If Chloe move	→ second bathroom
32.	Carl won't get a good job unless he starts getting up before 11 AM.	→ If Carl gets good job	→ up before 11
33.	All pets must be registered with the rental office.	→ If pet	→ registered
34.	Any student who masters Formal Logic will have an advantage on the LSAT.	→ If master FL	→ advantage on LSAT
35.	All students registering for Crafting 201 must have completed either Basket Weaving 101 or Pottery 101.	→ If registering for Crafting 201	→ taken Basket Weaving 101 OR taken Pottery 101
36.	If I'm not mistaken, this lo mein contains MSG.	→ If NOT mistaken	→ MSG in lo mein
37.	Paul will be able to afford his dream car only if he gives up his weekly laser-tag matches.	→ If Paul can afford car	→ gave up weekly laser tag
38.	Every plant that I've bought at Brown Thumb Nurseries has died.	→ If plant bought at BTN	→ plant died
39.	Only applicants with flawless driving records and no convictions will be considered for the position.	→ If considered for position	→ flawless driving record AND no convictions
40.	No snack food can be considered nutritious unless it contains either whole grains or essential vitamins.	→ If snack food considered nutritious	→ whole grains OR essential vitamins

Make Valid Deductions from Conditional Statements
Prepare

LEARNING OBJECTIVES

In this section, you'll learn to:

- Make deductions on the basis of conditional statements

LSAT STRATEGY

Any time the necessary or "result" clause of one statement matches the sufficient or "If" clause of another, the two statements can be combined. For example:

$$\text{If } N \longrightarrow \sim P$$

$$\text{If } \sim P \longrightarrow \sim Q$$

$$\text{If } N \longrightarrow \sim P \longrightarrow \sim Q$$

Deduction:

$$\text{If } N \longrightarrow \sim Q$$

Connecting Conditional Statements

Now that you understand conditional relationships and how to spot them, you're ready to think about how to combine them to make new deductions.

Formal Logic Statements		Analysis
If A then B If B then C	$\longrightarrow$	If A $\rightarrow$ B $\rightarrow$ C
If D then E If F then E	$\longrightarrow$	If D OR F $\rightarrow$ E
If G then H If G then I	$\longrightarrow$	If G $\rightarrow$ H AND I

Practice

Translate the given conditional statements and use them to create a chain of logic. Then, answer questions about what we must know, given the chain.

Formal Logic Statements	My Analysis
(1) If Patrick is selected, then so is Jane.	$\longrightarrow$
(2) If Jane is selected, then so is Eloise.	$\longrightarrow$
(3) If Eloise is selected, then so is Grace.	$\longrightarrow$
Chain of logic:	$\longrightarrow$

What do we know if ...

41. Patrick is selected?	$\longrightarrow$
42. Jane is selected?	$\longrightarrow$
43. Grace is selected?	$\longrightarrow$

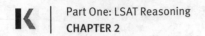

Expert Analysis

Here's how an LSAT expert would translate and combine the conditional statements in the previous exercise.

Formal Logic Statements		Analysis
(1) If Patrick is selected, then so is Jane.	$\longrightarrow$	If P $\longrightarrow$ J
(2) If Jane is selected, then so is Eloise.	$\longrightarrow$	If J $\longrightarrow$ E
(3) If Eloise is selected, then so is Grace.	$\longrightarrow$	If E $\longrightarrow$ G
Chain of logic:	$\longrightarrow$	If P $\longrightarrow$ J $\longrightarrow$ E $\longrightarrow$ G

What do we know if ...

41. Patrick is selected?	$\longrightarrow$ If Patrick is selected, then Jane is selected, Eloise is selected, and Grace is selected.
	If P $\longrightarrow$ J $\longrightarrow$ E $\longrightarrow$ G
42. Jane is selected?	$\longrightarrow$ If Jane is selected, then Eloise is selected and Grace is selected. Patrick may or may not be selected.
	If J $\longrightarrow$ E $\longrightarrow$ G
43. Grace is selected?	$\longrightarrow$ If Grace is selected, then it's not certain whether anyone else is selected. Selecting Grace does not trigger any other conditions.

Perform

Translate the given conditional statements and use them to create a chain of logic. Then, answer questions about what we must know, given the chain.

Formal Logic Statements	My Analysis
(1) If a store stocks bicycles, then it also stocks sofas. →	
(2) If a store stocks sofas, then it also stocks televisions and mattresses. →	
(3) If a store stocks televisions, then it also stocks dishwashers. →	
(4) If a store doesn't stock dishwashers, then it doesn't stock computers. →	

Chain of logic: →

What do we know if ...

44. the store stocks sofas?

→

45. the store stocks televisions?

→

46. the store stocks dishwashers?

→

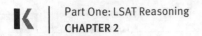
Expert Analysis

Here's how an LSAT expert would translate and combine the conditional statements in the previous exercise.

Formal Logic Statements		Analysis
(1) If a store stocks bicycles, then it also stocks sofas.	→	If B → S
(2) If a store stocks sofas, then it also stocks televisions and mattresses.	→	If S → T AND M
(3) If a store stocks televisions, then it also stocks dishwashers.	→	If T → D
(4) If a store doesn't stock dishwashers, then it doesn't stock computers.	→	If ~D → ~C
Chain of logic:	→	If B → S → T AND M ↗ D

What do we know if ...

44. the store stocks sofas?	→	If a store stocks sofas, then it also stocks televisions and mattresses. And stores that stock televisions also stock dishwashers. $$S \rightarrow T \ AND \ M \nearrow D$$
45. the store stocks televisions?	→	A store that stocks televisions also stocks dishwashers. $$T \rightarrow D$$
46. the store stocks dishwashers?	→	Nothing else can be determined if all that is known is that a store stocks dishwashers.

CONTRAPOSITIVES

Despite the many ways to express conditional statements, the logic underlying conditional statements is remarkably consistent. One more feature of these statements that is crucial for making deductions is the contrapositive.

LEARNING OBJECTIVES

In this section, you'll learn to:

· Translate a conditional statement into its contrapositive
· Make valid deductions from the contrapositive of a conditional statement
· Make valid deductions from conditional statements containing *And* and *Or*
· Make valid deductions from conditional statements containing an "Exclusive Or" provision

---

[handwritten margin notes:]
contrapositive
— reverse
— negate
— and ↔ or

if not B → not A

Translating "If ... Then" Statements into Contrapositives

The contrapositive of a conditional statement is just another way of phrasing the sufficient/necessary relationship described in that statement. Take the following statement as an example:

[handwritten margin note:]
if not fuel OR oil
then it wont run

> All overnight campers are required to obtain a permit from the park ranger.

> If camp overnight   →   obtain ranger permit

Now, what happens if you cannot obtain a permit from the ranger? Well, you can't camp overnight. That's the contrapositive of the statement. It looks like this:

> If NOT obtain ranger permit   →   NOT camp overnight

That's the basis for the contrapositive: What happens if the *necessary* condition is negated, if it cannot happen? In that case, the sufficient condition cannot happen either. Every contrapositive is formed in exactly that way.

Now consider a conditional statement with two terms in the necessary condition:

> No application will be processed unless it is accompanied by a signed form BE101 and the applicant presents valid identification.

Abbreviate that statement in Formal Logic shorthand:

> If application processed   →   signed BE101 AND valid ID

Now, what happens if either one of the two necessary conditions is not met?

> If NO signed BE101   →   application NOT processed

> If NO valid ID   →   application NOT processed

Thus, to form the contrapositive of the first statement, the *and* in the necessary condition must become *or* in the sufficient condition of the contrapositive:

> If NO signed BE101 OR NO valid ID   →   application NOT processed

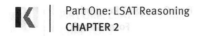

Expert Analysis

Here's how an LSAT expert might abbreviate the statements and form the contrapositives.

	Formal Logic Statement		Analysis	
47.	All new counselors are required to undergo two weeks of training.	→	If new counselor	→	2 wks train
			If ~2 wks train	→	~new counselor
48.	The company will consider purchasing any new technology that is proven to increase the productivity of its workers.	→	If tech increases prod	→	co consider
			If ~co consider	→	~tech increases prod
49.	Due to statistical anomalies, each vote from district nine was recounted.	→	If vote dist 9	→	recounted
			If ~recounted	→	~vote dist 9
50.	Deborah will agree to go kayaking if Jesse and Sara go as well.	→	If S kayaking AND J kayaking	→	D kayaking
			If ~D kayaking	→	~S kayaking OR ~J kayaking
51.	Megan only listens to hip-hop.	→	If M	→	hip-hop
			If ~hip-hop	→	~M
52.	No Liberty Head nickels were officially authorized for production in 1913.	→	If LHN auth	→	~1913
			If 1913	→	~LHN auth
53.	Patrick never attends classes on Tuesdays.	→	If P attends classes	→	~Tues
			If Tues	→	~P attend classes
54.	Anna will not go sledding unless Paul and Reid go with her.	→	If A sleds	→	P sleds AND R sleds
			If P ~sled OR R ~sled	→	A ~sled
55.	Her record will do well on the charts if and only if it is popular with her key demographic.	→	If rec does well on charts	→	pop key demo
			If ~pop key demo	→	rec ~do well on charts
			If pop key demo	→	rec do well on charts
			If rec ~do well on charts	→	~pop key demo

Perform

Translate each of the following statements into simple shorthand, and form the correct contrapositive of each.

Formal Logic Statement	My Analysis
56. Every bed sold today comes with free delivery.	$\longrightarrow$
57. Whenever James plays tennis, Kay goes rock climbing.	$\longrightarrow$
58. The car will run only if the radiator is replaced.	$\longrightarrow$
59. The only candidates admitted by the committee this year applied before April.	$\longrightarrow$
60. The watch is not on the nightstand.	$\longrightarrow$
61. None of the diners ordered today's special.	$\longrightarrow$
62. Scott doesn't go anywhere without a banjo.	$\longrightarrow$
63. The LSAT is a prerequisite for law school.	$\longrightarrow$
64. If the Lions win or the Bulldogs lose, then the Eagles will advance to the playoffs.	$\longrightarrow$

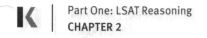

Practice

Review the deduction exercise you tried earlier, and then complete the practice on the next page.

Formal Logic Statements		Analysis
If Patrick is selected, then so is Jane.	→	If P → J
If Jane is selected, then so is Eloise.	→	If J → E
If Eloise is selected, then so is Grace.	→	If E → G
Chain of logic:	→	If P → J → E → G
What do we know if ...		
Patrick is selected?	→	If Patrick is selected, then Jane is selected, Eloise is selected, and Grace is selected. If P → J → E → G
Jane is selected?	→	If Jane is selected, then Eloise is selected and Grace is selected. Patrick may or may not be selected. If J → E → G
Grace is selected?	→	If Grace is selected, then it's not certain whether anyone else is selected. Selecting Grace does not trigger any other conditions.

For each of the following statements, form the contrapositive of the statement and add it to the My Analysis column. Then answer the questions that follow.

Formal Logic Statements		My Analysis
If Patrick is selected, then so is Jane.	→	If P → J
		If no J → no P
If Jane is selected, then so is Eloise.	→	If J → E
		If no E → no J
If Eloise is selected, then so is Grace.	→	If E → G
		If no G → no E
Chain of logic:	→	If P → J → E → G
		If no G → no E → no J → no P

What do we know if ...

65. Grace is not selected?

→ not E, J, ~~P~~

66. Eloise is not selected?

→ not J or P

67. Jane is not selected?

→ no P

68. Patrick is not selected?

→ nothing

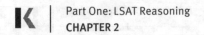

Expert Analysis

Here's how an LSAT expert would analyze the previous statements and answer the associated questions.

Formal Logic Statements		Analysis
If Patrick is selected, then so is Jane.	→	If P → J If ~J → ~P
If Jane is selected, then so is Eloise.	→	If J → E If ~E → ~J
If Eloise is selected, then so is Grace.	→	If E → G If ~G → ~E
Chain of logic:	→	If P → J → E → G If ~G → ~E → ~J → ~P

What do we know if ...

65. Grace is not selected?	→	If Grace is not selected, then Eloise, Jane, and Patrick will also not be selected.
66. Eloise is not selected?	→	If Eloise is not selected, then Jane and Patrick will also not be selected. We cannot determine whether Grace will or will not be selected based on Eloise's not being selected.
67. Jane is not selected?	→	If Jane is not selected, then Patrick will not be selected. Jane's not being selected, however, tells us nothing about Eloise or Grace.
68. Patrick is not selected?	→	We do not know anything additional from the fact that Patrick is not selected.

In the practice sets on the following pages, you will need to make the initial translations and abbreviations for the conditional statements, and then form the contrapositives before moving on to answer the questions.

Perform

For each of the following statements, turn it into shorthand, form the contrapositive, and then make notes about how each can be combined with other conditional statements in the same set to make deductions.

Formal Logic Statements	My Analysis
If Devin goes to the lecture, then he will not go to the movies. $\longrightarrow$	
If Devin goes to the movies, then he will buy popcorn. $\longrightarrow$	
If Devin does not get soda, then he will not buy popcorn. $\longrightarrow$	
Chain of logic: $\longrightarrow$	

What do we know if ...

69. Devin does not purchase popcorn? $\longrightarrow$

70. Devin does not go to the movies? $\longrightarrow$

71. Devin does not get soda? $\longrightarrow$

72. Devin does not go to the lecture? $\longrightarrow$

73. Devin goes to the movies? $\longrightarrow$

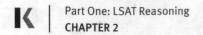

Expert Analysis

Here's how an LSAT expert would analyze the previous statements and answer the associated questions.

Formal Logic Statements		Analysis	
If Devin goes to the lecture, then he will not go to the movies.	→	If lecture If movies	→ ~movies → ~lecture
If Devin goes to the movies, then he will buy popcorn.	→	If movies If ~popcorn	→ popcorn → ~movies
If Devin does not get soda, then he will not buy popcorn.	→	If ~soda If popcorn	→ ~popcorn → soda
Chain of logic:	→	If movies → popcorn → soda If ~soda → ~popcorn → ~movies	

What do we know if . . .

69. Devin does not purchase popcorn?	→	He did not go to the movies.
70. Devin does not go to the movies?	→	Nothing additional.
71. Devin does not get soda?	→	He did not purchase popcorn, and he did not go to the movies.
72. Devin does not go to the lecture?	→	Nothing additional.
73. Devin goes to the movies?	→	He does not go to the lecture, he purchases popcorn, and he gets soda.

Make Valid Deductions from Conditional Statements Containing *And* and *Or*

Prepare

LEARNING OBJECTIVES

In this section, you'll learn to:

- Make valid deductions from conditional statements containing *And* and *Or*

Earlier in the chapter, you learned that when a conditional statement includes an *and* or an *or* in one of its conditions, you must swap *and* for *or* (and vice versa) when forming the contrapositive. Here's another example to refresh your memory.

> Whenever the country singer Joe Samson's mother is in the audience at one of his concerts, he always sings either "Mama Tried" or "Will the Circle Be Unbroken" during the encore.

In a Formal Logic abbreviation, that statement would become:

> If mother is in audience → MT OR WTCBU

To form the contrapositive, reverse and negate the terms and swap the *or* for *and*.

> If ~MT AND ~WTCBU → mother ~in audience

So, consider what you know in each of the following cases:

- When Joe's mother is in the audience
- When Joe's mother is not in the audience
- When Joe sings "Mama Tried" but does not sing "Will the Circle Be Unbroken"
- When Joe sings "Will the Circle Be Unbroken" but does not sing "Mama Tried"
- When Joe sings both "Mama Tried" and "Will the Circle Be Unbroken"
- When Joe sings neither "Mama Tried" nor "Will the Circle Be Unbroken"

...gic Statement					Contrapositive		
	$\rightarrow$	B OR C	$\rightarrow$		If ~B AND ~C	$\rightarrow$	~A
If D	$\rightarrow$	E AND F	$\rightarrow$		If ~E OR ~F	$\rightarrow$	~D
If G OR H	$\rightarrow$	J	$\rightarrow$		If ~J	$\rightarrow$	~G AND ~H
If K AND L	$\rightarrow$	M	$\rightarrow$		If ~M	$\rightarrow$	~K OR ~L
If N AND O	$\rightarrow$	P AND R	$\rightarrow$		If ~P OR ~R	$\rightarrow$	~N OR ~O
If S OR T	$\rightarrow$	U AND V	$\rightarrow$		If ~U OR ~V	$\rightarrow$	~S AND ~T
If W AND X	$\rightarrow$	Y OR Z	$\rightarrow$		If ~Y AND ~Z	$\rightarrow$	~W OR ~X
If AA OR BB	$\rightarrow$	CC OR DD	$\rightarrow$		If ~CC AND ~DD	$\rightarrow$	~AA AND ~BB

Conditional Statement		Analysis
Whenever Claudia goes to the health club, then Ann and Becky go as well.	$\rightarrow$	If C $\rightarrow$ A AND B If ~A OR ~B $\rightarrow$ ~C

Is each of the following an acceptable group of visitors to the health club?

Ann, Becky, and Claudia together	$\rightarrow$	Yes
Ann and Becky, but not Claudia	$\rightarrow$	Yes
Ann and Claudia, but not Becky	$\rightarrow$	No
Becky and Claudia, but not Ann	$\rightarrow$	No
Ann alone	$\rightarrow$	Yes
Becky alone	$\rightarrow$	Yes
Claudia alone	$\rightarrow$	No

Channels on LSAT

Black Tie Optional

Brain Me & my arrow

Practice

In this exercise, translate each of the conditional statements to Formal Logic abbreviations and form the correct contrapositive of each statement. Then, answer the questions beneath the statement using your work.

Conditional Statement	My Analysis
The forestry bill will not pass without the support of both Senator Brown and Senator Mendoza.	$\longrightarrow$
74. If both Senator Brown and Senator Mendoza support the forestry bill, will it pass?	$\longrightarrow$
75. If Senator Brown supports the forestry bill, but Senator Mendoza opposes it, will the bill pass?	$\longrightarrow$
76. If the forestry bill passes, what do you know?	$\longrightarrow$

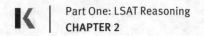

Expert Analysis

Here's how an LSAT expert would analyze the previous statements and answer the questions.

Conditional Statement		Analysis
The forestry bill will not pass without the support of both Senator Brown and Senator Mendoza. $\longrightarrow$		If bill passes $\rightarrow$ Brown supports AND Mendoza supports If Brown ~support OR Mendoza ~support $\rightarrow$ bill ~pass
74. If both Senator Brown and Senator Mendoza support the forestry bill, will it pass?	$\longrightarrow$	We don't know. Their mutual support is necessary, but not sufficient, to ensure passage.
75. If Senator Brown supports the forestry bill, but Senator Mendoza opposes it, will the bill pass?	$\longrightarrow$	No. The support of both Senators is necessary to passage.
76. If the forestry bill passes, what do you know?	$\longrightarrow$	Both Senators supported it. The support of both is necessary to passage.

Perform

In this exercise, translate each of the conditional statements to Formal Logic abbreviations and form the correct contrapositive of each statement. Then, answer the questions beneath the statement using your work.

Conditional Statement	My Analysis

If Tomoko sings and Garrett plays drums, then Juniper must play the saxophone solo.

$\longrightarrow$

77. If Tomoko sings, but Garrett does not play the drums, can Juniper play the saxophone solo?

$\longrightarrow$

78. If Juniper does not play the saxophone, what do you know?

$\longrightarrow$

79. If Juniper does play the saxophone solo, what do you know?

$\longrightarrow$

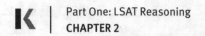

Expert Analysis

Here's how an LSAT expert would analyze the previous statements and answer the questions.

Conditional Statement		Analysis
If Tomoko sings and Garrett plays drums, then Juniper must play the saxophone solo.	→	If T sings AND G drums → J sax solo If J ~sax solo → T ~sing OR G ~drum
77. If Tomoko sings, but Garrett does not play the drums, can Juniper play the saxophone solo?	→	Yes. She is required to play the sax solo when BOTH sufficient conditions apply, but she may play it without those conditions.
78. If Juniper does not play the saxophone, what do you know?	→	Either Tomoko did not sing OR Garrett did not play the drums.
79. If Juniper does play the saxophone solo, what do you know?	→	Nothing additional. She might play the sax solo in any case; she's required to when Tomoko sings AND Garrett drums.

Make Valid Deductions from Conditional Statements Containing an "Exclusive Or" Provision

Prepare

So far, you've learned the fact that *or*, by itself, does not denote a relationship of mutual exclusivity in conditional Formal Logic statements. However, if the LSAT adds a phrase such as "but not both," then, and only then, does it become a case of mutual exclusivity. Such statements are rare on the LSAT, but they warrant enough practice that you won't be thrown by them on Test Day.

Formal Logic Statements			Analysis	
If X, then Y or Z, but not both		If X	$\rightarrow$	Y OR Z (but not both)
	$\rightarrow$	If ~Y AND ~Z	$\rightarrow$	~X
		If Y AND Z	$\rightarrow$	~X

Practice

Record each of the following statements in "If ... then" format, and form both parts of their contrapositive.

Formal Logic Statements	My Analysis
80. The radio edit of this song will feature either the drum solo or the guitar solo, but not both.	
	$\rightarrow$
81. Every Family Budget Pass includes admission to exactly one of the IMAX movie experience or the water park.	
	$\rightarrow$

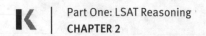
Expert Analysis

Here's how an LSAT expert might analyze the statements on the previous page.

	Formal Logic Statements			Analysis
80.	The radio edit of this song will feature either the drum solo or the guitar solo, but not both.		If radio edit	→	drum solo OR guitar solo (but not both)
		→	If ~drum solo AND ~guitar solo	→	~radio edit
			If drum solo AND guitar solo	→	~radio edit
81.	Every Family Budget Pass includes admission to exactly one of the IMAX movie experience or the water park.		If FBP	→	IMAX OR water park (but not both)
		→	If ~IMAX AND ~water park	→	~FBP
			If IMAX AND water park	→	~FBP

Perform

In this exercise, take each of the Formal Logic statements, turn it into If-Then format, and make both parts of the contrapositive.

Formal Logic Statements	My Analysis
82. Every shirt Norah wears is purple or yellow, but never both. $\longrightarrow$	
83. If Owen majors in economics, then he'll also major in finance or marketing, but not both. $\longrightarrow$	

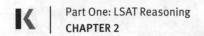

Expert Analysis

Here's how an LSAT expert might analyze the statements on the previous page.

Formal Logic Statements	Analysis
82. Every shirt Norah wears is purple or yellow, but never both.	If Norah's shirt → purple OR yellow (but not both) → If ~purple AND ~yellow → ~Norah's shirt If purple AND yellow → ~Norah's shirt
83. If Owen majors in economics, then he'll also major in finance or marketing, but not both.	If economics → finance OR marketing (but not both) → If ~finance AND ~marketing → ~economics If finance AND marketing → ~economics

NUMERICAL DEDUCTIONS FROM CONDITIONAL STATEMENTS

Numerical deductions are often rewarded on the LSAT, especially in Logic Games. This section highlights two such deductions that frequently arise from conditional Formal Logic statements.

Prepare

> ## LEARNING OBJECTIVES
>
> In this section, you'll learn to:
>
> · Determine the valid deduction from If X → ~Y and from If ~X → Y

[handwritten: if X → ~y / if y → ~X / never X Y / if no X, y could be there or not / if no y, X could be there or not]

Determining the Valid Deduction from If X → ~Y

The trigger involves something that *does* happen, and the result is something else that *cannot* happen. This reduces the number of terms by at least one.

In this case, the deduction is this: You cannot have both. (And you might have neither.)

If Duncan eats a cheeseburger, he won't also order a hot dog.

If cheeseburger → ~hot dog
If hot dog → ~cheeseburger

Duncan cannot order both. He can get just a hot dog, just a cheeseburger, or neither.

Determining the Valid Deduction from If ~X → Y

The trigger involves something that *doesn't* happen, and the result is something that *must* happen. This increases the number of terms chosen by at least one.

In this case, the deduction is this: You must have at least one. (And you might have both.)

[handwritten: if ~X → y / if ~y → X / at least 1, could be both]

If Margot doesn't read the book, then she'll watch the movie.

If ~book → movie
If ~movie → book

Margot will definitely do at least one of the activities. She'll watch the movie, read the book, or possibly do both.

> ## LSAT STRATEGY
>
> The triggers of a Formal Logic statement and its contrapositive can never occur simultaneously. You can have the sufficient and necessary terms of the original statement, the sufficient and necessary terms of the contrapositive, or both necessary terms—but never both sufficient terms at once.

[handwritten: if both rules in play, only 1 is possible]

Formal Logic Statements	Analysis
No X are Y	If X → ~Y You cannot have both X and Y. You may have X without Y, Y without X, or neither Y nor X.
If no U, then V.	If ~U → V You must have at least one of U or V. You can either have just U, just V, or both U and V.
All those with J don't have K	If J → ~K One cannot have both J and K. One may have J without K, have K without J, or have neither J nor K.
R unless S	If ~R → S You must have at least one of R and S. You can either have just R, just S, or both R and S.

Practice

For each of the following statements, write out the statement in shorthand, and indicate whether a numerical deduction can be made based on the statement.

Formal Logic Statements	My Analysis
84. Sylvia will serve either veggie burgers or falafel at her cookout. $\longrightarrow$	
85. If Vernon eats the potato salad, he won't eat the macaroni and cheese. $\longrightarrow$	
86. I can't meet my friend for lunch unless I skip my exercise class. $\longrightarrow$	
87. Any flowerbed that isn't planted with petunias must be planted with impatiens. $\longrightarrow$	

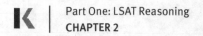
Expert Analysis

Here's how an LSAT expert might translate and analyze the statements in the exercise.

	Formal Logic Statements		Analysis
84.	Sylvia will serve either veggie burgers or falafel at her cookout.	→	If ~veggie burger → falafel If ~falafel → veggie burger This statement establishes a minimum of one of these menu options. Sylvia must serve at least one of the two foods; she may serve both.
85.	If Vernon eats the potato salad, he won't eat the macaroni and cheese.	→	If potato salad → ~mac & cheese If mac & cheese → ~potato salad In simpler terms: Vernon cannot eat both the potato salad and the mac & cheese. **Vernon never potato salad and mac & cheese** This statement reduces Vernon's maximum number of food choices by one.
86.	I can't meet my friend for lunch unless I skip my exercise class.	→	If lunch w/friend → ~exercise class If exercise class → ~lunch w/friend *Or* **Never lunch and exercise class** This rule decreases my maximum number of activities by one, because either of my activities definitely excludes another of my activities.
87.	Any flowerbed that isn't planted with petunias must be planted with impatiens.	→	If ~petunias → impatiens If ~impatiens → petunias At least one of petunias and impatiens must be included in each flower bed: This statement establishes a minimum of one of these flower types.

Perform

For each of the following statements, write out the statement in shorthand, and indicate whether a numerical deduction can be made based on the statement.

Formal Logic Statements	My Analysis
88. If the customer purchases the door, she will purchase at least two matching windows as well. $\longrightarrow$	
89. Keith bought six tickets to the concert, but if Darren doesn't go, then neither will Charles, so Keith could end up with extra tickets. $\longrightarrow$	
90. If Joanna is not selected for the varsity team, then Megan is selected for the varsity team. $\longrightarrow$	
91. Any bin that contains potatoes cannot contain onions. $\longrightarrow$	

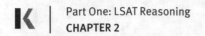
Expert Analysis

Here's how an LSAT expert might translate and analyze the statements in the exercise.

Formal Logic Statements		Analysis
88. If the customer purchases the door, she will purchase at least two matching windows as well.		If purchase door → purchase 2+ windows
		If ~purchase 2+ windows → ~purchase door
	→	This statement does not set a minimum or maximum because the purchase of windows *depends* on the purchase of a door. The customer could purchase neither a window nor a door, or the customer could purchase one or more windows, without triggering this rule.
89. Keith bought six tickets to the concert, but if Darren doesn't go, then neither will Charles, so Keith could end up with extra tickets.		If ~Darren go to concert → ~Charles go to concert
		If Charles go to concert → Darren go to concert
	→	This rule does not affect the minimum or maximum number of concert attendees, because we don't know at this point whether Charles is going or Darren is not going.
90. If Joanna is not selected for the varsity team, then Megan is selected for the varsity team.		If ~J varsity → M varsity
	→	If ~M varsity → J varsity
		At least one of Joanna or Megan will make the varsity team; it's possible that both do.
91. Any bin that contains potatoes cannot contain onions.		If potatoes → ~onions
		If onions → ~potatoes
	→	This reduces by one the maximum number of vegetables that can be stored in a bin; no bin may have potatoes and onions.

REFLECTION

Look back over your practice:

- Did you take the time to understand each conditional statement before noting it down in shorthand?
- If you couldn't immediately see how to write it down in one sentence, did you translate it into If-Then form and make the contrapositive? (If so, that's great!)
- When forming contrapositives, did you remember to always negate and reverse the terms?
- Did you always remember that the result (the necessary condition) can occur without the trigger (the sufficient condition), but not vice versa?

Now, take a moment to look back over all of Chapter 2. You may not have been thinking about it as you did your work, but you've now successfully employed a great many essential LSAT skills, skills you will continue to use in law school and in the practice of law. Now that you've built this foundation, you are ready for work in all of the other sections of the LSAT.

Come back to Chapter 2 any time you need a refresher on Formal Logic as it is presented and tested on the LSAT.

PART TWO

Logic Games

CHAPTER 3

The Kaplan Logic Games Method

A STRATEGIC APPROACH TO LOGIC GAMES

Prepare

LEARNING OBJECTIVES

In this section, you'll learn to:

- State the steps of the Kaplan Logic Games Method and the purpose of each step

While logic games may initially appear abstract and irrelevant to the skills necessary for a legal career, they actually test core LSAT skills. The ability to interpret, deconstruct, and combine individual rules to deduce what must, can, or cannot be true under various conditions is central to the work you'll do in law school.

In this chapter, you'll see the Logic Games Method, the approach an LSAT expert uses.

THE KAPLAN LOGIC GAMES METHOD

Step 1: Overview

Step 2: Sketch

Step 3: Rules

Step 4: Deductions

Step 5: Questions

3 3 3 3

Questions 18–23

From the 1st through the 7th of next month, seven nurses—Farnham, Griseldi, Heany, Juarez, Khan, Lightfoot, and Moreau—will each conduct one information session at a community center. Each nurse's session will fall on a different day. The nurses' schedule is governed by the following constraints:

At least two of the other nurses' sessions must fall in between Heany's session and Moreau's session.
Griseldi's session must be on the day before Khan's.
Juarez's session must be on a later day than Moreau's.
Farnham's session must be on an earlier day than Khan's but on a later day than Lightfoot's.
Lightfoot cannot conduct the session on the 2nd.

> The opening paragraph is called the Overview. It describes the game and presents the game's action(s).

18. Which one of the following could be the order of the nurses' sessions, from first to last?

(A) Farnham, Griseldi, Khan, Moreau, Juarez, Lightfoot, Heany
(B) Heany, Lightfoot, Farnham, Moreau, Juarez, Griseldi, Khan
(C) Juarez, Heany, Lightfoot, Farnham, Moreau, Griseldi, Khan
(D) Lightfoot, Moreau, Farnham, Juarez, Griseldi, Khan, Heany
(E) Moreau, Lightfoot, Heany, Juarez, Farnham, Griseldi, Khan

> These are the rules of the game. They establish what must, might, or cannot be true in the game.

F G H J K L M

```
 1   2   3   4   5   6   7      H/M ___ ... ᴹ/H
~K  ~L  ~K   L  ~L   L  ~L      L...F...GK
~G  ~K  ~G  ~K      ~F  ~F      M...J
 F  ~G           ~G
~J              ~M
```

> An LSAT expert creates a master sketch that visually displays the game's action(s) and restrictions.

> Experts translate the game's rules into a consistent visual shorthand.

3   **3**

19. Juarez's session CANNOT be on which one of the following days?

×CBT

(A) the 2nd
(B) the 3rd
(C) the 5th
(D) the 6th
(E) the 7th

20. If Juarez's session is on the 3rd, then which one of the following could be true?

(A) Moreau's session is on the 1st.
(B) Khan's session is on the 5th.
(C) Heany's session is on the 6th.
(D) Griseldi's session is on the 5th.
(E) Farnham's session is on the 2nd.

21. If Khan's session is on an earlier day than Moreau's, which one of the following could conduct the session on the 3rd?

(A) Griseldi
(B) Heany
(C) Juarez
(D) Lightfoot
(E) Moreau

L...F...GK...M...J
~2   H

22. If Griseldi's session is on the 5th, then which one of the following must be true?

(A) Farnham's session is on the 3rd.
(B) Heany's session is on the 7th.
(C) Juarez's session is on the 4th.
(D) Lightfoot's session is on the 1st.
(E) Moreau's session is on the 2nd.

23. Lightfoot's session coul[d]
following days?

(A) the 3rd
(B) the 4th
(C) the 5th
(D) the 6th
(E) the 7th

> Experts know that it is important to characterize the correct and incorrect answer choices in Logic Games.

> Experts don't try to keep all of the rules and deductions in their heads. They depict relationships on the page and continue to add new information.

S T O P

IF YOU FINISH BEFORE TIME IS CALLED, YOU MAY CHECK YOUR WORK ON THIS SECTION ONLY.
DO NOT WORK ON ANY OTHER SECTION IN THE TEST.

20. L MJ   F...GK
    1 2 3 4 5 6 7
              H

22. MJE
     ≠MJ
     mFJ
     L ⌢ GKH
    1 2 3 4 5 6 7
    MJ L F G K H

> Use the available space to create new sketches for questions that ask you to consider new information.

Practice

Step 1: Overview

The first thing an LSAT expert does is read a game's opening paragraph to understand the game's moving parts. The expert asks four questions while conducting this overview: the SEAL questions.

> ## STEP 1: OVERVIEW—THE SEAL QUESTIONS
>
> **S**ituation—What is the real-world scenario being described? What is the deliverable information—an ordered list, a calendar, a chart showing what's matched up?
>
> **E**ntities—Who or what are the "moving parts," the people or things I'm distributing, selecting, sequencing, or matching?
>
> **A**ction—What is the specific action—distribution, selection, sequencing, matching, or a combination of those—that I'm performing on the entities?
>
> **L**imitations—Does the game state parameters (e.g., select four of seven, sequence the entities one per day, or the like) that restrict how I'll set up and sketch the game?

Here's an example of the SEAL framework in action.

From the 1st through the 7th of next month, seven nurses—Farnham, Griseldi, Heany, Juarez, Khan, Lightfoot, and Moreau—will each conduct one information session at a community center. Each nurse's session will fall on a different day. The nurses' schedule is governed by the following constraints

PrepTest61 Sec3 Qs 18–23

What is this game's **Situation?** _nurse schedule_

What **Entities** are involved in this game? _7 nurses_

What is this game's **Action?** _schedule nurses_

Are there any **Limitations** to this game? _diff days_

```
 _   _   _   _   _   _   _
 1   2   3   4   5   6   7

     F G H J K L M
```

Step 2: Sketch

After conducting the overview, an LSAT expert creates a sketch based on the game's action (or actions) and limitations. A strong sketch is simple, easy to read, and often based on something familiar: If a game's action involves scheduling, for example, the sketch may mimic a calendar, or if the game involves putting people or items into different groups, the sketch might be a table.

STEP 2: SKETCH

· Create a sketch that depicts the game's action(s) and limitations.
· Aim for a sketch that is easy to read, quick to replicate, and able to account for what is certain and uncertain based on the game's rules.

Revisit the overview of the game you've seen before and create an appropriate sketch.

From the 1st through the 7th of next month, seven nurses—
Farnham, Griseldi, Heany, Juarez, Khan, Lightfoot, and
Moreau—will each conduct one information session at
a community center. Each nurse's session will fall on a
different day. The nurses' schedule is governed by the
following constraints:

PrepTest61 Sec3 Qs 18–23

My Sketch:

— — — — — — —
1 2 3 4 5 6 7
XJ XL XK XL XL XL XL
XF XG XG XK   XF XM
XG XK   XF
XK   XG

F G H J K L M

H/M . . . M/H

M . . . J

G K

L . . . F . . . K

L . . . F . . . G K

...the possible permutations of a game by establishing restrictions on the placement, order, or selection of entities, or by establishing relationships between entities.

STEP 3: RULES

- Whenever possible, add information directly to your Master Sketch.
- If you cannot build a rule directly into the Master Sketch, make a shorthand graphical representation of it.
- Write the rules in a way that matches the style and conventions of the Master Sketch.
- Consider both the positive and negative implications of a rule.
- Write similar rules consistently, the same way from game to game.

Now let's look at our game with the rules included.

From the 1st through the 7th of next month, seven nurses—Farnham, Griseldi, Heany, Juarez, Khan, Lightfoot, and Moreau—will each conduct one information session at a community center. Each nurse's session will fall on a different day. The nurses' schedule is governed by the following constraints:

At least two of the other nurses' sessions must fall in between Heany's session and Moreau's session.

Griseldi's session must be on the day before Khan's.

Juarez's session must be on a later day than Moreau's.

Farnham's session must be on an earlier day than Khan's but on a later day than Lightfoot's.

Lightfoot cannot conduct the session on the 2nd.

PrepTest61 Sec3 Qs 18–23

Blocs of entities
Limited options
Established entities
Numbers
Duplicates

Using the framework above, consider which of the given rules can be directly incorporated into your sketch. For those where that isn't possible, what kind of shorthand next to the sketch might be most efficient?

Rule 1: At least two of the other nurses' sessions must fall in between Heany's session and Moreau's session.

H . . M
or M . . H

Rule 2: Griseldi's session must be on the day before Khan's.

Rule 3: Juarez's session must be on a later day than Moreau's.

M . . J

Rule 4: Farnham's session must be on an earlier day than Khan's but on a later day than Lightfoot's.

Rule 5: Lightfoot cannot conduct the session on the 2nd.

Step 4: Deductions

This is the step that the majority of untrained test takers overlook. Even those who instinctively understand the value of making a sketch or depicting the rules visually often don't take the time to determine what must be true or must be false beyond what the rules explicitly state.

An LSAT expert, however, knows that in most games, it is possible to combine the rules with each other (or with the game's overall limitations) in a way that reveals greater certainty when she goes to tackle the questions. As you practice, you'll start to make valuable deductions almost instinctively, but learn to be systematic and rigorous in this step so that you get all of a game's potential deductions quickly and accurately.

The vast majority of deductions come from one of five patterns, easily remembered with the mnemonic BLEND. Use this as a checklist, not a series of steps. You don't look for Blocks of Entities first, necessarily.

STEP 4: DEDUCTIONS

Blocks of Entities—two or more players who are always grouped together

Limited Options—rules or restrictions that limit the overall setup to one of two acceptable arrangements

Established Entities—a player locked into a specific space or group

Number Restrictions—rules or limitations that provide guidance about the number of entities assigned to a group or space

Duplications—entities that appear in two or more rules and allow the rules to be combined

An LSAT expert's sketch and rule notations for the Nurses game appear on the next page.

Here is what an expert would have for a setup thus far. Try going through the BLEND checklist with this game to determine which, if any, of these restrictions you see here. How can they provide additional certainty in this game? Make sure to consider both positive and negative implications.

LSAT Question	Analysis

From the 1st through the 7th of next month, seven nurses—Farnham, Griseldi, Heany, Juarez, Khan, Lightfoot, and Moreau—will each conduct one information session at a community center. Each nurse's session will fall on a different day. The nurses' schedule is governed by the following constraints:
 	
At least two of the other nurses' sessions must fall in between Heany's session and Moreau's session.
Griseldi's session must be on the day before Khan's.
Juarez's session must be on a later day than Moreau's.
Farnham's session must be on an earlier day than Khan's but on a later day than Lightfoot's.
Lightfoot cannot conduct the session on the 2nd.
	F G H J K L M
	
	__ __ __ __ __ __ __
	1 2 3 4 5 6 7
	   ~L
	
	H/M __ __ ... M/H
	
	   G K
	
	M ... J
	
	L ... F ... K

PrepTest61 Sec3 Qs 18–23 →

Step 5: Questions

Making a useful sketch, writing out the rules, and making available deductions are necessary, but not sufficient for success in the Logic Games section. Experts know that the ultimate goal is to answer the questions correctly—and not just correctly, but also quickly.

STEP 5: QUESTIONS

· Be able to characterize both correct and incorrect answer choices.
· Know the different question types and how to approach each one.
· Don't hesitate to draw a new sketch in "If" questions.
· Use deductions and past work to eliminate wrong answers quickly.

Follow this order

LGQ's
1. Acceptability
2. If Q's
3. non - If Q's
4. rule replacement
~ completely determine
5. change the rules

Acceptability Question

The first question for this game (and the first question in most games' question sets) is an Acceptability question. In these questions, the correct answer is the one that breaks none of the rules. The expert's strategy is simple: Check the answers rule-by-rule, and eliminate choices that break the rules.

LSAT Question	My Analysis

From the 1st through the 7th of next month, seven nurses—Farnham, Griseldi, Heany, Juarez, Khan, Lightfoot, and Moreau—will each conduct one information session at a community center. Each nurse's session will fall on a different day. The nurses' schedule is governed by the following constraints:

$\longrightarrow$

At least two of the other nurses' sessions must fall in between Heany's session and Moreau's session.
Griseldi's session must be on the day before Khan's.
Juarez's session must be on a later day than Moreau's.
Farnham's session must be on an earlier day than Khan's but on a later day than Lightfoot's.
Lightfoot cannot conduct the session on the 2nd.

18. Which one of the following could be the order of the nurses' sessions, from first to last?

Rule 1 broken by answer choice: ___E___

Rule 2 broken by answer choice: _____

Rule 3 broken by answer choice: ___C___

Rule 4 broken by answer choice: ___A___

Rule 5 broken by answer choice: ___B___

(A) Farnham, Griseldi, Khan, Moreau, Juarez, Lightfoot, Heany $\longrightarrow$

(B) Heany, Lightfoot, Farnham, Moreau, Juarez, Griseldi, Khan $\longrightarrow$

(C) Juarez, Heany, Lightfoot, Farnham, Moreau, Griseldi, Khan $\longrightarrow$

(D) Lightfoot, Moreau, Farnham, Juarez, Griseldi, Khan, Heany $\longrightarrow$

(E) Moreau, Lightfoot, Heany, Juarez, Farnham, Griseldi, Khan

PrepTest61 Sec3 Q18 $\longrightarrow$

New-"If"/Could Be True Question

Here is another New-"If" question. NOTE: New-"If" conditions apply only to the question in which they appear. Do not carry over one question's New-"If" to another question. Keep your question-specific notes distinct and clearly labeled.

LSAT Question	My Analysis

From the 1st through the 7th of next month, seven nurses—Farnham, Griseldi, Heany, Juarez, Khan, Lightfoot, and Moreau—will each conduct one information session at a community center. Each nurse's session will fall on a different day. The nurses' schedule is governed by the following constraints:

  At least two of the other nurses' sessions must fall in between Heany's session and Moreau's session.
  Griseldi's session must be on the day before Khan's.
  Juarez's session must be on a later day than Moreau's.
  Farnham's session must be on an earlier day than Khan's but on a later day than Lightfoot's.
  Lightfoot cannot conduct the session on the 2nd.

21. If Khan's session is on an earlier day than Moreau's, which one of the following could conduct the session on the 3rd?

(A) Griseldi →

(B) Heany →

(C) Juarez →

(D) Lightfoot →

(E) Moreau →

PrepTest61 Sec3 Q21

HINT: How is the new condition in this question stem different from the one in question 20? What will you do differently in your notes?

New-"If"/Must Be True Question

Question 22 is another New-"If" question.

LSAT Question	My Analysis
From the 1st through the 7th of next month, seven nurses—Farnham, Griseldi, Heany, Juarez, Khan, Lightfoot, and Moreau—will each conduct one information session at a community center. Each nurse's session will fall on a different day. The nurses' schedule is governed by the following constraints: At least two of the other nurses' sessions must fall in between Heany's session and Moreau's session. Griseldi's session must be on the day before Khan's. Juarez's session must be on a later day than Moreau's. Farnham's session must be on an earlier day than Khan's but on a later day than Lightfoot's. Lightfoot cannot conduct the session on the 2nd.	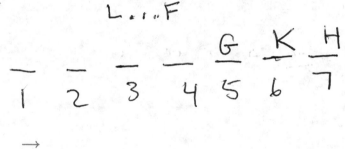

22. If Griseldi's session is on the 5th, then which one of the following must be true?

$$L \cdots F$$
$$\underline{}\ \underline{}\ \underline{}\ \underline{}\ \underline{G}\ \underline{K}\ \underline{H}$$
$$1 \quad 2 \quad 3 \quad 4 \quad 5 \quad 6 \quad 7$$

→

  (A)   Farnham's session is on the 3rd.   →

  (B)   Heany's session is on the 7th.   →

  (C)   Juarez's session is on the 4th.   →

  (D)   Lightfoot's session is on the 1st.   →

  (E)   Moreau's session is on the 2nd.   →

PrepTest61 Sec3 Q22

HINT: What is the characteristic of the one correct answer? How about the characteristics of the four wrong answers?

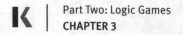

Could Be True Question

This next question is a Could be True question.

LSAT Question	My Analysis
From the 1st through the 7th of next month, seven nurses—Farnham, Griseldi, Heany, Juarez, Khan, Lightfoot, and Moreau—will each conduct one information session at a community center. Each nurse's session will fall on a different day. The nurses' schedule is governed by the following constraints:	

From the 1st through the 7th of next month, seven nurses—Farnham, Griseldi, Heany, Juarez, Khan, Lightfoot, and Moreau—will each conduct one information session at a community center. Each nurse's session will fall on a different day. The nurses' schedule is governed by the following constraints:

At least two of the other nurses' sessions must fall in between Heany's session and Moreau's session.
Griseldi's session must be on the day before Khan's.
Juarez's session must be on a later day than Moreau's.
Farnham's session must be on an earlier day than Khan's but on a later day than Lightfoot's.
Lightfoot cannot conduct the session on the 2nd.

→

F G H J K L M

1	2	3	4	5	6	7
~K	~L	~K	~L	~L	~L	~L
~G	~K	~G	~K		~F	~F
~F	~G					~G
~J						~M

```
                    J
H/M ___ ___ ... M/H

        J

L...F... G K
```

23. Lightfoot's session could be on which one of the following days?

→   1 or 3

(A) the 3rd

→

(B) the 4th

→

(C) the 5th

→

(D) the 6th

→

(E) the 7th

PrepTest61 Sec3 Q23   →

HINT: Where can you find help in answering this question? What alternative approaches are available to determine the correct answer or eliminate incorrect answers?

Back to Question 19

As you completed the other questions in this set, you were able to eliminate three of the wrong answers in question 19.

LSAT Question	My Analysis

From the 1st through the 7th of next month, seven nurses—Farnham, Griseldi, Heany, Juarez, Khan, Lightfoot, and Moreau—will each conduct one information session at a community center. Each nurse's session will fall on a different day. The nurses' schedule is governed by the following constraints:

- At least two of the other nurses' sessions must fall in between Heany's session and Moreau's session.
- Griseldi's session must be on the day before Khan's.
- Juarez's session must be on a later day than Moreau's.
- Farnham's session must be on an earlier day than Khan's but on a later day than Lightfoot's.
- Lightfoot cannot conduct the session on the 2nd.

F G H J K L M

1	2	3	4	5	6	7
~K	~L	~K	~L	~L	~L	~L
~G	~K	~G	~K		~F	~F
~F	~G					~G
~J						~M

H/M __ __ ... M/H

L...F... G K

19. Juarez's session CANNOT be on which one of the following days?

Rule 3 eliminates Juarez from day 1, but that doesn't help with any of the answer choices.

(A) the 2nd

Question 22 proved that Juarez could be second. Eliminate.

(B) the 3rd

Question 20 proved that Juarez could be third. Eliminate.

(C) the 5th

(D) the 6th

(E) the 7th

PrepTest61 Sec3 Q19

Question 21 proved that Juarez could be seventh. Eliminate.

HINT: How many of the remaining answers will you need to check before completing the question?

1

J cant be 5th

H/M	L	F	H/M	J	G	K
1	2	3	4	5	6	7

L F G K J H M

L...F
H...M

Perform

Fill in the blanks below, listing the steps and strategies associated with the Logic Games Method.

Kaplan Logic Games Method

Step 1: _____

    → 4 questions to ask before Step 2

- •
- •
- •
- •

Step 2: _____

Step 3: _____

Step 4: _____

    → 6 things to look for before Step 5

- •
- •
- •
- •
- •
- • Note any unused entities known as _____

Step 5: _____

Logic Games Questions

What is the strategy for Acceptability questions?

_____

What is the strategy for Must Be/Could Be questions?

_____

What is the strategy for New-"If" questions?

_____

Perform—Answer Key

Kaplan Logic Games Method

Step 1: _Overview_

→ 4 questions to ask before Step 2

- **_Situation_**
- **_Entities_**
- **_Action_**
- **_Limitations_**

Step 2: _Sketch_

Step 3: _Rules_

Step 4: _Deductions_

→ 6 things to look for before Step 5

- **_Blocks of Entities_**
- **_Limited Options_**
- **_Established Entities_**
- **_Numbers_**
- **_Duplication_**
- Note any unused entities known as **_Floaters_**

Step 5: _Questions_

Logic Games Questions

What is the strategy for Acceptability questions?

Go rule by rule to eliminate each answer choice that violates a rule.

What is the strategy for Must Be/Could Be questions?

Consult the Master Sketch to see if the question can be answered immediately. If not, use sketches from New-"If"s, as well as the Acceptability question correct answer, to eliminate answers. The sketch from a New-"If" could also help pick a Could Be True answer. If multiple answer choices still remain use trial and error.

What is the strategy for New-"If" questions?

Draw a new sketch that incorporates the new information.

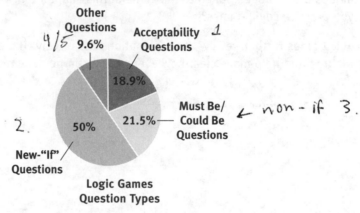

Relative Frequency of Logic Games Question Types

Other Questions 9.6%   4/5

Acceptability Questions   1

18.9%

Must Be/ Could Be Questions   ← non-if 3.

21.5%

50%   2.

New-"If" Questions

Logic Games Question Types

PrepTests 66–80; released 2012–2016

REFLECTION

Now that you've seen the Logic Games Method, take a few minutes to reflect on the following questions:

- What is the purpose of Step 1, and why does an expert always take that step?
- What is the purpose of Step 2, and why does an expert always take that step?
- What is the purpose of Step 3, and why does an expert always take that step?
- What is the purpose of Step 4, and why does an expert always take that step?
- What is the purpose of Step 5, and why does an expert always take that step?
- Did any part of the Logic Games Method surprise you?
- Are there specific steps in the Logic Games Method that excite you?
- Were any of the steps confusing? How will you get additional practice with those steps?
- How will you approach Logic Games differently the next time you practice them?
- What techniques did you see applied to the game in this chapter that you can immediately put to use the next time you practice Logic Games?

As you practice Logic Games further, review the explanations thoroughly. The explanations will cover each step in the Logic Games Method and help make clear how every game can be done most efficiently and effectively.

How an LSAT Expert Sees It

Step 1: Overview

From the 1st through the 7th of next month, seven nurses—
Farnham, Griseldi, Heany, Juarez, Khan, Lightfoot, and
Moreau—will each conduct one information session at
a community center. Each nurse's session will fall on a
different day. The nurses' schedule is governed by the
following constraints:

PrepTest61 Sec3 Qs 18–23

What is this game's **Situation?** *A schedule of nursing information sessions over the course of a week*

What **Entities** are involved in this game? *The nurses—F, G, H, J, K, L, and M*

What is this game's **Action?** *Sequencing: Determine the order of nurses' sessions*

Are there any **Limitations** to this game? *One nurse per day*

Step 2: Sketch

In this Sequencing game, the order of the sessions matters. Create a sketch of seven horizontal dashes. The earliest session will be day 1, the latest will be day 7. When the placement of nurses is determined, that information can be added directly to the sketch.

```
F G H J K L M

___ ___ ___ ___ ___ ___ ___
 1   2   3   4   5   6   7
```

Step 3: Rules

Rule 1: At least two of the other nurses' sessions must fall in between Heany's session and Moreau's session.

Can the information in this rule be placed directly into the sketch? NO

H/M __ __ . . . M/H
Or
H __ __ . . . M or M __ __ . . . H

Rule 2: Griseldi's session must be on the day before Khan's.

Can the information in this rule be placed directly into the sketch? NO

G̲ K̲

Rule 3: Juarez's session must be on a later day than Moreau's.

Can the information in this rule be placed directly into the sketch? NO

M . . . J

Rule 4: Farnham's session must be on an earlier day than Khan's but on a later day than Lightfoot's.

Can the information in this rule be placed directly into the sketch? NO

L . . . F . . . K

Rule 5: Lightfoot cannot conduct the session on the 2nd.

Can the information in this rule be placed directly into the sketch? YES

```
F G H J K L M

___ ___ ___ ___ ___ ___ ___
 1   2   3   4   5   6   7
    ~L
```

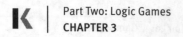

How an LSAT Expert Sees It

Step 4: Deductions

LSAT Question	Analysis

From the 1st through the 7th of next month, seven nurses—Farnham, Griseldi, Heany, Juarez, Khan, Lightfoot, and Moreau—will each conduct one information session at a community center. Each nurse's session will fall on a different day. The nurses' schedule is governed by the following constraints:
 	
At least two of the other nurses' sessions must fall in between Heany's session and Moreau's session.
Griseldi's session must be on the day before Khan's.
Juarez's session must be on a later day than Moreau's.
Farnham's session must be on an earlier day than Khan's but on a later day than Lightfoot's.
Lightfoot cannot conduct the session on the 2nd.
PrepTest61 Sec3 Qs 18–23
	F G H J K L M
	
	__ __ __ __ __ __ __
	 1 2 3 4 5 6 7
	    ~L
	
	→ H/M __ __ ... M/H
	
	     G K
	
	M ... J
	
	L ... F ... K

Deductions:

Duplication: Rules 1 and 3 share Moreau.

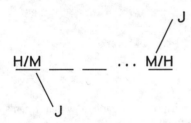

Duplication: Rules 2 and 4 share Khan.

L ... F ... G K

Deductions (cont.)

The string created by combining Rules 2 and 4 restricts four entities: L, F, G, and K. Given the order in the string, it has strong negative implications: K cannot conduct a session on days 1, 2, or 3; G cannot conduct a session on days 1, 2, or 7; F cannot conduct a session on days 1, 6, or 7; and L cannot conduct a session on days 5, 6, or 7 (and is forbidden already by Rule 5 from conducting a session on day 2).

1	2	3	4	5	6	7
~K	~L	~K		~L	~F	~G
~G	~K			~L	~F	
~F	~G				~L	

Rule 3's negative implications can likewise be entered into the sketch.

1	2	3	4	5	6	7
~K	~L	~K		~L	~F	~G
~G	~K			~L	~F	
~F	~G				~L	
~J					~M	

Because the L-F-GK string accounts for four days and because Rule 1 requires at least two days between H and M, it is impossible for either L or K to conduct a session on day 4. If either of them did so, there would be insufficient space for H and M to be properly spaced.

F G H J K L M

1	2	3	4	5	6	7
~K	~L	~K	~L	~L	~L	~L
~G	~K	~G	~K		~F	~F
~F	~G					~G
~J						~M

```
                            J
                           /
  H/M  ___  ___ ... M/H
                    \
                     J
  L...F... G  K
```

Note too, that since K cannot conduct a session on day 4, G cannot conduct a session on day 3. That is your final sketch.

How an LSAT Expert Sees It

Acceptability Question

LSAT Question	Analysis
From the 1st through the 7th of next month, seven nurses—Farnham, Griseldi, Heany, Juarez, Khan, Lightfoot, and Moreau—will each conduct one information session at a community center. Each nurse's session will fall on a different day. The nurses' schedule is governed by the following constraints:	Rule 1 broken by answer choice: **(E)**
	Rule 2 broken by answer choice: **None**
	Rule 3 broken by answer choice: **(C)**
At least two of the other nurses' sessions must fall in between Heany's session and Moreau's session.	→ Rule 4 broken by answer choice: **(A)**
Griseldi's session must be on the day before Khan's.	Rule 5 broken by answer choice: **(B)**
Juarez's session must be on a later day than Moreau's.	
Farnham's session must be on an earlier day than Khan's but on a later day than Lightfoot's.	
Lightfoot cannot conduct the session on the 2nd.	

18. Which one of the following could be the order of the nurses' sessions, from first to last?

(A)	Farnham, Griseldi, Khan, Moreau, Juarez, Lightfoot, Heany	Violates Rule 4. Eliminate.
(B)	Heany, Lightfoot, Farnham, Moreau, Juarez, Griseldi, Khan	Violates Rule 5. Eliminate.
(C)	Juarez, Heany, Lightfoot, Farnham, Moreau, Griseldi, Khan	Violates Rule 3. Eliminate.
(D)	Lightfoot, Moreau, Farnham, Juarez, Griseldi, Khan, Heany	Correct.
(E)	Moreau, Lightfoot, Heany, Juarez, Farnham, Griseldi, Khan	Violates Rule 1. Eliminate.

PrepTest61 Sec3 Q18 →

How an LSAT Expert Sees It
Must Be False Question

Because this question potentially requires testing four of the answers before arriving at the correct answer, the LSAT expert may choose to skip it and complete the rest of the question set. Then, he can check his notes for the remaining questions and eliminate any answer containing a day on which he found it was acceptable for Juarez to conduct a session.

LSAT Question	Analysis
From the 1st through the 7th of next month, seven nurses—Farnham, Griseldi, Heany, Juarez, Khan, Lightfoot, and Moreau—will each conduct one information session at a community center. Each nurse's session will fall on a different day. The nurses' schedule is governed by the following constraints: At least two of the other nurses' sessions must fall in between Heany's session and Moreau's session. Griseldi's session must be on the day before Khan's. Juarez's session must be on a later day than Moreau's. Farnham's session must be on an earlier day than Khan's but on a later day than Lightfoot's. Lightfoot cannot conduct the session on the 2nd.	F G H J K L M ___ ___ ___ ___ ___ ___ ___ J 1 2 3 4 5 6 7 / ~K ~L ~K ~L ~L ~L ~L H/M ___ ___ ... M/H ~G ~K ~G ~K ~F ~F \\ ~F ~G ~G J ~J ~M L...F... _G_ _K_
19. Juarez's session CANNOT be on which one of the following days?	Rule 3 eliminates Juarez from day 1, but that doesn't help with any of the answer choices.
(A) the 2nd	M-J-L-F-H-G-K and M-J-L-H-F-G-K are acceptable. Eliminate. Question 22 also proves that Juarez could be second.
(B) the 3rd	L-M-J-F-H-G-K is acceptable. Eliminate. Question 20 also proves that Juarez could be third.
(C) the 5th	Correct.
(D) the 6th	L-F-M-G-K-J-H and L-M-F-G-K-J-H are acceptable. Eliminate.
(E) the 7th *PrepTest61 Sec3 Q19*	L-H-F-G-K-M-J, L-F-H-G-K-M-J, L-M-F-G-K-H-J, and L-F-M-G-K-H-J are all acceptable. Eliminate. Question 21 also proves that Juarez could be seventh.

How an LSAT Expert Sees It
New-"If"/Could Be True Question

LSAT Question	Analysis

From the 1st through the 7th of next month, seven nurses—Farnham, Griseldi, Heany, Juarez, Khan, Lightfoot, and Moreau—will each conduct one information session at a community center. Each nurse's session will fall on a different day. The nurses' schedule is governed by the following constraints:

At least two of the other nurses' sessions must fall in between Heany's session and Moreau's session.

Griseldi's session must be on the day before Khan's.

Juarez's session must be on a later day than Moreau's.

Farnham's session must be on an earlier day than Khan's but on a later day than Lightfoot's.

Lightfoot cannot conduct the session on the 2nd.

→

F G H J K L M

1	2	3	4	5	6	7
~K	~L	~K	~L	~L	~L	~L
~G	~K	~G	~K		~F	~F
~F	~G					~G
~J						~M

```
          J
          /
H/M ___ ___ ... M/H
   /
  J
L...F... G K
```

---

20. If Juarez's session is on the 3rd, then which one of the following could be true?

→

Redraw the Master Sketch, and add J to spot 3:

___ ___ J ___ ___ ___ ___

With J placed, Rule 3 forces M into day 1 or 2. And, according to Rule 1, H must go at least 3 days later than M, and so, later than J. Now, work in the L-F-GK string. L must go earlier than J, but can't take day 2 (Rule 5), and so must take day 1. To obey Rule 1, F must take day 4. So, there are two possible arrangements.

L M J F H G K

L M J F G K H

(A)	Moreau's session is on the 1st.	→	Must be false. Moreau takes day 2. Eliminate.
(B)	Khan's session is on the 5th.	→	Must be false. Khan takes day 6 or 7. Eliminate.
(C)	Heany's session is on the 6th.	→	Must be false. Heany takes day 5 or 7. Eliminate.
(D)	Griseldi's session is on the 5th.	→	Correct.
(E)	Farnham's session is on the 2nd.	→	Must be false. Farnham takes day 4. Eliminate.

PrepTest61 Sec3 Q20

Note that, in this question's sketch, J can acceptably conduct a session on day 3. Return to question 19 and eliminate **(B)**.

How an LSAT Expert Sees It
New-"If"/Could Be True Question

LSAT Question	Analysis

From the 1st through the 7th of next month, seven nurses—Farnham, Griseldi, Heany, Juarez, Khan, Lightfoot, and Moreau—will each conduct one information session at a community center. Each nurse's session will fall on a different day. The nurses' schedule is governed by the following constraints:

F G H J K L M

1	2	3	4	5	6	7
~K	~L	~K	~L	~L	~L	~L
~G	~K	~G	~K		~F	~F
~F	~G					~G
~J						~M

H/M ___ ___ ... M/H (J top right)

J (below H/M arrow)

L...F... <u>G</u> <u>K</u>

At least two of the other nurses' sessions must fall in between Heany's session and Moreau's session.
Griseldi's session must be on the day before Khan's.
Juarez's session must be on a later day than Moreau's.
Farnham's session must be on an earlier day than Khan's but on a later day than Lightfoot's.
Lightfoot cannot conduct the session on the 2nd.

---

21. If Khan's session is on an earlier day than Moreau's, which one of the following could conduct the session on the 3rd?

Deductions:

Adding the new info to the L-F-GK string produces:

L . . . F . . . GK . . . M . . . J

The only entity not accounted for is H, which must be separated from M by at least two days (Rule 1).

<u>L</u> <u>H/F</u> <u>F/H</u> <u>G</u> <u>K</u> <u>M</u> <u>J</u>
~L

The correct answer could be true, while the four wrong answer choices all must be false under these conditions.

(A) Griseldi — Must be on day 4. Eliminate.

(B) Heany — Correct.

(C) Juarez — Must be on day 7. Eliminate.

(D) Lightfoot — Must be on day 1. Eliminate.

(E) Moreau — Must be on day 6. Eliminate.

PrepTest61 Sec3 Q21

Note that, in this New-"If" sketch, J can conduct a session on day 7. Return to question 19 and eliminate **(E)**.

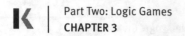

How an LSAT Expert Sees It
New-"If"/Must Be True Question

LSAT Question	Analysis

From the 1st through the 7th of next month, seven nurses—Farnham, Griseldi, Heany, Juarez, Khan, Lightfoot, and Moreau—will each conduct one information session at a community center. Each nurse's session will fall on a different day. The nurses' schedule is governed by the following constraints:

At least two of the other nurses' sessions must fall in between Heany's session and Moreau's session.

Griseldi's session must be on the day before Khan's.

Juarez's session must be on a later day than Moreau's.

Farnham's session must be on an earlier day than Khan's but on a later day than Lightfoot's.

Lightfoot cannot conduct the session on the 2nd.

F G H J K L M

1	2	3	4	5	6	7
~K	~L	~K	~L	~L	~L	~L
~G	~K	~G	~K		~F	~F
~F	~G					~G
~J						~M

H/M __ __ ... M/H

J ↘ ↙ J

L ... F ... G K

---

22. If Griseldi's session is on the 5th, then which one of the following must be true?

Placing G on day 5 affects the L-F-GK string.

L ... F ...

__ __ __ __ *G* K __
~L

Now, which of H, J, or M could take day 7? Not M (Rule 3). And not J, because either H and M would run afoul of Rule 1, or L would violate Rule 5. So, H takes day 7.

M ... J ...
L ... F ...

__ __ __ __ *G* K H
~L

(A)	Farnham's session is on the 3rd.	Could be false—F could take days 2 or 4. Eliminate.
(B)	Heany's session is on the 7th.	Correct.
(C)	Juarez's session is on the 4th.	Could be false—J could take days 2 or 3. Eliminate.
(D)	Lightfoot's session is on the 1st.	Could be false—L could take day 3. Eliminate.
(E)	Moreau's session is on the 2nd.	Could be false—M could take days 1 or 3. Eliminate.

PrepTest61 Sec3 Q22

Note that, in this New-"If" sketch, J can teach session 2. Return to question 19 and eliminate **(A)**.

How an LSAT Expert Sees It
Could Be True Question

LSAT Question	Analysis

From the 1st through the 7th of next month, seven nurses—Farnham, Griseldi, Heany, Juarez, Khan, Lightfoot, and Moreau—will each conduct one information session at a community center. Each nurse's session will fall on a different day. The nurses' schedule is governed by the following constraints:

At least two of the other nurses' sessions must fall in between Heany's session and Moreau's session.

Griseldi's session must be on the day before Khan's.

Juarez's session must be on a later day than Moreau's.

Farnham's session must be on an earlier day than Khan's but on a later day than Lightfoot's.

Lightfoot cannot conduct the session on the 2nd.

F G H J K L M

1	2	3	4	5	6	7
~K	~L	~K	~L	~L	~L	~L
~G	~K	~G	~K		~F	~F
~F	~G					~G
~J						~M

H/M ___ ___ ... M/H

J

L...F... G K

23. Lightfoot's session could be on which one of the following days?

You know from the Master Sketch that Lightfoot cannot conduct a session on day 4, 5, 6, or 7. That leaves only one possibility among the answer choices.

(A) the 3rd — Correct.

(B) the 4th — Must be false. Eliminate.

(C) the 5th — Must be false. Eliminate.

(D) the 6th — Must be false. Eliminate.

(E) the 7th — Must be false. Eliminate.

PrepTest61 Sec3 Q23

This question illustrates the value of making all available deductions in Step 4. With the complete Master Sketch in place, answering this question correctly takes only a few seconds.

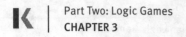

How an LSAT Expert Sees It
Could Be True Question

LSAT Question	Analysis

From the 1st through the 7th of next month, seven nurses—Farnham, Griseldi, Heany, Juarez, Khan, Lightfoot, and Moreau—will each conduct one information session at a community center. Each nurse's session will fall on a different day. The nurses' schedule is governed by the following constraints:

   At least two of the other nurses' sessions must fall in between Heany's session and Moreau's session.
   Griseldi's session must be on the day before Khan's.
   Juarez's session must be on a later day than Moreau's.
   Farnham's session must be on an earlier day than Khan's but on a later day than Lightfoot's.
   Lightfoot cannot conduct the session on the 2nd.

→

F G H J K L M

1	2	3	4	5	6	7
~K	~L	~K	~L	~L	~L	~L
~G	~K	~G	~K		~F	~F
~F	~G					~G
~J						~M

H/M ___ ___ . . . M/H ⟍J (J above right)

L . . . F . . . <u>G K</u>

---

19. Juarez's session CANNOT be on which one of the following days?

→ Rule 3 eliminates Juarez from day 1, but that doesn't help with any of the answer choices.

(A) the 2nd

→ Question 22 proved that Juarez could be second. Eliminate.

(B) the 3rd

→ Question 20 proved that Juarez could be third. Eliminate.

(C) the 5th

→ Correct—must be false. With J on day 5, a problem arises for the GK block. If G and K take days 6 and 7, H and M would need to take days 1 and 4, but that violates Rule 5 by placing L on day 2.

H/M ~~2~~ F M/H J G K

If the L-F-GK string takes days 1–4, H and M are forced to take days 6 and 7, violating Rule 1.

<u>L</u> <u>F</u> <u>G</u> <u>K</u> <u>J</u> <u>H/M͛M/H</u> (crossed out)

(D) the 6th

→ For the record: L-F-M-G-K-J-H and L-M-F-G-K-J-H are acceptable. Eliminate.

(E) the 7th

PrepTest61 Sec3 Q19

→ Question 21 also proved that Juarez could be seventh. Eliminate.

The LSAT expert is finished with the questions in this set and is ready to confidently move on to the next game or the next section.

CHAPTER 4

Logic Game Types

LOGIC GAME TYPES

Prepare

GAME TYPE ACTIONS

In this section, you'll learn to apply the Logic Games Method to games of the following types:

- Strict Sequencing: Ordering entities with respect to defined positions
- Loose Sequencing: Ordering entities with respect to each other
- Selection: Choosing a small group out of a large group
- Matching: Matching two kinds of entities to each other
- Distribution: Forming several small groups out of a large group
- Hybrid: Performing two or more of the other actions

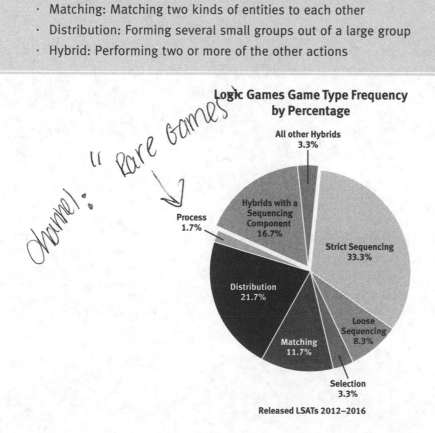

Logic Games Game Type Frequency by Percentage

All other Hybrids 3.3%

Hybrids with a Sequencing Component 16.7%

Strict Sequencing 33.3%

Process 1.7%

Distribution 21.7%

Matching 11.7%

Loose Sequencing 8.3%

Selection 3.3%

Released LSATs 2012–2016

(handwritten annotation: Channel: "Rare Games")

111

...ns that inform how we make sketches: Sequencing (putting entities in order); ...es and rejecting others); Matching (matching attributes to entities); and Distribution ...ketches should be easy to read and understand, quick to replicate, and able to

As you practice Logic Games, develop and maintain a library of common sketch formats for each game type. There are a limited number of game actions and basic sketch templates that are useful time after time.

Here are the basic sketches we recommend for each standard game action. Your individual sketches may vary, of course, but the examples here provide a tested foundation that should be useful for all test takers.

Strict Sequencing Games

Six magnetic letters—A, B, C, D, E, and F—are arranged from left to right by a child on a refrigerator. Each letter is used exactly once. The following conditions apply:

A is immediately to the left of B.
Exactly two letters separate C and D.

A B C D E F
— — — — — —
1 2 3 4 5 6

Loose Sequencing Games

Eight kickballers—A, B, C, D, E, F, G, and H—are sequenced for their position in a kicking order. Each kickballer appears in the order exactly once. The following conditions apply:

A is before B and C.
E is after B.
Both F and G are after C
F is before D.
G is after H.

Selection Games

A cook selects which of seven ingredients—A, B, C, D, E, F, and G—she'll use in her recipe. The following conditions apply:

If C is chosen, then G is chosen.
If A or B is chosen, then E is chosen.
If A is not chosen, C is chosen.
If D is chosen, then F is chosen.
E is not chosen.

A teacher chooses 4 of 6 books—A, B, C, D, E, and F—to put on a summer reading list for his students. The following conditions apply:

> B is not selected unless A is selected.
> If B is selected, then D is selected.
> F is selected only if E is not selected.
> If A is selected, then E is selected.

For Selection games defining a specific number of entities, some test takers prefer:

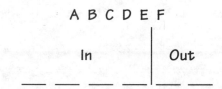

Matching Games

Six students—A, B, C, D, E, and F—each are learning between one and three new languages—X, Y, and Z. The following conditions apply:

> Anyone who learns X learns Y.
>
> ...

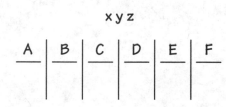

	A	B	C	D	E	F
x						
y						
z						

Distribution Games

Seven pieces of jewelry—L, M, N, O, P, R, and S—are each distributed among three different safes—1, 2, and 3. Each piece of jewelry is in exactly one safe, and each safe contains at least two pieces of jewelry. The following conditions apply:

> Safe 3 contains more pieces of jewelry than safe 2.
>
> ...

```
L M N O P R S
 1    2    3
___  ___  ___

___  ___  ___

          ___
```

Sequencing/Matching Hybrid Games

Six rodent enthusiasts—A, B, C, D, E, and F—are placed in order for a pet exhibition. Each enthusiast will show either a gerbil or a hamster. Each enthusiast shows exactly one animal. The following conditions apply:

> A will show an animal before B.
> D shows a hamster.
> Two gerbils are shown after E.

```
___ ___ ___ ___ ___ ___   A B C D E F

___ ___ ___ ___ ___ ___   g/h
 1   2   3   4   5   6
```

Sequencing Games

Prepare and Practice

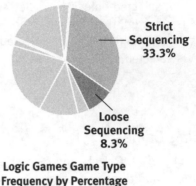

Strict
Sequencing
33.3%

Loose
Sequencing
8.3%

**Logic Games Game Type
Frequency by Percentage**

PrepTests 66–80; released 2012–2016

LEARNING OBJECTIVES
In this section, you'll learn to: · Apply the Logic Games Method to Sequencing games

---

Sequencing games are far and away the most common type of game on the LSAT. There are many variations on how Sequencing games can look. Here are sample overviews along with a possible rule or two that could accompany that type of setup.

STRICT

Six singers—A, B, C, D, E, and F—perform solos during a competition. Each singer performs exactly once. The following conditions apply:

A performs immediately before B.

C does not perform 4th.

Alejandro receives seven text messages, and each message is from exactly one of five people—G, H, I, J, and K. He receives at least one text message from each person. The order of the messages conforms to the following conditions:

Any message Alejandro receives from G is immediately preceded by a message from H.

A game show has six different prizes—L, M, N, O, P, and Q—behind one of four doors labeled in order 1, 2, 3, and 4. No door has more than two prizes behind it. The following conditions apply:

L is behind an earlier door than M.

O and P are behind consecutive doors.

LOOSE

Six hiking trails—R, S, T, U, W, and X—are ranked by an outdoor magazine from best to worst. Each hiking trail receives a different rank. The following conditions apply:

R is ranked lower than U and X.

T and W are ranked higher than U.

S is ranked lower than T.

Eight knights—A, B, C, D, E, F, G, and H—are seated around a circular table. Each of the eight chairs around the table are spaced evenly and occupied by exactly one of the knights. Each chair is directly across from another chair. The following conditions apply:

A and D sit directly across from one another.

F does not sit on either side of A.

Lena is thinking about switching up her morning routine. Each morning she has to complete five tasks—J, K, L, M, and N. This week on Monday, Tuesday, and Wednesday, she'll try out a different sequence of accomplishing those tasks. The following conditions apply:

Lena does L earlier than N all three days.

Lena does not do the same activity in the same position on consecutive days.

Jerome is scheduling six appointments with six clients—O, P, Q, R, S, and T. He'll have a morning, afternoon, and evening appointment on each of Saturday and Sunday. In each appointment he'll meet with only one client. The following conditions apply:

Jerome meets with Q in the afternoon.

Jerome meets with S and T on the same day.

Rules in Sequencing Games

Sequencing games are, by far, the most common games on recent LSATs. The testmaker uses several variati[on]
Sequencing, so practice with the rules of these games is essential to Logic Games mastery.

Deductions in Sequencing Games

As you practice, take note of the types of rules and restrictions that tend to produce deductions most often in various game types. Here are the most likely sources of deductions in Sequencing games.

...ns on

...mily law, health law,
...es, and tax law. The
...e floors—the bottom
...oor. Each floor can
..., and no department is to
...nt of departments to
floors is subj... ...straints:

Probate must be on the ... floor as tax law.
Health law must be on the floor immediately above injury
 law.
Labor law must occupy an entire floor by itself.

BMT

: up to 4

FHILPST

~~RPLT~~ P & T together

~~FHMP~~ H'I

116-121   L alone

dont go past 121

B	M	T
L	P	H
	T	F
	I	S

1. Which one of the following could be the assignment of
   departments to floors?

   (A) top floor: labor law
        middle floor: injury law, probate, tax law
        bottom floor: family law, health law, securities
   (B) top floor: family law, health law, probate
        middle floor: injury law, securities, tax law
        bottom floor: labor law
   (C) top floor: health law, probate, tax law
        middle floor: family law, injury law, securities
        bottom floor: labor law
   (D) top floor: health law, probate, tax law
        middle floor: injury law, securities
        bottom floor: family law, labor law
   (E) top floor: family law, health law, probate, tax law
        middle floor: labor law
        bottom floor: injury law, securities

GO ON TO THE NEXT PAGE.

116

2. If injury law and probate are both assigned to the middle floor, which one of the following could be true?

(A) Family law is assigned to the middle floor.
(B) Health law is assigned to the middle floor.
(C) Labor law is assigned to the top floor.
(D) Securities is assigned to the bottom floor.
(E) Tax law is assigned to the top floor.

3. Which one of the following CANNOT be the assignment for any of the floors?

(A) family law, health law, probate, and tax law
(B) family law, injury law, probate, and tax law
(C) family law, probate, securities, and tax law
(D) health law, probate, securities, and tax law
(E) injury law, probate, securities, and tax law

4. If family law is assigned to the same floor as securities, which one of the following could be true?

(A) Exactly one department is assigned to the middle floor.
(B) Exactly four departments are assigned to the middle floor.
(C) Exactly two departments are assigned to the bottom floor.
(D) Exactly three departments are assigned to the bottom floor.
(E) Exactly four departments are assigned to the bottom floor.

5. If probate is assigned to the middle floor along with exactly two other departments, then which one of the following must be true?

(A) Family law is assigned to the floor immediately above health law.
(B) Family law is assigned to the floor immediately below labor law.
(C) Family law is assigned to the same floor as securities.
(D) Probate is assigned to the same floor as health law.
(E) Probate is assigned to the same floor as injury law.

Preptest59 Sec1 Qs 1–5

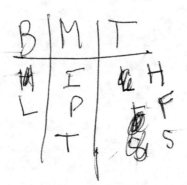

Questions 6–10

A museum curator is arranging seven photographs—*Fence, Gardenias, Hibiscus, Irises, Katydid, Lotus,* and *Magnolia*—on a gallery wall in accordance with the photographer's requirements. The photographs are to be hung along the wall in a row, in seven positions sequentially numbered from first to seventh. The photographer's requirements are as follows:

Gardenias must be immediately before *Katydid*.
Hibiscus must be somewhere before *Katydid* but cannot be the first photograph.
Irises and *Lotus* must be next to one another.
Magnolia must be one of the first three photographs.
Fence must be either first or seventh.

6. Which one of the following could be the positions, from first to seventh, in which the photographs are hung?

(A) Fence, Hibiscus, Gardenias, Magnolia, Katydid, Irises, Lotus
(B) Hibiscus, Magnolia, Gardenias, Katydid, Irises, Lotus, Fence
(C) Irises, Lotus, Magnolia, Hibiscus, Gardenias, Katydid, Fence
(D) Lotus, Magnolia, Irises, Hibiscus, Gardenias, Katydid, Fence
(E) Magnolia, Fence, Hibiscus, Gardenias, Katydid, Lotus, Irises

GO ON TO THE NEXT PAGE.

F G H I K L M

7. If *Irises* is immediately before *Gardenias*, which one of the following could be true?

   (A) *Gardenias* is fourth.
   (B) *Hibiscus* is fourth.
   (C) *Irises* is third.
   (D) *Lotus* is second.
   (E) *Magnolia* is third.

8. Where each photograph is hung is fully determined if which one of the following is true?

   (A) *Gardenias* is fourth.
   (B) *Hibiscus* is second.
   (C) *Irises* is second.
   (D) *Lotus* is first.
   (E) *Magnolia* is third.

9. If *Magnolia* is second, which one of the following CANNOT be true?

   (A) *Hibiscus* is third.
   (B) *Hibiscus* is fourth.
   (C) *Hibiscus* is fifth.
   (D) *Gardenias* is fourth.
   (E) *Gardenias* is sixth.

10. Which one of the following, if substituted for the condition that *Hibiscus* must be hung somewhere before *Katydid* but cannot be the first photograph, would have the same effect in determining the arrangement of the photographs?

    (A) If *Fence* is seventh, *Hibiscus* is second.
    (B) *Gardenias* is somewhere after *Hibiscus*, and either *Fence* or *Magnolia* is first.
    (C) *Hibiscus* must be somewhere between the first and sixth photographs.
    (D) Unless *Hibiscus* is second, it must be somewhere between *Magnolia* and *Gardenias*.
    (E) *Katydid* is somewhere after *Hibiscus*, which must be somewhere after *Fence*.

    PrepTest59 Sec1 Qs 6–10

Questions 11–15

On a particular Saturday, a student will perform six activities—grocery shopping, hedge trimming, jogging, kitchen cleaning, laundry, and motorbike servicing. Each activity will be performed once, one at a time. The order in which the activities are performed is subject to the following conditions:

Grocery shopping has to be immediately after hedge trimming.

Kitchen cleaning has to be earlier than grocery shopping.

Motorbike servicing has to be earlier than laundry.

Motorbike servicing has to be either immediately before or immediately after jogging.

11. Which one of the following could be the order, from first to last, of the student's activities?

(A) jogging, kitchen cleaning, hedge trimming, grocery shopping, motorbike servicing, laundry

(B) jogging, motorbike servicing, laundry, hedge trimming, grocery shopping, kitchen cleaning

(C) kitchen cleaning, hedge trimming, grocery shopping, laundry, motorbike servicing, jogging

(D) kitchen cleaning, jogging, motorbike servicing, laundry, hedge trimming, grocery shopping

(E) motorbike servicing, jogging, laundry, hedge trimming, kitchen cleaning, grocery shopping

GO ON TO THE NEXT PAGE.

G H J K L M

__ __ __ __ __ __
1 2 3 4 5 6

K...GH   K...G

M...L

JM or MJ

12. Which one of the following activities CANNOT be third?

    (A) grocery shopping
    (B) hedge trimming
    (C) jogging
    (D) kitchen cleaning
    (E) motorbike servicing

13. Which one of the following CANNOT be true?

    (A) Hedge trimming is fourth.
    (B) Jogging is fourth.
    (C) Kitchen cleaning is second.
    (D) Laundry is third.
    (E) Motorbike servicing is second.

14. Which one of the following activities CANNOT be fifth?

    (A) grocery shopping
    (B) hedge trimming
    (C) jogging
    (D) laundry
    (E) motorbike servicing

15. Which one of the following, if substituted for the condition that motorbike servicing has to be earlier than laundry, would have the same effect in determining the order of the student's activities?

    (A) Laundry has to be one of the last three activities.
    (B) Laundry has to be either immediately before or immediately after jogging.
    (C) Jogging has to be earlier than laundry.
    (D) Laundry has to be earlier than hedge trimming.
    (E) Laundry has to be earlier than jogging.

PrepTest57 Sec1 Qs 1–5

Questions 16–22

A courier delivers exactly eight parcels—G, H, J, K, L, M, N, and O. No two parcels are delivered at the same time, nor is any parcel delivered more than once. The following conditions must apply:

L is delivered later than H. ✓
K is delivered earlier than O. ✓
H is delivered earlier than M. ✓
O is delivered later than G. ✓
M is delivered earlier than G. ✓
Both N and J are delivered earlier than M. ✓

16. Which one of the following could be the order of deliveries from first to last?

(A) N, H, K, M, J, G, O, L
(B) H, N, J, K, G, O, L, M
(C) J, H, N, M, K, O, G, L
(D) N, J, H, L, M, K, G, O
(E) K, N, J, M, G, H, O, L

GO ON TO THE NEXT PAGE.

H, N, J, K could be first, 2nd, 3rd, 4th
O, L could be last

L could be 3rd

Highest G could be is 5th

M could be 4th

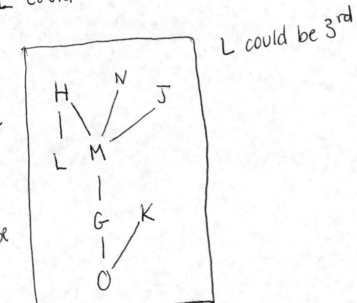

EX: A before B or before C but NOT both

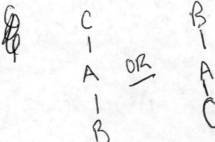

C
|
A   OR
|
B

B
|
A
|
C

← Refer to master sketch ↓

17. Which one of the following must be true?

(A) At least one parcel is delivered earlier than K is delivered.
(B) At least two parcels are delivered later than G is delivered.
(C) At least four parcels are delivered later than H is delivered. ✓
(D) At least four parcels are delivered later than J is delivered.
(E) At least four parcels are delivered earlier than M is delivered.

18. If M is the fourth parcel delivered, then which one of the following must be true?

(A) G is the fifth parcel delivered.
(B) O is the seventh parcel delivered.
(C) J is delivered later than H.
(D) K is delivered later than N.
(E) G is delivered later than L.

19. If H is the fourth parcel delivered, then each of the following could be true EXCEPT:

(A) K is the fifth parcel delivered.
(B) L is the sixth parcel delivered.
(C) M is the sixth parcel delivered.
(D) G is the seventh parcel delivered.
(E) O is the seventh parcel delivered.

20. Each of the following could be true EXCEPT:

(A) H is delivered later than K. ✓
(B) J is delivered later than G. ✗
(C) L is delivered later than O.
(D) M is delivered later than L.
(E) N is delivered later than H.

21. If K is the seventh parcel delivered, then each of the following could be true EXCEPT:

(A) G is the fifth parcel delivered. ✓
(B) M is the fifth parcel delivered. ✓
(C) H is the fourth parcel delivered.
(D) L is the fourth parcel delivered.
(E) J is the third parcel delivered.

22. If L is delivered earlier than K, then which one of the following must be false?

(A) N is the second parcel delivered. ✓
(B) L is the third parcel delivered.
(C) H is the fourth parcel delivered.
(D) K is the fifth parcel delivered.
(E) M is the sixth parcel delivered.

PrepTest51 Sec4 Qs 16–22

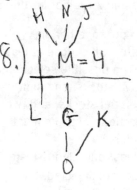

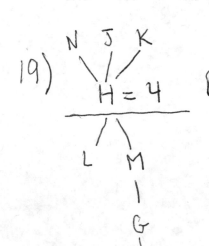

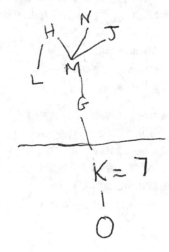

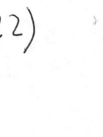

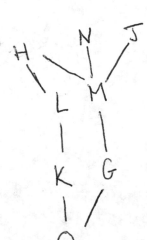

Selection Games

Prepare and Practice

LEARNING OBJECTIVES

In this section, you'll learn to:

· Apply the Logic Games Method to Selection games

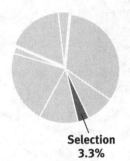

**Selection
3.3%**

**Logic Games Game Type
Frequency by Percentage**

PrepTests 66–80; released 2012–2016

Here are sample overviews of Selection Games along with a possible rule or two that could accompany that setup.

For a game night, the hosts are selecting exactly five of eight games—A, B, C, D, E, F, G, and H—to play with their guests. The selection meets the following restrictions:

If C is played, D is not played.   5/8
If F is not played, G must be played.
A will be played if B is played.

A student is choosing among seven courses—I, J, K, L, M, N, and O—to take during the next semester. The student selects at least one course. The selection of courses must meet the following restrictions:

If K and L are selected, M is not.
The student does not take both N and O.

From among nine food items, a parent picks six to include in his child's lunch. Three of the choices—P, Q, and R—are meats; three—S, T, and U—are fruits; and three—X, Y, and Z—are dairy products. The following conditions apply: 6/9

Exactly two fruits are included in the lunch.
If P is in the lunch, then U and Z are not included.

An investor is picking stocks to put together an investment portfolio. The investor will choose at least three and at most five stocks. The possible selections include three low-risk automotive stocks, one high-risk automotive stock, two low-risk retail stocks, and two high-risk retail stocks. The selection of stocks must conform to the following conditions:

The portfolio includes at least one high-risk stock.
If both low-risk retail stocks are selected, the high-risk automotive stock is also selected.

in   out

— — — — —|— — —

A B C D E F G H

Only works if exact #

Rules in Selection Games

Selection games are less common than Sequencing games and do not appear on every test. Because these games always involve choosing some entities and rejecting others, almost all Selection rules involve conditional Formal Logic statements.

LSAT STRATEGY

Selection rules tell you one or more of the following:

- One entity is dependent on another entity being selected.
- At least one of two entities must be rejected.
- At least one of two entities must be selected.
- Two entities must be selected or rejected as a pair (one cannot be selected or rejected without the other).

Deductions in Selection Games

Because the great majority of Selection rules involve Formal Logic, simply noting the valid contrapositive of each rule is a great source of deductions. Having the contrapositives down also helps you to see which rules trigger others.

LSAT STRATEGY

In Selection games, deductions are likely to stem from:

- **Duplications**—Entities shared by two or more rules; Selection games often feature "chains," or Formal Logic statements that can be linked by shared entities.
- **Numbers Restrictions**—Restrictions or limitations on the number of entities to be selected or determinations of the minimum and maximum numbers that can be selected given the game's rules

In Selection games, deductions may involve:

- **Limited Options**—The situation that arises when a rule specifies only one of two selection patterns is acceptable (e.g., G is selected and F is not selected, or F is selected and G is not selected)
- **Blocks of Entities**—Two or more entities that must be selected or rejected as a pair
- **Established Entities**—Entities that must be selected or rejected; this is very rare in Selection games where all or most rules are conditional; occasionally, the Numbers Restrictions will allow you to determine that a specific entity can never be selected.

Practice and Perform

Questions 23–28

Alicia will take exactly four courses this semester. She must choose from the following seven courses—Geography, Japanese, Macroeconomics, Psychology, Russian, Statistics (which is offered twice, once each on Tuesdays at 9 A.M. and 3 P.M.), and World History. No one is allowed to take any course more than once per semester. Because of university requirements and time conflicts, the following restrictions apply to Alicia's choices:

> She must take Japanese if she does not take Russian.
> She cannot take Japanese if she takes Macroeconomics.
> She cannot take World History if she takes Statistics at 9 A.M.
> She must take Statistics at 9 A.M. if she takes Psychology.
> She must take either Geography or World History but cannot take both.

23. Which one of the following could be the list of the four courses Alicia takes?

(A) Geography, Japanese, Psychology, Russian
(B) Geography, Macroeconomics, Psychology, Statistics
(C) Geography, Japanese, Macroeconomics, Russian
(D) Geography, Psychology, Russian, Statistics
   Macroeconomics, Psychology, Russian, Statistics

GO ON TO THE NEXT PAGE.

PICK (4)

G J M P R S₉ S₃ W   max 1

— — — —

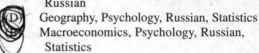

if ~R → J
~J → R

if M → ~J
J → ~M

if S₉ → ~W
W → ~S₉

if P → S₉
~S₉ → ~P

exactly 1 of G/W

Partial acceptability b/c 3 not 4

24. Which one of the following could be an accurate list of three of the courses Alicia takes?

   (A) Geography, Statistics, World History
   (B) Japanese, Macroeconomics, Statistics
   (C) Japanese, Psychology, World History
   (D) Psychology, Russian, World History
   (E) Russian, Statistics, World History

25. Which courses Alicia takes is fully determined if she takes Russian and which one of the following?

   (A) World History
   (B) Statistics
   (C) Psychology
   (D) Macroeconomics
   (E) Japanese

26. Alicia could take Statistics at either of the available times if she takes which one of the following pairs of courses?

   (A) Geography and Japanese
   (B) Geography and Psychology
   (C) Japanese and World History
   (D) Psychology and Russian
   (E) Russian and World History

27. If Alicia takes Statistics at 3 P.M. and Geography, then which one of the following courses must she also take?

   (A) Japanese
   (B) Macroeconomics
   (C) Psychology
   (D) Russian
   (E) World History

28. Suppose that Alicia must take Statistics if she takes Psychology, but rather than being restricted to taking Statistics at 9 A.M. she can take it at either 9 A.M. or at 3 P.M. If all the other restrictions remain the same, then which one of the following could be the list of the four courses Alicia takes?

   (A) Psychology, Russian, Statistics, World History
   (B) Macroeconomics, Psychology, Statistics, World History
   (C) Macroeconomics, Psychology, Russian, World History
   (D) Geography, Psychology, Russian, World History
   (E) Geography, Macroeconomics, Russian, World History

PrepTest59 Sec1 Qs 11–16

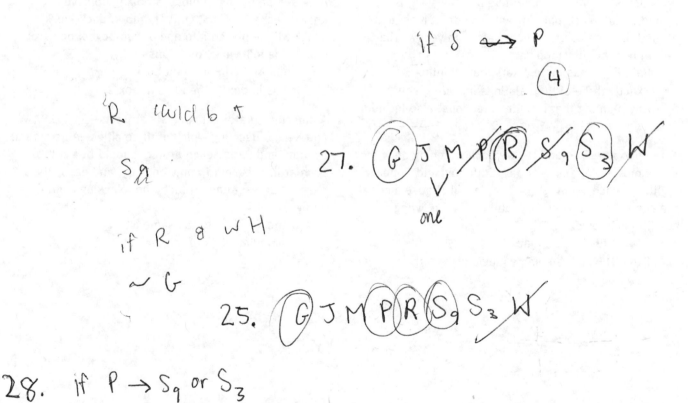

[handwritten: if 3rd element use a grid]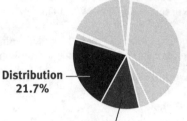

Matching and Distribution Games

Prepare and Practice

Distribution
21.7%

Matching
11.7%
Logic Games Game Type
Frequency by Percentage
PrepTests 66–80; released 2012–2016

Here are sample overviews of Matching and Distribution Games along with a possible rule or two that could accompany that setup.

Matching Games

[handwritten: can be repeated]

An artist is planning to paint five paintings—A, B, C, D, and E—and each painting will include at least one of the following colors: green, blue, and yellow. The following conditions apply:

Painting A has more colors than painting B.

Exactly three of the paintings include green.

Any painting that includes blue must also include green.

Three people—F, G, and H—are each watching an entire movie alone on a Friday, Saturday, and Sunday night. For each evening, the people will choose among the same three movies—I, J, and K. The following conditions apply:

G watches J on Sunday.

F and H watch the same movie on exactly two days.

Distribution Games

[handwritten: used only once]

A person preparing to move is boxing up seven knick-knacks—L, M, N, O, P, Q, and R. Each knick-knack will be placed into one of two boxes: box 1 or box 2. The following conditions apply:

L and M are in different boxes.

If O is in box 1, then P is in box 2.

A museum curator is taking six artifacts—S, T, U, V, W, and X—and deciding which of three cities—Amsterdam, London, and Paris—each artifact should be sent to. Each artifact is sent to only one city, and each city receives at least one artifact. The following conditions apply:

S and T will go to the same city.

Amsterdam will not receive X.

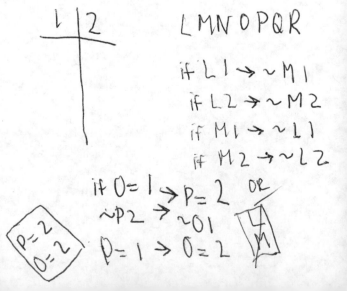

Rules in Matching and Distribution Games

The rules in Matching and Distribution games are similar. The primary difference between the two games is that entities, attributes, and characteristics can be used more than once in Matching games. Typically in Distribution games, once an entity is placed into a group, it cannot be placed into any other groups.

LSAT STRATEGY

Distribution rules tell you one or more of the following:

· Entities that must or cannot be assigned to the same group
· The number of entities that must, can, or cannot be assigned to a group, or the relative sizes among groups (e.g., the Blue Group must have more members than the Green Group)
· Conditions triggering the assignment of an entity to a particular group (e.g., if Rachel joins the marketing team, then Gar joins the service team)

Matching rules tell you one or more of the following:

· Attributes that must or cannot be matched to the same entity
· The number of attributes that must, can, or cannot be assigned to an entity, or the relative numbers among entities (e.g., Sascha must be assigned more of the tasks than Craig is assigned)
· Conditions triggering the assignment of an attribute to a particular entity (e.g., if Rebecca is assigned copyediting, then Jesse is assigned layout)

Deductions in Matching Games

> ### LSAT STRATEGY
>
> In Matching games, deductions are likely to stem from:
>
> - **Duplications**—Entities shared by two or more rules; one rule might match a certain attribute to entity X, and another might tell you that entity Y has more attributes matched to it than X does.
> - **Numbers Restrictions**—Limitations on the number of attributes that can be assigned to a given entity or limitations on the number of entities to which an attribute can be matched
> - **Established Entities**—Matches between entities and attributes that must be maintained throughout the game (e.g., Entity X wears the red jacket); Established Entities are quite common in Matching games.
>
> In Matching games, deductions may involve:
>
> - **Blocks of Entities**—Two or more entities that must be assigned a given attribute or two or more attributes that must be assigned to the same entity or entities; Blocks are somewhat rare in Matching games.
> - **Limited Options**—The situation that arises when a rule or combination of rules makes all acceptable arrangements fall into one of two patterns; Limited Options is a rare deduction to find in Matching games.

Deductions in Distribution Games

LSAT STRATEGY

In Distribution games, deductions are likely to stem from:

- **Numbers Restrictions**—Limitations on the number of entities per group or determinations of the minimum and maximum numbers of entities per group; in Distribution games, rules preventing entities from being assigned to the same group may act as *de facto* Numbers Restrictions (e.g., B and F must see different events; ergo, each event has at least one attendee). Another Number Restriction involves games with only two groups: The binary structure of such games means that if an entity is not in one group it must be in the other.
- **Blocks of Entities**—These are two or more entities that must be placed in the same group.
- **Limited Options**—The situation that arises when the game specifies only two possible patterns for the number of entities per group (e.g., Group A contains four students and Group B contains five students, or Group A contains five students and Group B contains four students); in Distribution games, you can sometimes determine a Limited Options numbers scenario by applying other rules to the game's overall framework. Limited Options sketches may also be created if a Block of Entities is influential enough to warrant two or three sketches.
- **Duplications**—Entities shared by two or more rules; a common occurrence in Distribution games is one rule that says A and B will be in the same group and another rule that says A and C cannot be in the same group—from this, you can deduce that B and C cannot be in the same group.

In Distribution games, deductions may involve:

- **Established Entities**—Entities that are assigned to one group for the entire game; this is not very common in Distribution games.

Practice and Perform

Questions 29–33

A clown will select a costume consisting of two pieces and no others: a jacket and overalls. One piece of the costume will be entirely one color, and the other piece will be plaid. Selection is subject to the following restrictions:

If the jacket is plaid, then there must be exactly three colors in it.

If the overalls are plaid, then there must be exactly two colors in them.

The jacket and overalls must have exactly one color in common.

Green, red, and violet are the only colors that can be in the jacket.

Red, violet, and yellow are the only colors that can be in the overalls.

29. Which one of the following could be a complete and accurate list of the colors in the costume?

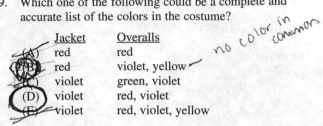

	Jacket	Overalls
(A)	red	red
(B)	red	violet, yellow
(C)	violet	green, violet
(D)	violet	red, violet
(E)	violet	red, violet, yellow

no color in common

GO ON TO THE NEXT PAGE.

J plaid | O solid | color
plaid

g | r/v
r |
v |

if J = p'aid → 3 colors
if O = p'aid → 2 colors
J & O = 1 color (only r or v)
g r v = J
r v y = O

J_s | O_p

r/v | r/v
| r/v/g

132

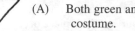
30. If there are exactly two colors in the costume, then which one of the following must be false?

   (A) At least part of the jacket is green.
   (B) At least part of the jacket is red.
   (C) The overalls are red and violet.
   (D) The overalls are red and yellow.
   (E) The overalls are violet and yellow.

31. If at least part of the jacket is green, then which one of the following could be true?

   (A) The overalls are plaid.
   (B) No part of the jacket is red.
   (C) No part of the jacket is violet.
   (D) At least part of the overalls are yellow.
   (E) At least part of the overalls are violet.

32. Which one of the following must be false?

   (A) Both green and red are colors used in the costume.
   (B) Both green and violet are colors used in the costume.
   (C) Both green and yellow are colors used in the costume.
   (D) Both red and violet are colors used in the costume.
   (E) Both violet and yellow are colors used in the costume.

33. If there are exactly three colors in the costume, the overalls must be

   (A) entirely red or else red and violet plaid
   (B) entirely yellow or else violet and yellow plaid
   (C) entirely violet or else red and violet plaid
   (D) entirely red or else entirely yellow
   (E) entirely red or else entirely violet

PrepTest51 Sec4 Qs 1–5

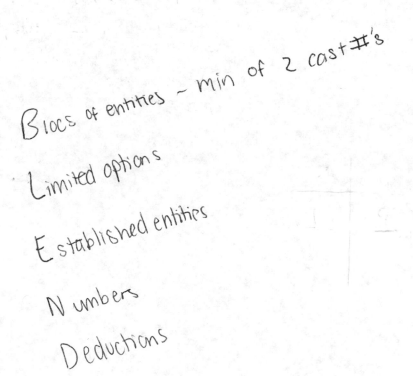

Distribution Game (handwritten)

2 grids if they give 2 options (handwritten)

Questions 34–38

There are exactly five pieces of mail in a mailbox: a flyer, a letter, a magazine, a postcard, and a survey. Each piece of mail is addressed to exactly one of three housemates: Georgette, Jana, or Rini. Each housemate has at least one of the pieces of mail addressed to her. The following conditions must apply:

Neither the letter nor the magazine is addressed to Georgette.

If the letter is addressed to Rini, then the postcard is addressed to Jana.

The housemate to whom the flyer is addressed has at least one of the other pieces of mail addressed to her as well.

34. Which one of the following could be a complete and accurate matching of the pieces of mail to the housemates to whom they are addressed?

(A) Georgette: the flyer, the survey
Jana: the letter
Rini: the magazine

(B) Georgette: the flyer, the postcard
Jana: the letter, the magazine
Rini: the survey

(C) Georgette: the magazine, the survey
Jana: the flyer, the letter
Rini: the postcard

(D) Georgette: the survey
Jana: the flyer, the magazine
Rini: the letter, the postcard

(E) Georgette: the survey
Jana: the letter, the magazine, the postcard
Rini: the flyer

GO ON TO THE NEXT PAGE.

(Handwritten notes:)

G | J | R
P/S | L | —

~L
~M

f L m p s

G ≠ L or m

if L = R → p = J
~~p~~ p ≠ J → L ≠ R ← 3 options

if f → at least 1 other
(F never alone)
G = f p or S

3 - 1 - 1, 2 - 2 - 1

if, then
contrapositive
& 1 options from
if, then & contra
(P = J
  L ≠ R)

G | J | R
S | P | L

~L
~M

35. Which one of the following is a complete and accurate list of the pieces of mail, any one of which could be the only piece of mail addressed to Jana?

(A) the postcard
(B) the letter, the postcard
(C) the letter, the survey
(D) the magazine, the survey
(E) the letter, the magazine, the postcard

36. Which one of the following CANNOT be a complete and accurate list of the pieces of mail addressed to Jana?

(A) the flyer, the letter, the magazine
(B) the flyer, the letter, the postcard
(C) the flyer, the letter, the survey
(D) the flyer, the magazine, the postcard
(E) the flyer, the magazine, the survey

37. Which one of the following CANNOT be a complete and accurate list of the pieces of mail addressed to Rini?

(A) the magazine, the postcard
(B) the letter, the survey
(C) the letter, the magazine ✓
(D) the flyer, the magazine ✓
(E) the flyer, the letter ✓

38. If the magazine and the survey are both addressed to the same housemate, then which one of the following could be true?

(A) The survey is addressed to Georgette.
(B) The postcard is addressed to Rini. ✓
(C) The magazine is addressed to Jana.
(D) The letter is addressed to Rini.
(E) The flyer is addressed to Jana.

PrepTest49 Sec1 Qs 8–12

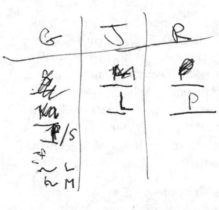

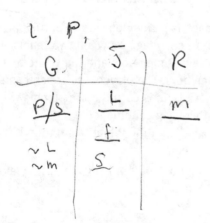

Hybrid Games

Prepare and Practice

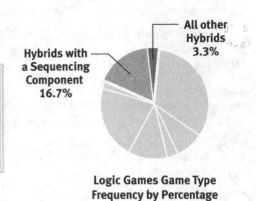

LEARNING OBJECTIVES

In this section, you'll learn to:

· Apply the Logic Games Method to Hybrid games

**Logic Games Game Type
Frequency by Percentage**

PrepTests 66–80; released 2012–2016

Here are sample overviews of Hybrid Games along with a possible rule or two that could accompany that setup.

Gene is ranking his favorite books from among a list of six total books—A, B, C, D, E, and F. He will make two sets of rankings: a ranking of his favorite fiction books and a ranking of his favorite nonfiction books. There are no ties within each set of rankings. The following conditions apply:

    A is ranked 1st on the nonfiction list.
    B and C are both fiction, and one of them is the lowest-ranked fiction book.

A neighborhood has six families—G, H, I, J, K, and L—living in six consecutive houses along Mason Street numbered 1 to 6 from left to right. Each family also has exactly one pet—a bird, a cat, or a dog. The following conditions apply:

    The families in the houses immediately to the left and to the right of family J's house have a cat.
    There is a dog living in the 5th house.

A traveler will visit five different European countries on five consecutive days, one country each day. She'll choose from the following eight countries—M, N, P, R, S, T, U, and V. The following conditions apply:

    If she visits M, she'll also visit N.
    If R is selected, it is the 4th country visited.

A coach is picking players to participate in an intra-squad scrimmage between two teams. The Red team will have 3 members and the White team will also have 3 members. The players the coach can select from are A, B, C, D, E, F, G, and H. The teams will conform to the following conditions:

    If A is on the White team, then B is on the Red team.
    E and F are both selected and play on different teams.

Handwritten notes:

1 2 3 4 5 6

GHIJKL
___ ___ ___ ___ ___ ___
~J   ~J   ~J

___ ___ ___ d ___

bcd ___ ___ ___ ___

c J c

J cant be 1 or 2 b/c need cat b4   J cant be 4 b/c dog

6 players

ABCDEFGH

R | W
E/F | E/F
___ | ___
___ | ___

if A=W → B=R
B≠R → A≠W

Rules in Hybrid Games

The rules in Hybrid games will be of the same type that you see in single-action games. The only difference is that within a Hybrid game, you will see a mix of different types of rules. For example, in a Distribution/Sequencing game, some rules will restrict or define which entities can go in which group (Distribution rules), while other rules will restrict or define the order in which entities can go (Sequencing rules).

> ### LSAT STRATEGY
>
> Hybrid rules tell you one of the following:
>
> · How the first of the actions is restricted
> · How the second of the actions is restricted
> · How the actions are restricted simultaneously

NOTE: Rarely, a Hybrid game will include three actions. The function of the rules is identical in that case.

Deductions in Hybrid Games

In Hybrid games, expect to see the same types of deductions you saw earlier in the chapter centering around individual game actions.

> ### LSAT STRATEGY
>
> In Hybrid games, deductions are likely to stem from:
>
> · **BLEND**—Because Hybrid games may involve any of the standard logic games actions, all five of the BLEND elements are on the table.
> · **"Cross Over" rules**—In Hybrid games, keep an eye out for rules that provide restrictions to both of the actions in the game.

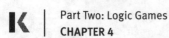

Hybrid: selection & sequence

Practice and Perform

Questions 39–44

The coach of a women's track team must determine which four of five runners—Quinn, Ramirez, Smith, Terrell, and Uzoma—will run in the four races of an upcoming track meet. Each of the four runners chosen will run in exactly one of the four races—the first, second, third, or fourth. The coach's selection is bound by the following constraints:

If Quinn runs in the track meet, then Terrell runs in the race immediately after the race in which Quinn runs.

Smith does not run in either the second race or the fourth race.

If Uzoma does not run in the track meet, then Ramirez runs in the second race.

If Ramirez runs in the second race, then Uzoma does not run in the track meet.

always need T. if no T no Q &
then only 3. need 4

Q R S ⊤ U   pick 4

39. Which one of the following could be the order in which the runners run, from first to fourth?

(A) Uzoma, Ramirez, Quinn, Terrell
(B) Terrell, Smith, Ramirez, Uzoma
(C) Smith, Ramirez, Terrell, Quinn
(D) Ramirez, Uzoma, Smith, Terrell
(E) Quinn, Terrell, Smith, Ramirez

GO ON TO THE NEXT PAGE.

if Q → QT

if ~U → R=2   } contrapositive
if R=2 → ~U   ~U + R=2

OR
U + R ≠ 2

↑
2 sketches

①
$\underline{S}$	$\underline{R}$	$\underline{Q}$	$\underline{\text{⊤}}$
1	2	3	4
	~S		~S
			~Q

②
$\overline{}$	$\overline{}$	$\overline{}$	$\overline{}$
1	2	3	4
	~S		~S
	~R		~Q

40. Which one of the following runners must the coach select to run in the track meet?

    (A) Quinn
    (B) Ramirez
    (C) Smith
    (D) Terrell
    (E) Uzoma

41. The question of which runners will be chosen to run in the track meet and in what races they will run can be completely resolved if which one of the following is true?

    (A) Ramirez runs in the first race.
    (B) Ramirez runs in the second race.
    (C) Ramirez runs in the third race.
    (D) Ramircz runs in the fourth race.
    (E) Ramirez does not run in the track meet.

42. Which one of the following CANNOT be true?

    (A) Ramirez runs in the race immediately before the race in which Smith runs.
    (B) Smith runs in the race immediately before the race in which Quinn runs.
    (C) Smith runs in the race immediately before the race in which Terrell runs.
    (D) Terrell runs in the race immediately before the race in which Ramirez runs.
    (E) Uzoma runs in the race immediately before the race in which Terrell runs.

43. If Uzoma runs in the first race, then which one of the following must be true?

    (A) Quinn does not run in the track meet.
    (B) Smith does not run in the track meet.
    (C) Quinn runs in the second race.
    (D) Terrell runs in the second race.
    (E) Ramirez runs in the fourth race.

44. If both Quinn and Smith run in the track meet, then how many of the runners are there any one of whom could be the one who runs in the first race?

    (A) one
    (B) two
    (C) three
    (D) four
    (E) five

PrepTest61 Sec3 Qs 12–17

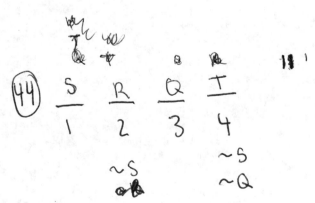

Questions 45–49

A locally known guitarist's demo CD contains exactly seven different songs—S, T, V, W, X, Y, and Z. Each song occupies exactly one of the CD's seven tracks. Some of the songs are rock classics; the others are new compositions. The following conditions must hold:

S occupies the fourth track of the CD. ✓
Both W and Y precede S on the CD.
T precedes W on the CD.
A rock classic occupies the sixth track of the CD. ✓
Each rock classic is immediately preceded on the CD by a new composition.
Z is a rock classic.

45. Which one of the following could be the order of the songs on the CD, from the first track through the seventh?

(A) T, W, V, S, Y, X, Z
(B) V, Y, T, S, W, Z, X
(C) X, Y, W, S, T, Z, S
(D) Y, T, W, S, X, Z, V   ✓
(E) Z, T, X, W, V, Y, S

GO ON TO THE NEXT PAGE.

46. Which one of the following is a pair of songs that must occupy consecutive tracks on the CD?

    (A) S and V
    (B) S and W
    (C) T and Z
    (D) T and Y
    (E) V and Z

47. Which one of the following songs must be a new composition?

    (A) S
    (B) T
    (C) W
    (D) X
    (E) Y

48. If W precedes Y on the CD, then which one of the following must be true?

    (A) S is a rock classic.
    (B) V is a rock classic.
    (C) Y is a rock classic.
    (D) T is a new composition.
    (E) W is a new composition.

49. If there are exactly two songs on the CD that both precede V and are preceded by Y, then which one of the following could be true?

    (A) V occupies the seventh track of the CD.
    (B) X occupies the fifth track of the CD.
    (C) Y occupies the third track of the CD.
    (D) T is a rock classic.
    (E) W is a rock classic.

PrepTest51 Sec4 Qs 11–15

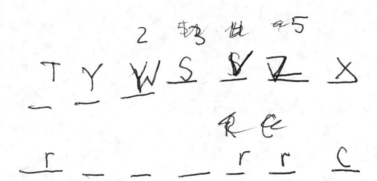

ANSWER KEY

Game 1—Law Firm Departments (pp. 116–117)

1. C
2. A
3. C
4. D
5. C

Game 2—Museum Photographs (pp. 118–119)

6. C
7. E
8. D
9. B
10. D

Game 3—Student Activities (pp. 120–121)

11. D
12. B
13. C
14. D
15. C

Game 4—Parcel Delivery (pp. 122–123)

16. D
17. C
18. D
19. A
20. B
21. C
22. C

Game 5—Alicia's Courses (pp. 126–127)

23. D
24. E
25. C
26. A
27. D
28. A

Game 6—Clown Costumes (pp. 132–133)

29. D
30. A
31. E
32. C
33. E

Game 7—Housemates & Mail (pp. 134–135)

34. B
35. B
36. E
37. B
38. E

Game 8—Track Team (pp. 138–139)

39. D
40. D
41. B
42. A
43. E
44. B

Game 9—Guitarist's Demo CD (pp. 140–141)

45. D
46. E
47. D
48. D
49. E

Complete explanations for these games can be found in your online resources.

CHAPTER 5

Logic Games Section Management

TIMING AND SECTION MANAGEMENT

Logic Games Section Timing: The Basics

The facts: Every Logic Games section has four games, each with 5–7 questions, for a total of 22–24 questions to be completed in 35 minutes.

The strategy: On average, then, you should take between eight and nine minutes for each game. Of that time, you'll usually take between three and four minutes to set up the game, analyze the rules, and make deductions, and then utilize the remaining four to five minutes to answer the questions. Don't rush steps 1–4 of the Logic Games Method. Approached strategically, the easiest games may take less than eight minutes. Bank that extra time for tougher games. When a game threatens to drag on much longer than nine minutes, however, be prepared to guess on its toughest questions and move on with ample time to solve the next game and answer its questions.

Here are a few of the principles of great section management that LSAT experts use to their advantage. Learn them and put them into practice whenever you undertake timed section or full test practice.

Efficiency, Not Speed—Being methodical does not mean being slow. Rushing through the setup will cost you dearly in both time and accuracy. Take the time to go through the Logic Games Method fully and you will find that it provides the shortest and most direct route to correct answers.

Triage the Section—Games within a section and questions within a game are rarely printed in order of difficulty. LSAT experts can use that knowledge to their advantage. You can decide the order in which to tackle the games and, within each game, the order in which to tackle the questions based on certain factors like question type and difficulty level. Be decisive and remember that you are in control of the situation.

Skip and Guess Strategically—An easy question is worth just as much as a difficult one. The key is to correctly answer the most questions from the section, not the most difficult or the most consecutive questions. You do not need to get every question to get a great score and skipping one or two difficult/ time-consuming questions will often allow you to correctly answer many easier ones in return. Skipping is not done because you can't get a question right, it's because given the timing of the test, it may be to your benefit to do so. Stay in control of the section and the test.

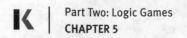

THE KAPLAN LOGIC GAMES METHOD

Step 1: Overview

Step 2: Sketch

Step 3: Rules

Step 4: Deductions

Step 5: Questions

TAKING THE TIMING SECTION

The Logic Games section that follows was originally Section 3 in PrepTest 45, administered in December 2004.

Proctoring

Complete this section under timed test-like conditions. Give yourself 35 minutes for the section and finish it in one uninterrupted sitting.

Scoring

After you finish the section, record your answers in the appropriate webgrid (PrepTest 45, Section 3) found in your online resources. This will make your results and percent correct easy to see, and the score report will contain links to the explanations for each game and question.

Review

For your convenience, an answer key is included at the end of this chapter. For complete answers and explanations, consult the explanations PDF in your online resources. Check that you consistently followed the Logic Games Method, set up each game with a helpful sketch, and made all of the available deductions as well.

PrepTest 45, Section 3

Time—35 minutes

22 Questions

this section is based on a set of conditions. In answering some of the questions, it may be
se the response that most accurately and completely answers each question and blacken the
heet.

Questions 1–6

On one afternoon, Patterson meets individually with each
of exactly five clients—Reilly, Sanchez, Tang, Upton, and
Yansky—and also goes to the gym by herself for a
workout. Patterson's workout and her five meetings each
start at either 1:00, 2:00, 3:00, 4:00, 5:00, or 6:00. The
following conditions must apply:

Patterson meets with Sanchez at some time before
her workout.

Patterson meets with Tang at some time after her
workout.

Patterson meets with Yansky either immediately
before or immediately after her workout.

Patterson meets with Upton at some time before she
meets with Reilly.

1. Which one of the following could be an acceptable
schedule of Patterson's workout and meetings, in
order from 1:00 to 6:00?

(A) Yansky, workout, Upton, Reilly, Sanchez, Tang
(B) Upton, Tang, Sanchez, Yansky, workout, Reilly
(C) Upton, Reilly, Sanchez, workout, Tang, Yansky
(D) Sanchez, Yansky, workout, Reilly, Tang, Upton
(E) Sanchez, Upton, workout, Yansky, Tang, Reilly

GO ON TO THE NEXT PAGE.

R S T U Y

Clients
WO

meetings

1   2   3   4   5   6

W

S (W)   YW or WY

WT   U...R

S √
R X
T X
U
Y

2. How many of the clients are there, any one of whom could meet with Patterson at 1:00?

   (A)   one
   (B)   two
   (C)   three
   (D)   four
   (E)   five

3. Patterson CANNOT meet with Upton at which one of the following times?

   (A)   1:00
   (B)   2:00
   (C)   3:00
   (D)   4:00
   (E)   5:00

4. If Patterson meets with Sanchez the hour before she meets with Yansky, then each of the following could be true EXCEPT:

   (A)   Patterson meets with Reilly at 2:00.
   (B)   Patterson meets with Yansky at 3:00.
   (C)   Patterson meets with Tang at 4:00.
   (D)   Patterson meets with Yansky at 5:00.
   (E)   Patterson meets with Tang at 6:00.

5. If Patterson meets with Tang a... of the following must be true?

   (A)   Patterson meets with Reilly at 5:00.
   (B)   Patterson meets with Upton at 5:00.
   (C)   Patterson meets with Yansky at 2:00.
   (D)   Patterson meets with Yansky at 3:00.
   (E)   Patterson's workout is at 2:00.

6. Which one of the following could be the order of Patterson's meetings, from earliest to latest?

   (A)   Upton, Yansky, Sanchez, Reilly, Tang
   (B)   Upton, Reilly, Sanchez, Tang, Yansky
   (C)   Sanchez, Yansky, Reilly, Tang, Upton
   (D)   Sanchez, Upton, Tang, Yansky, Reilly
   (E)   Sanchez, Upton, Reilly, Yansky, Tang

GO ON TO THE NEXT PAGE.

Questions 7–12

Exactly six people—Lulu, Nam, Ofelia, Pachai, Santiago, and Tyrone—are the only contestants in a chess tournament. The tournament consists of four games, played one after the other. Exactly two people play in each game, and each person plays in at least one game. The following conditions must apply:

Tyrone does not play in the first or third game.

Lulu plays in the last game.

Nam plays in only one game and it is not against Pachai.

Santiago plays in exactly two games, one just before and one just after the only game that Ofelia plays in.

7. Which one of the following could be an accurate list of the contestants who play in each of the four games?

(A) first game: Pachai, Santiago; second game: Ofelia, Tyrone; third game: Pachai, Santiago; fourth game: Lulu, Nam

(B) first game: Lulu, Nam; second game: Pachai, Santiago; third game: Ofelia, Tyrone; fourth game: Lulu, Santiago

(C) first game: Pachai, Santiago; second game: Lulu, Tyrone; third game: Nam, Ofelia; fourth game: Lulu, Nam

(D) first game: Nam, Santiago; second game: Nam, Ofelia; third game: Pachai, Santiago; fourth game: Lulu, Tyrone

(E) first game: Lulu, Nam; second game: Santiago, Tyrone; third game: Lulu, Ofelia; fourth game: Pachai, Santiago

GO ON TO THE NEXT PAGE.

L N O P S T

4 games
2 per game
at least 1

Games | 1 | 2 | 3 | 4

L

~T   ~T

N only 1 game
~ against P

P = 2 games

S O S

8. Which one of the following contestants could play in two consecutive games?

(A) Lulu
(B) Nam
(C) Ofelia
(D) Santiago
(E) Tyrone

9. If Tyrone plays in the fourth game, then which one of the following could be true?

(A) Nam plays in the second game.
(B) Ofelia plays in the third game.
(C) Santiago plays in the second game.
(D) Nam plays a game against Lulu.
(E) Pachai plays a game against Lulu.

10. Which one of the following could be true?

(A) Pachai plays against Lulu in the first game.
(B) Pachai plays against Nam in the second game.
(C) Santiago plays against Ofelia in the second game.
(D) Pachai plays against Lulu in the third game.
(E) Nam plays against Santiago in the fourth game.

11. Which one of the following is a complete and accurate list of the contestants who CANNOT play against Tyrone in any game?

(A) Lulu, Pachai
(B) Nam, Ofelia
(C) Nam, Pachai
(D) Nam, Santiago
(E) Ofelia, Pachai

12. If Ofelia plays in the third game, which one of the following must be true?

(A) Lulu plays in the third game.
(B) Nam plays in the third game.
(C) Pachai plays in the first game.
(D) Pachai plays in the third game.
(E) Tyrone plays in the second game.

GO ON TO THE NEXT PAGE.

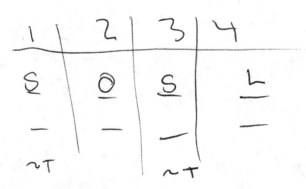

Questions 13–17

An album contains photographs picturing seven friends:
Raimundo, Selma, Ty, Umiko, Wendy, Yakira, Zack. The
friends appear either alone or in groups with one another,
in accordance with the following:

> Wendy appears in every photograph that Selma
> appears in.
> Selma appears in every photograph that Umiko
> appears in.
> Raimundo appears in every photograph that Yakira
> does not appear in.
> Neither Ty nor Raimundo appears in any photograph
> that Wendy appears in.

13. Which one of the following could be a complete and
accurate list of the friends who appear together in a
photograph?

   (A) Raimundo, Selma, Ty, Wendy
   (B) Raimundo, Ty, Yakira, Zack
   (C) Raimundo, Wendy, Yakira, Zack
   (D) Selma, Ty, Umiko, Yakira
   (E) Selma, Ty, Umiko, Zack

7 friends

GO ON TO THE NEXT PAGE.

R S T U W Y Z

1	2	3	4	5	6	7

WS
SU
if R → ~Y
if W → ~T or R

14. If Ty and Zack appear together in a photograph, then which one of the following must be true?

    (A) Selma also appears in the photograph.
    (B) Yakira also appears in the photograph.
    (C) Wendy also appears in the photograph.
    (D) Raimundo does not appear in the photograph.
    (E) Umiko does not appear in the photograph.

15. What is the maximum number of friends who could appear in a photograph that Yakira does not appear in?

    (A) six
    (B) five
    (C) four
    (D) three
    (E) two

16. If Umiko and Zack appear together in a photograph, then exactly how many of the other friends must also appear in that photograph?

    (A) four
    (B) three
    (C) two
    (D) one
    (E) zero

17. If exactly three friends appear together in a photograph, then each of the following could be true EXCEPT:

    (A) Selma and Zack both appear in the photograph.
    (B) Ty and Yakira both appcar in the photograph.
    (C) Wendy and Selma both appear in the photograph.
    (D) Yakira and Zack both appear in the photograph.
    (E) Zack and Raimundo both appear in the photograph.

GO ON TO THE NEXT PAGE.

Questions 18–22

The Export Alliance consists of exactly three nations: Nation X, Nation Y, and Nation Z. Each nation in the Alliance exports exactly two of the following five crops: oranges, rice, soybeans, tea, and wheat. Each of these crops is exported by at least one of the nations in the Alliance. The following conditions hold:

>None of the nations exports both wheat and oranges.
>Nation X exports soybeans if, but only if, Nation Y does also.
>If Nation Y exports rice, then Nations X and Z both export tea.
>Nation Y does not export any crop that Nation Z exports.

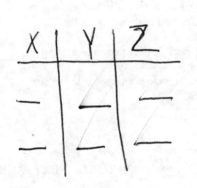

18. Which one of the following could be an accurate list, for each of the nations, of the crops it exports?

(A) Nation X: oranges, rice; Nation Y: oranges, tea; Nation Z: soybeans, wheat

(B) Nation X: oranges, tea; Nation Y: oranges, rice; Nation Z: soybeans, wheat

(C) Nation X: oranges, wheat; Nation Y: oranges, tea; Nation Z: rice, soybeans

(D) Nation X: rice, wheat; Nation Y: oranges, tea; Nation Z: oranges, soybeans

(E) Nation X: soybeans, rice; Nation Y: oranges, tea; Nation Z: soybeans, wheat

GO ON TO THE NEXT PAGE.

19. If Nation X exports soybeans and tea, then which one of the following could be true?

(A) Nation Y exports oranges.
(B) Nation Y exports rice.
(C) Nation Y exports tea.
(D) Nation Z exports soybeans.
(E) Nation Z exports tea.

20. If Nation Z exports tea and wheat, then which one of the following must be true?

(A) Nation X exports oranges.
(B) Nation X exports tea.
(C) Nation X exports wheat.
(D) Nation Y exports rice.
(E) Nation Y exports soybeans.

21. It CANNOT be the case that both Nation X and Nation Z export which one of the following crops?

(A) oranges
(B) rice
(C) soybeans
(D) tea
(E) wheat

22. Which one of the following pairs CANNOT be the two crops that Nation Y exports?

(A) oranges and rice
(B) oranges and soybeans
(C) rice and tea
(D) rice and wheat
(E) soybeans and wheat

S T O P

IF YOU FINISH BEFORE TIME IS CALLED, YOU MAY CHECK YOUR WORK ON THIS SECTION ONLY.
DO NOT WORK ON ANY OTHER SECTION IN THE TEST.

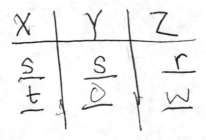

153

ANSWER KEY

Game 1—Meetings with Clients & Gym

1. E
2. B
3. C
4. D
5. B
6. E

Game 2—Chess Tournament

7. A
8. A
9. A
10. A
11. C
12. E

Game 3—Photographs

13. B
14. E
15. D
16. B
17. A

Game 4—Export Alliance

18. A
19. A
20. E
21. C
22. C

Complete explanations for this section can be found in your online resources.

PART THREE

Logical Reasoning

CHAPTER 6

The Kaplan Logical Reasoning Method

Prepare

LEARNING OBJECTIVES

In this section, you'll learn to:

- State the steps of the Kaplan Logical Reasoning Method and the purpose of each step

---

The Logical Reasoning sections of the LSAT test your ability to analyze and critique short arguments and to evaluate and apply factual statements. The skills associated with Logical Reasoning are the most important to your LSAT score. The reason is clear: Logical Reasoning accounts for roughly half of your LSAT score. Every administration of the LSAT contains exactly two scored Logical Reasoning sections of between 24 and 26 questions apiece. Among the 50 or so Logical Reasoning questions you'll see on each test, you will learn to identify the following question types, grouped here into the families of questions covered in the next three chapters.

LSAT Score Distribution by Section

LOGICAL REASONING QUESTION TYPES

Chapter 7
Argument-Based Questions

- Main Point
- Role of a Statement
- Method of Argument
- Point at Issue
- Parallel Reasoning

Chapter 8
Assumption Family Questions

- Assumption
- Flaw
- Strengthen/Weaken
- Assumption-Family Principle
- Parallel Flaw

Chapter 9
Non-Argument Questions

- Inference
- Paradox
- Inference-Based Principle

LOGICAL REASONING QUESTION FORMAT AND THE KAPLAN LOGICAL REASONING METHOD

Although Logical Reasoning questions ask for several different kinds of analyses, the LSAT expert uses a consistent approach on all of the questions.

THE KAPLAN LOGICAL REASONING METHOD

Step 1: Identify the Question Type

Step 2: Untangle the Stimulus

Step 3: Predict the Correct Answer

Step 4: Evaluate the Answer Choices

There is nothing abstract about this method. Take a look at it mapped onto a Logical Reasoning question. This is how the well-trained expert sees it.

5.   Studies reveal that most people select the foods they eat primarily on the basis of flavor, and that nutrition is usually a secondary concern at best. This suggests that <health experts would have more success in encouraging people to eat wholesome foods if they emphasized how flavorful those foods truly are rather than how nutritious they are.>

Which one of the following, if true, most strengthens the argument above?

(A)   Most people currently believe that wholesome foods are more flavorful, on average, than unwholesome foods are.

(B)   Few people, when given a choice between foods that are flavorful but not nutritious and foods that are nutritious but not flavorful, will choose the foods that are nutritious but not flavorful.

(C)   Health experts' attempts to encourage people to eat wholesome foods by emphasizing how nutritious those foods are have been moderately successful.

(D)   The studies that revealed that people choose the foods they eat primarily on the basis of flavor also revealed that people rated as most flavorful those foods that were least nutritious.

(E)   In a study, subjects who were told that a given food was very flavorful were more willing to try the food and more likely to enjoy it than were subjects who were told that the food was nutritious.

PrepTest57 Sec2 Q5

Step 1: Identify the Question Type

Start here, so you know what to look for in the stimulus.

Step 2: Untangle the Stimulus

Zero in on what is relevant. Here, the underlined and bracketed text helps you to predict the correct answer.

Step 3: Predict the Correct Answer

In your own words, state what the correct answer must say.

Step 4: Evaluate the Answer Choices

Identify the answer that matches your prediction. Eliminate those that do not.

Practice

Now, try applying the Logical Reasoning Method to that question one step at a time. Don't worry that you don't know all of the names and terminology that go along with various Logical Reasoning question types. You'll pick that up in subsequent chapters. At this point, just concentrate on what each step accomplishes and how it helps you anticipate what to look for in the subsequent step.

LSAT Question	My Analysis
Studies reveal that most people select the foods they eat primarily on the basis of flavor, and that nutrition is usually a secondary concern at best. This suggests that health experts would have more success in encouraging people to eat wholesome foods if they emphasized how flavorful those foods truly are rather than how nutritious they are. →	**Step 2:**
Which one of the following, if true, most strengthens the argument above? →	**Step 1:**
	Step 3:
(A) Most people currently believe that wholesome foods are more flavorful, on average, than unwholesome foods are. →	**Step 4:**
(B) Few people, when given a choice between foods that are flavorful but not nutritious and foods that are nutritious but not flavorful, will choose the foods that are nutritious but not flavorful. →	
(C) Health experts' attempts to encourage people to eat wholesome foods by emphasizing how nutritious those foods are have been moderately successful. →	
(D) The studies that revealed that people choose the foods they eat primarily on the basis of flavor also revealed that people rated as most flavorful those foods that were least nutritious. →	
(E) In a study, subjects who were told that a given food was very flavorful were more willing to try the food and more likely to enjoy it than were subjects who were told that the food was nutritious. →	

PrepTest57 Sec2 Q5

Compare your analysis to that of an LSAT expert. Did you select the correct answer? Was it clear to you why each wrong answer did not strengthen the argument?

LSAT Question	Analysis
Studies reveal that most people select the foods they eat primarily on the basis of flavor, and that nutrition is usually a secondary concern at best. This suggests that health experts would have more success in encouraging people to eat wholesome foods if they emphasized how flavorful those foods truly are rather than how nutritious they are.	**Step 2:** Conclusion—Experts will have more success selling people on how good a healthy food tastes than on how good it is for them. Evidence—Studies show people choose food based on taste more than on nutrition. Assumption—The author takes for granted that people will respond favorably to expert suggestions that correspond to their own preferences (flavor over nutrition).
Which one of the following, if true, most strengthens the argument above?	**Step 1:** The correct answer will be a fact that makes the argument stronger. That is, it will make the conclusion more likely to follow from the evidence.
	Step 3: The correct answer needs to supply a fact suggesting that people are more likely to be convinced by claims about flavor than by those about nutrition.
(A) Most people currently believe that wholesome foods are more flavorful, on average, than unwholesome foods are.	**Step 4:** 180. This is a benefit of emphasizing nutritiousness because people will associate that with flavorful too. Eliminate.
(B) Few people, when given a choice between foods that are flavorful but not nutritious and foods that are nutritious but not flavorful, will choose the foods that are nutritious but not flavorful.	Outside the Scope. The argument is about telling people that nutritious foods are tasty, not about foods that are wholesome but bad tasting. Eliminate.
(C) Health experts' attempts to encourage people to eat wholesome foods by emphasizing how nutritious those foods are have been moderately successful.	180. The argument is about encouraging people to choose wholesome foods by telling them that these foods taste good. Eliminate.
(D) The studies that revealed that people choose the foods they eat primarily on the basis of flavor also revealed that people rated as most flavorful those foods that were least nutritious.	180. This choice makes it less likely that people will be persuaded by the experts' suggestions. Eliminate.
(E) In a study, subjects who were told that a given food was very flavorful were more willing to try the food and more likely to enjoy it than were subjects who were told that the food was nutritious.	Correct. This introduces a new study that found that people were more likely to try and to like foods they are *told* are flavorful, exactly what the experts would be telling people in the author's conclusion.

PrepTest57 Sec2 Q5

Try applying the Logical Reasoning Method to another question. Once again, be mindful of going step-by-step.

LSAT Question	My Analysis
Engineers are investigating the suitability of Wantastiquet Pass as the site of a new bridge. Because one concern is whether erosion could eventually weaken the bridge's foundations, they contracted for two reports on erosion in the region. Although both reports are accurate, one claims that the region suffers relatively little erosion, while the other claims that regional erosion is heavy and a cause for concern. →	**Step 2:**
Which one of the following, if true, most helps to explain how both reports could be accurate? →	**Step 1:**
	Step 3:
(A) Neither report presents an extensive chemical analysis of the soil in the region. →	**Step 4:**
(B) Both reports include computer-enhanced satellite photographs. →	
(C) One report was prepared by scientists from a university, while the other report was prepared by scientists from a private consulting firm. →	
(D) One report focuses on regional topsoil erosion, while the other report focuses on riverbank erosion resulting from seasonal floods. →	
(E) One report cost nearly twice as much to prepare as did the other report. →	

PrepTest51 Sec3 Q8

LSAT Question	Analysis
Engineers are investigating the suitability of Wantastiquet Pass as the site of a new bridge. Because one concern is whether erosion could eventually weaken the bridge's foundations, they contracted for two reports on erosion in the region. Although both reports are accurate, one claims that the region suffers relatively little erosion, while the other claims that regional erosion is heavy and a cause for concern.	**Step 2:** Two studies looked at erosion near a bridge. Both are accurate. → Report 1—Relatively little erosion Report 2—Heavy erosion
Which one of the following, if true, most helps to explain how both reports could be accurate?	**Step 1:** The correct answer will provide a fact that explains how two (apparently contradictory) reports can both be true.
	Step 3: For two reports to be accurate, and yet reach opposite conclusions, they must be studying different things. The correct answer will explain this.
(A) Neither report presents an extensive chemical analysis of the soil in the region.	**Step 4:** 180. This is yet another way in which the studies are similar. Eliminate.
(B) Both reports include computer-enhanced satellite photographs.	180. This is yet another way in which the studies are similar. Eliminate.
(C) One report was prepared by scientists from a university, while the other report was prepared by scientists from a private consulting firm.	Irrelevant Comparison. The fact that different people ran the two studies doesn't explain how both can be accurate. Eliminate.
(D) One report focuses on regional topsoil erosion, while the other report focuses on riverbank erosion resulting from seasonal floods.	Correct. If the reports studied two different kinds of erosion, they may reach opposite conclusions without one being incorrect.
(E) One report cost nearly twice as much to prepare as did the other report. *PrepTest51 Sec3 Q8*	Irrelevant Comparison. The fact that the reports cost a different amount doesn't explain how both can be correct. Eliminate.

Common Logical Reasoning Wrong Answer Types

As you reviewed the analysis of the previous questions, you probably noticed that certain wrong answer types appeared several times. While not every wrong answer fits neatly into one of the following types identified (and, arguably, some wrong answers fit into more than one category), an LSAT expert can use the common wrong answer types to quickly and confidently eliminate dozens of wrong answers on Test Day.

LOGICAL REASONING: WRONG ANSWER TYPES

- **Outside the Scope**—a choice containing a statement that is too broad, too narrow, or beyond the purview of the stimulus
- **Irrelevant Comparison**—a choice that compares two items or attributes in a way not germane to the author's argument or statements
- **Extreme**—a choice containing language too emphatic to be supported by the stimulus; Extreme choices are often (though not always) characterized by words such as *all*, *never*, *every*, or *none*
- **Distortion**—a choice that mentions details from the stimulus but mangles or misstates what the author says or implies about those details
- **180**—a choice that directly contradicts what the correct answer must say (for example, a choice that strengthens the argument in a Weaken question)
- **Faulty Use of Detail**—a choice that accurately states something from the stimulus but in a manner that answers the question incorrectly; this type is rarely used in Logical Reasoning

The bottom line is that every wrong answer is wrong because it does not answer the question posed by the question stem. As you continue to study, practice, and review, make a point of explaining in your own words *why* each wrong answer is incorrect.

LSAT STRATEGY

Some wrong answers apply to specific question types. In Assumption and Main Point questions, for example, it is common to see wrong answers that simply repeat the author's evidence. You'll see more question-specific wrong answers as you move through the following chapters and learn why they are incorrect on the exam.

blanks listing the steps and strategies associated with the Logical Reasoning Method.

Kaplan Logical Reasoning Method

Step 1: _Read Question stem_

What is the purpose of Step 1?

Knowing type of a stem will tell you what to look for in stimulus

Step 2: _Untangle Stimulus_

What is the purpose of Step 2?

Zero in on what is relevant based on question type.

Step 3: _Make a prediction_

What is the purpose of Step 3?

Predictions help you focus on what to look for in right answer & keep you from picking wrong answer

Step 4: _Evaluate answer choices_

What is the purpose of Step 4?

Only one right answer, select one that matches prediction or eliminate wrong answers

164

Fill in the blanks listing the six common Logical Reasoning wrong answer traps, along with a brief description of each one.

Logical Reasoning Common Wrong Answer Traps

Wrong Answer Trap: *Outside Scope*

Description: _____

Wrong Answer Trap: *Irrelevant comparison*

Description: _____

Wrong Answer Trap: *Extreme*

Description: _____

Wrong Answer Trap: *Distortion*

Description: _____

Wrong Answer Trap: *180*

Description: _____

Wrong Answer Trap: *Faulty use of Detail*

Description: _____

Perform—Answer Key

Kaplan Logical Reasoning Method

Step 1: *Identify the Question Type*

What is the purpose of Step 1?

> *By starting here, you know what to look for in the stimulus.*

Step 2: *Untangle the Stimulus*

What is the purpose of Step 2?

> *Zero in on what is relevant based on the question type.*

Step 3: *Predict the Correct Answer*

What is the purpose of Step 3?

> *A prediction allows you to stay focused on what to look for in the answer choices and will keep you from being tempted by wrong answers.*

Step 4: *Evaluate the Answer Choices*

What is the purpose of Step 4?

> *Identify the answer that matches your prediction. Eliminate those that do not. Do not try to gauge which answer is better than another. There is only one right answer.*

Logical Reasoning Common Wrong Answer Traps

Wrong Answer Trap: _**Outside the Scope**_

Description: _An answer that is beyond the purview of the stimulus, making it irrelevant to the question stem._

Wrong Answer Trap: _**Irrelevant Comparison**_

Description: _A choice that compares two things in a way not relevant to the question stem._

Wrong Answer Trap: _**Extreme**_

Description: _A choice that contains language too strong to be supported by the stimulus._

Wrong Answer Trap: _**Distortion**_

Description: _An answer that mentions details from the stimulus but alters or misstates the relationship about those details._

Wrong Answer Trap: _**180**_

Description: _A choice that directly contradicts what the correct answer should say._

Wrong Answer Trap: _**Faulty Use of Detail**_

Description: _An answer that accurately states something from the stimulus, but in a manner that does not accurately answer the question stem._

REFLECTION

Take a moment and look back over the work you did in this chapter. Reflect on the following questions:

· How does the Logical Reasoning Method help you tackle questions more efficiently?
· Were you consistently predicting what the correct answer would say before evaluating the choices?
· How does predicting the correct answer help you eliminate wrong answer choices?
· If you have practiced LSAT Logical Reasoning questions before now, how will your approach to these questions change going forward?

In the following chapters, you will learn how to identify and answer all of the questions in the Logical Reasoning sections of the LSAT. Along the way, you'll build the skills that these questions are designed to reward. Some Logical Reasoning questions zero in on one skill, but most test several reading and thinking skills in combination. Chapters 7 and 8 are arranged so that you begin with the most fundamental skills and work your way to some of the most challenging and complex problems on the test.

CHAPTER 7

Argument-Based Questions

On the LSAT, the word *argument* does not refer to a dispute between two people. An LSAT argument is one person's attempt to convince the reader that some assertion is true or that some action is advisable. LSAT arguments are defined by two explicit components: the *conclusion* and the *evidence*.

LSAT STRATEGY

Every LSAT argument contains:

- A conclusion—The assertion, evaluation, or recommendation about which the author is trying to convince his readers
- Evidence—The facts, studies, or contentions the author believes support or establish the conclusion

---

The question types covered in this chapter—Main Point, Role of a Statement, Method of Argument, Point at Issue, and Parallel Reasoning questions—directly reward your ability to identify, paraphrase, and describe the explicit parts of the argument.

The Assumption Family questions covered in Chapter 8 are also argument-based questions, but they add the ability to determine the implicit part of an argument—the assumption—to the list of requisite skills. Because of their frequency, Assumption Family questions are the most important group of Logical Reasoning question types.

Taken together, Argument-Based and Assumption Family questions account for over 75 percent of Logical Reasoning questions on recent LSATs. That's more than one-third of your score on the entire test.

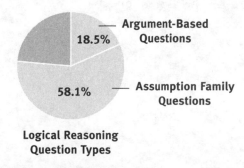

18.5% — Argument-Based Questions

58.1% — Assumption Family Questions

Logical Reasoning Question Types

PrepTests 66–80; released 2012–2016

CONCLUSIONS AND MAIN POINT QUESTIONS

Identify the Conclusion

Prepare

> ## LEARNING OBJECTIVES
>
> In this section, you'll learn to:
>
> · Identify the conclusion in an LSAT argument

All Argument-Based and Assumption Family questions reward your ability to identify an argument's conclusion. Main Point questions, like the one that follows, test this skill directly.

Editorial: Almost every year the Smithfield River floods the coastal fishing community of Redhook, which annually spends $3 million on the cleanup. Some residents have proposed damming the river, which would cost $5 million but would prevent the flooding. However, their position is misguided. A dam would prevent nutrients in the river from flowing into the ocean. Fish that now feed on those nutrients would start feeding elsewhere. The loss of these fish would cost Redhook $10 million annually.

Which one of the following most accurately expresses the main conclusion of the editorial's argument?

(A)   The Smithfield River should be dammed to prevent flooding.
(B)   Nutrients from the Smithfield River are essential to the local fish population.
(C)   Damming the Smithfield River is not worth the high construction costs for such a project.
(D)   For Redhook to build a dam on the Smithfield River would be a mistake.
(E)   The Smithfield River floods cost Redhook $3 million every year.

PrepTest51 Sec1 Q1

The conclusion of an argument is the author's main point: The statement she hopes to convince the reader is true.

Conclusion Keywords

Many LSAT arguments include Keywords that highlight the conclusion.

LSAT Question	Analysis
Vanwilligan: Some have argued that professional athletes receive unfairly high salaries. But in an unrestricted free market, such as the market these athletes compete in, salaries are determined by what someone else is willing to pay for their services. These athletes make enormous profits for their teams' owners, and that is why owners are willing to pay them extraordinary salaries. [Thus the salaries they receive are fair.] *PrepTest49 Sec2 Q19*	*Thus* signals the author's conclusion: *The salaries professional athletes receive are fair.*

LSAT STRATEGY

Conclusion Keywords include:

- Thus
- Therefore
- As a result
- It follows that

- Consequently
- So
- [Evidence] is evidence that [conclusion]

Now, you try it. Circle the conclusion Keyword and mark the conclusion in the following argument.

> Editorial: (Clearly) during the past two years, the
> unemployment situation in our city has been
> improving. Studies show that the number of
> unemployed people who are actively looking for
> jobs has steadily decreased during that period.
>
> *PrepTest49 Sec4 Q1*

TEST DAY TIP

Bracket the conclusion of an argument in your test booklet. Get in the habit of
doing this on all Argument-Based and Assumption Family questions.

Subsidiary Conclusions

Not every conclusion Keyword signals the author's main point or final conclusion. Some arguments on the LSAT
contain subsidiary or intermediate conclusions.

LSAT Question	Analysis
Economist: As should be obvious, raising the minimum wage significantly would make it more expensive for businesses to pay workers for minimum-wage jobs. Therefore, businesses could not afford to continue to employ as many workers for such jobs. So raising the minimum wage significantly will cause an increase in unemployment. *PrepTest57 Sec3 Q6*	Conclusion: *So* signals the author's main point: *Significantly increasing the minimum wage will increase unemployment.* *Therefore* signals a subsidiary conclusion that serves as evidence for the main point.

What is a subsidiary conclusion?

How can you distinguish a subsidiary conclusion from the argument's main point?

Evidence Keywords

In other LSAT arguments, evidence Keywords signal the support for the author's conclusion.

LSAT Question	Analysis
In a poll of a representative sample of a province's residents, the provincial capital was the city most often selected as the best place to live in that province. Since the capital is also the largest of that province's many cities, the poll shows that most residents of that province generally prefer life in large cities to life in small cities. *PrepTest51 Sec1 Q18*	The Keyword [s]*ince* signals the evidence in the argument. The conclusion begins after the comma in that sentence: [T]*he poll shows that most in the province prefer life in big cities to life in small cities.*

LSAT STRATEGY

Evidence Keywords include:

- Because
- Since
- [Evidence] is evidence of [conclusion]
- After all
- For

Now you try it. Circle the evidence Keyword(s) and mark the conclusion in the following argument.

There is a difference between beauty and truth. After all, if there were no difference, then the most realistic pieces of art would be the best as well, since the most realistic pieces are the most truthful. But many of the most realistic artworks are not among the best.

PrepTest49 Sec4 Q16

Conclusion from Context

Still other LSAT arguments contain neither conclusion nor evidence Keywords.

LSAT Question	Analysis
It is due to a misunderstanding that most modern sculpture is monochromatic. When ancient sculptures were exhumed years ago, they were discovered to be uncolored. No one at the time had reason to believe, as we now do, that the sculptures had originally been colorfully painted, but that centuries of exposure to moisture washed away the paint. *PrepTest49 Sec4 Q13*	Conclusion: *Modern sculpture is monochromatic due to a mistaken understanding.* → The facts in the rest of the argument are offered to support the first sentence.

How can you identify a conclusion when there are no Keywords to signal evidence or conclusion in an argument? Is the author's main point still clear?

Conclusion as a Negation of Opponent's Point

Be on the lookout for when an author asserts that another person's position is incorrect. This relatively common argument pattern on the LSAT will signal the author's conclusion.

LSAT Question	Analysis
Musicologist: Many critics complain of the disproportion between text and music in Handel's *da capo* arias. These texts are generally quite short and often repeated well beyond what is needed for literal understanding. Yet such criticism is refuted by noting that repetition serves a vital function: it frees the audience to focus on the music itself, which can speak to audiences whatever their language. *PrepTest61 Sec 4 Q6*	Conclusion: Those who say that the disproportion between text and music is a weakness in Handel's *da capo* arias are wrong. → The author's conclusion says that "such criticism is refuted," referring to those who criticize the disproportion between text and music in Handel's *da capo* arias.

How do you incorporate the author's opponent's position into a statement of the author's conclusion?

Practice

Circle conclusion and evidence Keywords and mark the conclusion in each of the following arguments.

	LSAT Question	My Analysis
1.	1990 editorial: Local pay phone calls have cost a quarter apiece ever since the 1970s, when a soft drink from a vending machine cost about the same. The price of a soft drink has more than doubled since, so phone companies should be allowed to raise the price of pay phone calls too. $\longrightarrow$	
	PrepTest49 Sec2 Q8	
2.	Eating garlic reduces the levels of cholesterol and triglycerides in the blood and so helps reduce the risk of cardiovascular disease. Evidence that eating garlic reduces these levels is that a group of patients taking a garlic tablet each day for four months showed a 12 percent reduction in cholesterol and a 17 percent reduction in triglycerides; over the same period, a group of similar patients taking a medically inert tablet showed only a 2 percent reduction in triglycerides and a 3 percent reduction in cholesterol. $\longrightarrow$	
	PrepTest49 Sec4 Q2	

Expert Analysis: Identify Conclusions

Here's how an LSAT expert might identify the conclusion in each of the previous arguments.

LSAT Question	Analysis
1. 1990 editorial: Local pay phone calls have cost a quarter apiece ever since the 1970s, when a soft drink from a vending machine cost about the same. The price of a soft drink has more than doubled since, so [phone companies should be allowed to raise the price of pay phone calls too.] *PrepTest49 Sec2 Q8*	*So* identifies the conclusion: Phone companies should be allowed to raise the price of pay phone calls.
2. Eating garlic reduces the levels of cholesterol and triglycerides in the blood and so [helps reduce the risk of cardiovascular disease.] Evidence that eating garlic reduces these levels is that a group of patients taking a garlic tablet each day for four months showed a 12 percent reduction in cholesterol and a 17 percent reduction in triglycerides; over the same period, a group of similar patients taking a medically inert tablet showed only a 2 percent reduction in triglycerides and a 3 percent reduction in cholesterol. *PrepTest49 Sec4 Q2*	[A]nd so signals the author's main point: Eating garlic helps reduce the risk of cardiovascular disease. The first part of the sentence indicates a direct result of eating garlic, and the word [e]vidence at the start of the second sentence indicates that the rest of the argument supports that direct result.

Perform

Circle conclusion and evidence Keywords and mark the conclusion in each of the following arguments.

LSAT Question	My Analysis
3. Scientist: A controversy in paleontology centers on the question of whether prehistoric human ancestors began to develop sophisticated tools before or after they came to stand upright. I argue that they stood upright first, simply because advanced toolmaking requires free use of the hands, and standing upright makes this possible. *PrepTest49 Sec2 Q14*	→
4. Letter to the editor: Middle-class families in wealthy nations are often criticized for the ecological damage resulting from their lifestyles. This criticism should not be taken too seriously, however, since its source is often a movie star or celebrity whose own lifestyle would, if widely adopted, destroy the environment and deplete our resources in a short time. *PrepTest49 Sec2 Q5*	→

Expert Analysis: Identify Conclusions

Here's how an LSAT expert might identify the conclusion in each of the previous arguments.

LSAT Question	Analysis
3. Scientist: A controversy in paleontology centers on the question of whether prehistoric human ancestors began to develop sophisticated tools before or after they came to stand upright. I argue that [they stood upright first,] simply because advanced toolmaking requires free use of the hands, and standing upright makes this possible. *PrepTest49 Sec2 Q14*	*I argue that* signals the conclusion: Human ancestors stood upright before developing sophisticated tools.
4. Letter to the editor: Middle-class families in wealthy nations are often criticized for the ecological damage resulting from their lifestyles. [This criticism should not be taken too seriously,] however, since its source is often a movie star or celebrity whose own lifestyle would, if widely adopted, destroy the environment and deplete our resources in a short time. *PrepTest49 Sec2 Q5*	The letter writer negates a common criticism. The idea that middle-class lifestyles damage the environment, the author says, "should not be taken too seriously."

Paraphrase and Characterize the Conclusion

Prepare

> **LEARNING OBJECTIVES**
>
> In this section, you'll learn to:
>
> · Paraphrase and characterize the conclusion

Once you can spot conclusions, the next skill is understanding what they mean. LSAT arguments don't always use the simplest or most succinct language. Paraphrasing the conclusion is important because, in some questions, the LSAT will paraphrase the author's conclusion in the answer choices. Moreover, paraphrasing simplifies the argument and makes it easier to zero in on the author's main point.

Here's how an LSAT expert might simplify a fairly complex conclusion.

LSAT Question	Analysis
From the fact that people who studied music as children frequently are quite proficient at mathematics, it cannot be concluded that the skills required for mathematics are acquired by studying music: it is equally likely that proficiency in mathematics and studying music are both the result of growing up in a family that encourages its children to excel at all intellectual and artistic endeavors. *PrepTest49 Sec4 Q17*	A colon usually signals evidence, because it leads to further explanation or examples. The author's conclusion is the first sentence. *Being good at music is correlated with being good at math, but that doesn't mean that the person's math skills came from studying music.*

Paraphrasing is made easier by knowing that nearly all LSAT conclusions fall into one of six categories.

> **CONCLUSION TYPES**
>
> In an LSAT argument, the conclusion almost always matches one or more of these six types:
>
> · Value Judgment (an evaluative statement; e.g., Action X is unethical or Y's recital was poorly sung)
> · If/Then (a conditional prediction, recommendation, or assertion; e.g., If X is true, then so is Y or If you are an M, you should do N)
> · Prediction (X *will* or *will not* happen in the future)
> · Comparison (X is taller/shorter/more common/less common/etc. than Y)
> · Assertion of Fact (X is true or X is false)
> · Recommendation (we *should* or *should not* do X)

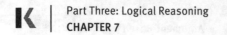

Identify the conclusion type in each of the following examples.

Conclusion	My Analysis
a. Therefore, these fat-free brownies are healthier than those cookies are. *PrepTest51 Sec3 Q22* →	[H]*ealthier than* makes this conclusion a[n]
b. This fact helps make large-animal species more vulnerable to extinction than small-animal species . . . . *PrepTest49 Sec2 Q9* →	[M]*ore . . . than* makes this conclusion a[n]
c. It is time to put a halt to this trivial journalism. *PrepTest49 Sec4 Q4* →	*It is time to* makes this conclusion a[n]
d. I maintain, however, that to save lives, automobile manufacturers ought to stop equipping cars with them. *PrepTest49 Sec4 Q11* →	[O]*ught* makes this conclusion a[n]
e. Thus, it is unlikely that the airport will be built. *PrepTest61 Sec4 Q11* →	[W]*ill* makes this conclusion a[n]
f. This shows that a decrease in humidity can make people ill. *PrepTest59 Sec3 Q12* →	[A] *. . . can* makes this conclusion a[n]
g. Thus the salaries they receive are fair. *PrepTest49 Sec2 Q19* →	[F]*air* makes this conclusion a[n]
h. So if the screen is to be a hedge, it will be a hemlock hedge. *PrepTest51 Sec1 Q5* →	[I]*f . . . will* makes this conclusion a[n]

Practice

Identify, characterize, and paraphrase the conclusion in each of the following arguments.

LSAT Question	My Analysis
5. Pundit: The average salary for teachers in our society is lower than the average salary for athletes. Obviously, our society values sports more than it values education. *PrepTest51 Sec3 Q4* →	Paraphrase: Type:
6. Engineer: Thermophotovoltaic generators are devices that convert heat into electricity. The process of manufacturing steel produces huge amounts of heat that currently go to waste. So if steel-manufacturing plants could feed the heat they produce into thermophotovoltaic generators, they would greatly reduce their electric bills, thereby saving money. *PrepTest61 Sec2 Q16* →	Paraphrase: Type:
7. Essayist: Lessing contended that an art form's medium dictates the kind of representation the art form must employ in order to be legitimate; painting, for example, must represent simultaneous arrays of colored shapes, while literature, consisting of words read in succession, must represent events or actions occurring in sequence. The claim about literature must be rejected, however, if one regards as legitimate the imagists' poems, which consist solely of amalgams of disparate images. *PrepTest57 Sec2 Q7* →	Paraphrase: Type:
8. Bethany: Psychologists have discovered a technique for replacing one's nightmares with pleasant dreams, and have successfully taught it to adults suffering from chronic nightmares. Studies have found that nightmare-prone children are especially likely to suffer from nightmares as adults. Thus, psychologists should direct efforts toward identifying nightmare-prone children so that these children can be taught the technique for replacing their nightmares with pleasant dreams. *PrepTest59 Sec2 Q13* →	Paraphrase: Type:
9. Sometimes one reads a poem and believes that the poem expresses contradictory ideas, even if it is a great poem. So it is wrong to think that the meaning of a poem is whatever the author intends to communicate to the reader by means of the poem. No one who is writing a great poem intends it to communicate contradictory ideas. *PrepTest57 Sec2 Q24* →	Paraphrase: Type:

Expert Analysis: Paraphrase and Characterize Conclusions

Here's how an LSAT expert might paraphrase and characterize the conclusions in the previous arguments.

LSAT Question	Analysis
5. Pundit: The average salary for teachers in our society is lower than the average salary for athletes. Obviously, our society values sports more than it values education. *PrepTest51 Sec3 Q4*	Paraphrase: Our society values sports more than it does education. Type: Comparison
6. Engineer: Thermophotovoltaic generators are devices that convert heat into electricity. The process of manufacturing steel produces huge amounts of heat that currently go to waste. So if steel-manufacturing plants could feed the heat they produce into thermophotovoltaic generators, they would greatly reduce their electric bills, thereby saving money. *PrepTest61 Sec2 Q16*	Paraphrase: If steel plants could cycle heat into TP generators, then they would save money. Type: If/Then, Prediction
7. Essayist: Lessing contended that an art form's medium dictates the kind of representation the art form must employ in order to be legitimate; painting, for example, must represent simultaneous arrays of colored shapes, while literature, consisting of words read in succession, must represent events or actions occurring in sequence. The claim about literature must be rejected, however, if one regards as legitimate the imagists' poems, which consist solely of amalgams of disparate images. *PrepTest57 Sec2 Q7*	Paraphrase: If imagist poems are literature, then literature does not have to depict events in sequence. Type: If/Then, Assertion of Fact
8. Bethany: Psychologists have discovered a technique for replacing one's nightmares with pleasant dreams, and have successfully taught it to adults suffering from chronic nightmares. Studies have found that nightmare-prone children are especially likely to suffer from nightmares as adults. Thus, psychologists should direct efforts toward identifying nightmare-prone children so that these children can be taught the technique for replacing their nightmares with pleasant dreams. *PrepTest59 Sec2 Q13*	Paraphrase: Psychologists should focus on identifying nightmare-prone children (so that the kids can benefit from the new technique). Type: Recommendation
9. Sometimes one reads a poem and believes that the poem expresses contradictory ideas, even if it is a great poem. So it is wrong to think that the meaning of a poem is whatever the author intends to communicate to the reader by means of the poem. No one who is writing a great poem intends it to communicate contradictory ideas. *PrepTest57 Sec2 Q24*	Paraphrase: A poem's meaning is *not* determined by the author's intent. Type: Assertion of Fact

Perform

Identify, characterize, and paraphrase the conclusion in each of the following arguments.

LSAT Question	My Analysis
10. In a poll of a representative sample of a province's residents, the provincial capital was the city most often selected as the best place to live in that province. Since the capital is also the largest of that province's many cities, the poll shows that most residents of that province generally prefer life in large cities to life in small cities. *PrepTest51 Sec1 Q18*	Paraphrase: Type:
11. Ecologists predict that the incidence of malaria will increase if global warming continues or if the use of pesticides is not expanded. But the use of pesticides is known to contribute to global warming, so it is inevitable that we will see an increase in malaria in the years to come. *PrepTest51 Sec3 Q24*	Paraphrase: Type:
12. Team captain: Winning requires the willingness to cooperate, which in turn requires motivation. So you will not win if you are not motivated. *PrepTest57 Sec2 Q19*	Paraphrase: Type:
13. Scientist: A controversy in paleontology centers on the question of whether prehistoric human ancestors began to develop sophisticated tools before or after they came to stand upright. I argue that they stood upright first, simply because advanced toolmaking requires free use of the hands, and standing upright makes this possible. *PrepTest49 Sec2 Q14*	Paraphrase: Type:
14. The typological theory of species classification, which has few adherents today, distinguishes species solely on the basis of observable physical characteristics, such as plumage color, adult size, or dental structure. However, there are many so-called "sibling species," which are indistinguishable on the basis of their appearance but cannot interbreed and thus, according to the mainstream biological theory of species classification, are separate species. Since the typological theory does not count sibling species as separate species, it is unacceptable. *PrepTest51 Sec1 Q15*	Paraphrase: Type:

Expert Analysis: Paraphrase and Characterize Conclusions

Here's how an LSAT expert might paraphrase and characterize the conclusions in the previous arguments.

LSAT Question	Analysis
10. In a poll of a representative sample of a province's residents, the provincial capital was the city most often selected as the best place to live in that province. Since the capital is also the largest of that province's many cities, the poll shows that most residents of that province generally prefer life in large cities to life in small cities. *PrepTest51 Sec1 Q18*	Paraphrase: Most residents of the province prefer big-city life to life in small cities. Type: Comparison
11. Ecologists predict that the incidence of malaria will increase if global warming continues or if the use of pesticides is not expanded. But the use of pesticides is known to contribute to global warming, so it is inevitable that we will see an increase in malaria in the years to come. *PrepTest51 Sec3 Q24*	Paraphrase: A rise in malaria is inevitable. Type: Prediction
12. Team captain: Winning requires the willingness to cooperate, which in turn requires motivation. So you will not win if you are not motivated. *PrepTest57 Sec2 Q19*	Paraphrase: Motivation is necessary for winning. If win → motivated. If not motivated → not win. Type: If/Then
13. Scientist: A controversy in paleontology centers on the question of whether prehistoric human ancestors began to develop sophisticated tools before or after they came to stand upright. I argue that they stood upright first, simply because advanced toolmaking requires free use of the hands, and standing upright makes this possible. *PrepTest49 Sec2 Q14*	Paraphrase: Human ancestors stood upright before they developed sophisticated tools. Type: Assertion of Fact
14. The typological theory of species classification, which has few adherents today, distinguishes species solely on the basis of observable physical characteristics, such as plumage color, adult size, or dental structure. However, there are many so-called "sibling species," which are indistinguishable on the basis of their appearance but cannot interbreed and thus, according to the mainstream biological theory of species classification, are separate species. Since the typological theory does not count sibling species as separate species, it is unacceptable. *PrepTest51 Sec1 Q15*	Paraphrase: The typological theory is unacceptable. Type: Value Judgment

Identify and Answer Main Point Questions

Prepare

Separating an author's main conclusion from her evidence is so critical on the LSAT that there is even a question type—Main Point questions—that asks you to do only that.

You can identify Main Point questions from question stems such as these:

Which one of the following most accurately expresses the main conclusion of the argument?

PrepTest59 Sec2 Q10

Which one of the following sentences best expresses the main point of the musicologist's reasoning?

PrepTest61 Sec4 Q6

Which one of the following most accurately expresses the conclusion of the argument as a whole?

PrepTest57 Sec3 Q3

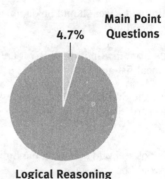

4.7% **Main Point Questions**

Logical Reasoning Question Types
PrepTests 66–80; released 2012–2016

MAIN POINT QUESTIONS AT A GLANCE

Task: Identify the argument's main conclusion.

Strategies: Use conclusion Keywords, evidence Keywords, subsidiary conclusions, and/or the argument's structure to distinguish the author's main point from her supporting evidence.

Frequency: Main Point questions are not prevalent; on LSAT tests released from 2012 through 2016, there were an average of 2.4 Main Point questions per test. But remember that being able to identify and understand an argument's conclusion is a skill involved in more than 75 percent of Logical Reasoning questions.

Here's how an LSAT expert might apply the Logical Reasoning Method to a Main Point question.

LSAT Question	Analysis
Editorial: Almost every year the Smithfield River floods the coastal fishing community of Redhook, which annually spends $3 million on the cleanup. Some residents have proposed damming the river, which would cost $5 million but would prevent the flooding. However, their position is misguided. A dam would prevent nutrients in the river from flowing into the ocean. Fish that now feed on those nutrients would start feeding elsewhere. The loss of these fish would cost Redhook $10 million annually. →	**Step 2:** Conclusion: Their [some residents'] position [damming the river] is misguided. The rest of the facts are offered to support the author's rebuttal of those who advocate for a dam or as background context to the debate.
Which one of the following most accurately expresses the main conclusion of the editorial's argument? →	**Step 1:** A Main Point question: The correct answer will paraphrase the argument's final conclusion.
	Step 3: The correct answer will paraphrase the main point: Damming the river is a bad idea.
(A) The Smithfield River should be dammed to prevent flooding. →	**Step 4:** 180. The author's conclusion rejects this view. Eliminate.
(B) Nutrients from the Smithfield River are essential to the local fish population. →	This is part of the author's evidence for why building a dam would be a bad idea. Eliminate.
(C) Damming the Smithfield River is not worth the high construction costs for such a project. →	The author mentions the cost of construction when describing the argument of "some residents," but his discussion of costs is in the evidence. Eliminate.
(D) For Redhook to build a dam on the Smithfield River would be a mistake. →	Correct. This matches the conclusion of the stimulus argument.
(E) The Smithfield River floods cost Redhook $3 million every year. →	This is background to the debate over damming the river. Eliminate.

PrepTest51 Sec1 Q1

Practice

Follow the Logical Reasoning Method to answer each of the following Main Point questions.

LSAT Question	My Analysis
15. Musicologist: Classification of a musical instrument depends on the mechanical action through which it produces music. So the piano is properly called a percussion instrument, not a stringed instrument. Even though the vibration of the piano's strings is what makes its sound, the strings are caused to vibrate by the impact of hammers.	**Step 2:**
Which one of the following most accurately expresses the main conclusion of the musicologist's argument? →	**Step 1:**
	Step 3:

(A) Musical instruments should be classified according to the mechanical actions through which they produce sound. →	**Step 4:**
(B) Musical instruments should not be classified based on the way musicians interact with them. →	
(C) Some people classify the piano as a stringed instrument because of the way the piano produces sound. →	
(D) The piano should be classified as a stringed instrument rather than as a percussion instrument. →	
(E) It is correct to classify the piano as a percussion instrument rather than as a stringed instrument. →	

PrepTest61 Sec2 Q9

LSAT Question		My Analysis
16. Chemical fertilizers not only create potential health hazards, they also destroy earthworms, which are highly beneficial to soil. For this reason alone the use of chemical fertilizers should be avoided. The castings earthworms leave behind are much richer than the soil they ingest, thus making a garden rich in earthworms much more fertile than a garden without them.	→	**Step 2:**
Which one of the following most accurately expresses the main conclusion of the argument?	→	**Step 1:**
		Step 3:
(A) Earthworms are highly beneficial to soil.	→	**Step 4:**
(B) Chemical fertilizers destroy earthworms.	→	
(C) The castings that earthworms leave behind are much richer than the soil they ingest.	→	
(D) The use of chemical fertilizers should be avoided.	→	
(E) A garden rich in earthworms is much more fertile than a garden that is devoid of earthworms.	→	

PrepTest59 Sec2 Q10

Expert Analysis: Main Point Questions

Here's how an LSAT expert might use the Logical Reasoning Method to answer the previous practice questions.

LSAT Question	Analysis
15. Musicologist: Classification of a musical instrument depends on the mechanical action through which it produces music. So the piano is properly called a percussion instrument, not a stringed instrument. Even though the vibration of the piano's strings is what makes its sound, the strings are caused to vibrate by the impact of hammers. →	**Step 2:** *So* signals the conclusion: The piano is properly categorized as a percussion instrument, not a string instrument. The rest of the argument explains why the author agrees with this categorization.
Which one of the following most accurately expresses the main conclusion of the musicologist's argument? →	**Step 1:** A Main Point question: The correct answer will paraphrase the argument's final conclusion.
	Step 3: The piano is properly categorized as a percussion instrument, not a string instrument.
(A) Musical instruments should be classified according to the mechanical actions through which they produce sound. →	**Step 4:** This is the rule about how to categorize instruments. The author applies the rule in order to reach his conclusion. Eliminate.
(B) Musical instruments should not be classified based on the way musicians interact with them. →	Outside the Scope. Not only is this not the author's conclusion, it actually disagrees with the rule he states in the evidence. Eliminate.
(C) Some people classify the piano as a stringed instrument because of the way the piano produces sound. →	Outside the Scope. How others classify the piano is not relevant to the author's conclusion, which expresses how it should be categorized. Eliminate.
(D) The piano should be classified as a stringed instrument rather than as a percussion instrument. →	180. The author concludes the opposite. Eliminate.
(E) It is correct to classify the piano as a percussion instrument rather than as a stringed instrument. *PrepTest61 Sec2 Q9* →	Correct. This paraphrases the author's main point.

LSAT Question	Analysis
16. Chemical fertilizers not only create potential health hazards, they also destroy earthworms, which are highly beneficial to soil. For this reason alone the use of chemical fertilizers should be avoided. The castings earthworms leave behind are much richer than the soil they ingest, thus making a garden rich in earthworms much more fertile than a garden without them. →	**Step 2:** [*T*]*his reason* refers to the first sentence, so the first sentence must be evidence, and not the main point. What follows [*f*]*or this reason* is a recommendation: Avoid chemical fertilizers. The final sentence contains another reason to avoid chemical fertilizers, so it must be a subsidiary conclusion.
Which one of the following most accurately expresses the main conclusion of the argument? →	**Step 1:** A Main Point question: The correct answer will paraphrase the argument's final conclusion.
	Step 3: Chemical fertilizers should not be used.
(A) Earthworms are highly beneficial to soil. →	**Step 4:** This is part of the first sentence, which is evidence. Eliminate.
(B) Chemical fertilizers destroy earthworms. →	This is evidence used to support the conclusion. Eliminate.
(C) The castings that earthworms leave behind are much richer than the soil they ingest. →	This is again evidence to support the conclusion. Eliminate.
(D) The use of chemical fertilizers should be avoided. →	Correct. This states the argument's conclusion word for word.
(E) A garden rich in earthworms is much more fertile than a garden that is devoid of earthworms. *PrepTest59 Sec2 Q10* →	This is a subsidiary conclusion that supports the author's recommendation. This choice is attractive to someone who jumps at the word *thus* without considering the author's main idea. Eliminate.

Perform

Follow the Logical Reasoning Method to answer each of the following Main Point questions.

LSAT Question	My Analysis
17. Although free international trade allows countries to specialize, which in turn increases productivity, such specialization carries risks. After all, small countries often rely on one or two products for the bulk of their exports. If those products are raw materials, the supply is finite and can be used up. If they are foodstuffs, a natural disaster can wipe out a season's production overnight.	**Step 2:**
Which one of the following most accurately expresses the conclusion of the argument as a whole?	**Step 1:** **Step 3:**

Specialization ↑ prod but also risk

(A)	Specialization within international trade comes with risks.	**Step 4:**
(B)	A natural disaster can destroy a whole season's production overnight, devastating a small country's economy.	
(C)	A small country's supply of raw materials can be used up in a short period.	
(D)	Some countries rely on a small number of products for the export-based sectors of their economies.	
(E)	When international trade is free, countries can specialize in what they export.	

PrepTest57 Sec3 Q3

LSAT Question	My Analysis
18. Musicologist: Many critics complain of the disproportion between text and music in Handel's *da capo* arias. These texts are generally quite short and often repeated well beyond what is needed for literal understanding. Yet such criticism is refuted by noting that repetition serves a vital function: it frees the audience to focus on the music itself, which can speak to audiences whatever their language.	**Step 2:** →
Which one of the following sentences best expresses the main point of the musicologist's reasoning?	**Step 1:** → *Repetition helps focus on music*
	Step 3:
(A) Handel's *da capo* arias contain a disproportionate amount of music.	**Step 4:** →
(B) Handel's *da capo* arias are superior to most in their accessibility to diverse audiences.	→
(C) At least one frequent criticism of Handel's *da capo* arias is undeserved.	→
(D) At least some of Handel's *da capo* arias contain unnecessary repetitions.	→
(E) Most criticism of Handel's *da capo* arias is unwarranted.	→

PrepTest61 Sec4 Q6

"Many" is in passage
only 1 complaint
MOST = extreme

Expert Analysis: Main Point Questions

Here's how an LSAT expert might use the Logical Reasoning Method to answer the previous questions.

LSAT Question	Analysis
17. Although free international trade allows countries to specialize, which in turn increases productivity, such specialization carries risks. After all, small countries often rely on one or two products for the bulk of their exports. If those products are raw materials, the supply is finite and can be used up. If they are foodstuffs, a natural disaster can wipe out a season's production overnight. →	**Step 2:** *After all* at the beginning of the second sentence signals the evidence. That indicates that the conclusion is located in the first sentence: The specialization enabled by international free trade carries risks. Everything following [a]*fter all* explains and provides examples of the risks the author recognizes in her conclusion.
Which one of the following most accurately expresses the conclusion of the argument as a whole? →	**Step 1:** A Main Point question: The correct answer will paraphrase the argument's final conclusion.
	Step 3: The specialization enabled by international free trade carries risks.
(A) Specialization within international trade comes with risks. →	**Step 4:** Correct. This closely paraphrases the conclusion in the argument.
(B) A natural disaster can destroy a whole season's production overnight, devastating a small country's economy. →	This is one of the hypothetical scenarios in the author's evidence. Eliminate.
(C) A small country's supply of raw materials can be used up in a short period. →	This is one of the hypothetical scenarios in the author's evidence. Eliminate.
(D) Some countries rely on a small number of products for the export-based sectors of their economies. →	This is the author's basic premise (or evidence) for why she believes her conclusion. Eliminate.
(E) When international trade is free, countries can specialize in what they export. *PrepTest57 Sec3 Q3* →	While the author would agree with this statement, it is just background information from the first sentence. The author's negative opinion about specialization at the end of the first sentence is her main point. Eliminate.

LSAT Question	Analysis
18. Musicologist: Many critics complain of the disproportion between text and music in Handel's *da capo* arias. These texts are generally quite short and often repeated well beyond what is needed for literal understanding. Yet such criticism is refuted by noting that repetition serves a vital function: it frees the audience to focus on the music itself, which can speak to audiences whatever their language. →	**Step 2:** Conclusion: Those who say that the disproportion between text and music is a weakness in Handel's *da capo* arias are wrong.
Which one of the following sentences best expresses the main point of the musicologist's reasoning? →	**Step 1:** A Main Point question: The correct answer will paraphrase the argument's final conclusion.
	Step 3: Those who say that the disproportion between text and music is a weakness in Handel's *da capo* arias are wrong.
(A) Handel's *da capo* arias contain a disproportionate amount of music. →	**Step 4:** Faulty Use of Detail. The author may agree with this statement, but his conclusion is about whether the arias should be criticized for their repetitiveness. Eliminate.
(B) Handel's *da capo* arias are superior to most in their accessibility to diverse audiences. →	Outside the Scope. The author doesn't compare Handel's arias to those of any other composer. Eliminate.
(C) At least one frequent criticism of Handel's *da capo* arias is undeserved. →	Correct. This paraphrases the author's conclusion by substituting [a]*t least one* for the specific criticism the author rejects.
(D) At least some of Handel's *da capo* arias contain unnecessary repetitions. →	180. This is part of the author's opponents' position. The author's evidence, however, actually finds merit in the repetition. Eliminate.
(E) Most criticism of Handel's *da capo* arias is unwarranted. *PrepTest61 Sec4 Q6* →	Extreme. The author rejects one criticism of the arias. He may or may not agree with [m]*ost* of the others. Eliminate.

EVIDENCE AND ARGUMENTS: ROLE OF A STATEMENT, POINT AT ISSUE, AND METHOD OF ARGUMENT QUESTIONS

On the LSAT, you will never be asked to defend the author's evidence. Frequently, however, you will need to analyze an argument's structure and characterize how the evidence interacts with the author's conclusion. Those skills are most directly rewarded on questions like these:

Role of a Statement

It would not be surprising to discover that the trade routes between China and the West were opened many centuries, even millennia, earlier than 200 B.C., contrary to what is currently believed. After all, what made the Great Silk Road so attractive as a trade route linking China and the West—level terrain, easily traversable mountain passes, and desert oases—would also have made it an attractive route for the original emigrants to China from Africa and the Middle East, and this early migration began at least one million years ago.

That a migration from Africa and the Middle East to China occurred at least one million years ago figures in the above reasoning in which one of the following ways?

(A) It is cited as conclusive evidence for the claim that trade links between China and the Middle East were established long before 200 B.C.

(B) It is an intermediate conclusion made plausible by the description of the terrain along which the migration supposedly took place.

(C) It is offered as evidence in support of the claim that trade routes between China and the West could easily have been established much earlier than is currently believed.

(D) It is offered as evidence against the claim that trade routes between China and Africa preceded those eventually established between China and the Middle East.

(E) It is the main conclusion that the argument attempts to establish about intercourse between China and the West.

PrepTest51 Sec1 Q14

Point at Issue

Talbert: Chess is beneficial for school-age children. It is enjoyable, encourages foresight and logical thinking, and discourages carelessness, inattention, and impulsiveness. In short, it promotes mental maturity.

Sklar: My objection to teaching chess to children is that it diverts mental activity from something with societal value, such as science, into something that has no societal value.

Talbert's and Sklar's statements provide the strongest support for holding that they disagree with each other over whether

(A) chess promotes mental maturity
(B) many activities promote mental maturity just as well as chess does
(C) chess is socially valuable and science is not
(D) children should be taught to play chess
(E) children who neither play chess nor study science are mentally immature

PrepTest61 Sec2 Q7

Method of Argument

Hernandez: I recommend that staff cars be replaced every four years instead of every three years. Three-year-old cars are still in good condition and this would result in big savings.

Green: I disagree. Some of our salespeople with big territories wear out their cars in three years.

Hernandez: I meant three-year-old cars subjected to normal use.

In the conversation, Hernandez responds to Green's objection in which one of the following ways?

(A) by explicitly qualifying a premise used earlier
(B) by criticizing salespeople who wear out their cars in three years
(C) by disputing the accuracy of Green's evidence
(D) by changing the subject to the size of sales territories
(E) by indicating that Green used a phrase Ambiguously

PrepTest57 Sec3 Q5

Identify the Evidence

Prepare

Once you've learned to identify the conclusion, the next step in analyzing an argument is to distinguish the relevant evidence from the conclusion and from any general background information.

LEARNING OBJECTIVES

In this section, you'll learn to:

· Distinguish evidence from background information

As a strategic reader, you should be able to describe the way each statement serves the argument. Take a look at how an LSAT expert might distinguish among the roles of various statements in an argument you've already seen.

LSAT Question	Analysis
Editorial: Almost every year the Smithfield River floods the coastal fishing community of Redhook, which annually spends $3 million on the cleanup. Some residents have proposed damming the river, which would cost $5 million but would prevent the flooding. However, their position is misguided. A dam would prevent nutrients in the river from flowing into the ocean. Fish that now feed on those nutrients would start feeding elsewhere. The loss of these fish would cost Redhook $10 million annually. *PrepTest51 Sec1 Q1*	**Step 2:** Sentence 1—**Background—the impetus for a debate:** Flood cleanup costs $3 million per year. Sentence 2—**Some residents' (not the author's) recommendation:** Build a dam for $5 million. → Sentence 3—**The author's conclusion:** *some residents'* recommendation is a mistake. Sentences 4, 5, and 6—**The author's evidence:** · A dam would stop nutrients. · Fish that need the nutrients would leave the area. · Losing the fish costs $10 million per year.

LSAT STRATEGY

One sentence does not always contain one "statement." A single sentence might contain two pieces of evidence or an evidentiary premise and the conclusion.

Practice

Identify how each statement functions in the following LSAT arguments. Identify the conclusion first, and then describe the roles played by the other statements.

LSAT Question	My Analysis
19. Most of the employees of the Compujack Corporation are computer programmers. Since most computer programmers receive excellent salaries from their employers, at least one Compujack employee must receive an excellent salary from Compujack. *PrepTest49 Sec4 Q24*	Conclusion: Roles of Other Statements:
20. An art critic, by ridiculing an artwork, can undermine the pleasure one takes in it; conversely, by lavishing praise upon an artwork, an art critic can render the experience of viewing the artwork more pleasurable. So an artwork's artistic merit can depend not only on the person who creates it but also on those who critically evaluate it. *PrepTest61 Sec4 Q13*	Conclusion: Roles of Other Statements:
21. Vanwilligan: Some have argued that professional athletes receive unfairly high salaries. But in an unrestricted free market, such as the market these athletes compete in, salaries are determined by what someone else is willing to pay for their services. These athletes make enormous profits for their teams' owners, and that is why owners are willing to pay them extraordinary salaries. Thus the salaries they receive are fair. *PrepTest49 Sec2 Q19*	Conclusion: Roles of Other Statements:
22. Columnist: It has been noted that attending a live musical performance is a richer experience than is listening to recorded music. Some say that this is merely because we do not see the performers when we listen to recorded music. However, there must be some other reason, for there is relatively little difference between listening to someone read a story over the radio and listening to someone in the same room read a story. *PrepTest59 Sec2 Q7*	Conclusion: Roles of Other Statements:

Expert Analysis: Distinguish Roles of Statements

Here's how an LSAT expert might characterize the roles of the statements in those practice arguments.

LSAT Question	Analysis
19. Most of the employees of the Compujack Corporation are computer programmers. Since most computer programmers receive excellent salaries from their employers, at least one Compujack employee must receive an excellent salary from Compujack. *PrepTest49 Sec4 Q24*	**Conclusion:** [last part of sentence 2] At least one CJ employee receives an excellent salary from CJ. Sentence 1 and first part of sentence 2—**Two separate pieces of evidence:** · Most employees of CJ are programmers. · Most programmers have great salaries.
20. An art critic, by ridiculing an artwork, can undermine the pleasure one takes in it; conversely, by lavishing praise upon an artwork, an art critic can render the experience of viewing the artwork more pleasurable. So an artwork's artistic merit can depend not only on the person who creates it but also on those who critically evaluate it. *PrepTest61 Sec4 Q13*	**Conclusion:** [second sentence] A work's artistic merit can depend on both the artist and the critics. Sentence 1—**Two contrasting pieces of evidence:** · Critics can decrease pleasure in art. · But critics can increase pleasure, too.
21. Vanwilligan: Some have argued that professional athletes receive unfairly high salaries. But in an unrestricted free market, such as the market these athletes compete in, salaries are determined by what someone else is willing to pay for their services. These athletes make enormous profits for their teams' owners, and that is why owners are willing to pay them extraordinary salaries. Thus the salaries they receive are fair. *PrepTest49 Sec2 Q19*	**Conclusion:** [fourth sentence] Professional athletes' salaries are fair. Sentence 1—**Author's opponents' position:** Pro athletes' salaries are unfair. Sentence 2—**Author's evidence:** Free markets set fair salaries at what employers are willing to pay. Sentence 3—**Author's evidence:** Owners are willing to pay pro athletes' salaries.
22. Columnist: It has been noted that attending a live musical performance is a richer experience than is listening to recorded music. Some say that this is merely because we do not see the performers when we listen to recorded music. However, there must be some other reason, for there is relatively little difference between listening to someone read a story over the radio and listening to someone in the same room read a story. *PrepTest59 Sec2 Q7*	**Conclusion:** [first part of Sentence 3] Seeing the musicians is *not* the reason live music is richer (my opponents' explanation is wrong). Sentence 1—**Background observation:** Live music is a richer experience than recorded music. Sentence 2—**The author's opponents' explanation for the observation:** Live music is richer because we see the musicians. Second part of Sentence 3—**Author's evidence:** An analogy showing why the opponents' explanation must be wrong.

Perform

Identify how each statement functions in the following LSAT arguments. Identify the conclusion first, and then describe the roles played by the other statements.

LSAT Question	My Analysis
23. Chiu: The belief that a person is always morally blameworthy for feeling certain emotions, such as unjustifiable anger, jealousy, or resentment, is misguided. Individuals are responsible for only what is under their control, and whether one feels such an emotion is not always under one's control. *PrepTest51 Sec1 Q16*	**Conclusion:** **Roles of Other Statements:**
24. Scientist: A controversy in paleontology centers on the question of whether prehistoric human ancestors began to develop sophisticated tools before or after they came to stand upright. I argue that they stood upright first, simply because advanced toolmaking requires free use of the hands, and standing upright makes this possible. *PrepTest49 Sec2 Q14*	**Conclusion:** **Roles of Other Statements:**
25. Bethany: Psychologists have discovered a technique for replacing one's nightmares with pleasant dreams, and have successfully taught it to adults suffering from chronic nightmares. Studies have found that nightmare-prone children are especially likely to suffer from nightmares as adults. Thus, psychologists should direct efforts toward identifying nightmare-prone children so that these children can be taught the technique for replacing their nightmares with pleasant dreams. *PrepTest59 Sec2 Q13*	**Conclusion:** **Roles of Other Statements:**
26. It is primarily by raising interest rates that central bankers curb inflation, but an increase in interest rates takes up to two years to affect inflation. Accordingly, central bankers usually try to raise interest rates before inflation becomes excessive, at which time inflation is not yet readily apparent either. But unless inflation is readily apparent, interest rate hikes generally will be perceived as needlessly restraining a growing economy. Thus, central bankers' success in temporarily restraining inflation may make it harder for them to ward off future inflation without incurring the public's wrath. *PrepTest49 Sec2 Q12*	**Conclusion:** **Roles of Other Statements:**

Expert Analysis: Distinguish Roles of Statements

Here's how an LSAT expert might characterize the roles of the statements in those arguments.

LSAT Question	Analysis
23. Chiu: The belief that a person is always morally blameworthy for feeling certain emotions, such as unjustifiable anger, jealousy, or resentment, is misguided. Individuals are responsible for only what is under their control, and whether one feels such an emotion is not always under one's control. *PrepTest51 Sec1 Q16*	**Conclusion:** [first sentence] People are not always blameworthy for feeling negative emotions. Sentence 2—**Two related pieces of evidence:** · People are responsible only for things under their control. · Feeling emotions is not always under a person's control.
24. Scientist: A controversy in paleontology centers on the question of whether prehistoric human ancestors began to develop sophisticated tools before or after they came to stand upright. I argue that they stood upright first, simply because advanced toolmaking requires free use of the hands, and standing upright makes this possible. *PrepTest49 Sec2 Q14*	**Conclusion:** [first part of Sentence 2] Humans stood upright before making advanced tools. Sentence 1—**Background description of a scientific debate:** Which came first—standing upright or making advanced tools? Second part of Sentence 2—**Author's evidence:** · Free hands are needed to make advanced tools. · Standing up frees up the hands.
25. Bethany: Psychologists have discovered a technique for replacing one's nightmares with pleasant dreams, and have successfully taught it to adults suffering from chronic nightmares. Studies have found that nightmare-prone children are especially likely to suffer from nightmares as adults. Thus, psychologists should direct efforts toward identifying nightmare-prone children so that these children can be taught the technique for replacing their nightmares with pleasant dreams. *PrepTest59 Sec2 Q13*	**Conclusion:** [first part of Sentence 3] Psychologists should focus on nightmare-prone kids. Sentence 1—**A scientific discovery that gives rise to the author's argument:** successful nightmare treatments Sentence 2—**A second discovery that makes the first important for one group:** nightmare-prone kids likely to become nightmare-prone adults Second part of Sentence 3—**The reason for the recommendation in the author's conclusion**
26. It is primarily by raising interest rates that central bankers curb inflation, but an increase in interest rates takes up to two years to affect inflation. Accordingly, central bankers usually try to raise interest rates before inflation becomes excessive, at which time inflation is not yet readily apparent either. But unless inflation is readily apparent, interest rate hikes generally will be perceived as needlessly restraining a growing economy. Thus, central bankers' success in temporarily restraining inflation may make it harder for them to ward off future inflation without incurring the public's wrath. *PrepTest49 Sec2 Q12*	**Conclusion:** [fourth sentence] Temporary success in halting inflation makes it harder to prevent future inflation without causing public anger. Sentences 1, 2, and 3 **are three related pieces of the author's evidence:** · The main way bankers try to halt inflation is by raising interest rates. · Bankers usually raise interest rates early, before it becomes apparent. · If inflation isn't apparent, the public gets angry at steps that slow the economy.

Identify and Answer Role of a Statement Questions

Prepare

Role of a Statement questions, which ask how a statement functions in an argument, reward your ability to identify the argument's conclusion, evidence, and other components.

You can identify Role of a Statement questions from question stems like these:

The statement that the educational use of computers enables schools to teach far more courses with far fewer teachers figures in the argument in which one of the following ways?

PrepTest57 Sec2 Q13

Which one of the following most accurately describes the role played in the argument by the claim that it is primarily by raising interest rates that central bankers curb inflation?

PrepTest49 Sec2 Q12

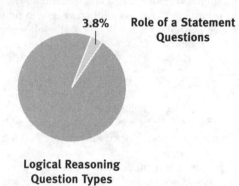

3.8% **Role of a Statement Questions**

Logical Reasoning Question Types

*PrepTests 66–80; released 2012–2016

ROLE OF A STATEMENT QUESTIONS AT A GLANCE

Task: Identify how a specified statement or idea functions within the argument.

Strategy: Note the statement cited in the question stem; then, analyze the argument to characterize the role played by the statement.

Frequency: Released LSATs between 2012 and 2016 featured an average of 1.9 Role of a Statement questions.

Here's how an expert LSAT test taker might proceed through a Role of a Statement question.

LSAT Question	Analysis
It would not be surprising to discover that the trade routes between China and the West were opened many centuries, even millennia, earlier than 200 B.C., contrary to what is currently believed. After all, what made the Great Silk Road so attractive as a trade route linking China and the West—level terrain, easily traversable mountain passes, and desert oases—would also have made it an attractive route for the original emigrants to China from Africa and the Middle East, and this early migration began at least one million years ago.	**Step 2:** Conclusion: Trade routes between China and the West may very well have opened long before 200 B.C. Evidence: *After all* is the evidence signal. · What made the GSR a desirable route would've made it desirable for the original emigrants to China. · The original emigrant migration began a million years ago or more. [This is the statement in the question stem.]
That a migration from Africa and the Middle East to China occurred at least one million years ago figures in the above reasoning in which one of the following ways?	**Step 1:** "Figures … in which one of the following ways"—Role of a Statement question.
	Step 3: One of two pieces of evidence included to support the conclusion.
(A) It is cited as conclusive evidence for the claim that trade links between China and the Middle East were established long before 200 B.C.	**Step 4:** The statement is one of two parts of evidence, so by itself it cannot be "conclusive evidence." Eliminate.
(B) It is an intermediate conclusion made plausible by the description of the terrain along which the migration supposedly took place.	The *and* before the statement means that it is another evidentiary fact, not an intermediate conclusion. Eliminate.
(C) It is offered as evidence in support of the claim that trade routes between China and the West could easily have been established much earlier than is currently believed.	Correct. The choice has the right role—"offered as evidence"—and the correct conclusion.
(D) It is offered as evidence against the claim that trade routes between China and Africa preceded those eventually established between China and the Middle East.	The author does not claim that routes between China and Africa came before those between China and the Middle East. Eliminate.
(E) It is the main conclusion that the argument attempts to establish about intercourse between China and the West.	The main conclusion is the first sentence, not the statement in question. Eliminate.

PrepTest51 Sec1 Q14

Practice

Apply the Logical Reasoning Method steps to answer each of the following Role of a Statement questions.

LSAT Question	My Analysis
27. It is primarily by raising interest rates that central bankers curb inflation, but an increase in interest rates takes up to two years to affect inflation. Accordingly, central bankers usually try to raise interest rates before inflation becomes excessive, at which time inflation is not yet readily apparent either. But unless inflation is readily apparent, interest rate hikes generally will be perceived as needlessly restraining a growing economy. Thus, central bankers' success in temporarily restraining inflation may make it harder for them to ward off future inflation without incurring the public's wrath.	**Step 2:**
Which one of the following most accurately describes the role played in the argument by the claim that it is primarily by raising interest rates that central bankers curb inflation?	**Step 1:**
	Step 3:
(A) It is presented as a complete explanation of the fact that central bankers' success in temporarily restraining inflation may make it harder for them to ward off future inflation without incurring the public's wrath.	**Step 4:**
(B) It is a description of a phenomenon for which the claim that an increase in interest rates takes up to two years to affect inflation is offered as an explanation.	
(C) It is a premise offered in support of the conclusion that central bankers' success in temporarily restraining inflation may make it harder for them to ward off future inflation without incurring the public's wrath.	
(D) It is a conclusion for which the statement that an increase in interest rates takes up to two years to affect inflation is offered as support.	
(E) It is a premise offered in support of the conclusion that unless inflation is readily apparent, interest rate hikes generally will be perceived as needlessly restraining a growing economy.	

PrepTest49 Sec2 Q12

LSAT Question	My Analysis
28. Columnist: It has been noted that attending a live musical performance is a richer experience than is listening to recorded music. Some say that this is merely because we do not see the performers when we listen to recorded music. However, there must be some other reason, for there is relatively little difference between listening to someone read a story over the radio and listening to someone in the same room read a story. →	Step 2:
Which one of the following most accurately expresses the role played in the argument by the observation that attending a live musical performance is a richer experience than is listening to recorded music? →	Step 1:
	Step 3:
(A) It is what the columnist's argument purports to show. →	Step 4:
(B) It is the reason given for the claim that the columnist's argument is attempting to undermine. →	
(C) It is what the columnist's argument purports to explain. →	
(D) It is what the columnist's argument purports to refute. →	
(E) It is what the position that the columnist tries to undermine is purported to explain. →	

PrepTest59 Sec2 Q7

Expert Analysis: Role of a Statement Questions

Here's how an LSAT expert might have approached those practice questions.

LSAT Question	Analysis
27. It is primarily by raising interest rates that central bankers curb inflation, but an increase in interest rates takes up to two years to affect inflation. Accordingly, central bankers usually try to raise interest rates before inflation becomes excessive, at which time inflation is not yet readily apparent either. But unless inflation is readily apparent, interest rate hikes generally will be perceived as needlessly restraining a growing economy. Thus, central bankers' success in temporarily restraining inflation may make it harder for them to ward off future inflation without incurring the public's wrath.	**Step 2:** Conclusion: [fourth sentence] Temporary success in halting inflation makes it harder to prevent future inflation without causing public anger. Sentences 1, 2, and 3 are three related pieces of the author's evidence: · The main way bankers try to halt inflation is by raising interest rates. [This is the statement in the question stem.] · Bankers usually raise interest rates early, before it becomes apparent. · If inflation isn't apparent, the public gets angry at steps that slow the economy.
Which one of the following most accurately describes the role played in the argument by the claim that it is primarily by raising interest rates that central bankers curb inflation?	**Step 1:** Role of a Statement question—the correct answer will describe how the statement fits into the argument.
	Step 3: One of the statements given as evidence for the author's conclusion.
(A) It is presented as a complete explanation of the fact that central bankers' success in temporarily restraining inflation may make it harder for them to ward off future inflation without incurring the public's wrath.	**Step 4:** Extreme. The statement in question is one of three pieces of evidence offered for the conclusion. *Complete explanation* is too strong. Eliminate.
(B) It is a description of a phenomenon for which the claim that an increase in interest rates takes up to two years to affect inflation is offered as an explanation.	Distortion. The *claim* referred to in this choice is just a detail about the statement in question, not an explanation of it. Eliminate.
(C) It is a premise offered in support of the conclusion that central bankers' success in temporarily restraining inflation may make it harder for them to ward off future inflation without incurring the public's wrath.	Correct. *Premise* means the same as evidence, and the paraphrase of the author's conclusion here is accurate. The statement in question was just evidence for the conclusion.
(D) It is a conclusion for which the statement that an increase in interest rates takes up to two years to affect inflation is offered as support.	Distortion. The statement in question was actually the first piece in a string of evidence. Eliminate.
(E) It is a premise offered in support of the conclusion that unless inflation is readily apparent, interest rate hikes generally will be perceived as needlessly restraining a growing economy.	Distortion. What this answer identifies as the conclusion is actually another piece of evidence for the author's main point. Eliminate.

PrepTest49 Sec2 Q12

LSAT Question	Analysis
28. Columnist: It has been noted that attending a live musical performance is a richer experience than is listening to recorded music. Some say that this is merely because we do not see the performers when we listen to recorded music. However, there must be some other reason, for there is relatively little difference between listening to someone read a story over the radio and listening to someone in the same room read a story.	**Step 2: Conclusion:** [first part of sentence 3] Seeing the musicians is *not the reason* live music is richer (my opponents' explanation is wrong). Sentence 1—Background observation: Live music is a richer experience than recorded music. [This is the statement in the question stem.] Sentence 2—The author's opponents' explanation for the observation: Live music is richer because we see the musicians. Second part of sentence 3—Author's evidence: an analogy showing why the opponents' explanation must be wrong.
Which one of the following most accurately expresses the role played in the argument by the observation that attending a live musical performance is a richer experience than is listening to recorded music?	**Step 1:** Role of a Statement question—the correct answer will describe how the statement fits into the argument.
	Step 3: The statement in question stipulates a fact. The author and his opponents fight about *the reason* it is true.
(A) It is what the columnist's argument purports to show.	**Step 4:** Distortion. The author wants to show that someone else's explanation for the statement is wrong. Eliminate.
(B) It is the reason given for the claim that the columnist's argument is attempting to undermine.	Distortion. The statement in question is not the reason for the claim; it *is* the claim. Moreover, the author is not trying to undermine the claim, but rather, his opponents' explanation of it. Eliminate.
(C) It is what the columnist's argument purports to explain.	Distortion. The author never offers his own explanation for why live music is richer; he just wants to show that his opponents' explanation is wrong. Eliminate.
(D) It is what the columnist's argument purports to refute.	The author does not want to refute the claim that live music is richer. Implicitly, he accepts that. He wants to show that seeing the musicians is not the reason it is richer. Eliminate.
(E) It is what the position that the columnist tries to undermine is purported to explain. *PrepTest59 Sec2 Q7*	Correct. The author and his opponents agree that live music is a richer experience. The opponents try to explain this by saying, "It is true because you see the musicians." The author rejects this explanation.

Perform

Apply the Logical Reasoning Method steps to answer each of the following Role of a Statement questions.

LSAT Question	My Analysis
29. Administrators of educational institutions are enthusiastic about the educational use of computers because they believe that it will enable schools to teach far more courses with far fewer teachers than traditional methods allow. Many teachers fear computers for the same reason. But this reason is mistaken. Computerized instruction requires more, not less, time of instructors, which indicates that any reduction in the number of teachers would require an accompanying reduction in courses offered. $\longrightarrow$	**Step 2:**
The statement that the educational use of computers enables schools to teach far more courses with far fewer teachers figures in the argument in which one of the following ways? $\longrightarrow$	**Step 1:**
	Step 3:
(A) It is presented as a possible explanation for an observation that follows it. $\longrightarrow$	**Step 4:**
(B) It is a statement of the problem the argument sets out to solve. $\longrightarrow$	
(C) It is a statement that the argument is designed to refute. $\longrightarrow$	
(D) It is a statement offered in support of the argument's main conclusion. $\longrightarrow$	
(E) It is the argument's main conclusion. *PrepTest57 Sec2 Q13* $\longrightarrow$	

LSAT Question	My Analysis
30. Software reviewer: Dictation software allows a computer to produce a written version of sentences that are spoken to it. Although dictation software has been promoted as a labor-saving invention, it fails to live up to its billing. The laborious part of writing is in the thinking and the editing, not in the typing. And proofreading the software's error-filled output generally squanders any time saved in typing. →	Step 2:
Which one of the following most accurately describes the role played in the software reviewer's argument by the claim that dictation software fails to live up to its billing? →	Step 1:
	Step 3:
(A) It is the argument's main conclusion but not its only conclusion. →	Step 4:
(B) It is the argument's only conclusion. →	
(C) It is an intermediate conclusion that is offered as direct support for the argument's main conclusion. →	
(D) It is a premise offered in support of the argument's conclusion. →	
(E) It is a premise offered as direct support for an intermediate conclusion of the argument. →	

PrepTest57 Sec2 Q16

Expert Analysis: Role of a Statement Questions

Here's how an LSAT expert might have approached those questions.

LSAT Question	Analysis
29. Administrators of educational institutions are enthusiastic about the educational use of computers because they believe that it will enable schools to teach far more courses with far fewer teachers than traditional methods allow. Many teachers fear computers for the same reason. But this reason is mistaken. Computerized instruction requires more, not less, time of instructors, which indicates that any reduction in the number of teachers would require an accompanying reduction in courses offered. →	**Step 2:** Conclusion: It isn't true that computers will let schools teach many more courses with way fewer teachers. Evidence: Computerized instruction needs more time from teachers, so if we lose teachers we would also lose courses. The statement in question is neither the conclusion nor the evidence. It's a belief that the author claims is wrong.
The statement that the educational use of computers enables schools to teach far more courses with far fewer teachers figures in the argument in which one of the following ways? →	**Step 1:** "[F]igures in the argument in which of the following ways" signals a Role of a Statement question.
	Step 3: This is the statement that the author attempts to contradict.
(A) It is presented as a possible explanation for an observation that follows it. →	**Step 4:** The statement in question is a belief; it doesn't explain or support anything. Eliminate.
(B) It is a statement of the problem the argument sets out to solve. →	While the teachers view this statement as a problem (and the administrators claim it as a benefit), the author accepts it as neither, refuting its validity. Eliminate.
(C) It is a statement that the argument is designed to refute. →	Correct. The author's conclusion and evidence try to prove that the belief is wrong.
(D) It is a statement offered in support of the argument's main conclusion. →	The statement cannot support a main conclusion that claims that statement itself is wrong! Eliminate.
(E) It is the argument's main conclusion. *PrepTest57 Sec2 Q13* →	The argument's main conclusion is the sentence that follows the statement in the question stem. Eliminate.

LSAT Question	Analysis
30. Software reviewer: Dictation software allows a computer to produce a written version of sentences that are spoken to it. Although dictation software has been promoted as a labor-saving invention, it fails to live up to its billing. The laborious part of writing is in the thinking and the editing, not in the typing. And proofreading the software's error-filled output generally squanders any time saved in typing.	**Step 2:** Conclusion (second part of second sentence): Dictation software hasn't lived up to the hype. [This is the statement from the question stem.]

Everything else supports the conclusion:

First sentence—Background: a definition of dictation software

→ First part of second sentence—More background: what was hyped about dictation software (it makes writing easier)

Third and fourth sentences—Two related pieces of evidence:

· What makes writing hard
· Why dictation software doesn't make it any easier |
Which one of the following most accurately describes the role played in the software reviewer's argument by the claim that dictation software fails to live up to its billing?	→ **Step 1:** Role of a Statement question—the correct answer will describe how the statement fits into the argument.
	Step 3: It is the argument's main point, the conclusion.
(A) It is the argument's main conclusion but not its only conclusion.	→ **Step 4:** Distortion. There are no subsidiary conclusions here. Eliminate.
(B) It is the argument's only conclusion.	→ Correct. There are no subsidiary conclusions and the statement in question is the author's main point.
(C) It is an intermediate conclusion that is offered as direct support for the argument's main conclusion.	→ There are no subsidiary conclusions. The statement in question *is* the main point. Eliminate.
(D) It is a premise offered in support of the argument's conclusion.	→ Distortion. It *is* the main point. The rest of the argument is evidence. Eliminate.
(E) It is a premise offered as direct support for an intermediate conclusion of the argument. *PrepTest57 Sec2 Q16*	→ Distortion. The statement in question is the main point, and there are no intermediate conclusions. Eliminate.

This chapter continues on the next page ▶ ▶ ▶

Outline Complete Arguments

Prepare

All LSAT arguments—even those written in the most complicated prose—can be reduced to the pattern of "conclusion *because* evidence."

LEARNING OBJECTIVES

In this section, you'll learn to:

· Outline complete arguments

When you distill an LSAT argument down to its essence, accept the background information as given, and focus on the conclusion and the evidence the author offers in direct support of her main point.

Here's how an LSAT expert might outline one of the complete arguments you saw earlier.

LSAT Question	Analysis
The typological theory of species classification, which has few adherents today, distinguishes species solely on the basis of observable physical characteristics, such as plumage color, adult size, or dental structure. However, there are many so-called "sibling species," which are indistinguishable on the basis of their appearance but cannot interbreed and thus, according to the mainstream biological theory of species classification, are separate species. Since the typological theory does not count sibling species as separate species, it is unacceptable. *PrepTest51 Sec1 Q15*	Conclusion: The typological theory of species classification is unacceptable. *because* → Evidence: The typological theory of species classification does not count sibling species as separate species (while the mainstream theory does).

An expert reader uses the background information—such as the definition of sibling species—to get the context she needs, but her analysis of the argument zeroes in on the author's conclusion and evidence.

LSAT STRATEGY

When a Logical Reasoning question includes two arguments, or when a single argument involves the author's response to someone else's position, paraphrase both arguments and be sure you understand how they relate to one another.

Practice

Outline the argument structure, using the "conclusion because evidence" format, in each of the following LSAT stimuli.

LSAT Question	My Analysis
31. A survey of clerical workers' attitudes toward their work identified a group of secretaries with very positive attitudes. They responded "Strongly agree" to such statements as "I enjoy word processing" and "I like learning new secretarial skills." These secretaries had been rated by their supervisors as excellent workers—far better than secretaries whose attitudes were identified as less positive. Clearly these secretaries' positive attitudes toward their work produced excellent job performance. *PrepTest49 Sec2 Q13*	Conclusion: *because* Evidence:
32. There can be no individual freedom without the rule of law, for there is no individual freedom without social integrity, and pursuing the good life is not possible without social integrity. *PrepTest61 Sec4 Q25*	Conclusion: *because* Evidence:
33. Ilana: Carver's stories are somber and pessimistic, which is a sure sign of inferior writing. I have never read a single story of his that ends happily. Gustav: Carver was one of the finest writers of the past 30 years. Granted, his stories are characterized by somberness and pessimism, but they are also wryly humorous, compassionate, and beautifully structured. *PrepTest49 Sec2 Q1*	**[Ilana]** Conclusion: *because* Evidence: **[Gustav]** Conclusion: *because* Evidence:
34. Politician: The huge amounts of money earned by oil companies elicit the suspicion that the regulations designed to prevent collusion need to be tightened. But just the opposite is true. If the regulations designed to prevent collusion are not excessively burdensome, then oil companies will make profits sufficient to motivate the very risky investments associated with exploration that must be made if society is to have adequate oil supplies. But recent data show that the oil industry's profits are not the highest among all industries. Clearly, the regulatory burden on oil companies has become excessive. *PrepTest49 Sec4 Q12*	Conclusion: *because* Evidence:

Expert Analysis: Outline Arguments

Here's how an LSAT expert might outline the argument structure in each of those LSAT stimuli.

LSAT Question	Analysis
31. A survey of clerical workers' attitudes toward their work identified a group of secretaries with very positive attitudes. They responded "Strongly agree" to such statements as "I enjoy word processing" and "I like learning new secretarial skills." These secretaries had been rated by their supervisors as excellent workers—far better than secretaries whose attitudes were identified as less positive. Clearly these secretaries' positive attitudes toward their work produced excellent job performance. *PrepTest49 Sec2 Q13*	Conclusion: The positive attitudes of secretaries in the positive group caused their excellent job performance. *because* Evidence: Secretaries in the positive group were rated excellent workers by their supervisors. Secretaries not in the positive group were rated lower.
32. There can be no individual freedom without the rule of law, for there is no individual freedom without social integrity, and pursuing the good life is not possible without social integrity. *PrepTest61 Sec4 Q25*	Conclusion: Individual freedom requires the rule of law. *because* Evidence: Individual freedom requires social integrity.
33. Ilana: Carver's stories are somber and pessimistic, which is a sure sign of inferior writing. I have never read a single story of his that ends happily. Gustav: Carver was one of the finest writers of the past 30 years. Granted, his stories are characterized by somberness and pessimism, but they are also wryly humorous, compassionate, and beautifully structured. *PrepTest49 Sec2 Q1*	**[Ilana]** Conclusion: Carver's writing is inferior. *because* Evidence: 1) Somberness and pessimism are sure signs of inferior writing. 2) I've never read a happy Carver story. **[Gustav]** Conclusion: Carver was one of the best writers of the last three decades. *because* Evidence: While somber and pessimistic, Carver's stories are nevertheless funny, compassionate, and well-structured.
34. Politician: The huge amounts of money earned by oil companies elicit the suspicion that the regulations designed to prevent collusion need to be tightened. But just the opposite is true. If the regulations designed to prevent collusion are not excessively burdensome, then oil companies will make profits sufficient to motivate the very risky investments associated with exploration that must be made if society is to have adequate oil supplies. But recent data show that the oil industry's profits are not the highest among all industries. Clearly, the regulatory burden on oil companies has become excessive. *PrepTest49 Sec4 Q12*	Conclusion: Oil companies are excessively burdened by regulation. *because* Evidence: Oil companies' profits are not the highest among all industries.

Perform

Outline the argument structure, using the "conclusion because evidence" format, in each of the following LSAT stimuli.

LSAT Question	My Analysis
35. Letter to the editor: Middle-class families in wealthy nations are often criticized for the ecological damage resulting from their lifestyles. This criticism should not be taken too seriously, however, since its source is often a movie star or celebrity whose own lifestyle would, if widely adopted, destroy the environment and deplete our resources in a short time. *PrepTest49 Sec2 Q5*	Conclusion: *because* Evidence:
36. Vanwilligan: Some have argued that professional athletes receive unfairly high salaries. But in an unrestricted free market, such as the market these athletes compete in, salaries are determined by what someone else is willing to pay for their services. These athletes make enormous profits for their teams' owners, and that is why owners are willing to pay them extraordinary salaries. Thus the salaries they receive are fair. *PrepTest49 Sec2 Q19*	Conclusion: *because* Evidence:
37. Talbert: Chess is beneficial for school-age children. It is enjoyable, encourages foresight and logical thinking, and discourages carelessness, inattention, and impulsiveness. In short, it promotes mental maturity. Sklar: My objection to teaching chess to children is that it diverts mental activity from something with societal value, such as science, into something that has no societal value. *PrepTest61 Sec2 Q7*	**[Talbert]** Conclusion: *because* Evidence: **[Sklar]** Conclusion: *because* Evidence:
38. A development company has proposed building an airport near the city of Dalton. If the majority of Dalton's residents favor the proposal, the airport will be built. However, it is unlikely that a majority of Dalton's residents would favor the proposal, for most of them believe that the airport would create noise problems. Thus, it is unlikely that the airport will be built. *PrepTest61 Sec4 Q11*	Conclusion: *because* Evidence:

Expert Analysis: Outline Arguments

Here's how an LSAT expert might outline the argument structure in each of those LSAT stimuli.

LSAT Question	Analysis
35. Letter to the editor: Middle-class families in wealthy nations are often criticized for the ecological damage resulting from their lifestyles. This criticism should not be taken too seriously, however, since its source is often a movie star or celebrity whose own lifestyle would, if widely adopted, destroy the environment and deplete our resources in a short time. *PrepTest49 Sec2 Q5*	Conclusion: The criticism that middle-class lifestyles cause ecological damage should not be taken seriously. *because* Evidence: Those making the criticism are often celebrities who live worse lifestyles.
36. Vanwilligan: Some have argued that professional athletes receive unfairly high salaries. But in an unrestricted free market, such as the market these athletes compete in, salaries are determined by what someone else is willing to pay for their services. These athletes make enormous profits for their teams' owners, and that is why owners are willing to pay them extraordinary salaries. Thus the salaries they receive are fair. *PrepTest49 Sec2 Q19*	Conclusion: Professional athletes' salaries are fair. *because* Evidence: 1) The free market sets salaries at what employers are willing to pay, and 2) team owners are willing to pay professional athletes' salaries.
37. Talbert: Chess is beneficial for school-age children. It is enjoyable, encourages foresight and logical thinking, and discourages carelessness, inattention, and impulsiveness. In short, it promotes mental maturity. Sklar: My objection to teaching chess to children is that it diverts mental activity from something with societal value, such as science, into something that has no societal value. *PrepTest61 Sec2 Q7*	[Talbert] Conclusion: Chess is good for school kids. *because* Evidence: Chess promotes mental maturity (in three specific ways). [Sklar] Conclusion: Teaching chess to school kids is objectionable. *because* Evidence: Chess diverts mental activity away from things with social value.
38. A development company has proposed building an airport near the city of Dalton. If the majority of Dalton's residents favor the proposal, the airport will be built. However, it is unlikely that a majority of Dalton's residents would favor the proposal, for most of them believe that the airport would create noise problems. Thus, it is unlikely that the airport will be built. *PrepTest61 Sec4 Q11*	Conclusion: The proposed Dalton airport probably will not be built. *because* Evidence: If a majority of Dalton's residents favor building the proposed airport it will be built, but a majority probably won't support building it.

This chapter continues on the next page ▶ ▶ ▶

Identify and Answer Point at Issue Questions

Prepare

LEARNING OBJECTIVES

In this section, you'll learn to:

· Identify and answer Point at Issue questions

Once you are able to summarize complete arguments, you have the skill necessary to answer Point at Issue questions. These questions require you to pinpoint the specific issue about which two speakers disagree. In rare cases, they will ask for a point of agreement between the speakers.

Point at Issue questions always present a dialogue stimulus, but not every dialogue stimulus represents a Point at Issue question. You can identify Point at Issue questions from question stems like these:

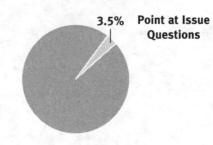

3.5% **Point at Issue Questions**

Talbert's and Sklar's statements provide the strongest support for holding that they disagree with each other over whether

PrepTest61 Sec2 Q7

Megan and Channen disagree over whether

PrepTest49 Sec2 Q10

Logical Reasoning Question Types

*PrepTests 66–80; released 2012–2016

On the basis of their statements, Ilana and Gustav are committed to disagreeing over whether

PrepTest49 Sec2 Q1

POINT AT ISSUE QUESTIONS AT A GLANCE

Task: Identify the specific claim, statement, or recommendation about which two speakers disagree (or rarely, about which they agree).

Strategy: Analyze both speakers' arguments and determine the point at issue between them, or use the Point at Issue Tree approach to identify the correct answer.

Frequency: On LSAT tests released from 2012 through 2016, there were an average of 1.8 Point at Issue questions.

Point at Issue Tree

In Point at Issue questions, one (and only one) answer choice will contain a statement about which the two speakers disagree. This provides a built-in way to evaluate the answer choices efficiently and effectively. It is depicted in the "decision tree" model that follows.

TEST DAY TIP

A great way to evaluate the answer choices in Point at Issue questions is to apply the questions from the Point at Issue Tree to the answer choices to identify the right answer.

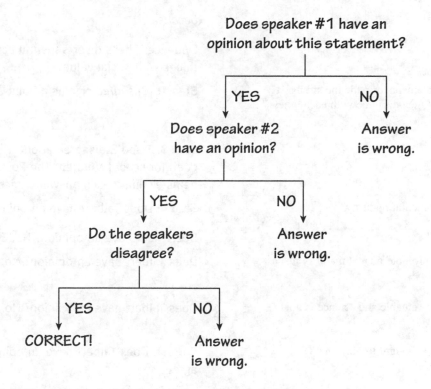

What are the characteristics of wrong answers in Point at Issue questions?

Here is how an LSAT expert might analyze a Point at Issue question.

LSAT Question	Analysis
Talbert: Chess is beneficial for school-age children. It is enjoyable, encourages foresight and logical thinking, and discourages carelessness, inattention, and impulsiveness. In short, it promotes mental maturity. Sklar: My objection to teaching chess to children is that it diverts mental activity from something with societal value, such as science, into something that has no societal value. →	**Step 2:** [Talbert] Conclusion: Chess is good for school kids. *because* Evidence: Chess promotes mental maturity (in three specific ways). [Sklar] Conclusion: Teaching chess to school kids is objectionable. *because* Evidence: Chess diverts mental activity away from things with social value.
Talbert's and Sklar's statements provide the strongest support for holding that they disagree with each other over whether →	**Step 1:** [D]*isagree* signals a Point at Issue question.
	Step 3: T and S disagree about whether chess is good for school children. The Point at Issue Tree helps evaluate each answer choice.
(A) chess promotes mental maturity →	**Step 4:** Does Talbert have an opinion? Yes. Does Sklar have an opinion? No. Eliminate.
(B) many activities promote mental maturity just as well as chess does →	Does Talbert have an opinion? No. Eliminate.
(C) chess is socially valuable and science is not →	Does Talbert have an opinion? No. Eliminate.
(D) children should be taught to play chess →	Correct. Does Talbert have an opinion? Yes. He agrees. Does Sklar have an opinion? Yes. He disagrees. Do Talbert and Sklar disagree? Yes.
(E) children who neither play chess nor study science are mentally immature *PrepTest61 Sec2 Q7* →	Does Talbert have an opinion? No. Eliminate.

Practice

Use the Logical Reasoning Method and the Point at Issue Tree to complete the following question.

LSAT Question	My Analysis
39. Ilana: Carver's stories are somber and pessimistic, which is a sure sign of inferior writing. I have never read a single story of his that ends happily. Gustav: Carver was one of the finest writers of the past 30 years. Granted, his stories are characterized by somberness and pessimism, but they are also wryly humorous, compassionate, and beautifully structured. $\longrightarrow$	Step 2:
On the basis of their statements, Ilana and Gustav are committed to disagreeing over whether $\longrightarrow$	Step 1:
	Step 3:
(A) Carver's stories are truly compassionate $\longrightarrow$	Step 4:
(B) Carver's stories are pessimistic in their vision $\longrightarrow$	
(C) stories that are characterized by somberness and pessimism can appropriately be called humorous $\longrightarrow$	
(D) stories that are well written can be somber and pessimistic $\longrightarrow$	
(E) there are some characteristics of a story that are decisive in determining its aesthetic value $\longrightarrow$	

PrepTest49 Sec2 Q1

Expert Analysis: Point at Issue Question

Here's how an LSAT expert might have approached that question.

LSAT Question	Analysis
39. Ilana: Carver's stories are somber and pessimistic, which is a sure sign of inferior writing. I have never read a single story of his that ends happily. Gustav: Carver was one of the finest writers of the past 30 years. Granted, his stories are characterized by somberness and pessimism, but they are also wryly humorous, compassionate, and beautifully structured.	**Step 2: [Ilana]** Conclusion: Carver's writing is inferior. *because* Evidence: 1) Somberness and pessimism are sure signs of inferior writing. 2) I've never read a happy Carver story. **[Gustav]** Conclusion: Carver was one of the best writers of the last three decades. *because* Evidence: While somber and pessimistic, Carver's stories are nevertheless funny, compassionate, and well-structured.
On the basis of their statements, Ilana and Gustav are committed to disagreeing over whether	**Step 1:** "[C]ommitted to disagreeing" signals a Point at Issue question.
	Step 3: I & G disagree about whether Carver's somberness and pessimism make him a bad writer. The Point at Issue Tree helps evaluate each answer choice.
(A) Carver's stories are truly compassionate	**Step 4:** Ilana expresses no opinion on this. Eliminate.
(B) Carver's stories are pessimistic in their vision	180. Ilana and Gustav *agree* that Carver's stories are pessimistic. Eliminate.
(C) stories that are characterized by somberness and pessimism can appropriately be called humorous	Ilana expresses no opinion about this. Eliminate.
(D) stories that are well written can be somber and pessimistic	Correct. Ilana has an opinion (she disagrees). Gustav has an opinion (he agrees). The two speakers disagree on this point.
(E) there are some characteristics of a story that are decisive in determining its aesthetic value *PrepTest49 Sec2 Q1*	Ilana would agree with this statement, but Gustav seems to think that stories can be good despite or because of various characteristics. Eliminate.

Perform

Use the Logical Reasoning Method and the Point at Issue Tree to complete the following question.

LSAT Question	My Analysis
40. Megan: People pursue wealth beyond what their basic needs require only if they see it as a way of achieving high status or prestige.	**Step 2:**
Channen: Not everybody thinks that way. After all, money is the universal medium of exchange. So, if you have enough of it, you can exchange it for whatever other material goods you may need or want even if you are indifferent to what others think of you. →	
Megan and Channen disagree over whether →	**Step 1:**
	Step 3:
(A) people ever pursue wealth beyond what is required for their basic needs →	**Step 4:**
(B) it is irrational to try to achieve high status or prestige in the eyes of one's society →	
(C) the pursuit of monetary wealth is irrational only when it has no further purpose →	
(D) it is rational to maximize one's ability to purchase whatever one wants only when the motive for doing so is something other than the desire for prestige →	
(E) the motive for pursuing wealth beyond what one's basic needs require is ever anything other than the desire for prestige or high status →	

PrepTest49 Sec2 Q10

Expert Analysis: Point at Issue Question

Here's how an LSAT expert might have approached that question.

LSAT Question	Analysis
40. Megan: People pursue wealth beyond what their basic needs require only if they see it as a way of achieving high status or prestige.	**Step 2: [Megan]** Conclusion: If people pursue wealth beyond their needs, then they see wealth as a means to status or prestige. [No evidence.]
Channen: Not everybody thinks that way. After all, money is the universal medium of exchange. So, if you have enough of it, you can exchange it for whatever other material goods you may need or want even if you are indifferent to what others think of you. →	**[Channen]** Conclusion: Status and prestige aren't the only motivations for acquiring wealth beyond one's needs. *because* Evidence: Wealth is money, and with enough, you can buy anything you want.
Megan and Channen disagree over whether →	**Step 1:** "[D]isagree over whether" signals a Point at Issue question.
	Step 3: M & C disagree about whether status and prestige are the only reasons people seek excess wealth. The Point at Issue Tree will help evaluate the answer choices.
(A) people ever pursue wealth beyond what is required for their basic needs →	**Step 4:** 180. At least implicitly, the two speakers *agree* that people pursue excess wealth. Eliminate.
(B) it is irrational to try to achieve high status or prestige in the eyes of one's society →	Neither speaker expresses an opinion on whether anything is *irrational*. Eliminate.
(C) the pursuit of monetary wealth is irrational only when it has no further purpose →	Neither speaker opines on whether the pursuit of wealth is *irrational* in any case. Eliminate.
(D) it is rational to maximize one's ability to purchase whatever one wants only when the motive for doing so is something other than the desire for prestige →	Megan says nothing about whether the pursuit of excess wealth is ever *rational*. Eliminate.
(E) the motive for pursuing wealth beyond what one's basic needs require is ever anything other than the desire for prestige or high status → *PrepTest49 Sec2 Q10*	Correct. Megan would disagree (status and prestige are the *only* motivators). Channen would agree (sometimes it's just about "things"). The two speakers disagree on this point.

Describe Argumentative Strategies

Prepare

Now that you have some practice outlining argument structures, you're ready to learn how to describe an author's argumentative strategy. In other words, you're ready to summarize *how* an author uses evidence to convince a reader that the conclusion is sound.

> ## LEARNING OBJECTIVES
>
> In this section, you'll learn to:
>
> · Describe an author's argumentative strategy

Describing an author's method of argument may, at first, seem somewhat generic and abstract. Instead of focusing on the content of the argument, you have to summarize the author's technique. Keywords help keep your focus on what the author does rather than what she says. Here's how an LSAT expert might describe the argumentative strategy in an argument you saw earlier in the chapter.

LSAT Question	Analysis
Columnist: It has been noted that attending a live musical performance is a richer experience than is listening to recorded music. Some say that this is merely because we do not see the performers when we listen to recorded music. However, there must be some other reason, for there is relatively little difference between listening to someone read a story over the radio and listening to someone in the same room read a story. *PrepTest59 Sec2 Q7*	The author offers an analogy (stories on the radio are like recorded music) as a supposed counterexample to a claim (live music is richer because you see the musicians).

It is impossible to anticipate exactly the argumentative strategies you'll see on Test Day, but a few methods of argument appear more regularly on the LSAT than others.

LSAT STRATEGY

Methods of argument common on the LSAT include:

- Analogy, in which an author draws parallels between two unrelated (but purportedly similar) situations
- Example, in which an author cites specific cases to justify a generalization
- Counterexample, in which an author seeks to discredit an opponent's argument by citing a specific case in which the opponent's conclusion appears to be invalid
- Appeal to authority, in which an author cites an expert or another figure as support for her conclusion
- Elimination of alternatives, in which an author lists possibilities and discredits all but one
- *Ad hominem*, in which an author attacks her opponent's personal credibility rather than the substance of her opponent's argument
- Means/Requirements, in which an author argues that something is needed to achieve a desired result
- Definition, in which an author defines a term in a way that helps to justify her argument or undermine/point out a contradiction in an opponent's argument

Practice

Describe the method of argument used in each of the following stimuli.

LSAT Question	My Analysis
41. The more modern archaeologists learn about Mayan civilization, the better they understand its intellectual achievements. Not only were numerous scientific observations and predictions made by Mayan astronomers, but the people in general seem to have had a strong grasp of sophisticated mathematical concepts. We know this from the fact that the writings of the Mayan religious scribes exhibit a high degree of mathematical competence. $\longrightarrow$	
PrepTest59 Sec3 Q8	
42. Archaeologist: After the last ice age, groups of paleohumans left Siberia and crossed the Bering land bridge, which no longer exists, into North America. Archaeologists have discovered in Siberia a cache of Clovis points—the distinctive stone spear points made by paleohumans. This shows that, contrary to previous belief, the Clovis point was not invented in North America. $\longrightarrow$	
PrepTest57 Sec2 Q22	
43. To predict that a device will be invented, one must develop a conception of the device that includes some details at least about how it will function and the consequences of its use. But clearly, then, the notion of predicting an invention is self-contradictory, for inventing means developing a detailed conception, and one cannot predict what has already taken place. $\longrightarrow$	
PrepTest59 Sec3 Q23	

Expert Analysis: Describe Argumentative Strategies

Here's how an LSAT expert might analyze those arguments.

LSAT Question	Analysis
41. The more modern archaeologists learn about Mayan civilization, the better they understand its intellectual achievements. Not only were numerous scientific observations and predictions made by Mayan astronomers, but the people in general seem to have had a strong grasp of sophisticated mathematical concepts. We know this from the fact that the writings of the Mayan religious scribes exhibit a high degree of mathematical competence. *PrepTest59 Sec3 Q8*	Examples. The author cites the knowledge of Mayan religious scribes in order to reach a conclusion about the Mayan people in general.
42. Archaeologist: After the last ice age, groups of paleohumans left Siberia and crossed the Bering land bridge, which no longer exists, into North America. Archaeologists have discovered in Siberia a cache of Clovis points—the distinctive stone spear points made by paleohumans. This shows that, contrary to previous belief, the Clovis point was not invented in North America. *PrepTest57 Sec2 Q22*	The author offers a supposed counterexample that he claims undermines a previous belief.
43. To predict that a device will be invented, one must develop a conception of the device that includes some details at least about how it will function and the consequences of its use. But clearly, then, the notion of predicting an invention is self-contradictory, for inventing means developing a detailed conception, and one cannot predict what has already taken place. *PrepTest59 Sec3 Q23*	The author uses two definitions to show that a certain type of prediction is a contradiction in terms.

Perform

Describe the method of argument used in each of the following stimuli.

LSAT Question	My Analysis
44. Letter to the editor: Middle-class families in wealthy nations are often criticized for the ecological damage resulting from their lifestyles. This criticism should not be taken too seriously, however, since its source is often a movie star or celebrity whose own lifestyle would, if widely adopted, destroy the environment and deplete our resources in a short time. $\longrightarrow$	
PrepTest49 Sec2 Q5	
45. Gilbert: This food label is mistaken. It says that these cookies contain only natural ingredients, but they contain alphahydroxy acids that are chemically synthesized by the cookie company at their plant. Sabina: The label is not mistaken. After all, alphahydroxy acids also are found occurring naturally in sugarcane. $\longrightarrow$	
PrepTest59 Sec2 Q5	
46. In modern deep-diving marine mammals, such as whales, the outer shell of the bones is porous. This has the effect of making the bones light enough so that it is easy for the animals to swim back to the surface after a deep dive. The outer shell of the bones was also porous in the ichthyosaur, an extinct prehistoric marine reptile. We can conclude from this that ichthyosaurs were deep divers. $\longrightarrow$	
PrepTest61 Sec4 Q21	

Expert Analysis: Describe Argumentative Strategies

Here's how an LSAT expert might analyze those arguments.

LSAT Question	Analysis
44. Letter to the editor: Middle-class families in wealthy nations are often criticized for the ecological damage resulting from their lifestyles. This criticism should not be taken too seriously, however, since its source is often a movie star or celebrity whose own lifestyle would, if widely adopted, destroy the environment and deplete our resources in a short time. *PrepTest49 Sec2 Q5*	*Ad hominem* attack. The author concludes that a social critique need not be taken seriously because many who make the critique act hypocritically.
45. Gilbert: This food label is mistaken. It says that these cookies contain only natural ingredients, but they contain alphahydroxy acids that are chemically synthesized by the cookie company at their plant. Sabina: The label is not mistaken. After all, alphahydroxy acids also are found occurring naturally in sugarcane. *PrepTest59 Sec2 Q5*	**[Gilbert]** Means/Requirement. Argues that an ingredient does not fit a definition. **[Sabina]** Means/Requirement. Argues that the ingredient does fit the definition.
46. In modern deep-diving marine mammals, such as whales, the outer shell of the bones is porous. This has the effect of making the bones light enough so that it is easy for the animals to swim back to the surface after a deep dive. The outer shell of the bones was also porous in the ichthyosaur, an extinct prehistoric marine reptile. We can conclude from this that ichthyosaurs were deep divers. *PrepTest61 Sec4 Q21*	Analogy. From the fact that a modern animal displays a characteristic, the author concludes that ancient animals with the same characteristic must have behaved in the same way.

Identify and Answer Method of Argument Questions

Prepare

> ### LEARNING OBJECTIVES
>
> In this section, you'll learn to:
>
> · Identify and answer Method of Argument questions

Method of Argument questions ask you to focus on an argument's structure more than its content. In this way, these questions are similar to many Reading Comprehension questions. In a Method of Argument question, the correct answer will describe the author's argumentative strategy, usually in generic, abstract terms.

You can identify Method of Argument questions from question stems such as these.

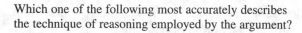

Which one of the following most accurately describes the technique of reasoning employed by the argument?

PrepTest59 Sec3 Q23

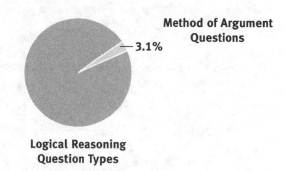

Method of Argument Questions

—3.1%

Logical Reasoning Question Types

PrepTests 66–80; released 2012–2016

In the conversation, Hernandez responds to Green's objection in which one of the following ways?

PrepTest57 Sec3 Q5

The columnist's argument proceeds by

PrepTest45 Sec4 Q12

Note how all of those question stems, despite their different wording, ask you to describe *how* the author makes her argument.

> ## METHOD OF ARGUMENT QUESTIONS AT A GLANCE
>
> **Task:** Describe the author's argumentative strategy, *how* she argues (not necessarily what she says).
>
> **Strategy:** Identify the author's conclusion and evidence; take note of Keywords indicating the author's purpose; and summarize the author's strategy in generic, descriptive terms.
>
> **Frequency:** Method of Argument questions are relatively rare in the Logical Reasoning sections of the test. LSAT tests released from 2012 through 2016 had an average of 1.6 Method of Argument questions.

Here's how an LSAT expert would attack a Method of Argument question.

LSAT Question	Analysis
Hernandez: I recommend that staff cars be replaced every four years instead of every three years. Three-year-old cars are still in good condition and this would result in big savings. Green: I disagree. Some of our salespeople with big territories wear out their cars in three years. Hernandez: I meant three-year-old cars subjected to normal use.	**Step 2:** Hernandez's response begins with "I meant," which suggests that she has to clarify something that she's said. Examining her original statement, we see that she is clarifying her comment regarding three-year-old cars.
In the conversation, Hernandez responds to Green's objection in which one of the following ways?	**Step 1:** "[R]esponds … in which … way" means the right answer will describe how Hernandez responds (not *what* she says in response). This is a Method of Argument question.
	Step 3: Clarifying an earlier statement
(A) by explicitly qualifying a premise used earlier	**Step 4:** Correct. Hernandez clarifies her original evidence, so "explicitly qualifying a premise" is a perfect description of *how* she responds.
(B) by criticizing salespeople who wear out their cars in three years	Hernandez doesn't criticize anyone. Moreover, she clarifies her statement to exclude the salespeople with big territories. Eliminate.
(C) by disputing the accuracy of Green's evidence	Hernandez seems to agree with Green's evidence; that's why she clarifies her statement to exclude cars driven by people with big territories. Eliminate.
(D) by changing the subject to the size of sales territories	Hernandez does not change the subject; Green is the one who mentions territory size. Eliminate.
(E) by indicating that Green used a phrase ambiguously *PrepTest57 Sec3 Q5*	Hernandez says nothing about how Green *used* a phrase (although she implies something about how Green may have understood the phrase Hernandez used). Eliminate.

Practice

Use the Logical Reasoning Method to complete the following Method of Argument question.

LSAT Question	My Analysis
47. To predict that a device will be invented, one must develop a conception of the device that includes some details at least about how it will function and the consequences of its use. But clearly, then, the notion of predicting an invention is self-contradictory, for inventing means developing a detailed conception, and one cannot predict what has already taken place. $\longrightarrow$	**Step 2:**
Which one of the following most accurately describes the technique of reasoning employed by the argument? $\longrightarrow$	**Step 1:**
	Step 3:
(A) constructing a counterexample to a general hypothesis about the future $\longrightarrow$	**Step 4:**
(B) appealing to definitions to infer the impossibility of a kind of occurrence $\longrightarrow$	
(C) countering a hypothesis by indicating the falsehood of the implications of that hypothesis $\longrightarrow$	
(D) pointing out how a problem is widely thought to be scientific yet is really conceptual $\longrightarrow$	
(E) attempting to show that predicting any event implies that it has in fact already taken place *PrepTest59 Sec3 Q23* $\longrightarrow$	

Expert Analysis: Method of Argument Question
Here's how an LSAT expert might approach that question.

LSAT Question	Analysis
47. To predict that a device will be invented, one must develop a conception of the device that includes some details at least about how it will function and the consequences of its use. But clearly, then, the notion of predicting an invention is self-contradictory, for inventing means developing a detailed conception, and one cannot predict what has already taken place. →	**Step 2:** Conclusion: The idea of predicting an invention is self-contradictory. *because* Evidence: 1) predicting an invention has to include details about the device's function and use, and 2) detailing a device's function and use is inventing. In short, if you've predicted an invention, then you have invented it, so you cannot *predict* what's already happened.
Which one of the following most accurately describes the technique of reasoning employed by the argument? →	**Step 1:** "[D]escribes the technique of reasoning" signals a Method of Argument question. The correct answer will accurately describe how the author makes his case.
	Step 3: The author shows how two definitions make it a contradiction to say you've done something.
(A) constructing a counterexample to a general hypothesis about the future →	**Step 4:** Outside the Scope. No general hypothesis about the future is discussed, and the author presents no counterexamples to anything. Eliminate.
(B) appealing to definitions to infer the impossibility of a kind of occurrence →	Correct. The author infers that one cannot predict an invention, because by the time one has sufficiently predicted it, then it is, by definition, invented.
(C) countering a hypothesis by indicating the falsehood of the implications of that hypothesis →	Distortion. Nothing indicates that to "predict a device will be invented" is anyone's hypothesis, and the author appeals to the definitions of terms (not the implications of a hypothesis) to make his case. Eliminate.
(D) pointing out how a problem is widely thought to be scientific yet is really conceptual →	Outside the Scope. The author does not say that most people treat the idea of predicting an invention as scientific. Eliminate.
(E) attempting to show that predicting any event implies that it has in fact already taken place *PrepTest59 Sec3 Q23* →	Extreme. The author's argument is about predicting inventions, not about predicting *any event*. Eliminate.

Perform

Use the Logical Reasoning Method to complete the following Method of Argument question.

LSAT Question		My Analysis
48. Economist: A country's trade deficit may indicate weakness in its economy, but it does not in itself weaken that economy. So restricting imports to reduce a trade deficit would be like sticking a thermometer into a glass of cold water in the hope of bringing down a patient's feverish temperature.	→	**Step 2:**
The economist's argument employs which one of the following techniques?	→	**Step 1:**
		Step 3:
(A) claiming that a crucial assumption entails a falsehood	→	**Step 4:**
(B) demonstrating that an analogy explicitly used to establish a certain conclusion is faulty	→	
(C) appealing to an analogy in order to indicate the futility of a course of action	→	
(D) calling into question the authority on the basis of which a claim is made	→	
(E) showing that a recommended course of action would have disastrous consequences	→	

PrepTest59 Sec3 Q14

Expert Analysis: Method of Argument Question

Here's how an LSAT expert might approach that question.

LSAT Question	Analysis
48. Economist: A country's trade deficit may indicate weakness in its economy, but it does not in itself weaken that economy. So restricting imports to reduce a trade deficit would be like sticking a thermometer into a glass of cold water in the hope of bringing down a patient's feverish temperature. →	**Step 2:** Conclusion: Restricting imports to fix a trade deficit is like chilling a thermometer to reduce a sick person's fever. *because* Evidence: A trade deficit reveals (but does not cause) economic weakness. The author uses an analogy to make her point.
The economist's argument employs which one of the following techniques? →	**Step 1:** "[E]mploys which … techniques": a Method of Argument question. The correct answer will accurately describe how the author makes her case.
	Step 3: The author uses an analogy to show why an action is misguided.
(A) claiming that a crucial assumption entails a falsehood →	**Step 4:** Distortion. The author says nothing about another argument's assumption. Eliminate.
(B) demonstrating that an analogy explicitly used to establish a certain conclusion is faulty →	180. It is the author who uses the analogy; she apparently thinks it is an apt one. Eliminate.
(C) appealing to an analogy in order to indicate the futility of a course of action →	Correct. This describes the author's argumentative strategy precisely: just as chilling the thermometer won't help the patient, slowing imports won't help the economy.
(D) calling into question the authority on the basis of which a claim is made →	The author doesn't question anyone's authority or expertise. Eliminate.
(E) showing that a recommended course of action would have disastrous consequences PrepTest59 Sec3 Q14 →	Extreme. The author simply says the action won't work, not that it would be disastrous. Eliminate.

PARALLEL REASONING QUESTIONS

Identify and Answer Parallel Reasoning Questions

Prepare

LEARNING OBJECTIVES

In this section, you'll learn to:

- Rule out incorrect answers in Parallel Reasoning questions based on conclusion type
- Identify similar argument structures

One more way in which the LSAT tests your ability to recognize argument structures is through Parallel Reasoning questions. Parallel Reasoning questions ask you to identify two arguments—on different subjects—that use the same pattern to reach the same kind of conclusion.

You can recognize Parallel Reasoning questions from question stems such as these:

The pattern of reasoning in which one of the following arguments is most parallel to that in the argument above?

PrepTest49 Sec4 Q17

In which one of the following is the pattern of reasoning most similar to that in the landscape architect's argument?

PrepTest51 Sec1 Q5

Parallel Reasoning Questions 3.3%

Logical Reasoning Question Types

PrepTests 66–80, released 2012–2016

The phrases "most closely parallels" or "most similar to" are associated with almost all Parallel Reasoning questions.

PARALLEL REASONING QUESTIONS AT A GLANCE

Task: Identify the answer choice in which the argument has the same structure and reaches the same type of conclusion as the argument in the stimulus.

Strategy: Use your knowledge of conclusion types, patterns of argument, Formal Logic, and/or principles to identify the answer containing an argument parallel to the one in the stimulus.

Frequency: On LSAT tests released from 2012 through 2016, there were an average of 1.7 Parallel Reasoning questions per test.

Parallel Reasoning questions are often very long; some have nearly as much text as a Reading Comprehension passage. Fortunately, there are a variety of tools and tactics to help you manage them efficiently and confidently.

Compare Conclusions. For two arguments to have parallel structures, they must reach the same kind of conclusion. For example, consider this conclusion:

> The company should decline the merger offer.

Here are the conclusions of two other arguments. Which one comes from an argument that could be parallel to the argument from which the sample conclusion was drawn?

> (1) Further consolidation will lead to layoffs at the plant.

> (2) The patient should avoid high cholesterol foods.

Compare Formal Logic. When a Parallel Reasoning argument features a clear application of Formal Logic, the best approach is often to abstract the argument into an "A, B, C" shorthand, and evaluate the answer choices by doing the same to them. Consider the following argument:

> Amanda is a strong legal writer. All strong legal writers are good analysts. So, Amanda must be a good analyst.

Here are two other arguments. Which is parallel to the argument in the example?

> (1) Bruno is a well-trained Labrador retriever. All well-trained Labrador retrievers are sweet-tempered. So, Bruno is a good dog for a family with children.

> (2) Erika must have good balance. After all, excellent surfers always have good balance, and Erika is an excellent surfer.

TEST DAY TIP

Parallel arguments will have the same argument structure, but the pieces of the argument need NOT appear in the same order. It's a Parallel *Reasoning* question, not a Parallel *Writing* question.

Compare Evidence. Evidence is not as easily categorized as are conclusions, but you can still compare features in the evidence of the stimulus argument to features of the evidence in each answer choice and eliminate answers in which the evidence is clearly not parallel. For example, imagine that you see a stimulus argument with the following evidence:

The larger a nation's manufacturing base, the more likely it is that its middle class will have economic mobility.

Here are pieces of evidence from two arguments. Which could be parallel to the argument from which the sample evidence came?

(1) Chicago has a larger manufacturing base than Omaha does.

(2) Greater artistic innovation is likely to be found in areas with greater population density.

Compare Principles. Rarely, a Parallel Reasoning argument illustrates an easily identifiable principle. Consider an argument like this one:

Policy A will strengthen the economy. Policy B will not. One goal of good government is to strengthen the economy. Therefore, Congress should vote for Policy A.

Here are two other arguments. Which is parallel to that in the example?

(1) Destination Q will be educational, but not relaxing. Destination P will be relaxing. Since the goal of a good family vacation is relaxation, the Miller family should choose Destination P.

(2) School X offers many in-state employment opportunities. School Y does not. Susan should choose School X because, above all, she wants in-state employment opportunities.

TEST DAY TIP

Parallel Reasoning questions sometimes feature complete, unflawed arguments.

Activate Prior Knowledge: Characterizing Conclusions

Before practicing on full Parallel Reasoning questions, refresh your conclusion types. You first learned the standard conclusion types earlier in this chapter. Take that work a step further here, by accounting for the strength and "charge" (positive/negative) of conclusions, as well.

Exercise: Characterizing Conclusions

For each of the following, identify the conclusion type; where applicable, characterize it as positive or negative; and designate each as "strong" or "qualified."

Conclusion		My Analysis
49. The higher than average rainfall this past winter will not significantly increase either the quantity or quality of this summer's wine grape harvest.	→	Type: +/–: Strength:
50. The actor has been unable to secure any new roles in the wake of multiple embarrassing incidents.	→	Type: +/–: Strength:
51. The most likely cause of the spate of deaths of various species of seals and dolphins in the harbor is a viral infection.	→	Type: +/–: Strength:
52. In cities, such as New York and San Francisco, with well-managed public water supply systems, there are few, if any, health benefits to purchasing bottled water rather than drinking from the tap.	→	Type: +/–: Strength:
53. The propriety of flaunting one's wealth, as with most matters of taste and manners, is dependent upon the circumstances.	→	Type: +/–: Strength:
54. Whenever El Niño conditions prevail, farmers in the south and southwest must prepare to deal with drought conditions.	→	Type: +/–: Strength:

Conclusion		My Analysis
55. Overcoming fears that she was not qualified to star in a dramatic role of such significance, the heretofore supporting actress in vapid teen comedies likely turned in the performance that will win this year's Oscar.	→	Type: +/–: Strength:
56. Rebuilding soil depth, structure, and organic matter content should be the focus of efforts in the agricultural industry to increase both yields and sustainability.	→	Type: +/–: Strength:
57. The raster data format in geographic information systems provides substantial advantages in processing speed and intuitive command structures over the alternative vector format.	→	Type: +/–: Strength:
58. If there are no further disruptions in the tourism sector due to unfavorable weather conditions, then the regional economy will not slip into recession, despite the claims to the contrary of other economists.	→	Type: +/–: Strength:
59. Simply eliminating daylight saving time throughout the world could increase global economic productivity by more than three percent per year.	→	Type: +/–: Strength:
60. All third year law students should be required to participate in a practical skills course or internship that will make them of more immediate value to employers upon graduation.	→	Type: +/–: Strength:

Expert Analysis: Characterizing Conclusions

Here's how an LSAT expert would characterize the conclusions in the preceding exercise. Compare your characterizations to those of the LSAT expert on the pages following this exercise. Make sure you accurately determined not only the conclusion type, but also the strength and "charge" of each conclusion.

	Conclusion		Analysis
49.	The higher than average rainfall this past winter will not significantly increase either the quantity or quality of this summer's wine grape harvest.	→	Type: Prediction +/–: Negative (will not) Strength: Strong
50.	The actor has been unable to secure any new roles in the wake of multiple embarrassing incidents.	→	Type: Assertion of Fact +/–: Negative Strength: Strong
51.	The most likely cause of the spate of deaths of various species of seals and dolphins in the harbor is a viral infection.	→	Type: Assertion of Fact +/–: Positive Strength: Qualified (most likely)
52.	In cities, such as New York and San Francisco, with well-managed public water supply systems, there are few, if any, health benefits to purchasing bottled water rather than drinking from the tap.	→	Type: Comparison +/–: Negative (few, if any) Strength: Strong
53.	The propriety of flaunting one's wealth, as with most matters of taste and manners, is dependent upon the circumstances.	→	Type: Value Judgment (propriety) +/–: Positive Strength: Qualified (dependent upon the circumstances)
54.	Whenever El Niño conditions prevail, farmers in the south and southwest must prepare to deal with drought conditions.	→	Type: Conditional, Assertion of Fact (whenever x, then y) +/–: Positive Strength: Strong

Conclusion		Analysis
55. Overcoming fears that she was not qualified to star in a dramatic role of such significance, the heretofore supporting actress in vapid teen comedies likely turned in the performance that will win this year's Oscar.	→	Type: Prediction (likely ... will) +/–: Positive Strength: Qualified (likely)
56. Rebuilding soil depth, structure, and organic matter content should be the focus of efforts in the agricultural industry to increase both yields and sustainability.	→	Type: Recommendation (should ... focus) +/–: Positive Strength: Strong
57. The raster data format in geographic information systems provides substantial advantages in processing speed and intuitive command structures over the alternative vector format.	→	Type: Comparison (advantages ... over) +/–: Positive Strength: Strong (substantial advantages)
58. If there are no further disruptions in the tourism sector due to unfavorable weather conditions, then the regional economy will not slip into recession, despite the claims to the contrary of other economists.	→	Type: Prediction, Conditional +/–: Negative (if not *x*, then will not *y*) Strength: Strong
59. Simply eliminating daylight saving time throughout the world could increase global economic productivity by more than three percent per year.	→	Type: Assertion of Fact +/–: Positive Strength: Qualified (could increase)
60. All third year law students should be required to participate in a practical skills course or internship that will make them of more immediate value to employers upon graduation.	→	Type: Recommendation (should be required) +/–: Positive Strength: Strong

Activate Prior Knowledge: Formal Logic

Exercise: Recognizing Equivalent Statements

In this exercise, enter the appropriate terms or phrases from the bolded conditional statement into the blanks in the statements beneath such that all of the statements are equivalent in meaning.

If Joey goes to the movies, then Jane goes to the movies.

61. Every time _____ goes to the movies, _____ must also go to the movies.

62. _____ does not go to the movies unless _____ also goes to the movies.

63. _____ goes to the movies only if _____ also goes to the movies.

64. _____ going to the movies is necessary for _____ to go to the movies.

Miguel plays hockey if Cindy goes to the movies.

65. _____ only if _____.

66. If _____, then _____.

67. _____ will not _____ unless _____.

68. Knowing that _____ is sufficient to know that _____.

All mollusks are invertebrates.

69. If a creature is a(n)_____, then it is a(n)_____.

70. A creature is a(n)_____ only if it is a(n)_____.

71. Only_____ are _____.

72. A creature is not a(n) _____ unless it is a(n) _____.

Only patrons at least 21 years of age will be admitted to the concert.

73. _____ is necessary for a patron _____.

74. If a patron is _____, then s/he is _____.

75. A patron _____ only if s/he _____.

76. A patron will not _____ unless s/he _____.

Being a good lawyer requires strong writing skills.

77. If someone _____, then s/he _____.

78. _____ is/are necessary for a person _____.

79. A person cannot _____ unless s/he _____.

80. Only a person who _____ can _____.

Running the school's summer program depends upon receiving generous contributions from the community.

81. Only if _____ will _____.

82. _____ will _____ unless _____.

83. If _____ are not _____, then _____.

84. _____ necessitates _____.

Only if it is sunny will Gail go to the beach.

85. Gail _____ only if _____.

86. Gail does not _____ unless _____.

87. If Gail _____, then _____.

88. Gail's _____ requires _____.

Unless she plays the viola, Linda cannot join the band.

89. If Linda _____, then _____.

90. Linda _____ only if _____.

91. If Linda does not _____, then _____.

92. Linda's _____ depends upon _____.

Every winning game included the team's all-star player.

93. If _____, then _____.

94. A _____ needed _____.

95. Only when _____ did _____.

96. The team _____ unless _____.

Whenever June eats a salty snack, she eats pretzels.

97. June _____ only if _____.

98. June does not _____ unless _____.

99. If June _____, then _____.

100. Every _____, she _____.

Expert Analysis: Recognizing Equivalent Statements

Check your work against that of an LSAT expert.

If Joey goes to the movies, then Jane goes to the movies.

61. Every time *Joey* goes to the movies, *Jane* must also go to the movies.

62. *Joey* does not go to the movies unless *Jane* also goes to the movies.

63. *Joey* goes to the movies only if *Jane* also goes to the movies.

64. *Jane's* going to the movies is necessary for *Joey* to go to the movies.

Miguel plays hockey if Cindy goes to the movies.

65. *Cindy goes to the movies* only if *Miguel plays hockey*.

66. If *Cindy goes to the movies*, then *Miguel plays hockey*.

67. *Cindy* will not *go to the movies* unless *Miguel plays hockey*.

68. Knowing that *Cindy goes to the movies* is sufficient to know that *Miguel plays hockey*.

All mollusks are invertebrates.

69. If a creature is a *mollusk*, then it is an *invertebrate*.

70. A creature is a *mollusk* only if it is an *invertebrate*.

71. Only *invertebrates* are *mollusks*.

72. A creature is not a *mollusk* unless it is an *invertebrate*.

Only patrons at least 21 years of age will be admitted to the concert.

73. *Being at least 21* is necessary for a patron *to be admitted to the concert*.

74. If a patron is *admitted to the concert*, then s/he is *at least 21*.

75. A patron *will be admitted to the concert* only if s/he *is at least 21*.

76. A patron will not *be admitted to the concert* unless s/he *is at least 21*.

Being a good lawyer requires strong writing skills.

77. If someone *is a good lawyer*, then s/he *has strong writing skills*.

78. *Strong writing skills* are necessary for a person *to be a good lawyer*.

79. A person cannot *be a good lawyer* unless s/he *has strong writing skills*.

80. Only a person who *has strong writing skills* can *be a good lawyer*.

Running the school's summer program depends upon receiving generous contributions from the community.

81. Only if *the school receives generous contributions from the community* will *the school's summer program run*.

82. *The school's summer program* will *not run* unless *it receives generous contributions from the community*.

83. If *contributions from the community* are not *generous*, then *the school's summer program will not run*. (Or If *generous contributions from the community* are not *received*, then *the school's summer program will not run*.)

84. *Running the school's summer program* necessitates *receiving generous contributions from the community*.

Only if it is sunny will Gail go to the beach.

85. Gail *goes to the beach* only if *it is sunny*.

86. Gail does not *go to the beach* unless *it is sunny*.

87. If Gail *goes to the beach*, then *it is sunny*.

88. Gail's *going to the beach* requires *it to be sunny*.

Unless she plays the viola, Linda cannot join the band.

89. If Linda *joins the band*, then *she plays the viola*.

90. Linda *joins the band* only if *she plays the viola*.

91. If Linda does not *play the viola*, then *she does not join the band*.

92. Linda's *joining the band* depends upon *her playing the viola*.

Every winning game included the team's all-star player.

93. If *the team won a game*, then *it included the team's all-star player*.

94. A *winning game* needed *the team's all-star player*.

95. Only when *the team included the all-star player* did *it win*.

96. The team *did not win* unless *it included the team's all-star player*.

Whenever June eats a salty snack, she eats pretzels.

97. June *eats a salty snack* only if *she eats pretzels*.

98. June does not *eat a salty snack* unless *she eats pretzels*.

99. If June *eats a salty snack*, then *she eats pretzels*.

100. Every *time June eats a salty snack,* she *eats pretzels*.

Here's how an LSAT expert might analyze and answer a Parallel Reasoning question. Note: Italics indicate where the argument structures in the answer choices differ from that of the argument in the stimulus.

LSAT Question	Analysis
Ecologists predict that the incidence of malaria will increase if global warming continues or if the use of pesticides is not expanded. But the use of pesticides is known to contribute to global warming, so it is inevitable that we will see an increase in malaria in the years to come.	**Step 2:** Conclusion: A *strong positive prediction* ("it is inevitable") that there will be an increase in malaria incidence.
	because
	Evidence (if needed): If global warming continues or if pesticide use is not expanded, then malaria incidence will increase. Pesticide use contributes to global warming.
The pattern of reasoning in which one of the following is most similar to that in the argument above?	**Step 1:** The phrase "most similar to" indicates a Parallel Reasoning question.
	Step 3: Rule out choices in which the conclusion is not a strong positive prediction that something will get worse and/or compare the overall argument structure: If A or not B, then C; but if B, then A. Therefore, C.
(A) The crime rate will increase if the economy does not improve or if we do not increase the number of police officers. But we will be able to hire more police officers if the economy does improve. Therefore, the crime rate will not increase.	**Step 4:** Conclusion is a *negative* prediction: the crime rate *will not* go up. Structure: If *not* A or not B, then C; but if *A*, then *D*. Therefore, *not* C. Eliminate.
(B) If educational funds remain at their current level or if we fail to recruit qualified teachers, student performance will worsen. But we will fail to recruit qualified teachers. Therefore, student performance will worsen.	Conclusion is parallel, a strong positive prediction that student performance will get worse. Structure: If A or not B, then C; but *not B will happen*. Therefore, C. The second part of the evidence does not match. Eliminate.
(C) If interest rates increase or demand for consumer goods does not decline, inflation will rise. But if there is a decline in the demand for consumer goods that will lead to higher interest rates. Therefore, inflation will rise.	Correct. Conclusion is a strong prediction that inflation will get worse. Structure: If A or not B, then C; but if B, then A. Therefore, C.
(D) If global warming continues or if the rate of ozone depletion is not reduced, there will be an increase in the incidence of skin cancer. But reduced use of aerosols ensures both that global warming will not continue and that ozone depletion will be reduced. Thus, the incidence of skin cancer will not increase.	Conclusion is a *negative* prediction: Skin cancer *will not* get worse. Structure: If A or not B, then C; but if B, then *not A and not D*. Therefore, *not* C. Eliminate.

LSAT Question (cont.)	Analysis (cont.)
(E) If deforestation continues at the current rate and the use of chemicals is not curtailed, wildlife species will continue to become extinct. But because of increasing population worldwide, it is inevitable that the current rate of deforestation will continue and that the use of chemicals will not be curtailed. Thus, wildlife species will continue to become extinct. *PrepTest51 Sec3 Q24*	→ Conclusion is a prediction that extinction will continue, not that it will get worse. Structure: If A *and* not B, then C; but *A and not B will happen.* Therefore, C. Eliminate.

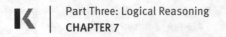

Practice

Now, practice some Parallel Reasoning questions. Use any of the tools and tactics discussed earlier in this section.

LSAT Question	My Analysis
101. Judicial punishment's power to deter people from committing crimes is a function of the severity of the penalty and the likelihood of one's actually receiving the penalty. Occasionally, juries decide that a crime's penalty is too severe and so refuse to convict a person they are convinced has committed that crime. Thus, increasing the penalty may decrease the deterrent power of judicial punishment. $\longrightarrow$	**Step 2:**
The pattern of reasoning in which one of the following arguments is most similar to the pattern of reasoning in the argument above? $\longrightarrow$	**Step 1:**
	Step 3:
(A) Success in attaining one's first academic job depends on the quality of one's dissertation and the amount of time spent working on it in graduate school. But sometimes, so much time is spent on a dissertation that it becomes too lengthy to be coherent and its quality suffers. So spending more time working on a dissertation can lead to less success in attaining a first academic job. $\longrightarrow$	**Step 4:**
(B) People who drive cars having many safety features are likely to drive more aggressively than do people who drive cars having few safety features. Thus, the people who drive the safest cars are likely to be the most dangerous drivers on the road. $\longrightarrow$	
(C) A new surgical technique is developed to treat a dangerous condition. This technique enables people to live longer than does an older form of surgery. But the new surgery's mortality rate is also slightly higher. Thus, if more people choose to undergo the new surgery, more people may die from the dangerous condition than previously. $\longrightarrow$	
(D) To be attractive to tourists, it is best for a city to have both wide appeal and sufficient hotel space. Though a sufficient number of hotel rooms alone cannot attract tourists, it is much harder for city governments to affect the appeal of their city than for them to affect its amount of hotel space. Thus, governments of cities that want to increase their attractiveness to tourists should put their energies into increasing their hotel space. $\longrightarrow$	
(E) Many young, talented artists, because they are unknown, decide to charge low prices for their work. As their reputations grow, the prices they can charge for their work increase. Thus, raising the price of an artist's work can improve that artist's reputation. $\longrightarrow$	

PrepTest49 Sec2 Q24

LSAT Question	My Analysis
102. Team captain: Winning requires the willingness to cooperate, which in turn requires motivation. So you will not win if you are not motivated. →	**Step 2:**
The pattern of reasoning in which one of the following is most similar to that in the argument above? →	**Step 1:**
	Step 3:
(A) Being healthy requires exercise. But exercising involves risk of injury. So, paradoxically, anyone who wants to be healthy will not exercise. →	**Step 4:**
(B) Learning requires making some mistakes. And you must learn if you are to improve. So you will not make mistakes without there being a noticeable improvement. →	
(C) Our political party will retain its status only if it raises more money. But raising more money requires increased campaigning. So our party will not retain its status unless it increases its campaigning. →	
(D) You can repair your own bicycle only if you are enthusiastic. And if you are enthusiastic, you will also have mechanical aptitude. So if you are not able to repair your own bicycle, you lack mechanical aptitude. →	
(E) Getting a ticket requires waiting in line. Waiting in line requires patience. So if you do not wait in line, you lack patience. →	

PrepTest57 Sec2 Q19

Expert Analysis: Parallel Reasoning Questions

Compare your work to that of an LSAT expert. Which tools did you use to evaluate the answer choices? Where did the expert use a different tool?

LSAT Question	Analysis
101. Judicial punishment's power to deter people from committing crimes is a function of the severity of the penalty and the likelihood of one's actually receiving the penalty. Occasionally, juries decide that a crime's penalty is too severe and so refuse to convict a person they are convinced has committed that crime. Thus, increasing the penalty may decrease the deterrent power of judicial punishment. →	**Step 2:** Conclusion—*A weak assertion* that an increase in one thing (the severity of a penalty) may cause a decrease in another (deterrence). *because* Evidence—*Two requirements* (deterrence needs severity of penalty and chance of receiving penalty) *subject to a dilemma* (if severity of penalty increases, chance of receiving penalty may decrease).
The pattern of reasoning in which one of the following arguments is most similar to the pattern of reasoning in the argument above? →	**Step 1:** "Most similar to" indicates a Parallel Reasoning question.
	Step 3: Start by ruling out choices in which the conclusion is not a weak assertion that an increase in one thing may cause a decrease in something else; if necessary, compare the evidence.
(A) Success in attaining one's first academic job depends on the quality of one's dissertation and the amount of time spent working on it in graduate school. But sometimes, so much time is spent on a dissertation that it becomes too lengthy to be coherent and its quality suffers. So spending more time working on a dissertation can lead to less success in attaining a first academic job. →	**Step 4:** Correct. Conclusion is a weak assertion that increasing time spent on dissertation may lower chances of success. (No other choice has a matching conclusion!) Evidence is two requirements subject to a dilemma.
(B) People who drive cars having many safety features are likely to drive more aggressively than do people who drive cars having few safety features. Thus, the people who drive the safest cars are likely to be the most dangerous drivers on the road. →	Conclusion is a probable assertion due to the word *likely*. Also, the superlatives "safest" and "most dangerous" are not parallel to the stimulus. Eliminate.

LSAT Question (cont.)		Analysis (cont.)
(C)	A new surgical technique is developed to treat a dangerous condition. This technique enables people to live longer than does an older form of surgery. But the new surgery's mortality rate is also slightly higher. Thus, if more people choose to undergo the new surgery, more people may die from the dangerous condition than previously.	Conclusion is a conditional If/Then statement. The evidence presents a dilemma, but not one between two requirements. Eliminate.
(D)	To be attractive to tourists, it is best for a city to have both wide appeal and sufficient hotel space. Though a sufficient number of hotel rooms alone cannot attract tourists, it is much harder for city governments to affect the appeal of their city than for them to affect its amount of hotel space. Thus, governments of cities that want to increase their attractiveness to tourists should put their energies into increasing their hotel space.	Conclusion is a recommendation, a piece of advice to city governments that want to increase their attractiveness to tourists. The evidence presents a comparison, not a dilemma. Eliminate.
(E)	Many young, talented artists, because they are unknown, decide to charge low prices for their work. As their reputations grow, the prices they can charge for their work increase. Thus, raising the price of an artist's work can improve that artist's reputation. *PrepTest49 Sec2 Q24*	Conclusion is a weak assertion that an increase in one thing (price) can lead to an *increase,* not a decrease, in something else (reputation). The conclusion presents neither requirements nor a dilemma. Eliminate.

LSAT Question	Analysis
102. Team captain: Winning requires the willingness to cooperate, which in turn requires motivation. So you will not win if you are not motivated.	**Step 2:** Conclusion is conditional (*If/Then*): If you are not motivated, then you won't win. → *because* Evidence (if needed): If you win, then you cooperated; and if you cooperated, then you had motivation.
The pattern of reasoning in which one of the following is most similar to that in the argument above? →	**Step 1:** The phrase "most similar to" indicates a Parallel Reasoning question.
	Step 3: A scan of the choices reveals that all have conditional conclusions, so compare the Formal Logic structures: If A (win), then B (cooperate); if B, then C (motivation). Therefore, if no C, then no A.
(A) Being healthy requires exercise. But exercising involves risk of injury. So, paradoxically, anyone who wants to be healthy will not exercise.	**Step 4:** Structure: If A (healthy), then B (exercise); but if B, then *risk of C* (injury). Therefore, if *want* A, then *not* B. Eliminate.
(B) Learning requires making some mistakes. And you must learn if you are to improve. So you will not make mistakes without there being a noticeable improvement.	Structure: If A (improve), then B (learn). If B, then C (make mistakes). Therefore, *if not A, then not C*. Eliminate.
(C) Our political party will retain its status only if it raises more money. But raising more money requires increased campaigning. So our party will not retain its status unless it increases its campaigning.	Correct. The structure is identical to that in the stimulus: if A (retain status), then B (raise more money); if B, then C (more campaigning); therefore, if not C, then not A.
(D) You can repair your own bicycle only if you are enthusiastic. And if you are enthusiastic, you will also have mechanical aptitude. So if you are not able to repair your own bicycle, you lack mechanical aptitude.	Structure: If A (repair bike), then B (enthusiastic); if B, then C (mechanical aptitude). Therefore, *if not A, then not C*. Eliminate.
(E) Getting a ticket requires waiting in line. Waiting in line requires patience. So if you do not wait in line, you lack patience. *PrepTest57 Sec2 Q19*	Structure: If A (get ticket), then B (wait in line); if B, then C (patience). Therefore, *If not B, then not C*. Eliminate.

Perform

Use the Logical Reasoning Method and the Parallel Reasoning tactics to complete the following questions.

LSAT Question	My Analysis
103. Landscape architect: If the screen between these two areas is to be a hedge, that hedge must be of either hemlocks or Leyland cypress trees. However, Leyland cypress trees cannot be grown this far north. So if the screen is to be a hedge, it will be a hemlock hedge. →	**Step 2:**
In which one of the following is the pattern of reasoning most similar to that in the landscape architect's argument? →	**Step 1:**
	Step 3:
(A) If there is to be an entrance on the north side of the building, it will have to be approached by a ramp. However, a ramp would become impossibly slippery in winter, so there will be no entrance on the north side. →	**Step 4:**
(B) If visitors are to travel to this part of the site by automobile, there will be a need for parking spaces. However, no parking spaces are allowed for in the design. So if visitors are likely to come by automobile, the design will be changed. →	
(C) The subsoil in these five acres either consists entirely of clay or consists entirely of shale. Therefore, if one test hole in the area reveals shale, it will be clear that the entire five acres has a shale subsoil. →	
(D) Any path along this embankment must be either concrete or stone. But a concrete path cannot be built in this location. So if there is to be a path on the embankment, it will be a stone path. →	
(E) A space the size of this meadow would be suitable for a playground or a picnic area. However, a playground would be noisy and a picnic area would create litter. So it will be best for the area to remain a meadow. →	

PrepTest51 Sec1 Q5

LSAT Question	My Analysis
104. From the fact that people who studied music as children frequently are quite proficient at mathematics, it cannot be concluded that the skills required for mathematics are acquired by studying music: it is equally likely that proficiency in mathematics and studying music are both the result of growing up in a family that encourages its children to excel at all intellectual and artistic endeavors. →	**Step 2:**
The pattern of reasoning in which one of the following arguments is most parallel to that in the argument above? →	**Step 1:**
	Step 3:
(A) Although children who fail to pay attention tend to perform poorly in school, it should not necessarily be thought that their poor performance is caused by their failure to pay attention, for it is always possible that their failure to pay attention is due to undiagnosed hearing problems that can also lead to poor performance in school. →	**Step 4:**
(B) People who attend a university in a foreign country are usually among the top students from their native country. It would therefore be wrong to conclude from the fact that many foreign students perform better academically than others in this country that secondary schools in other countries are superior to those in this country; it may be that evaluation standards are different. →	
(C) People whose diet includes relatively large quantities of certain fruits and vegetables have a slightly lower than average incidence of heart disease. But it would be premature to conclude that consuming these fruits and vegetables prevents heart disease, for this correlation may be merely coincidental. →	
(D) Those who apply to medical school are required to study biology and chemistry. It would be a mistake, however, to conclude that those who have mastered chemistry and biology will succeed as physicians, for the practical application of knowledge is different from its acquisition. →	
(E) Those who engage in vigorous exercise tend to be very healthy. But it would be silly to conclude that vigorous exercise is healthful simply because people who are healthy exercise vigorously, since it is possible that exercise that is less vigorous also has beneficial results. →	

PrepTest49 Sec4 Q17

Expert Analysis: Parallel Reasoning Questions

Compare your work to that of an LSAT expert. Which tools did you use to evaluate the answer choices? Where did the expert use a different tool?

LSAT Question	Analysis
103. Landscape architect: If the screen between these two areas is to be a hedge, that hedge must be of either hemlocks or Leyland cypress trees. However, Leyland cypress trees cannot be grown this far north. So if the screen is to be a hedge, it will be a hemlock hedge. →	**Step 2:** Conclusion—A *strong conditional prediction*—if A (the screen is a hedge), then it must be B (hemlock). *because* Evidence (if needed)—If A (the screen is a hedge), then it must be B (hemlock) or C (cypress), but C is impossible (cypress doesn't grow this far north).
In which one of the following is the pattern of reasoning most similar to that in the landscape architect's argument? →	**Step 1:** The phrase "most similar to" identifies this as a Parallel Reasoning question.
	Step 3: Compare conclusions and/or overall structures of the answer choices with those in the stimulus.
(A) If there is to be an entrance on the north side of the building, it will have to be approached by a ramp. However, a ramp would become impossibly slippery in winter, so there will be no entrance on the north side. →	**Step 4:** Conclusion is a strong negative prediction ("there will be no entrance … "), but is not conditional. Eliminate.
(B) If visitors are to travel to this part of the site by automobile, there will be a need for parking spaces. However, no parking spaces are allowed for in the design. So if visitors are likely to come by automobile, the design will be changed. →	Conclusion is a conditional prediction, but it introduces a qualifier in the sufficient condition: "likely" is not parallel to the stimulus. Moreover, the evidence does not match the "B or C, but C is impossible" structure of the stimulus. Eliminate.
(C) The subsoil in these five acres either consists entirely of clay or consists entirely of shale. Therefore, if one test hole in the area reveals shale, it will be clear that the entire five acres has a shale subsoil. →	Conclusion lacks the structure "If there will be A then it will be a special kind of A." Moreover, the evidence does not match the "B or C, but C is impossible" structure of the stimulus. Eliminate.
(D) Any path along this embankment must be either concrete or stone. But a concrete path cannot be built in this location. So if there is to be a path on the embankment, it will be a stone path. →	Correct. Only this choice has a conclusion that is parallel to the one in the stimulus: "If there's a path then it will be a special kind of path." The evidence also matches the "B or C, but C is impossible" structure of the stimulus.
(E) A space the size of this meadow would be suitable for a playground or a picnic area. However, a playground would be noisy and a picnic area would create litter. So it will be best for the area to remain a meadow. →	Conclusion is a recommendation: "it will be best … " Moreover, the evidence does not match the "B or C, but C is impossible" structure of the stimulus. Eliminate.

PrepTest51 Sec1 Q5

LSAT Question	Analysis
104. From the fact that people who studied music as children frequently are quite proficient at mathematics, it cannot be concluded that the skills required for mathematics are acquired by studying music: it is equally likely that proficiency in mathematics and studying mus ic are both the result of growing up in a family that encourages its children to excel at all intellectual and artistic endeavors. →	**Step 2:** Conclusion—A *qualified negative assertion* that correlation does not prove causation—specifically, math skills are not necessarily acquired by studying music. *because* Evidence (if needed)—Proficiency in math and music may both be the result of growing up in a certain type of family.
The pattern of reasoning in which one of the following arguments is most parallel to that in the argument above? →	**Step 1:** The phrase "most parallel to" identifies this as a Parallel Reasoning question.
	Step 3: The argument's structure is easily summarized: A (musical ability) and B (math skills) are correlated, but both A and B may be the result of C (family encouragement). Therefore, A cannot be said to cause B. Compare the argument structures in the answer choices.
(A) Although children who fail to pay attention tend to perform poorly in school, it should not necessarily be thought that their poor performance is caused by their failure to pay attention, for it is always possible that their failure to pay attention is due to undiagnosed hearing problems that can also lead to poor performance in school. →	**Step 4:** Correct. This argument has a structure identical to that in the stimulus. A (poor attention) and B (poor performance) are correlated, but A and B may be the result of C (hearing problems). Therefore, A cannot be said to cause B.
(B) People who attend a university in a foreign country are usually among the top students from their native country. It would therefore be wrong to conclude from the fact that many foreign students perform better academically than others in this country that secondary schools in other countries are superior to those in this country; it may be that evaluation standards are different. →	This argument includes too many terms. A (attend foreign university) and B (top scholar in home country) are correlated, but C (foreign evaluation standards may be different). Therefore, *D* (the fact that foreign students outperform some domestic students) *does not imply E* (superiority of foreign high schools). Eliminate.
(C) People whose diet includes relatively large quantities of certain fruits and vegetables have a slightly lower than average incidence of heart disease. But it would be premature to conclude that consuming these fruits and vegetables prevents heart disease, for this correlation may be merely coincidental. →	This argument is parallel but for one problem: instead of introducing a possible third factor, it says the correlation may be mere coincidence. Eliminate.
(D) Those who apply to medical school are required to study biology and chemistry. It would be a mistake, however, to conclude that those who have mastered chemistry and biology will succeed as physicians, for the practical application of knowledge is different from its acquisition. →	This argument does not attempt to refute a correlation versus causation argument. Rather, it says that the fact that A (apply to med school) requires B (study chem and bio) does not mean that B is sufficient for C (being a doctor). Eliminate.

LSAT Question (cont.)	**Analysis (cont.)**
(E) Those who engage in vigorous exercise tend to be very healthy. But it would be silly to conclude that vigorous exercise is healthful simply because people who are healthy exercise vigorously, since it is possible that exercise that is less vigorous also has beneficial results. *PrepTest49 Sec4 Q17*	The conclusion is a strong assertion that correlation does not prove causation. But the evidence is all wrong: instead of proposing a third factor that might cause both A (vigorous exercise) and B (health), the author states that another type of A (less vigorous exercise) might be generally beneficial. Eliminate.

REFLECTION

Look back over the arguments you saw in the chapter. Consider the various analytical skills that the LSAT rewarded.

- · How do you now look at arguments differently?
- · When you see an argument, can you zero in on the conclusion directly?
- · Is it easier to spot what the author considers to be the direct and relevant evidence for the conclusion?
- · Are you able to spot the actual points of disagreement between two speakers?
- · Can you separate the author's argumentative strategy from the content of the argument? Do you think you could spot arguments with similar argumentative strategies even if they are on different subjects?

Arguments occur everywhere in the real world: television news and commentary, advertisements, debate over music, and claims about sports teams. In the coming days, read and listen to arguments very carefully. Apply the analytical skills you practiced in this chapter.

- · What is the author's main point? Does she offer any subsidiary conclusions in the argument?
- · What kind of conclusion is the author offering: a recommendation? a prediction? a comparison? an assertion of fact?
- · Is the conclusion conditional?
- · What is the author's evidence? Is it relevant to the conclusion?
- · If two people are arguing, what is their actual disagreement over? Do they have points of agreement? Are the two actually making different points?
- · What argumentative strategies are being used? Does the speaker or advertiser offer an analogy? A counterexample?
- · What is the role of necessity and sufficiency in the arguments you read or hear?

In the next chapter, you'll take your analytical skills to the next level, learning to identify the assumption(s) an author is making (of which he or she may not even be aware). The skill of identifying assumptions opens the door to several of the most important—and most challenging—question types on the LSAT: Assumption, Strengthen, Weaken, and Flaw.

CHAPTER 8

Assumption Family Questions

This chapter builds on Chapter 7 by adding another layer to your skills in the analysis of arguments: determining the author's assumption(s), or unstated premise(s). Every argument you'll encounter in this chapter is incomplete as written. There is an essential premise that the author has left unsaid. Developing an ability to quickly, calmly, and accurately put your finger on an author's key assumption is the foundational skill tested by more than half of all Logical Reasoning questions, and thus accounts for more than one-quarter of your LSAT score.

LSAT STRATEGY

Every Assumption Family argument contains the following:

- A conclusion—The author's main point: an assertion, evaluation, or recommendation
- Evidence—The facts and information the author presents in support of the conclusion
- An assumption—The unstated premise that logically connects the evidence to the conclusion

---

As you analyzed the explicit parts of arguments in Chapter 7, it's likely that you felt that most of these arguments were not entirely convincing. Here's a good example:

Pundit: The average salary for teachers in our society is lower than the average salary for athletes. Obviously, our society values sports more than it values education.

PrepTest51 Sec3 Q4

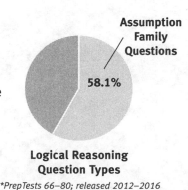

Assumption Family Questions

58.1%

Logical Reasoning Question Types

PrepTests 66–80; released 2012–2016

As you see it again now, what's your reaction? Do you have the sense that there is more to this argument than what the author has presented? Can you think of things the author may be overlooking or failing to take into account? Can you think of other facts that would strengthen or weaken this argument, or that you would at least like to know to evaluate it? If so, you are anticipating all of the key question types in the Assumption Family of Logical Reasoning questions.

On LSAT tests released from 2012 to 2016, there were approximately 30 Assumption Family questions per test.

There are three main Assumption Family question types:

Assumption Questions: These ask directly for an unstated premise in the argument.

Flaw Questions: These ask you to describe the error in the author's reasoning; the error is most often related to what the author has overlooked, or how the evidence fails to establish the conclusion.

Strengthen/Weaken Questions: These ask for facts that, if true, would make the argument more or less likely to be valid; you'll need to understand what the author is assuming to answer most of these questions accurately and efficiently.

Here are examples of each of those question types:

Assumption Question

There can be no individual freedom without the rule of law, for there is no individual freedom without social integrity, and pursuing the good life is not possible without social integrity.

The conclusion drawn above follows logically if which one of the following is assumed?

(A) There can be no rule of law without social integrity.

(B) There can be no social integrity without the rule of law.

(C) One cannot pursue the good life without the rule of law.

(D) Social integrity is possible only if individual freedom prevails.

(E) There can be no rule of law without individual freedom.

PrepTest61 Sec4 Q25

Flaw Question

The more modern archaeologists learn about Mayan civilization, the better they understand its intellectual achievements. Not only were numerous scientific observations and predictions made by Mayan astronomers, but the people in general seem to have had a strong grasp of sophisticated mathematical concepts. We know this from the fact that the writings of the Mayan religious scribes exhibit a high degree of mathematical competence.

The argument's reasoning is most vulnerable to criticism on the grounds that the argument

(A) fails to provide an adequate definition of the term "intellectual achievement"

(B) bases a generalization on a sample that is likely to be unrepresentative

(C) overlooks the impressive achievements of other past civilizations

(D) relies on two different senses of the term "scientific"

(E) takes a mere correlation to be evidence of a causal relationship

PrepTest59 Sec3 Q8

Weaken Question

We can now dismiss the widely held suspicion that sugar consumption often exacerbates hyperactivity in children with attention deficit disorder. A scientific study of the effects of three common sugars— sucrose, fructose, and glucose—on children who have attention deficit disorder, with experimental groups each receiving a type of sugar in their diets and a control group receiving a sugar substitute instead of sugar, showed no statistically significant difference between the groups in thinking or behavior.

Which one of the following, if true, would most weaken the argument above?

(A) Only one of the three types of sugar used in the study was ever widely suspected of exacerbating hyperactivity.

(B) The consumption of sugar actually has a calming effect on some children.

(C) The consumption of some sugar substitutes exacerbates the symptoms of hyperactivity.

(D) The study included some observations of each group in contexts that generally tend to make children excited and active.

(E) Some children believe that they can tell the difference between the taste of sugar and that of sugar substitutes.

PrepTest51 Sec1 Q8

Strengthen Question

A recent study confirms that nutritious breakfasts make workers more productive. For one month, workers at Plant A received free nutritious breakfasts every day before work, while workers in Plant B did not. The productivity of Plant A's workers increased, while that of Plant B's workers did not.

Which one of the following, if true, most strengthens the argument?

(A) Few workers in Plant B consumed nutritious breakfasts during the month of the study.

(B) Workers in the study from Plant A and Plant B started work at the same time of day.

(C) During the month before the study, workers at Plant A and Plant B were equally productive.

(D) Workers from Plant A took fewer vacation days per capita during the month than did workers from Plant B.

(E) Workers in Plant B were more productive during the month of the study than were workers from Plant A.

PrepTest59 Sec2 Q22

TEST DAY TIP

Do not confuse the truth of a conclusion with the logical validity of an argument. Remember:

· A conclusion can be true even if the evidence for it is incomplete or the argument's reasoning is flawed.

· A logically valid argument can produce a false conclusion.

MISMATCHED CONCEPTS AND OVERLOOKED POSSIBILITIES

There are two broad categories of assumptions in LSAT arguments: Mismatched Concepts and Overlooked Possibilities. The categories are not mutually exclusive. As you will see, some arguments can be described in both ways. The first broad category of LSAT arguments is one in which the author assumes a relationship between terms or concepts of two different *kinds*; we'll refer to these assumptions as Mismatched Concepts.

Mismatched Concepts: The Basics

Prepare

LEARNING OBJECTIVES

In this section, you'll learn to:

- Identify Mismatched Concepts in a simple argument

Have you ever made an argument like one of these?

> "She likes bananas, so she will like plantains, too."
> "Joseph must watch his diet. All professional dancers are diet conscious."

If so, you've made an argument with a Mismatched Concepts assumption. You've assumed (and perhaps your audience has, too) that two terms or concepts were related in such a way that you could draw a conclusion about something different than what is in your evidence. Your argument may have been right given additional information that you and your audience had and therefore both took for granted (i.e., you both know your friend Joseph is a professional dancer and therefore didn't need to state the obvious). However, if an argument doesn't tell you this additional information, it is incomplete.

LSAT STRATEGY

How can you tell an argument contains mismatched concepts?

- The terms or concepts in the evidence appear unrelated to those in the conclusion.
- A new term or concept—not related to the evidence—appears in the conclusion.

Most arguments containing Mismatched Concepts fall into one of two patterns. In the first, the evidence and conclusion make different claims about the same subject.

> Socrates is human. Therefore, Socrates is mortal.

Here, the author assumes that what is claimed in the conclusion is entailed by what is claimed in the evidence: "Humans are mortal." In the second pattern, the same claim is made about two different subjects.

> Humans are mortal. Therefore, Socrates is mortal.

In this type of Mismatched Concepts argument, the author assumes that the subject of the conclusion is logically related to the subject of the evidence: "Socrates is human." Although LSAT arguments are longer, wordier, and more complex than those examples, you may be surprised to find that many of them boil down to one of those two patterns.

LSAT STRATEGY

When tackling an argument containing mismatched concepts:

· Separate concepts in the evidence from concepts in the conclusion.
· Identify the mismatched concepts that the author *assumes* are related.
· Find the assumption by forming a sentence that logically bridges—i.e., connects—the mismatched concepts—this sentence serves to make the evidence relevant to the conclusion.

Mismatched Concepts: Sample Arguments

Here are a handful of representative examples of Mismatched Concepts arguments.

Argument		Analysis
Bobby is a championship swimmer. Hence, he trains every day.	→	**Conclusion:** Bobby trains every day. *because* **Evidence:** Bobby is a championship swimmer. **Assumption:** Championship swimmers train every day.
Cats are cleaner animals than dogs. Therefore, cats make better pets than dogs make.	→	**Conclusion:** Cats make better pets than dogs make. *because* **Evidence:** Cats are cleaner animals than dogs are. **Assumption:** Cleaner animals make better pets.
Every kid loves ice cream, so Judy loves ice cream.	→	**Conclusion:** Judy loves ice cream. *because* **Evidence:** Every kid loves ice cream. **Assumption:** Judy is a kid.
Susan doesn't eat her vegetables. So Susan will not grow big and strong.	→	**Conclusion:** Susan will not grow big and strong. *because* **Evidence:** Susan doesn't eat her vegetables. **Assumption:** Susan needs to eat her vegetables to grow big and strong.
This package weighs more than 50 pounds. Therefore, the post office cannot ship it.	→	**Conclusion:** The post office cannot ship this package. *because* **Evidence:** This package weighs more than 50 pounds. **Assumption:** The post office cannot ship packages that weigh more than 50 pounds.

Practice

Now, analyze some arguments similar to those in the preceding examples. When you're done, compare your work to that of an LSAT expert on the pages following this exercise.

Argument	My Analysis
1. Lena has final exams so she must not be an English major.	**Conclusion:** *because* **Evidence:** **Assumption:**
2. Jeremy cannot come up with more than $500 per month. Therefore, he cannot rent an apartment in Brentwood.	**Conclusion:** *because* **Evidence:** **Assumption:**
3. Since tigers are heavy animals, they cannot run fast.	**Conclusion:** *because* **Evidence:** **Assumption:**
4. Julie's handbag costs more than Karen's handbag. Clearly, Julie's handbag is softer to the touch.	**Conclusion:** *because* **Evidence:** **Assumption:**
5. On Friday night, the local newspaper surveyed moviegoers and found that 75 percent of them were seeing an action movie or a romantic comedy. This proves that action and romantic comedy are the most popular movie genres.	**Conclusion:** *because* **Evidence:** **Assumption:**

Expert Analysis: Mismatched Concepts

Here's how an LSAT expert would analyze those arguments.

Argument	Analysis
1. Lena has final exams so she must not be an English major.	**Conclusion:** Lena must not be an English major. *because* **Evidence:** Lena has final exams. **Assumption:** "English majors do not have final exams." The phrases "English major" and "have final exams" are mutually exclusive.
2. Jeremy cannot come up with more than $500 per month. Therefore, he cannot rent an apartment in Brentwood.	**Conclusion:** Jeremy cannot rent an apartment in Brentwood. *because* **Evidence:** Jeremy cannot come up with more than $500 per month. **Assumption:** "An apartment in Brentwood costs more than $500 per month to rent." The phrases "apartment in Brentwood" and "$500 or less per month" are mutually exclusive. (Or, the phrases "apartment in Brentwood" and "more than $500 per month" are equivalent.)
3. Since tigers are heavy animals, they cannot run fast.	**Conclusion:** Tigers cannot run fast. *because* **Evidence:** Tigers are heavy animals. **Assumption:** "Heavy animals cannot run fast." The terms "heavy animals" and "run fast" are mutually exclusive.
4. Julie's handbag costs more than Karen's handbag. Clearly, Julie's handbag is softer to the touch.	**Conclusion:** Julie's handbag is softer to the touch. *because* **Evidence:** Julie's handbag costs more than Karen's handbag. **Assumption:** "Handbags that cost more are softer to the touch." The terms "cost more" and "softer to the touch" are equivalent.
5. On Friday night, the local newspaper surveyed moviegoers and found that 75 percent of them were seeing an action movie or a romantic comedy. This proves that action and romantic comedy are the most popular movie genres.	**Conclusion:** Action movies and romantic comedies are the most popular movie genres. *because* **Evidence:** Seventy-five percent of local moviegoers on Friday night were seeing an action movie or a romantic comedy. **Assumption:** "Local moviegoers on Friday night are representative of all moviegoers." The sample in the evidence is representative of that in the conclusion.

Perform

Identify the conclusion, evidence, and assumption in each of these arguments containing Mismatched Concepts.

Argument	My Analysis
6. This raspberry lemonade is a very sour drink. Hence, it will not pair well with the pasta dish. →	**Conclusion:** *because* **Evidence:** **Assumption:**
7. Sam will not eat at least three plates of food. Therefore, the buffet option will not be worth it for Sam. →	**Conclusion:** *because* **Evidence:** **Assumption:**
8. Digital flashcards are a more convenient study aid than traditional textbooks. Consequently, Sophia prefers digital flashcards for studying. →	**Conclusion:** *because* **Evidence:** **Assumption:**
9. Airport security will not allow any passenger carrying more than 3 ounces of liquid to board the plane. Clearly, Sandra will not be permitted to board the plane. →	**Conclusion:** *because* **Evidence:** **Assumption:**
10. Nearly everyone in urban areas would like to pass the referendum. Therefore, the people of this state support passing the referendum. →	**Conclusion:** *because* **Evidence:** **Assumption:**

Expert Analysis: Mismatched Concepts

Here's how an LSAT expert would analyze those arguments.

Argument	Analysis
6. This raspberry lemonade is a very sour drink. Hence, it will not pair well with the pasta dish.	**Conclusion:** This raspberry lemonade will not pair well with the pasta dish. *because* → **Evidence:** This raspberry lemonade is a very sour drink. **Assumption:** "A very sour drink will not pair well with the pasta dish." The terms "very sour drink" and "pair well with the pasta" are mutually exclusive.
7. Sam will not eat at least three plates of food. Therefore, the buffet option will not be worth it for Sam.	**Conclusion:** The buffet option will not be worth it for Sam. *because* → **Evidence:** Sam will not eat at least three plates of food. **Assumption:** "A diner needs to eat at least three plates of food to make the buffet worth it." The evidence term is necessary for the conclusion.
8. Digital flashcards are a more convenient study aid than traditional textbooks. Consequently, Sophia prefers digital flashcards for studying.	**Conclusion:** Sophia prefers digital flashcards for studying. *because* **Evidence:** Digital flashcards are a more convenient study aid than traditional textbooks. → **Assumption:** "Sophia prefers to study with study aids that are more convenient." The terms "prefers" and "more convenient" are equivalent (at least in Sophia's case).
9. Airport security will not allow any passenger carrying more than 3 ounces of liquid to board the plane. Clearly, Sandra will not be permitted to board the plane.	**Conclusion:** Sandra will not be permitted to board the plane. *because* **Evidence:** Airport security will not allow any passenger carrying more than 3 ounces of liquid to board the plane. → **Assumption:** "Sandra is a passenger carrying more than 3 ounces of liquid." The term "Sandra" is equivalent to the phrase "a passenger carrying more than 3 ounces of liquid" (at least right now).
10. Nearly everyone in urban areas would like to pass the referendum. Therefore, the people of this state support passing the referendum.	**Conclusion:** The people of the state support passing the referendum. *because* **Evidence:** The urban areas support it. **Assumption:** "The state's urban residents are representative of all residents." The sample in the evidence is representative of that in the conclusion.

Overlooked Possibilities: The Basics

The other common pattern in LSAT arguments involves those in which the author assumes a difference in *scale*, *degree*, or *level of certainty*, rather than a difference of kind; we'll refer to these assumptions as containing Overlooked Possibilities.

Prepare

> ### LEARNING OBJECTIVES
>
> In this section, you'll learn to:
>
> · Identify Overlooked Possibilities in a simple argument

Have you ever made an argument like this, maybe to a sibling or a roommate?

> The sandwich I was saving is gone. You must have eaten it.

Now, it is certainly possible that the accused party ate your sandwich. But, by concluding that he or she *must* have eaten it, you're overlooking several possibilities. Maybe someone else ate the sandwich. Maybe it wasn't eaten at all, but was thrown out because it was getting moldy. Maybe something was accidentally spilled on it and your roommate kindly disposed of it for you.

> ### LSAT STRATEGY
>
> You can identify Overlooked Possibilities as follows:
>
> · The terms or concepts in the evidence are related to the conclusion.
> · The conclusion reached is too strong or extreme to follow logically from the evidence.
> · The author has failed to consider possible objections to the conclusion.

What sort of overlooked possibilities do you spot in this argument?

> The city budget surplus is large enough to build a new park or to repave streets in the financial district. A recent study shows that the city has an abundance of parks, so the only viable project on which to spend the surplus is the repaving of streets in the financial district.

Here, the author has given a false dichotomy. There may be any number of other projects that are viable and perhaps even preferable to his recommendation.

> ### LSAT STRATEGY
>
> When tackling an argument with overlooked possibilities:
>
> · Focus on the conclusion.
> · Determine possible objections to that conclusion.
> · Understand the assumption in negative terms: The author assumes that the possible objections are *not* present or did *not* happen.

Overlooked Possibilities: Sample Arguments

Argument	Analysis
Samson does not have a ticket stub so he must have sneaked into the movie without paying.	**Conclusion:** Samson must have sneaked into the movie. *because* → **Evidence:** Samson has no ticket stub. **Assumption:** Since Samson doesn't have a ticket stub, he must have sneaked in; the *only way* to be in the theater without a ticket stub is to have sneaked in.
Sarah was late to work this morning and her boss fired her. Therefore, she must have been fired over her lateness.	**Conclusion:** Lateness is the reason for Sarah's firing. *because* → **Evidence:** Sarah was late and got fired. **Assumption:** There was no other reason for Sarah's firing; lateness is the *only* reason Sarah got fired.
George is a better race car driver than Jeff. Clearly, George will beat Jeff in the upcoming car race.	**Conclusion:** George will beat Jeff in the car race. *because* → **Evidence:** George is a better driver than Jeff. **Assumption:** There is no other factor that could cause George to lose; driver skill is the *only* relevant factor to who will win.
Jonah's marketing plan will save the company money. Therefore, the company should adopt Jonah's plan.	**Conclusion:** The company should adopt Jonah's plan. *because* → **Evidence:** Jonah's plan has one advantage: It saves money. **Assumption:** There are no overlooked disadvantages to Jonah's plan; saving money is the *only* factor relevant to the company's decision.
My balcony gets direct sunlight all summer and all of my plants on the balcony died. Clearly, the direct sunlight must be responsible for my plants dying.	**Conclusion:** Direct sunlight caused the plants to die. *because* → **Evidence:** Direct sunlight was correlated with the plants dying. **Assumption:** There was no other reason (over- or under-watering, bad soil, plant disease) that the plants died; direct sunlight was the ONLY cause of the plants' deaths.

Practice

Now, analyze some arguments similar to those in the preceding examples. When you're done, compare your work to that of an LSAT expert on the pages following this exercise.

Argument	My Analysis
11. Roger is not playing on the swing set today. Therefore, he must be in the sandbox. →	**Conclusion:** *because* **Evidence:** **Assumption:**
12. Jules held a commanding lead over Esteban in the first 20 minutes of the race. Clearly, Jules will defeat Esteban in this race. →	**Conclusion:** *because* **Evidence:** **Assumption:**
13. To qualify for the university's science prize, a student must publish original research. Neither Becky nor Ahmed have published original research this year, so unfortunately, none of Dr. Iglesias's students will receive the university science prize. →	**Conclusion:** *because* **Evidence:** **Assumption:**
14. Taking the school bus ensures that one gets to school on time. Jason missed the bus this morning, so he will definitely be late to school. →	**Conclusion:** *because* **Evidence:** **Assumption:**
15. In May, gasoline prices skyrocketed, driving up transportation costs. Shortly thereafter, produce prices at local grocery stores spiked. Rising transportation costs must have caused the spike in produce prices. →	**Conclusion:** *because* **Evidence:** **Assumption:**

Expert Analysis: Overlooked Possibilities

Argument	Analysis
11. Roger is not playing on the swing set today. Therefore, he must be in the sandbox. →	**Conclusion:** Roger *must* be in the sandbox. *because* **Evidence:** Roger is not playing on the swing set. **Assumption:** There is no place other than the sandbox or the swing set that Roger could be; there are *only* two places Roger could be.
12. Jules held a commanding lead over Esteban in the first 20 minutes of the race. Clearly, Jules will defeat Esteban in this race. →	**Conclusion:** Jules *will* defeat Esteban in this race. *because* **Evidence:** Jules held a commanding lead over Esteban in the first 20 minutes of the race. **Assumption:** Nothing could happen that would allow Esteban to defeat Jules; *only* the runner with the commanding lead early in the race can win.
13. To qualify for the university's science prize, a student must publish original research. Neither Becky nor Ahmed have published original research this year, so unfortunately, none of Dr. Iglesias's students will receive the university science prize. →	**Conclusion:** *None* of Dr. Iglesias's students will receive the university's science prize. *because* **Evidence:** 1) The university's science prize requires publication of original research, and 2) neither Becky nor Ahmed have published original research. **Assumption:** Dr. Iglesias has no students other than Becky or Ahmed who might have published original research; Becky and Ahmed are the *only* students of Dr. Iglesias who might have published original research.
14. Taking the school bus ensures that one gets to school on time. Jason missed the bus this morning, so he will definitely be late to school. →	**Conclusion:** Jason will not be at school on time. *because* **Evidence:** 1) Taking the bus is *sufficient* to get one to school on time, and 2) Jason did not take the bus. **Assumption:** The author has confused a sufficient condition for a necessary one. That means she overlooks the possibility of any other condition sufficient to get Jason to school on time; the author (perhaps mistakenly) assumes that taking the bus is the *only* way to get to school on time.
15. In May, gasoline prices skyrocketed, driving up transportation costs. Shortly thereafter, produce prices at local grocery stores spiked. Rising transportation costs must have caused the spike in produce prices. →	**Conclusion:** Rising transportation costs caused the spike in produce prices. *because* **Evidence:** Produce prices rose shortly after transportation costs shot up. **Assumption:** No factor other than transportation costs caused the spike in produce prices; increased transportation costs are the *only* reason produce prices went up.

Perform

Argument	My Analysis
16. The house on the near side of the street has better lighting than the house on the far side of the street. Clearly, Inga should buy the house on the near side of the street. →	**Conclusion:** *because* **Evidence:** **Assumption:**
17. Beth has been working for ABG Corp. longer than Antonio. Obviously, Beth will make assistant manager before Antonio does. →	**Conclusion:** *because* **Evidence:** **Assumption:**
18. My doctor charged me 35 percent more for an X-ray this year than last. As the X-ray procedure hasn't changed over the last year, my doctor must be overcharging me out of greed. →	**Conclusion:** *because* **Evidence:** **Assumption:**
19. Infant mortality rates are lower in country M than they are In country N. Country M must have a better medical system and better doctors than country N has. →	**Conclusion:** *because* **Evidence:** **Assumption:**
20. My snow blower refuses to start this morning, so I must have forgotten to charge the batteries. →	**Conclusion:** *because* **Evidence:** **Assumption:**

Expert Analysis: Overlooked Possibilities

Argument	Analysis
16. The house on the near side of the street has better lighting than the house on the far side of the street. Clearly, Inga should buy the house on the near side of the street.	**Conclusion:** Inga should buy the house on the near side of the street. *because* **Evidence:** The house on the near side of the street has better lighting than the house on the far side of the street. **Assumption:** There is no other factor that should sway Inga's decision; lighting is the *only* factor Inga should consider when buying the house.
17. Beth has been working for ABG Corp. longer than Antonio. Obviously, Beth will make assistant manager before Antonio does.	**Conclusion:** Beth *will* make assistant manager before Antonio does. *because* **Evidence:** Beth has been working for ABG Corp. longer than Antonio. **Assumption:** There is no other factor that could influence the promotion to assistant manager; seniority is the *only* factor relevant to the promotion to assistant manager.
18. My doctor charged me 35 percent more for an X-ray this year than last. As the X-ray procedure hasn't changed over the last year, my doctor must be overcharging me out of greed.	**Conclusion:** My doctor *must* be overcharging me out of greed. *because* **Evidence:** 1) My doctor charged me 35 percent more for an X-ray this year than last. 2) The X-ray procedure hasn't changed over the last year. **Assumption:** There is no reason other than greed for the X-ray to cost 35 percent more this year than last year; greed is the *only* reason to charge that much more than last year.
19. Infant mortality rates are lower in country M than they are in country N. Country M must have a better medical system and better doctors than country N has.	**Conclusion:** Country M must have a better medical system and better doctors than country N has. *because* **Evidence:** Infant mortality rates are lower in country M than they are in country N. **Assumption:** Nothing other than a better medical system and better doctors could be responsible for a lower infant mortality rate; a better medical system and better doctors are the *only* reasons for a lower infant mortality rate.

Argument	Analysis
20. My snow blower refuses to start this morning, so I must have forgotten to charge the batteries.	**Conclusion:** I must have forgotten to charge the snow blower's batteries. *because*
	Evidence: The snow blower won't start this morning.
$\longrightarrow$	**Assumption:** There is no reason other than an uncharged battery for my snow blower to refuse to start; a dead battery is the *only* reason my snow blower won't start.

Introduction to Assumption Family Question Types

Try applying the Logical Reasoning Method to a few questions. As you complete each step, think about how it prepares you to tackle the subsequent step more efficiently and effectively.

Assumption Questions

LSAT Question	My Analysis
21. Some political thinkers hope to devise a form of government in which every citizen's rights are respected. But such a form of government is impossible. For any government must be defined and controlled by laws that determine its powers and limits; and it is inevitable that some individuals will learn how to interpret these laws to gain a greater share of political power than others have. $\longrightarrow$	**Step 2:** Conclusion— *because* Evidence—
Which one of the following is an assumption required by the argument? $\longrightarrow$	**Step 1:**
	Step 3:
(A) In any form of government that leads to unequal distribution of political power, the rights of the majority of people will be violated. $\longrightarrow$	**Step 4:**
(B) A government can ensure that every citizen's rights are respected by keeping the citizens ignorant of the laws. $\longrightarrow$	
(C) Not all the laws that define a government's power and limits can be misinterpreted. $\longrightarrow$	
(D) In any form of government, if anybody gains a greater share of political power than others have, then somebody's rights will be violated. $\longrightarrow$	
(E) People who have more political power than others have tended to use it to acquire an even greater share of political power. $\longrightarrow$	

PrepTest51 Sec3 Q2

Flaw Questions

LSAT Question	My Analysis

22. Politician: Most of those at the meeting were not persuaded by Kuyler's argument, nor should they have been, for Kuyler's argument implied that it would be improper to enter into a contract with the government; and yet—as many people know—Kuyler's company has had numerous lucrative contracts with the government.

→ **Step 2:** Conclusion—

because

Evidence—

Which one of the following describes a flaw in the politician's argument?

→ **Step 1:**

Step 3:

(A) It concludes that an argument is defective merely on the grounds that the argument has failed to persuade anyone of the truth of its conclusion.

→ **Step 4:**

(B) It relies on testimony that is likely to be biased.

→

(C) It rejects an argument merely on the grounds that the arguer has not behaved in a way that is consistent with the argument.

→

(D) It rejects a position merely on the grounds that an inadequate argument has been given for it.

→

(E) It rejects an argument on the basis of an appeal to popular opinion.

PrepTest57 Sec3 Q2 →

Strengthen/Weaken Questions

LSAT Question	My Analysis
23. Over the last five years, every new major alternative-energy initiative that initially was promised government funding has since seen that funding severely curtailed. In no such case has the government come even close to providing the level of funds initially earmarked for these projects. Since large corporations have made it a point to discourage alternative-energy projects, it is likely that the corporations' actions influenced the government's funding decisions. $\longrightarrow$	**Step 2:** Conclusion— *because* Evidence—
Which one of the following, if true, most strengthens the reasoning above? $\longrightarrow$	**Step 1:** **Step 3:**
(A) For the past two decades, most alternative-energy initiatives have received little or no government funding. $\longrightarrow$	**Step 4:**
(B) The funding initially earmarked for a government project is always subject to change, given the mechanisms by which the political process operates. $\longrightarrow$	
(C) The only research projects whose government funding has been severely curtailed are those that large corporations have made it a point to discourage. $\longrightarrow$	
(D) Some projects encouraged by large corporations have seen their funding severely curtailed over the last five years. $\longrightarrow$	
(E) All large corporations have made it a point to discourage some forms of research. $\longrightarrow$	

PrepTest61 Sec2 Q6

This chapter continues on the next page ▶ ▶ ▶

Expert Analysis: Assumption Family Question Types

Compare your work to that of an LSAT expert. As you review the following analysis, pay special attention to how the expert characterized each of the wrong answers.

LSAT Question	Analysis
21. Some political thinkers hope to devise a form of government in which every citizen's rights are respected. But such a form of government is impossible. For any government must be defined and controlled by laws that determine its powers and limits; and it is inevitable that some individuals will learn how to interpret these laws to gain a greater share of political power than others have.	**Step 2:** Conclusion—A form of government respecting every citizen's rights is impossible. Evidence—1) Government must be defined and controlled by laws, and 2) some people will learn how to use the laws to gain more political power than others.
Which one of the following is an assumption required by the argument?	**Step 1:** The correct answer will be an unstated premise ("assumption") that must be true in order for the conclusion to be drawn from the evidence.
	Step 3: This argument contains Mismatched Concepts. The author must assume that if some people have more political power, then not every citizen's rights can be respected.
(A) In any form of government that leads to unequal distribution of political power, the rights of the majority of people will be violated.	**Step 4:** Extreme. The argument assumes only that some citizen's rights will be violated, not that a majority of people's rights will. Eliminate.
(B) A government can ensure that every citizen's rights are respected by keeping the citizens ignorant of the laws.	Distortion. The author makes clear that some individuals will learn how to manipulate the laws. Moreover, there is no assumption about how to make sure everyone's rights are respected because the argument concludes that it is impossible to do so. Eliminate.
(C) Not all the laws that define a government's power and limits can be misinterpreted.	Extreme/Distortion. The evidence states that individuals will learn to distort laws to their own advantage. Whether that involves some or all of the laws is irrelevant. Eliminate.
(D) In any form of government, if anybody gains a greater share of political power than others have, then somebody's rights will be violated.	Correct. This assumption is necessary to the argument. If (D) is not true, then the evidence in the argument does not support the conclusion.
(E) People who have more political power than others have tend to use it to acquire an even greater share of political power. *PrepTest51 Sec3 Q2*	Outside the Scope. Whether an initial imbalance in political power leads to greater imbalance is beyond the purview of the argument. Eliminate.

LSAT Question	Analysis
22. Politician: Most of those at the meeting were not persuaded by Kuyler's argument, nor should they have been, for Kuyler's argument implied that it would be improper to enter into a contract with the government; and yet—as many people know—Kuyler's company has had numerous lucrative contracts with the government.	**Step 2:** Conclusion—Kuyler is wrong to imply that entering into a government contract would be improper. Evidence—Kuyler's company has entered into many lucrative government contracts.
Which one of the following describes a flaw in the politician's argument?	**Step 1:** The correct answer describes a mistake in the politician's reasoning.
	Step 3: The politician assumes that Kuyler's conclusion is incorrect because Kuyler is a hypocrite. This overlooks the possibility that someone's point can be valid even though that person doesn't follow his own advice.
(A) It concludes that an argument is defective merely on the grounds that the argument has failed to persuade anyone of the truth of its conclusion.	**Step 4:** Distortion. The politician states that "*most* of those at the meeting were not persuaded." Moreover, the politician doesn't attack Kuyler for his failure to persuade but for his hypocrisy. Eliminate.
(B) It relies on testimony that is likely to be biased.	Outside the Scope. The politician's argument is not supported by any testimony. Eliminate.
(C) It rejects an argument merely on the grounds that the arguer has not behaved in a way that is consistent with the argument.	Correct. This summarizes the flaw of arguing *ad hominem*. Kuyler's conclusion may be right even though his behavior is hypocritical.
(D) It rejects a position merely on the grounds that an inadequate argument has been given for it.	Outside the Scope. The politician doesn't even say what Kuyler's argument was; he just attacks Kuyler's conclusion because of Kuyler's behavior. Eliminate.
(E) It rejects an argument on the basis of an appeal to popular opinion. *PrepTest57 Sec3 Q2*	Distortion. While the politician references many people's knowledge of Kuyler's contracts, he does not cite any opinions regarding them. Eliminate.

LSAT Question	Analysis
23. Over the last five years, every new major alternative-energy initiative that initially was promised government funding has since seen that funding severely curtailed. In no such case has the government come even close to providing the level of funds initially earmarked for these projects. Since large corporations have made it a point to discourage alternative-energy projects, it is likely that the corporations' actions influenced the government's funding decisions. →	**Step 2:** Conclusion—Corporate influence is the likely reason the government has cut alternative energy funding. Evidence—Corporations have worked to discourage alternative energy projects, and funding for those projects has been cut.
Which one of the following, if true, most strengthens the reasoning above? →	**Step 1:** The correct answer provides a fact that strengthens the argument; it will make the conclusion more likely to follow from the evidence.
	Step 3: This argument contains Overlooked Possibilities. The author assumes that corporate influence (and not some other factor) is the likely cause of the reduction in government funding. The correct answer will make it more likely that corporate influence was the cause of the funding cuts, or will rule out some other possible reason.
(A) For the past two decades, most alternative-energy initiatives have received little or no government funding. →	**Step 4:** Outside the Scope. The argument is about *why* alternative energy research has been cut. The fact that it has not been funded for a long time doesn't make the author's assertion that corporate opposition is the cause any more or any less likely. Eliminate.
(B) The funding initially earmarked for a government project is always subject to change, given the mechanisms by which the political process operates. →	Outside the Scope. A general statement about the uncertainties of government funding doesn't make the author's assertion about the cause of alternative energy program funding cuts any more or any less likely. Eliminate.
(C) The only research projects whose government funding has been severely curtailed are those that large corporations have made it a point to discourage. →	Correct. If research projects not opposed by corporations have continued to be funded, it is less likely that the alternative energy programs were simply victims of overall cost cutting measures.
(D) Some projects encouraged by large corporations have seen their funding severely curtailed over the last five years. →	180. This suggests that corporate influence is not all powerful. If even projects that corporations support have been cut, maybe the alternative energy programs were cut for other reasons, too. Eliminate.
(E) All large corporations have made it a point to discourage some forms of research. *PrepTest61 Sec2 Q6* →	Extreme. This blanket statement about corporate behavior does not make it more likely that corporate influence was the cause of these research cuts. Eliminate.

REFLECTION

Look back over the arguments you've seen so far in the chapter. Consider the various analytical skills that the LSAT rewarded.

- How do you now look at arguments differently?
- When you see an argument, can you determine the author's assumption?
- Are you able to determine the type of assumption the author is making?

IDENTIFYING ASSUMPTIONS IN LSAT ARGUMENTS

Prepare

LEARNING OBJECTIVES

In this section, you'll learn to:

- Identify the assumption in LSAT arguments

Activate Prior Knowledge: Common Relationships Between Mismatched Concepts

Alike/Equivalent is the assumption that two terms/concepts are similar enough to justify the conclusion.

Example: "This house is decorated with antiques and memorabilia. It will, therefore, appeal to a sentimental person." The assumption here is that antiques and memorabilia appeal to sentimental people.

Mutually Exclusive is the assumption that two terms/concepts are incompatible.

Example: "These dwellings are built using adobe materials. Thus, while they are excellent examples of adobe construction, they cannot be said to represent the native architecture of the region." The assumption here is that the native architecture of the region *did not* use adobe materials.

One Term/Concept Needed for the Other is the assumption that A cannot happen without B. In other words, B is necessary for A.

Example: "I cannot vote because I am not registered." The assumption here is that voting *requires* registration.

LSAT arguments sometimes present a closely related argument with this structure: Something is necessary for something else; therefore, something else won't happen.

Example: "Voters are required to register. Therefore, I cannot vote." The assumption here is that a necessary condition (registration) was not—and will not be—fulfilled.

One Term/Concept Representative of the Other is the assumption that the group or sample in the evidence is representative of the group or sample in the conclusion.

Example: "Doctors are unlikely to prescribe the new drug. We know this from a survey of recent medical school graduates in which over 70 percent of those surveyed said they would not prescribe the new drug." The assumption here is recent medical school graduates are representative of doctors in general.

Lit is A
A isn't B
∴ not isn't B

Practice

Analyze the following LSAT arguments. Identify the conclusion and evidence, and determine the author's assumption. Categorize the assumption according to the common relationships on the previous page.

LSAT Argument	My Analysis
24. Chiu: The belief that a person is always morally blameworthy for feeling certain emotions, such as unjustifiable anger, jealousy, or resentment, is misguided. Individuals are responsible for only what is under their control, and whether one feels such an emotion is not always under one's control. *PrepTest51 Sec1 Q16*	**Conclusion:** People not always blameworthy for feeling certain emotions *because* **Evidence:** ◄ **Assumption:** Not always responsible for emotions **Assumption type:** ~~can only be able to be blamed~~ to be blamed for something requires responsibility
25. Critic: Photographers, by deciding which subjects to depict and how to depict them, express their own worldviews in their photographs, however realistically those photographs may represent reality. Thus, photographs are interpretations of reality. *PrepTest61 Sec2 Q13*	**Conclusion:** Photo interpretations of reality *because* **Evidence:** Photographers express their own world views in photographs **Assumption:** **Assumption type:** Photographers worldviews are interpretations of reality
26. Essayist: Lessing contended that an art form's medium dictates the kind of representation the art form must employ in order to be legitimate; painting, for example, must represent simultaneous arrays of colored shapes, while literature, consisting of words read in succession, must represent events or actions occurring in sequence. The claim about literature must be rejected, however, if one regards as legitimate the imagists' poems, which consist solely of amalgams of disparate images. *PrepTest57 Sec2 Q7*	**Conclusion:** Lit doesn't have to represent events in sequence *because* **Evidence:** Imagists poems are type of lit which are amalgams of disparate images **Assumption:** Amalgams of disparate images **Assumption type:** dont represent events in sequence
27. The more modern archaeologists learn about Mayan civilization, the better they understand its intellectual achievements. Not only were numerous scientific observations and predictions made by Mayan astronomers, but the people in general seem to have had a strong grasp of sophisticated mathematical concepts. We know this from the fact that the writings of the Mayan religious scribes exhibit a high degree of mathematical competence. *PrepTest59 Sec3 Q8*	**Conclusion:** Mayans had grasp on math concepts *because* **Evidence:** Mayan religious scribes knew a lot of math **Assumption:** Because some people in Mayan culture mathematically intelligent, whole pop was **Assumption type:**

Expert Analysis: Mismatched Concepts

Here's how an LSAT expert would analyze the arguments from that exercise. Compare your work.

LSAT Argument	Analysis
24. Chiu: The belief that a person is always morally blameworthy for feeling certain emotions, such as unjustifiable anger, jealousy, or resentment, is misguided. Individuals are responsible for only what is under their control, and whether one feels such an emotion is not always under one's control. *PrepTest51 Sec1 Q16* →	**Conclusion:** A person is not always blameworthy for feeling certain emotions. *because* **Evidence:** 1) Feeling emotions is not always under one's control, and 2) a person is responsible only for what is under his control. **Assumption:** If a person is not responsible for something, he isn't blameworthy for doing it. (Blameworthiness *requires* responsibility.) **Assumption type:** Mismatched Concepts—Need
25. Critic: Photographers, by deciding which subjects to depict and how to depict them, express their own worldviews in their photographs, however realistically those photographs may represent reality. Thus, photographs are interpretations of reality. *PrepTest61 Sec2 Q13* →	**Conclusion:** Photographs are interpretations of reality. *because* **Evidence:** Photographers express their worldviews in photographs. **Assumption:** The expression of a worldview is an interpretation of reality. **Assumption type:** Mismatched Concepts—Alike/Equivalent

LSAT Argument	**Analysis**
26. Essayist: Lessing contended that an art form's medium dictates the kind of representation the art form must employ in order to be legitimate; painting, for example, must represent simultaneous arrays of colored shapes, while literature, consisting of words read in succession, must represent events or actions occurring in sequence. The claim about literature must be rejected, however, if one regards as legitimate the imagists' poems, which consist solely of amalgams of disparate images. *PrepTest57 Sec2 Q7*	**Conclusion:** If imagist poems are literature, then literature does not have to represent events in sequence. *because* **Evidence:** If imagist poems are literature, they are just amalgams of disparate images. **Assumption:** An amalgam of disparate images does not represent events in sequence. **Assumption type:** Mismatched Concepts—Mutually Exclusive
27. The more modern archaeologists learn about Mayan civilization, the better they understand its intellectual achievements. Not only were numerous scientific observations and predictions made by Mayan astronomers, but the people in general seem to have had a strong grasp of sophisticated mathematical concepts. We know this from the fact that the writings of the Mayan religious scribes exhibit a high degree of mathematical competence. *PrepTest59 Sec3 Q8*	**Conclusion:** Mayan people in general had a strong understanding of mathematical concepts. *because* **Evidence:** Mayan religious scribes exhibited strong mathematical competence. **Assumption:** What's true of Mayan religious scribes is likely to be true of the Mayan people in general. **Assumption type:** Mismatched Concepts—Representativeness

Prepare

Activate Prior Knowledge: Common Patterns in Overlooked Possibilities

Assuming There is No Other Explanation, Reason, or Outcome

Example: "Sheila has enough money for a comfortable retirement. She must have regularly put a portion of her salary into savings." The assumption here is that regularly putting a portion of her salary is the *only* way Sheila could have enough money for a comfortable retirement. The author has overlooked any number of possible objections to this argument. Finding an alternative method of acquiring money for retirement would weaken this argument.

Assuming That What Is Sufficient Is Actually Necessary or Vice Versa

Example: "Booking during the week of February 1st ensures a stateroom on the summer jazz cruise. Nathan did not book during the week of February 1st, so he won't be able to get a stateroom on the summer jazz cruise." The author mistakes a condition sufficient to book a stateroom for one necessary to get a stateroom. The author (perhaps mistakenly) assumes that there is no other way to book a stateroom.

Assuming That a Correlation Proves Causation

Example: "I notice that whenever the store has a poor sales month, employee tardiness is higher. It must be that employee tardiness causes the store to lose sales." The author assumes no factor other than tardiness causes the store's lost sales.

There are three ways in which an argument conflating correlation with causation could be wrong. Think of a correlation versus causation argument like this: *X and Y are correlated, so X must cause Y.*

1) It could be that a third factor is responsible for both the author's purported cause and effect. *Maybe Z causes both X and Y.* (In the previous example, maybe the manager goes on vacation or is out of the store during months when sales decrease and employees are tardy.)
2) It could be that the author confuses an effect for a cause. *Maybe Y causes X.* (In the previous example, maybe employees are showing up late because sales are so poor.)
3) It could be that the correlation is simply a coincidence. *Maybe X and Y are unrelated.* (In the previous example, maybe it is just by chance that poor sales and tardiness have happened to occur at the same time.)

Assuming Changed or Unchanged Circumstances to Make a Prediction

Example: "For the past ten years, the winner of *Moviestar*'s best actor award has starred in a serious political drama. Hap Studley only appeared in romantic comedies this year, so he will not be named *Moviestar*'s best actor." The author assumes that the past trend will continue, thus overlooking any possibility that *Moviestar* could break from it. He assumes that the same conditions that have applied for the past decade *will* apply again this year.

Assuming That There Are No Overlooked Advantages or Disadvantages to a Recommendation

Example: "You really ought to buy the new Brand Q minivan. After all, it is the safest family vehicle currently produced." The author assumes that there are no factors that could trump safety in her listener's buying decision. She overlooks any number of considerations: price, appearance, gas mileage, and so on. Pointing out any one of those as a possible concern of the listener would weaken this argument.

Assuming That Something That Can Occur, Will (or Should) Occur

Example: "A popular proposal before the city council has the potential to balance the city's budget next fiscal year. Thus, for the first time in nearly a decade, the city will not run a budget deficit next year." Not only does the author assume that the popular proposal will be enacted, but also assumes that nothing else will happen that could cause the city to run a deficit even with the proposal in place.

Practice

Analyze the following LSAT arguments. Identify the conclusion and evidence, and determine the author's assumption. Categorize the assumption according to the common relationships on the previous page.

LSAT Argument	My Analysis
28. Scientist: While studying centuries-old Antarctic ice deposits, I found that several years of relatively severe atmospheric pollution in the 1500s coincided with a period of relatively high global temperatures. So it is clear in this case that atmospheric pollution did cause global temperatures to rise. *PrepTest59 Sec2 Q4*	**Conclusion:** Atmospheric pollution caused temps to rise *because* **Evidence:** **Assumption:** no other causes for temp rise **Assumption type:**
29. Economist: As should be obvious, raising the minimum wage significantly would make it more expensive for businesses to pay workers for minimum-wage jobs. Therefore, businesses could not afford to continue to employ as many workers for such jobs. So raising the minimum wage significantly will cause an increase in unemployment. *PrepTest57 Sec3 Q6*	**Conclusion:** Raising min wage will raise unemployment *because* **Evidence:** **Assumption:** **Assumption type:**
30. Recently discovered bird fossils are about 20 million years older than the fossils of the birdlike dinosaurs from which the birds are generally claimed to have descended. So these newly discovered fossils show, contrary to the account espoused by most paleontologists, that no bird descended from any dinosaur. *PrepTest51 Sec3 Q6*	**Conclusion:** Birds didn't descend from dinos *because* **Evidence:** recently discovered fossils **Assumption:** no other evidence exists that shows birds descended from dinos **Assumption type:**
31. Scientist: A controversy in paleontology centers on the question of whether prehistoric human ancestors began to develop sophisticated tools before or after they came to stand upright. I argue that they stood upright first, simply because advanced toolmaking requires free use of the hands, and standing upright makes this possible. *PrepTest49 Sec2 Q14*	**Conclusion:** ancestors stood upright before tool *because* **Evidence:** **Assumption:** **Assumption type:**

Expert Analysis: Overlooked Possibilities

Here's how an LSAT expert would analyze the arguments from that exercise. Compare your work.

LSAT Argument	Analysis
28. Scientist: While studying centuries-old Antarctic ice deposits, I found that several years of relatively severe atmospheric pollution in the 1500s coincided with a period of relatively high global temperatures. So it is clear in this case that atmospheric pollution did cause global temperatures to rise. *PrepTest59 Sec2 Q4* →	**Conclusion:** In the 1500s, air pollution caused global warming. *because* **Evidence:** In the 1500s, air pollution coincided with (was correlated with) global warming. **Assumption:** In the 1500s: 1) Global warming did not cause air pollution; 2) there was no third factor that caused both air pollution and global warming; and 3) air pollution and global warming were not merely coincidental. **Assumption type:** Overlooked Possibilities—Correlation versus Causation
29. Economist: As should be obvious, raising the minimum wage significantly would make it more expensive for businesses to pay workers for minimum-wage jobs. Therefore, businesses could not afford to continue to employ as many workers for such jobs. So raising the minimum wage significantly will cause an increase in unemployment. *PrepTest57 Sec3 Q6* →	**Conclusion:** Raising the minimum wage will increase unemployment. *because* **Evidence:** 1) Raising the minimum wage will make paying minimum-wage workers more expensive, and so 2) businesses will cut the number of minimum-wage jobs. **Assumption:** There is no way other than by keeping minimum-wage job numbers steady for businesses to keep employment numbers steady. The author overlooks both an increase in the number of non-minimum wage jobs and other ways in which businesses might afford to keep employment numbers up. **Assumption type:** Overlooked Possibilities—No Other Outcome/No Change in Circumstances

LSAT Argument	Analysis
30. Recently discovered bird fossils are about 20 million years older than the fossils of the birdlike dinosaurs from which the birds are generally claimed to have descended. So these newly discovered fossils show, contrary to the account espoused by most paleontologists, that no bird descended from any dinosaur. *PrepTest51 Sec3 Q6* ⟶	**Conclusion:** No bird descended from any dinosaur. *because* **Evidence:** Scientists have discovered bird fossils older than those of one dinosaur thought to be the ancestor of birds. **Assumption:** 1) The existence of the dinosaur claimed to be the ancestor of birds does not predate the earliest known fossils of that dinosaur. 2) There is no other dinosaur that might have been the ancestor of birds; this one dinosaur is the only dinosaur that might have been the ancestor of birds. **Assumption type:** Overlooked Possibilities—No Other Explanation
31. Scientist: A controversy in paleontology centers on the question of whether prehistoric human ancestors began to develop sophisticated tools before or after they came to stand upright. I argue that they stood upright first, simply because advanced toolmaking requires free use of the hands, and standing upright makes this possible. *PrepTest49 Sec2 Q14* ⟶	**Conclusion:** Early humans stood upright prior to developing sophisticated tools. *because* **Evidence:** 1) Free use of the hands is necessary for making sophisticated tools, and 2) standing upright is sufficient for free use of the hands. **Assumption:** There is no way other than standing upright to allow for free use of the hands; standing upright is the *only* way to allow for free use of the hands. **Assumption type:** Overlooked Possibilities—Necessary versus Sufficient

Perform

Analyze each of the following arguments. Identify the author's conclusion and evidence. Use them to determine the key assumption(s). Note the type of argument, and where applicable, the common pattern to which it conforms.

LSAT Argument	My Analysis
32. A recent study confirms that nutritious breakfasts make workers more productive. For one month, workers at Plant A received free nutritious breakfasts every day before work, while workers in Plant B did not. The productivity of Plant A's workers increased, while that of Plant B's workers did not. *PrepTest 59 Sec2 Q22*	**Conclusion:** *nutritious bfasts workers more prod* *because* → **Evidence:** *Plant A got nutr bfast Plant B did not* **Assumption:** *Assuming they ate it "received free"* **Assumption type:**
33. A development company has proposed building an airport near the city of Dalton. If the majority of Dalton's residents favor the proposal, the airport will be built. However, it is unlikely that a majority of Dalton's residents would favor the proposal, for most of them believe that the airport would create noise problems. Thus, it is unlikely that the airport will be built. *PrepTest61 Sec4 Q11*	**Conclusion:** *because* → **Evidence:** **Assumption:** **Assumption type:**
34. Although Jaaks is a respected historian, her negative review of Yancey's new book on the history of coastal fisheries in the region rests on a mistake. Jaaks's review argues that the book inaccurately portrays the lives of fishery workers. However, Yancey used the same research methods in this book as in her other histories, which have been very popular. This book is also very popular in local bookstores. *PrepTest59 Sec2 Q6*	**Conclusion:** *because* → **Evidence:** **Assumption:** **Assumption type:**
35. 1990 editorial: Local pay phone calls have cost a quarter apiece ever since the 1970s, when a soft drink from a vending machine cost about the same. The price of a soft drink has more than doubled since, so phone companies should be allowed to raise the price of pay phone calls too. *PrepTest49 Sec2 Q8*	**Conclusion:** *Phone comp. should raise price* *because* → **Evidence:** *soft drink ↑* **Assumption:** *whatever happens to 1 should* **Assumption type:** *happen to other*
36. Sometimes one reads a poem and believes that the poem expresses contradictory ideas, even if it is a great poem. So it is wrong to think that the meaning of a poem is whatever the author intends to communicate to the reader by means of the poem. No one who is writing a great poem intends it to communicate contradictory ideas. *PrepTest57 Sec2 Q24*	**Conclusion:** *because* → **Evidence:** **Assumption:** **Assumption type:**

LSAT Argument		My Analysis
37. A survey of clerical workers' attitudes toward their work identified a group of secretaries with very positive attitudes. They responded "Strongly agree" to such statements as "I enjoy word processing" and "I like learning new secretarial skills." These secretaries had been rated by their supervisors as excellent workers—far better than secretaries whose attitudes were identified as less positive. Clearly these secretaries' positive attitudes toward their work produced excellent job performance. *PrepTest49 Sec2 Q13*	→	**Conclusion:** *because* **Evidence:** **Assumption:** **Assumption type:**
38. There can be no individual freedom without the rule of law, for there is no individual freedom without social integrity, and pursuing the good life is not possible without social integrity. *PrepTest61 Sec4 Q25*	→	**Conclusion:** *because* **Evidence:** **Assumption:** **Assumption type:**
39. Vanwilligan: Some have argued that professional athletes receive unfairly high salaries. But in an unrestricted free market, such as the market these athletes compete in, salaries are determined by what someone else is willing to pay for their services. These athletes make enormous profits for their teams' owners, and that is why owners are willing to pay them extraordinary salaries. Thus the salaries they receive are fair. *PrepTest49 Sec2 Q19*	→	**Conclusion:** *because* **Evidence:** **Assumption:** **Assumption type:**
40. Eating garlic reduces the levels of cholesterol and triglycerides in the blood and so helps reduce the risk of cardiovascular disease. Evidence that eating garlic reduces these levels is that a group of patients taking a garlic tablet each day for four months showed a 12 percent reduction in cholesterol and a 17 percent reduction in triglycerides; over the same period, a group of similar patients taking a medically inert tablet showed only a 2 percent reduction in triglycerides and a 3 percent reduction in cholesterol. *PrepTest49 Sec4 Q2*	→	**Conclusion:** *because* **Evidence:** **Assumption:** **Assumption type:**
41. To cut costs, a high school modified its air-conditioning system to increase its efficiency. The modified system, however, caused the humidity in the school air to decrease by 18 percent. Twenty-four hours after the decrease in air humidity, a 25 percent increase in the number of visits to the school nurse was reported. This shows that a decrease in humidity can make people ill. *PrepTest59 Sec3 Q12*	→	**Conclusion:** *because* **Evidence:** **Assumption:** **Assumption type:**

Expert Analysis: Mismatched Concepts and Overlooked Possibilities

Here's how an LSAT expert would analyze the arguments from that exercise. Compare your work.

LSAT Argument	Analysis
32. A recent study confirms that nutritious breakfasts make workers more productive. For one month, workers at Plant A received free nutritious breakfasts every day before work, while workers in Plant B did not. The productivity of Plant A's workers increased, while that of Plant B's workers did not. *PrepTest59 Sec2 Q22* ⟶	**Conclusion:** Nutritious breakfasts make workers more productive. *because* **Evidence:** A study: Plant A workers given free nutritious breakfast; Plant B workers not. Result: Plant A workers more productive; Plant B workers not. **Assumption:** More Plant A workers than Plant B workers *ate* a nutritious breakfast. Also, the increased productivity was neither a coincidence nor caused by something else other than the nutritious breakfast. **Assumption type:** Mismatched Concepts— Representativeness (You could say the author overlooks the possibility that Plant B workers ate breakfast as often as Plant A workers did and get at the same assumption.) Overlooked Possibilities— Correlation versus Causation
33. A development company has proposed building an airport near the city of Dalton. If the majority of Dalton's residents favor the proposal, the airport will be built. However, it is unlikely that a majority of Dalton's residents would favor the proposal, for most of them believe that the airport would create noise problems. Thus, it is unlikely that the airport will be built. *PrepTest61 Sec4 Q11* ⟶	**Conclusion:** It is unlikely that the Dalton airport will be built. *because* **Evidence:** 1) A majority vote in favor of building the airport is sufficient for the Dalton airport to be built, but 2) it is unlikely that building the airport will receive a majority vote. **Assumption:** The author assumes that the airport will be built *only* if building the airport receives a majority vote. Said another way, the author assumes the airport won't be built without a majority vote in its favor. **Assumption type:** Overlooked Possibilities— Necessary versus Sufficient

LSAT Argument	Analysis
34. Although Jaaks is a respected historian, her negative review of Yancey's new book on the history of coastal fisheries in the region rests on a mistake. Jaaks's review argues that the book inaccurately portrays the lives of fishery workers. However, Yancey used the same research methods in this book as in her other histories, which have been very popular. This book is also very popular in local bookstores. *PrepTest59 Sec2 Q6* →	**Conclusion:** Yancey's new book portrays the lives of fishery workers accurately (a reviewer who says otherwise is mistaken). *because* **Evidence:** 1) Yancey's new book is very popular, and 2) she used the same research methods in her other popular books. **Assumption:** The popularity of Yancey's new book assures its accuracy. **Assumption type:** Mismatched Concepts—Alike/ Equivalent
35. 1990 editorial: Local pay phone calls have cost a quarter apiece ever since the 1970s, when a soft drink from a vending machine cost about the same. The price of a soft drink has more than doubled since, so phone companies should be allowed to raise the price of pay phone calls too. *PrepTest49 Sec2 Q8* →	**Conclusion:** Phone companies should be allowed to raise pay phone call prices. *because* **Evidence:** 1) In 1970, pay phone calls and soft drinks were the same price, but 2) now, soft drink prices have doubled. **Assumption:** There are no relevant factors to account for the difference between the current price of soft drinks and that of pay phone calls. The current price of a soda is (for some reason) a good indication of what the price of a pay phone call should be. **Assumption type:** Overlooked Possibilities—No Other Reason or Explanation (You could also see this argument as an example of Mismatched Concepts—Alike/Equivalent.)

LSAT Argument	**Analysis**
36. Sometimes one reads a poem and believes that the poem expresses contradictory ideas, even if it is a great poem. So it is wrong to think that the meaning of a poem is whatever the author intends to communicate to the reader by means of the poem. No one who is writing a great poem intends it to communicate contradictory ideas. *PrepTest57 Sec2 Q24*	**Conclusion:** An author's intentions do not determine the meaning of a poem. *because* **Evidence:** 1) No author of a great poem intends it to have contradictory ideas, but 2) readers of great poems sometimes believe them to express contradictory ideas. **Assumption:** A reader's beliefs about what a poem expresses are a part of the poem's meaning. **Assumption type:** Mismatched Concepts—Alike/ Equivalent
37. A survey of clerical workers' attitudes toward their work identified a group of secretaries with very positive attitudes. They responded "Strongly agree" to such statements as "I enjoy word processing" and "I like learning new secretarial skills." These secretaries had been rated by their supervisors as excellent workers—far better than secretaries whose attitudes were identified as less positive. Clearly these secretaries' positive attitudes toward their work produced excellent job performance. *PrepTest49 Sec2 Q13*	**Conclusion:** The positive attitudes of excellent secretaries caused their excellent performance. *because* **Evidence:** Secretaries with excellent performance were more likely to have positive attitudes. **Assumption:** 1) The excellent performance did not cause the positive attitudes; 2) there was no third factor that caused both excellent performance and positive attitudes; and 3) the excellent performance and positive attitudes are not merely coincidental. **Assumption type:** Overlooked Possibilities— Correlation versus Causation

LSAT Argument	Analysis
38. There can be no individual freedom without the rule of law, for there is no individual freedom without social integrity, and pursuing the good life is not possible without social integrity. *PrepTest61 Sec4 Q25*	**Conclusion:** Individual freedom requires the rule of law. If individual freedom → rule of law *because* **Evidence:** Individual freedom requires social integrity. If individual freedom → social integrity **Assumption:** Social integrity requires the rule of law. If social integrity → rule of law **Assumption type:** Mismatched Concepts—One Concept Needed for the Other
39. Vanwilligan: Some have argued that professional athletes receive unfairly high salaries. But in an unrestricted free market, such as the market these athletes compete in, salaries are determined by what someone else is willing to pay for their services. These athletes make enormous profits for their teams' owners, and that is why owners are willing to pay them extraordinary salaries. Thus the salaries they receive are fair. *PrepTest49 Sec2 Q19*	**Conclusion:** Professional athletes' salaries are fair. *because* **Evidence:** Owners are willing to pay professional athletes' salaries. **Assumption:** What owners are willing to pay constitutes a fair salary. **Assumption type:** Mismatched Concepts—Alike/Equivalent

LSAT Argument	Analysis
40. Eating garlic reduces the levels of cholesterol and triglycerides in the blood and so helps reduce the risk of cardiovascular disease. Evidence that eating garlic reduces these levels is that a group of patients taking a garlic tablet each day for four months showed a 12 percent reduction in cholesterol and a 17 percent reduction in triglycerides; over the same period, a group of similar patients taking a medically inert tablet showed only a 2 percent reduction in triglycerides and a 3 percent reduction in cholesterol. *PrepTest49 Sec4 Q2*	**Conclusion:** Eating garlic helps reduce the risk of cardiovascular disease. *because* **Evidence:** A study: Test group given a garlic tablet; control group given placebo. Results: The test group had a larger drop in cholesterol (12%) and triglycerides (17%) than did the control group, 2% and 3%, respectively. → **Assumption:** The groups were alike in every relevant respect other than the amount of garlic they consumed. The author overlooks 1) that the test group may have been different in terms of exercise, diet, smoking, etc., and 2) that the control group may have consumed garlic in another way. In drawing a conclusion about "eating garlic," the author also assumes that garlic has the same effect whether taken as a tablet or as food. **Assumption type:** Overlooked Possibilities—No Other Reason or Explanation
41. To cut costs, a high school modified its air conditioning system to increase its efficiency. The modified system, however, caused the humidity in the school air to decrease by 18 percent. Twenty-four hours after the decrease in air humidity, a 25 percent increase in the number of visits to the school nurse was reported. This shows that a decrease in humidity can make people ill. *PrepTest59 Sec3 Q12*	**Conclusion:** A decrease in humidity can make people ill. *because* **Evidence:** A school decreased humidity and saw a subsequent spike in visits to the school nurse. → **Assumption:** The visits to the nurse were due to illness (and not due to injury, accident, etc.) and that illness was caused by the decrease in humidity (and not due to food poisoning, allergic reactions, etc.) **Assumption type:** Overlooked Possibilities—No Other Cause or Explanation

ASSUMPTION QUESTIONS

The most direct application of the work you've been doing on the analysis of arguments is the Assumption question type. These questions reward you for being able to determine an author's unstated premise(s). While that task is relatively straightforward, Assumption questions are consistently among the hardest on the test.

Prepare

LEARNING OBJECTIVES

In this section, you'll learn to:

· Identify and answer Sufficient Assumption and Necessary Assumption questions

---

You can identify Assumption questions from question stems like these:

The argument's conclusion follows logically if which one of the following is assumed?

PrepTest57 Sec3 Q24

Which one of the following, if assumed, enables the essayist's conclusion to be properly drawn?

PrepTest57 Sec2 Q7

Which one of the following is an assumption on which the argument depends?

PrepTest51 Sec1 Q7

Which one of the following is an assumption required by the argument?

PrepTest49 Sec4 Q16

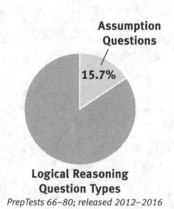

Assumption Questions

15.7%

Logical Reasoning Question Types
PrepTests 66–80; released 2012–2016

ASSUMPTION QUESTIONS AT A GLANCE

Task: Determine the unstated premise that is either 1) sufficient to guarantee that the conclusion follows logically from the evidence or 2) necessary for the conclusion to follow logically from the evidence.

Strategy: Analyze the argument, identifying the author's conclusion and evidence. Consider what the author has taken for granted in making the argument.

Frequency: LSAT tests released from 2012 to 2016 had an average of 8.0 Assumption questions per test.

Over that 2012–2016 stretch, Assumption questions were split about 65%–35% between those calling for a necessary assumption and those asking for a sufficient assumption.

Sufficient Assumption Questions

Look again at the question stems indicating Sufficient Assumption questions.

> The argument's conclusion follows logically if which one of the following is assumed?
>
> *PrepTest57 Sec3 Q24*

> Which one of the following, if assumed, enables the essayist's conclusion to be properly drawn?
>
> *PrepTest57 Sec2 Q7*

These questions seek an assumption strong enough to ensure that the conclusion is true on the basis of the evidence. The correct answer can, and often will, be stronger than what is merely necessary for the argument's validity. Consider a simple argument:

> Plovers are short-billed wading birds. Therefore, plovers hunt by sight, rather than by feel.

Now, examine two assumptions. Which one is sufficient to guarantee the conclusion in that argument?

(1) All short-billed wading birds hunt by sight.
(2) At least some short-billed wading birds hunt by sight.

LSAT STRATEGY

Some facts to remember about Sufficient Assumption questions:

- Recognize these questions from the phrases "if assumed" or "the conclusion follows logically if" in the question stem.
- The correct answer, when added to the evidence, guarantees the conclusion.
- Mismatched Concepts arguments (often with Formal Logic) dominate the Sufficient Assumption question type, although other argument patterns appear as well.

Here's how an LSAT expert might identify, analyze, and answer a Sufficient Assumption question.

LSAT Question	Analysis
There can be no individual freedom without the rule of law, for there is no individual freedom without social integrity, and pursuing the good life is not possible without social integrity.	**Step 2:** Conclusion—The rule of law is necessary for individual freedom. If individual freedom → rule of law *because* Evidence—Social integrity is necessary for individual freedom. If individual freedom → social integrity [NOTE: The statement that social integrity is necessary for pursuit of the good life is irrelevant to the conclusion.]
The conclusion drawn above follows logically if which one of the following is assumed?	**Step 1:** "[F]ollows logically if"—a Sufficient Assumption question. The correct answer will establish the conclusion on the basis of the evidence. The four wrong answers will not.
	Step 3: The author assumes that the rule of law is necessary for social integrity. If social integrity → rule of law If ~rule of law → ~social integrity
(A) There can be no rule of law without social integrity.	**Step 4:** Distortion. The author assumes that the rule of law is necessary to social integrity; this choice says the rule of law is sufficient. Eliminate.
(B) There can be no social integrity without the rule of law.	Correct. Adding this statement makes the argument complete and logical.
(C) One cannot pursue the good life without the rule of law.	Outside the Scope. This doesn't establish the relationship of the evidence to the conclusion, which is about social integrity. Eliminate.
(D) Social integrity is possible only if individual freedom prevails.	Distortion. This statement mistakes the sufficient term for the necessary one in the evidence. Eliminate.
(E) There can be no rule of law without individual freedom. *PrepTest61 Sec4 Q25*	Distortion. This statement mistakes the sufficient term for the necessary one in the conclusion. Eliminate.

Necessary Assumption Questions

Look again at the question stems indicating Necessary Assumption questions.

Which one of the following is an assumption on which
the argument depends?

PrepTest51 Sec1 Q7

Which one of the following is an assumption required
by the argument?

PrepTest49 Sec4 Q16

In these questions, the correct answer will be an unstated premise without which the conclusion cannot follow logically from the evidence. The author *needs* the correct answer to be true, although it might not, even when combined with the evidence, be sufficient to unequivocally establish the conclusion.

Mismatched Concepts in Necessary Assumption Questions

To understand how to predict the correct answer to a Necessary Assumption question with a Mismatched Concepts argument, consider the following:

> At State College, a freshman athlete who is on academic probation may not try out for one of the school's sports teams. Therefore, Mark, a freshman athlete at State College, may try out for the football team.

Here are two assumptions. Which is necessary for the argument above to be valid?

(1) Mark has the strongest academic record of any freshman athlete at State College.
(2) Mark is not on academic probation.

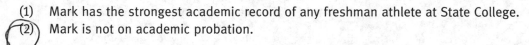

Overlooked Possibilities in Necessary Assumption Questions

For an author's Overlooked Possibilities argument to be valid, she must assume that any and all of the potential objections to her argument are not true. That means that it is necessary that each individual objection is not true. To see how that plays out in a Necessary Assumption question with an Overlooked Possibilities argument, consider the following:

> Since ServCo instituted its green energy program last quarter, the company's costs are down 8 percent. Cleary, the green energy program is saving ServCo money.

Here are two assumptions. Which one is necessary for the argument above to be valid?

(1) ServCo's reduction in expenses was not the result of reducing payroll.

(2) Every company instituting the green energy program used at ServCo has seen a cost reduction of at least 8 percent as a result.

The Denial Test

Because the correct answer to a Necessary Assumption question must be true for the argument to be valid, it can be useful to evaluate the answer choices by denying them. When you deny the correct answer to a Necessary Assumption question, the argument falls apart. Denying an incorrect answer does not destroy the argument. See what happens when you deny the two statements from two pages ago associated with Mark.

(1) Mark **does not have** the strongest academic record of any freshman athlete at State College.

(2) Mark **is** ~~not~~ on academic probation.

Try it again on the two statements you just evaluated in light of the ServCo argument.

(1) ServCo's reduction in expenses **was** ~~not~~ the result of reducing payroll.

(2) **Not** every company instituting the green energy program used at ServCo has seen a cost reduction of at least 8 percent as a result.

LSAT STRATEGY

Some facts to remember about Necessary Assumption questions:

· Recognize these questions from the phrases "required by the argument" or "the argument depends on" in the question stem.

· The correct answer does not have to guarantee the conclusion, but the conclusion cannot logically follow from the evidence if the correct answer is not true.

· Both Mismatched Concepts and Overlooked Possibilities arguments will appear.

· The Denial Test can help distinguish the correct answer.

necessary assumption question ↘

Here's how an LSAT expert might identify, analyze, and answer a Necessary Assumption question.

LSAT Question	Analysis
It is due to a misunderstanding that most modern sculpture is monochromatic. When ancient sculptures were exhumed years ago, they were discovered to be uncolored. No one at the time had reason to believe, as we now do, that the sculptures had originally been colorfully painted, but that centuries of exposure to moisture washed away the paint.	**Step 2:** Conclusion—Modern sculpture is monochromatic (all one color) due to a misunderstanding of historical sculpture. → *because* Evidence—Ancient sculptures were originally painted, but by the time they were discovered, the paint had washed away.
Which one of the following is an assumption on which the argument depends?	**Step 1:** "[A]ssumption on which the argument depends"—the correct answer is a statement without which the conclusion cannot follow from the evidence. The four wrong answers are not needed for the argument.
	Step 3: The author must assume that modern sculptors were trying to imitate their ancient counterparts. If not, she couldn't claim that modern sculpture's monochromatic style was *due to* a misunderstanding of historical sculpture.
(A) The natural beauty of the materials out of which modern sculptures are made plays a part in their effect.	**Step 4:** Outside the Scope or 180. This statement has no effect on the author's argument. If anything, it might harm the argument, suggesting that modern sculpture is monochromatic to show off its pretty materials. Eliminate.
(B) Modern sculpture has been influenced by beliefs about ancient sculpture.	Correct. Without this statement being true, the author's conclusion does not follow from the evidence.
(C) Ancient sculptures were more susceptible to moisture damage than are modern sculptures.	Irrelevant Comparison. Whether true or false, this statement has no impact on the argument. Eliminate.
(D) Some ancient paintings known to early archaeologists depicted sculptures.	180. This undermines the author's evidence ("[n]o one at the time had reason to believe"), so it is certainly not necessary to his argument. Eliminate.
(E) As modern sculptors come to believe that ancient sculpture was painted, they will begin to create polychromatic works. *PrepTest49 Sec4 Q13*	Outside the Scope. Whether ancient sculpture's influence will continue in the future is irrelevant. Eliminate.

Practice

Practice the following Assumption questions. In Step 1, determine whether the question asks for an assumption sufficient or necessary to establish the conclusion. In Step 2, analyze the argument: Identify the conclusion and evidence. In Step 3, determine the author's assumption and use it as your prediction of the correct answer. In Step 4, evaluate the answer choices: Choose the answer that matches your prediction and/or eliminate those that do not state the author's assumption.

LSAT Question	My Analysis
42. It is widely believed that lancelets—small, primitive sea animals—do not have hearts. Each lancelet has a contracting vessel, but this vessel is considered an artery rather than a heart. However, this vessel is indeed a heart. After all, it strongly resembles the structure of the heart of certain other sea animals. Moreover, the muscular contractions in the lancelet's vessel closely resemble the muscular contractions of other animals' hearts.	**Step 2:** Conclusion— *vessel is a heart* → *because* Evidence— *resembles structure & contractions*
The argument's conclusion follows logically if which one of the following is assumed? →	**Step 1:**
	Step 3:
(A) Only animals that have contracting vessels have hearts. →	**Step 4:**
(B) Some primitive animals other than lancelets have what is widely held to be a heart. →	
(C) A vessel whose structure and actions closely resemble those of other animal hearts is a heart. →	
(D) For a vessel in an animal to be properly considered a heart, that vessel must undergo muscular contractions. →	
(E) No animal that has a heart lacks an artery.	

PrepTest57 Sec3 Q24 →

LSAT Question	My Analysis
43. To cut costs, a high school modified its air-conditioning system to increase its efficiency. The modified system, however, caused the humidity in the school air to decrease by 18 percent. Twenty-four hours after the decrease in air humidity, a 25 percent increase in the number of visits to the school nurse was reported. This shows that a decrease in humidity can make people ill.	**Step 2:** Conclusion— *because* Evidence— ↓ humidity ↑ reported visits to school nurse
The argument depends on assuming which one of the following?	**Step 1:**
	Step 3:
(A) At least some of the visits to the school nurse after the system was modified were due to illness.	**Step 4:**
(B) Most of the students at the high school suffered from the decrease in air humidity.	language too strong
(C) It takes 24 hours after a person is infected with a virus for that person to exhibit symptoms.	
(D) A decrease of 18 percent in air humidity causes an increase of 25 percent in one's probability of becoming ill.	not same as becoming ill
(E) Modifying the air-conditioning system proved to be an ineffective way to cut costs. *PrepTest59 Sec3 Q12*	

LSAT Question	My Analysis
44. Critic: Photographers, by deciding which subjects to depict and how to depict them, express their own worldviews in their photographs, however realistically those photographs may represent reality. Thus, photographs are interpretations of reality.	**Step 2:** Conclusion— → *because* Evidence—
The argument's conclusion is properly drawn if which one of the following is assumed?	**Step 1:** →
	Step 3:
(A) Even representing a subject realistically can involve interpreting that subject.	**Step 4:** →
(B) To express a worldview is to interpret reality.	→
(C) All visual art expresses the artist's worldview.	→
(D) Any interpretation of reality involves the expression of a worldview.	→
(E) Nonrealistic photographs, like realistic photographs, express the worldviews of the photographers who take them.	→

PrepTest61 Sec2 Q13

LSAT Question	My Analysis
45. Essayist: Lessing contended that an art form's medium dictates the kind of representation the art form must employ in order to be legitimate; painting, for example, must represent simultaneous arrays of colored shapes, while literature, consisting of words read in succession, must represent events or actions occurring in sequence. The claim about literature must be rejected, however, if one regards as legitimate the imagists' poems, which consist solely of amalgams of disparate images. →	**Step 2:** Conclusion— *because* Evidence—
Which one of the following, if assumed, enables the essayist's conclusion to be properly drawn? →	**Step 1:**
	Step 3:
(A) An amalgam of disparate images cannot represent a sequence of events or actions. →	**Step 4:**
(B) Poems whose subject matter is not appropriate to their medium are illegitimate. →	
(C) Lessing was not aware that the imagists' poetry consists of an amalgam of disparate images. →	
(D) All art, even the imagists' poetry, depicts or represents some subject matter. →	
(E) All art represents something either as simultaneous or as successive. *PrepTest57 Sec2 Q7* →	

LSAT Question	My Analysis
46. Vanwilligan: Some have argued that professional athletes receive unfairly high salaries. But in an unrestricted free market, such as the market these athletes compete in, salaries are determined by what someone else is willing to pay for their services. These athletes make enormous profits for their teams' owners, and that is why owners are willing to pay them extraordinary salaries. Thus the salaries they receive are fair.	**Step 2:** Conclusion— → *because* Evidence—
Vanwilligan's conclusion follows logically if which one of the following is assumed?	**Step 1:** →
	Step 3:
(A) The fairest economic system for a society is one in which the values of most goods and services are determined by the unrestricted free market. →	**Step 4:**
(B) If professional athletes were paid less for their services, then the teams for which they play would not make as much money. →	
(C) The high level of competition in the marketplace forces the teams' owners to pay professional athletes high salaries. →	
(D) Any salary that a team owner is willing to pay for the services of a professional athlete is a fair salary. →	
(E) If a professional athlete's salary is fair, then that salary is determined by what an individual is willing to pay for the athlete's services in an unrestricted free market. →	

PrepTest49 Sec2 Q19

LSAT Question	My Analysis
47. Sometimes one reads a poem and believes that the poem expresses contradictory ideas, even if it is a great poem. So it is wrong to think that the meaning of a poem is whatever the author intends to communicate to the reader by means of the poem. No one who is writing a great poem intends it to communicate contradictory ideas.	**Step 2:** Conclusion— → *because* Evidence—
Which one of the following is an assumption on which the argument depends? →	**Step 1:**
	Step 3:
(A) Different readers will usually disagree about what the author of a particular poem intends to communicate by means of that poem. →	**Step 4:**
(B) If someone writes a great poem, he or she intends the poem to express one primary idea. →	
(C) Readers will not agree about the meaning of a poem if they do not agree about what the author of the poem intended the poem to mean. →	
(D) Anyone reading a great poem can discern every idea that the author intended to express in the poem. →	
(E) If a reader believes that a poem expresses a particular idea, then that idea is part of the meaning of the poem. →	

PrepTest57 Sec2 Q24

LSAT Question	My Analysis
48. Engineer: Thermophotovoltaic generators are devices that convert heat into electricity. The process of manufacturing steel produces huge amounts of heat that currently go to waste. So if steel-manufacturing plants could feed the heat they produce into thermophotovoltaic generators, they would greatly reduce their electric bills, thereby saving money.	**Step 2:** Conclusion— *because* Evidence—
Which one of the following is an assumption on which the engineer's argument depends?	**Step 1:**
	Step 3:
(A) There is no other means of utilizing the heat produced by the steel-manufacturing process that would be more cost effective than installing thermophotovoltaic generators.	**Step 4:**
(B) Using current technology, it would be possible for steel-manufacturing plants to feed the heat they produce into thermophotovoltaic generators in such a way that those generators could convert at least some of that heat into electricity.	
(C) The amount steel-manufacturing plants would save on their electric bills by feeding heat into thermophotovoltaic generators would be sufficient to cover the cost of purchasing and installing those generators.	
(D) At least some steel-manufacturing plants rely on electricity as their primary source of energy in the steel-manufacturing process.	
(E) There are at least some steel-manufacturing plants that could greatly reduce their electricity bills only if they used some method of converting wasted heat or other energy from the steel-manufacturing process into electricity.	

PrepTest61 Sec2 Q16

313

Expert Analysis: Assumption Questions

Compare your work to that of an LSAT expert. Did you identify the type of assumption called for? Was your analysis of the argument thorough and accurate? Were you able to predict the correct answer? Which answer choices gave you trouble, and which were easier to evaluate?

LSAT Question	Analysis
42. It is widely believed that lancelets—small, primitive sea animals—do not have hearts. Each lancelet has a contracting vessel, but this vessel is considered an artery rather than a heart. However, this vessel is indeed a heart. After all, it strongly resembles the structure of the heart of certain other sea animals. Moreover, the muscular contractions in the lancelet's vessel closely resemble the muscular contractions of other animals' hearts.	**Step 2:** Conclusion—The lancelet's contracting vessel **is** a heart. *because* Evidence—(1) It **looks like** a heart found in other sea creatures, and (2) it **acts like** a heart.
The argument's conclusion follows logically if which one of the following is assumed?	**Step 1:** "[F]ollows logically if"—a Sufficient Assumption question. The correct answer will establish the conclusion on the basis of the evidence. The four wrong answers will not.
	Step 3: The author assumes that something that looks and acts like a heart is a heart, and not something else.
(A) Only animals that have contracting vessels have hearts.	**Step 4:** Distortion. The issue is whether the lancelet's vessel is a heart, not what else is required to have a heart. Eliminate.
(B) Some primitive animals other than lancelets have what is widely held to be a heart.	Outside the Scope. The anatomy of other primitive creatures is irrelevant. Eliminate.
(C) A vessel whose structure and actions closely resemble those of other animal hearts is a heart.	Correct. Taken together with the evidence, this statement guarantees the validity of the conclusion.
(D) For a vessel in an animal to be properly considered a heart, that vessel must undergo muscular contractions.	Distortion. Whether contraction is necessary for something to be considered a heart is irrelevant. Eliminate.
(E) No animal that has a heart lacks an artery. *PrepTest57 Sec3 Q24*	Outside the Scope. The definition of the lancelet's artery/heart is at issue, not whether arteries always accompany hearts. Eliminate.

LSAT Question	Analysis
43. To cut costs, a high school modified its air-conditioning system to increase its efficiency. The modified system, however, caused the humidity in the school air to decrease by 18 percent. Twenty-four hours after the decrease in air humidity, a 25 percent increase in the number of visits to the school nurse was reported. This shows that a decrease in humidity can make people ill.	**Step 2:** Conclusion—Reducing humidity can make people ill. *because* Evidence—Twenty-four hours after the school's modified air-conditioning lowered humidity, there was a 25 percent uptick in visits to the school nurse.
The argument depends on assuming which one of the following?	**Step 1:** "[D]epends on assuming"—the correct answer is a statement without which the conclusion cannot follow from the evidence. The four wrong answers are not needed for the argument.
	Step 3: Overlooked Possibilities—The author must assume that nothing else was responsible for all these visits to the school nurse (e.g., sports injuries, a chemical spill in the chem lab, etc.).
(A) At least some of the visits to the school nurse after the system was modified were due to illness.	**Step 4:** Correct. Using the Denial Test, if *none* of the visits were due to illness, the author's argument would fall apart. That is, if all of the visits to the nurse were due to injury or accident, the increased humidity was not responsible for the increased visits.
(B) Most of the students at the high school suffered from the decrease in air humidity.	Extreme. The author's evidence is a 25 percent increase in visits to the nurse. He need not assume *most* students were impacted. Eliminate.
(C) It takes 24 hours after a person is infected with a virus for that person to exhibit symptoms.	Too specific to be necessary to the argument. First, the author doesn't claim that the illness was a virus. Second, 24 hours is the time after which people went to the nurse; they may have felt *symptoms* earlier. Eliminate.
(D) A decrease of 18 percent in air humidity causes an increase of 25 percent in one's probability of becoming ill.	Distortion. Even though there was a 25% increase in the number of visits, nothing in the argument suggests that the probability of each person going to the nurse increased by exactly 25%. Eliminate.
(E) Modifying the air-conditioning system proved to be an ineffective way to cut costs. *PrepTest59 Sec3 Q12*	Outside of the Scope. Cost cutting happened to be the initial impetus for the air-conditioning modifications. That has no impact on the argument about humidity and illness. Eliminate.

LSAT Question	Analysis
44. Critic: Photographers, by deciding which subjects to depict and how to depict them, express their own worldviews in their photographs, however realistically those photographs may represent reality. Thus, photographs are interpretations of reality.	**Step 2:** Conclusion—Photographs are **interpretations of reality**. *because* Evidence—Photographers **express their own worldviews** in photographs.
The argument's conclusion is properly drawn if which one of the following is assumed?	**Step 1:** "The … conclusion is properly drawn if"—a Sufficient Assumption question. The correct answer will establish the conclusion on the basis of the evidence. The four wrong answers will not.
	Step 3: The author assumes that expressing one's worldview constitutes an interpretation of reality.
(A) Even representing a subject realistically can involve interpreting that subject.	**Step 4:** Distortion. This is not inconsistent with the argument, but doesn't complete it either. It doesn't link interpretation to the expression of a worldview. Eliminate.
(B) To express a worldview is to interpret reality.	Correct. Adding this statement completes the argument logically.
(C) All visual art expresses the artist's worldview.	Extreme/Outside the Scope. Knowing that the evidence applies to *all* visual artists doesn't help to establish the conclusion. Eliminate.
(D) Any interpretation of reality involves the expression of a worldview.	Distortion. This confuses necessity and sufficiency. The author assumes that expressing a worldview is always an interpretation of reality, but there may be interpretations of reality other than the expression of worldviews. Who knows? Eliminate.
(E) Nonrealistic photographs, like realistic photographs, express the worldviews of the photographers who take them. *PrepTest61 Sec2 Q13*	Distortion. This adds nothing to the evidence, which already covers all photographs "however realistic." It certainly doesn't link the evidence to the interpretation of reality. Eliminate.

LSAT Question	Analysis
45. Essayist: Lessing contended that an art form's medium dictates the kind of representation the art form must employ in order to be legitimate; painting, for example, must represent simultaneous arrays of colored shapes, while literature, consisting of words read in succession, must represent events or actions occurring in sequence. The claim about literature must be rejected, however, if one regards as legitimate the imagists' poems, which consist solely of amalgams of disparate images.	**Step 2:** Conclusion—If imagist poems are literature, then literature need **not represent actions in sequence** (i.e., Lessing is wrong about literature). *because* Evidence—Imagist poems (for example) are literature, but they're just **"amalgams of disparate images."**
Which one of the following, if assumed, enables the essayist's conclusion to be properly drawn?	**Step 1:** "[I]f assumed ... the ... conclusion is properly drawn"–a Sufficient Assumption question. The correct answer will establish the conclusion on the basis of the evidence. The four wrong answers will not.
	Step 3: The author assumes that amalgams of disparate images do **not** represent actions in sequence.
(A) An amalgam of disparate images cannot represent a sequence of events or actions.	**Step 4:** Correct. Adding this statement completes the argument logically and unequivocally.
(B) Poems whose subject matter is not appropriate to their medium are illegitimate.	180. The author states that imagist poems must be taken as legitimate to work as his evidence. If they aren't legitimate, his evidence fails. Eliminate.
(C) Lessing was not aware that the imagists' poetry consists of an amalgam of disparate images.	Outside the Scope. The stimulus doesn't say whether Lessing knew about imagist poems or whether Lessing considered them legitimate literature. Eliminate.
(D) All art, even the imagists' poetry, depicts or represents some subject matter.	Extreme/Outside the Scope. Knowing this is true of *all* art (including, say, music) adds nothing to the argument. The argument is about form, *not* subject matter. Eliminate.
(E) All art represents something either as simultaneous or as successive. *PrepTest57 Sec2 Q7*	Extreme/Outside the Scope. Knowing this is true of *all* art (including, say, music) adds nothing to the argument. Whether Lessing had other criteria for other types of art is irrelevant. Eliminate.

LSAT Question	Analysis
46. Vanwilligan: Some have argued that professional athletes receive unfairly high salaries. But in an unrestricted free market, such as the market these athletes compete in, salaries are determined by what someone else is willing to pay for their services. These athletes make enormous profits for their teams' owners, and that is why owners are willing to pay them extraordinary salaries. Thus the salaries they receive are fair.	**Step 2:** Conclusion—Professional athletes' salaries are **fair**. *because* Evidence—**Owners are willing to pay** professional athletes' salaries.
Vanwilligan's conclusion follows logically if which one of the following is assumed?	**Step 1:** "[F]ollows logically if"—a Sufficient Assumption question. The correct answer will establish the conclusion on the basis of the evidence. The four wrong answers will not.
	Step 3: Assuming that whatever owners are willing to pay is fair completes this argument unequivocally.
(A) The fairest economic system for a society is one in which the values of most goods and services are determined by the unrestricted free market.	**Step 4:** Extreme/Outside the Scope. The author makes no claim that the free market is the *fairest* of all systems. He's interested in the definition of a *fair salary* within the free market system. Eliminate.
(B) If professional athletes were paid less for their services, then the teams for which they play would not make as much money.	Distortion. While this indicates a benefit to the owners of paying the higher salaries, it doesn't prove the salaries are *fair*. Eliminate.
(C) The high level of competition in the marketplace forces the teams' owners to pay professional athletes high salaries.	180. This contradicts the evidence that the enormous profits provided by the athletes is the reason owners are willing to pay the high salaries. Eliminate.
(D) Any salary that a team owner is willing to pay for the services of a professional athlete is a fair salary.	Correct. Adding this assumption to the argument makes the author's conclusion assuredly follow from his evidence.
(E) If a professional athlete's salary is fair, then that salary is determined by what an individual is willing to pay for the athlete's services in an unrestricted free market. *PrepTest49 Sec2 Q19*	Distortion. The author assumes that the owner's willingness to pay is sufficient for fairness; this choice says the owner's willingness is necessary for fairness. Eliminate.

LSAT Question	Analysis

47. Sometimes one reads a poem and believes that the poem expresses contradictory ideas, even if it is a great poem. So it is wrong to think that the meaning of a poem is whatever the author intends to communicate to the reader by means of the poem. No one who is writing a great poem intends it to communicate contradictory ideas.

→ **Step 2:** Conclusion—A poem's **meaning is not** determined by the **author's intentions**.

because

Evidence—(1) A **reader can believe he's found contradictory ideas** in a great poem, and (2) **no author** of a great poem **intends contradictory ideas**.

Which one of the following is an assumption on which the argument depends?

→ **Step 1:** "[A]ssumption on which the argument depends"—the correct answer is a statement without which the conclusion cannot follow from the evidence. The four wrong answers are not needed for the argument.

Step 3: The author must assume that a poem's meaning is determined, at least in part, by what a reader believes the poem says.

(A) Different readers will usually disagree about what the author of a particular poem intends to communicate by means of that poem.

→ **Step 4:** Extreme/Distortion. Whether readers will *usually* disagree is irrelevant. Moreover, this choice does not link the evidence to the poem's *meaning*. Eliminate.

(B) If someone writes a great poem, he or she intends the poem to express one primary idea.

→ Extreme. The authors of great poems do not intend contradictory ideas; that doesn't mean they're limited to "one primary idea." Eliminate.

(C) Readers will not agree about the meaning of a poem if they do not agree about what the author of the poem intended the poem to mean.

→ Distortion. Nothing in the argument hinges on the reader being aware of the author's intentions. Eliminate.

(D) Anyone reading a great poem can discern every idea that the author intended to express in the poem.

→ Extreme/Distortion. Whether *any* reader can discern *every* idea is irrelevant. Moreover, this choice does not link the evidence to the poem's *meaning*. Eliminate.

(E) If a reader believes that a poem expresses a particular idea, then that idea is part of the meaning of the poem.

PrepTest57 Sec2 Q24

→ Correct. If this statement is not added to the argument, then the evidence about readers' beliefs cannot support the conclusion about a poem's meaning.

LSAT Question	Analysis
48. Engineer: Thermophotovoltaic generators are devices that convert heat into electricity. The process of manufacturing steel produces huge amounts of heat that currently go to waste. So if steel-manufacturing plants could feed the heat they produce into thermophotovoltaic generators, they would greatly reduce their electric bills, thereby saving money.	**Step 2:** Conclusion—If steel manufacturing plants could feed heat into TPV generators (to cut electricity costs), the plants would save money. *because* Evidence—Steel manufacturing plants waste a lot of heat.
Which one of the following is an assumption on which the engineer's argument depends?	**Step 1:** "[A]ssumption on which the argument depends"—the correct answer is a statement without which the conclusion cannot follow from the evidence. The four wrong answers are not needed for the argument.
	Step 3: The author must assume that the money saved in electricity would more than offset whatever costs are associated with TPV generators.
(A) There is no other means of utilizing the heat produced by the steel-manufacturing process that would be more cost effective than installing thermophotovoltaic generators.	**Step 4:** Irrelevant Comparison. The argument needs to prove that TPV generators would save money, not that they save the most money possible. Eliminate.
(B) Using current technology, it would be possible for steel-manufacturing plants to feed the heat they produce into thermophotovoltaic generators in such a way that those generators could convert at least some of that heat into electricity.	Not necessary because the author's conclusion is conditional: "[I]f steel-manufacturing plants could feed the heat they produce into thermophotovoltaic generators …" Current feasibility is not an issue for the author. Eliminate.
(C) The amount steel-manufacturing plants would save on their electric bills by feeding heat into thermophotovoltaic generators would be sufficient to cover the cost of purchasing and installing those generators.	Correct. If the cost of TPV generators is higher than the amount of money by which their use would reduce electric bills, the plants will not save money, and the author's conclusion is shot.
(D) At least some steel-manufacturing plants rely on electricity as their primary source of energy in the steel-manufacturing process.	Outside the Scope/Extreme. Whether electricity is the *primary source* of energy is irrelevant. Eliminate.
(E) There are at least some steel-manufacturing plants that could greatly reduce their electricity bills only if they used some method of converting wasted heat or other energy from the steel-manufacturing process into electricity. *PrepTest61 Sec2 Q16*	Extreme. The argument does not require that use of TPV generators be the *only* way steel plants can save money on electricity. Eliminate.

Perform

LSAT Question	My Analysis
49. Global ecological problems reduce to the problem of balancing supply and demand. Supply is strictly confined by the earth's limitations. Demand, however, is essentially unlimited, as there are no limits on the potential demands made by humans. The natural tendency for there to be an imbalance between demand and sustainable supply is the source of these global problems. Therefore, any solutions require reducing current human demand. →	**Step 2:** Conclusion— *because* Evidence—
Which one of the following is an assumption on which the argument depends? →	**Step 1:**
	Step 3:
(A) Supply and demand tend to balance themselves in the long run. →	**Step 4:**
(B) It is possible to determine the limitations of the earth's sustainable supply. →	
(C) Actual human demand exceeds the earth's sustainable supply. →	
(D) It is never possible to achieve a balance between the environmental supply and human demand. →	
(E) Human consumption does not decrease the environmental supply. *PrepTest51 Sec1 Q7* →	

LSAT Question	My Analysis
50. An art critic, by ridiculing an artwork, can undermine the pleasure one takes in it; conversely, by lavishing praise upon an artwork, an art critic can render the experience of viewing the artwork more pleasurable. So an artwork's artistic merit can depend not only on the person who creates it but also on those who critically evaluate it. →	**Step 2:** Conclusion— *because* Evidence—
The conclusion can be properly drawn if which one of the following is assumed? →	**Step 1:**
	Step 3:
(A) The merit of an artistic work is determined by the amount of pleasure it elicits. →	**Step 4:**
(B) Most people lack the confidence necessary for making their own evaluations of art. →	
(C) Art critics understand what gives an artwork artistic merit better than artists do. →	
(D) Most people seek out critical reviews of particular artworks before viewing those works. →	
(E) The pleasure people take in something is typically influenced by what they think others feel about it. →	

PrepTest61 Sec4 Q13

LSAT Question	My Analysis

51. Chiu: The belief that a person is always morally blameworthy for feeling certain emotions, such as unjustifiable anger, jealousy, or resentment, is misguided. Individuals are responsible for only what is under their control, and whether one feels such an emotion is not always under one's control.

→

Step 2: Conclusion—

because

Evidence—

Chiu's conclusion follows logically if which one of the following is assumed?

→

Step 1:

Step 3:

(A) Individuals do not have control over their actions when they feel certain emotions.

→

Step 4:

(B) If a person is morally blameworthy for something, then that person is responsible for it.

→

(C) Although a person may sometimes be unjustifiably angry, jealous, or resentful, there are occasions when these emotions are appropriate.

→

(D) If an emotion is under a person's control, then that person cannot hold others responsible for it.

→

(E) The emotions for which a person is most commonly blamed are those that are under that person's control.

→

PrepTest51 Sec1 Q16

LSAT Question	My Analysis
52. There is a difference between beauty and truth. After all, if there were no difference, then the most realistic pieces of art would be the best as well, since the most realistic pieces are the most truthful. But many of the most realistic artworks are not among the best.	**Step 2:** Conclusion— → *because* Evidence—
Which one of the following is an assumption required by the argument? →	**Step 1:**
	Step 3:
(A) The most beautiful artworks are the best artworks. →	**Step 4:**
(B) If an artwork contains nonrealistic elements, then it is not at all truthful. →	
(C) None of the best artworks are realistic. →	
(D) Only the best artworks are beautiful. →	
(E) An artwork's beauty is inherently subjective and depends on who is viewing it. *PrepTest49 Sec4 Q16* →	

LSAT Question	My Analysis
53. Human beings can exhibit complex, goal-oriented behavior without conscious awareness of what they are doing. Thus, merely establishing that nonhuman animals are intelligent will not establish that they have consciousness.	**Step 2:** Conclusion— *because* $\longrightarrow$ Evidence—
Which one of the following is an assumption on which the argument depends? $\longrightarrow$	**Step 1:**
	Step 3:
(A) Complex, goal-oriented behavior requires intelligence. $\longrightarrow$	**Step 4:**
(B) The possession of consciousness does not imply the possession of intelligence. $\longrightarrow$	
(C) All forms of conscious behavior involve the exercise of intelligence. $\longrightarrow$	
(D) The possession of intelligence entails the possession of consciousness. $\longrightarrow$	
(E) Some intelligent human behavior is neither complex nor goal-oriented. *PrepTest49 Sec2 Q17* $\longrightarrow$	

LSAT Question	My Analysis
54. Any fruit that is infected is also rotten. No fruit that was inspected is infected. Therefore, any fruit that was inspected is safe to eat.	**Step 2:** Conclusion— *because* → Evidence—
The conclusion of the argument follows logically if which one of the following is assumed? →	**Step 1:**
	Step 3:
(A) It is not safe to eat any fruit that is rotten. →	**Step 4:**
(B) It is safe to eat any fruit that is not rotten. →	
(C) It would have been safe to eat infected fruit if it had been inspected. →	
(D) It is not safe to eat any fruit that is infected. →	
(E) It is safe to eat any fruit that is uninfected. *PrepTest49 Sec2 Q7* →	

Expert Analysis: Assumption Questions

Compare your work to that of an LSAT expert. Did you identify the type of assumption called for? Was your analysis of the argument thorough and accurate? Were you able to predict the correct answer? Which answer choices gave you trouble, and which were easier to evaluate?

LSAT Question	Analysis
49. Global ecological problems reduce to the problem of balancing supply and demand. Supply is strictly confined by the earth's limitations. Demand, however, is essentially unlimited, as there are no limits on the potential demands made by humans. The natural tendency for there to be an imbalance between demand and sustainable supply is the source of these global problems. Therefore, any solutions require reducing current human demand.	**Step 2:** Conclusion—Solutions to problems in supply and demand require reducing current human demand. *because* Evidence—(1) Supply is limited by Earth's resources; (2) potential demand is essentially unlimited; and (3) it's natural to find imbalance between sustainable supply and demand.
Which one of the following is an assumption on which the argument depends?	**Step 1:** "[A]ssumption on which the argument depends"—the correct answer is a statement without which the conclusion cannot follow from the evidence. The four wrong answers are not needed for the argument.
	Step 3: While the evidence indicates that future, *potential* demand could outstrip supply, the conclusion assumes that *current* demand does.
(A) Supply and demand tend to balance themselves in the long run.	**Step 4:** 180. Undermines the need for action to reduce demand. Eliminate.
(B) It is possible to determine the limitations of the earth's sustainable supply.	Extreme. It is not necessary to determine the overall supply in order to know what solutions to imbalance require. Eliminate.
(C) Actual human demand exceeds the earth's sustainable supply.	Correct. Without this statement being true, the author's conclusion would not be logical in light of his evidence.
(D) It is never possible to achieve a balance between the environmental supply and human demand.	Extreme/180. The author does not require complete, permanent balance. This suggests the author's call to action is futile. Eliminate.
(E) Human consumption does not decrease the environmental supply. *PrepTest51 Sec1 Q7*	180. Undermines any need to reduce human demand. Eliminate.

LSAT Question	Analysis
50. An art critic, by ridiculing an artwork, can undermine the pleasure one takes in it; conversely, by lavishing praise upon an artwork, an art critic can render the experience of viewing the artwork more pleasurable. So an artwork's artistic merit can depend not only on the person who creates it but also on those who critically evaluate it.	**Step 2:** Conclusion—An artwork's **merit** depends on its creator and its critics. *because* Evidence—(1) A critics' ridicule can reduce a viewer's **pleasure** in an artwork. (2) A critic's praise can increase a viewer's **pleasure** in an artwork.
The conclusion can be properly drawn if which one of the following is assumed?	**Step 1:** "The conclusion can be properly drawn if"—a Sufficient Assumption question. The correct answer will establish the conclusion on the basis of the evidence. The four wrong answers will not.
	Step 3: The author assumes that the amount of pleasure viewers take in an artwork is the measure of the artwork's merit.
(A) The merit of an artistic work is determined by the amount of pleasure it elicits.	**Step 4:** Correct. Adding this to the argument establishes the conclusion absolutely from the evidence.
(B) Most people lack the confidence necessary for making their own evaluations of art.	Extreme/Outside the Scope. Whether some (let alone *most*) viewers trust their own judgment in evaluating art is beside the point. The evidence that critics can influence art viewers' pleasure must be accepted as true, so explaining why they can does nothing to support, let alone prove, the conclusion. Eliminate.
(C) Art critics understand what gives an artwork artistic merit better than artists do.	Irrelevant Comparison. Which group *better* understands artistic merit is beside the point. The conclusion says both groups influence an artwork's value. Eliminate.
(D) Most people seek out critical reviews of particular artworks before viewing those works.	Extreme/Outside the Scope. While the argument does assume some exposure to critical reviews, this does not prove the connection to those reviews affecting the artistic merit. Eliminate.
(E) The pleasure people take in something is typically influenced by what they think others feel about it. *PrepTest61 Sec4 Q13*	Extreme. Again, the evidence regarding the influence of critics on art viewers must already be taken as true; this choice does nothing to make a connection to the conclusion regarding the subsequent effect on artistic merit. Eliminate.

LSAT Question	Analysis
51. Chiu: The belief that a person is always morally blameworthy for feeling certain emotions, such as unjustifiable anger, jealousy, or resentment, is misguided. Individuals are responsible for only what is under their control, and whether one feels such an emotion is not always under one's control.	**Step 2:** Conclusion—People are not always **blameworthy** for feeling certain emotions. *because* Evidence—(1) Feeling certain emotions is not always under one's control, and (2) people are **responsible** only **for** what's under their control.
Chiu's conclusion follows logically if which one of the following is assumed?	**Step 1:** "[F]ollows logically if"—a Sufficient Assumption question. The correct answer will establish the conclusion on the basis of the evidence. The four wrong answers will not.
	Step 3: The author assumes that if a person's feelings are blameworthy, then the feelings are ones for which the person is responsible. Or, phrased negatively, if a feeling is not one for which a person is responsible, then the feeling cannot be blameworthy.
(A) Individuals do not have control over their actions when they feel certain emotions.	**Step 4:** Extreme/Outside the Scope. The author says that feeling emotions is *not always* under one's control. Moreover, the argument does not touch at all upon one's ability to control their *actions* when feeling certain emotions. Eliminate.
(B) If a person is morally blameworthy for something, then that person is responsible for it.	Correct. Adding this statement to the argument makes the argument complete and logical.
(C) Although a person may sometimes be unjustifiably angry, jealous, or resentful, there are occasions when these emotions are appropriate.	Distortion. The author's argument doesn't hinge on when certain emotions are appropriate, but on whether feeling them is blameworthy. Eliminate.
(D) If an emotion is under a person's control, then that person cannot hold others responsible for it.	Outside the Scope. When a person can blame others for emotions that person feels doesn't enter into this argument. Eliminate.
(E) The emotions for which a person is most commonly blamed are those that are under that person's control.	Outside the Scope. How *often* someone is blamed for an action is irrelevant. Eliminate.

PrepTest51 Sec1 Q16

LSAT Question	Analysis
52. There is a difference between beauty and truth. After all, if there were no difference, then the most realistic pieces of art would be the best as well, since the most realistic pieces are the most truthful. But many of the most realistic artworks are not among the best.	**Step 2:** Conclusion—Beauty and truth are not the same thing (there's a difference between them). *because* Evidence—[Author attempts to show a contradiction if his conclusion were not true]: → If beauty and truth were the same, then the most realistic art would be the best art. *and that's because* The most realistic art is the most truthful. *but* The most realistic (i.e., the most truthful) art isn't always the best.
Which one of the following is an assumption required by the argument?	**Step 1:** "[A]n assumption required"—the correct answer is a statement without which the conclusion cannot follow from the evidence. The four wrong answers are not needed for the argument.
	Step 3: The author has shown a contradiction between the most truthful (the most realistic) art and the best art, but his conclusion is that truth is distinct from beauty. He must be assuming that the *most beautiful* art is the best art.
(A) The most beautiful artworks are the best artworks.	**Step 4:** Correct. Without this connection, the author's evidence (best art) doesn't relate to his conclusion (beauty).
(B) If an artwork contains nonrealistic elements, then it is not at all truthful.	Extreme. The author requires a connection between beauty and quality. What makes art not at all truthful is irrelevant. Eliminate.
(C) None of the best artworks are realistic.	Extreme. The author's evidence has established that the most realistic aren't always the best. Eliminate.
(D) Only the best artworks are beautiful.	Distortion. This answer choice states that anything that is beautiful is one of the best artworks. That is not supported by the argument. Eliminate.
(E) An artwork's beauty is inherently subjective and depends on who is viewing it. *PrepTest49 Sec4 Q16*	180. The author requires a relationship between the most beautiful art and the best. This statement suggests that no consistent evaluation of beauty is possible. Eliminate.

LSAT Question	**Analysis**
53. Human beings can exhibit complex, goal-oriented behavior without conscious awareness of what they are doing. Thus, merely establishing that nonhuman animals are intelligent will not establish that they have consciousness.	**Step 2:** Conclusion—Knowing a creature is **intelligent** is not sufficient to know that the creature has consciousness. Why not? *because* Evidence—Humans exhibit **complex, goal-oriented behavior** without having conscious awareness of doing so.
Which one of the following is an assumption on which the argument depends?	**Step 1:** "[A]ssumption on which the argument depends"—the correct answer is a statement without which the conclusion cannot follow from the evidence. The four wrong answers are not needed for the argument.
	Step 3: The author must assume that intelligence is necessary for complex, goal-oriented behavior. If she doesn't, her evidence doesn't support her conclusion.
(A) Complex, goal-oriented behavior requires intelligence.	**Step 4:** Correct. Without this assumption, the evidence does not relate to the conclusion.
(B) The possession of consciousness does not imply the possession of intelligence.	Distortion. This is a mistaken paraphrase of the conclusion. It does not link to the evidence at all. Eliminate.
(C) All forms of conscious behavior involve the exercise of intelligence.	180. This contradicts the conclusion. Eliminate.
(D) The possession of intelligence entails the possession of consciousness.	180. This contradicts the conclusion. Eliminate.
(E) Some intelligent human behavior is neither complex nor goal-oriented. *PrepTest49 Sec2 Q17*	Distortion. The author must assume that complex, goal-oriented behavior requires intelligence. Whether there are other types of intelligent behavior is irrelevant. Eliminate.

LSAT Question	Analysis
54. Any fruit that is infected is also rotten. No fruit that was inspected is infected. Therefore, any fruit that was inspected is safe to eat.	**Step 2:** Conclusion—If a fruit was inspected, then that fruit is safe to eat. If inspected → safe *because* Evidence—If a fruit was inspected, then that fruit is not infected. If inspected → ~infected [NOTE: The terms in the statement that infected fruits are rotten are unrelated to the terms in the conclusion.]
The conclusion of the argument follows logically if which one of the following is assumed?	**Step 1:** "[F]ollows logically if"—a Sufficient Assumption question. The correct answer will establish the conclusion on the basis of the evidence. The four wrong answers will not.
	Step 3: The author assumes that any uninfected fruit is safe to eat. If ~infected → safe
(A) It is not safe to eat any fruit that is rotten.	**Step 4:** Outside the Scope. The author tells you what is safe (inspected, uninfected fruits). What is unsafe is not defined here, and many things could make fruit unsafe to eat. Eliminate.
(B) It is safe to eat any fruit that is not rotten.	Distortion. Knowing that fruit is not rotten means it is not infected. That, however, doesn't mean that inspected fruits are safe to eat, and so does not establish the conclusion. Eliminate.
(C) It would have been safe to eat infected fruit if it had been inspected.	Distortion. This introduces a contradiction into the argument, which tells you that inspected fruits are *not* infected, and therefore safe to eat. Eliminate.
(D) It is not safe to eat any fruit that is infected.	Outside the Scope. The argument is about fruits that *are* safe to eat. Eliminate.
(E) It is safe to eat any fruit that is uninfected. *PrepTest49 Sec2 Q7*	Correct. This completes the argument logically.

FLAW QUESTIONS

The second major Assumption Family question type is the Flaw question. These will directly reward your skills in understanding and summarizing the kinds of reasoning errors you've learned to identify in LSAT arguments.

Prepare

LEARNING OBJECTIVES

In this section, you'll learn to:

· Identify and answer Flaw questions

You can identify Flaw questions from question stems such as these:

> The argument's reasoning is most vulnerable to criticism on the grounds that the argument
>
> *PrepTest59 Sec3 Q8*

> Which of the following identifies a reasoning error in the argument?
>
> *PrepTest49 Sec2 Q13*

> The reasoning in the pundit's argument is questionable because the argument
>
> *PrepTest51 Sec3 Q4*

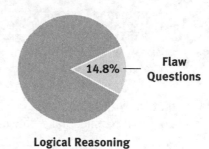

14.8% — **Flaw Questions**

Logical Reasoning Question Types
PrepTests 66–80; released 2012–2016

FLAW QUESTIONS AT A GLANCE

Task: Describe the author's reasoning error.

Strategy: Analyze the argument, identifying the author's conclusion and evidence; determine the author's assumption and use it to help you describe the logical fallacy or reasoning error the author has committed.

Frequency: LSAT tests released from 2012 to 2016 had an average of 7.5 Flaw questions per test.

Common Flaw Types

Your performance on Flaw questions will benefit from your familiarity with the common argument structures on the LSAT. In fact, the majority of Flaw questions feature a limited set of inherently flawed arguments.

LSAT STRATEGY

Flaw questions are dominated by these common argument types:

- Overlooked Possibilities (general)—A failure to consider alternative explanations or possible objections
- Overlooked Possibilities (correlation versus causation)—A conclusion of causation based on evidence of correlation
- Overlooked Possibilities (necessity versus sufficiency)—A conclusion treating a sufficient term in the evidence as if it were necessary
- Mismatched Concepts (including alike/equivalent, mutually exclusive, and representation)—A conclusion the scope or terms of which are unwarranted given the evidence

---

The way that Flaw question answer choices are worded provides evidence of just how common these reasoning errors are. As you practice, take note of answer choices like these, describing Overlooked Possibilities:

The argument is most vulnerable to the criticism that it

overlooks the possibility that …
ignores the possibility that …

And note the difference between those and answer choices that describe arguments in which the author makes an unreasonable leap between Mismatched Concepts.

The argument is most vulnerable to the criticism that it

presumes, without providing justification …
presumes, without warrant …

LSAT STRATEGY

Some facts to remember about Flaw questions:

- The correct answer will describe the error in the author's reasoning.
- You will be tested on your ability to identify flaws in both Mismatched Concepts and Overlooked Possibilities arguments.
- Correct answer choices are often written in abstract terms; form a prediction and match it to the most appropriate answer choice.

Less-Common Flaws

While the majority of arguments in Flaw questions fit into the categories on the previous page, you should be prepared to see examples of a few less-common flaws as well.

Mismatched Concepts—Equivocation: This reasoning error occurs when someone uses the same word or term inconsistently in the conclusion and evidence. For example: "The president of Bill's wine club said that Bill is a discriminating individual. But the president must be mistaken. Bill would never discriminate against anyone." The correct answer will say something along the lines of "The argument allows a key term to shift meaning illicitly."

Mismatched Concepts—Part versus Whole: When this flaw shows up on the LSAT, it usually involves the author assuming that what is true of something's parts is true of its whole. For example: "Each of the chapters in this novel is short, so the novel must be short." The correct answer usually describes this flaw clearly: "... assumes, without warrant, that what is true of an object's parts is true of the whole object."

Circular Reasoning: This form of argument goes wrong because the evidence provided simply assumes the truth of the conclusion. For example: "Without Jim, our team is incomplete, because even with everyone other than Jim on the team, it will still be incomplete." LSAT versions of the argument can be subtle, but you will recognize the correct answer from language like: "The purported evidence presumes the truth of the conclusion."

Evidence Contradicts Conclusion: This blatant flaw draws a conclusion that is the opposite of what its evidence implies. For example: "Management's position in the negotiations is strong. You can see this from the numerous concessions they've made to labor." The correct answer describes this error plainly: "The argument's conclusion conflicts with the evidence provided." Don't confuse this flaw with Overlooked Possibilities arguments in which the evidence is equally likely to support or contradict the conclusion. For example: "Our football team has a new quarterback. Therefore, the team must be stronger." Who knows? Maybe the new quarterback is weaker than the old one.

LSAT STRATEGY

Some extremely rare reasoning flaws you may see on the LSAT:

- Conflating numerical values with percent values
- Using evidence of belief to draw a conclusion of fact
- Attacking the person making the argument instead of the argument (*ad hominem*)
- Stating that absence of evidence is evidence of absence
- Making an inappropriate appeal to authority ("Professor Y says it's true, so it must be true.")
- Concluding that something does or will happen simply because it is possible for it to happen
- Indicating that what is true of a group is also true of its members (essentially the reverse of Part versus Whole)

Learning to recognize language describing rare flaws is valuable even when the argument in question is not flawed in one of these ways; you may find descriptions of these rare flaws among the *wrong answers*, and you will want to be confident that they do not match the argument in the stimulus.

LSAT Question	My Analysis
56. Editorial: Clearly, during the past two years, the unemployment situation in our city has been improving. Studies show that the number of unemployed people who are actively looking for jobs has steadily decreased during that period. $\longrightarrow$	**Step 2:** Conclusion— *because* Evidence—
The editorial's reasoning is most vulnerable to criticism on the grounds that it $\longrightarrow$	**Step 1:**
	Step 3:
(A) presumes, without providing justification, that the government is at least partly responsible for the improvement in the employment situation $\longrightarrow$	**Step 4:**
(B) relies on data from a period that is too short to justify an inference about a general trend $\longrightarrow$	
(C) fails to take into account the possibility that many unemployed workers who still desire jobs may have stopped looking for jobs $\longrightarrow$	
(D) fails to take into account that the sorts of governmental efforts that reduce unemployment may not be effective in creating more high-paying jobs $\longrightarrow$	
(E) ignores other economic indicators, which may not have improved during the past two years $\longrightarrow$ *PrepTest49 Sec4 Q1*	

LSAT Question	My Analysis

57. Scientist: While studying centuries-old Antarctic ice deposits, I found that several years of relatively severe atmospheric pollution in the 1500s coincided with a period of relatively high global temperatures. So it is clear in this case that atmospheric pollution did cause global temperatures to rise.

⟶

Step 2: Conclusion—

because

Evidence—

The reasoning in the scientist's argument is most vulnerable to criticism on the grounds that the argument ⟶

Step 1:

Step 3:

(A) presumes, without providing justification, that a rise in global temperatures is harmful ⟶

Step 4:

(B) draws a general conclusion based on a sample that is likely to be unrepresentative ⟶

(C) inappropriately generalizes from facts about a specific period of time to a universal claim ⟶

(D) takes for granted that the method used for gathering data was reliable ⟶

(E) infers, merely from a claim that two phenomena are associated, that one phenomenon causes the other ⟶

PrepTest59 Sec2 Q4

LSAT Question	My Analysis
58. Recently discovered bird fossils are about 20 million years older than the fossils of the birdlike dinosaurs from which the birds are generally claimed to have descended. So these newly discovered fossils show, contrary to the account espoused by most paleontologists, that no bird descended from any dinosaur.	**Step 2:** Conclusion— *because* Evidence—
The reasoning in the argument is flawed in that the argument	**Step 1:**
	Step 3:
(A) draws a generalization that is broader than is warranted by the findings cited	**Step 4:**
(B) rejects the consensus view of experts in the field without providing any counterevidence	
(C) attacks the adherents of the opposing view personally instead of addressing any reason for their view	
(D) fails to consider the possibility that dinosaurs descended from birds	
(E) ignores the possibility that dinosaurs and birds descended from a common ancestor	

PrepTest51 Sec3 Q6

LSAT Question	My Analysis
59. A development company has proposed building an airport near the city of Dalton. If the majority of Dalton's residents favor the proposal, the airport will be built. However, it is unlikely that a majority of Dalton's residents would favor the proposal, for most of them believe that the airport would create noise problems. Thus, it is unlikely that the airport will be built. $\longrightarrow$	**Step 2:** Conclusion— *because* Evidence—
The reasoning in the argument is flawed in that the argument $\longrightarrow$	**Step 1:**
	Step 3:
(A) treats a sufficient condition for the airport's being built as a necessary condition $\longrightarrow$	**Step 4:**
(B) concludes that something must be true, because most people believe it to be true $\longrightarrow$	
(C) concludes, on the basis that a certain event is unlikely to occur, that the event will not occur $\longrightarrow$	
(D) fails to consider whether people living near Dalton would favor building the airport $\longrightarrow$	
(E) overlooks the possibility that a new airport could benefit the local economy *PrepTest61 Sec4 Q11* $\longrightarrow$	

LSAT Question	My Analysis
60. Politician: The huge amounts of money earned by oil companies elicit the suspicion that the regulations designed to prevent collusion need to be tightened. But just the opposite is true. If the regulations designed to prevent collusion are not excessively burdensome, then oil companies will make profits sufficient to motivate the very risky investments associated with exploration that must be made if society is to have adequate oil supplies. But recent data show that the oil industry's profits are not the highest among all industries. Clearly, the regulatory burden on oil companies has become excessive.	**Step 2:** Conclusion— *because* → Evidence—
The reasoning in the politician's argument is most vulnerable to criticism on the grounds that the argument →	**Step 1:**
	Step 3: →
(A) fails to justify its presumption that profits sufficient to motivate very risky investments must be the highest among all industries →	**Step 4:**
(B) attacks the character of the oil companies rather than the substance of their conduct →	
(C) fails to justify its presumption that two events that are correlated must also be causally related →	
(D) treats the absence of evidence that the oil industry has the highest profits among all industries as proof that the oil industry does not have the highest profits among all industries →	
(E) illicitly draws a general conclusion from a specific example that there is reason to think is atypical →	

PrepTest49 Sec4 Q12

This chapter continues on the next page ▶ ▶ ▶

Expert Analysis: Flaw Questions

Compare your work to that of an LSAT expert. After analyzing the argument, were you able to describe the author's error in reasoning? Where was your prediction helpful in spotting the correct answer? When it was less helpful, can you see how you could have better phrased it?

LSAT Question	Analysis
55. Although Jaaks is a respected historian, her negative review of Yancey's new book on the history of coastal fisheries in the region rests on a mistake. Jaaks's review argues that the book inaccurately portrays the lives of fishery workers. However, Yancey used the same research methods in this book as in her other histories, which have been very popular. This book is also very popular in local bookstores.	**Step 2:** Conclusion—Yancey's book is accurate (i.e., Jaaks is wrong to say Yancey's book is inaccurate). *because* Evidence—Yancey's book is popular and uses the same methods as her other popular books.
The reasoning above is flawed in that it	**Step 1:** "[F]lawed in that ... " The correct answer will describe the author's flaw.
	Step 3: The author assumes that the book's popularity is evidence of its accuracy—a classic Mismatched Concepts mistake.
(A) relies on the word of a scholar who is unqualified in the area in question	**Step 4:** Distortion. The author relies on no other scholar's opinion in the argument. Eliminate.
(B) attacks the person making the claim at issue rather than addressing the claim	180. The author is, in fact, respectful of Jaaks, but still feels her to be mistaken in this case. Eliminate.
(C) takes for granted that the popularity of a book is evidence of its accuracy	Correct. This matches the prediction and describes the flaw perfectly.
(D) bases a general conclusion on a sample that is likely to be unrepresentative	Distortion. The conclusion is specific, not general: it deals with one historian's opinion of one book. Eliminate.
(E) presumes, without providing justification, that the methods used by Yancey are the only methods that would produce accurate results *PrepTest59 Sec2 Q6*	Outside the Scope. The author asserts that Yancey's methods have been sound, but does not offer any opinion about other methods. Eliminate.

LSAT Question	Analysis
56. Editorial: Clearly, during the past two years, the unemployment situation in our city has been improving. Studies show that the number of unemployed people who are actively looking for jobs has steadily decreased during that period.	**Step 2:** Conclusion—The city's unemployment situation is better. *because* Evidence—Fewer unemployed people are actively seeking work.
The editorial's reasoning is most vulnerable to criticism on the grounds that it	**Step 1:** "[V]ulnerable to criticism on the grounds"—the correct answer will describe a flaw in the argument's reasoning.
	Step 3: The author assumes fewer people are looking for jobs because they now have jobs, but this overlooks the possibility that they have just given up on finding work, and so aren't actively searching for jobs.
(A) presumes, without providing justification, that the government is at least partly responsible for the improvement in the employment situation	**Step 4:** Outside the Scope. There is no claim—good or bad—about the government's role here. Eliminate.
(B) relies on data from a period that is too short to justify an inference about a general trend	Distortion. The conclusion is a specific comparison (not a general trend), and the data cover precisely the time period discussed in the conclusion. Eliminate.
(C) fails to take into account the possibility that many unemployed workers who still desire jobs may have stopped looking for jobs	Correct. This cites the overlooked possibility that makes the author's assumption questionable.
(D) fails to take into account that the sorts of governmental efforts that reduce unemployment may not be effective in creating more high-paying jobs	Outside the Scope. The argument doesn't make any claims about the government's role here; nor does it imply that people have been able to get high-paying jobs. Eliminate.
(E) ignores other economic indicators, which may not have improved during the past two years *PrepTest49 Sec4 Q1*	Outside the Scope. The conclusion is specifically about unemployment; the author need not examine other economic indicators. Eliminate.

LSAT Question	Analysis
57. Scientist: While studying centuries-old Antarctic ice deposits, I found that several years of relatively severe atmospheric pollution in the 1500s coincided with a period of relatively high global temperatures. So it is clear in this case that atmospheric pollution did cause global temperatures to rise. →	**Step 2:** Conclusion—Atmospheric pollution caused global warming in the 1500s. *because* Evidence—Atmospheric pollution was correlated with global warming in the 1500s.
The reasoning in the scientist's argument is most vulnerable to criticism on the grounds that the argument →	**Step 1:** "[V]ulnerable to criticism on the grounds"—the correct answer will describe a flaw in the argument's reasoning.
	Step 3: The author assumes that because two phenomena coincided, one of them caused the other.
(A) presumes, without providing justification, that a rise in global temperatures is harmful →	**Step 4:** Outside the Scope. The author does not claim that global warming is harmful. Eliminate.
(B) draws a general conclusion based on a sample that is likely to be unrepresentative →	Extreme. The author draws a specific conclusion about the 1500s based on evidence about the 1500s. Eliminate.
(C) inappropriately generalizes from facts about a specific period of time to a universal claim →	Distortion. The author is careful to claim causation only "in this case," not universally. Eliminate.
(D) takes for granted that the method used for gathering data was reliable →	Outside the Scope. The argument's flaw is not in the reliability of its data. Even if its data are flawless, the author makes a reasoning error by claiming causation on the basis of correlation. Eliminate.
(E) infers, merely from a claim that two phenomena are associated, that one phenomenon causes the other →	Correct. This describes the "correlation versus causation" mistake that the author makes.

PrepTest59 Sec2 Q4

LSAT Question	Analysis
58. Recently discovered bird fossils are about 20 million years older than the fossils of the birdlike dinosaurs from which the birds are generally claimed to have descended. So these newly discovered fossils show, contrary to the account espoused by most paleontologists, that no bird descended from any dinosaur.	**Step 2:** Conclusion—*No* bird descended from *any* dinosaur. *because* Evidence—We've found bird fossils older than the fossils of birdlike dinosaurs thought generally to be the birds' ancestors.
The reasoning in the argument is flawed in that the argument	**Step 1:** A straightforward Flaw question stem—the correct answer will describe an error in the author's reasoning.
	Step 3: The conclusion is a blanket statement: No bird came from any dinosaur. Period. But all the evidence suggests is that at least one type of bird didn't come from the dinosaurs thought to be the ancestors of that type of bird. Even that assumption is questionable because the birdlike dinosaur may have existed earlier than its earliest known fossil. There is an overlooked possibility: It may still be that some birds came from the later birdlike dinosaurs or even from entirely other dinosaurs.
(A) draws a generalization that is broader than is warranted by the findings cited	**Step 4:** Correct. The findings show an exception to what was generally thought; they don't prove a blanket rejection of the idea.
(B) rejects the consensus view of experts in the field without providing any counterevidence	180. The author provides counterevidence to the authorities; it's just not strong enough to support his blanket conclusion. Eliminate.
(C) attacks the adherents of the opposing view personally instead of addressing any reason for their view	Outside the Scope. The author doesn't attack the paleontologists personally and does provide evidence against their position. Eliminate.
(D) fails to consider the possibility that dinosaurs descended from birds	The author is under no obligation to consider this possibility; his conclusion is simply that birds didn't descend from dinosaurs. Eliminate.
(E) ignores the possibility that dinosaurs and birds descended from a common ancestor *PrepTest51 Sec3 Q6*	The author is under no obligation to consider this possibility; his conclusion is simply that birds didn't descend from dinosaurs. Eliminate.

LSAT Question	Analysis
59. A development company has proposed building an airport near the city of Dalton. If the majority of Dalton's residents favor the proposal, the airport will be built. However, it is unlikely that a majority of Dalton's residents would favor the proposal, for most of them believe that the airport would create noise problems. Thus, it is unlikely that the airport will be built.	**Step 2:** Conclusion—The new Dalton airport probably won't be built. *because* Evidence—1) A majority vote is *sufficient* to get the new Dalton airport built. 2) The new airport probably won't get a majority vote.
The reasoning in the argument is flawed in that the argument	**Step 1:** "The reasoning is flawed in that … "—the correct answer will describe a logical error in the argument.
	Step 3: The author confuses necessity and sufficiency. His conclusion treats a majority vote as *necessary* for airport construction although his evidence states only that a condition *sufficient* for construction is unlikely to occur.
(A) treats a sufficient condition for the airport's being built as a necessary condition	**Step 4:** Correct. This matches the prediction and describes the author's reasoning error.
(B) concludes that something must be true, because most people believe it to be true	Distortion. The conclusion is a prediction (something probably won't happen), not an assertion of fact (something is true). Eliminate.
(C) concludes, on the basis that a certain event is unlikely to occur, that the event will not occur	Distortion. The author *concludes* that airport construction is "unlikely" from evidence that something is "unlikely." Eliminate.
(D) fails to consider whether people living near Dalton would favor building the airport	180. The author explicitly states that a vote in favor of construction is unlikely to pass. Eliminate.
(E) overlooks the possibility that a new airport could benefit the local economy *PrepTest61 Sec4 Q11*	Outside the Scope. The reasons why voters should favor the airport are irrelevant to the argument about whether the airport is likely to be built. Eliminate.

LSAT Question	Analysis
60. Politician: The huge amounts of money earned by oil companies elicit the suspicion that the regulations designed to prevent collusion need to be tightened. But just the opposite is true. If the regulations designed to prevent collusion are not excessively burdensome, then oil companies will make profits sufficient to motivate the very risky investments associated with exploration that must be made if society is to have adequate oil supplies. But recent data show that the oil industry's profits are not the highest among all industries. Clearly, the regulatory burden on oil companies has become excessive.	**Step 2:** Conclusion—Regulation of oil companies is excessive. *because* Evidence—1) If regulation is not excessive, then oil companies will make profits high enough to motivate risky investment, but 2) the oil industry is not the most profitable of all industries.
The reasoning in the politician's argument is most vulnerable to criticism on the grounds that the argument	**Step 1:** "[V]ulnerable to criticism on the grounds"— the correct answer will describe a flaw in the argument's reasoning.
	Step 3: Mismatched Concepts in the evidence— the author assumes that in order to make profits sufficient to spark risky investments, oil must be the most profitable of all industries. That is an unwarranted leap of logic.
(A) fails to justify its presumption that profits sufficient to motivate very risky investments must be the highest among all industries	**Step 4:** Correct. This answer summarizes the author's unwarranted assumption.
(B) attacks the character of the oil companies rather than the substance of their conduct	180. The author is *supporting* the oil companies. Eliminate.
(C) fails to justify its presumption that two events that are correlated must also be causally related	Extreme. While assuming that excessive regulation has affected industry profits, the author does not assume that all correlations imply causation. Eliminate.
(D) treats the absence of evidence that the oil industry has the highest profits among all industries as proof that the oil industry does not have the highest profits among all industries	Distortion. The author *has* data showing that oil is not the most profitable industry. The problem is his assumption that such data show excessive regulation. Eliminate.
(E) illicitly draws a general conclusion from a specific example that there is reason to think is atypical *PrepTest49 Sec4 Q12*	Distortion. There's no reason to suspect the author's evidence is atypical. Eliminate.

LSAT STRATEGY

Common Flaw Question Answer Choices by Argument Pattern

Overlooked Possibilities— General	"overlooks the possibility that"/"ignores the possibility that"/"fails to consider"
	"assumes only one possibility when more exist"
	"treats one explanation of many as though it were the only one"
Overlooked Possibilities— Causation	"mistakes a correlation for causation"
	"presumes that because one event was followed by another, the first event caused the second"
	"ignores the possibility that two things that occur together may be only coincidentally related"
Overlooked Possibilities— Nec vs Suff	"confuses a result with a condition that is required to bring about that result"
	"mistakes something that is necessary for a particular outcome for something that is merely sufficient for that outcome"
	"ignores the possibility that a particular outcome may be sufficient but not necessary for another"
Mismatched Concepts— General	"relies on irrelevant evidence"
	"facts that are not directly related to the case are used to support a conclusion about it"
	"draws an analogy between two things that are not alike enough in the ways they would need to be in order for the conclusion to be properly drawn"
Mismatched Concepts— Representation	"draws a general conclusion from a few isolated instances"
	"generalizes from an unrepresentative sample"
	"treats the children living in County X as though they were representative of all children that age living in State Y"
Mismatched Concepts— Equivocation	"relies on an ambiguity in the term *plant*"
	"allows a key phrase to shift in meaning from one use to the next"
Circular Reasoning	"the conclusion is no more than a restatement of the evidence used to support it"
	"restates its conclusion without providing sufficient justification for accepting it"
	"presupposes the truth of what it seeks to establish"
Evidence Contradicts the Conclusion	"the evidence given actually undermines the argument's conclusion"
	"some of the evidence given is inconsistent with other evidence presented"
	"draws a recommendation that is inconsistent with the evidence given to support it"

Drill: Identifying Argument Types in Flaw Question Answer Choices

For each of the following, name the flaw described in the answer choice.

Answer Choices	My Analysis
The argument is vulnerable to criticism on the grounds that the argument:	
61. presumes, without justification, that retirement benefits are used primarily for purchases of essential goods $\longrightarrow$	
62. treats a characteristic known to be true of one class of things as if that characteristic were unique to that class $\longrightarrow$	
63. mistakes a condition sufficient for bringing about a result for a condition necessary for doing so $\longrightarrow$	
64. takes the failure of evidence to establish the truth of a statement as evidence that that statement is false $\longrightarrow$	
65. concludes that two things that occur at the same time have a common cause $\longrightarrow$	
66. overlooks the possibility that most star systems are uninhabited $\longrightarrow$	
67. treats as similar two cases that are different in a critical respect $\longrightarrow$	
68. confuses the percentage of the budget spent on a program with the overall amount spent on the program $\longrightarrow$	
69. assumes the truth of what it attempts to demonstrate $\longrightarrow$	
70. bases its conclusion about a group on survey results that may not be representative of the group $\longrightarrow$	
71. assumes that because something is true of each of an object's parts, it is true of the object $\longrightarrow$	
72. improperly exploits an ambiguity in the phrase "public interest" $\longrightarrow$	

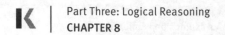

Expert Analysis: Argument Types in Flaw Questions

Here's how an LSAT expert would denominate the flaws described by the answer choices in that exercise.

Answer Choices		Analysis
The argument is vulnerable to criticism on the grounds that the argument:		
61. presumes, without justification, that retirement benefits are used primarily for purchases of essential goods	→	Mismatched Concepts. "Presumes, without justification" signals a problem in the author's assumption. The author's conclusion relies on the connection between retirement benefits and the purchase of essential goods, but the argument gives us no reason to know that this is true.
62. treats a characteristic known to be true of one class of things as if that characteristic were unique to that class	→	Overlooked Possibilities: Necessity versus Sufficiency. The author treats a characteristic necessary to a group of things as if it is sufficient to designate things as being in that group.
63. mistakes a condition sufficient for bringing about a result for a condition necessary for doing so	→	Overlooked Possibilities: Necessity versus Sufficiency. The author has treated a sufficient condition as though it were a necessary one.
64. takes the failure of evidence to establish the truth of a statement as evidence that that statement is false	→	Overlooked Possibilities. The specific flaw here is often described as "an absence of evidence is the same as evidence of absence." For example, absence of evidence for the existence of aliens is NOT evidence for the absence of aliens.
65. concludes that two things that occur at the same time have a common cause	→	Overlooked Possibilities: Correlation versus Causation
66. overlooks the possibility that most star systems are uninhabited	→	Overlooked Possibilities. Arguments in which the author assumes only one possibility without giving a reason to rule out others are inherently flawed.
67. treats as similar two cases that are different in a critical respect	→	Mismatched Concepts: Alike/Equivalent. The author assumes a shared property between two different things. The argument in this case might contain a faulty analogy.
68. confuses the percentage of the budget spent on a program with the overall amount spent on the program	→	Mismatched Concepts: Numbers versus Percents
69. assumes the truth of what it attempts to demonstrate	→	Circular Reasoning
70. bases its conclusion about a group on survey results that may not be representative of the group	→	Mismatched Concepts: Representativeness. The author relies on a sample that differs in some critical respect from the group in the conclusion.
71. assumes that because something is true of each of an object's parts, it is true of the object	→	Mismatched Concept: Part/Whole. The part or whole can have properties that are lacking in the other.
72. improperly exploits an ambiguity in the phrase "public interest"	→	Mismatched Concepts: Equivocation. This flaw occurs when one word or term is used in two incompatible senses in the argument.

Perform

LSAT Question	My Analysis
73. Pundit: The average salary for teachers in our society is lower than the average salary for athletes. Obviously, our society values sports more than it values education.	**Step 2:** Conclusion— *because* ⟶ Evidence—
The reasoning in the pundit's argument is questionable because the argument ⟶	**Step 1:**
	Step 3:
(A) presumes, without providing justification, that sports have some educational value ⟶	**Step 4:**
(B) fails to consider that the total amount of money spent on education may be much greater than the total spent on sports ⟶	
(C) fails to consider both that most teachers are not in the classroom during the summer and that most professional athletes do not play all year ⟶	
(D) compares teachers' salaries only to those of professional athletes rather than also to the salaries of other professionals ⟶	
(E) fails to compare salaries for teachers in the pundit's society to salaries for teachers in other societies ⟶	

PrepTest51 Sec3 Q4

LSAT Question	My Analysis
74. A survey of clerical workers' attitudes toward their work identified a group of secretaries with very positive attitudes. They responded "Strongly agree" to such statements as "I enjoy word processing" and "I like learning new secretarial skills." These secretaries had been rated by their supervisors as excellent workers—far better than secretaries whose attitudes were identified as less positive. Clearly these secretaries' positive attitudes toward their work produced excellent job performance. $\longrightarrow$	**Step 2:** Conclusion— *because* Evidence—
Which one of the following identifies a reasoning error in the argument? $\longrightarrow$	**Step 1:**
	Step 3:
(A) It attempts to prove a generalization about job performance by using the single example of clerical workers. $\longrightarrow$	**Step 4:**
(B) It restates the claim that the secretaries' positive attitudes produced their excellent job performance instead of offering evidence for it. $\longrightarrow$	
(C) It does not consider the possibility that secretaries with very positive attitudes toward their work might also have had very positive attitudes toward other activities. $\longrightarrow$	
(D) It uses the term "positive attitudes" to mean two different things. $\longrightarrow$	
(E) It identifies the secretaries' positive attitudes as the cause of their excellent job performance although their attitudes might be an effect of their performance. $\longrightarrow$	

PrepTest49 Sec2 Q13

LSAT Question	My Analysis
75. In a poll of a representative sample of a province's residents, the provincial capital was the city most often selected as the best place to live in that province. Since the capital is also the largest of that province's many cities, the poll shows that most residents of that province generally prefer life in large cities to life in small cities.	**Step 2:** Conclusion— *because* Evidence—
The argument is most vulnerable to the criticism that it	**Step 1:**
	Step 3:
(A) overlooks the possibility that what is true of the residents of the province may not be true of other people	**Step 4:**
(B) does not indicate whether most residents of other provinces also prefer life in large cities to life in small cities	
(C) takes for granted that when people are polled for their preferences among cities, they tend to vote for the city that they think is the best place to live	
(D) overlooks the possibility that the people who preferred small cities over the provincial capital did so not because of their general feelings about the sizes of cities, but because of their general feelings about capital cities	
(E) overlooks the possibility that most people may have voted for small cities even though a large city received more votes than any other single city	E

PrepTest51 Sec1 Q18

LSAT Question	My Analysis

76. The typological theory of species classification, which has few adherents today, distinguishes species solely on the basis of observable physical characteristics, such as plumage color, adult size, or dental structure. However, there are many so-called "sibling species," which are indistinguishable on the basis of their appearance but cannot interbreed and thus, according to the mainstream biological theory of species classification, are separate species. Since the typological theory does not count sibling species as separate species, it is unacceptable.

→

Step 2: Conclusion—

because

Evidence—

The reasoning in the argument is most vulnerable to criticism on the grounds that

→

Step 1:

Step 3:

(A) the argument does not evaluate all aspects of the typological theory

→

Step 4:

(B) the argument confuses a necessary condition for species distinction with a sufficient condition for species distinction

→

(C) the argument, in its attempt to refute one theory of species classification, presupposes the truth of an opposing theory

→

(D) the argument takes a single fact that is incompatible with a theory as enough to show that theory to be false

→

(E) the argument does not explain why sibling species cannot interbreed

PrepTest51 Sec1 Q15

→

LSAT Question	My Analysis
77. One is likely to feel comfortable approaching a stranger if the stranger is of one's approximate age. Therefore, long-term friends are probably of the same approximate age as each other since most long-term friendships begin because someone felt comfortable approaching a stranger. →	**Step 2:** Conclusion— *because* Evidence—
The reasoning in the argument is flawed in that it →	**Step 1:**
	Step 3:
(A) presumes, without warrant, that one is likely to feel uncomfortable approaching a person only if that person is a stranger →	**Step 4:**
(B) infers that a characteristic is present in a situation from the fact that that characteristic is present in most similar situations →	
(C) overlooks the possibility that one is less likely to feel comfortable approaching someone who is one's approximate age if that person is a stranger than if that person is not a stranger →	
(D) presumes, without warrant, that one never approaches a stranger unless one feels comfortable doing so →	
(E) fails to address whether one is likely to feel comfortable approaching a stranger who is not one's approximate age →	

PrepTest61 Sec4 Q24

LSAT Question	My Analysis
78. Counselor: Constantly comparing oneself to those one sees as more able or more successful almost invariably leads to self-disparagement. Conversely, constantly comparing oneself to those one sees as less able or less successful almost invariably leads to being dismissive of others. So, those who for the most part refrain from comparing themselves to others will most likely be, on the whole, self-accepting and accepting of others.	**Step 2:** Conclusion— *because* Evidence—
The counselor's reasoning is most vulnerable to criticism because it	**Step 1:**
	Step 3:
(A) overlooks the possibility that one can compare oneself both to those one perceives to be more able and more successful than oneself and to those one perceives to be less able and less successful than oneself	**Step 4:**
(B) overlooks the possibility that constantly comparing oneself to others may have beneficial effects that those who refrain from making such comparisons are deprived of	
(C) takes for granted that if one is both dismissive of others and self-disparaging, one will not be self-accepting and accepting of others	
(D) overlooks the possibility that self-disparagement and being dismissive of others can result from something other than comparing oneself to others	
(E) takes for granted that whenever one compares oneself to others one sees them as more successful and more able than oneself or less successful and less able than oneself	

PrepTest49 Sec4 Q23

LSAT Question	My Analysis
79. Deirdre: Many philosophers have argued that the goal of every individual is to achieve happiness—that is, the satisfaction derived from fully living up to one's potential. They have also claimed that happiness is elusive and can be achieved only after years of sustained effort. But these philosophers have been unduly pessimistic, since they have clearly exaggerated the difficulty of being happy. Simply walking along the seashore on a sunny afternoon causes many people to experience feelings of happiness.	**Step 2:** Conclusion— *because* Evidence—
Which one of the following most accurately describes a reasoning flaw in Deirdre's argument?	**Step 1:**
	Step 3:
(A) It dismisses a claim because of its source rather than because of its content.	**Step 4:**
(B) It fails to take into account that what brings someone happiness at one moment may not bring that person happiness at another time.	
(C) It allows the key term "happiness" to shift in meaning illicitly in the course of the argument.	
(D) It presumes, without providing justification, that happiness is, in fact, the goal of life.	
(E) It makes a generalization based on the testimony of a group whose views have not been shown to be representative. *PrepTest51 Sec1 Q6*	

LSAT Question	My Analysis
80. Letter to the editor: Middle-class families in wealthy nations are often criticized for the ecological damage resulting from their lifestyles. This criticism should not be taken too seriously, however, since its source is often a movie star or celebrity whose own lifestyle would, if widely adopted, destroy the environment and deplete our resources in a short time.	**Step 2:** Conclusion— *because* Evidence—
The reasoning in the letter to the editor is vulnerable to criticism in that it	**Step 1:**
	Step 3:
(A) criticizes a characteristic of the people giving an argument rather than criticizing the argument itself	**Step 4:**
(B) takes failure to act consistently with a belief as an indication of the sincerity with which that belief is held	
(C) presumes that a viewpoint must be unreasonable to accept simply because some of the grounds advanced to support it do not adequately do so	
(D) fails to recognize that evidence advanced in support of a conclusion actually undermines that conclusion	
(E) generalizes about the behavior of all people on the basis of the behavior of a few *PrepTest49 Sec2 Q5*	

Expert Analysis: Flaw Questions

Compare your work to that of an LSAT expert. After analyzing the argument, were you able to describe the author's error in reasoning? Where was your prediction helpful in spotting the correct answer? When it was less helpful, can you see how you could have better phrased it?

	LSAT Question	Analysis
73.	Pundit: The average salary for teachers in our society is lower than the average salary for athletes. Obviously, our society values sports more than it values education. $\longrightarrow$	**Step 2:** Conclusion—Society values sports more than it values education. *because* Evidence—Professional athletes' salaries are higher on average than those of teachers.
	The reasoning in the pundit's argument is questionable because the argument $\longrightarrow$	**Step 1:** "The reasoning is questionable because"—a Flaw question.
		Step 3: The author assumes that overall societal value placed on sports and education can be compared on the basis of athletes' and teachers' salaries. This overlooks all the other spending on the two institutions and any other factors related to how societal priorities could be measured.
(A)	presumes, without providing justification, that sports have some educational value $\longrightarrow$	**Step 4:** Outside the Scope. The author makes no such claim. Eliminate.
(B)	fails to consider that the total amount of money spent on education may be much greater than the total spent on sports $\longrightarrow$	Correct. This may be the most obvious of the many measures the author ignores.
(C)	fails to consider both that most teachers are not in the classroom during the summer and that most professional athletes do not play all year $\longrightarrow$	Irrelevant Comparison. That both teachers and athletes have "off seasons" makes the two groups comparable, so the pundit's failure to mention this isn't a weakness in his argument. Eliminate.
(D)	compares teachers' salaries only to those of professional athletes rather than also to the salaries of other professionals $\longrightarrow$	Irrelevant Comparison. The conclusion is only about sports and education, so the salaries of other professionals is a non-issue. Eliminate.
(E)	fails to compare salaries for teachers in the pundit's society to salaries for teachers in other societies *PrepTest51 Sec3 Q4* $\longrightarrow$	Irrelevant Comparison. The conclusion is about "our society" (meaning the pundit's society), so he's under no obligation to consider other societies. Eliminate.

LSAT Question	Analysis
74. A survey of clerical workers' attitudes toward their work identified a group of secretaries with very positive attitudes. They responded "Strongly agree" to such statements as "I enjoy word processing" and "I like learning new secretarial skills." These secretaries had been rated by their supervisors as excellent workers—far better than secretaries whose attitudes were identified as less positive. Clearly these secretaries' positive attitudes toward their work produced excellent job performance.	**Step 2:** Conclusion—Positive attitudes cause highly rated secretaries' excellent job performance. *because* Evidence—Secretaries with positive attitudes were more likely to be rated highly than those with less positive attitudes were.
Which one of the following identifies a reasoning error in the argument?	**Step 1:** The right answer "identifies a reasoning error"—Flaw question.
	Step 3: On the basis of a correlation (positive attitude and excellence) the author assumes causation (positive attitudes are the reason for the excellence). The author overlooks three possibilities: 1) the causation is reversed (excellent performance brings about positive attitudes); 2) alternative reasons for excellence; and 3) mere coincidence. The first seems most likely in this case; the third, least likely here.
(A) It attempts to prove a generalization about job performance by using the single example of clerical workers.	**Step 4:** Extreme. The author limits his conclusion to secretaries and does not try to prove a generalization. Eliminate.
(B) It restates the claim that the secretaries' positive attitudes produced their excellent job performance instead of offering evidence for it.	Distortion. The author offers evidence: the correlation between secretaries' survey results and their performance ratings. Eliminate.
(C) It does not consider the possibility that secretaries with very positive attitudes toward their work might also have had very positive attitudes toward other activities.	Irrelevant Comparison. The author has no need to investigate attitudes toward anything other than work; his conclusion is limited to the effect of positive attitudes on job performance. Eliminate.
(D) It uses the term "positive attitudes" to mean two different things.	Distortion. The term "positive attitudes" appears to be used the same way throughout the argument. Eliminate.
(E) It identifies the secretaries' positive attitudes as the cause of their excellent job performance although their attitudes might be an effect of their performance.	Correct. This describes the first of the three "causation versus correlation" overlooked possibilities.

PrepTest49 Sec2 Q13

LSAT Question	Analysis
75. In a poll of a representative sample of a province's residents, the provincial capital was the city most often selected as the best place to live in that province. Since the capital is also the largest of that province's many cities, the poll shows that most residents of that province generally prefer life in large cities to life in small cities.	**Step 2:** Conclusion—Most residents prefer life in large cities to life in small cities. *because* Evidence—The province's largest city received more "best place to live" votes than did any other city in the province.
The argument is most vulnerable to the criticism that it	**Step 1:** "[V]ulnerable to criticism in that it"—the correct answer will describe a flaw in the argument's reasoning.
	Step 3: The author bases her conclusion about "most residents" on evidence that the largest city received more votes than any other place. But what about all other places in aggregate? It's possible that *most* residents voted for small cities. To simplify this, imagine that the largest city received 100 votes, while 20 small cities received 10 votes apiece.
(A) overlooks the possibility that what is true of the residents of the province may not be true of other people	**Step 4:** Outside the Scope. The entire argument is about *this* province and its residents. Eliminate.
(B) does not indicate whether most residents of other provinces also prefer life in large cities to life in small cities	Outside the Scope. The entire argument is about *this* province. Eliminate.
(C) takes for granted that when people are polled for their preferences among cities, they tend to vote for the city that they think is the best place to live	180. The author does not take this for granted; she states it. Eliminate.
(D) overlooks the possibility that the people who preferred small cities over the provincial capital did so not because of their general feelings about the sizes of cities, but because of their general feelings about capital cities	Outside the Scope. Why residents stated they preferred life in small cities is irrelevant to the author's conclusion regarding people who prefer life in large cities. Eliminate.
(E) overlooks the possibility that most people may have voted for small cities even though a large city received more votes than any other single city	Correct. This summarizes the author's flaw nicely.

PrepTest51 Sec1 Q18

LSAT Question	Analysis
76. The typological theory of species classification, which has few adherents today, distinguishes species solely on the basis of observable physical characteristics, such as plumage color, adult size, or dental structure. However, there are many so-called "sibling species," which are indistinguishable on the basis of their appearance but cannot interbreed and thus, according to the mainstream biological theory of species classification, are separate species. Since the typological theory does not count sibling species as separate species, it is unacceptable. →	**Step 2:** Conclusion—The typological theory of species classification is unacceptable. *because* Evidence—The typological theory does not account for sibling species (as the mainstream theory does).
The reasoning in the argument is most vulnerable to criticism on the grounds that →	**Step 1:** "[V]ulnerable to criticism on the grounds"— the correct answer will describe a flaw in the argument's reasoning.
	Step 3: The author concludes that typological theory is inadequate on the grounds that it doesn't account for one thing mainstream theory accounts for. But what makes mainstream theory right?
(A) the argument does not evaluate all aspects of the typological theory →	**Step 4:** Extreme. The author need not find more reasons typological theory is inadequate; he needs to establish that his one reason is a decisive reason. Eliminate.
(B) the argument confuses a necessary condition for species distinction with a sufficient condition for species distinction →	Distortion. The author assumes that accounting for sibling species is necessary and draws his conclusion in a way consistent with that. The problem is that his only reason for thinking this way is that mainstream theory does it. Eliminate.
(C) the argument, in its attempt to refute one theory of species classification, presupposes the truth of an opposing theory →	Correct. The author just asserts the inadequacy of typological theory, but does nothing to establish the adequacy of mainstream theory.
(D) the argument takes a single fact that is incompatible with a theory as enough to show that theory to be false →	Distortion. The author doesn't show a *fact* that is incompatible with the typological theory. He introduces a contradictory classification from another *theory*, which, by definition, is not fact. Eliminate.
(E) the argument does not explain why sibling species cannot interbreed *PrepTest51 Sec1 Q15* →	Outside the Scope. The author doesn't need to explain the actual mechanics of sibling species interbreeding in order to make his argument in favor of the typological theory. Thus not doing so is not a flaw. Eliminate.

LSAT Question	Analysis
77. One is likely to feel comfortable approaching a stranger if the stranger is of one's approximate age. Therefore, long-term friends are probably of the same approximate age as each other since most long-term friendships begin because someone felt comfortable approaching a stranger. →	**Step 2:** Conclusion—Long-term friends are probably age mates. *because* Evidence—1) Long-term friendships start because one person is comfortable approaching a stranger, and 2) people are usually comfortable approaching their age mates.
The reasoning in the argument is flawed in that it →	**Step 1:** "The reasoning is flawed in that ... "—the correct answer will describe a logical error in the argument.
	Step 3: The author gives one reason we're comfortable approaching strangers, but couldn't there be others (similar dress, jobs, schooling, hobbies, tone of voice, facial expression, etc.)? Similar age is sufficient, but may not be necessary.
(A) presumes, without warrant, that one is likely to feel uncomfortable approaching a person only if that person is a stranger →	**Step 4:** Outside the Scope. This answer choice, by way of contrapositive, says that one is comfortable approaching any non-stranger. However, the argument is only concerned with strangers one might approach, not one's comfort in approaching non-strangers. Eliminate.
(B) infers that a characteristic is present in a situation from the fact that that characteristic is present in most similar situations →	Distortion. The author assumes that a sufficient characteristic (similar age) is the most common one. Eliminate.
(C) overlooks the possibility that one is less likely to feel comfortable approaching someone who is one's approximate age if that person is a stranger than if that person is not a stranger →	Outside the Scope. Premise: Long-term friendships begin because someone approaches a stranger. Whether we're more comfortable approaching acquaintances is irrelevant. Eliminate.
(D) presumes, without warrant, that one never approaches a stranger unless one feels comfortable doing so →	Extreme. The author starts from the premise that most long-term friendships start this way; she's not guilty of saying we *never* approach others unless we're comfortable. Eliminate.
(E) fails to address whether one is likely to feel comfortable approaching a stranger who is not one's approximate age *PrepTest61 Sec4 Q24* →	Correct. Until the author rules out other reasons to feel comfortable approaching a stranger, her conclusion that age is the reason we start friendships is suspect.

LSAT Question	Analysis
78. Counselor: Constantly comparing oneself to those one sees as more able or more successful almost invariably leads to self-disparagement. Conversely, constantly comparing oneself to those one sees as less able or less successful almost invariably leads to being dismissive of others. So, those who for the most part refrain from comparing themselves to others will most likely be, on the whole, self-accepting and accepting of others.	**Step 2:** Conclusion—If a person does not compare herself to others, then she will likely be self-accepting and accepting of others. *because* Evidence—1) If a person compares herself negatively to others, then she will be self-disparaging. 2) If a person compares herself positively to others, then she will be disparaging of others.
The counselor's reasoning is most vulnerable to criticism because it	**Step 1:** "[V]ulnerable to criticism because"—the correct answer will describe a flaw in the argument's reasoning.
	Step 3: Classic *sufficient* evidence versus *necessary* conclusion flaw: The author overlooks the possibility that there are other sufficient reasons for disparaging oneself and others.
(A) overlooks the possibility that one can compare oneself both to those one perceives to be more able and more successful than oneself and to those one perceives to be less able and less successful than oneself	**Step 4:** 180. The author does *not* overlook this; indeed, the effects of these two types of comparisons *are* her two pieces of evidence. Eliminate.
(B) overlooks the possibility that constantly comparing oneself to others may have beneficial effects that those who refrain from making such comparisons are deprived of	Outside the Scope. The effects, good or bad, of comparison on characteristics other than the acceptance of self and others are irrelevant to the author's conclusion. Eliminate.
(C) takes for granted that if one is both dismissive of others and self-disparaging, one will not be self-accepting and accepting of others	180. The terms listed here *are* opposites; the author doesn't take this for granted. Eliminate.
(D) overlooks the possibility that self-disparagement and being dismissive of others can result from something other than comparing oneself to others	Correct. There may be other factors sufficient to make one self-disparaging or disparaging of others.
(E) takes for granted that whenever one compares oneself to others one sees them as more successful and more able than oneself or less successful and less able than oneself *PrepTest49 Sec4 Q23*	Extreme. The author's evidence applies to cases of unequal comparison, and her conclusion is qualified ("most likely be, on the whole"). She's not guilty of ignoring neutral comparisons. Eliminate.

LSAT Question	Analysis
79. Deirdre: Many philosophers have argued that the goal of every individual is to achieve happiness—that is, the satisfaction derived from fully living up to one's potential. They have also claimed that happiness is elusive and can be achieved only after years of sustained effort. But these philosophers have been unduly pessimistic, since they have clearly exaggerated the difficulty of being happy. Simply walking along the seashore on a sunny afternoon causes many people to experience feelings of happiness.	**Step 2:** Conclusion—Philosophers exaggerate the difficulty of being happy (where "happy" is defined as "the satisfaction derived from fully living up to one's potential"). *because* Evidence—A walk on the beach can make people feel happy.
Which one of the following most accurately describes a reasoning flaw in Deirdre's argument?	**Step 1:** Flaw question—The correct answer "describes a reasoning flaw" in the argument.
	Step 3: Equivocation: The definition of happiness in the conclusion is far more specific than the "feelings of happiness" in the evidence.
(A) It dismisses a claim because of its source rather than because of its content.	**Step 4:** Distortion. The author doesn't say the philosophers are wrong because of *who* they are. Eliminate.
(B) It fails to take into account that what brings someone happiness at one moment may not bring that person happiness at another time.	180. The idea that certain things might cause someone a momentary feeling of happiness is something that Deirdre would agree with, according to the last sentence. So this is not something that she fails to take into account. Eliminate.
(C) It allows the key term "happiness" to shift in meaning illicitly in the course of the argument.	Correct. The author equivocates over the meaning of "happiness."
(D) It presumes, without providing justification, that happiness is, in fact, the goal of life.	Outside the Scope. Neither the philosophers nor Deirdre make this claim. Eliminate.
(E) It makes a generalization based on the testimony of a group whose views have not been shown to be representative. *PrepTest51 Sec1 Q6*	Distortion. The evidence does not consist of testimony, and the author offers the experience of "many people" to counter a generalization, not to make one. Eliminate.

LSAT Question	Analysis
80. Letter to the editor: Middle-class families in wealthy nations are often criticized for the ecological damage resulting from their lifestyles. This criticism should not be taken too seriously, however, since its source is often a movie star or celebrity whose own lifestyle would, if widely adopted, destroy the environment and deplete our resources in a short time.	**Step 2:** Conclusion—Criticism of middle-class families' lifestyles' impact on the environment should be ignored. *because* Evidence—The lifestyles of those making the criticism are often worse on the environment.
The reasoning in the letter to the editor is vulnerable to criticism in that it	**Step 1:** "[V]ulnerable to criticism in that it"—the correct answer will describe a flaw in the argument's reasoning.
	Step 3: The author wants us to ignore the criticism because those making it act hypocritically. This is an *ad hominem* flaw—attacking the motives or behavior of the person making the argument instead of the argument itself.
(A) criticizes a characteristic of the people giving an argument rather than criticizing the argument itself	**Step 4:** Correct. This describes an *ad hominem* flaw.
(B) takes failure to act consistently with a belief as an indication of the sincerity with which that belief is held	Distortion. The letter writer doesn't say the celebrities are insincere, just that they shouldn't be taken seriously. Eliminate.
(C) presumes that a viewpoint must be unreasonable to accept simply because some of the grounds advanced to support it do not adequately do so	Outside the Scope. We can't say the author claims that the celebrities' evidence is inadequate; he doesn't comment on their evidence at all. Eliminate.
(D) fails to recognize that evidence advanced in support of a conclusion actually undermines that conclusion	Outside the Scope. The author doesn't include anyone's substantive evidence, so there is no way to say what he does or does not recognize about it. Eliminate.
(E) generalizes about the behavior of all people on the basis of the behavior of a few *PrepTest49 Sec2 Q5*	Extreme. The author doesn't say all people behave hypocritically, just the ones making this argument. Eliminate.

This chapter continues on the next page ▶ ▶ ▶

STRENGTHEN AND WEAKEN QUESTIONS

The third major Assumption Family question type is Strengthen/Weaken questions. These are very practical, "lawyerly" questions. The correct answer provides a piece of evidence that would help convince someone that the argument is more (Strengthen) or less (Weaken) likely to be true.

Prepare

LEARNING OBJECTIVES

In this section, you'll learn to:

- Identify and answer Strengthen/Weaken questions

You can identify Strengthen/Weaken questions from question stems such as these:

Which one of the following, if true, most strengthens the argument above?

PrepTest57 Sec2 Q5

Which one of the following, if true, provides the most support for the argument?

PrepTest45 Sec4 Q7

Which one of the following, if true, would most weaken the argument above?

PrepTest51 Sec1 Q8

Which one of the following, if true, most calls into question the claim above?

PrepTest57 Sec2 Q9

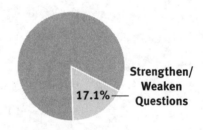

17.1% — Strengthen/ Weaken Questions

Logical Reasoning Question Types
PrepTests 66–80; released 2012–2016

STRENGTHEN/WEAKEN QUESTIONS AT A GLANCE

Task: Provide a fact that would make the conclusion more (Strengthen) or less (Weaken) likely to follow from the evidence.

Strategy: Analyze the argument, determine the author's assumption, and then choose the answer containing a fact that supports or undermines the author's reasoning.

Frequency: LSAT tests released from 2012 through 2016 had an average of 8.7 Strengthen/Weaken questions.

Representation of Strengthen and Weaken questions is slightly tilted toward Strengthen questions. On LSAT tests released from 2012 through 2016, Weaken questions made up 38.5 percent of the questions in this type. Strengthen questions accounted for 52.3 percent. Other Strengthen/Weaken questions, such as Evaluate questions, represented 9.2 percent (less than one per test, on average).

Strengthening or Weakening Overlooked Possibilities

Overlooked Possibilities arguments are more common than Mismatched Concepts in Strengthen/Weaken questions. The characteristically overbroad conclusions in Overlooked Possibilities arguments lend themselves easily to Strengthen/Weaken questions. Consider the following argument:

> The health of the city's economy is threatened by traffic congestion in the downtown business area. Petrucci's traffic plan would reduce congestion downtown. Therefore, the city should adopt Petrucci's plan. *recommendation*

Here are two facts. Which strengthens, and which weakens, the argument?

(1) Petrucci's plan would not increase the city's expenses. *strengthen*

(2) Petrucci's plan would increase traffic and speed limits near schools and residential areas. *weaken*

Strengthening or Weakening Mismatched Concepts

Mismatched Concepts are less common than Overlooked Possibilities, especially in Weaken questions. When you do encounter a Mismatched Concepts argument here, look for the fact that supports or undermines the assumed connection. Consider the following argument:

> The team captain's primary goal is to enhance team morale and enthusiasm. Thus, one of the captain's responsibilities is the continual development and training of less skilled players.

Here are two facts. Which strengthens and which weakens the argument?

(1) The ability and performance of all players affects a team's morale and enthusiasm. *strengthen*

(2) A team's morale and enthusiasm typically follow from the example set by the team's most skilled players. *weakens*

LSAT STRATEGY

Some facts to remember about Strengthen and Weaken questions:

- A correct answer does not have to prove or disprove the conclusion; it just has to make the conclusion more or less likely to follow from the evidence.
- Overlooked Possibilities is the most common argument type, especially in Weaken questions.
- To strengthen an argument containing Overlooked Possibilities, choose the answer that rules out a possible objection; to weaken such an argument, look for a fact that introduces an overlooked objection.
- To strengthen an argument containing Mismatched Concepts, choose the answer that helps to affirm the author's assumption; to weaken such an argument, look for a fact that undermines the assumption.

Less Common Strengthen/Weaken Questions

Strengthen/Weaken EXCEPT Questions

These questions are quite rare. The key to answering these questions is to characterize the one right and four wrong answers before evaluating the choices.

Each of the following, if true, strengthens the psychiatrist's argument EXCEPT:

PrepTest61 Sec2 Q22

[handwritten: Except Q's? weakens or irrelevant]

> ### LSAT STRATEGY
>
> Some facts to remember about Strengthen and Weaken EXCEPT questions:
>
> · Always slow down and characterize the one right and four wrong answer choices.
> · The correct answer in a Strengthen EXCEPT question will either weaken the argument or have no impact.
> · The correct answer in a Weaken EXCEPT question will either strengthen the argument or have no impact.

Evaluate Questions

Occasionally, the LSAT asks a question about a fact's relevance to the argument. Think of these as Strengthen-or-Weaken questions, because the disposition of the correct answer will impact the argument either positively or negatively. All four wrong answers will contain issues irrelevant to the argument.

It would be most important to determine which one of the following in evaluating the argument?

PrepTest49 Sec4 Q2

> ### LSAT STRATEGY
>
> Some facts to remember about Evaluate questions:
>
> · These questions are similar to Strengthen and Weaken questions.
> · Untangle the stimulus; then find the assumption.
> · The correct answer will often present a question, the answer to which has either a positive or a negative impact on the argument.

Principle-Application Stimuli

This unusual-looking question is really just a Strengthen question. Treat the Principle as evidence and the Application as the conclusion if you happen to see one of these.

Principle: When none of the fully qualified candidates for a new position at Arvue Corporation currently works for that company, it should hire the candidate who would be most productive in that position.

Application: Arvue should not hire Krall for the new position, because Delacruz is a candidate and is fully qualified.

Which one of the following, if true, justifies the above application of the principle?

PrepTest61 Sec4 Q19

"Claim" Stimuli

From time to time, the testmaker asks you to strengthen or weaken a "claim" rather than an argument. In these cases, treat the entire stimulus as a conclusion and seek the answer that directly supports or attacks the author's claim, depending on the question stem.

The cattle egret is a bird that lives around herds of cattle. The only available explanation of the fact that the cattle egret follows cattle herds is that the egrets consume the insects stirred up from the grasses as the cattle herds graze.

Which one of the following, if true, would most seriously undermine the claim that the explanation given above is the only available one?

PrepTest49 Sec2 Q6

Here's how an LSAT expert might analyze, predict, and answer a Strengthen question.

LSAT Question	Analysis
A recent study confirms that nutritious breakfasts make workers more productive. For one month, workers at Plant A received free nutritious breakfasts every day before work, while workers in Plant B did not. The productivity of Plant A's workers increased, while that of Plant B's workers did not. →	**Step 2:** Conclusion—Eating a nutritious breakfast increases productivity. *because* Evidence—A study. Methodology: Workers in Plant A received a free nutritious breakfast; workers in Plant B did not. Result: Workers' productivity increased in Plant A; workers' productivity in Plant B did not increase.
Which one of the following, if true, most strengthens the argument? →	**Step 1:** "[S]trengthens"—the correct answer will make the author's conclusion more likely to follow from her evidence. The four wrong answers will weaken the argument *or* do nothing.
	Step 3: The author concludes that *eating* breakfast increases productivity on the basis of evidence saying that one group *received* breakfast. He must be assuming that, during the study, more Plant A workers than Plant B workers *ate* breakfast. Additionally, the author states the productivity was caused by eating a nutritious breakfast. So he assumes that the increased productivity was not a coincidence or due to a third factor.
(A) Few workers in Plant B consumed nutritious breakfasts during the month of the study. →	**Step 4:** Correct. The conclusion is about eating a nutritious breakfast (not receiving one free). To strengthen the argument, we need to know that more workers in Plant A ate breakfast than did workers in Plant B.
(B) Workers in the study from Plant A and Plant B started work at the same time of day. →	Outside the Scope. Whether this contributes to more workers at one plant eating breakfast is unclear. Eliminate.
(C) During the month before the study, workers at Plant A and Plant B were equally productive. →	Outside the Scope. The author doesn't care which group was more productive, but whether eating a nutritious breakfast made a particular group *more* productive than they were. Eliminate.
(D) Workers from Plant A took fewer vacation days per capita during the month than did workers from Plant B. →	Outside the Scope. This tells us nothing about the effects of eating breakfast on worker productivity. Eliminate.
(E) Workers in Plant B were more productive during the month of the study than were workers from Plant A. *PrepTest59 Sec2 Q22* →	Outside the Scope. The question is not which group was more productive, but whether a group eating breakfast was more productive than they had been when not eating breakfast. Eliminate.

Here's how an LSAT expert might analyze, predict, and answer a Weaken question.

LSAT Question	Analysis
We can now dismiss the widely held suspicion that sugar consumption often exacerbates hyperactivity in children with attention deficit disorder. A scientific study of the effects of three common sugars—sucrose, fructose, and glucose—on children who have attention deficit disorder, with experimental groups each receiving a type of sugar in their diets and a control group receiving a sugar substitute instead of sugar, showed no statistically significant difference between the groups in thinking or behavior.	**Step 2:** Conclusion—Consuming sugar does not increase hyperactivity in children. *because* Evidence—A study. Methodology: Test groups—ADD children got three kinds of sugars. Control groups—ADD children got sugar substitutes. Result: No difference in thinking or behavior.
Which one of the following, if true, would most weaken the argument above?	**Step 1:** "[M]ost weakens"—the correct answer makes the conclusion less likely to follow from the evidence. The four wrong answers either strengthen or do nothing.
	Step 3: The author assumes that the study was sound. That means he thinks that if sugar exacerbates hyperactivity, the control group should have shown a difference in thinking and behavior from the test groups. So, the correct answer will suggest a reason that the two groups would act the same.
(A) Only one of the three types of sugar used in the study was ever widely suspected of exacerbating hyperactivity.	**Step 4:** Irrelevant Comparison. That test group, at least, should have shown differences in thinking and behavior if sugar makes hyperactivity worse. But they didn't. Eliminate.
(B) The consumption of sugar actually has a calming effect on some children.	Extreme/180. The author's claim is simply that sugar doesn't make hyperactivity worse. If anything, this helps the author's case. Eliminate.
(C) The consumption of some sugar substitutes exacerbates the symptoms of hyperactivity.	Correct. This undermines the validity of the study. If the sugar substitutes also make hyperactivity worse, then sugar may have made hyperactivity worse, too, without the groups showing any differences.
(D) The study included some observations of each group in contexts that generally tend to make children excited and active.	180. This makes the study even more sound as a test of the effects of sugar on hyperactivity. Eliminate.
(E) Some children believe that they can tell the difference between the taste of sugar and that of sugar substitutes.	Outside the Scope. Without more information, we can't tell what effect, if any, this had on the study's results. Eliminate.

PrepTest51 Sec1 Q8

Practice

Try the following Strengthen/Weaken questions. In each, read the question stem and characterize the one right and four wrong answers; analyze the argument by identifying the conclusion and evidence, and determine the author's assumption; consider the types of facts that would make the assumption more or less likely to be true and use that as your prediction; then, evaluate the answer choices.

LSAT Question	My Analysis
81. 1990 editorial: Local pay phone calls have cost a quarter apiece ever since the 1970s, when a soft drink from a vending machine cost about the same. The price of a soft drink has more than doubled since, so phone companies should be allowed to raise the price of pay phone calls too. →	**Step 2:** Conclusion— *because* Evidence—
Which one of the following, if true, most weakens the editorial's argument? →	**Step 1:**
	Step 3:
(A) A pay phone typically cost less than a soft-drink machine in the 1970s. →	**Step 4:**
(B) Due to inflation, the prices of most goods more than doubled between the 1970s and 1990. →	
(C) Government regulation of phone call prices did not become more stringent between the 1970s and 1990. →	
(D) Between the 1970s and 1990 the cost of ingredients for soft drinks increased at a greater rate than the cost of telephone equipment. →	
(E) Technological advances made telephone equipment more sophisticated between the 1970s and 1990. →	

PrepTest49 Sec2 Q8

LSAT Question	My Analysis
82. Eating garlic reduces the levels of cholesterol and triglycerides in the blood and so helps reduce the risk of cardiovascular disease. Evidence that eating garlic reduces these levels is that a group of patients taking a garlic tablet each day for four months showed a 12 percent reduction in cholesterol and a 17 percent reduction in triglycerides; over the same period, a group of similar patients taking a medically inert tablet showed only a 2 percent reduction in triglycerides and a 3 percent reduction in cholesterol.	**Step 2:** Conclusion— *because* Evidence—
It would be most important to determine which one of the following in evaluating the argument?	**Step 1:** *Need to know if any other differences in study*
	Step 3:
(A) whether the garlic tablets are readily available to the public	**Step 4:**
(B) what the diets of the two groups were during the period	
(C) what effect taking the garlic tablets each day for a period of less than four months had on the levels of cholesterol and triglycerides	
(D) whether large amounts of garlic are well tolerated by all patients	
(E) whether the manufacturer of the garlic tablets cites the study in its advertising *PrepTest49 Sec4 Q2*	

LSAT Question	My Analysis
83. Economist: As should be obvious, raising the minimum wage significantly would make it more expensive for businesses to pay workers for minimum-wage jobs. Therefore, businesses could not afford to continue to employ as many workers for such jobs. So raising the minimum wage significantly will cause an increase in unemployment. →	**Step 2:** Conclusion— *because* Evidence—
Which one of the following, if true, most weakens the economist's argument? →	**Step 1:**
	Step 3:
(A) Businesses typically pass the cost of increased wages on to consumers without adversely affecting profits. →	**Step 4:**
(B) When the difference between minimum wage and a skilled worker's wage is small, a greater percentage of a business's employees will be skilled workers. →	
(C) A modest increase in unemployment is acceptable because the current minimum wage is not a livable wage. →	
(D) Most workers are earning more than the current minimum wage. →	
(E) The unemployment rate has been declining steadily in recent years. *PrepTest57 Sec3 Q6* →	

LSAT Question	My Analysis
84. Scientist: A controversy in paleontology centers on the question of whether prehistoric human ancestors began to develop sophisticated tools before or after they came to stand upright. I argue that they stood upright first, simply because advanced toolmaking requires free use of the hands, and standing upright makes this possible. →	**Step 2:** Conclusion— *because* Evidence—
Which one of the following statements, if true, most weakens the scientist's argument? →	**Step 1:**
	Step 3:
(A) Many animals that do not stand upright have learned to make basic tools. →	**Step 4:**
(B) Advanced hunting weapons have been discovered among the artifacts belonging to prehistoric human ancestors who did not stand upright. →	
(C) Many prehistoric human ancestors who stood upright had no sophisticated tools. →	
(D) Those prehistoric human ancestors who first came to stand upright had no more dexterity with their hands than did those who did not stand upright. →	
(E) Many of the earliest sophisticated tools did not require their users to be able to stand upright. *PrepTest49 Sec2 Q14* →	

LSAT Question	My Analysis
85. Archaeologist: After the last ice age, groups of paleohumans left Siberia and crossed the Bering land bridge, which no longer exists, into North America. Archaeologists have discovered in Siberia a cache of Clovis points—the distinctive stone spear points made by paleohumans. This shows that, contrary to previous belief, the Clovis point was not invented in North America. →	**Step 2:** Conclusion— *because* Evidence—
Which one of the following, if true, would most strengthen the archaeologist's argument? →	**Step 1:**
	Step 3:
(A) The Clovis points found in Siberia are older than any of those that have been found in North America. →	**Step 4:**
(B) The Bering land bridge disappeared before any of the Clovis points found to date were made. →	
(C) Clovis points were more effective hunting weapons than earlier spear points had been. →	
(D) Archaeologists have discovered in Siberia artifacts that date from after the time paleohumans left Siberia. →	
(E) Some paleohuman groups that migrated from Siberia to North America via the Bering land bridge eventually returned to Siberia. →	

PrepTest57 Sec2 Q22

LSAT Question	My Analysis
86. Gilbert: This food label is mistaken. It says that these cookies contain only natural ingredients, but they contain alphahydroxy acids that are chemically synthesized by the cookie company at their plant. →	**Step 2:** Conclusion– *because* Evidence–
Sabina: The label is not mistaken. After all, alphahydroxy acids also are found occurring naturally in sugarcane.	
Which one of the following, if true, would most strengthen Sabina's argument? →	**Step 1:**
	Step 3:
(A) The cookie company has recently dropped alphahydroxy acids from its cookie ingredients. →	**Step 4:**
(B) Not all chemicals that are part of the manufacturing process are ingredients of the cookies. →	
(C) The label was printed before the cookie company decided to switch from sugarcane alphahydroxy acids to synthesized ones. →	
(D) Many other foods advertising all natural ingredients also contain some ingredients that are chemically synthesized. →	
(E) All substances except those that do not occur naturally in any source are considered natural. *PrepTest59 Sec2 Q5* →	

Expert Analysis: Strengthen and Weaken Questions

Compare your work to that of an LSAT expert. Were you able to turn your understanding of the argument into a solid prediction of the type of fact the correct answer would contain? Did you remember to characterize the right and wrong answers before evaluating the answer choices?

LSAT Question	Analysis
81. 1990 editorial: Local pay phone calls have cost a quarter apiece ever since the 1970s, when a soft drink from a vending machine cost about the same. The price of a soft drink has more than doubled since, so phone companies should be allowed to raise the price of pay phone calls too. →	**Step 2:** Conclusion—Phone companies should be allowed to increase the cost of pay phone calls (circa 1990). *because* Evidence—1) In the 1970s, vending-machine soft drinks and pay phone calls cost the same, and 2) vending-machine soft drinks are now (circa 1990) more expensive.
Which one of the following, if true, most weakens the editorial's argument? →	**Step 1:** "[M]ost weakens"—the correct answer makes the conclusion less likely to follow from the evidence. The four wrong answers either strengthen or do nothing.
	Step 3: The author assumes that the overhead for providing pay phone calls has increased proportionately to that for providing soft drinks. Weaken this by finding a fact suggesting a way in which the increase in soft drink prices is justified while the increase in pay phone call prices is not.
(A) A pay phone typically cost less than a soft-drink machine in the 1970s. →	**Step 4:** Outside the Scope. Equipment cost is one factor, but to be relevant, this would need to compare equipment costs circa 1990, too. Eliminate.
(B) Due to inflation, the prices of most goods more than doubled between the 1970s and 1990. →	180. Are these other goods relevant to pay phone service? To the extent they could be relevant, this strengthens the argument by pointing out an overall inflationary trend. Eliminate.
(C) Government regulation of phone call prices did not become more stringent between the 1970s and 1990. →	Outside the Scope. The author doesn't care whether regulation is stricter or looser than it was, just that prices be allowed to increase now. Eliminate.
(D) Between the 1970s and 1990 the cost of ingredients for soft drinks increased at a greater rate than the cost of telephone equipment. →	Correct. This damages the author's analogy between soft drinks and pay phone calls.
(E) Technological advances made telephone equipment more sophisticated between the 1970s and 1990. *PrepTest49 Sec2 Q8* →	Outside the Scope. Did these advances make pay phone calls more or less expensive to deliver? Were there similar advances in vending machine technology? Who knows? Eliminate.

LSAT Question	Analysis
82. Eating garlic reduces the levels of cholesterol and triglycerides in the blood and so helps reduce the risk of cardiovascular disease. Evidence that eating garlic reduces these levels is that a group of patients taking a garlic tablet each day for four months showed a 12 percent reduction in cholesterol and a 17 percent reduction in triglycerides; over the same period, a group of similar patients taking a medically inert tablet showed only a 2 percent reduction in triglycerides and a 3 percent reduction in cholesterol.	**Step 2:** Conclusion—Eating garlic helps reduce the risk of CV disease. *because* Evidence—1) Reducing the levels of cholesterol and triglycerides in the blood helps reduce the risk of CV disease, and 2) a study. Methodology: The test group took a garlic tablet every day; control group took placebo. Results: Test group—cholesterol down 12 percent and triglycerides down 17 percent; control group—cholesterol down 3 percent and triglycerides down 2 percent.
It would be most important to determine which one of the following in evaluating the argument?	**Step 1:** "[M]ost important ... in evaluating the argument"—the correct answer will be a fact relevant to the argument; the four wrong answers will be irrelevant. While there is information about what tablets each group consumed, nothing is stated about whether the groups differed in any other factors that might affect cardiovascular disease.
	Step 3: The author's primary evidence is the study. The correct answer will cite information relevant to the validity of the study. While there is information about what tablets each group consumed, nothing is stated about whether the groups differed in any other factors that might affect cardiovascular disease.
(A) whether the garlic tablets are readily available to the public	**Step 4:** Outside the Scope. How quickly the tablets could get to the general public has no impact on the study results. Eliminate.
(B) what the diets of the two groups were during the period	Correct. Knowing what else the two groups were eating is relevant to the legitimacy of the study.
(C) what effect taking the garlic tablets each day for a period of less than four months had on the levels of cholesterol and triglycerides	Irrelevant Comparison. Knowing this would tell us *how fast* the garlic treatment works, not whether it works. Eliminate.
(D) whether large amounts of garlic are well tolerated by all patients	Outside the Scope/Distortion. The argument does not address side effects. Moreover, we don't know whether the tablet contains "large amounts of garlic." Eliminate.
(E) whether the manufacturer of the garlic tablets cites the study in its advertising	Outside the Scope. The business implications of the study are irrelevant to the argument. Eliminate.

PrepTest49 Sec4 Q2

LSAT Question	Analysis
83. Economist: As should be obvious, raising the minimum wage significantly would make it more expensive for businesses to pay workers for minimum-wage jobs. Therefore, businesses could not afford to continue to employ as many workers for such jobs. So raising the minimum wage significantly will cause an increase in unemployment. →	**Step 2:** Conclusion—Raising the minimum wage will increase unemployment. *because* Evidence—1) Raising the minimum wage makes it more expensive to pay minimum-wage workers, and 2) businesses could not afford as many minimum-wage workers.
Which one of the following, if true, most weakens the economist's argument? →	**Step 1:** "[M]ost weakens"—the correct answer makes the conclusion less likely to follow from the evidence. The four wrong answers either strengthen or do nothing.
	Step 3: The author overlooks the possibilities that employers might find other ways to pay their minimum-wage workforce, or that they might increase their revenue to offset higher payroll. The right answer will point out one of these overlooked possibilities.
(A) Businesses typically pass the cost of increased wages on to consumers without adversely affecting profits. →	**Step 4:** Correct. This describes one of the author's overlooked possibilities, thereby weakening his argument.
(B) When the difference between minimum wage and a skilled worker's wage is small, a greater percentage of a business's employees will be skilled workers. →	Outside the Scope. It's unclear whether this situation has any effect on the overall level of unemployment, or if so, what effect. Eliminate.
(C) A modest increase in unemployment is acceptable because the current minimum wage is not a livable wage. →	Outside the Scope. This may be a good justification for raising the minimum wage, but it does not impact the author's argument about the level of unemployment. Eliminate.
(D) Most workers are earning more than the current minimum wage. →	Irrelevant Comparison. The author's argument is solely about minimum-wage workers and unemployment. Eliminate.
(E) The unemployment rate has been declining steadily in recent years. *PrepTest57 Sec3 Q6* →	Outside the Scope. The author's argument is prospective, not retrospective. Eliminate.

LSAT Question	Analysis
84. Scientist: A controversy in paleontology centers on the question of whether prehistoric human ancestors began to develop sophisticated tools before or after they came to stand upright. I argue that they stood upright first, simply because advanced toolmaking requires free use of the hands, and standing upright makes this possible.	**Step 2:** Conclusion—Human ancestors stood upright before they made sophisticated tools. *because* Evidence—1) If advanced toolmaking, then free use of hands, and 2) if stand upright, then free use of hands.
Which one of the following statements, if true, most weakens the scientist's argument?	**Step 1:** "[M]ost weakens"—the correct answer makes the conclusion less likely to follow from the evidence. The four wrong answers either strengthen or do nothing.
	Step 3: The author assumes humans stood upright before making advanced tools because standing upright is sufficient to allow one characteristic (free use of hands) necessary for making advanced tools. The author overlooks other ways to get free use of the hands, like sitting down. The right answer will suggest that humans didn't need to stand upright to make advanced tools.
(A) Many animals that do not stand upright have learned to make basic tools.	**Step 4:** Outside the Scope. The argument is about *advanced* tools. Eliminate.
(B) Advanced hunting weapons have been discovered among the artifacts belonging to prehistoric human ancestors who did not stand upright.	Correct. If human ancestors who could not stand upright had advanced tools, they must have found another way to free up their hands.
(C) Many prehistoric human ancestors who stood upright had no sophisticated tools.	Distortion. The author stipulates that free use of hands is *necessary* (not sufficient) for advanced toolmaking. Eliminate.
(D) Those prehistoric human ancestors who first came to stand upright had no more dexterity with their hands than did those who did not stand upright.	Irrelevant Comparison. Without more information, we don't know how manual dexterity impacts the argument. Eliminate.
(E) Many of the earliest sophisticated tools did not require their users to be able to stand upright. *PrepTest49 Sec2 Q14*	Distortion. The author is arguing that standing enabled human ancestors to *make* the tools, not to *use* them. Eliminate.

385

LSAT Question	Analysis
85. Archaeologist: After the last ice age, groups of paleohumans left Siberia and crossed the Bering land bridge, which no longer exists, into North America. Archaeologists have discovered in Siberia a cache of Clovis points—the distinctive stone spear points made by paleohumans. This shows that, contrary to previous belief, the Clovis point was not invented in North America.	**Step 2:** Conclusion—Clovis points were not invented in North America. *because* Evidence—1) Clovis points have been found in Siberia, and 2) paleohumans left Siberia and crossed into North America after the last ice age.
Which one of the following, if true, would most strengthen the archaeologist's argument?	**Step 1:** "[S]trengthens"—the correct answer will make the author's conclusion more likely to follow from her evidence. The four wrong answers will weaken the argument *or* do nothing.
	Step 3: The author assumes that paleohumans invented the Clovis points in Siberia before leaving; she overlooks the possibility that the paleohumans invented the Clovis points in North America and carried them back to Siberia. The correct answer will help rule out this overlooked possibility.
(A) The Clovis points found in Siberia are older than any of those that have been found in North America.	**Step 4:** Correct. This makes it less likely that the paleohumans carried the Clovis points back to Siberia, and thus, more likely that the points were invented there.
(B) The Bering land bridge disappeared before any of the Clovis points found to date were made.	180. Undermines the assumption that the Clovis points were carried across the land bridge. So the Clovis points found on the two continents may have been independently invented, or there are yet undiscovered Clovis points that pre-date the disappearance of the bridge. Eliminate.
(C) Clovis points were more effective hunting weapons than earlier spear points had been.	Outside the Scope. Without more information, this doesn't tell us anything about where the points were invented. Eliminate.
(D) Archaeologists have discovered in Siberia artifacts that date from after the time paleohumans left Siberia.	Outside the Scope. There's not enough information to know if this statement is even relevant to the argument. Did these later artifacts include Clovis points? Eliminate.
(E) Some paleohuman groups that migrated from Siberia to North America via the Bering land bridge eventually returned to Siberia. *PrepTest57 Sec2 Q22*	180. This weakens the author's argument, explaining how the points could have returned to Siberia even if they were invented in North America. Eliminate.

LSAT Question	Analysis
86. Gilbert: This food label is mistaken. It says that these cookies contain only natural ingredients, but they contain alphahydroxy acids that are chemically synthesized by the cookie company at their plant. Sabina: The label is not mistaken. After all, alphahydroxy acids also are found occurring naturally in sugarcane. →	**Step 2:** [Gilbert] Conclusion—These cookies do not contain all natural ingredients. *because* Evidence—The alphahydroxy acids in these cookies are synthesized. [**Sabina**] Conclusion—The cookies do contain all natural ingredients. *because* Evidence—Alphahydroxy acids occur in nature.
Which one of the following, if true, would most strengthen Sabina's argument? →	**Step 1:** "[S]trengthen Sabina's argument"—the correct answer will present a fact that supports Sabina's conclusion or perhaps that weakens Gilbert's.
	Step 3: The two speakers argue over whether chemicals found in nature can be listed as "natural ingredients" even when they are synthesized in a particular case. Look for an answer choice that suggests substances found in nature are always considered natural.
(A) The cookie company has recently dropped alphahydroxy acids from its cookie ingredients. →	**Step 4:** Outside the Scope. They're arguing about the cookie label from the time when the company included alphahydroxy acids. Eliminate.
(B) Not all chemicals that are part of the manufacturing process are ingredients of the cookies. →	Outside the Scope. Alphahydroxy acids *are* listed as an ingredient. Eliminate.
(C) The label was printed before the cookie company decided to switch from sugarcane alphahydroxy acids to synthesized ones. →	Irrelevant Comparison. Gilbert claims that the alphahydroxy acids in his cookies are synthesized. Sabina doesn't dispute that. Eliminate.
(D) Many other foods advertising all natural ingredients also contain some ingredients that are chemically synthesized. →	Outside the Scope. Gilbert and Sabina could have the same argument about those foods and their ingredients. Eliminate.
(E) All substances except those that do not occur naturally in any source are considered natural. *PrepTest59 Sec2 Q5* →	Correct. This statement supports Sabina's definition of "natural ingredients."

Perform

LSAT Question	My Analysis
87. On the Caribbean island of Guadeloupe, a researcher examined 35 patients with atypical Parkinson's disease and compared their eating habits to those of 65 healthy adults. She found that all of the patients with atypical Parkinson's regularly ate the tropical fruits soursop, custard apple, and pomme cannelle, whereas only 10 of the healthy adults regularly ate these fruits. From this, she concluded that eating these fruits causes atypical Parkinson's.	**Step 2:** Conclusion— → *because* Evidence—
Which one of the following, if true, most strengthens the researcher's reasoning? →	**Step 1:**
	Step 3:
(A) For many of the atypical Parkinson's patients, their symptoms stopped getting worse, and in some cases actually abated, when they stopped eating soursop, custard apple, and pomme cannelle. →	**Step 4:** A
(B) Of the healthy adults who did not regularly eat soursop, custard apple, and pomme cannelle, most had eaten each of these fruits on at least one occasion. →	
(C) In areas other than Guadeloupe, many people who have never eaten soursop, custard apple, and pomme cannelle have contracted atypical Parkinson's. →	
(D) The 10 healthy adults who regularly ate soursop, custard apple, and pomme cannelle ate significantly greater quantities of these fruits, on average, than did the 35 atypical Parkinson's patients. →	
(E) Soursop, custard apple, and pomme cannelle contain essential vitamins not contained in any other food that is commonly eaten by residents of Guadeloupe. →	

PrepTest59 Sec2 Q1

LSAT Question	My Analysis

88. Essayist: Politicians deserve protection from a prying press. No one wants his or her private life spread across the pages of the newspapers. Furthermore, the press's continual focus on politicians' private lives dissuades talented people from pursuing a career in politics and turns reporters into character cops who walk their beats looking for minute and inconsequential personality flaws in public servants. It is time to put a halt to this trivial journalism.

⟶

Step 2: Conclusion—

because

Evidence—

Each of the following, if true, strengthens the essayist's argument EXCEPT: ⟶ **Step 1:**

Step 3:

(A) The press is unusually inaccurate when it reports on people's private lives.   ⟶   **Step 4:**

(B) Reporting on politicians' private lives distracts voters from more important issues in a campaign.   ⟶

(C) Much writing on politicians' private lives consists of rumors circulated by opposing candidates.   ⟶

(D) In recent elections, the best local politicians have refused to run for national office because of the intrusiveness of press coverage.   ⟶

(E) Politicians' personality flaws often ultimately affect their performance on the job.
PrepTest49 Sec4 Q4   ⟶

E

LSAT Question	My Analysis

89. The cattle egret is a bird that lives around herds of cattle. The only available explanation of the fact that the cattle egret follows cattle herds is that the egrets consume the insects stirred up from the grasses as the cattle herds graze. →

Step 2: Conclusion—

because

Evidence—

Which one of the following, if true, would most seriously undermine the claim that the explanation given above is the only available one? →

Step 1:

Step 3:

(A) Birds other than cattle egrets have been observed consuming insects stirred up by the movement of cattle. →

Step 4:

(B) Cattle egrets are known to follow other slow-moving animals, such as rhinoceroses and buffalo. →

(C) The presence of cattle dissuades many would-be predators of the cattle egret. →

(D) Cattle egrets are not generally known to live outside the range of large, slow-moving animals. →

(E) Forests are generally inhospitable to cattle egrets because of a lack of insects of the kind egrets can consume.
PrepTest49 Sec2 Q6 →

LSAT Question	My Analysis

90. In modern deep-diving marine mammals, such as whales, the outer shell of the bones is porous. This has the effect of making the bones light enough so that it is easy for the animals to swim back to the surface after a deep dive. The outer shell of the bones was also porous in the ichthyosaur, an extinct prehistoric marine reptile. We can conclude from this that ichthyosaurs were deep divers.

Step 2: Conclusion—

→ *because*

Evidence—

Which one of the following, if true, most weakens the argument?

→ **Step 1:**

Step 3:

(A) Some deep-diving marine species must surface after dives but do not have bones with porous outer shells.

→ **Step 4:**

(B) In most modern marine reptile species, the outer shell of the bones is not porous.

→

(C) In most modern and prehistoric marine reptile species that are not deep divers, the outer shell of the bones is porous.

→

(D) In addition to the porous outer shells of their bones, whales have at least some characteristics suited to deep diving for which there is no clear evidence whether these were shared by ichthyosaurs.

→

(E) There is evidence that the bones of ichthyosaurs would have been light enough to allow surfacing even if the outer shells were not porous.

PrepTest61 Sec4 Q21 →

LSAT Question	My Analysis
91. On average, corporations that encourage frequent social events in the workplace show higher profits than those that rarely do. This suggests that the EZ Corporation could boost its profits by having more staff parties during business hours.	**Step 2:** Conclusion— *because* Evidence—
Which one of the following, if true, most weakens the argument above?	**Step 1:**
	Step 3:
(A) The great majority of corporations that encourage frequent social events in the workplace do so at least in part because they are already earning above-average profits.	**Step 4:**
(B) Corporations that have frequent staff parties after business hours sometimes have higher profits than do corporations that have frequent staff parties during business hours.	
(C) The EZ Corporation already earns above-average profits, and it almost never brings play into the workplace.	
(D) Frequent social events in a corporate workplace leave employees with less time to perform their assigned duties than they would otherwise have.	
(E) At one time the EZ Corporation encouraged social events in the workplace more frequently than it currently does, but it has not always been one of the most profitable corporations of its size.	

PrepTest51 Sec1 Q25

LSAT Question	My Analysis
92. The supernova event of 1987 is interesting in that there is still no evidence of the neutron star that current theory says should have remained after a supernova of that size. This is in spite of the fact that many of the most sensitive instruments ever developed have searched for the tell-tale pulse of radiation that neutron stars emit. Thus, current theory is wrong in claiming that supernovas of a certain size always produce neutron stars	**Step 2:** Conclusion— *because* Evidence—
Which one of the following, if true, most strengthens the argument?	**Step 1:**
	Step 3:
(A) Most supernova remnants that astronomers have detected have a neutron star nearby.	**Step 4:**
(B) Sensitive astronomical instruments have detected neutron stars much farther away than the location of the 1987 supernova.	
(C) The supernova of 1987 was the first that scientists were able to observe in progress.	
(D) Several important features of the 1987 supernova are correctly predicted by the current theory.	
(E) Some neutron stars are known to have come into existence by a cause other than a supernova explosion.	

PrepTest51 Sec1 Q24

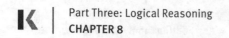

Expert Analysis: Strengthen and Weaken Questions

Compare your work to that of an LSAT expert. Were you able to turn your understanding of the argument into a solid prediction of the type of fact the correct answer would contain? Did you remember to characterize the right and wrong answers before evaluating the answer choices?

LSAT Question	Analysis
87. On the Caribbean island of Guadeloupe, a researcher examined 35 patients with atypical Parkinson's disease and compared their eating habits to those of 65 healthy adults. She found that all of the patients with atypical Parkinson's regularly ate the tropical fruits soursop, custard apple, and pomme cannelle, whereas only 10 of the healthy adults regularly ate these fruits. From this, she concluded that eating these fruits causes atypical Parkinson's.	**Step 2:** Conclusion—Eating certain fruits causes atypical Parkinson's disease. → *because* Evidence—Study: Thirty-five Parkinson's sufferers all ate the fruits. Of 65 unaffected adults, only 10 ate the fruits.
Which one of the following, if true, most strengthens the researcher's reasoning?	**Step 1:** "[S]trengthens"—the correct answer will make the author's conclusion more likely to follow from her evidence. The four wrong answers will weaken the argument *or* do nothing.
	Step 3: Correlation versus causation. To strengthen this argument, we need a fact that 1) *rules out* an alternative cause; 2) shows that the causation is *not* reversed (unlikely here); or 3) suggests the correlation is *not* coincidence.
(A) For many of the atypical Parkinson's patients, their symptoms stopped getting worse, and in some cases actually abated, when they stopped eating soursop, custard apple, and pomme cannelle.	**Step 4:** Correct. If the disease halted or reversed when the patients stopped eating these fruits, it is somewhat less likely that the correlation is mere coincidence.
(B) Of the healthy adults who did not regularly eat soursop, custard apple, and pomme cannelle, most had eaten each of these fruits on at least one occasion.	Extreme. The author doesn't claim that having eaten the fruits a few times would be enough to cause the disease. Eliminate.
(C) In areas other than Guadeloupe, many people who have never eaten soursop, custard apple, and pomme cannelle have contracted atypical Parkinson's.	Outside the Scope. The author's conclusion is that eating these fruits causes Parkinson's, not that it's the only cause. Eliminate.
(D) The 10 healthy adults who regularly ate soursop, custard apple, and pomme cannelle ate significantly greater quantities of these fruits, on average, than did the 35 atypical Parkinson's patients.	180. This makes it less likely that the fruits are the causal agents. Why aren't these 10 even worse off, after all? Eliminate.
(E) Soursop, custard apple, and pomme cannelle contain essential vitamins not contained in any other food that is commonly eaten by residents of Guadeloupe.	Outside the Scope. This might be a good reason to eat the fruits, but makes them no more or less likely to be the cause of Parkinson's. Eliminate.

PrepTest59 Sec2 Q1

LSAT Question	Analysis
88. Essayist: Politicians deserve protection from a prying press. No one wants his or her private life spread across the pages of the newspapers. Furthermore, the press's continual focus on politicians' private lives dissuades talented people from pursuing a career in politics and turns reporters into character cops who walk their beats looking for minute and inconsequential personality flaws in public servants. It is time to put a halt to this trivial journalism. →	**Step 2:** Conclusion—"Trivial" journalism focused on politicians' personal lives should end. *because* Evidence—Three negative effects of such journalism: 1) private lives exposed; 2) qualified people dissuaded from public service; and 3) journalists look for inconsequential character flaws.
Each of the following, if true, strengthens the essayist's argument EXCEPT: →	**Step 1:** "[S]trengthens … EXCEPT"—the right answer will either weaken the argument or will be irrelevant. The four wrong answers strengthen the argument.
	Step 3: The author points out three negatives of journalism that investigates politicians' private lives. What about the positives? The four wrong answers will add to the negatives or rule out potential positives. The correct answer is likely to point out one of the positives of such journalism the author has overlooked.
(A) The press is unusually inaccurate when it reports on people's private lives. →	**Step 4:** Strengthener. This points out another negative aspect of journalism that investigates politicians' personal lives. Eliminate.
(B) Reporting on politicians' private lives distracts voters from more important issues in a campaign. →	Strengthener. This points out another negative aspect of journalism that investigates politicians' personal lives. Eliminate.
(C) Much writing on politicians' private lives consists of rumors circulated by opposing candidates. →	Strengthener. This points out another negative aspect of journalism that investigates politicians' personal lives. Eliminate.
(D) In recent elections, the best local politicians have refused to run for national office because of the intrusiveness of press coverage. →	Strengthener. This points out another negative aspect of journalism that investigates politicians' personal lives. Eliminate.
(E) Politicians' personality flaws often ultimately affect their performance on the job. *PrepTest49 Sec4 Q4* →	Correct. This answer points out a potential positive effect of journalism that investigates politicians' personal lives.

LSAT Question	Analysis
89. The cattle egret is a bird that lives around herds of cattle. The only available explanation of the fact that the cattle egret follows cattle herds is that the egrets consume the insects stirred up from the grasses as the cattle herds graze.	**Step 2:** This stimulus is a "claim," not an argument. The claim is that the only explanation for egrets following cattle is that they can eat the insects the cattle stir up when grazing.
Which one of the following, if true, would most seriously undermine the claim that the explanation given above is the only available one?	**Step 1:** The correct answer will suggest that other explanations are available. The four wrong answers will make it more likely that the explanation in the stimulus is the only one, or will do nothing.
	Step 3: The correct answer will suggest a benefit that the egret derives from following cattle herds other than having insects to eat.
(A) Birds other than cattle egrets have been observed consuming insects stirred up by the movement of cattle.	**Step 4:** 180. This makes the author's claim even more likely. Eliminate.
(B) Cattle egrets are known to follow other slow-moving animals, such as rhinoceroses and buffalo.	Irrelevant Comparison. Presumably, rhinos and buffalo stir up insects, too. Eliminate.
(C) The presence of cattle dissuades many would-be predators of the cattle egret.	Correct. Receiving protection is a distinct benefit for the egrets. Maybe having bugs stirred up isn't the only explanation.
(D) Cattle egrets are not generally known to live outside the range of large, slow-moving animals.	Outside the Scope. *Why* they follow cattle herds is the question, not whether they live elsewhere, too. Eliminate.
(E) Forests are generally inhospitable to cattle egrets because of a lack of insects of the kind egrets can consume. *PrepTest49 Sec2 Q6*	Outside the Scope. The author claims to know why egrets follow cattle herds, not why they don't live in the forest. Eliminate.

LSAT Question	Analysis
90. In modern deep-diving marine mammals, such as whales, the outer shell of the bones is porous. This has the effect of making the bones light enough so that it is easy for the animals to swim back to the surface after a deep dive. The outer shell of the bones was also porous in the ichthyosaur, an extinct prehistoric marine reptile. We can conclude from this that ichthyosaurs were deep divers.	**Step 2:** Conclusion—Ichthyosaurs were deep divers. *because* Evidence—1) Ichthyosaurs had a porous outer shell of bone, and 2) modern deep-diving animals have a porous outer shell of bones (which make it easier to dive deep).
Which one of the following, if true, most weakens the argument?	**Step 1:** "[M]ost weakens"—the correct answer makes the conclusion less likely to follow from the evidence. The four wrong answers either strengthen or do nothing.
	Step 3: The author tells us that modern deep-diving animals have a porous outer shell of bone, but he doesn't tell us that *only* deep divers have this feature. If non-deep divers also have porous outer shells of bones, or if this feature has other benefits, the author's argument is suspect.
(A) Some deep-diving marine species must surface after dives but do not have bones with porous outer shells.	**Step 4:** Irrelevant Comparison. It must be harder for these deep divers to resurface, but that has no impact on the argument. The author needs to show that *only deep divers have porous outer shells*, not that only those with porous outer shells dive deep. Eliminate.
(B) In most modern marine reptile species, the outer shell of the bones is not porous.	Outside the Scope. Perhaps most modern reptiles are not deep divers. Eliminate.
(C) In most modern and prehistoric marine reptile species that are not deep divers, the outer shell of the bones is porous.	Correct. If non-deep divers have the same bone structure, then it is just as likely that ichthyosaurs were non-deep divers, too.
(D) In addition to the porous outer shells of their bones, whales have at least some characteristics suited to deep diving for which there is no clear evidence whether these were shared by ichthyosaurs.	Irrelevant Comparison. Whales may be better deep divers than ichthyosaurs, but that doesn't suggest that ichthyosaurs were not deep divers. Eliminate.
(E) There is evidence that the bones of ichthyosaurs would have been light enough to allow surfacing even if the outer shells were not porous.	180. This makes it more likely that ichthyosaurs were deep divers, not less. Eliminate.

PrepTest61 Sec4 Q21

LSAT Question	Analysis
91. On average, corporations that encourage frequent social events in the workplace show higher profits than those that rarely do. This suggests that the EZ Corporation could boost its profits by having more staff parties during business hours. →	**Step 2:** Conclusion—More staff parties during business hours causes increased corporate profits. *because* Evidence—Frequent social events for employees correlate to higher profits.
Which one of the following, if true, most weakens the argument above? →	**Step 1:** "[M]ost weakens"—the correct answer makes the conclusion less likely to follow from the evidence. The four wrong answers either strengthen or do nothing.
	Step 3: The author assumes a causal conclusion from evidence of correlation. This can be weakened by showing 1) alternate causes; 2) reversed causation (likely here); or 3) mere coincidence.
(A) The great majority of corporations that encourage frequent social events in the workplace do so at least in part because they are already earning above-average profits. →	**Step 4:** Correct. This shows reversed causation. Already profitable companies are more likely to fete their employees.
(B) Corporations that have frequent staff parties after business hours sometimes have higher profits than do corporations that have frequent staff parties during business hours. →	Irrelevant Comparison. Maybe parties after work hours are *even better*, but that certainly doesn't damage the author's argument. The author said "on average" the correlation proves true, so even if corporations with after hours parties *sometimes* have higher profits, that doesn't undermine that correlation "on average." Eliminate.
(C) The EZ Corporation already earns above-average profits, and it almost never brings play into the workplace. →	Irrelevant Comparison. The author concludes that more staff parties could *boost* profitability even more, not that EZ isn't profitable now. Eliminate.
(D) Frequent social events in a corporate workplace leave employees with less time to perform their assigned duties than they would otherwise have. →	Distortion. Accepting the evidence as true, even if employees have less time for assigned duties, there is still a positive correlation between social events and profitability. Eliminate.
(E) At one time the EZ Corporation encouraged social events in the workplace more frequently than it currently does, but it has not always been one of the most profitable corporations of its size. *PrepTest51 Sec1 Q25* →	Extreme. Many factors influence whether EZ is *"one of the most* profitable corporations." The relevant question for the author would be: Was EZ more profitable when it encouraged more parties than it is now? Eliminate.

LSAT Question	Analysis
92. The supernova event of 1987 is interesting in that there is still no evidence of the neutron star that current theory says should have remained after a supernova of that size. This is in spite of the fact that many of the most sensitive instruments ever developed have searched for the tell-tale pulse of radiation that neutron stars emit. Thus, current theory is wrong in claiming that supernovas of a certain size always produce neutron stars.	**Step 2:** Conclusion—Supernovas of a certain size do not always produce neutron stars (the current theory is wrong). *because* Evidence—Despite searching with sensitive instruments, scientists have found no trace of a neutron star following from the 1987 supernova.
Which one of the following, if true, most strengthens the argument?	**Step 1:** "[S]trengthens"—the correct answer will make the author's conclusion more likely to follow from her evidence. The four wrong answers will weaken the argument *or* do nothing.
	Step 3: The author assumes an absence of evidence (we haven't found the neutron star) is evidence of absence (there was no neutron star). The correct answer will be a fact that makes it more likely that absence of evidence really proves that there was no neutron star.
(A) Most supernova remnants that astronomers have detected have a neutron star nearby.	**Step 4:** 180. This observation is the basis of the current theory that the author opposes. Eliminate.
(B) Sensitive astronomical instruments have detected neutron stars much farther away than the location of the 1987 supernova.	Correct. If the same instruments have discovered neutron stars even farther away, it is more likely that a failure to find a neutron star following the 1987 supernova means that there is no such star, and not that the instruments simply cannot search far enough.
(C) The supernova of 1987 was the first that scientists were able to observe in progress.	Outside the Scope. Without more information, this makes it neither more nor less likely that the neutron star exists. Eliminate.
(D) Several important features of the 1987 supernova are correctly predicted by the current theory.	180. This supports the current theory, and makes it more likely that the 1987 supernova produced a neutron star that hasn't been found. Eliminate.
(E) Some neutron stars are known to have come into existence by a cause other than a supernova explosion. *PrepTest51 Sec1 Q24*	Outside the Scope. Other ways neutron stars can be produced are irrelevant. Eliminate.

ASSUMPTION-FAMILY PRINCIPLE QUESTIONS

Principle questions mimic other question types, including Assumption and Strengthen questions from the Assumption Family. These will be covered in this section. Later in this chapter, you'll see Principle questions that test Parallel Reasoning, and in Chapter 9, those that test Inference question skills.

Prepare

> ## LEARNING OBJECTIVES
>
> In this section, you'll learn to:
>
> · Recognize Principle question stems, and distinguish Identify the Principle questions from other Principle question types

Recognizing Principle Question Stems

On the LSAT, think of a *principle* like you would a law, a general rule applicable to all relevant cases. A question that asks you to either identify or apply a general rule is a Principle question. These question stems often use the word *principle*, but they may also use words like *proposition* or *policy*. Be on the lookout for tasks such as "most closely conforms to," "best illustrates," and "helps to justify."

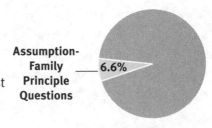

Assumption-Family Principle Questions — 6.6%

Logical Reasoning Question Types

PrepTests 66–80, released 2012–2016

LSAT Principle Q Stem	Analysis
Which one of the following most accurately expresses the principle underlying the reasoning above? *PrepTest51 Sec3 Q7*	"[E]xpresses the principle underlying the reasoning" indicates a Principle question that acts like an Assumption question.
Which one of the following principles, if valid, most helps to justify drawing the conclusion in the argument above? *PrepTest49 Sec2 Q15*	"[P]rinciple ... most helps to justify"—a Principle question that acts like a Strengthen question.
Which one of the following is best illustrated by the statements above? *PrepTest48 Sec1 Q11*	"[B]est illustrated by the statements" indicates that this is a Principle question that tests Inference skills.
Of the following, which one illustrates a principle that is most similar to the principle illustrated by the passage? *PrepTest61 Sec2 Q2*	"[A] principle ... most similar to the principle illustrated by the passage" is a Parallel Principle question that rewards the analysis seen in Parallel Reasoning questions.

(handwritten margin notes: "Assumption / clarify", "Strengthen", "Parallel Principle")

Distinguishing Types of Principle Questions

Identify the Principle questions will present a specific argument or set of events in the question stem, then ask you to identify a more general principle that underlies or strengthens the stimulus. These question types can mimic Assumption, Strengthen, or even Inference questions.

Apply the Principle questions operate in the opposite direction: They present a general rule or definition in the stimulus (often, but not always, expressed as a Formal Logic statement), then ask you to identify a specific situation that conforms to that rule or definition.

Parallel Principle questions ask you to perform both actions: Identify the general principle illustrated by the specific situation in the stimulus, and then apply that same principle to a specific situation in the answer choices.

Practice

Classify the Principle question type in each of the following question stems. Pay attention to whether you're asked to find a specific situation from a general rule, a general rule from a specific situation, or both.

	LSAT Question	My Analysis
93.	Which one of the following principles, if valid, most helps to justify the reasoning above? *PrepTest61 Sec2 Q21*	→ Identify
94.	Which one of the following judgments conforms most closely to the principles described by the industrial adviser? *Principle in stimulus* *PrepTest51 Sec1 Q17*	→ Apply
95.	The situation described above most closely conforms to which one of the following generalizations? *identify principle* *PrepTest59 Sec2 Q23*	→ Identify
96.	Which one of the following most closely conforms to the principle to which the reasoning in the passage conforms? *PrepTest59 Sec3 Q6*	→ Parallel
97.	Which one of the following most accurately expresses the principle underlying the argument above? *PrepTest59 Sec3 Q18*	→ Identify

Expert Analysis: Principle Question Stems

Here's how an LSAT expert would characterize each of the question stems in that exercise.

LSAT Question	Analysis
93. Which one of the following principles, if valid, most helps to justify the reasoning above? *PrepTest61 Sec2 Q21* →	"[M]ost helps to justify the reasoning" sounds a lot like a Strengthen question. Because the question asks for "the following principle," though, this is an Identify the Principle question that mimics a Strengthen question.
94. Which one of the following judgments conforms most closely to the principles described by the industrial adviser? *PrepTest51 Sec1 Q17* →	This question asks for a specific "judgment" that "conforms most closely to the principles described [above]." This is an Apply the Principle question similar to an Inference question.
95. The situation described above most closely conforms to which one of the following generalizations? *PrepTest59 Sec2 Q23* →	This question asks for a generalization that "most closely conforms to" the specific situation above. It is an Identify the Principle question that operates like an Inference question.
96. Which one of the following most closely conforms to the principle to which the reasoning in the passage conforms? *PrepTest59 Sec3 Q6* →	In this question, *both* the stimulus above *and* the correct answer "closely conform" to the same principle. This is a Parallel Principle question.
97. Which one of the following most accurately expresses the principle underlying the argument above? *PrepTest59 Sec3 Q18* →	"[P]rinciple underlying the argument above"—this is like an Assumption question. In this Identify the Principle question, the right answer states a general rule that connects the argument's evidence to its conclusion.

ASSUMPTION-FAMILY PRINCIPLE QUESTIONS AT A GLANCE

Task: Identify whether the question is asking for the principle that acts as the argument's assumption ("underlies the argument") or as a strengthener ("most justifies").

Strategy: Use the same skills you would to answer an Assumption or Strengthen question, but phrase your prediction of the correct answer as a broad general rule.

Frequency: On LSAT tests released between 2012 and 2016, there were an average of 5.0 Principle questions per test, of which 3.0 were Assumption-Family Principle questions.

Prepare

LEARNING OBJECTIVES

In this section, you'll learn to:

· Use your knowledge of Assumption Family questions to answer Principle questions that mimic Assumption and Strengthen questions

Here's how an LSAT expert might analyze and answer a Principle question that acts as a Strengthen question.

LSAT Question	Analysis
Philosopher: Some of the most ardent philosophical opponents of democracy have rightly noted that both the inherently best and the inherently worst possible forms of government are those that concentrate political power in the hands of a few. Thus, since democracy is a consistently mediocre form of government, it is a better choice than rule by the few.	**Step 2:** Conclusion—Democracy is a better choice than rule by the few. *because* Evidence: The best and worst forms of government concentrate power in the hands of a few, and democracy is a consistently mediocre form of government.
Which one of the following principles, if valid, most helps to justify the philosopher's argument?	**Step 1:** The phrase "following principles" indicates an Identify the Principle question. The word "justify" signifies that this acts as a Strengthen question.
	Step 3: The correct answer will provide a broad, general rule that strengthens the author's reasoning. The author assumes that a mediocre form of government is preferable to one that could be the best but carries the risk of being the worst.
(A) A society should adopt a democratic form of government if and only if most members of the society prefer a democratic form of government.	**Step 4:** What most members of a society *prefer* is Outside the Scope. Eliminate.
(B) In choosing a form of government, it is better for a society to avoid the inherently worst than to seek to attain the best.	Correct. This choice summarizes the author's assumption: Don't risk the worst form of government, even if it might turn out to be the best; play it safe and go with mediocrity instead.
(C) The best form of government is the one that is most likely to produce an outcome that is on the whole good.	Distortion. The only criterion the philosopher gives for the best form of government is that it "concentrate[s] political power in the hands of the few." Eliminate.
(D) Democratic governments are not truly equitable unless they are designed to prevent interest groups from exerting undue influence on the political process.	Outside the Scope. The philosopher does not attempt to define *equitable* government. Eliminate.
(E) It is better to choose a form of government on the basis of sound philosophical reasons than on the basis of popular preference. *PrepTest51 Sec3 Q13*	Outside the Scope. The philosopher says nothing about the role of *popular preference* in choosing a form of government. Eliminate.

Practice

Practice the following Assumption-Family Principle questions. Use the question stem to identify whether the question acts like an Assumption or Strengthen question and then apply the same skills you would use for those. But keep in mind that the correct answer will be a broad rule rather than a specific statement of the assumption or a helpful fact.

LSAT Question	My Analysis
98. Bethany: Psychologists have discovered a technique for replacing one's nightmares with pleasant dreams, and have successfully taught it to adults suffering from chronic nightmares. Studies have found that nightmare-prone children are especially likely to suffer from nightmares as adults. Thus, psychologists should direct efforts toward identifying nightmare-prone children so that these children can be taught the technique for replacing their nightmares with pleasant dreams.	**Step 2:** Conclusion— *because* Evidence—
Which one of the following principles, if valid, most helps to justify drawing the conclusion in Bethany's argument?	**Step 1:**
	Step 3:
(A) Psychologists should make an effort to determine why certain children are especially prone to nightmares while other children are not.	**Step 4:**
(B) Any psychological technique that can be successfully taught to a child can also be successfully taught to an adult.	
(C) Psychologists should do everything they can to minimize the number of adults troubled by chronic nightmares.	
(D) Identifying nightmare-prone children is generally more difficult than teaching adults the technique for replacing nightmares with pleasant dreams.	
(E) Psychologists should not teach the technique for replacing nightmares with pleasant dreams to children who are unlikely to suffer from nightmares as adults.	

PrepTest59 Sec2 Q13

LSAT Question	My Analysis
99. Those who claim that governments should not continue to devote resources to space exploration are wrong. Although most people's lives are relatively unaffected by the direct consequences of space exploration, many modern technologies that have a tremendous impact on daily life—e.g., fiber optics, computers, and lasers—are unexpected consequences of it. Society might have missed the benefits of these technologies if governments had not devoted resources to space exploration.	**Step 2:** Conclusion— *because* Evidence—
Which one of the following most accurately expresses the principle underlying the argument above?	**Step 1:**
	Step 3:
(A) Governments should not be prevented from allocating resources to projects whose intended consequences do not directly benefit most people.	**Step 4:**
(B) One can never underestimate the beneficial consequences of government support of ambitious technological undertakings.	
(C) The less practical the goal of a government-supported project, the more unexpected the consequences of that project.	
(D) Governments should continue to support those projects that have, in the past, produced unintended benefits.	
(E) In attempting to advance the welfare of society, governments should continue to dedicate resources to ambitious technological undertakings. *PrepTest59 Sec3 Q18*	

Expert Analysis: Assumption-Family Principle Questions

Compare your work to that of an LSAT expert. Were you able to identify whether each of the questions acted like an Assumption or Strengthen question? Did you apply what you know about analyzing and evaluating LSAT arguments?

LSAT Question	Analysis
98. Bethany: Psychologists have discovered a technique for replacing one's nightmares with pleasant dreams, and have successfully taught it to adults suffering from chronic nightmares. Studies have found that nightmare-prone children are especially likely to suffer from nightmares as adults. Thus, psychologists should direct efforts toward identifying nightmare-prone children so that these children can be taught the technique for replacing their nightmares with pleasant dreams.	**Step 2:** Conclusion—Psychologists should identify nightmare-prone children so that these children can learn to replace nightmares with pleasant dreams. *because* Evidence—Nightmare-prone children are especially likely to suffer from nightmares as adults.
Which one of the following principles, if valid, most helps to justify drawing the conclusion in Bethany's argument?	**Step 1:** The phrase "following principles" indicates an Identify the Principle question, and "justify ... the conclusion" signals a Strengthen-type question.
	Step 3: Bethany concludes that nightmare-prone children should be identified because such children are likely to become nightmare-prone adults, and there are now ways to reduce nightmares in adults. The correct answer will contain a broad rule that supports this recommendation.
(A) Psychologists should make an effort to determine why certain children are especially prone to nightmares while other children are not.	**Step 4:** Outside the Scope. *Why* certain children are nightmare-prone is irrelevant to Bethany's argument about identifying them for treatment. Eliminate.
(B) Any psychological technique that can be successfully taught to a child can also be successfully taught to an adult.	180. If anything, Bethany assumes that a technique that can be taught to an adult can also be taught to a child. Eliminate.
(C) Psychologists should do everything they can to minimize the number of adults troubled by chronic nightmares.	Correct. If this broad rule is valid, then Bethany's assumption is justified. The reason she wants to identify childhood sufferers is to prevent them from becoming nightmare-prone adults.
(D) Identifying nightmare-prone children is generally more difficult than teaching adults the technique for replacing nightmares with pleasant dreams.	Irrelevant Comparison. The relative difficulty of these things has no bearing on Bethany's argument that nightmare-prone children should in fact be identified. If anything, this undermines Bethany's conclusion by suggesting her proposal may not be easy. Eliminate.
(E) Psychologists should not teach the technique for replacing nightmares with pleasant dreams to children who are unlikely to suffer from nightmares as adults.	Outside the Scope. Bethany's objective is to identify children who *are* likely to be nightmare-prone as adults. Eliminate.

PrepTest59 Sec2 Q13

LSAT Question	**Analysis**
99. Those who claim that governments should not continue to devote resources to space exploration are wrong. Although most people's lives are relatively unaffected by the direct consequences of space exploration, many modern technologies that have a tremendous impact on daily life—e.g., fiber optics, computers, and lasers—are unexpected consequences of it. Society might have missed the benefits of these technologies if governments had not devoted resources to space exploration. →	**Step 2:** Conclusion—Governments *should* continue to devote resources to space exploration (those who say otherwise are wrong). *because* Evidence—Although people's lives are not affected by the direct consequences of space exploration, their lives are affected by technologies that have emerged as unexpected consequences of space exploration.
Which one of the following most accurately expresses the principle underlying the argument above? →	**Step 1:** The word *principle* signals a Principle question, while the word *underlying* indicates that this acts as an Assumption question.
	Step 3: The author assumes that space exploration should receive continued support because it provides unexpected technological benefits to society. The correct answer will state this assumption as a broad, general rule.
(A) Governments should not be prevented from allocating resources to projects whose intended consequences do not directly benefit most people. →	**Step 4:** Space exploration's *un*intended benefits, not its intended consequences, are at issue here. Eliminate.
(B) One can never underestimate the beneficial consequences of government support of ambitious technological undertakings. →	Extreme. Although the author is concerned that we *have* underestimated (or even ignored) the unintended benefits of space exploration, it goes too far to say one can *never* underestimate the benefits of government tech projects. Eliminate.
(C) The less practical the goal of a government-supported project, the more unexpected the consequences of that project. →	Outside the Scope. A rule stating that the predictability of consequences is inversely related to the practicality of goals does not necessarily support the author's recommendation to continue space exploration. Eliminate.
(D) Governments should continue to support those projects that have, in the past, produced unintended benefits. →	Correct. This choice broadly states the author's assumption about space exploration.
(E) In attempting to advance the welfare of society, governments should continue to dedicate resources to ambitious technological undertakings. *PrepTest59 Sec3 Q18* →	Distortion. This choice misses the point: It is not the fact that a technological undertaking is *ambitious*, but rather the fact that it has produced unexpected benefits that is important. Eliminate.

Perform

LSAT Question	My Analysis
100. A government study indicates that raising speed limits to reflect the actual average speeds of traffic on level, straight stretches of high-speed roadways reduces the accident rate. Since the actual average speed for level, straight stretches of high-speed roadways tends to be 120 kilometers per hour (75 miles per hour), that should be set as a uniform national speed limit for level, straight stretches of all such roadways. ⟶	**Step 2:** Conclusion— *because* Evidence—
Which one of the following principles, if valid, most helps to justify the reasoning above? ⟶	**Step 1:**
	Step 3:
(A) Uniform national speed limits should apply only to high-speed roadways. ⟶	**Step 4:**
(B) Traffic laws applying to high-speed roadways should apply uniformly across the nation. ⟶	
(C) A uniform national speed limit for high-speed roadways should be set only if all such roadways have roughly equal average speeds of traffic. ⟶	
(D) Long-standing laws that are widely violated are probably not good laws. ⟶	
(E) Any measure that reduces the rate of traffic accidents should be implemented. *PrepTest61 Sec2 Q21* ⟶	

LSAT Question	My Analysis
101. Ethicist: People who avoid alcoholic beverages simply because they regard them as a luxury beyond their financial means should not be praised for their abstinence. Similarly, those who avoid alcohol simply because they lack the desire to partake should not be praised, unless this disinclination has somehow resulted from an arduous process of disciplining oneself to refrain from acting indiscriminately on one's desires.	**Step 2:** Conclusion— *because* Evidence—
Which one of the following principles, if valid, most helps to justify the ethicist's claims?	**Step 1:**
	Step 3:
(A) Whether behavior should be regarded as praiseworthy is a function of both its consequences and the social context in which the agent acts.	**Step 4:**
(B) A person should be blamed for an action only if that action was not motivated by a desire to be virtuous or if the person did not have to overcome any obstacles in order to perform that action.	
(C) A person is praiseworthy for a particular behavior only if, in order to adopt that behavior, the person at some point had to overcome a desire to do something that she or he felt able to afford to do.	
(D) The extent to which the process of acquiring self-discipline is arduous for a person is affected by that person's set of desires and aversions.	
(E) The apportionment of praise and blame should be commensurate with the arduousness or ease of the lives of those who receive praise or blame.	

PrepTest49 Sec4 Q21

Expert Analysis: Assumption-Family Principle Questions

Compare your work to that of an LSAT expert. Were you able to identify whether each of the questions acted like an Assumption or Strengthen question? Did you apply what you know about analyzing and evaluating LSAT arguments?

LSAT Question	Analysis
100. A government study indicates that raising speed limits to reflect the actual average speeds of traffic on level, straight stretches of high-speed roadways reduces the accident rate. Since the actual average speed for level, straight stretches of high-speed roadways tends to be 120 kilometers per hour (75 miles per hour), that should be set as a uniform national speed limit for level, straight stretches of all such roadways. →	**Step 2:** Conclusion—The speed limit for all level, straight stretches of roadways should be 75 mph. *because* Evidence—A government study indicates that raising the speed limit to drivers' actual average speed on level, straight roadways reduces the accident rate. The actual average speed on such roadways is currently about 75 mph.
Which one of the following principles, if valid, most helps to justify the reasoning above? →	**Step 1:** The phrase "following principles" signals an Identify the Principle question. The word *justify* indicates that this is also a Strengthen question.
	Step 3: The argument assumes that an action that reduces the number of accidents should be taken. The correct answer will be in line with this assumption and will be a recommendation phrased in broad, general terms.
(A) Uniform national speed limits should apply only to high-speed roadways. →	**Step 4:** Roadways other than high-speed roadways are Outside the Scope. Eliminate.
(B) Traffic laws applying to high-speed roadways should apply uniformly across the nation. →	Outside the Scope. The only law the author is interested in is the speed limit on high-speed roadways because it reduces traffic accidents. Eliminate.
(C) A uniform national speed limit for high–speed roadways should be set only if all such roadways have roughly equal average speeds of traffic. →	This choice commits a necessity-sufficiency error. The argument in the stimulus says that if (*not only* if) the speed limit on high-speed roadways tends to be the same, there should be a uniform speed limit. Eliminate.
(D) Long-standing laws that are widely violated are probably not good laws. →	Outside the Scope. This answer mentions laws that are widely violated—a concept that is never discussed in the argument. The author advocates for a change to reduce accidents, not just because the law may not be consistently followed now. Eliminate.
(E) Any measure that reduces the rate of traffic accidents should be implemented. *PrepTest61 Sec2 Q21* →	Correct. In light of the evidence that a uniform speed limit would help reduce accidents, this principle supports the conclusion that the speed limit on level, straight roadways should be raised to 75 mph.

LSAT Question	Analysis
101. Ethicist: People who avoid alcoholic beverages simply because they regard them as a luxury beyond their financial means should not be praised for their abstinence. Similarly, those who avoid alcohol simply because they lack the desire to partake should not be praised, unless this disinclination has somehow resulted from an arduous process of disciplining oneself to refrain from acting indiscriminately on one's desires.	**Step 2:** [No argument; just two claims] Those who cannot afford alcoholic beverages should not be praised for abstaining from them. Likewise, those who do not desire alcohol should not be praised for abstinence, unless the lack of desire is the result of tough self-discipline.
Which one of the following principles, if valid, most helps to justify the ethicist's claims?	**Step 1:** The phrase "following principles" signals an Identify the Principle question. The word "justify" indicates that this is also a Strengthen question.
	Step 3: The correct answer will be a broad rule that strengthens the ethicist's claims. The ethicist allows praise only in cases where self-discipline has changed one's behavior, so the correct answer will state a rule to the effect that no behavior is praiseworthy unless there was self-discipline involved.
(A) Whether behavior should be regarded as praiseworthy is a function of both its consequences and the social context in which the agent acts.	**Step 4:** Consequences and social context are both Outside the Scope. Eliminate.
(B) A person should be blamed for an action only if that action was not motivated by a desire to be virtuous or if the person did not have to overcome any obstacles in order to perform that action.	Outside the Scope. The ethicist does not discuss blameworthy actions. He gives guidelines about praiseworthy actions. Eliminate.
(C) A person is praiseworthy for a particular behavior only if, in order to adopt that behavior, the person at some point had to overcome a desire to do something that she or he felt able to afford to do.	Correct. This general rule governs what the ethicist says about abstinence from alcohol: Praise is merited only for behavior produced through self-discipline.
(D) The extent to which the process of acquiring self-discipline is arduous for a person is affected by that person's set of desires and aversions.	Outside the Scope. This choice does not impact the concept of which behaviors are praiseworthy. Eliminate.
(E) The apportionment of praise and blame should be commensurate with the arduousness or ease of the lives of those who receive praise or blame.	The general "arduousness or ease" of someone's *life* is Outside the Scope. What is important to the ethicist is the difficulty of performing a specific *action*. Eliminate.

PrepTest49 Sec4 Q21

PARALLEL FLAW QUESTIONS

Compared to Parallel Reasoning questions, the strategy for Parallel Flaw questions is relatively straightforward. That's because you already know from the question stem that the argument will be flawed.

Prepare

LEARNING OBJECTIVES

In this section, you'll learn to:

· Identify and Answer Parallel Flaw questions

You can recognize Parallel Flaw questions from question stems such as these:

The pattern of flawed reasoning exhibited by the argument above is most similar to that exhibited by which one of the following?

PrepTest51 Sec1 Q20

Which one of the following most closely parallels the questionable reasoning cited above?

PrepTest57 Sec2 Q8

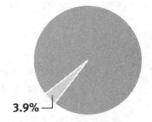

Parallel Flaw Questions

3.9% ⌐

Logical Reasoning Question Types
PrepTests 66–80, released 2012–2016

PARALLEL FLAW QUESTIONS AT A GLANCE

Task: Identify the answer choice in which the argument makes the same error(s) in reasoning that the argument in the stimulus commits.

Strategy: Analyze the argument in the stimulus and identify the author's reasoning error(s). Evaluate the answer choices to find the one containing an argument in which the author commits the same error(s) as did the author of the stimulus.

Frequency: On LSAT tests released from 2012 through 2016, there were an average of 2.0 Parallel Flaw questions per test.

Parallel Flaw is slightly more common than Parallel Reasoning.

When attacking Parallel Flaw questions, use one of these approaches.

Compare Flaws. After all of the work you did earlier in the section on Flaw questions, this tactic should feel familiar. Analyze the argument in the stimulus and describe the error in reasoning. Evaluate the answer choices by looking for the only one that contains exactly the same flaw. Consider this argument:

> A certain species of otter lives only in the vicinity of Midland Bay, which is also the only place a particular species of mussel grows. It must be the case that the otter of this specific species eats the mussels of this specific species.

Here are two other arguments. Which one is parallel to that in the example?

> (1) If two species are found exclusively in proximity to one another, then they must be part of an interconnected ecosystem. A certain bird and a certain snake are part of an interconnected wetlands ecosystem; therefore, the bird and the snake must be found exclusively in proximity to one another.

> (2) We can conclude that a certain species of snail consumes a certain species of mushroom from the fact that this species of mushroom grows exclusively in the shade of oak trees which are the exclusive home of the snail.

TEST DAY TIP

A Parallel Flaw argument may commit more than one reasoning error. If that's the case, then the argument in the correct answer will commit all of the same flaws.

Compare Conclusions. This is the same technique used in Parallel Reasoning questions. Keep in mind that qualifying or softening a conclusion often makes an Overlooked Possibilities argument's reasoning sound. That is, softening the conclusion removes the flaw.

Compare Formal Logic. Just as in Parallel Reasoning, when a Parallel Flaw argument is easily diagrammed in Formal Logic shorthand, comparing the argument structures can be even more efficient than describing the conclusion. Consider this argument:

> Whenever Craig goes shopping, Anne goes shopping too. Craig isn't shopping today, so Anne must not be shopping either.

Here are two more arguments. Which one is flawed in exactly the same way as the one in the example?

> (1) The zookeeper must not be feeding the penguins. This is obvious from the fact that he is not feeding the seals. Whenever the zookeeper feeds the seals, he also feeds the penguins.

> (2) Joan is not taking calculus this semester. Joan will take only classes also taken by Barbara, and Barbara is not taking calculus this semester.

TEST DAY TIP

If an answer choice contains an argument with sound reasoning, it cannot be the correct answer to a Parallel Flaw question.

Here's how an LSAT expert might analyze and answer a Parallel Flaw question.

LSAT Question	Analysis
Most of the employees of the Compujack Corporation are computer programmers. Since most computer programmers receive excellent salaries from their employers, at least one Compujack employee must receive an excellent salary from Compujack.	**Step 2:** Conclusion—A *strong assertion of fact* that at least one CJ employee must receive an excellent salary. *because* Evidence—(1) Most CJ employees are computer programmers, and (2) most computer programmers receive excellent salaries.
Which one of the following arguments exhibits a flawed pattern of reasoning most similar to the flawed pattern of reasoning exhibited by the argument above?	**Step 1:** The words "most similar to" and "flawed" identify this question as a Parallel Flaw question.
	Step 3: The stimulus wrongly assumes that at least one excellently salaried computer programmer works for CJ. Argument is structured like this: Most A are B; most B are C. Thus, at least one A is C.
(A) Most gardeners are people with a great deal of patience. Since most of Molly's classmates are gardeners, at least one of Molly's classmates must be a person with a great deal of patience.	**Step 4:** Correct. This choice has a structure identical to the one in the stimulus: most A (classmates) are B (gardeners); most B are C (patient). Thus, at least one A is C.
(B) Most of Molly's classmates are gardeners. Since most gardeners are people with a great deal of patience, some of Molly's classmates could be people with a great deal of patience.	Conclusion is qualified ("could be") in a way that removes any flaws. Most A are B; most B are C. Thus, *some* A *could be* C. Eliminate.
(C) Most gardeners are people with a great deal of patience. Since most of Molly's classmates are gardeners, at least one of Molly's classmates who is a gardener must be a person with a great deal of patience.	The conclusion does not match: Most A (classmates) are B (gardeners); most B are C (patient). Thus, at least one A is *B and C*. Eliminate.
(D) Most gardeners are people with a great deal of patience. Since most of Molly's classmates who garden are women, at least one female classmate of Molly's must be a person with a great deal of patience.	This choice introduces an additional term: women/female. Diagram the structure here and you need a D term. Eliminate.
(E) Most of Molly's classmates are gardeners with a great deal of patience. Since most of Molly's classmates are women, at least one female classmate of Molly's must be a gardener with a great deal of patience. *PrepTest49 Sec4 Q24*	Most A (classmates) are B (patient gardeners); most A are C (female). [*That piece of evidence doesn't match.*] Thus, at least one C and A is B. [*Conclusion doesn't match, either.*] Eliminate.

Practice

Practice some Parallel Flaw questions. In each, analyze the argument in the stimulus to determine if you want to evaluate the choices by comparing flaws, comparing structures, or a combination of the two.

LSAT Question		My Analysis
102. Only experienced salespeople will be able to meet the company's selling quota. Thus, I must not count as an experienced salesperson, since I will be able to sell only half the quota.	→	**Step 2:** Conclusion— *because* Evidence—
The pattern of flawed reasoning exhibited by the argument above is most similar to that exhibited by which one of the following?	→	**Step 1:**
		Step 3:
(A) Only on Fridays are employees allowed to dress casually. Today is Friday but Hector is dressed formally. So he must not be going to work.	→	**Step 4:**
(B) Only music lovers take this class. Thus, since Hillary is not taking this class, she apparently does not love music.	→	
(C) Only oceanographers enjoy the Atlantic in midwinter. Thus, we may expect that Gerald does not enjoy the Atlantic in midwinter, since he is not an oceanographer.	→	
(D) As this tree before us is a giant redwood, it follows that we must be in a northern latitude, since it is only in northern latitudes that one finds giant redwoods.	→	
(E) Only accomplished mountain climbers can scale El Capitan. Thus, Michelle must be able to scale El Capitan, since she is an accomplished mountain climber.	→	

PrepTest51 Sec1 Q20

LSAT Question	My Analysis
103. There are circumstances in which it is not immoral to make certain threats, and there are circumstances in which it is not immoral to ask for money or some other favor. Therefore, there are circumstances in which it is not immoral to ask for money or a favor while making a threat. →	**Step 2:** Conclusion— *because* Evidence—
Which one of the following exhibits a flawed pattern of reasoning most similar to that in the argument above? →	**Step 1:**
	Step 3:
(A) There are many business events for which casual dress is appropriate, and there are many social events for which casual dress is appropriate; therefore, if an occasion is neither a business event nor a social event, casual dress is not likely to be appropriate. →	**Step 4:**
(B) It is usually easy to move a piano after you have convinced five people to help you, provided that you do not need to take it up or down stairs. Therefore, it is usually easy to move a piano. →	
(C) It is healthful to take drug A for a headache, and it is healthful to take drug B for a headache; therefore, it is healthful to take drug A together with drug B for a headache. →	
(D) Heavy trucks are generally operated in a safe manner, but the ability to drive a truck safely can be impaired by certain prescription drugs. Therefore, heavy trucks cannot be operated safely while the driver is under the effect of a prescription drug. →	
(E) The mountain roads are treacherous after it rains, and the mountain streams are full after a rain. So, if the roads in the mountains are treacherous, and the mountain streams are full, it surely has rained recently. →	

PrepTest59 Sec3 Q15

Expert Analysis: Parallel Flaw Questions

Compare your work to that of an LSAT expert. Where did your approaches align? Were you as efficient and confident in eliminating wrong answers as you could have been?

LSAT Question	Analysis
102. Only experienced salespeople will be able to meet the company's selling quota. Thus, I must not count as an experienced salesperson, since I will be able to sell only half the quota.	**Step 2:** Conclusion—*Strong assertion* that I must not be an experienced salesperson. → *because* Evidence—I will only be able to sell half the quota, and only experienced salespeople will be able to meet the quota.
The pattern of flawed reasoning exhibited by the argument above is most similar to that exhibited by which one of the following?	→ **Step 1:** The words "flawed" and "most similar to" indicate a Parallel Flaw question.
	Step 3: The author confuses necessity for sufficiency by negating without reversing. If *meet quota* (X) → *experienced* (Y) If *~meet quota* (~X) → *~experienced* (~Y) The correct answer will contain this same flawed algebraic structure.
(A) Only on Fridays are employees allowed to dress casually. Today is Friday but Hector is dressed formally. So he must not be going to work.	→ **Step 4:** Assumes that Hector would be dressing casually for work at any time he was permitted to do so. This is not the same necessity-sufficiency error in the stimulus. Eliminate.
(B) Only music lovers take this class. Thus, since Hillary is not taking this class, she apparently does not love music.	→ Correct. This argument assumes that all music lovers will take the class Hillary has chosen to skip. It follows the same flawed algebraic structure as the stimulus.
(C) Only oceanographers enjoy the Atlantic in midwinter. Thus, we may expect that Gerald does not enjoy the Atlantic in midwinter, since he is not an oceanographer.	→ This argument contains no flaw, just a properly formed contrapositive. Eliminate.
(D) As this tree before us is a giant redwood, it follows that we must be in a northern latitude, since it is only in northern latitudes that one finds giant redwoods.	→ This argument contains no flaw, just properly analyzed Formal Logic. Eliminate.
(E) Only accomplished mountain climbers can scale El Capitan. Thus, Michelle must be able to scale El Capitan, since she is an accomplished mountain climber. *PrepTest51 Sec1 Q20*	→ Assumes that all accomplished mountain climbers can scale El Capitan, but unlike the stimulus, this choice concludes that Michelle must be able to do something based on the group she is a member of, rather than concluding that she is *not* a member of that group based on evidence of something that she *cannot* do. Eliminate.

LSAT Question	Analysis
103. There are circumstances in which it is not immoral to make certain threats, and there are circumstances in which it is not immoral to ask for money or some other favor. Therefore, there are circumstances in which it is not immoral to ask for money or a favor while making a threat.	**Step 2:** Conclusion—A *strong assertion* that it is not immoral to ask for money or a favor while making a threat. *because* Evidence—There are circumstances in which it is not immoral to make a threat, and there are circumstances in which it is not immoral to ask for money or a favor.
Which one of the following exhibits a flawed pattern of reasoning most similar to that in the argument above?	**Step 1:** The phrase "most similar to" indicates a Parallel Reasoning question. The word "flawed" identifies this question more specifically as a Parallel Flaw question.
	Step 3: The flawed assumption is that if two things are each okay to do independently, it is okay to do them in combination. The correct answer will contain this same faulty assumption.
(A) There are many business events for which casual dress is appropriate, and there are many social events for which casual dress is appropriate; therefore, if an occasion is neither a business event nor a social event, casual dress is not likely to be appropriate.	**Step 4:** Conclusion is phrased as a conditional statement. Eliminate.
(B) It is usually easy to move a piano after you have convinced five people to help you, provided that you do not need to take it up or down stairs. Therefore, it is usually easy to move a piano.	Conclusion contains the qualifier "usually." Eliminate.
(C) It is healthful to take drug A for a headache, and it is healthful to take drug B for a headache; therefore, it is healthful to take drug A together with drug B for a headache.	Correct. This argument contains the same flawed assumption as the argument in the stimulus: if two things are okay individually, then combining them must also be okay.
(D) Heavy trucks are generally operated in a safe manner, but the ability to drive a truck safely can be impaired by certain prescription drugs. Therefore, heavy trucks cannot be operated safely while the driver is under the effect of a prescription drug.	Conclusion states that combining two things (operating a truck and taking prescription medication) is *not* a good idea. Eliminate.
(E) The mountain roads are treacherous after it rains, and the mountain streams are full after a rain. So, if the roads in the mountains are treacherous, and the mountain streams are full, it surely has rained recently. *PrepTest59 Sec3 Q15*	Conclusion is phrased as a conditional statement. Eliminate.

Perform

Try some more Parallel Flaw questions. In each, analyze the argument in the stimulus to determine if you want to evaluate the choices by comparing flaws, comparing structures, or a combination of the two.

LSAT Question	My Analysis
104. A psychiatrist argued that there is no such thing as a multiple personality disorder on the grounds that in all her years of clinical practice, she had never encountered one case of this type. →	**Step 2:** Conclusion— *because* Evidence—
Which one of the following most closely parallels the questionable reasoning cited above? →	**Step 1:**
	Step 3:
(A) Anton concluded that colds are seldom fatal on the grounds that in all his years of clinical practice, he never had a patient who died of a cold. →	**Step 4:**
(B) Lyla said that no one in the area has seen a groundhog and so there are probably no groundhogs in the area. →	
(C) Sauda argued that because therapy rarely had an effect on her patient's type of disorder, therapy was not warranted. →	
(D) Thomas argued that because Natasha has driven her car to work every day since she bought it, she would probably continue to drive her car to work. →	
(E) Jerod had never spotted a deer in his area and concluded from this that there are no deer in the area. *PrepTest57 Sec2 Q8* →	

LSAT Question	My Analysis
105. Food that is very high in fat tends to be unhealthy. These brownies are fat-free, while those cookies contain a high percentage of fat. Therefore, these fat-free brownies are healthier than those cookies are. →	**Step 2:** Conclusion— *because* Evidence—
Which one of the following exhibits flawed reasoning most similar to the flawed reasoning exhibited by the argument above? →	**Step 1:**
	Step 3:
(A) Canned foods always contain more salt than frozen foods do. Therefore, these canned peas contain more salt than those frozen peas do. →	**Step 4:**
(B) Vegetables that are overcooked generally have few vitamins. Therefore, these carrots, which are overcooked, contain fewer vitamins than those peas, which are uncooked. →	
(C) The human body needs certain amounts of many minerals to remain healthy. Therefore, this distilled water, which has no minerals, is unhealthy. →	
(D) Some types of nuts make Roy's throat itch. These cookies contain a greater percentage of nuts than that pie contains. Therefore, these cookies are more likely to make Roy's throat itch. →	
(E) Eating at a restaurant costs more than eating food prepared at home. Therefore, this home-cooked meal is less expensive than a restaurant meal of the same dishes would be. *PrepTest51 Sec3 Q22* →	

Expert Analysis: Parallel Flaw Questions

Compare your work to that of an LSAT expert. Where did your approaches align? Were you as efficient and confident in eliminating wrong answers as you could have been?

LSAT Question	Analysis
104. A psychiatrist argued that there is no such thing as a multiple personality disorder on the grounds that in all her years of clinical practice, she had never encountered one case of this type.	**Step 2:** Conclusion—The psychiatrist concludes that there is no such thing as a multiple personality disorder. This is a *strong assertion of fact*. *because* Evidence—The psychiatrist has never seen a case of multiple personality disorder.
Which one of the following most closely parallels the questionable reasoning cited above?	**Step 1:** The words "parallels" and "questionable" signal a Parallel Flaw question.
	Step 3: The flaw boils down to "I've never seen it, so it doesn't exist."
(A) Anton concluded that colds are seldom fatal on the grounds that in all his years of clinical practice, he never had a patient who died of a cold.	**Step 4:** Conclusion is not parallel: "seldom fatal" is qualified. Eliminate.
(B) Lyla said that no one in the area has seen a groundhog and so there are probably no groundhogs in the area.	Conclusion is qualified ("probably"). Eliminate.
(C) Sauda argued that because therapy rarely had an effect on her patient's type of disorder, therapy was not warranted.	Conclusion is a recommendation: therapy is "not warranted," that is, it should not be done. Eliminate.
(D) Thomas argued that because Natasha has driven her car to work every day since she bought it, she would probably continue to drive her car to work.	Conclusion is a weak prediction that Natasha will "probably" continue to drive her car to work. Eliminate.
(E) Jerod had never spotted a deer in his area and concluded from this that there are no deer in the area. *PrepTest57 Sec2 Q8*	Correct. This is the only choice with a conclusion that is a strong assertion ("there are no deer in this area"). The flaw is the same: Jerod hasn't seen a deer in the area, so deer must not exist there.

LSAT Question	Analysis
105. Food that is very high in fat tends to be unhealthy. These brownies are fat-free, while those cookies contain a high percentage of fat. Therefore, these fat-free brownies are healthier than those cookies are.	**Step 2:** Conclusion—These fat-free brownies are healthier than those cookies. This is a *strong comparison*. → *because* Evidence—Food high in fat tends to be unhealthy. These brownies are fat-free; those cookies are high in fat.
Which one of the following exhibits flawed reasoning most similar to the flawed reasoning exhibited by the argument above? →	**Step 1:** The phrases "most similar to" and "flawed reasoning" signal a Parallel Flaw question.
	Step 3: The author overlooks the possibility that there might be some other factor that might make the brownies less healthy overall than the cookies, despite their respective fat contents.
(A) Canned foods always contain more salt than frozen foods do. Therefore, these canned peas contain more salt than those frozen peas do. →	**Step 4:** The problem with this argument is that we don't know the relative quantities of the two foods. If the quantities of canned and frozen peas are the same, there is no flaw. But there's no way to establish this. Note the difference between *always* in this answer choice versus "tends to be" in the stimulus. Eliminate.
(B) Vegetables that are overcooked generally have few vitamins. Therefore, these carrots, which are overcooked, contain fewer vitamins than those peas, which are uncooked. →	Correct. This argument overlooks the possibility that the overcooked carrots actually have more vitamins than the uncooked peas. Perhaps the carrots have *so* many more vitamins to begin with that even a diminished quantity after cooking is still more than uncooked peas.
(C) The human body needs certain amounts of many minerals to remain healthy. Therefore, this distilled water, which has no minerals, is unhealthy. →	Conclusion is not a comparison. Eliminate.
(D) Some types of nuts make Roy's throat itch. These cookies contain a greater percentage of nuts than that pie contains. Therefore, these cookies are more likely to make Roy's throat itch. →	This choice distinguishes between different types of nuts, only "some" of which make Roy's throat itch. The stimulus does not distinguish different types of fat, only *some* of which are unhealthy. The evidence here is not parallel to that in the stimulus. Eliminate.
(E) Eating at a restaurant costs more than eating food prepared at home. Therefore, this home-cooked meal is less expensive than a restaurant meal of the same dishes would be. → *PrepTest51 Sec3 Q22*	There is no flaw in this argument. Eliminate.

PARALLEL PRINCIPLE QUESTIONS

Parallel Principle questions ask you to identify the principle underlying the argument in the stimulus, and then, find the answer in which the argument has a similar principle underlying it. Much like Parallel Reasoning, the answer choices are likely to contain subject matter different than that in the stimulus argument.

You can identify Parallel Principle questions from question stems such as these:

Of the following, which one illustrates a principle that is
most similar to the principle illustrated by the passage?

PrepTest61 Sec2 Q2

Which one of the following most closely conforms to
the principle to which the reasoning in the passage
conforms?

PrepTest59 Sec3 Q6

PARALLEL PRINCIPLE QUESTIONS AT A GLANCE

Task: Identify the principle underlying the argument in the stimulus and use that principle to distinguish the one answer containing an argument with a similar principle underlying it.

Strategy: Analyze the stimulus argument and identify the principle underlying its assumption. Evaluate the choices by spotting the one with a principle paralleling that of the argument in the stimulus.

Frequency: Parallel Principle questions are extremely rare. On LSAT tests released between 2012 and 2016, there were just five total (an average of one per year).

Here's how an LSAT expert approached one Parallel Principle question.

LSAT Question	Analysis
Since there is no survival value in an animal's having an organ that is able to function when all its other organs have broken down to such a degree that the animal dies, it is a result of the efficiency of natural selection that no organ is likely to evolve in such a way that it greatly outlasts the body's other organs.	**Step 2:** Conclusion—No animal organ likely to evolve to outlast the other organs. *because* Evidence—Having one organ that outlasts the others doesn't increase survival value.
Of the following, which one illustrates a principle that is most similar to the principle illustrated by the passage?	**Step 1:** The stimulus illustrates a principle. The correct answer illustrates the same principle. This is an Identify and Apply the Principle question. It works much like Parallel Reasoning.
	Step 3: The right answer will argue that there is no reason to have one part outlast other parts if the part in question doesn't add value in outlasting others.
(A) A store in a lower-income neighborhood finds that it is unable to sell its higher-priced goods and so stocks them only when ordered by a customer.	**Step 4:** Outside the Scope. Having a plan for when to deploy overpriced items has nothing in common with the argument in the stimulus. Eliminate.
(B) The body of an animal with a deficient organ is often able to compensate for that deficiency when other organs perform the task the deficient one normally performs.	Distortion. This is about compensating for an underdeveloped organ, not whether there is an advantage to having an overdeveloped one. Eliminate.
(C) One car model produced by an automobile manufacturer has a life expectancy that is so much longer than its other models that its great popularity requires the manufacturer to stop producing some of the other models.	Distortion/180. This argument is about different models, not parts of a whole. Moreover, the overdeveloped part is beneficial. Eliminate.
(D) Athletes occasionally overdevelop some parts of their bodies to such a great extent that other parts of their bodies are more prone to injury as a result.	180. Here the overdevelopment of one part is detrimental to the other parts. Eliminate.
(E) Automotive engineers find that it is not cost-effective to manufacture a given automobile part of such high quality that it outlasts all other parts of the automobile, as doing so would not raise the overall quality of the automobile.	Correct. There is no reason to design one part to outlast others since it isn't cost effective to do so. This matches the original argument's principle in a different context.

PrepTest61 Sec2 Q2

REFLECTION

Look back over the arguments you saw in the chapter. Consider the various analytical skills that the LSAT rewarded.

- How do you now look at arguments differently?
- When you see an argument, can you determine the author's assumption?
- Are you able to determine the type of assumption the author is making?
- Once you have determined the author's assumption, can you establish the types of facts that would make his reasoning more or less likely to be valid?
- Can you identify and describe the flaws in an author's argument more efficiently and effectively?

Arguments occur everywhere in the real world: television news and commentary, advertisements, debate over music, and claims about sports teams. In the coming days, read and listen to arguments very carefully. Apply the analytical skills you practiced in this chapter.

- What is the author's assumption?
- What assumptions are necessary for her conclusion to follow from her evidence?
- What assumption would be sufficient to establish her conclusion from her evidence?
- Is the author's argument sound? If flawed, does her error in reasoning match one or more of the flaws commonly tested on the LSAT?
- Can I describe her flaw in general language without reference to the argument's content?
- Am I able to think of facts that would strengthen or weaken the reasoning in the argument?

In the next chapter, you'll leave argument-based questions behind temporarily and focus on LSAT questions that ask you to make valid inferences from one or more statements. Essentially, you'll be given evidence and then asked for a conclusion that can be deduced from it. Making valid inferences from pieces of text is also an important skill in the Reading Comprehension section, so as you work in Chapter 9, remember that you are building strengths that will add to your LSAT score even beyond the specific Logical Reasoning questions you are learning.

Non-Argument Questions

Though most Logical Reasoning questions test your ability to analyze arguments, a significant number do not. Instead, these Non-Argument questions reward your ability to make valid deductions and inferences from a set of statements (Inference questions and some Principle questions) or to resolve an apparent discrepancy (Paradox questions). The best way to see the fundamental difference between Argument-Based and Non-Argument questions is to set questions of each type side by side.

Inference Question

Baxe Interiors, one of the largest interior design companies in existence, currently has a near monopoly in the corporate market. Several small design companies have won prestigious awards for their corporate work, while Baxe has won none. Nonetheless, the corporate managers who solicit design proposals will only contract with companies they believe are unlikely to go bankrupt, and they believe that only very large companies are unlikely to go bankrupt.

The **statements above, if true**, most strongly support which one of the following?

(A)   There are other very large design companies besides Baxe, but they produce designs that are inferior to Baxe's.

(B)   Baxe does not have a near monopoly in the market of any category of interior design other than corporate interiors.

(C)   For the most part, designs that are produced by small companies are superior to the designs produced by Baxe.

(D)   At least some of the corporate managers who solicit design proposals are unaware that there are designs that are much better than those produced by Baxe.

(E)   The existence of interior designs that are superior to those produced by Baxe does not currently threaten its near monopoly in the corporate market.

PrepTest61 Sec4 Q7

Strengthen Question

A recent study confirms that nutritious breakfasts make workers more productive. For one month, workers at Plant A received free nutritious breakfasts every day before work, while workers in Plant B did not. The productivity of Plant A's workers increased, while that of Plant B's workers did not.

Which one of **the following, if true**, most strengthens the argument?

(A)   Few workers in Plant B consumed nutritious breakfasts during the month of the study.

(B)   Workers in the study from Plant A and Plant B started work at the same time of day.

(C)   During the month before the study, workers at Plant A and Plant B were equally productive.

(D)   Workers from Plant A took fewer vacation days per capita during the month than did workers from Plant B.

(E)   Workers in Plant B were more productive during the month of the study than were workers from Plant A.

PrepTest59 Sec2 Q22

Notice that in the Non-Argument Inference question, the statements in the stimulus lead to the correct answer; in the Assumption Family Strengthen question, on the other hand, the correct answer supports—or supplements the argument in the stimulus. This pattern holds true for all questions in these families.

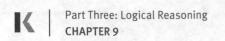
inference = must be true

contradiction = MBF

outside scope = CB T/F

MAKING DEDUCTIONS AND INFERENCE QUESTIONS

Inference questions present a stimulus containing a number of related factual statements. You are then asked to find an answer choice that must, could, or cannot be true based on those statements.

Prepare

LEARNING OBJECTIVES

In this section, you'll learn to:

· Identify and answer Inference questions

You can recognize Inference questions from question stems such as these:

If all of the statements above are true, then which one
of the following must be true?

PrepTest61 Sec2 Q3

Which one of the following can be properly inferred
from the information above?

PrepTest61 Sec2 Q10

If the statements above are true, then each of the
following could also be true EXCEPT:

PrepTest49 Sec2 Q21

Which one of the following is most strongly supported
by the information above?

PrepTest59 Sec3 Q3

The statements above, if true, most support which one
of the following?

PrepTest49 Sec2 Q9

The facts described above provide the strongest
evidence against which one of the following?

PrepTest57 Sec2 Q23

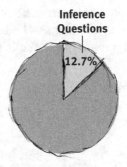

**Inference
Questions**

12.7%

**Logical Reasoning
Question Types**

PrepTests 66–80; released 2012–2016

INFERENCE QUESTIONS AT A GLANCE

Task: Identify the statement that must, could, or cannot be true based on a set of statements.

Strategy: Catalogue the statements in the stimulus: Identify the most concrete statement; combine related statements; note relationships indicated by Keywords; and/or use Formal Logic to evaluate the answer choices.

Frequency: LSAT tests released from 2012 to 2016 had an average of 6.5 Inference questions per test.

Incidentally, on most tests, the Inference questions are split just about 50-50 between those calling for a correct answer that must be true based on the stimulus and those calling for the answer most strongly supported by the stimulus.

Activate Prior Knowledge: Inference Questions and Levels of Truth

Use your knowledge of truth values from Chapter 1 to characterize the correct and incorrect answer choices called for by each of the following question stems. The expert analyses follow on the next page.

LSAT Question Stem	My Analysis
1. If all of the statements above are true, then which one of the following must be true? *PrepTest61 Sec2 Q3* →	**1 Right:** **4 Wrong:**
2. Which one of the following can be properly inferred from the information above? *PrepTest61 Sec2 Q10* →	**1 Right:** **4 Wrong:**
3. Which one of the following is most strongly supported by the information above? *PrepTest59 Sec3 Q3* →	**1 Right:** **4 Wrong:**
4. Which one of the following statements would most reasonably complete the argument? *PrepTest57 Sec2 Q18* →	**1 Right:** **4 Wrong:**
5. If all of the statements above are true, which one of the following CANNOT be true? *PrepTest49 Sec4 Q5* →	**1 Right:** **4 Wrong:**
6. The statements above, if true, provide support for each of the following EXCEPT: *PrepTest61 Sec4 Q3* →	**1 Right:** **4 Wrong:**
7. If the statements above are true, then each of the following could also be true EXCEPT: *PrepTest49 Sec2 Q21* →	**1 Right:** **4 Wrong:**
8. The facts described above provide the strongest evidence against which one of the following? *PrepTest57 Sec2 Q23* →	**1 Right:** **4 Wrong:**

Expert Analysis: Inference Question Stems

LSAT Question Stem	Analysis
1. If all of the statements above are true, then which one of the following must be true? *PrepTest61 Sec2 Q3*	**1 Right:** Must be true **4 Wrong:** Could be false
2. Which one of the following can be properly inferred from the information above? *PrepTest61 Sec2 Q10*	**1 Right:** Must be true **4 Wrong:** Could be false
3. Which one of the following is most strongly supported by the information above? *PrepTest59 Sec3 Q3*	**1 Right:** Is supported by the stimulus **4 Wrong:** Is not supported by the stimulus
4. Which one of the following statements would most reasonably complete the argument? *PrepTest57 Sec2 Q18*	**1 Right:** Represents the conclusion that follows closely from the stimulus's evidence **4 Wrong:** Is not a direct conclusion from the stimulus's evidence
5. If all of the statements above are true, which one of the following CANNOT be true? *PrepTest49 Sec4 Q5*	**1 Right:** Must be false **4 Wrong:** Could be true
6. The statements above, if true, provide support for each of the following EXCEPT: *PrepTest61 Sec4 Q3*	**1 Right:** Is NOT supported by the stimulus **4 Wrong:** Is supported by the stimulus
7. If the statements above are true, then each of the following could also be true EXCEPT: *PrepTest49 Sec2 Q21*	**1 Right:** Must be false **4 Wrong:** Could be true
8. The facts described above provide the strongest evidence against which one of the following? *PrepTest57 Sec2 Q23*	**1 Right:** Is WEAKENED by the stimulus **4 Wrong:** Is not weakened by the stimulus (could be strengthened by or outside the scope of the stimulus)

LSAT STRATEGY

Some facts to remember about LSAT inferences:

- An inference follows only from the facts given. No outside knowledge is required.
- An inference need not be mind-blowing. Sometimes it will be simple, even obvious.
- An inference may come from a single fact, or it may require combining multiple facts. It may not be necessary to take into account all the facts given in the stimulus.

If the Inference question stems on the previous page reminded you of Logic Games questions, your instincts are correct. Your task in Inference questions is much like that in the Logic Games section, except here, you are working with sets of statements rather than with rules.

> ## TEST DAY TIP
>
> Just as it does in Logic Games, the test gives you everything you need to distinguish the one correct answer from the four wrong answers in Inference questions.

Apply the same discipline to Inference questions that you've learned to exercise in Logic Games. Answer the question directly from the statements. Make sure you consider what the statements do and do not mean. Consider the following:

> Most members of Alpha Beta Chi are in-state students, and most members of Alpha Beta Chi enjoy playing basketball.

Which of the following statements is a valid inference based on those statements?

Most A are B.
Most A are C.

> (1) Most members of Alpha Beta Chi are in-state students who enjoy playing basketball.
> (2) At least one member of Alpha Beta Chi is an in-state student who enjoys playing basketball.

Some A are B+C (at least 1)

In Inference questions, it is essential that you avoid adding statements based on outside knowledge or on your own assumptions. What is your first reaction to the following statements?

> The school cafeteria managers surveyed 500 female and 500 male students on their preference between honeydew melon and cantaloupe. The results were surprising. The female students overwhelmingly preferred honeydew.

Cataloging and Paraphrasing Statements in the Stimulus

Without an argument in the stimulus to analyze, untrained test takers may have difficulty knowing where to focus their attention in Inference stimuli. Expert test takers read strategically, paraphrasing the statements, and then catalog them according to five criteria.

To make valid inferences, LSAT experts:

1. Note the most concrete statements

2. Combine statements

3. Use Keywords

4. Use Formal Logic

5. Use uncertain statements

Here's how an LSAT expert might analyze and answer an Inference question.

LSAT Question	Analysis
In a vast ocean region, phosphorus levels have doubled in the past few decades due to agricultural runoff pouring out of a large river nearby. The phosphorus stimulates the growth of plankton near the ocean surface. Decaying plankton fall to the ocean floor, where bacteria devour them, consuming oxygen in the process. Due to the resulting oxygen depletion, few fish can survive in this region. $\longrightarrow$	**Step 2:** The statements in the stimulus describe a chain of events: 1) Agricultural runoff from a nearby river causes phosphorus levels to rise. 2) The phosphorous causes plankton to grow near the ocean surface. 3) Increased plankton leads to less oxygen. 4) Less oxygen leads to fewer fish.
Which one of the following can be properly inferred from the information above? $\longrightarrow$	**Step 1:** "[C]an be properly inferred from the information above" indicates an Inference question.
	Step 3: The correct answer must be true based on the statements above.
(A) The agricultural runoff pouring out of the river contributes to the growth of plankton near the ocean surface. $\longrightarrow$	**Step 4:** Correct. This inference is supported by combining the information in the first two sentences.
(B) Before phosphorus levels doubled in the ocean region, most fish were able to survive in that region. $\longrightarrow$	Outside the Scope. What happened before the phosphorous levels doubled is not discussed. Other problems could have killed fish, too. Eliminate.
(C) If agricultural runoff ceased pouring out of the river, there would be no bacteria on the ocean floor devouring decaying plankton. $\longrightarrow$	Outside the Scope. What happens once the agricultural runoff stops pouring out of the river is not discussed. Eliminate.
(D) The quantity of agricultural runoff pouring out of the river has doubled in the past few decades. $\longrightarrow$	This is a distortion of the first sentence. Phosphorous levels have doubled, but that doesn't mean that runoff has doubled. Eliminate.
(E) The amount of oxygen in a body of water is in general inversely proportional to the level of phosphorus in that body of water. *PrepTest61 Sec2 Q10* $\longrightarrow$	A tempting answer choice, but be careful: The statements in the stimulus refer to one river flowing into a particular part of the ocean. Drawing an inference about bodies of water *in general* goes too far. Additionally, although more phosphorus may result in less oxygen generally, nothing indicates the relationship is "inversely proportional." Eliminate.

handwritten annotation: (A) circled

handwritten annotation beside (B) and (C): outside scope

handwritten annotation beside (D): distort

Practice

Note the Most Concrete Statements to Make Valid Inferences

LSAT Question	My Analysis
9. Commentator: Recently, articles criticizing the environmental movement have been appearing regularly in newspapers. According to Winslow, this is due not so much to an antienvironmental bias among the media as to a preference on the part of newspaper editors for articles that seem "daring" in that they seem to challenge prevailing political positions. It is true that editors like to run antienvironmental pieces mainly because they seem to challenge the political orthodoxy. But serious environmentalism is by no means politically orthodox, and antienvironmentalists can hardly claim to be dissidents, however much they may have succeeded in selling themselves as renegades.	Step 2:
The commentator's statements, if true, most strongly support which one of the following? →	Step 1:
	Step 3:
(A) Winslow is correct about the preference of newspaper editors for controversial articles. →	Step 4:
(B) Critics of environmentalism have not successfully promoted themselves as renegades. →	
(C) Winslow's explanation is not consonant with the frequency with which critiques of environmentalism are published. →	
(D) The position attacked by critics of environmentalism is actually the prevailing political position. →	never said prevailing political position
(E) Serious environmentalism will eventually become a prevailing political position. →	

PrepTest51 Sec3 Q12

LSAT Question	My Analysis

10 Hemoglobin, a substance in human blood, transports oxygen from the lungs to the rest of the body. With each oxygen molecule it picks up, a hemoglobin molecule becomes more effective at picking up additional oxygen molecules until its maximum capacity of four oxygen molecules is reached. Grabbing an oxygen molecule changes the shape of the hemoglobin molecule, each time causing it literally to open itself to receive more oxygen.

Step 2: →

Which one of the following is most strongly supported by the information above? →

Step 1:

Step 3:

(A) A hemoglobin molecule that has picked up three oxygen molecules will probably acquire a fourth oxygen molecule. →

Step 4:

(B) The only factor determining how effective a hemoglobin molecule is at picking up oxygen molecules is how open the shape of that hemoglobin molecule is. →

(C) A hemoglobin molecule that has picked up three oxygen molecules will be more effective at picking up another oxygen molecule than will a hemoglobin molecule that has picked up only one oxygen molecule. →

(D) A hemoglobin molecule that has picked up four oxygen molecules will have the same shape as a hemoglobin molecule that has not picked up any oxygen molecules →

(E) Each hemoglobin molecule in human blood picks up between one and four oxygen molecules in or near the lungs and transports them to some other part of the body. →

too extreme

PrepTest59 Sec3 Q3

Combine Statements to Make Valid Inferences

LSAT Question	My Analysis
11. Market analyst: According to my research, 59 percent of consumers anticipate paying off their credit card balances in full before interest charges start to accrue, intending to use the cards only to avoid carrying cash and writing checks. This research also suggests that in trying to win business from their competitors, credit card companies tend to concentrate on improving the services their customers are the most interested in. Therefore, my research would lead us to expect that _____.	**Step 2:**
Which one of the following most logically completes the market analyst's argument?	**Step 1:**
	Step 3:
(A) most customers would be indifferent about which company's credit card they use	**Step 4:**
(B) credit card companies would not make the interest rates they charge on cards the main selling point	
(C) most consumers would prefer paying interest on credit card debts over borrowing money from banks	
(D) most consumers would ignore the length of time a credit card company allows to pay the balance due before interest accrues	
(E) the most intense competition among credit card companies would be over the number of places that they can get to accept their credit card	

PrepTest59 Sec2 Q24

LSAT Question	My Analysis
12. Members of large-animal species must consume enormous amounts of food to survive. When climatic conditions in their environment deteriorate, such animals are often unable to find enough food. This fact helps make large-animal species more vulnerable to extinction than small-animal species, which can maintain greater populations on smaller amounts of food. →	**Step 2:**
The statements above, if true, most support which one of the following? →	**Step 1:**
	Step 3:
(A) The maximum population size that an animal species could maintain on any given amount of food is the main factor determining whether that species will become extinct. →	**Step 4:**
(B) The vulnerability of an animal species to extinction depends at least in part on how much food individuals of that species must consume to survive. →	
(C) When conditions deteriorate in a given environment, no small-animal species will become extinct unless some large-animal species also becomes extinct. →	
(D) Within any given species, the prospects for survival of any particular individual depend primarily on the amount of food that individual requires. →	
(E) Whenever climatic conditions in a given environment are bad enough to threaten large-animal species with extinction, small-animal species are able to find enough food to survive. →	

PrepTest49 Sec2 Q9

LSAT Question	My Analysis

13. Historian: The standard "QWERTY" configuration of the keys on typewriters and computer keyboards was originally designed to be awkward and limit typing speed. This was because early typewriters would jam frequently if adjacent keys were struck in quick succession. Experiments have shown that keyboard configurations more efficient than QWERTY can double typing speed while tremendously reducing typing effort. However, the expense and inconvenience of switching to a new keyboard configuration prevent any configuration other than QWERTY from attaining widespread use.

Step 2:

Which one of the following is most strongly supported by the historian's statements?

Step 1:

Step 3:

(A) Most people who have tried typing with non-QWERTY keyboards have typed significantly more quickly using those keyboards than they usually have done using QWERTY keyboards.

Step 4:

(B) Early QWERTY typewriters were less likely to jam than were at least some more recent typewriters if adjacent keys were struck in quick succession.

(C) If the designers of early typewriters had foreseen the possibility that technology would make it possible for adjacent keyboard keys to be struck in rapid succession without jamming, then they would not have proposed the QWERTY configuration.

(D) The benefit to society that would result from switching to a keyboard configuration other than QWERTY is significantly greater than the overall cost of such a switch.

(E) If the keyboard had been designed for computers, then it would not have been designed to limit typing speed.

PrepTest59 Sec3 Q21

437

Use Keywords to Make Valid Inferences

LSAT Question	My Analysis

14. Baxe Interiors, one of the largest interior design companies in existence, currently has a near monopoly in the corporate market. Several small design companies have won prestigious awards for their corporate work, while Baxe has won none. Nonetheless, the corporate managers → who solicit design proposals will only contract with companies they believe are unlikely to go bankrupt, and they believe that only very large companies are unlikely to go bankrupt.

Step 2:

The statements above, if true, most strongly support which one of the following? →

Step 1:

Step 3:

(A) There are other very large design companies besides Baxe, but they produce designs that → are inferior to Baxe's.

Step 4: *outside scope*

(B) Baxe does not have a near monopoly in the market of any category of interior design other → than corporate interiors.

(C) For the most part, designs that are produced by small companies are superior to the designs → produced by Baxe.

(D) At least some of the corporate managers who solicit design proposals are unaware that there → are designs that are much better than those produced by Baxe.

(E) The existence of interior designs that are superior to those produced by Baxe does not → currently threaten its near monopoly in the corporate market.

PrepTest61 Sec4 Q7

LSAT Question	My Analysis

15. A theoretical framework facilitates conceptual organization of material and fruitful expansions of research. Many historians argue that historical analysis is therefore done best within a theoretical framework. But the past is too complex for all of its main trends to be captured within a theoretical framework. Therefore, _____.

$\longrightarrow$

Step 2:

Which one of the following most logically completes the argument?

$\longrightarrow$

Step 1:

Step 3:

(A) there is no benefit ever to be gained in recommending to historians that they place their work within a theoretical framework $\longrightarrow$

Step 4:

(B) theoretical frameworks are less useful in history than they are in any other discipline $\longrightarrow$

(C) even the best historical analysis done within a theoretical framework fails to capture all of history's main trends $\longrightarrow$

(D) the value of theoretical work in extending research has been emphasized by historians who recommend doing historical analysis within a theoretical framework $\longrightarrow$

(E) there is no difference between historical analysis that is placed within a theoretical framework and historical analysis that is not $\longrightarrow$

PrepTest59 Sec2 Q12

Use Formal Logic to Make Valid Inferences

It is important that you know how to spot Formal Logic in all of its forms, including those that use terms such as *only*, *only if*, and *unless*. It's also important to be comfortable making Formal Logic contrapositives. Formal Logic appears in many forms in Inference stimuli. Conditional statements in Inference questions are often long and complex.

Review the following examples of conditional statements, convert them to Formal Logic abbreviations, and determine their contrapositives.

Sentence from LSAT Question	My Analysis
16. No one who is fully informed about the diseases caused by microorganisms will ever fall victim to those diseases. *PrepTest45 Sec4 Q9* →	If informed about diseases caused by microorganisms → you will not fall victim to disease
17. To be great, an artwork must express a deep emotion, such as sorrow or love. *PrepTest49 Sec4 Q10* →	If Artwork great → expresses deep emotion
18. A computer can create an artwork that expresses sorrow or love ~~only if~~ it has actually experienced such an emotion. *PrepTest49 Sec4 Q10* →	draw arrow through "only if" which means "then"

TEST DAY TIP

LSAT experts vary in how much Formal Logic they write out in their test booklets. In practice, get used to jotting down translations and contrapositives so that you'll be ready to do so when it is helpful on Test Day.

LSAT Question	My Analysis
19. To be great, an artwork must express a deep emotion, such as sorrow or love. But an artwork cannot express an emotion that the artwork's creator is incapable of experiencing. →	**Step 2:** If great art → express deep emotion if creator can't experience emotions → art wont express them
Which one of the following can be properly inferred from the statements above? →	**Step 1:** if great art → creator capable of experiencing emotion
	Step 3:
(A) A computer can create an artwork that expresses sorrow or love only if it has actually experienced such an emotion. →	**Step 4:**
(B) The greatest art is produced by those who have experienced the deepest emotions. →	
(C) An artwork that expresses a deep emotion of its creator is a great artwork. →	
(D) As long as computers are constructed so as to be incapable of experiencing emotions they will not create great artworks. →	
(E) Only artworks that succeed in expressing deep emotions are the products of great artists.	

PrepTest49 Sec4 Q10 →

LSAT Question	My Analysis
20. Commentator: If a political administration is both economically successful and successful at protecting individual liberties, then it is an overall success. Even an administration that fails to care for the environment may succeed overall if it protects individual liberties. So far, the present administration has not cared for the environment but has successfully protected individual liberties. →	**Step 2:**
If all of the statements above are true, then which one of the following must be true? →	**Step 1:**
	Step 3:
(A) The present administration is economically successful. →	**Step 4:**
(B) The present administration is not an overall success. →	
(C) If the present administration is economically successful, then it is an overall success. →	
(D) If the present administration had been economically successful, it would have cared for the environment. →	
(E) If the present administration succeeds at environmental protection, then it will be an overall success →	

PrepTest61 Sec2 Q3

LSAT Question	My Analysis
21. At a gathering at which bankers, athletes, and lawyers are present, all of the bankers are athletes and none of the lawyers are bankers.	**Step 2:** bankers = athletes if lawyer → ~banker if banker → athlete if banker → ~lawyer if ~ath → ~banker
If the statements above are true, which one of the following statements must also be true?	**Step 1:**
	Step 3:

(A) All of the athletes are bankers.	**Step 4:**
(B) Some of the lawyers are not athletes.	→
(C) Some of the athletes are not lawyers.	→
(D) All of the bankers are lawyers.	→
(E) None of the lawyers are athletes. *PrepTest59 Sec2 Q19*	don't know how lawyers relate to athletes

443

Use Uncertain Statements to Make Valid Inferences

Not all Inference question stimuli present concrete, or even conditional, statements. Terms such as *most, many, often, several,* and *some* indicate statements that lack absolute certainty.

Consider the following statements:

· Many of the birds that live near this lake are ducks.

· Some of the marbles in this jar are cracked.

· I go running often.

· Most of the restaurants in this town close before midnight.

Uncertain statements can't always be combined to make deductions. The LSAT will test you on your knowledge of when it is appropriate to combine information and when it is not appropriate.

In this set of statements, can you combine the information to make a further deduction? *NO*

at least 1 Some of the books in this library were written by French authors.
Some of the books in this library were written on a typewriter.

What about these statements—can you combine them to make a further deduction?

Most of the cars in this parking lot are red.
Most of the cars in this parking lot are over ten years old.

some of cars in lot are red
& over 10 yrs

2 "mosts" ≠ an "all" or "most"

LSAT STRATEGY

Levels of Certainty

Here are the types of statements you'll encounter in Inference stimuli, arranged from most concrete to least:

· **Unqualified Assertions** (e.g., *Bob is an attorney* or *Monday will be a rainy day*)
· **Conditional Statements/Formal Logic** (e.g., *If the company hopes to meet its budget, then it must cut travel costs* or *McLaren will lose the election unless the county sees record voter turnout*)
· **Statements with *most*—**This means *more than half* but could include *all* (e.g., *Most of Company Y's employees are college graduates* or *A majority of the respondents preferred the new logo*).
· **Statements with *some* or *few*—**This means anywhere from one to all, just not zero (e.g., *Some architects are painters*).

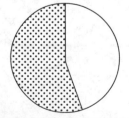

MOST of the circle has dots

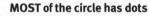
MOST of the circle has lines

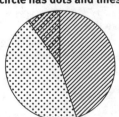
At least SOME of the circle has dots and lines

LSAT Question	My Analysis
22. Most veterinarians, and especially those at university veterinary research centers, have a devoted interest in the biological sciences. But most veterinarians choose their profession primarily because they love animals. Among persons who are seriously interested in biological science but lack any special love for animals, one does not find any prominent veterinarians. $\longrightarrow$	**Step 2:**
If all of the statements above are true, which one of the following CANNOT be true? $\longrightarrow$	**Step 1:**
	Step 3:
(A) Some veterinarians have a greater love for biological science than for individual animals. $\longrightarrow$	**Step 4:**
(B) Most veterinarians love animals and have an interest in biological science. $\longrightarrow$	
(C) Prominent veterinarians at some veterinary research centers are intensely devoted to the biological sciences but do not feel any pronounced affection for animals. $\longrightarrow$	*contradicts last sentence*
(D) Few veterinarians at university research centers chose their profession primarily because they love animals. $\longrightarrow$	
(E) Most veterinarians who are not prominent regard an understanding of the biological sciences as the most important quality for success in their profession. $\longrightarrow$	

PrepTest49 Sec4 Q5

LSAT Question	**My Analysis**

23. Most opera singers who add demanding roles to their repertoires at a young age lose their voices early. It has been said that this is because their voices have not yet matured and hence lack the power for such roles. But young singers with great vocal power are the most likely to ruin their voices. The real problem is that most young singers lack the technical training necessary to avoid straining their vocal cords—especially when using their full vocal strength. Such misuse of the cords inevitably leads to a truncated singing career.

→ **Step 2:**

Which one of the following does the information above most strongly support?

→ **Step 1:**

Step 3:

(A) Young opera singers without great vocal power are unlikely to ruin their voices by singing demanding roles. → **Step 4:**

(B) Some young opera singers ruin their voices while singing demanding roles because their vocal cords have not yet matured. →

(C) Only opera singers with many years of technical training should try to sing demanding roles. →

(D) Only mature opera singers can sing demanding roles without undue strain on their vocal cords. →

(E) Most young opera singers who sing demanding roles strain their vocal cords. →

PrepTest51 Sec3 Q21

LSAT Question	**My Analysis**
24. Forester: The great majority of the forests remaining in the world are only sickly fragments of the fully functioning ecosystems they once were. These fragmented forest ecosystems have typically lost their ability to sustain themselves in the long term, yet they include the last refuges for some of the world's most endangered species. To maintain its full complement of plant and animal species, a fragmented forest requires regular interventions by resource managers.	Step 2:
The forester's statements, if true, most strongly support which one of the following?	Step 1:
	Step 3:
(A) Most of the world's forests will lose at least some of their plant or animal species if no one intervenes.	Step 4:
(B) Unless resource managers regularly intervene in most of the world's remaining forests, many of the world's most endangered species will not survive.	
(C) A fragmented forest ecosystem cannot sustain itself in the long term if it loses any of its plant or animal species.	
(D) A complete, fully functioning forest ecosystem can always maintain its full complement of plant and animal species even without interventions by resource managers.	
(E) At present, resource managers intervene regularly in only some of the world's fragmented forest ecosystems.	

PrepTest49 Sec4 Q19

Expert Analysis: Inference Questions

LSAT Question	Analysis
9. Commentator: Recently, articles criticizing the environmental movement have been appearing regularly in newspapers. According to Winslow, this is due not so much to an antienvironmental bias among the media as to a preference on the part of newspaper editors for articles that seem "daring" in that they seem to challenge prevailing political positions. It is true that editors like to run antienvironmental pieces mainly because they seem to challenge the political orthodoxy. But serious environmentalism is by no means politically orthodox, and antienvironmentalists can hardly claim to be dissidents, however much they may have succeeded in selling themselves as renegades.	**Step 2:** Background: 1) Newspapers' anti-EM articles ↑ 2) Winslow's reason: Editors want to *appear* "daring"/unorthodox Commentator's view: 3) Winslow is right! *but* 4) Serious EM is not orthodox, and 5) Anti-EM aren't dissidents (even if they convince people they are)
The commentator's statements, if true, most strongly support which one of the following?	**Step 1:** The statements above "most strongly support" the correct answer—Inference question.
	Step 3: The commentator agrees with Winslow—editors attack EM to appear "daring"; but "serious" EM is not orthodox, and anti-EM isn't daring or unorthodox. The right answer follows from those views.
(A) Winslow is correct about the preference of newspaper editors for controversial articles.	**Step 4:** Correct. One of the definitive statements confirms this preference.
(B) Critics of environmentalism have not successfully promoted themselves as renegades.	180. This contradicts the last clause: Antienvironmentalists may have succeeded at least a little bit. Eliminate.
(C) Winslow's explanation is not consonant with the frequency with which critiques of environmentalism are published.	180. In fact, Winslow is right about why the critiques are so common. Eliminate.
(D) The position attacked by critics of environmentalism is actually the prevailing political position.	180/Distortion. The commentator thinks "serious" environmentalism is unorthodox. However, it's not clear whether the anti-EM critics are attacking the "prevailing" position. Either way, eliminate.
(E) Serious environmentalism will eventually become a prevailing political position. *PrepTest51 Sec3 Q12*	Outside the Scope. The commentator makes no predictions about future events. Eliminate.

NOTE: The correct answer came directly from the commentator's clearest position: Winslow is right. Three of the wrong answers contradicted or distorted one or more of the commentator's stronger statements.

LSAT Question	Analysis
10. Hemoglobin, a substance in human blood, transports oxygen from the lungs to the rest of the body. With each oxygen molecule it picks up, a hemoglobin molecule becomes more effective at picking up additional oxygen molecules until its maximum capacity of four oxygen molecules is reached. Grabbing an oxygen molecule changes the shape of the hemoglobin molecule, each time causing it literally to open itself to receive more oxygen. $\longrightarrow$	**Step 2:** Three definitive statements: 1) Hemoglobin transports oxygen through the body. 2) More oxygen molecules = hemoglobin more effective at getting oxygen molecules (max 4). 3) Hemoglobin changes shape each time it grabs an oxygen molecule.
Which one of the following is most strongly supported by the information above? $\longrightarrow$	**Step 1:** "[M]ost supported by the information above" indicates an Inference question.
	Step 3: Each statement is definitive and clear. Check each answer choice against the statements: The four wrong answer choices are not supported by the statements; the correct answer choice is.
(A) A hemoglobin molecule that has picked up three oxygen molecules will probably acquire a fourth oxygen molecule. $\longrightarrow$	**Step 4:** Close, but Extreme. The second statement does not say how likely it is that hemoglobin will reach its maximum of four molecules. Maybe there aren't any available molecules to pick up. Eliminate.
(B) The only factor determining how effective a hemoglobin molecule is at picking up oxygen molecules is how open the shape of that hemoglobin molecule is. $\longrightarrow$	The word *only* makes this Extreme. There could be factors other than shape. Eliminate.
(C) A hemoglobin molecule that has picked up three oxygen molecules will be more effective at picking up another oxygen molecule than will a hemoglobin molecule that has picked up only one oxygen molecule. $\longrightarrow$	Correct. This follows directly from the author's second statement.
(D) A hemoglobin molecule that has picked up four oxygen molecules will have the same shape as a hemoglobin molecule that has not picked up any oxygen molecules. $\longrightarrow$	180. The last sentence states that the hemoglobin molecule changes shape each time it picks up an oxygen molecule. Eliminate.
(E) Each hemoglobin molecule in human blood picks up between one and four oxygen molecules in or near the lungs and transports them to some other part of the body. *PrepTest59 Sec3 Q3* $\longrightarrow$	Extreme. It's reasonable to infer that some hemoglobin molecules follow this process, but to say that *each* molecule does so goes too far. They can pick up oxygen, but it is not required that *each* one does so—perhaps some pick up none at all. Eliminate.

LSAT Question	Analysis
11. Market analyst: According to my research, 59 percent of consumers anticipate paying off their credit card balances in full before interest charges start to accrue, intending to use the cards only to avoid carrying cash and writing checks. This research also suggests that in trying to win business from their competitors, credit card companies tend to concentrate on improving the services their customers are the most interested in. Therefore, my research would lead us to expect that _____.	**Step 2:** Two statements: 1) Research shows that most credit card customers intend to pay off cards before they begin to accrue interest. 2) "This research also suggests" that, to win customers, credit card companies tend to focus on services in which customers are most interested.
Which one of the following most logically completes the market analyst's argument?	**Step 1:** The correct answer "completes the . . . argument." It serves as a conclusion to the stimulus's evidence, so this is an Inference question.
	Step 3: Consumers don't plan to carry balances, so they likely aren't too concerned with interest rates. Because credit card companies tend to focus on features in which customers are interested, *they will focus on something other than interest rates.*
(A) most customers would be indifferent about which company's credit card they use	**Step 4:** Distortion. The research findings indicate that customers decide which credit card to carry mostly based on the features in which they are interested. So although interest rates may not matter, other features might. Eliminate.
(B) credit card companies would not make the interest rates they charge on cards the main selling point	Correct. This is the answer that follows from combining the analyst's two findings.
(C) most consumers would prefer paying interest on credit card debts over borrowing money from banks	Irrelevant Comparison. The stimulus does not discuss preferences in *paying* interest (rather, a desire to *avoid* interest) and says nothing at all about borrowing from banks. Eliminate.
(D) most consumers would ignore the length of time a credit card company allows to pay the balance due before interest accrues	Outside the Scope. The length of time allowed before interest begins to accrue is not discussed. Eliminate.
(E) the most intense competition among credit card companies would be over the number of places that they can get to accept their credit card *PrepTest59 Sec2 Q24*	Outside the Scope. The stimulus does not even hint at a discussion of places where a credit card is accepted. Eliminate.

LSAT Question	Analysis
12. Members of large-animal species must consume enormous amounts of food to survive. When climatic conditions in their environment deteriorate, such animals are often unable to find enough food. This fact helps make large-animal species more vulnerable to extinction than small-animal species, which can maintain greater populations on smaller amounts of food.	**Step 2:** Four related statements: 1) Large animals need a lot of food to survive. 2) Changes in climate make it harder for large animals to find enough food. 3) Small animals need less food. 4) Statement 2 makes large animals more vulnerable to extinction than small animals are.
The statements above, if true, most support which one of the following?	**Step 1:** Statements in the stimulus "support" the correct answer choice—an Inference question.
	Step 3: The correct answer is supported by the statements above.
(A) The maximum population size that an animal species could maintain on any given amount of food is the main factor determining whether that species will become extinct.	**Step 4:** Outside the Scope/Extreme. The stimulus never discusses maximum population, only greater population size. Moreover, calling food availability the *main* factor in extinction goes too far. Eliminate.
(B) The vulnerability of an animal species to extinction depends at least in part on how much food individuals of that species must consume to survive.	Correct. This is a summary of all four statements in the stimulus. "[A]t least in part" ensures that this answer is not too extreme to follow from the stimulus.
(C) When conditions deteriorate in a given environment, no small-animal species will become extinct unless some large-animal species also becomes extinct.	Extreme. Small-animal species don't need as much food, but there could be other factors leading to a small-animal species's extinction before any large-animal species's extinctions. Eliminate.
(D) Within any given species, the prospects for survival of any particular individual depend primarily on the amount of food that individual requires.	This choice narrows the scope to individual animals within specific species. The stimulus compares only small- and large-animal species, not individual animals. Eliminate.
(E) Whenever climatic conditions in a given environment are bad enough to threaten large-animal species with extinction, small-animal species are able to find enough food to survive. *PrepTest49 Sec2 Q9*	Extreme. If conditions were severe enough, perhaps no species could find enough food to survive. Eliminate.

LSAT Question	Analysis
13. Historian: The standard "QWERTY" configuration of the keys on typewriters and computer keyboards was originally designed to be awkward and limit typing speed. This was because early typewriters would jam frequently if adjacent keys were struck in quick succession. Experiments have shown that keyboard configurations more efficient than QWERTY can double typing speed while tremendously reducing typing effort. However, the expense and inconvenience of switching to a new keyboard configuration prevent any configuration other than QWERTY from attaining widespread use.	**Step 2:** Five related statements: 1) QWERTY keyboards originally designed to make typing slower and harder. *because* 2) Old typewriters would jam. 3) Faster, easier keyboards could be designed for computers now. *but* 4) They probably won't be used. *because* 5) Everyone is familiar with QWERTY keyboards, and switching is expensive and difficult.
Which one of the following is most strongly supported by the historian's statements?	**Step 1:** The correct answer is "strongly supported by" the stimulus—an Inference question.
	Step 3: The statements combine to allow for several possible inferences focusing on the differences between old typewriters and computers. The correct answer will follow from the stimulus statements.
(A) Most people who have tried typing with non-QWERTY keyboards have typed significantly more quickly using those keyboards than they usually have done using QWERTY keyboards.	**Step 4:** Extreme. Faster typing is possible with new keyboards, but that doesn't mean that over half of those who have used them typed significantly faster. Eliminate.
(B) Early QWERTY typewriters were less likely to jam than were at least some more recent typewriters if adjacent keys were struck in quick succession.	Distortion/180. Because all typewriters used QWERTY, which was designed to prevent jamming, there's no reason to believe this statement. If anything, one would suspect that newer typewriters solved jamming problems in other ways. Eliminate.
(C) If the designers of early typewriters had foreseen the possibility that technology would make it possible for adjacent keyboard keys to be struck in rapid succession without jamming, then they would not have proposed the QWERTY configuration.	Distortion. The need for a keyboard that worked well with old typewriters might still have prompted the use of QWERTY; it's unlikely that the world would have gone decades without typing. The stimulus doesn't give us enough information to draw this inference. Eliminate.
(D) The benefit to society that would result from switching to a keyboard configuration other than QWERTY is significantly greater than the overall cost of such a switch.	180. The passage suggests that the difficulty of learning a new keyboard will deter a switch to new faster, easier keyboards. Eliminate.
(E) If the keyboard had been designed for computers, then it would not have been designed to limit typing speed. *PrepTest59 Sec3 Q21*	Correct. Computers don't have problems with jamming, so faster, easier keyboards can be used, and so we wouldn't have developed the familiarity with QWERTY that deters the use of faster, easier keyboards now.

LSAT Question	Analysis
14. Baxe Interiors, one of the largest interior design companies in existence, currently has a near monopoly in the corporate market. Several small design companies have won prestigious awards for their corporate work, while Baxe has won none. Nonetheless, the corporate managers who solicit design proposals will only contract with companies they believe are unlikely to go bankrupt, and they believe that only very large companies are unlikely to go bankrupt.	**Step 2:** Three facts about Baxe: 1) It's large; 2) it has a near monopoly on the corporate market; and 3) it has *not* won any design awards. One fact about small design companies: Several have won design awards. *Nevertheless* Corporate managers will only use large companies, the only ones they believe are unlikely to go bankrupt.
The statements above, if true, most strongly support which one of the following?	**Step 1:** The statements above "strongly support" an answer choice below—an Inference question.
	Step 3: The author explicitly contrasts his belief that corporate managers will continue to use large companies with the fact that Baxe (a large company) has no design awards while several small companies have won such awards. These statements support the correct answer.
(A) There are other very large design companies besides Baxe, but they produce designs that are inferior to Baxe's.	**Step 4:** The stimulus states only that Baxe is one of the largest interior design companies; there is no information about other large companies or the quality of their designs. Eliminate.
(B) Baxe does not have a near monopoly in the market of any category of interior design other than corporate interiors.	Outside the Scope. The stimulus says nothing about categories of interior design other than corporate interiors. Eliminate.
(C) For the most part, designs that are produced by small companies are superior to the designs produced by Baxe.	Extreme. Several small companies have won awards for their corporate work, but this says nothing about small companies overall. Eliminate.
(D) At least some of the corporate managers who solicit design proposals are unaware that there are designs that are much better than those produced by Baxe.	Outside the Scope. Corporate managers may or may not be aware of design quality; even if they are, they contract with companies they consider stable. Eliminate.
(E) The existence of interior designs that are superior to those produced by Baxe does not currently threaten its near monopoly in the corporate market. *PrepTest61 Sec4 Q7*	Correct. Baxe should continue to get business from corporate managers because of its large size (and perceived stability), and should thus hold onto its monopoly despite not winning awards.

LSAT Question	Analysis
15. A theoretical framework facilitates conceptual organization of material and fruitful expansions of research. Many historians argue that historical analysis is therefore done best within a theoretical framework. But the past is too complex for all of its main trends to be captured within a theoretical framework. Therefore, _____. →	**Step 2:** Background about theoretical frameworks followed by two contrasting assertions: 1) Many historians say that historical analysis is best done within a theoretical framework. *but* 2) The past is too complex for all of its main trends to be captured in a theoretical framework. *So, _____.*
Which one of the following most logically completes the argument? →	**Step 1:** "[M]ost logically completes the argument" indicates an Inference question. This stimulus ends with "Therefore, _____," so the correct answer represents the conclusion of an argument based on the evidence in the stimulus.
	Step 3: Predict the author's conclusion. The Keyword *but* indicates that the author disagrees with historians who prefer a theoretical framework because such frameworks cannot capture all of history's main trends.
(A) there is no benefit ever to be gained in recommending to historians that they place their work within a theoretical framework →	**Step 4:** Extreme. Just because it has one disadvantage (it can't capture all main trends) does not mean that a theoretical framework has *no* benefit. Eliminate.
(B) theoretical frameworks are less useful in history than they are in any other discipline →	Irrelevant Comparison/Extreme. Whether (and to what extent) theoretical frameworks are useful in other disciplines is irrelevant here. Eliminate.
(C) even the best historical analysis done within a theoretical framework fails to capture all of history's main trends →	Correct. If the author's statements are accurate, this must be true.
(D) the value of theoretical work in extending research has been emphasized by historians who recommend doing historical analysis within a theoretical framework →	This combines the background information about theoretical frameworks with the statement that some historians like them. However, it misses entirely the statement following [b]ut in the stimulus, so it cannot be the author's conclusion. Eliminate.
(E) there is no difference between historical analysis that is placed within a theoretical framework and historical analysis that is not *PrepTest59 Sec2 Q12* →	Irrelevant Comparison. The stimulus does not discuss other types of analyses. They may or may not differ from theoretical frameworks. Eliminate.

Sentence from LSAT Question	Analysis	
16. No one who is fully informed about the diseases caused by microorganisms will ever fall victim to those diseases. *PrepTest45 Sec4 Q9* →	If fully informed about diseases	→ not fall victim to those diseases
	If fall victim to those diseases	→ not fully informed about diseases
17. To be great, an artwork must express a deep emotion, such as sorrow or love. *PrepTest49 Sec4 Q10* →	If great art	→ express deep emotion
	If not express deep emotion	→ not great art
18. A computer can create an artwork that expresses sorrow or love only if it has actually experienced such an emotion. *PrepTest49 Sec4 Q10* →	If expresses sorrow OR love	→ has actually experienced such an emotion
	If has not actually experienced such an emotion	→ cannot express sorrow AND cannot express love

LSAT Question	Analysis
19. To be great, an artwork must express a deep emotion, such as sorrow or love. But an artwork cannot express an emotion that the artwork's creator is incapable of experiencing.	**Step 2:** Two Formal Logic statements: 1) If *great art* → *express a deep emotion* If *not express a deep emotion* → *not great art* 2) If *art expresses an emotion* → *creator capable of experiencing that emotion* If *creator incapable of experiencing an emotion* → *art cannot express that emotion*
Which one of the following can be properly inferred from the statements above?	**Step 1:** The correct answer is "properly inferred" from the statements above—Inference question. The correct answer must be true based on the stimulus.
	Step 3: Combine the statements: If *a creator is incapable of experiencing deep emotion* → *art cannot be great*

LSAT Question (cont.)	**Analysis (cont.)**
(A) A computer can create an artwork that expresses sorrow or love only if it has actually experienced such an emotion. $\longrightarrow$	**Step 4:** If *computer can* $\longrightarrow$ *has experienced that* *create art* *emotion* *expressing* *sorrow/love* For art to express an emotion, its creator must be *capable* of experiencing an emotion. This answer choice distorts that into "*has* experienced" an emotion. Eliminate.
(B) The greatest art is produced by those who have experienced the deepest emotions. $\longrightarrow$	Extreme. The stimulus says nothing about the *greatest* art. Eliminate.
(C) An artwork that expresses a deep emotion of its creator is a great artwork. $\longrightarrow$	If *art expresses* $\longrightarrow$ *great art* *deep emotion* This flips the necessary and sufficient terms in the Formal Logic of the first sentence. Being able to express deep emotion is necessary, not sufficient, for great artwork. Eliminate.
(D) As long as computers are constructed so as to be incapable of experiencing emotions they will not create great artworks. $\longrightarrow$	Correct. If *incapable of* $\longrightarrow$ *won't create great art* *experiencing* *emotions* This matches the prediction perfectly.
(E) Only artworks that succeed in expressing deep emotions are the products of great artists. *PrepTest49 Sec4 Q10* $\longrightarrow$	*Only* signifies a necessary condition. If *product of great* $\longrightarrow$ *succeeds in expressing* *artist* *deep emotion* Outside the Scope. Great art must express deep emotions, but perhaps not everything produced by a great artist is great art. Eliminate.

LSAT Question	Analysis

20. Commentator: If a political administration is both economically successful and successful at protecting individual liberties, then it is an overall success. Even an administration that fails to care for the environment may succeed overall if it protects individual liberties. So far, the present administration has not cared for the environment but has successfully protected individual liberties. →	**Step 2:** A principle expressed in Formal Logic and an assessment of the current administration:
	
	If *political admin.* → *overall success*
	  successful at econ.
	  AND at protecting
	  indiv. liberties
	
	Present administration: successful at protecting indiv. liberties
	
	The second sentence makes the present administration's failure to care for the environment irrelevant to an assessment of overall success.

If all of the statements above are true, then which one of the following must be true? →	**Step 1:** The correct answer "must be true" based on the stimulus—a classic Inference question stem.
	Step 3: Combine the Formal Logic statement and the statement in the last sentence: The present administration has met one of two conditions sufficient for overall success. The correct answer must be true based on these statements.
(A) The present administration is economically successful. →	**Step 4:** This cannot be inferred from the statements above. Eliminate.
(B) The present administration is not an overall success. →	This depends on whether the present administration is economically successful, and that is unknown here. Eliminate.
(C) If the present administration is economically successful, then it is an overall success. →	Correct. If this is true, then both sufficient conditions have been met, and the administration would be an overall success.
(D) If the present administration had been economically successful, it would have cared for the environment. →	Outside the Scope. We do not know what would have made the administration care or not care for the environment. Eliminate.
(E) If the present administration succeeds at environmental protection, then it will be an overall success.	The second half of the sufficient condition is a successful economy, not success protecting the environment. Eliminate.

PrepTest61 Sec2 Q3

LSAT Question	Analysis
21. At a gathering at which bankers, athletes, and lawyers are present, all of the bankers are athletes and none of the lawyers are bankers.	**Step 2:** Two Formal Logic statements about a meeting at which bankers, athletes, and lawyers are present: If banker → athlete If ~athlete → ~banker If lawyer → ~banker If banker → ~lawyer
If the statements above are true, which one of the following statements must also be true?	**Step 1:** The correct answer must be true if the statements in the stimulus are true—an Inference question.
	Step 3: None of the necessary terms in either statement matches a sufficient term in the other, so the statements cannot be combined to remove a redundant term. But note that *banker* is a sufficient term in both statements, thus: All of the bankers at the gathering are athletes and *not* lawyers. Because bankers are present at the gathering, there is at least one person in attendance who is a banker, an athlete, and not a lawyer.
(A) All of the athletes are bankers.	**Step 4:** The fact that all the bankers are athletes doesn't mean that all the athletes are bankers. This confuses sufficient and necessary terms. Eliminate.
(B) Some of the lawyers are not athletes.	The only thing we know about lawyers is that they are not bankers. But we don't know anything about people who are not bankers. Eliminate.
(C) Some of the athletes are not lawyers.	Correct. Based on the statements, you can deduce that there is at least one banker-athlete who is not a lawyer attending the gathering. This answer choice describes (at least) that person.
(D) All of the bankers are lawyers.	180. The bankers are *not* lawyers. Eliminate.
(E) None of the lawyers are athletes. *PrepTest59 Sec2 Q19*	The fact that some of the athletes in the crowd (those who are bankers) are not lawyers does not mean that all lawyers in attendance are not athletes. Eliminate.

LSAT Question	Analysis
22. Most veterinarians, and especially those at university veterinary research centers, have a devoted interest in the biological sciences. But most veterinarians choose their profession primarily because they love animals. Among persons who are seriously interested in biological science but lack any special love for animals, one does not find any prominent veterinarians. →	**Step 2:** Two uncertain statements followed by a conditional statement: 1) Most (over half of) vets are devoted to bio. 2) Most (over half of) vets love animals. 3) If *devoted to* → ~*prominent vet* *bio* AND ~*love animals* If *prominent* → ~*devoted to bio* *vet* OR *love animals*
If all of the statements above are true, which one of the following CANNOT be true? →	**Step 1:** Based on the statements, the correct answer cannot be true—a negative Inference question. The correct answer will directly contradict the stimulus; the four wrong answers could be true in light of the stimulus.
	Step 3: Because both uncertain statements involve over half of the vet population, there must be some overlap. At least one vet must be devoted to bio and love animals. The Formal Logic statement applies to any *prominent* vet.
(A) Some veterinarians have a greater love for biological science than for individual animals. →	**Step 4:** Irrelevant Comparison. Most vets have at least one of these characteristics; the stimulus doesn't compare the characteristics, however. Eliminate.
(B) Most veterinarians love animals and have an interest in biological science. →	Could be true. Most vets have one of these characteristics; it might be true that most have both. Eliminate.
(C) Prominent veterinarians at some veterinary research centers are intensely devoted to the biological sciences but do not feel any pronounced affection for animals. →	Correct. This choice contradicts the final sentence: There are no prominent vets who are seriously interested in bio but don't care intensely for animals.
(D) Few veterinarians at university research centers chose their profession primarily because they love animals. →	Could be true. Most vets overall choose their profession primarily because of their love of animals. This may not be true of those at research centers. Eliminate.
(E) Most veterinarians who are not prominent regard an understanding of the biological sciences as the most important quality for success in their profession. →	Could be true. The stimulus is silent on vets' opinions about what leads to *success* in the profession. Eliminate.

PrepTest49 Sec4 Q5

LSAT Question	Analysis
23. Most opera singers who add demanding roles to their repertoires at a young age lose their voices early. It has been said that this is because their voices have not yet matured and hence lack the power for such roles. But young singers with great vocal power are the most likely to ruin their voices. The real problem is that most young singers lack the technical training necessary to avoid straining their vocal cords—especially when using their full vocal strength. Such misuse of the cords inevitably leads to a truncated singing career. →	**Step 2:** Catalogue the statements: 1) [uncertain] Most (over half of) young opera singers with demanding roles will lose voice prematurely. 2) [a popular explanation] Some say this is because they don't have the power for the roles. *but* 3) [author's observation] Those with the most power are the ones most likely to ruin their voices. 4) [author's reason—"the real problem"] Most (over half of) young singers lack technical training *and* 5) [Formal Logic] Training is *necessary* to avoid straining the vocal cords. *and* 6) Strained vocal cords shorten singing careers.
Which one of the following does the information above most strongly support? →	**Step 1:** The information above strongly supports the correct answer—an Inference question.
	Step 3: Combine statements and make deductions: Most young opera singers with demanding roles lack the training *necessary* to avoid vocal strain. The correct answer is supported by these statements.
(A) Young opera singers without great vocal power are unlikely to ruin their voices by singing demanding roles. →	**Step 4:** Young singers with great vocal power are *most likely* to ruin their voices. Young singers without power may ruin their voices, too. Eliminate.
(B) Some young opera singers ruin their voices while singing demanding roles because their vocal cords have not yet matured. →	Distortion. This is what "has been said" by others. The author disagrees and presents an alternative theory (the "real problem"). Eliminate.
(C) Only opera singers with many years of technical training should try to sing demanding roles. →	Extreme. The author does not say technical training requires many years. Eliminate.
(D) Only mature opera singers can sing demanding roles without undue strain on their vocal cords. →	Extreme. Young singers *could* take on demanding roles without straining their vocal cords if they were properly trained. Eliminate.
(E) Most young opera singers who sing demanding roles strain their vocal cords. *PrepTest51 Sec3 Q21* →	Correct. The "real problem" is that most young singers lack the training required to avoid straining vocal cords when singing demanding roles.

LSAT Question	Analysis
24. Forester: The great majority of the forests remaining in the world are only sickly fragments of the fully functioning ecosystems they once were. These fragmented forest ecosystems have typically lost their ability to sustain themselves in the long term, yet they include the last refuges for some of the world's most endangered species. To maintain its full complement of plant and animal species, a fragmented forest requires regular interventions by resource managers. ⟶	**Step 2:** Catalogue the statements: 1) [uncertain] Most (over half of) remaining forests are just fragments of what they once were. 2) [uncertain] These fragmented forests have "typically" lost their ability to sustain themselves. 3) [uncertain] Fragmented forests are refuges for some of the world's endangered species. 4) [Formal Logic] Regular intervention by resource managers is *necessary* for fragmented forest to maintain all plant/animal species.
The forester's statements, if true, most strongly support which one of the following? ⟶	**Step 1:** The correct answer is supported by the statements in the stimulus—an Inference question.
	Step 3: The Formal Logic statement is the strongest here: If ~regular ⟶ fragmented intervention by resource managers forests will lose some plant/ animal species. Combined with the first sentence, you can deduce: Without regular intervention by resource managers, most forests will lose *some* species.
(A) Most of the world's forests will lose at least some of their plant or animal species if no one intervenes. ⟶	**Step 4:** Correct. This matches the deduction above.
(B) Unless resource managers regularly intervene in most of the world's remaining forests, many of the world's most endangered species will not survive. ⟶	Extreme. Fragmented forests contain *some* of the world's most endangered species. It is impossible to determine whether many such species would be lost without intervention in *most* of these forests. Eliminate.
(C) A fragmented forest ecosystem cannot sustain itself in the long term if it loses any of its plant or animal species. ⟶	Distortion. It is not clear that the loss of a single plant or animal species would make a forest unsustainable. Eliminate.
(D) A complete, fully functioning forest ecosystem can always maintain its full complement of plant and animal species even without interventions by resource managers. ⟶	Extreme ("always") and Outside the Scope. It's not known what complete, fully functioning forest ecosystems can do. Eliminate.
(E) At present, resource managers intervene regularly in only some of the world's fragmented forest ecosystems. ⟶	Outside the Scope. We have no way of knowing what resource managers are currently doing. Eliminate.

PrepTest49 Sec4 Q19

Perform

Now, complete some Inference questions on your own. In each of the following, look for opportunities to use any or all of the strategies you've learned in this section. Make inferences from concrete statements, combined statements, Keywords, Formal Logic, and uncertain statements.

LSAT Question	My Analysis
25. Although most people know what their bad habits are and want to rid themselves of them, a majority of these people find it very difficult to do so. This is because cessation of habitual behavior is immediately and vividly painful, while whatever benefit is to be gained by the absence of the habit is perceived only dimly because it is remote. →	Step 2:
The information above most strongly supports the statement that the people who are most successful at ending their bad habits are those who →	Step 1:
	Step 3:
(A) can vividly imagine remote but attainable benefit →	Step 4:
(B) can vividly imagine their present pain being felt in the future →	
(C) have succeeded in the past at modifying their behavior →	
(D) are relatively unaware of their own behavioral characteristics →	
(E) can vividly remember the pain caused them in the past by their bad habits →	

PrepTest59 Sec3 Q7

LSAT Question	My Analysis
26. Cable TV stations have advantages that enable them to attract many more advertisers than broadcast networks attract. For example, cable stations are able to target particular audiences with 24-hour news, sports, or movies, whereas broadcast networks must offer a variety of programming. Cable can also offer lower advertising rates than any broadcast network can, because it is subsidized by viewers through subscriber fees. Additionally, many cable stations have expanded worldwide with multinational programming.	**Step 2:** →
The statements above, if true, provide support for each of the following EXCEPT:	**Step 1:** →
	Step 3:
(A) Some broadcast networks can be viewed in several countries.	**Step 4:** *first sentence says cable TVs have advantages broadcast doesnt* →
(B) Broadcast networks do not rely on subscriber fees from viewers.	→
(C) Low costs are often an important factor for advertisers in selecting a station or network on which to run a TV ad.	→
(D) Some advertisers prefer to have the opportunity to address a worldwide audience.	→
(E) The audiences that some advertisers prefer to target watch 24-hour news stations.	→

PrepTest61 Sec4 Q3

LSAT Question	My Analysis
27. Often a type of organ or body structure is the only physically feasible means of accomplishing a given task, so it should be unsurprising if, like eyes or wings, that type of organ or body structure evolves at different times in a number of completely unrelated species. After all, whatever the difference of heritage and habitat, as organisms animals have fundamentally similar needs and so _____. →	**Step 2:**
Which one of the following most logically completes the last sentence of the passage? →	**Step 1:**
	Step 3:
(A) will often live in the same environment as other species quite different from themselves →	**Step 4:**
(B) will in many instances evolve similar adaptations enabling them to satisfy these needs →	
(C) will develop adaptations allowing them to satisfy these needs →	
(D) will resemble other species having different biological needs →	
(E) will all develop eyes or wings as adaptations →	

PrepTest61 Sec2 Q15

465

LSAT Question	My Analysis

28. The law of the city of Weston regarding contributions to mayoral campaigns is as follows: all contributions to these campaigns in excess of $100 made by nonresidents of Weston who are not former residents of Weston must be registered with the city council. Brimley's mayoral campaign clearly complied with this law since it accepted contributions only from residents and former residents of Weston.

Step 2:
→

If all the statements above are true, which one of the following statements must be true?

Step 1:
→

Step 3:

(A) No nonresident of Weston contributed in excess of $100 to Brimley's campaign.

Step 4:
→

(B) Some contributions to Brimley's campaign in excess of $100 were registered with the city council.

→

(C) No contributions to Brimley's campaign needed to be registered with the city council.

→

(D) All contributions to Brimley's campaign that were registered with the city council were in excess of $100.

→

(E) Brimley's campaign did not register any contributions with the city council.

PrepTest57 Sec2 Q25 →

LSAT Question	My Analysis
29. Most successful entrepreneurs work at least 18 hours a day, and no one who works at least 18 hours a day has time for leisure activities. But all happy entrepreneurs have time for leisure activities.	**Step 2:**

successful ent → 18 hr day
18 hrs → no leisure
happy ent → leisure

if no time for leisure →
not happy
entrep.

| If the statements above are true, each of the following could be true EXCEPT: | **Step 1:** |

Step 3:

| (A) Anyone who has no time for leisure activities works at least 18 hours a day. | **Step 4:** |

could be true

(B) Some entrepreneurs who work at least 18 hours a day are successful.

(C) Some happy entrepreneurs are successful.

(D) Some entrepreneurs who work at least 18 hours a day are happy.

(E) Some successful entrepreneurs work less than 18 hours a day.

PrepTest49 Sec2 Q16 →

LSAT Question	My Analysis
30. Art historian: More than any other genre of representational painting, still-life painting lends itself naturally to art whose goal is the artist's self-expression, rather than merely the reflection of a preexisting external reality. This is because in still-life painting, the artist invariably chooses, modifies, and arranges the objects to be painted. Thus, the artist has considerably more control over the composition and subject of a still-life painting than over those of a landscape painting or portrait, for example. ⟶	**Step 2:**
Which one of the following is most strongly supported by the art historian's statements? ⟶	**Step 1:**
	Step 3:
(A) Landscape painting and portraiture are the artistic genres that lend themselves most naturally to the mere reflection of a preexisting ⟶ external reality.	**Step 4:**
(B) The only way in which artists control the composition and subject of a painting is by choosing, modifying, and arranging the objects ⟶ to be represented in that painting.	
(C) Nonrepresentational painting does not lend itself as naturally as still-life painting does to the goal of the artist's self-expression. ⟶	
(D) In genres of representational painting other than still-life painting, the artist does not always choose, modify, and arrange the objects to be ⟶ painted.	
(E) When painting a portrait, artists rarely attempt to express themselves through the choice, modification, or arrangement of the background elements against which the subject of the portrait ⟶ is painted.	

PrepTest57 Sec3 Q13

Expert Analysis: Inference Questions

Compare your work to that of an LSAT expert. Note the strategies the expert employed in each of these questions. Were you able to make inferences from concrete statements, combined statements, Keywords, Formal Logic, and uncertain statements?

LSAT Question	Analysis
25. Although most people know what their bad habits are and want to rid themselves of them, a majority of these people find it very difficult to do so. This is because cessation of habitual behavior is immediately and vividly painful, while whatever benefit is to be gained by the absence of the habit is perceived only dimly because it is remote.	**Step 2:** Two uncertain statements and an explanation: 1) Most (over half of) people know their bad habits and want to end them. 2) Most (over half of) people who know their bad habits and want to end them, find it hard to end their bad habits. *This is because* 3) The pain of ending bad habits is tangible. *but* 4) The benefits of ending bad habits are remote and hard to perceive.
The information above most strongly supports the statement that the people who are most successful at ending their bad habits are those who	**Step 1:** The stimulus "strongly supports" the correct answer—an Inference question. Here, the correct answer will define the characteristic(s) of people successful at ending bad habits.
	Step 3: Those who succeed at breaking bad habits must be either less susceptible to the pain of withdrawal or better at perceiving distant/hard to imagine benefits. The correct answer will follow from these statements.
(A) can vividly imagine remote but attainable benefit	**Step 4:** Correct. This follows directly from statement 4 in the stimulus.
(B) can vividly imagine their present pain being felt in the future	Distortion. It is withdrawal that causes pain. And it is the future benefit of quitting that must be imagined. Eliminate.
(C) have succeeded in the past at modifying their behavior	Outside the Scope. The stimulus says nothing about those who have modified their behavior previously. Eliminate.
(D) are relatively unaware of their own behavioral characteristics	Distortion/180. The stimulus says that most people are aware of their bad habits and the difficulty of ending them, but says nothing to suggest that being unaware would help a person succeed in quitting. Eliminate.
(E) can vividly remember the pain caused them in the past by their bad habits *PrepTest59 Sec3 Q7*	Distortion. The stimulus mentions the pain of *withdrawal,* not pain caused by engaging in bad habits. Eliminate.

LSAT Question	Analysis
26. Cable TV stations have advantages that enable them to attract many more advertisers than broadcast networks attract. For example, cable stations are able to target particular audiences with 24-hour news, sports, or movies, whereas broadcast networks must offer a variety of programming. Cable can also offer lower advertising rates than any broadcast network can, because it is subsidized by viewers through subscriber fees. Additionally, many cable stations have expanded worldwide with multinational programming.	**Step 2:** An assertion illustrated by three examples: Cable TV stations have advantages over broadcast networks in attracting advertisers. *Examples*: 1) Cable can target specific demographics *better* than broadcast. 2) Cable can offer advertising rates *lower* than broadcast (because cable charges subscribers and broadcast doesn't). 3) Many cable stations are global.
The statements above, if true, provide support for each of the following EXCEPT:	**Step 1:** Inference question: the stimulus "provide[s] support" for each of the four wrong answers; the stimulus either contradicts or is irrelevant to the correct answer.
	Step 3: The wrong answers follow from the stimulus. The correct answer does not, so what is unknown is important. NOTE: The only example that is not comparative is the third; it implies, but does not state, that broadcast networks are not global.
(A) Some broadcast networks can be viewed in several countries.	**Step 4:** Correct. There is no support for this statement in the stimulus. It may even contradict the implication of the third example. If global reach is an advantage for cable stations, then it's unlikely that networks are multinational.
(B) Broadcast networks do not rely on subscriber fees from viewers.	This is supported by the second example. Eliminate.
(C) Low costs are often an important factor for advertisers in selecting a station or network on which to run a TV ad.	The second example of cable's advantages in attracting advertisers is low rates, so it must be a factor in advertisers' decisions. Eliminate.
(D) Some advertisers prefer to have the opportunity to address a worldwide audience.	Cable's global reach is the third example of cable's advantages in attracting advertisers. Eliminate.
(E) The audiences that some advertisers prefer to target watch 24-hour news stations.	The first example advantage supports this statement. Eliminate.

PrepTest61 Sec4 Q3

LSAT Question	Analysis
27. Often a type of organ or body structure is the only physically feasible means of accomplishing a given task, so it should be unsurprising if, like eyes or wings, that type of organ or body structure evolves at different times in a number of completely unrelated species. After all, whatever the difference of heritage and habitat, as organisms animals have fundamentally similar needs and so _____.	**Step 2**: Two statements describing a phenomenon and a statement of similarity: 1) Often an organ/body part is the only way to accomplish a task, *so* 2) different species naturally evolve similar organs/body parts. *Since* 3) animals have similar needs, *It follows that _____.*
Which one of the following most logically completes the last sentence of the passage?	**Step 1**: "[L]ogically completes" indicates an Inference question. The correct answer will provide a conclusion to the stimulus's evidence.
	Step 3: The statements build on one another and point to the conclusion that animals will likely develop similar organs/body parts.
(A) will often live in the same environment as other species quite different from themselves	**Step 4**: Outside the Scope. The stimulus doesn't address whether those living in the same environment all have similar needs. Eliminate.
(B) will in many instances evolve similar adaptations enabling them to satisfy these needs	Correct. This matches the prediction, substituting the word "adaptations" for "organs/body parts."
(C) will develop adaptations allowing them to satisfy these needs	This is already implied by the evidence. The conclusion logically entails the development of *similar* adaptations, not just any adaptation. Eliminate.
(D) will resemble other species having different biological needs	180. The stimulus suggests that similar needs produce similar adaptations. If anything, this implies that animals with different needs will develop different body parts. Eliminate.
(E) will all develop eyes or wings as adaptations *PrepTest61 Sec2 Q15*	Distortion. This would work if the stimulus said "all animals need either to see or to fly," but it is nowhere near that specific. Eliminate.

LSAT Question	Analysis
28. The law of the city of Weston regarding contributions to mayoral campaigns is as follows: all contributions to these campaigns in excess of $100 made by nonresidents of Weston who are not former residents of Weston must be registered with the city council. Brimley's mayoral campaign clearly complied with this law since it accepted contributions only from residents and former residents of Weston.	**Step 2:** A principle and a purported application: 1) [principle] Weston campaign law: Registration with the city council is *required* for contributions >$100 from nonresidents who are not former residents. 2) [application] Brimley accepted contributions only from residents and former residents, and so complies with the law.
If all the statements above are true, which one of the following statements must be true?	**Step 1:** The correct answer "must be true" based on the stimulus—an Inference question.
	Step 3: If the stimulus contains the complete law and the facts it provides about Brimley are correct, then he adhered to the law and need not register any contributions with the city council. The correct answer must be true based on these statements.
(A) No nonresident of Weston contributed in excess of $100 to Brimley's campaign.	**Step 4:** Distortion. No nonresident *who is not a former resident* contributed >$100 to Brimley. This choice is too broad. Eliminate.
(B) Some contributions to Brimley's campaign in excess of $100 were registered with the city council.	Outside the Scope. Brimley was not *required* to register any contributions; he may have registered some anyway, but that's beside the point. Eliminate.
(C) No contributions to Brimley's campaign needed to be registered with the city council.	Correct. Registration is required for $100+ contributions from nonresidents who are not former residents. Brimley had no contributors in that category.
(D) All contributions to Brimley's campaign that were registered with the city council were in excess of $100.	Distortion. From the stimulus, it's unclear that any of Brimley's contributions were registered. None needed to be. Eliminate.
(E) Brimley's campaign did not register any contributions with the city council. *PrepTest57 Sec2 Q25*	Outside the Scope. Brimley was not *required* to register any contributions; he may have registered some anyway, but that's beside the point. Eliminate.

LSAT Question	Analysis
29. Most successful entrepreneurs work at least 18 hours a day, and no one who works at least 18 hours a day has time for leisure activities. But all happy entrepreneurs have time for leisure activities.	**Step 2:** One uncertain statement and two conditional statements: 1) Most (over half of) successful entrepreneurs work ≥ 18 hours/day. 2) If work ≥ 18 hours/day → no time for leisure If time for leisure → work < 18 hours/day 3) If happy entrepreneur → time for leisure If no time for leisure → not happy entrepreneur
If the statements above are true, each of the following could be true EXCEPT:	**Step 1:** An Inference question: Based on the stimulus, the correct answer must be false, while each of the four wrong answers could be true.
	Step 3: The two conditional statements combine to tell you that no happy entrepreneurs work ≥ 18 hours/day. Combine that with the first statement about most successful entrepreneurs—they are not happy. Remember, the correct answer must be false given these statements.
(A) Anyone who has no time for leisure activities works at least 18 hours a day.	**Step 4:** This confuses necessity and sufficiency. Working ≥ 18 hours/day is one reason you may not have time for leisure, but there could be any number of other reasons. Eliminate.
(B) Some entrepreneurs who work at least 18 hours a day are successful.	Must be true based on the first statement in the stimulus. Eliminate.
(C) Some happy entrepreneurs are successful.	Could be true. Most successful entrepreneurs work too much to be happy, but that means that a minority may work less. Eliminate.
(D) Some entrepreneurs who work at least 18 hours a day are happy.	Correct. The two conditional statements combine to say: "If a person works ≥ 18 hours/day, then he or she is not a happy entrepreneur." The statement in this answer must be false.
(E) Some successful entrepreneurs work less than 18 hours a day. *PrepTest49 Sec2 Q16*	Could be true. Most successful entrepreneurs work more, so it's possible that some work less. Eliminate.

LSAT Question	Analysis
30. Art historian: More than any other genre of representational painting, still-life painting lends itself naturally to art whose goal is the artist's self-expression, rather than merely the reflection of a preexisting external reality. This is because in still-life painting, the artist invariably chooses, modifies, and arranges the objects to be painted. Thus, the artist has considerably more control over the composition and subject of a still-life painting than over those of a landscape painting or portrait, for example. →	**Step 2**: A concrete statement and a two-part explanation for it: 1) Still-life painting lends itself to self-expression (as opposed to reflecting reality) more than any other representational genre does. *because* 2) In still-life, the painter *always* chooses, modifies, and arranges the objects. *and so* 3) The artist has more control over the composition of a still-life than over, for example, a landscape or a portrait.
Which one of the following is most strongly supported by the art historian's statements? →	**Step 1**: The correct answer is "strongly supported by" the stimulus—an Inference question.
	Step 3: For the author's explanation to apply to the concrete statement, it must be the case that still-life is unique in having the painter invariably choose, modify, and arrange the subject matter, and that doing those things is tantamount to self-expression.
(A) Landscape painting and portraiture are the artistic genres that lend themselves most naturally to the mere reflection of a preexisting external reality. →	**Step 4**: Outside the Scope. The stimulus does not address what, if anything, landscape and portraiture are best for. Eliminate.
(B) The only way in which artists control the composition and subject of a painting is by choosing, modifying, and arranging the objects to be represented in that painting. →	Extreme. There may be other ways in which artists can control a painting's composition; the author finds still-life better for self-expression because, in still-life, painters *always* choose, modify, and arrange the objects. Eliminate.
(C) Nonrepresentational painting does not lend itself as naturally as still-life painting does to the goal of the artist's self-expression. →	Outside the Scope. The stimulus is concerned exclusively with representational painting. Eliminate.
(D) In genres of representational painting other than still-life painting, the artist does not always choose, modify, and arrange the objects to be painted. →	Correct. If this is the quality that explains still-life's superiority, it follows that other representational painting styles do not share this quality.
(E) When painting a portrait, artists rarely attempt to express themselves through the choice, modification, or arrangement of the background elements against which the subject of the portrait is painted. *PrepTest57 Sec3 Q13* →	Distortion. Artists' attempts to control some or all of the composition in portraits need not be *rare* in order for still-life to be a superior genre for self-expression. After all, painters *always* choose, modify, and arrange the objects in a still-life. Eliminate.

INFERENCE-BASED PRINCIPLE QUESTIONS

Some Principle question stems—those you learned about in Chapter 8—mimic the skills associated with Assumption, Strengthen, and Parallel Reasoning questions. Other Principle questions test Inference question skills. These Principle questions ask you either to identify a general rule from a specific case or to determine which specific case follows from a general rule.

Prepare

LEARNING OBJECTIVES

In this section, you'll learn to:

· Identify and answer Inference-Based Principle questions

You can identify Inference-Based Principle questions from question stems such as these:

Identify the Principle

Which one of the following is best illustrated by the examples presented above?

PrepTest51 Sec3 Q5

The situation described above most closely conforms to which of the following generalizations?

PrepTest59 Sec2 Q23

Apply the Principle

Which one of the following judgments conforms most closely to the principles described by the industrial adviser?

PrepTest51 Sec1 Q17

Which of the following situations violates the food labeling regulation?

PrepTest57 Sec3 Q14

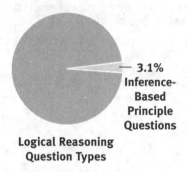

— 3.1%
Inference-
Based
Principle
Questions

**Logical Reasoning
Question Types**

PrepTests 66–80; released 2012–2016

INFERENCE-BASED PRINCIPLE QUESTIONS AT A GLANCE

Task: Identify the principle illustrated by the specific case in the stimulus, or apply the principle stated in the stimulus to the specific case in the correct answer.

Strategy: In Identify the Principle questions, summarize the broad rule illustrated by the situation or example and use your summary to find the answer choice with a matching principle; in Apply the Principle questions, note each element in the principle and find the situation or example that conforms to each and every element.

Frequency: LSAT tests released from 2012 to 2016 had an average of 5.0 Principle questions per test.

Out of those, the typical test featured three Assumption-Family Principle questions, usually one Inference-Based Apply the Principle question, and one or two Inference-Based Identify the Principle questions.

Here's how an LSAT expert might analyze and answer a Principle question asking for an inference.

LSAT Question	Analysis
Philosopher: Effective tests have recently been developed to predict fatal diseases having a largely genetic basis. Now, for the first time, a person can be warned well in advance of the possibility of such life-threatening conditions. However, medicine is not yet able to prevent most such conditions. Simply being informed that one will get a disease that is both fatal and incurable can itself be quite harmful to some people. This raises the question of whether such "early warning" tests should be made available at all..	**Step 2:** The philosopher explains a new medical technology, and then points out an issue that technology creates. With new genetic testing, it is now possible to warn patients in advance about their risk for contracting potentially fatal illnesses for which no cure yet exists. This leads to an ethical dilemma for medical professionals: Should patients be given such tests when finding out that one will get an incurable disease is, in and of itself, harmful to some people?
Which one of the following statements is best illustrated by the state of affairs described by the philosopher?	**Step 1:** A Principle question asking you to identify the principle illustrated by the situation outlined in the stimulus. The correct answer will be a broad principle that matches the stimulus; the four wrong answers will be too broad or too narrow, will distort the stimulus, or will be outside the scope.
	Step 3: The correct answer will broadly state that technological breakthroughs can lead to dilemmas. The wrong answers will each, in some way, fail to match up to the specific case described by the philosopher.
(A) The advance of medicine fails to provide solutions to every problem.	**Step 4:** Too broad. The philosopher doesn't claim that medical science can or should solve "every problem." Eliminate.
(B) The advance of medicine creates new contexts in which ethical dilemmas can arise.	Correct. The philosopher describes one case in which an advance has created a moral or ethical dilemma for doctors.
(C) Medical technologies continue to advance, increasing our knowledge and understanding of disease.	Too narrow. This misses the part of the philosopher's case outlining the dilemma created by the tests. Eliminate..
(D) The more we come to learn, the more we realize how little we know.	This distorts the case described in the stimulus. The problem is not that the new tests reveal our ignorance, but that they raise an issue about what patients should learn about their genetic predispositions. Eliminate.
(E) The advance of technology is of questionable value. *PrepTest46 Sec2 Q3*	Too broad. The philosopher does not question the value of advancing medical technology in general, but rather, identifies a dilemma caused by one such advance. Eliminate.

Identify a Principle from a Specific Case That Illustrates It

Practice

Cases That Describe Actions and Outcomes

In these questions, the stimulus describes a specific, detailed example that you can broaden to fit similar scenarios.

LSAT Question	My Analysis
31. Among Trinidadian guppies, males with large spots are more attractive to females than are males with small spots, who consequently are presented with less frequent mating opportunities. Yet guppies with small spots are more likely to avoid detection by predators, so in waters where predators are abundant only guppies with small spots live to maturity. →	**Step 2:**
The situation described above most closely conforms to which one of the following generalizations? →	**Step 1:** *Principle Question*
	Step 3:
(A) A trait that helps attract mates is sometimes more dangerous to one sex than to another. →	**Step 4:**
(B) Those organisms that are most attractive to the opposite sex have the greatest number of offspring. →	
(C) Those organisms that survive the longest have the greatest number of offspring. →	
(D) Whether a trait is harmful to the organisms of a species can depend on which sex possesses it. →	
(E) A trait that is helpful to procreation can also hinder it in certain environments. →	

PrepTest61 Sec4 Q1

LSAT Question	My Analysis
32. Students asked by a psychologist to tell a lie before discussion groups vastly overestimated how many people in the discussion groups could tell they were lying. Other research has found that when volleyball players perform unusually poorly on the court, teammates notice this far less often than the players expect. Finally, in one research experiment a student wearing a funny T-shirt entered a room full of people. Questioning revealed that only a small fraction of the people in the room noticed the shirt, contrary to the student's expectations.	Step 2:
Which one of the following is best illustrated by the statements above?	Step 1:
	Step 3:
(A) People tend to be far less aware of their own appearance and behavior than are other people.	Step 4:
(B) People tend not to notice the appearance or behavior of others.	
(C) We are actually less observant of the appearance and behavior of others than we think ourselves to be.	
(D) People will notice the appearance or behavior of others only if it is specifically highlighted in some way.	
(E) People tend to believe their appearance and behavior are noticed by others more often than is actually the case.	

PrepTest48 Sec1 Q11

Apply a Principle to a Specific Case

Practice

LSAT Question	My Analysis
33. Most employees spend their time completing unimportant tasks for which they have been given firm schedules and deadlines. Efficient employees know how to ignore such demands and instead spend their time on projects that will yield big rewards for their employers if successful, even when such projects carry the risk of significant loss if unsuccessful. $\longrightarrow$	Step 2:
Which one of the following is an example of efficiency as described above? $\longrightarrow$	Step 1:
	Step 3:
(A) spending the entire afternoon working on a report that a supervisor has ordered completed by the following day $\longrightarrow$	Step 4:
(B) instead of working on a report that a supervisor has ordered completed by the following day, spending the entire afternoon completing routine correspondence that could be delayed $\longrightarrow$	
(C) deciding to take an urgent call from a major customer instead of being punctual at a monthly sales meeting $\longrightarrow$	
(D) meeting daily with other staff members to discuss workloads and schedules $\longrightarrow$	
(E) spending time each morning scheduling tasks according to the most immediate deadlines $\longrightarrow$	

PrepTest49 Sec2 Q3

Identify the Principle and Apply the Principle Question Stems

Practice

When you're dealing with a Principle question that rewards a valid inference, you will first need to determine your task. Either you'll be asked to identify or infer a broad principle from a specific example in the stimulus (Identify the Principle) or you'll be asked to apply a broad rule or definition to a specific situation in the answer choices (Apply the Principle).

Use the following stems, along with their analysis, to check your ability to make this important distinction.

LSAT Question Stem	My Analysis
i. The situation described above most closely conforms to which one of the following generalizations? → *PrepTest59 Sec2 Q23*	
ii. Which one of the following judgments most closely conforms to the principle cited by the philosopher? → *PrepTest51 Sec1 Q9*	
iii. Which one of the following principles is best illustrated by the information above? → *PrepTest46 Sec3 Q8*	
iv. Which of the following situations violates the food labeling regulation? → *PrepTest57 Sec3 Q14*	

Expert Analysis: Inference-Based Principle Questions

LSAT Question	Analysis
31. Among Trinidadian guppies, males with large spots are more attractive to females than are males with small spots, who consequently are presented with less frequent mating opportunities. Yet guppies with small spots are more likely to avoid detection by predators, so in waters where predators are abundant only guppies with small spots live to maturity.	**Step 2:** The Keyword *yet* is central to the rule this situation illustrates: While large spots help male guppies mate, the large spots can also cause the guppies to be detected by predators.
The situation described above most closely conforms to which one of the following generalizations?	**Step 1:** "Generalizations" is an LSAT synonym for principles. The "situation described above" means that the stimulus is a specific situation, while the answer choices will be broader in scope.
	Step 3: The correct answer will take the specific situation in the stimulus and broaden the scope beyond the specific case of guppies: A physical feature that helps an animal mate might also end up causing that animal harm.
(A) A trait that helps attract mates is sometimes more dangerous to one sex than to another.	**Step 4:** Irrelevant Comparison. The stimulus says nothing about females facing more or less danger than the males due to large spots. Eliminate.
(B) Those organisms that are most attractive to the opposite sex have the greatest number of offspring.	Distortion. This may be true, but it is not the general rule illustrated in the stimulus. Eliminate.
(C) Those organisms that survive the longest have the greatest number of offspring.	Outside the Scope. The stimulus doesn't mention a relationship between life span and reproductive success, let alone illustrate a principle about it. Eliminate.
(D) Whether a trait is harmful to the organisms of a species can depend on which sex possesses it.	Irrelevant Comparison. The stimulus makes no sex-based distinction about the dangers of large spots. Eliminate.
(E) A trait that is helpful to procreation can also hinder it in certain environments. *PrepTest61 Sec4 Q1*	Correct. This general rule matches the specific example above.

LSAT Question	Analysis
32. Students asked by a psychologist to tell a lie before discussion groups vastly overestimated how many people in the discussion groups could tell they were lying. Other research has found that when volleyball players perform unusually poorly on the court, teammates notice this far less often than the players expect. Finally, in one research experiment a student wearing a funny T-shirt entered a room full of people. Questioning revealed that only a small fraction of the people in the room noticed the shirt, contrary to the student's expectations.	**Step 2:** The stimulus describes people in three potentially embarrassing situations. In all three, the person performing the potentially embarrassing action overestimates the percentage of witnesses who will actually notice the action. The person's behavior is noticed less often than the person thinks it will be.
Which one of the following is best illustrated by the statements above?	**Step 1:** A Principle question asking you to identify the principle illustrated by the situation outlined in the stimulus. The correct answer will be a broad principle that matches the stimulus; the four wrong answers will be too broad or too narrow, will distort the stimulus, or will be outside the scope.
	Step 3: The correct answer will state that people overestimate the amount of attention paid by others. The four wrong answers will each, in some way, fail to match the situations outlined in the stimulus.
(A) People tend to be far less aware of their own appearance and behavior than are other people.	**Step 4:** 180. The stimulus describes cases in which a person is more aware of his or her actions than others are. Eliminate.
(B) People tend not to notice the appearance or behavior of others.	Too narrow. The point of the examples in the stimulus is that a person believes others will pay more attention than they do. This choice misses the misperception angle. Eliminate.
(C) We are actually less observant of the appearance and behavior of others than we think ourselves to be.	Distortion. The point of the examples in the stimulus is that others pay less attention than we think they do, not that we pay less attention than we think we do. Eliminate.
(D) People will notice the appearance or behavior of others only if it is specifically highlighted in some way.	Outside the scope. Nothing in the stimulus addresses situations in which others <u>do</u> pay attention; rather, it describes situations in which others pay less attention than anticipated. Eliminate.
(E) People tend to believe their appearance and behavior are noticed by others more often than is actually the case. *PrepTest48 Sec1 Q11*	Correct. This statement broadly summarizes the points illustrated by the three cases described in the stimulus.

LSAT Question	Analysis
33. Most employees spend their time completing unimportant tasks for which they have been given firm schedules and deadlines. Efficient employees know how to ignore such demands and instead spend their time on projects that will yield big rewards for their employers if successful, even when such projects carry the risk of significant loss if unsuccessful.	**Step 2:** The stimulus defines "efficiency" as: 1) Ignoring unimportant tasks with firm schedules and deadlines, and 2) spending time on high-risk, high-reward projects.
Which one of the following is an example of efficiency as described above?	**Step 1:** The correct answer is an "example of" a definition in the stimulus—an Apply the Principle question asking for an inference.
	Step 3: The answer choices will describe employee actions. The correct answer will describe "efficient" behavior as defined in the stimulus. The four wrong answers will describe inefficient behaviors.
(A) spending the entire afternoon working on a report that a supervisor has ordered completed by the following day	**Step 4:** 180. Focusing on a menial task with a hard deadline is what an efficient employee should ignore. Eliminate.
(B) instead of working on a report that a supervisor has ordered completed by the following day, spending the entire afternoon completing routine correspondence that could be delayed	180. Routine correspondence that could be delayed is an example of a menial task with little reward. Eliminate.
(C) deciding to take an urgent call from a major customer instead of being punctual at a monthly sales meeting	Correct. The employee here is putting off a menial task so she can focus on a potentially high-yield project.
(D) meeting daily with other staff members to discuss workloads and schedules	180. This fits the "unimportant tasks" category defined in the stimulus as inefficient and best ignored. Eliminate.
(E) spending time each morning scheduling tasks according to the most immediate deadlines *PrepTest49 Sec2 Q3*	180. This employee is not ignoring trivial, deadline-driven work in order to focus on a high-yield project. Eliminate.

LSAT Question Stem	Analysis
i. The situation described above most closely conforms to which one of the following generalizations? *PrepTest59 Sec2 Q23* →	Identify the Principle
ii. Which one of the following judgments most closely conforms to the principle cited by the philosopher? *PrepTest51 Sec1 Q9* →	Apply the Principle
iii. Which one of the following principles is best illustrated by the information above? *PrepTest46 Sec3 Q8* →	Identify the Principle
iv. Which of the following situations violates the food labeling regulation? *PrepTest57 Sec3 Q14* →	Apply the Principle (NOTE: Find the one case that violates the principle; the wrong answers in this case will either conform to the principle or will be irrelevant to it.)

Perform

LSAT Question	My Analysis
34. Philosopher: An action is morally good if it both achieves the agent's intended goal and benefits someone other than the agent. →	**Step 2:**
Which one of the following judgments most closely conforms to the principle cited by the philosopher? →	**Step 1:** Applied Question
	Step 3:
(A) Colin chose to lie to the authorities questioning him, in an attempt to protect his friends. The authorities discovered his deception and punished Colin and his friends severely. But because he acted out of love for his friends, Colin's action was morally good. →	**Step 4:**
(B) Derek prepared a steak dinner to welcome his new neighbors to the neighborhood. When they arrived for dinner, Derek found out that the newcomers were strict vegetarians. Though the new neighbors were still grateful for Derek's efforts to welcome them, Derek's action was not morally good. →	
(C) Ellen worked overtime hoping to get a promotion. The extra money she earned allowed her family to take a longer vacation that year, but she failed to get the promotion. Nevertheless, Ellen's action was morally good. →	
(D) Louisa tried to get Henry into serious trouble by making it appear that he stole some expensive clothes from a store. But the store's detective realized what Louisa did, and so Louisa was punished rather than Henry. Since she intended to harm Henry, Louisa's action was not morally good. →	
(E) Yolanda took her children to visit their grandfather because she wanted her children to enjoy their vacation and she knew they adored their grandfather. The grandfather and the children all enjoyed the visit. Though Yolanda greatly enjoyed the visit, her action was morally good. →	

PrepTest51 Sec1 Q9

LSAT Question	My Analysis

35. Critic: As modern methods of communication and transportation have continued to improve, the pace of life today has become faster than ever before. This speed has created feelings of impermanence and instability, making us feel as if we never have enough time to achieve what we want—or at least what we think we want. → **Step 2:**

The critic's statements most closely conform to which one of the following assessments? → **Step 1:**

Step 3:

(A) The fast pace of modern life has made it difficult for people to achieve their goals. → **Step 4:**

(B) The disadvantages of technological progress often outweigh the advantages. →

(C) Changes in people's feelings about life can result from technological changes. →

(D) The perception of impermanence in contemporary life makes it more difficult for people to know what they want. →

(E) Changes in people's feelings fuel the need for technological advancement. →

PrepTest57 Sec3 Q16 →

Expert Analysis: Inference-Based Principle Questions

LSAT Question	Analysis
34. Philosopher: An action is morally good if it both achieves the agent's intended goal and benefits someone other than the agent.	**Step 2:** A conditional statement: If an action achieves the agent's intended goal AND the action benefits someone other than the agent → the action is morally good If an action is not morally good → the action did not achieve the agent's goal OR the action didn't benefit anyone else besides the agent
Which one of the following judgments most closely conforms to the principle cited by the philosopher?	**Step 1:** The correct answer is a specific judgment that "conforms to the principle cited" in the stimulus—an Apply the Principle question.
	Step 3: The correct answer will correctly apply the Formal Logic rule; the four wrong answers will misapply or fall outside the scope of the rule.
(A) Colin chose to lie to the authorities questioning him, in an attempt to protect his friends. The authorities discovered his deception and punished Colin and his friends severely. But because he acted out of love for his friends, Colin's action was morally good.	**Step 4:** Colin's action did not achieve its intended goal, so it does not fulfill the conditions sufficient to establish an action as morally good. Eliminate.
(B) Derek prepared a steak dinner to welcome his new neighbors to the neighborhood. When they arrived for dinner, Derek found out that the newcomers were strict vegetarians. Though the new neighbors were still grateful for Derek's efforts to welcome them, Derek's action was not morally good.	Outside the Scope. The stimulus rule does not define actions or outcomes sufficient to make an action *not* morally good. Eliminate.
(C) Ellen worked overtime hoping to get a promotion. The extra money she earned allowed her family to take a longer vacation that year, but she failed to get the promotion. Nevertheless, Ellen's action was morally good.	Ellen's action did not achieve its intended goal and did not benefit anyone else, so the conditions sufficient to make her action morally good were not met. Eliminate.
(D) Louisa tried to get Henry into serious trouble by making it appear that he stole some expensive clothes from a store. But the store's detective realized what Louisa did, and so Louisa was punished rather than Henry. Since she intended to harm Henry, Louisa's action was not morally good.	Outside the Scope. The stimulus rule does not define actions or outcomes sufficient to make an action *not* morally good. Eliminate.

LSAT Question (cont.)	Analysis (cont.)
(E) Yolanda took her children to visit their grandfather because she wanted her children to enjoy their vacation and she knew they adored their grandfather. The grandfather and the children all enjoyed the visit. Though Yolanda greatly enjoyed the visit, her action was morally good. *PrepTest51 Sec1 Q9*	Correct. Yolanda's action achieved its intended goal AND it benefited someone other than Yolanda, so according to the rule presented in the stimulus, it is a morally good action.

LSAT Question	Analysis
35. Critic: As modern methods of communication and transportation have continued to improve, the pace of life today has become faster than ever before. This speed has created feelings of impermanence and instability, making us feel as if we never have enough time to achieve what we want—or at least what we think we want. →	**Step 2:** The statements describe a chain of causes and effects: Improved communication and transportation *caused* faster pace of life *causing* feelings of impermanence and instability *causing* the feeling that we don't have the time to achieve what we think we want.
The critic's statements most closely conform to which one of the following assessments? →	**Step 1:** The stimulus statements "most closely conform to" the correct answer—an Identify the Principle question asking for an inference.
	Step 3: The correct answer must take into account all of the statements. Connect the first statement to the last: Technological improvements can cause people to have different feelings about their lives and goals.
(A) The fast pace of modern life has made it difficult for people to achieve their goals. →	**Step 4:** Distortion. The last sentence in the stimulus says that the fast pace of life has caused us to *feel* as though we don't have time to achieve what we want. Eliminate.
(B) The disadvantages of technological progress often outweigh the advantages. →	Outside the Scope. The statements in the stimulus never talk about the advantages of technological progress. Eliminate.
(C) Changes in people's feelings about life can result from technological changes. →	Correct. This ties together all of the statements in the stimulus and sums them up succinctly.
(D) The perception of impermanence in contemporary life makes it more difficult for people to know what they want. →	Distortion. Feelings of impermanence and instability have led to the feeling that we don't have time to achieve what we think we want. This choice says we don't know what we want. Eliminate.
(E) Changes in people's feelings fuel the need for technological advancement. *PrepTest57 Sec3 Q16* →	Outside the Scope. The stimulus never discusses what fuels the need for technological advancement. Eliminate.

RESOLVING DISCREPANCIES AND PARADOX QUESTIONS

Paradox questions present two facts that appear to be in conflict, and then ask you to select the answer presenting information that, if true, helps to resolve or reconcile the apparent contradiction.

Prepare

LEARNING OBJECTIVES

In this section, you'll learn to:

· Identify and answer Paradox questions

You can identify Paradox questions from question stems such as these:

> Which one of the following, if true, most helps to explain how both reports could be accurate?
>
> *PrepTest51 Sec3 Q8*

> Which one of the following, if true, most helps to resolve the apparent conflict in the consumer activist's statements?
>
> *PrepTest49 Sec4 Q11*

> Each of the following, if true, would contribute to an explanation of the apparent discrepancy in the information above EXCEPT:
>
> *PrepTest59 Sec3 Q17*

> Which one of the following, if true, most helps to account for the apparent discrepancy in the students' preferences?
>
> *PrepTest61 Sec2 Q25*

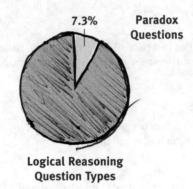

7.3%   **Paradox Questions**

**Logical Reasoning
Question Types**

PrepTests 66–80; released 2012–2016

PARADOX QUESTIONS AT A GLANCE

Task: Select the one answer containing a fact that would help explain or resolve an apparent discrepancy.

Strategy: Identify the apparent contradiction or inexplicable situation in the stimulus. Make a general prediction of the type of fact needed to resolve the paradox. Use your paraphrase of the paradox and your broad prediction to evaluate the answer choices.

Frequency: On LSAT tests released from 2012 through 2016, there were an average of 3.7 Paradox questions per test.

Anticipating the sort(s) of fact that would resolve an apparent discrepancy provides the generalized prediction you'll use to evaluate the answer choices.

Review an LSAT expert's work on the question featuring apparently contradictory erosion reports.

LSAT Question	Analysis
Engineers are investigating the suitability of Wantastiquet Pass as the site of a new bridge. Because one concern is whether erosion could eventually weaken the bridge's foundations, they contracted for two reports on erosion in the region. Although both reports are accurate, one claims that the region suffers relatively little erosion, while the other claims that regional erosion is heavy and a cause for concern.	**Step 2:** "Although" and "while" reveal contradictory ideas: Fact 1: Both reports on erosion in the region are accurate. *but* Fact 2: One says that the region suffers little erosion, and the other says that the region suffers heavy erosion.
Which one of the following, if true, most helps to explain how both reports could be accurate?	**Step 1:** "Most helps to explain" indicates that a contradiction needs resolution.
	Step 3: How could it be that studies with contradictory results are both accurate? Resolve this paradox by showing that the studies looked at two different kinds of erosion or at erosion in two different contexts.
(A) Neither report presents an extensive chemical analysis of the soil in the region.	**Step 4:** 180. This states a similarity between the studies, making it even harder to understand how both could be accurate and yet report seemingly opposite findings. Eliminate.
(B) Both reports include computer-enhanced satellite photographs.	180. This states a similarity between the studies, making it even harder to understand how both could be accurate and yet report seemingly opposite findings. Eliminate.
(C) One report was prepared by scientists from a university, while the other report was prepared by scientists from a private consulting firm.	A difference in researchers' employers doesn't explain how both reports could be accurate while giving apparently contradictory results. Eliminate.
(D) One report focuses on regional topsoil erosion, while the other report focuses on riverbank erosion resulting from seasonal floods.	Correct. If true, this explains why the reports, while both correct, got different results.
(E) One report cost nearly twice as much to prepare as did the other report. *PrepTest51 Sec3 Q8*	A difference in cost does nothing to explain how both reports could be accurate while giving apparently contradictory results. Eliminate.

Practice

Identify and paraphrase the anomaly in the following LSAT Paradox stimuli, and anticipate the kind of fact that would help provide a resolution for each one.

LSAT Question	My Analysis
36. Human settlement of previously uninhabited areas tends to endanger species of wildlife. However, the Mississippi kite, a bird found on the prairies of North America, flourishes in areas that people have settled. In fact, during the five years since 1985 its population has risen far more rapidly in towns than in rural areas. *PrepTest51 Sec3 Q10* →	*why does the kite do better in settled areas when typically human settlement leads to endangerment*
37. Scientists removed all viruses from a seawater sample and then measured the growth rate of the plankton population in the water. They expected the rate to increase dramatically, but the population actually got smaller. *PrepTest57 Sec3 Q7* →	
38. Consumer activist: When antilock brakes were first introduced, it was claimed that they would significantly reduce the incidence of multiple-car collisions, thereby saving lives. Indeed, antilock brakes have reduced the incidence of multiple-car collisions. I maintain, however, that to save lives, automobile manufacturers ought to stop equipping cars with them. *PrepTest49 Sec4 Q11* →	

LSAT Question	**My Analysis**

39. The number of automobile thefts has declined steadily during the past five years, and it is more likely now than it was five years ago that someone who steals a car will be convicted of the crime.

PrepTest61 Sec4 Q14

$\longrightarrow$

40. A recent study of major motion pictures revealed that the vast majority of their plots were simply variations on plots that had been used many times before. Despite this fact, many people enjoy seeing several new movies each year.

PrepTest59 Sec3 Q17

$\longrightarrow$

Expert Analysis: Paradox Stimuli

LSAT Question	Analysis
36. Human settlement of previously uninhabited areas tends to endanger species of wildlife. However, the Mississippi kite, a bird found on the prairies of North America, flourishes in areas that people have settled. In fact, during the five years since 1985 its population has risen far more rapidly in towns than in rural areas. *PrepTest51 Sec3 Q10* ⟶	*However* indicates the conflicting ideas. Fact 1: New human settlement usually endangers wildlife. *but* Fact 2: The Mississippi kite (a prairie bird) seems to do better in settled than in unsettled areas. Paradox: Even though most species are negatively affected by human settlement, the Mississippi kite seems to thrive in settled areas. Why would this prairie bird do better in town?

Prediction: The correct answer will provide a fact that explains why settled environments are preferable for the Mississippi kite.

LSAT Question	Analysis
37. Scientists removed all viruses from a seawater sample and then measured the growth rate of the plankton population in the water. They expected the rate to increase dramatically, but the population actually got smaller. *PrepTest57 Sec3 Q7* ⟶	[B]*ut* indicates the conflict: Fact 1: Scientists expected plankton population to grow rapidly upon removal of viruses from seawater. *instead* Fact 2: The plankton population shrank. Why would removing viruses from seawater cause the plankton population to decline?

Prediction: Resolve this unexpected result by providing evidence that the plankton unexpectedly benefit from the viruses.

LSAT Question	Analysis
38. Consumer activist: When antilock brakes were first introduced, it was claimed that they would significantly reduce the incidence of multiple-car collisions, thereby saving lives. Indeed, antilock brakes have reduced the incidence of multiple-car collisions. I maintain, however, that to save lives, automobile manufacturers ought to stop equipping cars with them. *PrepTest49 Sec4 Q11* ⟶	[H]*owever* indicates the conflict: Fact 1: Antilock brakes have reduced the incidence of multi-car collisions. *but* Fact 2: To save lives, automakers should stop equipping cars with antilock brakes. Why would the author maintain that ceasing use of something that reduces the number of multi-car accidents would save lives?

Prediction: Resolve this with evidence that equipping cars with antilock brakes makes a car or its driver less safe.

LSAT Question	Analysis
39. The number of automobile thefts has declined steadily during the past five years, and it is more likely now than it was five years ago that someone who steals a car will be convicted of the crime. *PrepTest61 Sec4 Q14* →	Here, the facts are not necessarily in conflict; *and* indicates the relevant relationship: Fact 1: The number of auto thefts is down over the past five years. *and* Fact 2: Car thieves are more likely to be convicted now than they were five years ago. What would account for a higher conviction rate for car thieves despite a decline in the number of car thefts?

Prediction: To explain both facts, provide a reason that car thieves are now more likely to be apprehended or why the cases against them are more likely to result in convictions.

LSAT Question	Analysis
40. A recent study of major motion pictures revealed that the vast majority of their plots were simply variations on plots that had been used many times before. Despite this fact, many people enjoy seeing several new movies each year. *PrepTest59 Sec3 Q17* →	"Despite this fact" indicates the conflict: Fact 1: Most motion pictures have derivative plots that have been used many times before. *but* Fact 2: People enjoy seeing several new movies per year. Why would people enjoy seeing movies that just recycle well-worn plots?

Prediction: Resolve this paradox by showing that people enjoy familiar plots, that they are unaware that the plots of new movies have been used before, or that other factors are more important than plot.

Practice

In each of the following Paradox questions, use your general predictions about the stimuli from the previous practice exercise to pick the answer choice that provides a specific fact that would resolve the paradox.

LSAT Question	My Analysis
41. Human settlement of previously uninhabited areas tends to endanger species of wildlife. However, the Mississippi kite, a bird found on the prairies of North America, flourishes in areas that people have settled. In fact, during the five years since 1985 its population has risen far more rapidly in towns than in rural areas. →	**Step 2:**
Which one of the following, if true, most helps to explain why the Mississippi kite population does not follow the usual pattern? →	**Step 1:**
	Step 3:
(A) Residents of prairie towns have been setting off loud firecrackers near kites' roosting spots because of the birds' habit of diving at people and frightening them. →	**Step 4:**
(B) Towns on the prairies tend to be small, with a low density of human population and large numbers of wild birds and animals →	
(C) Since the international migratory bird protection treaty of 1972, it has been illegal to shoot kites, and the treaty has been effectively enforced. →	
(D) Wildlife such as pigeons and raccoons had already adapted successfully to towns and cities long before there were towns on the North American prairies. →	
(E) Trees are denser in towns than elsewhere on the prairie, and these denser trees provide greater protection from hail and windstorms for kites' nests and eggs. →	

PrepTest51 Sec3 Q10

LSAT Question	My Analysis

42. Scientists removed all viruses from a seawater sample and then measured the growth rate of the plankton population in the water. They expected the rate to increase → dramatically, but the population actually got smaller.

Step 2:

Which one of the following, if true, most helps to → explain the unexpected result described above?

Step 1:

Step 3:

(A) Viruses in seawater help to keep the plankton population below the maximum level that the → resources in the water will support.

Step 4:

(B) Plankton and viruses in seawater compete for some of the same nutrients.

→

(C) Plankton utilize the nutrients released by the death of organisms killed by viruses.

→

(D) The absence of viruses can facilitate the flourishing of bacteria that sometimes → *not told anything about bacteria* damage other organisms.

(E) At any given time, a considerable portion of the plankton in seawater are already infected by → viruses.

LSAT Question	My Analysis
43. Consumer activist: When antilock brakes were first introduced, it was claimed that they would significantly reduce the incidence of multiple-car collisions, thereby saving lives. Indeed, antilock brakes have reduced the incidence of multiple-car collisions. I maintain, however, that to save lives, automobile manufacturers ought to stop equipping cars with them.	**Step 2:**
Which one of the following, if true, most helps to resolve the apparent conflict in the consumer activist's statements?	**Step 1:**
	Step 3:
(A) Drivers and passengers in automobiles with antilock brakes feel less vulnerable, and are thus less likely to wear seat belts.	**Step 4:**
(B) Under some circumstances, automobiles with traditional brakes stop just as quickly as do automobiles with antilock brakes.	
(C) For inexperienced drivers, antilock brakes are easier to use correctly than are traditional brakes.	
(D) Antilock brakes are considerably more expensive to manufacture than are traditional brakes.	
(E) Antilock brakes are no more effective in preventing multiple-car accidents than in preventing other kinds of traffic accidents.	

PrepTest49 Sec4 Q11

LSAT Question	My Analysis

44. The number of automobile thefts has declined steadily during the past five years, and it is more likely now than it was five years ago that someone who steals a car will be convicted of the crime. ⟶

Step 2:

Which one of the following, if true, most helps to explain ⟶ the facts cited above?

Step 1:

Step 3:

(A) Although there are fewer car thieves now than there were five years ago, the proportion of thieves who tend to abandon cars before their owners notice that they have been stolen has also decreased. ⟶

Step 4:

(B) Car alarms are more common than they were five years ago, but their propensity to be triggered in the absence of any criminal activity ⟶ has resulted in people generally ignoring them when they are triggered.

(C) An upsurge in home burglaries over the last five years has required police departments to ⟶ divert limited resources to investigation of these cases.

(D) Because of the increasingly lucrative market for stolen automobile parts, many stolen cars are ⟶ quickly disassembled and the parts are sold to various buyers across the country.

(E) There are more adolescent car thieves now than there were five years ago, and the sentences given to young criminals tend to be far more ⟶ lenient than those given to adult criminals.

PrepTest61 Sec4 Q14

LSAT Question	My Analysis
45. A recent study of major motion pictures revealed that the vast majority of their plots were simply variations on plots that had been used many times before. Despite this fact, many people enjoy seeing several new movies each year. →	**Step 2:**
Each of the following, if true, would contribute to an explanation of the apparent discrepancy in the information above EXCEPT: →	**Step 1:**
	Step 3:
(A) Movies based on standard plots are more likely to be financially successful than are ones based on original plots. →	**Step 4:**
(B) If the details of their stories are sufficiently different, two movies with the same basic plot will be perceived by moviegoers as having different plots. →	
(C) Because of the large number of movies produced each year, the odds of a person seeing two movies with the same general plot structure in a five-year period are fairly low. →	
(D) A certain aesthetic pleasure is derived from seeing several movies that develop the same plot in slightly different ways. →	
(E) Although most modern movie plots have been used before, most of those previous uses occurred during the 1940s and 1950s. →	

PrepTest59 Sec3 Q17

Expert Analysis: Paradox Questions

How do your analyses compare to those of an LSAT expert?

LSAT Question	Analysis
41. Human settlement of previously uninhabited areas tends to endanger species of wildlife. However, the Mississippi kite, a bird found on the prairies of North America, flourishes in areas that people have settled. In fact, during the five years since 1985 its population has risen far more rapidly in towns than in rural areas. →	**Step 2**: *However* indicates the conflicting ideas. Fact 1: New human settlement usually endangers wildlife. *but* Fact 2: The Mississippi kite (a prairie bird) seems to do better in settled than in unsettled areas.
Which one of the following, if true, most helps to explain why the Mississippi kite population does not follow the usual pattern? →	**Step 1**: The correct answer helps explain a deviation from the "usual pattern"—a Paradox question.
	Step 3: Most species are negatively affected by human settlement, so why would this prairie bird do better in town? The correct answer will provide a fact that explains why settled environments are preferable for the Mississippi kite.
(A) Residents of prairie towns have been setting off loud firecrackers near kites' roosting spots because of the birds' habit of diving at people and frightening them. →	**Step 4**: 180. This is a reason that the kites would not want to live near humans. Eliminate.
(B) Towns on the prairies tend to be small, with a low density of human population and large numbers of wild birds and animals. →	Outside the Scope. This may be true, but it does not explain why kites are the exception to the rule that settlement tends to decrease animal and bird populations. Eliminate.
(C) Since the international migratory bird protection treaty of 1972, it has been illegal to shoot kites, and the treaty has been effectively enforced. →	Outside the Scope. This might explain an overall increase in the kite population, but not a disproportionate rise near human settlements. Eliminate.
(D) Wildlife such as pigeons and raccoons had already adapted successfully to towns and cities long before there were towns on the North American prairies. →	Irrelevant Comparison. To resolve the paradox, the answer must show a benefit to kites from living near humans. The fact that other species did it too doesn't explain *this* exception to the general rule. Eliminate.
(E) Trees are denser in towns than elsewhere on the prairie, and these denser trees provide greater protection from hail and windstorms for kites' nests and eggs. →	Correct. Protection is the benefit that the kites get from living near humans. This explains why they are exceptions to the usual pattern.

PrepTest51 Sec3 Q10

LSAT Question	Analysis
42. Scientists removed all viruses from a seawater sample and then measured the growth rate of the plankton population in the water. They expected the rate to increase dramatically, but the population actually got smaller. →	**Step 2:** [B]*ut* indicates the conflict: Fact 1: Scientists expected plankton population to grow rapidly upon removal of viruses from seawater. *instead* Fact 2: The plankton population shrank.
Which one of the following, if true, most helps to explain the unexpected result described above? →	**Step 1:** The correct answer will "explain the unexpected results" described in the stimulus—a Paradox question.
	Step 3: Why would removing viruses from seawater cause the plankton population to decline? Resolve this unexpected result by providing evidence that the plankton unexpectedly benefit from the viruses.
(A) Viruses in seawater help to keep the plankton population below the maximum level that the resources in the water will support. →	**Step 4:** 180. If this were true, then at least initially, the plankton population would increase when the viruses were removed. Eliminate.
(B) Plankton and viruses in seawater compete for some of the same nutrients. →	180. If this were true, then the plankton population, which would no longer have to compete for resources, would increase when the viruses were removed. Eliminate.
(C) Plankton utilize the nutrients released by the death of organisms killed by viruses. →	Correct. If plankton use nutrients provided by viruses, then it is reasonable that plankton would decrease after viruses are removed.
(D) The absence of viruses can facilitate the flourishing of bacteria that sometimes damage other organisms. →	Without more information, it's not clear that bacteria harm plankton, so this doesn't clear up the unexpected results. Eliminate.
(E) At any given time, a considerable portion of the plankton in seawater are already infected by viruses. *PrepTest57 Sec3 Q7* →	180. Presuming that infection is bad for plankton, this provides a reason to expect the plankton population to rise once viruses are removed. Eliminate.

LSAT Question	Analysis
43. Consumer activist: When antilock brakes were first introduced, it was claimed that they would significantly reduce the incidence of multiple-car collisions, thereby saving lives. Indeed, antilock brakes have reduced the incidence of multiple-car collisions. I maintain, however, that to save lives, automobile manufacturers ought to stop equipping cars with them.	**Step 2:** [*H*]*owever* indicates the conflict: Fact 1: Antilock brakes have reduced the incidence of multi-car collisions. *but* Fact 2: To save lives, automakers should stop equipping cars with antilock brakes.
Which one of the following, if true, most helps to resolve the apparent conflict in the consumer activist's statements?	**Step 1:** The correct answer "helps to resolve the apparent conflict" in the activist's statements—a Paradox question.
	Step 3: Why would the author maintain that ceasing use of something that reduces the number of multi-car accidents would save lives? Resolve this with evidence that equipping cars with antilock brakes make a car or its driver less safe.
(A) Drivers and passengers in automobiles with antilock brakes feel less vulnerable, and are thus less likely to wear seat belts.	**Step 4:** Correct. If drivers and passengers behave less safely when in cars with antilock brakes, it helps explain why the activist might think removing them would save lives.
(B) Under some circumstances, automobiles with traditional brakes stop just as quickly as do automobiles with antilock brakes.	Irrelevant Comparison. This gives us no reason to think removing antilock brakes from cars would save lives. Eliminate.
(C) For inexperienced drivers, antilock brakes are easier to use correctly than are traditional brakes.	180. This is a reason to think cars with antilock brakes are safer. Eliminate.
(D) Antilock brakes are considerably more expensive to manufacture than are traditional brakes.	Irrelevant Comparison. We might save money this way, but the answer needs to explain why the activist thinks we will save *lives*. Eliminate.
(E) Antilock brakes are no more effective in preventing multiple-car accidents than in preventing other kinds of traffic accidents. *PrepTest49 Sec4 Q11*	Irrelevant Comparison/180. Knowing that antilock brakes help prevent other kinds of accidents doesn't explain why removing them would save lives. If anything, it just makes them seem safer overall. Eliminate.

LSAT Question	Analysis
44. The number of automobile thefts has declined steadily during the past five years, and it is more likely now than it was five years ago that someone who steals a car will be convicted of the crime. →	**Step 2:** [A]*nd* indicates the relevant relationship: Fact 1: The number of auto thefts is down over the past five years. *and* Fact 2: Car thieves are more likely to be convicted now than they were five years ago.
Which one of the following, if true, most helps to explain the facts cited above? →	**Step 1:** The correct answer helps "explain the facts . . . above"—a Paradox question (although here, the two facts may not appear contradictory).
	Step 3: There are fewer thefts, but a greater rate of convictions. To explain both facts, provide a reason that car thieves are now more likely to be apprehended or why the cases against them are more likely to result in convictions.
(A) Although there are fewer car thieves now than there were five years ago, the proportion of thieves who tend to abandon cars before their owners notice that they have been stolen has also decreased. →	**Step 4:** Correct. This provides an explanation for the increased conviction rate despite the overall decline in thefts.
(B) Car alarms are more common than they were five years ago, but their propensity to be triggered in the absence of any criminal activity has resulted in people generally ignoring them when they are triggered. →	This explains neither the lower number of thefts nor the increased conviction rate. Eliminate.
(C) An upsurge in home burglaries over the last five years has required police departments to divert limited resources to investigation of these cases. →	180. If anything, this would provide a reason why fewer car thieves are caught, making an increased conviction rate even more inexplicable. Eliminate.
(D) Because of the increasingly lucrative market for stolen automobile parts, many stolen cars are quickly disassembled and the parts are sold to various buyers across the country. →	This does not explain the decline in the number of thefts nor why a higher rate of thieves is convicted. Eliminate.
(E) There are more adolescent car thieves now than there were five years ago, and the sentences given to young criminals tend to be far more lenient than those given to adult criminals. *PrepTest61 Sec4 Q14* →	Without more evidence, there is no reason to believe that adolescent thieves are caught or convicted more often. Eliminate.

LSAT Question	Analysis
45. A recent study of major motion pictures revealed that the vast majority of their plots were simply variations on plots that had been used many times before. Despite this fact, many people enjoy seeing several new movies each year.	**Step 2**: "Despite this fact" indicates the conflict: Fact 1: Most motion pictures have derivative plots that have been used many times before. *but* Fact 2: People enjoy seeing several new movies per year. Why would people enjoy seeing movies that just recycle well-worn plots?
Each of the following, if true, would contribute to an explanation of the apparent discrepancy in the information above EXCEPT:	**Step 1**: Paradox EXCEPT question: The four wrong answers help explain the apparent discrepancy; the correct answer does not.
	Step 3: Answers that resolve the paradox—by showing that people enjoy familiar plots, that they are unaware that plots are recycled, or that other factors are more important than plot—are *wrong* answers. The correct answer does *not* help explain the situation.
(A) Movies based on standard plots are more likely to be financially successful than are ones based on original plots.	**Step 4**: Correct. This does nothing to explain why people enjoy seeing the well-worn plots again and again.
(B) If the details of their stories are sufficiently different, two movies with the same basic plot will be perceived by moviegoers as having different plots.	This helps explain the discrepancy—people are often not aware that they've seen the plot before. Eliminate.
(C) Because of the large number of movies produced each year, the odds of a person seeing two movies with the same general plot structure in a five-year period are fairly low.	This helps explain the discrepancy—people may be unaware that plots are recycled. Eliminate.
(D) A certain aesthetic pleasure is derived from seeing several movies that develop the same plot in slightly different ways.	This helps explain the discrepancy—people may actually enjoy seeing familiar plots. Eliminate.
(E) Although most modern movie plots have been used before, most of those previous uses occurred during the 1940s and 1950s. *PrepTest59 Sec3 Q17*	This helps explain the discrepancy—unless people know very old movies, they are unlikely to be aware of similarities in plots between movies. Eliminate.

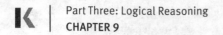

Perform

In each of the following Paradox questions, separate Fact A from Fact B in the stimulus, paraphrase the apparent contradiction, make a broad prediction of what could be true to resolve it, and select the answer choice that gives a specific fact that explains the paradox.

LSAT Question	My Analysis
46. After the rush-hour speed limit on the British M25 motorway was lowered from 70 miles per hour (115 kilometers per hour) to 50 miles per hour (80 kilometers per hour), rush-hour travel times decreased by approximately 15 percent.	Step 2:
Which one of the following, if true, most helps to explain the decrease in travel times described above?	Step 1:
	Step 3:
(A) After the decrease in the rush-hour speed limit, the average speed on the M25 was significantly lower during rush hours than at other times of the day.	Step 4:
(B) Travel times during periods other than rush hours were essentially unchanged after the rush-hour speed limit was lowered.	
(C) Before the rush-hour speed limit was lowered, rush-hour accidents that caused lengthy delays were common, and most of these accidents were caused by high-speed driving.	
(D) Enforcement of speed limits on the M25 was quite rigorous both before and after the rush-hour speed limit was lowered.	
(E) The number of people who drive on the M25 during rush hours did not increase after the rush-hour speed limit was lowered.	

PrepTest61 Sec4 Q12

	LSAT Question	My Analysis
47.	New technologies that promise to extend life and decrease pain involve innovations that require extensive scientific research. Therefore, investment in such technologies is very risky, because innovations requiring extensive scientific research also require large amounts of capital but are unlikely to provide any financial return. Nonetheless, some people are willing to invest in these new technologies. $\longrightarrow$	**Step 2:**
	Which one of the following, if true, most helps to explain why some people are willing to invest in new technologies that promise to extend life and decrease pain? $\longrightarrow$	**Step 1:**
		Step 3:
(A)	When investments in new technologies that promise to extend life and decrease pain do provide financial return, they generally return many times the original investment, which is much more than the return on safer investments. $\longrightarrow$	**Step 4:**
(B)	A large variety of new technologies that promise to extend life and decrease pain have been developed in the last decade. $\longrightarrow$	
(C)	The development of certain new technologies other than those that promise to extend life and decrease pain is also very risky, because these technologies require large amounts of capital but are unlikely to provide any financial return. $\longrightarrow$	
(D)	Some investments that initially seem likely to provide reasonably large financial return ultimately provide no financial return. $\longrightarrow$	
(E)	The scientific research necessary to develop new technologies that promise to extend life and decrease pain sometimes leads to no greater understanding of the natural world. $\longrightarrow$	

PrepTest59 Sec3 Q1

507

LSAT Question	My Analysis
48. A recent poll revealed that most students at our university prefer that the university, which is searching for a new president, hire someone who has extensive experience as a university president. However, in the very same poll, the person most students chose from among a list of leading candidates as the one they would most like to see hired was someone who has never served as a university president.	**Step 2:**
Which one of the following, if true, most helps to account for the apparent discrepancy in the students' preferences?	**Step 1:**
	Step 3:
(A) Because several of the candidates listed in the poll had extensive experience as university presidents, not all of the candidates could be differentiated on this basis alone.	**Step 4:**
(B) Most of the candidates listed in the poll had extensive experience as university presidents.	
(C) Students taking the poll had fewer candidates to choose from than were currently being considered for the position.	
(D) Most of the students taking the poll did not know whether any of the leading candidates listed in the poll had ever served as a university president.	
(E) Often a person can be well suited to a position even though they have relatively little experience in such a position.	

PrepTest61 Sec2 Q25

LSAT Question	My Analysis
49. A study conducted over a 6-month period analyzed daily attendance and average length of visit at the local art museum. The results showed that when the museum was not featuring a special exhibition, attendance tended to be lower but patrons spent an average of 45 minutes longer in the museum than when it was featuring a special exhibition. →	**Step 2:**
Each of the following, if true, could help to explain the differing average lengths of visits to the museum EXCEPT: →	**Step 1:**
	Step 3:
(A) Visitors to the museum during special exhibitions tend to have narrower artistic interests, and do not view as many different exhibits during their visit. →	**Step 4:**
(B) A plan to extend normal museum hours during special exhibitions was considered but not enacted during the period studied. →	
(C) Many people who go to special exhibitions go simply for the prestige of having been there. →	
(D) Admission tickets to the special exhibitions at the museum are issued for a specific 1-hour period on a specific day. →	
(E) Many people who go to special exhibitions are on organized tours and do not have the opportunity to browse. →	

PrepTest49 Sec4 Q25

509

Expert Analysis: Paradox Questions

LSAT Question	Analysis
46. After the rush-hour speed limit on the British M25 motorway was lowered from 70 miles per hour (115 kilometers per hour) to 50 miles per hour (80 kilometers per hour), rush-hour travel times decreased by approximately 15 percent. →	**Step 2:** Two facts occurring in sequence: Fact 1: The rush-hour speed limit was lowered on the M25 motorway. *but then* Fact 2: Rush-hour travel times on the M25 decreased.
Which one of the following, if true, most helps to explain the decrease in travel times described above? →	**Step 1:** "[M]ost helps to explain" indicates a Paradox question. The correct answer will explain or resolve the apparent discrepancy above.
	Step 3: How is it that speed limits were reduced (with cars presumably going slower), yet travel time has gone down? The correct answer will help explain the strange result. Perhaps fewer people are taking the road, or the decrease in the speed limit has increased the efficiency of driving on that road.
(A) After the decrease in the rush-hour speed limit, the average speed on the M25 was significantly lower during rush hours than at other times of the day. →	**Step 4:** Irrelevant Comparison. Differences between average speed and rush hour speed don't explain why a lower speed limit at rush hour is making for a faster rush-hour commute. Eliminate.
(B) Travel times during periods other than rush hours were essentially unchanged after the rush-hour speed limit was lowered. →	Outside the Scope. Travel times during other periods of the day don't help explain why rush-hour travel time has decreased. Eliminate.
(C) Before the rush-hour speed limit was lowered, rush-hour accidents that caused lengthy delays were common, and most of these accidents were caused by high-speed driving. →	Correct. This explains why rush-hour travel time is down despite slower speeds: The road is no longer clogged by accidents caused by faster drivers.
(D) Enforcement of speed limits on the M25 was quite rigorous both before and after the rush-hour speed limit was lowered. →	180. Showing a similarity between conditions before and after the new speed limit makes it even more confusing why there would have been a decrease in travel time. Eliminate.
(E) The number of people who drive on the M25 during rush hours did not increase after the rush-hour speed limit was lowered. *PrepTest61 Sec4 Q12* →	Distortion. Knowing that the number of people who drive on the M25 during rush hour *did not* increase does not explain why travel time has decreased. Eliminate.

LSAT Question	Analysis
47. New technologies that promise to extend life and decrease pain involve innovations that require extensive scientific research. Therefore, investment in such technologies is very risky, because innovations requiring extensive scientific research also require large amounts of capital but are unlikely to provide any financial return. Nonetheless, some people are willing to invest in these new technologies.	**Step 2:** *Nonetheless* signals the seemingly contradictory facts: Fact 1: Investing in new technologies that promise to extend life and decrease pain is risky, because such investments require much capital and are unlikely to be profitable. *but* Fact 2: There are people who do invest in these technologies.
Which one of the following, if true, most helps to explain why some people are willing to invest in new technologies that promise to extend life and decrease pain?	**Step 1:** "[M]ost helps to explain" indicates that this is a Paradox question. Select an answer choice that explains or resolves the apparent discrepancy above.
	Step 3: Why are some people investing in technology that appears to carry significant financial risk? Find an answer choice that helps explain the strange result. Perhaps people are investing for reasons other than monetary gain, or there is something that justifies investment despite the slim chance of profit.
(A) When investments in new technologies that promise to extend life and decrease pain do provide financial return, they generally return many times the original investment, which is much more than the return on safer investments.	**Step 4:** Correct. This provides a reason why people would be willing to assume the risk of the investment: high-risk, but high-reward. The potential payout is much greater than on safer investments.
(B) A large variety of new technologies that promise to extend life and decrease pain have been developed in the last decade.	Outside the Scope. According to the stimulus, all such technology is high-risk, so variety doesn't explain why people would invest. Eliminate.
(C) The development of certain new technologies other than those that promise to extend life and decrease pain is also very risky, because these technologies require large amounts of capital but are unlikely to provide any financial return.	Outside the Scope. The fact that other technologies carry similar risks doesn't help explain why people are investing in these technologies. Eliminate.
(D) Some investments that initially seem likely to provide reasonably large financial return ultimately provide no financial return.	Outside the Scope. The fact that some seemingly safe investments don't pan out doesn't explain why some people are investing in these high-risk technologies. Eliminate.
(E) The scientific research necessary to develop new technologies that promise to extend life and decrease pain sometimes leads to no greater understanding of the natural world.	180. This just deepens the paradox, because it removes a possible alternative reason why people would invest in this technology. Eliminate.

PrepTest59 Sec3 Q1

LSAT Question	Analysis
48. A recent poll revealed that most students at our university prefer that the university, which is searching for a new president, hire someone who has extensive experience as a university president. However, in the very same poll, the person most students chose from among a list of leading candidates as the one they would most like to see hired was someone who has never served as a university president. →	**Step 2:** *However* signals the paradox: Fact 1: Recently polled students said they wanted the new university president to have previous experience as a university president. *but* Fact 2: The same students' top choice on a list of candidates was someone with no experience as a university president.
Which one of the following, if true, most helps to account for the apparent discrepancy in the students' preferences? →	**Step 1:** The correct answer "helps to account for the apparent discrepancy" in the stimulus—a Paradox question.
	Step 3: Why would the students pick a candidate with no experience when they said they preferred candidates with experience? The correct answer will resolve this paradox. Maybe none of the candidates on the list had experience, or perhaps some other criterion trumps experience in students' minds.
(A) Because several of the candidates listed in the poll had extensive experience as university presidents, not all of the candidates could be differentiated on this basis alone. →	**Step 4:** 180. The students went with a candidate who had no experience. Knowing that other candidates had experience deepens the paradox. Eliminate.
(B) Most of the candidates listed in the poll had extensive experience as university presidents. →	180. The students went with a candidate who had no experience. Knowing that other candidates had experience deepens the paradox. Eliminate.
(C) Students taking the poll had fewer candidates to choose from than were currently being considered for the position. →	Without knowing whether any candidate had experience, this does not explain the students' seemingly contradictory choice. Eliminate.
(D) Most of the students taking the poll did not know whether any of the leading candidates listed in the poll had ever served as a university president. →	Correct. This essentially matches the first prediction. If students don't know that any candidate on the list has experience, then experience cannot be a differentiator among those on the list.
(E) Often a person can be well suited to a position even though they have relatively little experience in such a position. *PrepTest61 Sec2 Q25* →	This may be true, but it doesn't explain why students seemingly ignored their own criterion in choosing a favorite candidate from the list. Eliminate.

LSAT Question	Analysis
49. A study conducted over a 6-month period analyzed daily attendance and average length of visit at the local art museum. The results showed that when the museum was not featuring a special exhibition, attendance tended to be lower but patrons spent an average of 45 minutes longer in the museum than when it was featuring a special exhibition.	**Step 2**: Focus on *but*, which signals a contrast. When the museum has a special exhibit: Fact 1: Attendance was higher. *but* Fact 2: Patrons stayed a shorter time.
Each of the following, if true, could help to explain the differing average lengths of visits to the museum EXCEPT:	**Step 1**: A Paradox EXCEPT question: Here, the four wrong answers "help to explain" an apparent discrepancy; the correct answer will either deepen the confusion or will be irrelevant.
	Step 3: The four wrong answers *will help explain* the discrepant patterns in attendance. The correct answer will fail to give a reason why special exhibits tend to attract more visitors who stay for a shorter time.
(A) Visitors to the museum during special exhibitions tend to have narrower artistic interests, and do not view as many different exhibits during their visit.	**Step 4**: If people coming for the special exhibit have less interest in other exhibits, then there is some explanation for the shorter visits. Eliminate.
(B) A plan to extend normal museum hours during special exhibitions was considered but not enacted during the period studied.	Correct. The museum's rejected plans don't help us understand its actual attendance patterns.
(C) Many people who go to special exhibitions go simply for the prestige of having been there.	If people go to special exhibits to "see and be seen," then this would explain why they spend less time at the museum. Eliminate.
(D) Admission tickets to the special exhibitions at the museum are issued for a specific 1-hour period on a specific day.	If people have to come to special exhibits during prescribed windows of time, this would help explain why they spend less time at the museum (especially if their tickets were for just one or two hours before closing time). Eliminate.
(E) Many people who go to special exhibitions are on organized tours and do not have the opportunity to browse. *PrepTest49 Sec4 Q25*	If people have no opportunity to browse, it helps explain why they would spend less time at the museum. Eliminate.

REFLECTION

Think back over the work you've done in this chapter. Ask yourself the following questions.

- Are you able to recognize Inference questions and Principle questions calling for an inference?
- What patterns in Inference question stimuli should you be able to recognize?
- Can you remember and use the five tools that help to untangle Inference stimuli?
- Why are Extreme, 180, and Outside the Scope wrong answers so often associated with Inference questions? Can you recognize these wrong answer types when you see them?
- What do Paradox question stimuli always contain?
- Why are Keywords so helpful in untangling Paradox stimuli?
- How can you most effectively predict the correct answer to a Paradox question?

Every day, you hear people make inferences and deductions from one or more facts. The next time you encounter this in the "real world," ask yourself the following questions.

- In everyday life, we tend to use the term *inference* loosely. Sometimes we mean something closer to *guess*. Would this person's inference pass muster on the LSAT?
- If you encounter a flawed inference or deduction, does it match one of the LSAT wrong answer types? Is it, perhaps, too extreme to follow from the facts? Is it irrelevant? Or is it even contradictory to the facts given?

Likewise, if you encounter a person expressing confusion over what appears to him or her to be a paradox, pay attention.

- What are the two facts that appear to this person as contradictory?
- If someone offers an explanation, is it really a fact that helps resolve the paradox? Or is it perhaps outside the scope of the first person's question?

Practicing your LSAT skills is something you can learn to do almost any time because the skills tested on the LSAT are so central to the kinds of thinking, reading, and reasoning we do every day.

SUMMARY

Congratulations! Over the last three chapters, you've learned how to answer all of the Logical Reasoning question types on the LSAT. You will, of course, encounter all of the Logical Reasoning question types—Argument-Based, Assumption Family, and Non-Argument questions—in the full sections and tests you practice between now and Test Day. Return to Chapters 6, 7, 8, and 9 from time to time to brush up on strategies that may get rusty and to refresh your memory about all of the tools and tactics you've learned.

CHAPTER 10

Logical Reasoning Section Management

save to later:
parallel reasoning
parallel flawed

TIMING AND SECTION MANAGEMENT

Logical Reasoning Section Timing: The Basics

The facts: Every Logical Reasoning section contains 24–26 questions to be completed in 35 minutes.

The strategy: On average, then, you should take roughly 1 minute 20 seconds per question. You may be able to answer some easier questions correctly in less time. Some of the hardest or densest questions will take you longer. When you answer a question quickly, bank that time for tougher questions to come. If a question threatens to drag on for over a minute and a half, cross out those answers you've confidently eliminated, mark the question as incomplete, and move on. If you have time to come back to the question, that's great. If not, mark your score sheet with a guess from among the answer choices you were still considering. Always remember that your goal in timed section practice is to get as many correct answers as possible in 35 minutes. Don't overinvest in one or two tough questions to the detriment of your overall performance.

Here are a few of the principles of great section management that LSAT experts use to their advantage. Learn them and put them into practice whenever you undertake timed section or full-test practice.

Efficiency, Not Speed

The facts: Rereading several times (even if you do so quickly) will cost you more time than reading strategically once. A strong prediction of the correct answer increases the likelihood that you'll spot the right choice as you evaluate the answers.

egy: Follow the Logical Reasoning Method. In the preceding chapters, you've seen how identifying the
on, untangling the stimulus, and predicting the correct answer provide everything you need to answer
stions quickly and accurately. Don't let "clock anxiety" tempt you into abandoning the most efficient approach.
eing methodical *does not* mean being slow. When you have practiced enough that the Logical Reasoning Method
is second nature, you'll find that it provides the shortest and most direct route to correct answers, the single goal
of all the work you do on the LSAT.

Triage: Take Control of the Section

The facts: You are under no obligation to do the questions in the order in which they are presented. Typically, the
Logical Reasoning sections of the LSAT follow the pattern you see in the following chart. The early questions are
generally easier, although there is often one difficult question among the first 8–10 questions in the section. The
latter third of the section usually contains the highest concentration of hard questions, but there are often one or
two fairly easy questions near the very end of the section.

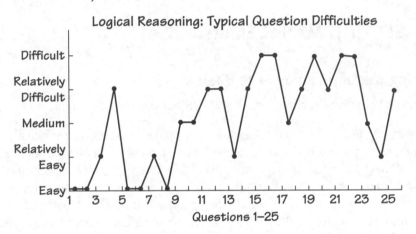

The strategy: It would be unreasonably time-consuming to try to evaluate the difficulty of 25 distinct items before
starting your work on the questions. In the Logical Reasoning section, "triage" needs to be done on a question-
by-question basis. Move through the section in order, but be willing to skip a question when it is to your benefit
to do so. To make time-management decisions in your own best interest, you must be able to 1) identify questions
quickly, 2) know your own strengths and weaknesses in Logical Reasoning, and 3) be fearless in looking for and
prioritizing the questions most likely to turn into correct answers for you.

Some LSAT experts find it most helpful to manage the Logical Reasoning sections by working straight through from
Question 1 to Question 25, skipping or guessing on problematic questions as they go. Others, taking their cue
from the pattern in the previous chart, work from Question 1 through Question 15, and then turn to the end of the
section and work backward from Question 25 to Question 16. The latter pattern ensures that the test taker will get
to the easier questions likely found at the end of the section.

Regardless of any grand plan or approach you take, your battle in the Logical Reasoning sections will be won step by step,
question by question. You will have to know the question types, what they ask for, and the most strategic approaches to
them to maximize your score. Consistent practice will lead to real efficiency: getting as many points as you can in
35 minutes.

Skip and Guess Strategically

The facts: You do not need to answer every question to get a great score. The features of certain questions are
time-consuming (e.g., long stimuli in Parallel Reasoning questions or dense Formal Logic in Inference questions) for
most test takers. There is no bonus for solving the hardest question(s) in the section.

The strategy: Remember that you are in control of how much time and effort you dedicate to any particular question. Allowing yourself to get into an "ego battle" with particular questions—"I *will* figure this one out no matter what!"—can take precious minutes away from other questions you could be answering quickly and accurately. Be willing to skip one or two difficult or very time-consuming questions if doing so will allow you to get more questions correct subsequently. Preempt situations in which you are guessing out of frustration—"Okay, I give up. I've already given this two minutes; I'll never get it!"—by learning to guess strategically—"I'll guess on this long Method of Argument question and give myself an extra two minutes for the next two pages." In other words, guess when it is in your benefit to do so. Stay in control of the section and the test.

TAKING THE TIMING SECTION

After the question stem exercise on the next few pages, there is a Logical Reasoning section that was originally Section 4 of PrepTest 45, administered in December 2004.

Proctoring

Complete this section under timed, test-like conditions. Give yourself 35 minutes, and finish in one uninterrupted sitting.

Scoring

After you finish the section, record your answers in the appropriate webgrid (PrepTest 45, Section 4) found in your online resources. This will make your results and percent correct easy to see, and the score report will contain links to the explanations for each question.

Review

When you review a section, review it completely, even those questions you got right. Check that you consistently followed the Logical Reasoning Method, identifying each question, untangling its stimulus effectively, using your analyses to predict the correct answers, and evaluating the choices quickly and accurately.

Activate Prior Knowledge: Identifying Logical Reasoning Question Stems

You've now seen the variety of ways in which the LSAT rewards both your ability to analyze and evaluate arguments, as well as your ability to make deductions from a set of statements. On Test Day, you must be able to quickly and accurately identify the question types so that you can apply all of the skills you've been mastering appropriately. LSAT experts know that a key component of success in Logical Reasoning sections is to be familiar with each question type and know immediately which skills and strategies they'll need.

Practice

For each of the following question stems, identify the question type and characterize the one right and four wrong answers.

Question Stem	My Analysis
1. If the above statements are true, then which of the following must also be true? →	Question Type: Inference 1 Right: 4 Wrong:
2. Which of the following principles most helps to justify the conclusion above? →	Question Type: Principle 1 Right: 4 Wrong:
3. Which of the following, if true, most contributes to a resolution of the apparent anomaly above? →	Question Type: Paradox 1 Right: 4 Wrong:
4. Which of the following best expresses the argument's error in reasoning? →	Question Type: Flaw 1 Right: 4 Wrong:
5. The argument above uses which of the following argumentative techniques? →	Question Type: Method of argument 1 Right: 4 Wrong:
6. Which of the following arguments contains an error in reasoning most similar to that in the argument above? →	Question Type: Parallel Flaw 1 Right: 4 Wrong:

Question Stem		My Analysis
7. The argument above relies on which of the following presuppositions?	→	Question Type: Assumption (Necessary) 1 Right: 4 Wrong:
8. Which of the following, if true, casts the most doubt on the conclusion above?	→	Question Type: Weaken 1 Right: 4 Wrong:
9. Each of the following, if true, supports the argument EXCEPT:	→	Question Type: Strengthen EXCEPT 1 Right: 4 Wrong:
10. The primary issue in dispute between Jax and Connor is	→	Question Type: Pointed Issue 1 Right: 4 Wrong:
11. Each of the following contributes to an explanation of the apparent discrepancy above EXCEPT:	→	Question Type: Paradox 1 Right: 4 Wrong:
12. If the above statements are true, then all of the following must be false EXCEPT:	→	Question Type: Inference 1 Right: inference or outside scope 4 Wrong: contradict

Expert Analysis: Logical Reasoning Question Stems

Here's how an LSAT expert would identify the question types and characterize the correct and incorrect answers for the question stems in that exercise.

Question Stem	Analysis
1. If the above statements are true, then which of the following must also be true?	Question Type: Inference—signal is "must … be true" → 1 Right: Statement that must be true based on the stimulus 4 Wrong: Statements that could be false based on the stimulus
2. Which of the following principles most helps to justify the conclusion above?	Question Type: Principle—but *justify* makes this similar to a Strengthen question → 1 Right: A general rule that makes the conclusion more likely to follow from the evidence 4 Wrong: General rules irrelevant to the conclusion, or rules that weaken it
3. Which of the following, if true, most contributes to a resolution of the apparent anomaly above?	Question Type: Paradox—signal is *anomaly* → 1 Right: Statement that resolves the apparent contradiction 4 Wrong: Statements that make the apparent contradiction worse or that have no effect on it
4. Which of the following best expresses the argument's error in reasoning?	Question Type: Flaw—tag is "error in reasoning" → 1 Right: Description of why the conclusion does not logically follow from the evidence 4 Wrong: Descriptions of flaw types not present in the argument, or descriptions of unflawed aspects of the argument
5. The argument above uses which of the following argumentative techniques?	Question Type: Method of Argument—tag is "argumentative technique" → 1 Right: Description of the argument's structure 4 Wrong: Descriptions of argument structures not found in the stimulus
6. Which of the following arguments contains an error in reasoning most similar to that in the argument above?	Question Type: Parallel Reasoning—"error in reasoning most similar to" indicates Parallel Flaw → 1 Right: Argument with the same flaw as the one in the stimulus 4 Wrong: Arguments with different flaw types, or unflawed arguments

Question Stem	Analysis
7. The argument above relies on which of the following presuppositions?	Question Type: Assumption—tag word is *presupposit...* *relies* signals Necessary Assumption question
	→ 1 Right: Description of the unstated fact or idea required for the conclusion to follow logically from the evidence
	4 Wrong: Restatements of evidence, statements irrelevant to the conclusion, or statements that weaken the conclusion
8. Which of the following, if true, casts the most doubt on the conclusion above?	Question Type: Weaken—tag is "casts doubt"
	→ 1 Right: Statement that makes the conclusion less likely to follow from the evidence
	4 Wrong: Statements that make the conclusion more likely to follow from the evidence or that have no effect on the conclusion
9. Each of the following, if true, supports the argument EXCEPT:	Question Type: Strengthen EXCEPT
	→ 1 Right: Statement irrelevant to the conclusion or statement that makes the conclusion less likely to follow from the evidence
	4 Wrong: Statements that make the conclusion more likely to follow from the evidence
10. The primary issue in dispute between Jax and Connor is	Question Type: Point at Issue—signal is *dispute*
	→ 1 Right: Description of the point of disagreement between the two speakers
	4 Wrong: Points of agreement between the speakers or issues about which one or both speakers have no opinion
11. Each of the following contributes to an explanation of the apparent discrepancy above EXCEPT:	Question Type: Paradox EXCEPT—key phrase is "apparent discrepancy"
	→ 1 Right: Statement that makes the apparent contradiction in the stimulus worse or that has no effect on it
	4 Wrong: Statements that resolve the apparent contradiction in the stimulus
12. If the above statements are true, then all of the following must be false EXCEPT:	Question Type: Inference EXCEPT
	→ 1 Right: Statement that could be true based on the stimulus
	4 Wrong: Statements that must be false based on the stimulus

PrepTest 45, Section 4

Time—35 minutes

25 Questions

section are based on the reasoning contained in brief statements or passages. For some
oices could conceivably answer the question. However, you are to choose the best answer; that
tely and completely answers the question. You should not make assumptions that are by
commonsense standards implausible, superfluous, or incompatible with the passage. After you have chosen the best answer,
blacken the corresponding space on your answer sheet.

1. Mayor McKinney's policies have often been criticized
    on the grounds that they benefit only wealthy city
    residents, but that is not a fair evaluation. Some of
    McKinney's policies have clearly benefited the city's
    less affluent residents. McKinney actively supported
    last year's proposal to lower the city's high property
    taxes. Because of this tax decrease, more
    development is taking place in the city, helping to
    end the housing shortage and stabilize the rents in
    the city.

    Which one of the following most accurately expresses
    the main conclusion of the argument?

    (A) It is impossible to tell whether McKinney is
         more committed to the interests of the
         wealthy than to those of the poor.
    (B) McKinney's policies have often been criticized
         for benefiting only wealthy city residents.
    (C) The decrease in property taxes that McKinney
         supported caused more development to take
         place in the city.
    (D) The criticism that McKinney's policies benefit
         only the wealthy is unjustified.
    (E) McKinney's efforts helped end the housing
         shortage and stabilize the rents in the city.

2. A factory spokesperson argued that the factory
    should not be required to clean up the water in the
    nearby wetlands, maintaining that although
    wastewater from the factory polluted the wetlands
    over the past several years, the factory is not to blame
    for this, since the disposal of the factory's wastewater
    is handled entirely by an independent contractor.

    Which one of the following arguments most closely
    conforms to the principle underlying the reasoning
    in the spokesperson's argument?

    (A) A recent survey revealed that over two-thirds
         of the teachers in the district are permitted to
         teach classes on subjects in which they have
         received no formal training. Thus parents of
         students in the district should check the
         qualifications of their children's teachers.
    (B) I object to the policy of making parents
         responsible for the offenses of their older
         adolescent children. After all, these
         adolescents have minds of their own and
         freely choose to act as they do, often in ways
         that do not reflect the wishes of their parents.
    (C) The students are justified in their objection to
         the reading assignment. Many of the topics
         concern material that is not covered in class,
         and students should not be required to do
         such reading in order to do well in the course.
    (D) The most recent appointee to the prize
         committee should not be permitted to
         participate in the selection of this year's
         winner. Unlike each of the other committee
         members, the appointee has a relative in the
         contest.
    (E) Despite all the publicity, I am skeptical of the
         politician's claims of having just returned
         from the remote village. Just two days ago a
         reporter spoke with the villagers and said that
         not a single one reported seeing the politician
         in the past several months.

GO ON TO THE NEXT PAGE.

3. Nylon industry spokesperson: Even though cotton and nylon are used for similar purposes, some people have the mistaken notion that cotton is natural but nylon is not. However, nylon's main components come from petroleum and from the nitrogen in the atmosphere. Clearly the atmosphere is natural. And petroleum comes from oil, which in turn comes from ancient plants—a natural source.

Which one of the following principles, if valid, most helps to justify the nylon industry spokesperson's reasoning?

(A) A substance is unnatural only if the function it serves is unnatural.

(B) A substance is no less natural than the processes used in its production.

(C) A substance is no more natural than its least natural component.

(D) One substance can be more natural than another if only one is wholly derived from natural substances.

(E) A substance is natural if the origins of its main components are natural.

4. Computer manufacturers and retailers tell us that the complexity involved in connecting the various components of personal computers is not a widespread obstacle to their use, but this is wrong. Customers who install accessories to their personal computers have to take full responsibility for the setting of jumpers and switches to satisfy mysterious specifications. Many accessories require extra software that can cause other accessories to stop working; adding a modem, for instance, may disable a printer.

Which one of the following, if true, most seriously weakens the argument?

(A) Personal computer instruction manuals usually explain the purposes of the jumpers and switches.

(B) Software for accessories can often be obtained for free.

(C) Installing an accessory will become extremely easy in the foreseeable future.

(D) A personal computer is usually sold as part of a package that includes accessories and free installation.

(E) Computer manufacturers rarely take into account ease of installation when they are designing programs or accessories.

5. Rats fed high doses of the artificial sweetener saccharin develop silicate crystals that are toxic to cells lining the bladder. When the cells regenerate, some are cancerous and form tumors. Unlike rats, mice fed high doses of saccharin do not get bladder cancer.

Which one of the following, if true, does the most to resolve the apparent discrepancy in the information above?

(A) Urine proteins that react with saccharin to form silicate crystals are found in rats but not in mice.

(B) Cells in the bladder regenerate more quickly in mice than they do in rats.

(C) High doses of saccharin are much more likely to produce silicate crystals than lower doses are.

(D) The silicate crystals are toxic only to the cells lining the bladder and not to other bladder cells.

(E) High doses of other artificial sweeteners have been shown to produce silicate crystals in mice but not in rats.

6. Although we could replace the beautiful—but dilapidated—old bridge across Black River with a concrete skyway, we should instead replace it with a cable bridge even though this would be more expensive than building a concrete skyway. The extra cost is clearly justified by the importance of maintaining the beauty of our river crossing.

Which one of the following is an assumption on which the argument depends?

(A) It is no more costly to maintain a cable bridge than a concrete skyway.

(B) A concrete skyway would not have any practical advantages over a cable bridge.

(C) The beauty of the river crossing must be preserved.

(D) If the new cable bridge is built, most people who see it will think the extra money well spent.

(E) Building a cable bridge across Black River would produce a more aesthetically pleasing result than building a concrete skyway.

GO ON TO THE NEXT PAGE.

7. A typical gasoline-powered lawn mower emits about as much air-polluting material per hour of use as does an automobile. Collectively, such mowers contribute significantly to summer air pollution. Since electric mowers emit no air pollutants, people can help reduce air pollution by choosing electric mowers over gasoline ones whenever feasible.

    Which one of the following, if true, provides the most support for the argument?

    (A) Lawns help to clean the air, replacing pollutants with oxygen.
    (B) Electric lawn mowers are more expensive to purchase and maintain than are gasoline mowers.
    (C) Producing the power to run an electric mower for an hour causes less air pollution than does running an automobile for an hour.
    (D) Most manufacturers of gasoline lawn mowers are trying to redesign their mowers to reduce the emission of air pollutants.
    (E) Lawn mowers are used for fewer hours per year than are automobiles.

8. Ariel: Government art subsidies never benefit art, for art's role is to challenge society's values. A society's values, however, are expressed by its government, and artists cannot challenge the very institution upon which they depend.

    Sasha: I agree that art should challenge society's values. However, by its very nature, a democratic government respects dissent and encourages challenges to its own values. Therefore, in a democratic society, government art subsidies ensure that artists can be fully committed to their work while expressing themselves freely.

    The dialogue most supports the claim that Ariel and Sasha disagree with each other about whether

    (A) art's role is to challenge society's values
    (B) a society's values are expressed by its government
    (C) artists can express themselves freely in a nondemocratic society
    (D) art subsidies provided by a democratic government benefit art
    (E) only governments that respect dissent ensure that art subsidies are fairly distributed

9. Public health expert: Until recently people believed that applications of biochemical research would eventually achieve complete victory over the microorganisms that cause human disease. However, current medical research shows that those microorganisms reproduce so rapidly that medicines developed for killing one variety will only spur the evolution of other varieties that are immune to those medicines. The most rational public health strategy, therefore, would place much more emphasis than at present on fully informing people about the transmission of diseases caused by microorganisms, with a view to minimizing the incidence of such diseases.

    Of the following, which one most accurately expresses the conclusion drawn by the public health expert?

    (A) A medicine that kills one variety of disease-causing microorganism can cause the evolution of a drug-resistant variety.
    (B) A patient who contracts a disease caused by microorganisms cannot be effectively cured by present methods.
    (C) There is good reason to make a particular change to public health policy.
    (D) No one who is fully informed about the diseases caused by microorganisms will ever fall victim to those diseases.
    (E) Some previous approaches to public health policy ignored the fact that disease-causing microorganisms reproduce at a rapid rate.

10. The enthusiastic acceptance of ascetic lifestyles evidenced in the surviving writings of monastic authors indicates that medieval societies were much less concerned with monetary gain than are contemporary Western cultures.

    The reasoning in the argument is most vulnerable to criticism on the grounds that the argument

    (A) employs the imprecise term "ascetic"
    (B) generalizes from a sample that is likely to be unrepresentative
    (C) applies contemporary standards inappropriately to medieval societies
    (D) inserts personal opinions into what purports to be a factual debate
    (E) advances premises that are inconsistent

GO ON TO THE NEXT PAGE.

11. Between 1976 and 1985, chemical wastes were dumped into Cod Bay. Today, 3 percent of the bay's bluefin cod population have deformed fins, and wary consumers have stopped buying the fish. In seeking financial reparations from companies that dumped the chemicals, representatives of Cod Bay's fishing industry have claimed that since the chemicals are known to cause genetic mutations, the deformity in the bluefin cod must have been caused by the presence of those chemicals in Cod Bay.

The answer to each of the following questions would be helpful in evaluating the representatives' claim EXCEPT:

(A) What is the incidence of deformed fins in blucfin cod that are not exposed to chemicals such as those dumped into Cod Bay?

(B) What was the incidence of deformed fins in bluefin cod in Cod Bay before the chemical dumping began?

(C) Has the consumption of the bluefin cod from Cod Bay that have deformed fins caused any health problems in the people who ate them?

(D) Are bluefin cod prone to any naturally occurring diseases that can cause fin deformities of the same kind as those displayed by the bluefin cod of Cod Bay?

(E) Are there gene-altering pollutants present in Cod Bay other than the chemical wastes that were dumped by the companies?

12. Columnist: If you received an unsigned letter, you would likely have some doubts about the truth of its contents. But news stories often include statements from anonymous sources, and these are usually quoted with the utmost respect. It makes sense to be skeptical of these sources, for, as in the case of the writer ofan unsigned letter, their anonymity makes it possible for them to plant inaccurate or slanted statements without ever having to answer for them.

The columnist's argument proceeds by

(A) pointing out that a certain attitude would presumably be adopted in one situation, in order to support the claim that a similar attitude would be justified in an analogous situation

(B) drawing an analogy between an attitude commonly adopted in one situation and a different attitude commonly adopted in another situation, and establishing that the latter attitude is better justified than the former

(C) inferring that an attitude would be justified in all situations of a given type on the grounds that this attitude is justified in a hypothetical situation of that type

(D) calling into question a certain type of evidence by drawing an analogy between that evidence and other evidence that the argument shows is usually false

(E) calling into question the motives of those presenting certain information, and concluding for this reason that the information is likely to be false

13. Art theft from museums is on the rise. Most stolen art is sold to wealthy private collectors. Consequently, since thieves steal what their customers are most interested in buying, museums ought to focus more of their security on their most valuablc pieces.

The argument depends on assuming which one of the following?

(A) Art thieves steal both valuable and not-so-valuable art.

(B) Art pieces that are not very valuable are not very much in demand by wealthy private collectors.

(C) Art thieves steal primarily from museums that are poorly secured.

(D) Most museums provide the same amount of security for valuable and not-so-valuable art.

(E) Wealthy private collectors sometimes sell their stolen art to other wealthy private collectors.

GO ON TO THE NEXT PAGE.

14. Insufficient rain can cause crops to falter and agricultural prices to rise. Records indicate that during a certain nation's recent crisis, faltering crops and rising agricultural prices prompted the government to take over food distribution in an effort to prevent starvation. Thus, the weather must have played an important role in bringing about the crisis.

The argument's reasoning is most vulnerable to criticism on the grounds that the argument

(A) concludes, merely from the fact that the period of insufficient rain occurred before the nation's crisis, that insufficient rain caused the nation's crisis

(B) fails to take into account the possibility that the scarcity was not severe enough to justify the government's taking over food distribution

(C) uses the term "crisis" equivocally in the reasoning, referring to both a political crisis and an economic crisis

(D) infers, merely from the fact that one event could have caused a second event, that the first event in fact caused the second

(E) takes for granted that any condition that is necessary for an increase in agricultural prices is also sufficient for such an increase

15. The cost of a semester's tuition at a certain university is based on the number of courses in which a student enrolls that semester. Although the cost per course at that university has not risen in four years, many of its students who could afford the tuition when they first enrolled now claim they can no longer afford it.

Each of the following, if true, helps to resolve the apparent discrepancy above EXCEPT:

(A) Faculty salaries at the university have risen slightly over the past four years.

(B) The number of courses per semester for which full-time students are required to enroll is higher this year than any time in the past.

(C) The cost of living in the vicinity of the university has risen over the last two years.

(D) The university awards new students a large number of scholarships that are renewed each year for the students who maintain high grade averages.

(E) The university has turned many of its part-time office jobs, for which students had generally been hired, into full-time, nonstudent positions.

16. People are not happy unless they feel that they are needed by others. Most people in modern society, however, can achieve a feeling of indispensability only within the sphere of family and friendship, because almost everyone knows that his or her job could be done by any one of thousands of others.

The statements above most strongly support which one of the following?

(A) People who realize that others could fill their occupational roles as ably as they do themselves cannot achieve any happiness in their lives.

(B) The nature of modern society actually undermines the importance of family life to an individual's happiness.

(C) Most people in modern society are happy in their private lives even if they are not happy in their jobs.

(D) A majority of people in modern society do not appreciate having the jobs that they do have.

(E) Fewer than a majority of people in modern society can find happiness outside the sphere of private interpersonal relationships.

17. Art critic: Criticism focuses on two issues: first, whether the value of an artwork is intrinsic to the work; and second, whether judgments about an artwork's quality are objective rather than merely matters of taste. These issues are related, for if an artwork's value is not intrinsic, then it must be extrinsic, and thus judgments about the quality of the work can only be a matter of taste.

The art critic's reasoning is most vulnerable to the criticism that it takes for granted that

(A) judgments about the quality of an artwork are always a matter of taste

(B) people sometimes agree about judgments that are only matters of taste

(C) judgments about extrinsic value cannot be objective

(D) judgments about intrinsic value are always objective

(E) an artwork's value is sometimes intrinsic to it

GO ON TO THE NEXT PAGE.

18. Decentralization enables divisions of a large institution to function autonomously. This always permits more realistic planning and strongly encourages innovation, since the people responsible for decision making are directly involved in implementing the policies they design. Decentralization also permits the central administration to focus on institution-wide issues without being overwhelmed by the details of daily operations.

    The statements above most strongly support which one of the following?

    (A) In large institutions whose divisions do not function autonomously, planning is not maximally realistic.

    (B) Innovation is not always encouraged in large centralized institutions.

    (C) For large institutions the advantages of decentralization outweigh its disadvantages.

    (D) The central administrations of large institutions are usually partially responsible for most of the details of daily operations.

    (E) The people directly involved in implementing policies are always able to make innovative and realistic policy decisions.

19. According to some astronomers, Earth is struck by a meteorite large enough to cause an ice age on an average of once every 100 million years. The last such incident occurred nearly 100 million years ago, so we can expect that Earth will be struck by such a meteorite in the near future. This clearly warrants funding to determine whether there is a means to protect our planet from such meteorite strikes.

    The reasoning in the argument is most subject to criticism on the grounds that the argument

    (A) makes a bold prescription on the basis of evidence that establishes only a high probability for a disastrous event

    (B) presumes, without providing justification, that the probability of a chance event's occurring is not affected by whether the event has occurred during a period in which it would be expected to occur

    (C) moves from evidence about the average frequency of an event to a specific prediction about when the next such event will occur

    (D) fails to specify the likelihood that, if such a meteorite should strike Earth, the meteorite would indeed cause an ice age

    (E) presumes, without providing justification, that some feasible means can be found to deter large meteorite strikes

20. Polling data reveal that an overwhelming majority of nine-year-olds can correctly identify the logos of major cigarette brands. However, of those nine-year-olds who recognize such logos, less than 1 percent smoke. Therefore, there is little or no connection between recognition of cigarette brand logos and smoking.

    Which one of the following uses flawed reasoning most similar to the flawed reasoning above?

    (A) The concern about the long-term effect on dolphins of small quantities of mercury in the ocean is unfounded. During a three-month observation period, 1,000 dolphins were exposed to small quantities of mercury in seawater, with no effect on the animals.

    (B) Many ten-year-olds dream of becoming actors. Yet it is not likely they will seriously consider becoming actors, because most parents discourage their children from pursuing such a highly competitive career.

    (C) Most dentists recommend using fluoride to reduce the incidence of cavities, but few recommend giving up candy entirely; so, using fluoride is probably more effective in preventing cavities than is avoiding sweets.

    (D) A large percentage of men exercise moderately throughout their lives, but the average life span of those who do so is not significantly greater than of those who get little or no exercise. So there is little or no correlation between moderate exercise and good health.

    (E) Most people cannot name their legislative representatives. Nonetheless, this is insignificant, for when queried, most of them displayed an adequate command of current political issues.

GO ON TO THE NEXT PAGE.

21. Etiquette firmly opposes both obscene and malicious talk, but this does not imply that speech needs to be restricted by law. Etiquette does not necessarily even oppose the expression of offensive ideas. Rather, it dictates that there are situations in which the expression of potentially offensive, disturbing, or controversial ideas is inappropriate and that, where appropriate, the expression and discussion of such ideas is to be done in a civil manner.

    Which one of the following judgments most closely corresponds to the principles of etiquette stated above?

    (A) Neighbors should not be gruff or unfriendly to one another when they meet on the street.
    (B) When prosecutors elicit testimony from a cooperative witness they should do so without intensive questioning.
    (C) There should be restrictions on speech only if a large majority of the population finds the speech offensive and hateful.
    (D) The journalists at a news conference should not ask a politician potentially embarrassing questions about a controversial policy issue.
    (E) The moderator of a panel discussion of a divisive moral issue should not allow participants to engage in name-calling.

22. The only preexisting recordings that are transferred onto compact disc are those that record companies believe will sell well enough on compact disc to be profitable. So, most classic jazz recordings will not be transferred onto compact disc, because few classic jazz recordings are played on the radio.

    The conclusion above follows logically if which one of the following is assumed?

    (A) Few of the preexisting recordings that record companies believe can be profitably transferred to compact disc are classic jazz recordings.
    (B) Few compact discs featuring classic jazz recordings are played on the radio.
    (C) The only recordings that are played on the radio are ones that record companies believe can be profitably sold as compact discs.
    (D) Most record companies are less interested in preserving classic jazz recordings than in making a profit.
    (E) No recording that is not played on the radio is one that record companies believe would be profitable if transferred to compact disc.

23. Agricultural economist: Over the past several years, increases in worldwide grain production have virtually ceased. Further increases will be extremely difficult; most usable farmland is already being farmed with near-maximal efficiency. But worldwide demand for grain has been increasing steadily, due largely to continuing population growth. Hence, a severe worldwide grain shortage is likely.

    Which one of the following most accurately describes the role played in the agricultural economist's argument by the claim that further increases in worldwide grain production will be extremely difficult?

    (A) It is one of the two conclusions drawn by the agricultural economist, neither of which is used to provide support for the other.
    (B) It is a description of a phenomenon, a causal explanation of which is the main conclusion of the argument.
    (C) It is the only premise offered in support of the argument's main conclusion.
    (D) It is a prediction for which the agricultural economist's first claim is offered as the primary justification.
    (E) It is an intermediate conclusion that is presented as evidence for the argument's main conclusion.

GO ON TO THE NEXT PAGE.

24. Bardis: Extensive research shows that television advertisements affect the buying habits of consumers. Some people conclude from this that violent television imagery sometimes causes violent behavior. But the effectiveness of television advertisements could be a result of those televised images being specifically designed to alter buying habits, whereas television violence is not designed to cause violent behavior. Hence we can safely conclude that violent television imagery does not cause violence.

The reasoning in Bardis's argument is flawed because that argument

(A) relies on an illegitimate inference from the fact that advertisements can change behavior to the claim that advertisements can cause violent behavior

(B) fails to distinguish a type of behavior from a type of stimulus that may or may not affect behavior

(C) undermines its own position by questioning the persuasive power of television advertising

(D) concludes that a claim is false on the basis of one purported fault in an argument in favor of that claim

(E) fails to consider the possibility that the argument it disputes is intended to address a separate issue

25. Sarah: Our regulations for staff review are vague and thus difficult to interpret. For instance, the regulations state that a staff member who is performing unsatisfactorily will face dismissal, but they fail to define unsatisfactory performance. Thus, some staff may be dismissed merely because their personal views conflict with those of their supervisors.

Which one of the following generalizations, if applicable to Sarah's company, most helps to justify her reasoning?

(A) Performance that falls only somewhat below expectations results in disciplinary measures short of dismissal.

(B) Interpreting regulations is a prerogative that belongs solely to supervisors.

(C) A vague regulation can be used to make those subject to it answer for their performance.

(D) A vague regulation can be used to keep those subject to it in subordinate positions.

(E) Employees usually consider specific regulations to be fairer than vague regulations.

S T O P

IF YOU FINISH BEFORE TIME IS CALLED, YOU MAY CHECK YOUR WORK ON THIS SECTION ONLY.
DO NOT WORK ON ANY OTHER SECTION IN THE TEST.

ANSWER KEY

1. D
2. B
3. E
4. D
5. A
6. E
7. C
8. D
9. C
10. B
11. C
12. A
13. B
14. D
15. A
16. E
17. C
18. A
19. C
20. A
21. E
22. E
23. E
24. D
25. B

Complete explanations for this section can be found in your online resources.

PART FOUR

Reading Comprehension

CHAPTER 11

The Kaplan Reading Comprehension Method

A STRATEGIC APPROACH TO READING COMPREHENSION

Prepare

> ### LEARNING OBJECTIVES
>
> In this section, you'll learn to:
>
> - State the steps of the Kaplan Reading Comprehension Method and the purpose of each step

The structure and, to some extent, content of Reading Comprehension passages remains virtually unchanged from test to test. More importantly, the questions in this section consistently test and reward the same reading and reasoning skills. LSAT experts use this predictability to their advantage, and their goal in each passage is simple: Read the passage strategically, with an eye focused on opinions and structure, and then refer back to the text to answer specific questions.

As an example, take a look at this question stem from an LSAT Reading Comprehension section:

The information in the passage suggests that the author would most likely agree with which one of the following statements regarding training in statutory law?

PrepTest59 Sec4 Q14

The question stem asks the reader to identify the statement with which the author would most likely agree. But, based on what information? The stem is clear: based on the information *in the passage*.

> ### LSAT STRATEGY
>
> LSAT experts rely only on information presented in the passages to answer Reading Comprehension questions.

In this chapter, you'll see how an expert works through a passage and the accompanying questions using the Reading Comprehension Method. In Chapter 12, you'll see a more detailed discussion of each of the five steps involved.

Reading Comprehension as an Expert Sees It

5 –28– **5** **5**

> Identify signals in question stems that indicate question type.

5

A proficiency in understanding, applying, and even formulating statutes—the actual texts of laws enacted by legislative bodies—is a vital aspect of the practice of law, but statutory law is often given too little
(5) attention by law schools. Much of legal education, with its focus on judicial decisions and analysis of cases, can give a law student the impression that the practice of law consists mainly in analyzing past cases to determine their relevance to a client's situation and speculative interpretation of the law client's legal problem.

> *too little attn to statutory law in law school*

> *focus on cases misleading*

> Circle or underline Keywords to identify and organize structural elements and big-picture ideas in a passage.

discover fairly soon, however, that much does not depend on the kind of analysis of cases that is performed in law example, a lawyer representing the owner often find an explicit answer as to what the client should do about a certain tax-related
(20) issue by consulting the relevant statutes. In such a case the facts are clear and the statutes' relation to them transparent, so that the client's question can be answered by direct reference to the wording of the statutes. But statutes' meanings and their applicability to relevant situations are not always so obvious, and that is one reason that the ability to interpret them
(25) accurately is an essential skill for law students to learn. Another skill that teaching statutory law would improve is synthesis. Law professors work hard at developing their students' ability to analyze individual cases, but in so doing they favor the ability to apply
(30) law in particular cases over the ability to understand the interrelations among all the statutes of a legal of the law would enable laws form a coherent w
(35) able to apply this abilit statutory law that they practice. This is especia students intend to speci of the law.
(40) One possible argument against including training in statutory law as a standard part of law school curricula is that many statutes vary from region to region within a nation, so that the mastery of a set of statutes would usually not be generally applicable. There is some truth
(45) to this objection; law schools that currently provide some training in statutes generally intend it as a preparation for practice in their particular region, but for schools that are nationally oriented, this could seem to be an inappropriate investment of time and
(50) resources. But while the knowledge of a particular region's statutory law is not generally transferable to other regions, the skills acquired in mastering a particular set of statutes are, making the study of statutory law an important undertaking even for law
(55) schools with a national orientation.

> *ex: lawyer and shop owner*

> *statutes not always cut and dry—must learn to interpret them*

> *must learn statutory synthesis*

> Margin notes summarize content and opinions for quick research while answering questions. *(Hint: Don't shy away from using symbols you already use in everyday life.)*

> *Dissent—regional variation prevents gen. application*

> *Au: still ok for nat'lly oriented schools b/c skills are the value, not specific stat. knowledge*

9. Which one of the following most accurately expresses the main point of the passage?

(A) In spite of the reservations that nationally oriented law schools can be expected to have, law schools can serve the overall needs of law students better by implementing a standard national curriculum in statutory law.

(B) Since the skills promoted by the study of statutory law are ultimately more important than those promoted by case analysis, the relative emphasis that law schools place on these two areas should be reversed.

(C) Although statutes typically vary from region to region, law schools should provide training in statutory law in order to develop students' ability interpret

(D) I   ning,
                                              most
   important assets that students can have.

(E) Law schools generally are deficient in their attention to statutory law training and therefore fail to impart the skills necessary for the analysis of legal information.

> *Always circle the correct answer to a question before moving on.*

10. Which one of the following is cited in the passage as a reason that might be given for not including statutory law training in law school curricula?

(A) Such training wou   the far more imp   ability to analyze

(B) Such training is n   what is already p   school education

(C) The goals of such training can better be achieved by other means, most of which are more directly related to the actual practice of law.

(D) Such training would be irrelevant for those students who do not plan to specialize.

(E) The lack of geographic uniformity among statutory laws makes expertise in the statutes of any particular region generally nontransferable.

> In addition to question type, pay attention to key information in a question stem that tells you where or what to research.

> Circle or underline the words that clearly identify a *wrong* answer before crossing it out and evaluating the next answer choice.

5   (5)   5   -29- 5

inf.

> Make a note of the question type if the question stem does not explicitly state the question's task.

11. Which one of the following would, if true, most weaken the author's argument as expressed in the passage?

(A) Many law school administrators recommend the i...
curri...

> Cross out answer choices that are definitely incorrect, but leave challenging or ambiguous-sounding answer choices unmarked so you can reevaluate them later. Returning to debate between two potential answer choices is preferable to debating among five.

(B) Most ...
profi...
expe...

(C) Mo...
geog...
scho...

(D) The c...
scho...

(E) Most ...
statutory law are thoroughly familiar with only a narrow range of statutes.

12. The author discusses the skill of synthesis in the third paragraph primarily in order to

(A) identify and describe one of the benefits that the author says would result from the change that is advocated in the passage

(B) indi...
oth...
this...

> Don't hesitate to circle an answer choice that perfectly matches your prediction and then move on without reading the remaining choices. The LSAT rewards this type of bold behavior.

(C) argu...
co...
ear...

(D) expl...
of ...

(E) prov...
typ...

13. Which one of the following questions can be most clearly and directly answered by reference to information in the passage?

(A) What are some ways in which synthetic skills are strengthened or encouraged through the analysis of cases and judicial decisions?

(B) In which areas of legal practice is a proficiency in case analysis more valuable than a proficiency in statutory law?

(C) What skills are common to the study of both statutory law and judicial decisions?

(D) What are some objections that have been raised against including the regionally oriented ...

What is the primary ...
currently offered i...

> Identify particulary challenging or time-consuming questions. To maximize the number of questions you get correct, you may need to sacrifice a hard question early on to have time for two or three questions later.

14. The information in the passage suggests that the author would most likely agree with which one of the following statements regarding training in statutory law?

(A) While nationally oriented law schools have been deficient in statutory law training, most regionally oriented law schools have been equally deficient in the teaching of case law.

(B) Training in statutory law would help lawyers resolve legal questions for which the answers are not immediately apparent in the relevant statutes.

(C) Lawyers who are trained in statutory law typically also develop a higher level of efficiency in manipulating details of past cases as compared with lawyers who are not trained in this way.

(D) Courses in statutory l...
focus specifically on ...
region or in a particu...

(E) Lawyers who do not ...
little need for trainin...
brief introduction to ...

> Always note words in question stems that appear in all caps. These words can be easy to overlook or forget.

15. Each of the following conforms to the kinds of educational results that the author would expect from the course of action proposed in the passage EXCEPT:

(A) skill in locating references to court decisions on an issue involving a particular statute regarding taxation

(B) an understanding of the ways in which certain underl...
interrelated gr...

(C) a knowledge of ...
formulated

(D) familiarity with ...
of laws applyi...
region or loca...

(E) an appreciation ...
involved in dr...

> After choosing an answer, circle challenging questions that you may want to come back to once all the other questions in a section have been answered.

PrepTest59 Sec4 Qs 9–15

GO ON TO THE NEXT PAGE.

~e Kaplan Reading Comprehension Method

The work modeled on the preceding pages is the result of an LSAT expert using the Reading Comprehension Method. This approach provides a consistent, strategic way to approach each passage and every question you will see in an LSAT Reading Comprehension section.

THE KAPLAN READING COMPREHENSION METHOD

Step 1: Read the Passage Strategically—Circle Keywords and jot down margin notes to summarize the portions of the passage relevant to LSAT questions; summarize the author's Topic/Scope/Purpose/Main Idea.

Step 2: Read the Question Stem—Identify the question type, characterize the correct and incorrect answers, and look for clues to guide your research.

Step 3: Research the Relevant Text—Based on the clues in the question stem, consult your Roadmap; for open-ended questions, refer to your Topic/Scope/Purpose/Main Idea summaries.

Step 4: Predict the Correct Answer—Based on research (or, for open-ended questions, your Topic/Scope/Purpose/Main Idea summaries) predict the correct answer.

Step 5: Evaluate the Answer Choices—Select the choice that matches your prediction of the correct answer or eliminate the four wrong answer choices.

Practice

Step 1: Read the Passage Strategically

To do well in the Reading Comprehension section of the LSAT, it's imperative to read strategically.

> **Strategic reading:** focusing on Keywords and phrases to determine the structure of a passage and to identify the author's Purpose and Main Idea.

Contrast this approach to the way you typically read academic materials for a college course. You won't answer many LSAT Reading Comprehension questions by focusing on details in a passage; instead, you win points by understanding *why* details are used.

When tackling the passages in the Reading Comprehension section, experts focus on two things:

1) Creating a **Roadmap** for each passage that highlights the main points of each paragraph, as well as areas of conflict or contrast
2) Understanding a passage's **big picture** by noting the Topic, Scope, Purpose, and Main Idea of each passage

The Physical Roadmap—Keywords and Margin Notes

The LSAT expert reads with pencil in hand. As she reads, she circles or underlines Keywords that indicate the passage's structure and the author's purpose. Keywords fall into six categories.

READING COMPREHENSION: KEYWORD CATEGORIES

Emphasis/Opinion—words that signal that the author finds a detail noteworthy or has a positive or negative opinion about it, or any subjective or evaluative language on the author's part (e.g., *especially, crucial, unfortunately, disappointing, I suggest, it seems likely*)

Contrast—words indicating that the author thinks two details or ideas are incompatible or illustrate conflicting points (e.g., *but, yet, despite, on the other hand*)

Logic—words that indicate an argument, either the author's or someone else's (e.g., *thus, therefore, because*)

Illustration—words indicating an example offered to clarify or support another point (e.g., *for example, this shows, to illustrate*)

Sequence/Chronology—words showing steps in a process or developments over time (e.g., *traditionally, in the past, recently, today, first, second, finally, earlier, since*)

Continuation—words indicating that a subsequent example or detail supports the same point or illustrates the same idea (e.g., *moreover, in addition, also, further*)

in order of importance

As the LSAT expert reads a passage strategically, she also makes brief, abbreviated notes to indicate important points in the text, points to which she is likely to return when answering the questions.

The Mental Roadmap—Summarizing Topic/Scope/Purpose/Main Idea

While the expert's pencil is circling Keywords and jotting down margin notes, her mind is also keeping track of the author's big picture, building a summary of the passage as she reads. There are four concepts involved in the big picture.

READING COMPREHENSION: THE BIG PICTURE

Topic—the overall subject of the passage

Scope—the particular aspect of the Topic that the author is focusing on

Purpose—the author's reason for writing the passage (express this as a verb—e.g., *to refute, to outline, to evaluate, to critique*)

Main Idea—the author's conclusion or overall takeaway; if you combine the author's Purpose and Scope, you'll usually have a good sense of the Main Idea

---

On Test Day, there is no reason to write down your big-picture summaries. Just make sure you can articulate the author's Purpose and Main Idea within the Scope of the passage so that you can predict the correct answers to Global questions and Inference questions that reward an understanding of the author's overall point of view.

Try reading a passage strategically, focusing on Keywords and the big-picture summaries. Don't worry if you're not fast or confident with this approach yet. You'll have many opportunities to practice and refine this approach as you learn to master Reading Comprehension.

A proficiency in understanding, applying, and even formulating statutes—the actual texts of laws enacted by legislative bodies—is a vital aspect of the practice of law, but statutory law is often given too little

(5) attention by law schools. Much of legal education, with its focus on judicial decisions and analysis of cases, can give a law student the impression that the practice of law consists mainly in analyzing past cases to determine their relevance to a client's situation and

(10) arriving at a speculative interpretation of the law relevant to the client's legal problem.

Lawyers discover fairly soon, however, that much of their practice does not depend on the kind of painstaking analysis of cases that is performed in law

(15) school. For example, a lawyer representing the owner of a business can often find an explicit answer as to what the client should do about a certain tax-related issue by consulting the relevant statutes. In such a case the facts are clear and the statutes' relation to them

(20) transparent, so that the client's question can be answered by direct reference to the wording of the statutes. But statutes' meanings and their applicability to relevant situations are not always so obvious, and that is one reason that the ability to interpret them

(25) accurately is an essential skill for law students to learn. Another skill that teaching statutory law would improve is synthesis. Law professors work hard at developing their students' ability to analyze individual cases, but in so doing they favor the ability to apply the

(30) law in particular cases over the ability to understand the interrelations among laws. In contrast, the study of all the statutes of a legal system in a certain small area of the law would enable the student to see how these laws form a coherent whole. Students would then be

(35) able to apply this ability to synthesize in other areas of statutory law that they encounter in their study or practice. This is especially important because most students intend to specialize in a chosen area, or areas, of the law.

(40) One possible argument against including training in statutory law as a standard part of law school curricula is that many statutes vary from region to region within a nation, so that the mastery of a set of statutes would usually not be generally applicable. There is some truth

(45) to this objection; law schools that currently provide some training in statutes generally intend it as a preparation for practice in their particular region, but for schools that are nationally oriented, this could seem to be an inappropriate investment of time and

(50) resources. But while the knowledge of a particular region's statutory law is not generally transferable to other regions, the skills acquired in mastering a particular set of statutes are, making the study of statutory law an important undertaking even for law

(55) schools with a national orientation.

Handwritten annotations:

statutes important - not enough in law school

focusing just on case law is misleading

cases not so important in practice of law

ex.

not always so clear - need to learn to interpret

- skill = synthesis
- student able to analyze individ cases but need to be able to understand intent.
Author thinks study statutes in small area help see laws as whole → synthesis

seeing coherent whole

most students specialize in law → imp. b/c of specialization

argument against: statutes vary regionally

concession not nationally oriented

skills of mastering set of statutes imp.

> On the next page, review an LSAT expert's work on this passage. In Reading Comprehension expert analyses, the Analysis column will reflect the expert's internal monologue as he reads, paraphrases, and summarizes.

PrepTest59 Sec4 Qs 9–15

A proficiency in understanding, applying, and even formulating statutes—the actual texts of laws enacted by legislative bodies—is a vital aspect of the practice of law, but statutory law is often given too little
(5) attention by law schools. Much of legal education, with its focus on judicial decisions and analysis of cases, can give a law student the impression that the practice of law consists mainly in analyzing past cases to determine their relevance to a client's situation and
(10) arriving at a speculative interpretation of the law relevant to the client's legal problem.

Too little attn to statutory law in law school

Focus on cases misleading

Proficiency with statutes is very important for the practice of law, *but* law schools pay them little attention. Law schools focus on case law, giving students the impression that applying past cases is what legal practice is all about. **Topic:** legal education. **Scope:** the (too limited) role of statutory law. The passage is likely to further explain the importance of statutory law and may suggest how legal education should emphasize it.

Lawyers discover fairly soon, however, that much of their practice does not depend on the kind of painstaking analysis of cases that is performed in law
(15) school. For example, a lawyer representing the owner of a business can often find an explicit answer as to what the client should do about a certain tax-related issue by consulting the relevant statutes. In such a case the facts are clear and the statutes' relation to them
(20) transparent, so that the client's question can be answered by direct reference to the wording of the statutes. But statutes' meanings and their applicability to relevant situations are not always so obvious, and that is one reason that the ability to interpret them
(25) accurately is an essential skill for law students to learn.

Ex. lawyer and shop owner

Statutes not always so cut and dried – must learn to interpret them

Despite the focus on case law in law school, lawyers in practice soon discover statutes are crucial. A lengthy example: A lawyer uses statutes to advise a client with tax issues. Statutes are not always clear; law students should learn how to interpret them.

Another skill that teaching statutory law would improve is synthesis. Law professors work hard at developing their students' ability to analyze individual cases, but in so doing they favor the ability to apply the
(30) law in particular cases over the ability to understand the interrelations among laws. In contrast, the study of all the statutes of a legal system in a certain small area of the law would enable the student to see how these laws form a coherent whole. Students would then be
(35) able to apply this ability to synthesize in other areas of statutory law that they encounter in their study or practice. This is especially important because most students intend to specialize in a chosen area, or areas, of the law.

Must learn statutory synthesis

Seeing coherent whole is beneficial

b/c of specialization

Synthesis is another skill that would be improved by learning statutory law. Law professors emphasize application of cases *instead of* interrelationship among laws. Author: Law schools should, in contrast, teach statutory interpretation in a small area of law to teach the skill; then students will learn to apply it in other areas, and this is *especially important* because most students intend to specialize in practice.

(40)   One possible argument against including training in statutory law as a standard part of law school curricula is that many statutes vary from region to region within a nation, so that the mastery of a set of statutes would usually not be generally applicable. There is some truth
(45) to this objection; law schools that currently provide some training in statutes generally intend it as a preparation for practice in their particular region, but for schools that are nationally oriented, this could seem to be an inappropriate investment of time and
(50) resources. But while the knowledge of a particular region's statutory law is not generally transferable to other regions, the skills acquired in mastering a particular set of statutes are, making the study of statutory law an important undertaking even for law
(55) schools with a national orientation.

Dissent– regional variation prevents general application

Auth – still Ok for nat'lly oriented schools b/c skills are the value, not the specific statutory knowledge

A possible argument against teaching more statutory law: Statutes vary regionally or state-to-state. The author acknowledges *some truth* to this objection, particularly for national law schools. Author: *But* the objection is limited to the content of local statutes, *not* to the *skills* involved in interpreting and synthesizing statutes. Thus, the author's **Purpose** is to discuss/outline the value of increasing statutory law curricula in law school, and his **Main Idea** is that skills acquired in studying statutory law are, even acknowledging reasonable objections, important enough to justify a greater emphasis in law school.

Steps 2 through 5: Answering Reading Comprehension Questions

After an LSAT expert has read a Reading Comprehension passage, noting the structure and summarizing the big picture, she turns to Steps 2 through 5 of the Reading Comprehension Method for a consistent, effective, and efficient approach to the questions.

Take a look at how an LSAT expert would approach the first question associated with the Statutory Law passage.

LSAT Question	Analysis
Which one of the following most accurately expresses the main point of the passage? →	**Step 2:** This asks for the Main Idea of the entire passage, so it's a Global question.
	Step 3: Consult the big picture Main Idea summary.
	Step 4: The author's Main Idea was identified in paragraph 4: Despite some objections, statutory law should be a larger focus of curricula in both regional and national law schools. Find a match in the answer choices.
(A) In spite of the reservations that nationally oriented law schools can be expected to have, law schools can serve the overall needs of law students better by implementing a standard national curriculum in statutory law. →	**Step 5:** The author never suggests that statutory law curricula need to be *standardized* nationally. Eliminate.
(B) Since the skills promoted by the study of statutory law are ultimately more important than those promoted by case analysis, the relative emphasis that law schools place on these two areas should be reversed. →	Distortion. Although the author would like to see law schools teach more statutory law, he never suggests a flip in curricula from case analysis to statutory law. Eliminate.
(C) Although statutes typically vary from region to region, law schools should provide training in statutory law in order to develop students' ability to synthesize legal information and interpret individual statutes. →	Correct. This matches the prediction.
(D) In the theoretical world of law school training, as opposed to the actual practice of law, a proficiency in case law is often one of the most important assets that students can have. →	Outside the Scope. The author is focused on the actual practice of law. So, his recommendation to increase training in statutory law is not concerned with the "theoretical world." Eliminate.
(E) Law schools generally are deficient in their attention to statutory law training and therefore fail to impart the skills necessary for the analysis of legal information. →	Extreme. Law schools "fail to impart the skills necessary" is excessive. Eliminate.

PrepTest59 Sec4 Q9

A proficiency in understanding, applying, and even
formulating statutes—the actual texts of laws enacted
by legislative bodies—is a vital aspect of the practice
of law, but statutory law is often given too little
(5) attention by law schools. Much of legal education, with
its focus on judicial decisions and analysis of cases,
can give a law student the impression that the practice
of law consists mainly in analyzing past cases to
determine their relevance to a client's situation and
(10) arriving at a speculative interpretation of the law
relevant to the client's legal problem.

Lawyers discover fairly soon, however, that much
of their practice does not depend on the kind of
painstaking analysis of cases that is performed in law
(15) school. For example, a lawyer representing the owner
of a business can often find an explicit answer as to
what the client should do about a certain tax-related
issue by consulting the relevant statutes. In such a case
the facts are clear and the statutes' relation to them
(20) transparent, so that the client's question can be
answered by direct reference to the wording of the
statutes. But statutes' meanings and their applicability
to relevant situations are not always so obvious, and
that is one reason that the ability to interpret them
(25) accurately is an essential skill for law students to learn.

Another skill that teaching statutory law would
improve is synthesis. Law professors work hard at
developing their students' ability to analyze individual
cases, but in so doing they favor the ability to apply the
(30) law in particular cases over the ability to understand
the interrelations among laws. In contrast, the study of
all the statutes of a legal system in a certain small area
of the law would enable the student to see how these
laws form a coherent whole. Students would then be
(35) able to apply this ability to synthesize in other areas of
statutory law that they encounter in their study or
practice. This is especially important because most
students intend to specialize in a chosen area, or areas,
of the law.

(40) One possible argument against including training in
statutory law as a standard part of law school curricula
is that many statutes vary from region to region within
a nation, so that the mastery of a set of statutes would
usually not be generally applicable. There is some truth
(45) to this objection; law schools that currently provide
some training in statutes generally intend it as a
preparation for practice in their particular region, but
for schools that are nationally oriented, this could seem
to be an inappropriate investment of time and
(50) resources. But while the knowledge of a particular
region's statutory law is not generally transferable to
other regions, the skills acquired in mastering a
particular set of statutes are, making the study of
statutory law an important undertaking even for law
(55) schools with a national orientation.

PrepTest59 Sec4 Qs 9–15

Topic: Legal education

Scope: The limited coverage of statutory law in law school curricula

Purpose: To discuss or illustrate the value of increasing the emphasis on statutory law in law school curricula

Main Idea: The skills gained in studying statutory law are important enough to legal practice to overcome objections and justify an increased emphasis on statutory law in law school.

THE KAPLAN READING COMPREHENSION METHOD

Step 1: Read the passage strategically

Step 2: Identify the question type

Step 3: Research a specific part of the passage or the big picture summaries

Step 4: Make an informed prediction

Step 5: Select the closest match

Only a handful of questions in a Reading Comprehension section will ask you for a passage's Main Point or Purpose. Most questions will ask you to research specific parts of the passage. And some, like this one, will ask you about specific information included in the passage. Luckily, the LSAT is an open-book test. In Step 3, refer back to the passage. Try that now.

LSAT Question	My Analysis
1. Which one of the following is cited in the passage as a reason that might be given for not including statutory law training in law school curricula? →	**Step 2:**
	Step 3:
	Step 4:
(A) Such training would divert resources away from the far more important development of the ability to analyze cases. →	**Step 5:** E.
(B) Such training is not essentially different from what is already provided in the core areas of law school education. →	
(C) The goals of such training can better be achieved by other means, most of which are more directly related to the actual practice of law. →	
(D) Such training would be irrelevant for those students who do not plan to specialize. →	
(E) The lack of geographic uniformity among statutory laws makes expertise in the statutes of any particular region generally nontransferable. →	

PrepTest59 Sec4 Q10

Practice

Now answer the rest of the questions associated with this passage. Refer to the Roadmap and big-picture summaries on this page, and use Steps 2 through 5 to tackle each question.

A proficiency in understanding, applying, and even formulating statutes—the actual texts of laws enacted by legislative bodies—is a vital aspect of the practice of law, but statutory law is often given too little
(5) attention by law schools. Much of legal education, with its focus on judicial decisions and analysis of cases, can give a law student the impression that the practice of law consists mainly in analyzing past cases to determine their relevance to a client's situation and
(10) arriving at a speculative interpretation of the law relevant to the client's legal problem.

Too little attn to statutory law in law school

Focus on cases misleading

Lawyers discover fairly soon, however, that much of their practice does not depend on the kind of painstaking analysis of cases that is performed in law
(15) school. For example, a lawyer representing the owner of a business can often find an explicit answer as to what the client should do about a certain tax-related issue by consulting the relevant statutes. In such a case the facts are clear and the statutes' relation to them
(20) transparent, so that the client's question can be answered by direct reference to the wording of the statutes. But statutes' meanings and their applicability to relevant situations are not always so obvious, and that is one reason that the ability to interpret them
(25) accurately is an essential skill for law students to learn.

Ex. lawyer and shop owner

Statutes not always so cut and dried — must learn to interpret them

Another skill that teaching statutory law would improve is synthesis. Law professors work hard at developing their students' ability to analyze individual cases, but in so doing they favor the ability to apply the
(30) law in particular cases over the ability to understand the interrelations among laws. In contrast, the study of all the statutes of a legal system in a certain small area of the law would enable the student to see how these laws form a coherent whole. Students would then be
(35) able to apply this ability to synthesize in other areas of statutory law that they encounter in their study or practice. This is especially important because most students intend to specialize in a chosen area, or areas, of the law.

Must learn statutory synthesis

Seeing coherent whole is beneficial

b/c of specialization

(40) One possible argument against including training in statutory law as a standard part of law school curricula is that many statutes vary from region to region within a nation, so that the mastery of a set of statutes would usually not be generally applicable. There is some truth
(45) to this objection; law schools that currently provide some training in statutes generally intend it as a preparation for practice in their particular region, but for schools that are nationally oriented, this could seem to be an inappropriate investment of time and
(50) resources. But while the knowledge of a particular region's statutory law is not generally transferable to other regions, the skills acquired in mastering a particular set of statutes are, making the study of statutory law an important undertaking even for law
(55) schools with a national orientation.

Dissent — regional variation prevents general application

Auth — still OK for nat'lly oriented schools b/c skills are the value, not the specific statutory knowledge

Topic: Legal education

Scope: The limited coverage of statutory law in law school curricula

Purpose: To discuss or illustrate the value of increasing the emphasis on statutory law in law school curricula

Main Idea: The skills gained in studying statutory law are important enough to legal practice to overcome objections and justify an increased emphasis on statutory law in law school.

PrepTest59 Sec4 Qs 9–15

LSAT Question	My Analysis

2. Which one of the following would, if true, most weaken the author's argument as expressed in the passage? →

Step 2:

weaken: doesnt need to be taught in law school

Step 3:

Step 4:

(A) Many law school administrators recommend the inclusion of statutory law training in the curricula of their schools. →

Step 5: ฿.

(B) Most lawyers easily and quickly develop proficiency in statutory law through their work → experiences after law school.

(C) Most lawyers do not practice law in the same geographic area in which they attended law → school.

(D) The curricula of many regionally oriented law schools rely primarily on analysis of cases. →

(E) Most lawyers who have undergone training in statutory law are thoroughly familiar with only a → narrow range of statutes.

PrepTest59 Sec4 Q11

3. The author discusses the skill of synthesis in the third paragraph primarily in order to →

Step 2:

Step 3:

Step 4:

(A) identify and describe one of the benefits that the author says would result from the change that is → advocated in the passage

Step 5: A.

(B) indicate that law schools currently value certain other skills over this skill and explain why this → is so

(C) argue for the greater importance of this skill as compared with certain others that are discussed → earlier in the passage

(D) explain why this skill is necessary for the study of → statutory law

(E) provide an example of the type of problem typically encountered in the practice of law →

PrepTest59 Sec4 Q12

A proficiency in understanding, applying, and even formulating statutes—the actual texts of laws enacted by legislative bodies—is a vital aspect of the practice of law, but statutory law is often given too little
(5) attention by law schools. Much of legal education, with its focus on judicial decisions and analysis of cases, can give a law student the impression that the practice of law consists mainly in analyzing past cases to determine their relevance to a client's situation and
(10) arriving at a speculative interpretation of the law relevant to the client's legal problem.

Lawyers discover fairly soon, however, that much of their practice does not depend on the kind of painstaking analysis of cases that is performed in law
(15) school. For example, a lawyer representing the owner of a business can often find an explicit answer as to what the client should do about a certain tax-related issue by consulting the relevant statutes. In such a case the facts are clear and the statutes' relation to them
(20) transparent, so that the client's question can be answered by direct reference to the wording of the statutes. But statutes' meanings and their applicability to relevant situations are not always so obvious, and that is one reason that the ability to interpret them
(25) accurately is an essential skill for law students to learn.

Another skill that teaching statutory law would improve is synthesis. Law professors work hard at developing their students' ability to analyze individual cases, but in so doing they favor the ability to apply the
(30) law in particular cases over the ability to understand the interrelations among laws. In contrast, the study of all the statutes of a legal system in a certain small area of the law would enable the student to see how these laws form a coherent whole. Students would then be
(35) able to apply this ability to synthesize in other areas of statutory law that they encounter in their study or practice. This is especially important because most students intend to specialize in a chosen area, or areas, of the law.
(40) One possible argument against including training in statutory law as a standard part of law school curricula is that many statutes vary from region to region within a nation, so that the mastery of a set of statutes would usually not be generally applicable. There is some truth
(45) to this objection; law schools that currently provide some training in statutes generally intend it as a preparation for practice in their particular region, but for schools that are nationally oriented, this could seem to be an inappropriate investment of time and
(50) resources. But while the knowledge of a particular region's statutory law is not generally transferable to other regions, the skills acquired in mastering a particular set of statutes are, making the study of statutory law an important undertaking even for law
(55) schools with a national orientation.

Too little attn to statutory law in law school

Focus on cases misleading

Ex. lawyer and shop owner

Statutes not always so cut and dried — must learn to interpret them

Must learn statutory synthesis

Seeing coherent whole is beneficial

b/c of specialization

Dissent — regional variation prevents general application

Auth – still OK for nat'lly oriented schools b/c skills are the value, not the specific statutory knowledge

Topic: Legal education

Scope: The limited coverage of statutory law in law school curricula

Purpose: To discuss or illustrate the value of increasing the emphasis on statutory law in law school curricula

Main Idea: The skills gained in studying statutory law are important enough to legal practice to overcome objections and justify an increased emphasis on statutory law in law school.

LSAT Question	My Analysis

4. Which one of the following questions can be most clearly and directly answered by reference to information in the passage? → **Step 2:**

Step 3:

Step 4:

(A) What are some ways in which synthetic skills are strengthened or encouraged through the analysis → of cases and judicial decisions?   **Step 5:** E.

(B) In which areas of legal practice is a proficiency in case analysis more valuable than a proficiency in → statutory law?

(C) What skills are common to the study of both statutory law and judicial decisions? →

(D) What are some objections that have been raised against including the study of statutes in → regionally oriented law schools?   — only 1 objection in passage so dump

(E) What is the primary focus of the curriculum currently offered in most law schools? →

PrepTest59 Sec4 Q13

5. Each of the following conforms to the kinds of educational results that the author would expect from the → course of action proposed in the passage EXCEPT: **Step 2:**

Step 3:

Step 4:

(A) skill in locating references to court decisions on an issue involving a particular statute regarding → taxation   **Step 5:** — nothing to do w/ statutory law

(B) an understanding of the ways in which certain underlying purposes are served by an → interrelated group of environmental laws

(C) a knowledge of how maritime statutes are → formulated

(D) familiarity with the specific wordings of a group of laws applying to businesses in a particular → region or locality   A.

(E) an appreciation of the problems of wording involved in drafting antiterrorism laws →

PrepTest59 Sec4 Q15

A proficiency in understanding, applying, and even formulating statutes—the actual texts of laws enacted by legislative bodies—is a vital aspect of the practice of law, but statutory law is often given too little

(5) attention by law schools. Much of legal education, with its focus on judicial decisions and analysis of cases, can give a law student the impression that the practice of law consists mainly in analyzing past cases to determine their relevance to a client's situation and

(10) arriving at a speculative interpretation of the law relevant to the client's legal problem.

Too little attn to statutory law in law school

Focus on cases misleading

Lawyers discover fairly soon, however, that much of their practice does not depend on the kind of painstaking analysis of cases that is performed in law

(15) school. For example, a lawyer representing the owner of a business can often find an explicit answer as to what the client should do about a certain tax-related issue by consulting the relevant statutes. In such a case the facts are clear and the statutes' relation to them

(20) transparent, so that the client's question can be answered by direct reference to the wording of the statutes. But statutes' meanings and their applicability to relevant situations are not always so obvious, and that is one reason that the ability to interpret them

(25) accurately is an essential skill for law students to learn.

Ex. lawyer and shop owner

Statutes not always so cut and dried — must learn to interpret them

Another skill that teaching statutory law would improve is synthesis. Law professors work hard at developing their students' ability to analyze individual cases, but in so doing they favor the ability to apply the

(30) law in particular cases over the ability to understand the interrelations among laws. In contrast, the study of all the statutes of a legal system in a certain small area of the law would enable the student to see how these laws form a coherent whole. Students would then be

(35) able to apply this ability to synthesize in other areas of statutory law that they encounter in their study or practice. This is especially important because most students intend to specialize in a chosen area, or areas, of the law.

Must learn statutory synthesis

Seeing coherent whole is beneficial

b/c of specialization

(40) One possible argument against including training in statutory law as a standard part of law school curricula is that many statutes vary from region to region within a nation, so that the mastery of a set of statutes would usually not be generally applicable. There is some truth

(45) to this objection; law schools that currently provide some training in statutes generally intend it as a preparation for practice in their particular region, but for schools that are nationally oriented, this could seem to be an inappropriate investment of time and

(50) resources. But while the knowledge of a particular region's statutory law is not generally transferable to other regions, the skills acquired in mastering a particular set of statutes are, making the study of statutory law an important undertaking even for law

(55) schools with a national orientation.

Dissent — regional variation prevents general application

Auth — still OK for nat'lly oriented schools b/c skills are the value, not the specific statutory knowledge

PrepTest59 Sec4 Qs 9–15

Topic: Legal education

Scope: The limited coverage of statutory law in law school curricula

Purpose: To discuss or illustrate the value of increasing the emphasis on statutory law in law school curricula

Main Idea: The skills gained in studying statutory law are important enough to legal practice to overcome objections and justify an increased emphasis on statutory law in law school.

LSAT Question	My Analysis
6. The information in the passage suggests that the author would most likely agree with which one of the following statements regarding training in statutory law? →	**Step 2:**
	Step 3:
	Step 4:
(A) While nationally oriented law schools have been deficient in statutory law training, most regionally oriented law schools have been equally deficient in the teaching of case law. →	**Step 5:**
(B) Training in statutory law would help lawyers resolve legal questions for which the answers are not immediately apparent in the relevant statutes. →	B.
(C) Lawyers who are trained in statutory law typically also develop a higher level of efficiency in manipulating details of past cases as compared with lawyers who are not trained in this way. →	
(D) Courses in statutory law are less effective if they focus specifically on the statutes of a particular region or in a particular area of the law. →	
(E) Lawyers who do not specialize probably have little need for training in statutory law beyond a brief introduction to the subject. →	

PrepTest59 Sec4 Q14

Common Reading Comprehension Wrong Answer Types

The previous questions illustrated how having a solid prediction is a key to success in the Reading Comprehension section. But note that, as elsewhere on the LSAT, the expert has another tool for evaluating the answer choices: recognizing wrong answer types.

The common wrong answers in Reading Comprehension are generally quite similar to those in Logical Reasoning.

READING COMPREHENSION: WRONG ANSWER TYPES

Outside the Scope—a choice containing a statement that is too broad, too narrow, or beyond the purview of the passage

Extreme—a choice containing language too emphatic (*all, never, every, none*) to be supported by the passage

Distortion—a choice that mentions details or ideas from the passage but mangles or misstates what the author says or implies about those details

180—a choice that directly contradicts what the correct answer must say

Faulty Use of Detail—a choice that accurately states something from the passage but in a manner that incorrectly answers the question

Half-Right/Half-Wrong—a choice in which one clause follows from the passage but another clause contradicts or distorts the passage

---

Expert Analysis: Reading Comprehension Questions

LSAT Question	Analysis
1. Which one of the following is cited in the passage as a reason that might be given for not including statutory law training in law school curricula? →	**Step 2:** "Which of the following is cited in the passage," indicates that this is a Detail question.
	Step 3: Paragraph 4 introduces a possible objection to teaching statutory law (lines 40–50): A focus on regional statutes may not be appropriate for national law schools.
	Step 4: Look for an answer choice that restates the objection raised in lines 40–50.
(A) Such training would divert resources away from the far more important development of the ability to analyze cases. →	**Step 5:** Outside the Scope. The author doesn't mention this concern at all in the passage. Eliminate.
(B) Such training is not essentially different from what is already provided in the core areas of law school education. →	180. This contradicts the primary scope of the entire passage. Eliminate.
(C) The goals of such training can better be achieved by other means, most of which are more directly related to the actual practice of law. →	"[O]ther means" are Outside the Scope, so this is unsupported by the passage. Eliminate.
(D) Such training would be irrelevant for those students who do not plan to specialize. →	Extreme/Distortion. The use of the word "irrelevant" is stronger than warranted by the passage, which notes regional differences in statutes. In Paragraph 3, the author says learning statutory analysis would benefit those who plan to specialize. Eliminate.
(E) The lack of geographic uniformity among statutory laws makes expertise in the statutes of any particular region generally nontransferable. →	Correct. This choice hews closely to the prediction and accurately paraphrases the objection raised in Paragraph 4.

PrepTest59 Sec4 Q10

LSAT Question	Analysis
2. Which one of the following would, if true, most weaken the author's argument as expressed in the passage? →	**Step 2:** The word "weaken" denotes a Logic Reasoning (Weaken) question.
	Step 3: Use the Topic/Scope/Purpose/Main Idea summaries to determine the author's main argument.
	Step 4: The author spends the entire passage arguing for more statutory law in the legal education system. He argues that this will give students a skill they do not obtain currently. Any answer choice that provides a reason why law schools either should not or do not need to teach statutory law will weaken the author's argument.
(A) Many law school administrators recommend the inclusion of statutory law training in the curricula of their schools. →	**Step 5:** 180. This strengthens the author's argument for including statutory law. Eliminate.
(B) Most lawyers easily and quickly develop proficiency in statutory law through their work experiences after law school. →	Correct. This reduces the value of teaching the subject in law schools because a newly minted lawyer will learn these lessons in actual practice. This matches the prediction.
(C) Most lawyers do not practice law in the same geographic area in which they attended law school. →	Faulty Use of Detail. This paraphrases the objection found in paragraph 4, but the author acknowledges and overcomes this objection by focusing on the skills acquired when learning how statutes fit together. Eliminate.
(D) The curricula of many regionally oriented law schools rely primarily on analysis of cases. →	Faulty Use of Detail. This choice merely applies a fact suggested in the passage. Eliminate.
(E) Most lawyers who have undergone training in statutory law are thoroughly familiar with only a narrow range of statutes. *PrepTest59 Sec4 Q11* →	Outside the Scope. Even if this is true, the author's argument focuses on skills (not knowledge of laws) gained in statutory law training. Eliminate.

LSAT Question	Analysis
3. The author discusses the skill of synthesis in the third paragraph primarily in order to	**Step 2:** The phrase "primarily in order to" signals a Logic Function question. The question asks *why* the author cites the "skill of synthesis" in paragraph 3.
	Step 3: The word *synthesis* comes up in the first sentence of the third paragraph, where it is cited as "[a]nother skill" fostered by learning statutory law in law school.
	Step 4: The word [a]*nother* signals the continuation of an argument, so the author discusses synthesis as yet *another* reason why statutory law should be taught in law schools.
(A) identify and describe one of the benefits that the author says would result from the change that is advocated in the passage	**Step 5:** Correct. Synthesis is "one of the benefits" of the "change [more statutory law courses] ... advocated."
(B) indicate that law schools currently value certain other skills over this skill and explain why this is so	Distortion. This is true according to the passage but does not describe *why* synthesis is discussed in paragraph 3. Eliminate.
(C) argue for the greater importance of this skill as compared with certain others that are discussed earlier in the passage	Distortion. Nowhere does the author say that synthesis is *more* important than any other skill developed by studying statutory law. Eliminate.
(D) explain why this skill is necessary for the study of statutory law	Distortion. This is a skill *gained by* the study of statutory law, not a skill *necessary for* its study. Eliminate.
(E) provide an example of the type of problem typically encountered in the practice of law *PrepTest59 Sec4 Q12*	Faulty Use of Detail. Mentions an example provided in paragraph 2, not paragraph 3. Eliminate.

LSAT Question	Analysis
4. Which one of the following questions can be most clearly and directly answered by reference to information in the passage? →	**Step 2:** A Detail question—The answer corresponds to explicit text in the passage.
	Step 3: This question does not include a research clue. Research each answer choice separately.
	Step 4: It is impossible to make an exact prediction for this open-ended question, so keep the big picture in mind: The author thinks statutory law should be taught in law schools because case analysis is insufficient to impart all required skills to budding lawyers.
(A) What are some ways in which synthetic skills are strengthened or encouraged through the analysis → of cases and judicial decisions?	**Step 5:** Distortion. According to the author, synthesis is a skill learned by studying statutes, not through case analysis. Eliminate.
(B) In which areas of legal practice is a proficiency in case analysis more valuable than a proficiency in → statutory law?	Outside the Scope. The passage does not address areas of law in which case analysis provides the more central skills. Eliminate.
(C) What skills are common to the study of both statutory law and judicial decisions? →	Distortion. The author emphasizes skills unique to statutory law analysis, not those it has in common with case analysis of judicial decisions. Eliminate.
(D) What are some objections that have been raised against including the study of statutes in → regionally oriented law schools?	Faulty Use of Detail. The only objection to increasing statutory law education was applicable to national programs, not regional ones. Eliminate.
(E) What is the primary focus of the curriculum currently offered in most law schools? *PrepTest59 Sec4 Q13* →	Correct. The author mentions in paragraph 1 that schools focus too little on statutory law and mostly use case analysis. The question in this choice can be answered directly from the passage.

LSAT Question	Analysis
5. Each of the following conforms to the kinds of educational results that the author would expect from the course of action proposed in the passage EXCEPT: →	**Step 2:** An Inference EXCEPT question—The four wrong answers will each describe a result the author would expect from his proposed change; the correct answer will either contradict the author's expectations or will be Outside the Scope.
	Step 3: Although this is an open-ended question (with no specific research clues), the first sentence of the passage states that law students currently lack proficiency in "understanding, applying, and even formulating statutes."
	Step 4: The author anticipates that statutory law training will improve students' proficiency in understanding, applying, and formulating statutes, along with the skill of synthesis (paragraph 3). These will appear in the wrong answers here.
(A) skill in locating references to court decisions on an issue involving a particular statute regarding taxation →	**Step 5:** Correct. This choice refers to cases ("court decisions") ruling on statutes. That distorts the author's point and is not, therefore, a valid inference from the passage.
(B) an understanding of the ways in which certain underlying purposes are served by an interrelated group of environmental laws →	This describes the skill of synthesizing statutes; something the author believes will result from his proposed change. Eliminate.
(C) a knowledge of how maritime statutes are formulated →	Knowledge of how statutes are formulated would be a result of training in statutory law. Eliminate.
(D) familiarity with the specific wordings of a group of laws applying to businesses in a particular region or locality →	Familiarity with specific statutes (although a minor point in the author's argument) would result from training in statutory law. Eliminate.
(E) an appreciation of the problems of wording involved in drafting antiterrorism laws →	This is a specific example of understanding how to formulate a set of statutes. Eliminate.

PrepTest59 Sec4 Q15

LSAT Question	Analysis
6. The information in the passage suggests that the author would most likely agree with which one of the following statements regarding training in statutory law? →	**Step 2:** An Inference question—The correct answer is a statement with which "the author would most likely agree" given what he wrote in the passage.
	Step 3: The question is fairly open-ended, referring to "training in statutory law," the subject of the entire passage.
	Step 4: It is difficult to predict precise wording, but the correct answer must agree with the author's position: He is in favor of statutory law training because 1) lawyers in practice regularly interpret statutes, and 2) statutory law training improves the skills of understanding and synthesizing statutes.
(A) While nationally oriented law schools have been deficient in statutory law training, most regionally oriented law schools have been equally deficient in the teaching of case law. →	**Step 5:** Half-Right/Half-Wrong. According to the author, regional schools are also deficient in statutory law training, not in case analysis. Eliminate.
(B) Training in statutory law would help lawyers resolve legal questions for which the answers are not immediately apparent in the relevant statutes. →	Correct. An accurate assessment of the author's lengthy example in paragraph 2.
(C) Lawyers who are trained in statutory law typically also develop a higher level of efficiency in manipulating details of past cases as compared with lawyers who are not trained in this way. →	Outside the Scope. The passage simply provides no support for this statement. Eliminate.
(D) Courses in statutory law are less effective if they focus specifically on the statutes of a particular region or in a particular area of the law. →	180. The author argues that the skills acquired trump the problems of regional differences in statutory law. Eliminate.
(E) Lawyers who do not specialize probably have little need for training in statutory law beyond a brief introduction to the subject. *PrepTest59 Sec4 Q14* →	Extreme. Paragraph 3 states that the skill of synthesis is especially important for those who intend to specialize; that does not mean that it is unimportant for the nonspecialist. Eliminate.

Perform

Fill in the blanks below listing the steps and strategies associated with the Reading Comprehension Method.

Kaplan Reading Comprehension Method

Step 1: _____

    Physical Roadmap:

    • Circling six types of _____

        ○

        ○

        ○

        ○

        ○

        ○

    • Summarizing paragraphs with _____

    Mental Roadmap:

    • 4 concepts to summarize

        ○

        ○

        ○

        ○

Step 2: _____

Step 3: _____

Step 4: _____

Step 5: _____

Reading Comprehension Wrong Answer Types

    • _____   • _____

    • _____   • _____

    • _____   • _____

Perform—Answer Key

Kaplan Reading Comprehension Method

Step 1: _Read the Passage Strategically_

> **Physical Roadmap:**
>
> - Circling six types of **_Keywords_**
>   - _Emphasis/Opinion_
>   - _Contrast_
>   - _Logic_
>   - _Illustration_
>   - _Sequence/Chronology_
>   - _Continuation_
> - Summarizing paragraphs with **_Margin Notes_**
>
> **Mental Roadmap:**
>
> - 4 concepts to summarize
>   - _Topic_
>   - _Scope_
>   - _Purpose_
>   - _Main Idea_

Step 2: _Read the Question Stem_

Step 3: _Research the Relevant Text_

Step 4: _Predict the Correct Answer_

Step 5: _Evaluate the Answer Choices_

Reading Comprehension Wrong Answer Types

- _Outside the Scope_
- _Extreme_
- _Distortion_
- _180_
- _Faulty Use of Detail_
- _Half-Right/Half-Wrong_

REFLECTION

Most students intuitively grasp the value of a clear, helpful Roadmap when they see an LSAT expert use one to answer questions quickly and confidently. That said, most students also struggle initially to know whether they are making the "right" Roadmap for themselves and whether they are taking too much time to do so.

Here are a few guidelines and questions you can ask yourself to become a better Roadmapper.

- A Roadmap is a tool—It is either helpful or unhelpful to you, *not* right or wrong.

- A strong Roadmap distinguishes the parts of the text that will help you answer LSAT questions. If you circle or underline *nothing*, you're not highlighting the valuable text; if you circle or underline *everything*, you're not highlighting what's important, either.

- A helpful Roadmap shows you *where* important details are and *how* they are used, but does not attempt to restate in detail *what* the passage says.

- LSAT experts typically read and Roadmap a passage in 3–4 minutes, leaving 4½–5½ minutes to answer the questions.

As you practice making Roadmaps, reflect on how helpful they were by asking the following questions as you review the passage and questions.

- How well were you able to navigate the passage as you researched the questions? Did you know where to find the text relevant to the question?

- Could you summarize the passage accurately with a glance back over your Roadmap?

- Did you know what the author was trying to say in each paragraph?

- Did you have to reread substantial portions of the text, or could you zero in on the piece(s) you would need to answer the questions?

Sample Roadmaps

Each test taker's Roadmap will look a little different, but all effective Roadmaps share a focus on passage structure and the author's Purpose. The sample passage maps included in the book and those that accompany Kaplan Reading Comprehension explanations are just that: *samples* of an expert's work. To illustrate the range of styles that effective Roadmaps might cover, the following pages present four more expert Roadmaps from the Statutory Law passage. As you review them, keep an eye on the characteristics they share as well as the differences you see among their circling, underlining, and margin notes.

TEST DAY TIP

No one other than you ever sees the Roadmap (or any other notes in your test booklet, for that matter). Don't aspire to some undefined perfection or worry that your work looks somewhat different than someone else's. Your goal is useful, accurate, succinct, and strategic scratch work.

Sample Roadmap A

A proficiency in understanding, applying, and even formulating statutes—the actual texts of laws enacted by legislative bodies—is a vital aspect of the practice of law, but statutory law is often given too little
(5) attention by law schools. Much of legal education, with its focus on judicial decisions and analysis of cases, can give a law student the impression that the practice of law consists mainly in analyzing past cases to determine their relevance to a client's situation and
(10) arriving at a speculative interpretation of the law relevant to the client's legal problem.

M.I. = l.s. needs to do more taking of how to "read" laws, not just apply precedents (Not Law Reading)

Wrong impression

Lawyers discover fairly soon, however, that much of their practice does not depend on the kind of painstaking analysis of cases that is performed in law
(15) school. For example, a lawyer representing the owner of a business can often find an explicit answer as to what the client should do about a certain tax-related issue by consulting the relevant statutes. In such a case the facts are clear and the statutes' relation to them
(20) transparent, so that the client's question can be answered by direct reference to the wording of the statutes. But statutes' meanings and their applicability to relevant situations are not always so obvious, and that is one reason that the ability to interpret them
(25) accurately is an essential skill for law students to learn.

Ex. of how a lawyer needs to understand the laws' wording.

MI again

Another skill that teaching statutory law would improve is synthesis. Law professors work hard at developing their students' ability to analyze individual cases, but in so doing they favor the ability to apply the
(30) law in particular cases over the ability to understand the interrelations among laws. In contrast, the study of all the statutes of a legal system in a certain small area of the law would enable the student to see how these laws form a coherent whole. Students would then be
(35) able to apply this ability to synthesize in other areas of statutory law that they encounter in their study or practice. This is especially important because most students intend to specialize in a chosen area, or areas, of the law.

"Put it all together"

another reason for policy

(40) One possible argument against including training in statutory law as a standard part of law school curricula is that many statutes vary from region to region within a nation, so that the mastery of a set of statutes would usually not be generally applicable. There is some truth
(45) to this objection; law schools that currently provide some training in statutes generally intend it as a preparation for practice in their particular region, but for schools that are nationally oriented, this could seem to be an inappropriate investment of time and
(50) resources. But while the knowledge of a particular region's statutory law is not generally transferable to other regions, the skills acquired in mastering a particular set of statutes are, making the study of statutory law an important undertaking even for law
(55) schools with a national orientation.

Counter-Arg.

Laws vary all over US; could hurt nat'l schools

Counter. Counter-Arg. Nah-learning to "read" laws is helpful everywhere

Sample Roadmap B

A proficiency in understanding, applying, and even formulating statutes—the actual texts of laws enacted by legislative bodies—is a vital aspect of the practice of law, but statutory law is often given too little
(5) attention by law schools. Much of legal education, with its focus on judicial decisions and analysis of cases, can give a law student the impression that the practice of law consists mainly in analyzing past cases to determine their relevance to a client's situation and
(10) arriving at a speculative interpretation of the law relevant to the client's legal problem.

Stat. law—insufficient attention in law school

Instead case analysis

Lawyers discover fairly soon, however, that much of their practice does not depend on the kind of painstaking analysis of cases that is performed in law
(15) school. For example, a lawyer representing the owner of a business can often find an explicit answer as to what the client should do about a certain tax-related issue by consulting the relevant statutes. In such a case the facts are clear and the statutes' relation to them
(20) transparent, so that the client's question can be answered by direct reference to the wording of the statutes. But statutes' meanings and their applicability to relevant situations are not always so obvious, and that is one reason that the ability to interpret them
(25) accurately is an essential skill for law students to learn.

Actual practice: just look up statutes

Must know how to interpret

Another skill that teaching statutory law would improve is synthesis. Law professors work hard at developing their students' ability to analyze individual cases, but in so doing they favor the ability to apply the
(30) law in particular cases over the ability to understand the interrelations among laws. In contrast, the study of all the statutes of a legal system in a certain small area of the law would enable the student to see how these laws form a coherent whole. Students would then be
(35) able to apply this ability to synthesize in other areas of statutory law that they encounter in their study or practice. This is especially important because most students intend to specialize in a chosen area, or areas, of the law.

Teaching stat. law good for synthesis

(40) One possible argument against including training in statutory law as a standard part of law school curricula is that many statutes vary from region to region within a nation, so that the mastery of a set of statutes would usually not be generally applicable. There is some truth
(45) to this objection; law schools that currently provide some training in statutes generally intend it as a preparation for practice in their particular region, but for schools that are nationally oriented, this could seem to be an inappropriate investment of time and
(50) resources. But while the knowledge of a particular region's statutory law is not generally transferable to other regions, the skills acquired in mastering a particular set of statutes are, making the study of statutory law an important undertaking even for law
(55) schools with a national orientation.

Critics

Concession

Au: skills transferable, even if statutes aren't

Sample Roadmap C

A proficiency in understanding, applying, and even formulating statutes—the actual texts of laws enacted by legislative bodies—is a |vital| aspect of the practice of law, |but| statutory law is often given too little
(5) attention by law schools. Much of legal education, with its focus on judicial decisions and analysis of cases, can give a law student the impression that the practice of law consists mainly in analyzing past cases to determine their relevance to a client's situation |and|
(10) arriving at a speculative interpretation of the law relevant to the client's legal problem.

L-schools need to teach statutes too!

Lawyers discover fairly soon, |however,| that much of their practice does not depend on the kind of painstaking analysis of cases that is performed in law
(15) school. |For example,| a lawyer representing the owner of a business can often find an explicit answer as to what the client should do about a certain tax-related issue by consulting the relevant statutes. In |such| a case the facts are clear and the statutes' relation to them
(20) transparent, |so that| the client's question can be answered by direct reference to the wording of the statutes. |But| statutes' meanings and their applicability to relevant situations are not always so obvious, |and| that is one reason that the ability to interpret them
(25) accurately is an essential skill for law students to learn.

Legal practice not just about cases

|Another| skill that teaching statutory law would improve is synthesis. Law professors work hard at developing their students' ability to analyze individual cases, |but| in so doing they favor the ability to apply the
(30) law in particular cases over the ability to understand the interrelations among laws. |In contrast,| the study of all the statutes of a legal system in a certain small area of the law would enable the student to see how these laws form a coherent whole. Students would |then| be
(35) able to apply this ability to synthesize in other areas of statutory law that they encounter in their study or practice. This is |especially| important because most students intend to specialize in a chosen area, or areas, of the law.

Stat interp. would also help to synth.

(40)   One possible argument against including training in statutory law as a standard part of law school curricula is that many statutes vary from region to region within a nation, so that the mastery of a set of statutes would usually not be generally applicable. There is |some truth|
(45) to this objection; law schools that currently provide some training in statutes generally intend it as a preparation for practice in their particular region, |but| for schools that are nationally oriented, this could seem to be an inappropriate investment of time and
(50) resources. |But| while the knowledge of a particular region's statutory law is not generally transferable to other regions, the skills acquired in mastering a particular set of statutes are, making the study of statutory law an important undertaking |even| for law
(55) schools with a national orientation.

Despite regional variance, stat. interp. skills are import.

Sample Roadmap D

A proficiency in understanding, applying, and even formulating statutes—the actual texts of laws enacted by legislative bodies—is a vital aspect of the practice of law, but statutory law is often given too little
(5) attention by law schools. Much of legal education, with its focus on judicial decisions and analysis of cases, can give a law student the impression that the practice of law consists mainly in analyzing past cases to determine their relevance to a client's situation and
(10) arriving at a speculative interpretation of the law relevant to the client's legal problem.

Statutes: -vital -neglected by law schools

false impression

Lawyers discover fairly soon, however, that much of their practice does not depend on the kind of painstaking analysis of cases that is performed in law
(15) school. For example, a lawyer representing the owner of a business can often find an explicit answer as to what the client should do about a certain tax-related issue by consulting the relevant statutes. In such a case the facts are clear and the statutes' relation to them
(20) transparent, so that the client's question can be answered by direct reference to the wording of the statutes. But statutes' meanings and their applicability to relevant situations are not always so obvious, and that is one reason that the ability to interpret them
(25) accurately is an essential skill for law students to learn.

law ≠ case analysis

Another skill that teaching statutory law would improve is synthesis. Law professors work hard at developing their students' ability to analyze individual cases, but in so doing they favor the ability to apply the
(30) law in particular cases over the ability to understand the interrelations among laws. In contrast, the study of all the statutes of a legal system in a certain small area of the law would enable the student to see how these laws form a coherent whole. Students would then be
(35) able to apply this ability to synthesize in other areas of statutory law that they encounter in their study or practice. This is especially important because most students intend to specialize in a chosen area, or areas, of the law.

synthesis

(40)   One possible argument against including training in statutory law as a standard part of law school curricula is that many statutes vary from region to region within a nation, so that the mastery of a set of statutes would usually not be generally applicable. There is some truth
(45) to this objection; law schools that currently provide some training in statutes generally intend it as a preparation for practice in their particular region, but for schools that are nationally oriented, this could seem to be an inappropriate investment of time and
(50) resources. But while the knowledge of a particular region's statutory law is not generally transferable to other regions, the skills acquired in mastering a particular set of statutes are, making the study of statutory law an important undertaking even for law
(55) schools with a national orientation.

possible arg. against auth:

some truth

but wrong

PrepTest59 Sec4 Qs 9–15

CHAPTER 12

Reading Comprehension Passage Types and Question Types

Success in Reading Comprehension is the result of an active, methodical approach. As you read each passage, engage with the material by asking questions and attempting to determine the author's purpose. When you get to the questions, be equally strategic. Know exactly what the question is asking, then return to the passage or your Roadmap to research the correct answer.

In this chapter, we'll walk through each step of the Reading Comprehension Method in more depth.

THE KAPLAN READING COMPREHENSION METHOD

Step 1: Read the Passage Strategically—Circle Keywords and jot down margin notes to summarize the portions of the passage relevant to LSAT questions; summarize the author's Topic/Scope/Purpose/Main Idea.

Step 2: Read the Question Stem—Identify the question type, characterize the correct and incorrect answers, and look for clues to guide your research.

Step 3: Research the Relevant Text—Based on the clues in the question stem, consult your Roadmap; for open-ended questions, refer to your Topic/Scope/Purpose/Main Idea summaries.

Step 4: Predict the Correct Answer—Based on research (or, for open-ended questions, your Topic/Scope/Purpose/Main Idea summaries) predict the correct answer.

Step 5: Evaluate the Answer Choices—Select the choice that matches your prediction of the correct answer or eliminate the four wrong answer choices.

STRATEGIC READING AND READING COMPREHENSION PASSAGE TYPES

The first step in the Reading Comprehension Method is to read the passage strategically. Untrained test takers read passages with little interest or curiosity and, in turn, find it difficult to identify the author's Purpose or Main Idea. In contrast, LSAT experts focus on areas of contrast and emphasis within a passage, and they always keep in mind the author's intent.

Prepare

LEARNING OBJECTIVES

In this portion of the chapter, you'll learn to:

- Read a passage strategically and Roadmap the passage

LSAT STRATEGY

Strategic Reading and Roadmapping skills include the following:

Use Keywords

- Identify Keywords from six categories (Emphasis/Opinion, Contrast, Logic, Illustration, Sequence/Chronology, and Continuation).
- Use Keywords to accurately paraphrase the text (author's Purpose, method of argument, etc.).
- Use Keywords to accurately predict where the passage will go (Scope and Purpose of remaining paragraphs, for example).
- Use Keywords to predict points in the passage to which LSAT questions will refer.

Use Margin Notes

- Identify text that warrants a margin note.
- Capture key content in a brief, accurate margin note.

Use Big Picture Summaries—Topic/Scope/Purpose/Main Idea

- Read a passage and identify the author's Topic and Scope.
- Read a passage and identify the author's Purpose.
- Read a passage and identify the author's Main Idea.

Why Use Keywords?

Keywords indicate differences in opinion and structure. Consider two facts and an LSAT-style question:

> Type X coffee beans grow at very high altitudes. Type X coffee beans produce a dark, mellow coffee when brewed.

With which one of the following statements would the author most likely agree?

> 1) Coffee beans that grow at high altitudes typically produce dark, mellow coffee when brewed.
>
> 2) Coffee beans that grow at high altitudes typically produce light, acidic coffee when brewed.

You cannot answer that question from the facts alone. To understand the author's point of view, you must be given Keywords by the author. Keywords will logically connect the statements in a specific way. Observe:

> Type X coffee beans grow at very high altitudes, *but* produce a *surprisingly* dark, mellow coffee when brewed.

Which answer would be correct now?

Change the Keyword, and you change the correct answer on the LSAT. For example:

> Type X coffee beans grow at very high altitudes, *and so* produce a dark, mellow coffee when brewed.

READING COMPREHENSION: KEYWORD CATEGORIES

Emphasis/Opinion—words that signal that the author finds a detail noteworthy or has a positive or negative opinion about it, or any subjective or evaluative language on the author's part (e.g., *especially, crucial, unfortunately, disappointing, I suggest, it seems likely*)

Contrast—words indicating that the author thinks two details or ideas are incompatible or illustrate conflicting points (e.g., *but, yet, despite, on the other hand*)

Logic—words that indicate an argument, either the author's or someone else's (e.g., *thus, therefore, because*)

Illustration—words indicating an example offered to clarify or support another point (e.g., *for example, this shows, to illustrate*)

Sequence/Chronology—words showing steps in a process or developments over time (e.g., *traditionally, in the past, recently, today, first, second, finally, earlier, since*)

Continuation—words indicating that a subsequent example or detail supports the same point or illustrates the same idea (e.g., *moreover, in addition, also, further*)

Read the passage below, and note how attention to structure, and not details, allows an LSAT expert to focus on the broad concepts discussed in a dense passage about a mathematical concept.

Fractal geometry is a mathematical theory devoted to the study of complex shapes called fractals. Although an exact definition of fractals has not been established, fractals commonly exhibit the property of self-similarity:
(5) the reiteration of irregular details or patterns at progressively smaller scales so that each part, when magnified, looks basically like the object as a whole. The Koch curve is a significant fractal in mathematics and examining it provides some insight into fractal
(10) geometry. To generate the Koch curve, one begins with a straight line. The middle third of the line is removed and replaced with two line segments, each as long as the removed piece, which are positioned so as to meet and form the top of a triangle. At this stage,
(15) the curve consists of four connected segments of equal length that form a pointed protrusion in the middle. This process is repeated on the four segments so that all the protrusions are on the same side of the curve, and then the process is repeated indefinitely on the
(20) segments at each stage of the construction.

Self-similarity is built into the construction process by treating segments at each stage the same way as the original segment was treated. Since the rules for getting from one stage to another are fully
(25) explicit and always the same, images of successive stages of the process can be generated by computer. Theoretically, the Koch curve is the result of infinitely many steps in the construction process, but the finest image approximating the Koch curve will be limited
(30) by the fact that eventually the segments will get too short to be drawn or displayed. However, using computer graphics to produce images of successive stages of the construction process dramatically illustrates a major attraction of fractal geometry:
(35) simple processes can be responsible for incredibly complex patterns.

A worldwide public has become captivated by fractal geometry after viewing astonishing computer-generated images of fractals; enthusiastic practitioners
(40) in the field of fractal geometry consider it a new language for describing complex natural and mathematical forms. They anticipate that fractal geometry's significance will rival that of calculus and expect that proficiency in fractal geometry will allow
(45) mathematicians to describe the form of a cloud as easily and precisely as an architect can describe a house using the language of traditional geometry. Other mathematicians have reservations about the fractal geometers' preoccupation with computer-generated
(50) graphic images and their lack of interest in theory. These mathematicians point out that traditional mathematics consists of proving theorems, and while many theorems about fractals have already been proven using the notions of pre-fractal mathematics,

(55) fractal geometers have proven only a handful of theorems that could not have been proven with pre-fractal mathematics. According to these mathematicians, fractal geometry can attain a lasting role in mathematics only if it becomes a precise
(60) language supporting a system of theorems and proofs.

PrepTest57 Sec4 Qs 20–27

Why Take Margin Notes?

Margin notes prompt you to make mental paraphrases of a passage as you read. This is important because, on Test Day, it is easy to lose focus and gloss over an entire paragraph or passage. Margin notes also serve as valuable reference points for locating the facts and opinions you need to answer the questions.

Having a strong Roadmap will allow you to research questions that refer to specific selections from the passage. Take a look at the following question stems and consider where in the passage you would find the answers to them.

Which one of the following is closest to the meaning of the phrase "fully explicit" as used in lines 24–25?

According to the description in the passage, each one of the following illustrates the concept of self-similarity EXCEPT:

The explanation of how a Koch curve is generated (lines 10–20) serves primarily to

Which one of the following does the author present as a characteristic of fractal geometry?

Each of the following statements about the Koch curve can be properly deduced from the information given in the passage EXCEPT:

The enthusiastic practitioners of fractal geometry mentioned in lines 39–40 would be most likely to agree with which one of the following statements?

PrepTest57 Sec4 Qs 21–26

Take a look at the notes added to the first paragraph below. Add your own margin notes for paragraphs 2 and 3. Focus on opinions, contrast, and points of emphasis.

Fractal geometry is a mathematical theory devoted to the study of complex shapes called fractals. Although an exact definition of fractals has not been established, fractals commonly exhibit the property of self-similarity:
(5) the reiteration of irregular details or patterns at progressively smaller scales so that each part, when magnified, looks basically like the object as a whole. The Koch curve is a significant fractal in mathematics and examining it provides some insight into fractal
(10) geometry. To generate the Koch curve, one begins with a straight line. The middle third of the line is removed and replaced with two line segments, each as long as the removed piece, which are positioned so as to meet and form the top of a triangle. At this stage,
(15) the curve consists of four connected segments of equal length that form a pointed protrusion in the middle. This process is repeated on the four segments so that all the protrusions are on the same side of the curve, and then the process is repeated indefinitely on the
(20) segments at each stage of the construction.

Fractal def.

Koch curve— how generated

Self-similarity is built into the construction process by treating segments at each stage the same way as the original segment was treated. Since the rules for getting from one stage to another are fully
(25) explicit and always the same, images of successive stages of the process can be generated by computer. Theoretically, the Koch curve is the result of infinitely many steps in the construction process, but the finest image approximating the Koch curve will be limited
(30) by the fact that eventually the segments will get too short to be drawn or displayed. However, using computer graphics to produce images of successive stages of the construction process dramatically illustrates a major attraction of fractal geometry:
(35) simple processes can be responsible for incredibly complex patterns.

self similarity -each segment same as original

get too small to draw, computers do it

simple → complex

A worldwide public has become captivated by fractal geometry after viewing astonishing computer-generated images of fractals; enthusiastic practitioners
(40) in the field of fractal geometry consider it a new language for describing complex natural and mathematical forms. They anticipate that fractal geometry's significance will rival that of calculus and expect that proficiency in fractal geometry will allow
(45) mathematicians to describe the form of a cloud as easily and precisely as an architect can describe a house using the language of traditional geometry. Other mathematicians have reservations about the fractal geometers' preoccupation with computer-generated
(50) graphic images and their lack of interest in theory. These mathematicians point out that traditional mathematics consists of proving theorems, and while many theorems about fractals have already been proven using the notions of pre-fractal mathematics,

public captivated by comp. images practioners love

others think should have more theorems reservations about comp. graphics

(55) fractal geometers have proven only a handful of theorems that could not have been proven with pre-fractal mathematics. According to these mathematicians, fractal geometry can attain a lasting role in mathematics only if it becomes a precise
(60) language supporting a system of theorems and proofs.

PrepTest57 Sec4 Qs 20–27

Why Summarize the Author's Topic, Scope, Purpose, and Main Idea?

On most passages, anywhere from one to four of the questions ask for the author's "main idea" or "primary purpose," or ask in an open-ended way for a statement with which the author would "most likely agree." To answer these, the LSAT expert keeps track of four big picture categories as he reads.

READING COMPREHENSION: THE BIG PICTURE

Topic—the overall subject of the passage

Scope—the particular aspect of the Topic that the author is focusing on

Purpose—the author's reason for writing the passage (express this as a verb—e.g., *to refute, to outline, to evaluate, to critique*)

Main Idea—the author's conclusion or overall takeaway; if you combine the author's Purpose and Scope, you'll usually have a good sense of the Main Idea

---

With the entire passage summed up in that way, consider how you would anticipate evaluating the answer choices to the following question stems.

Which one of the following most accurately expresses the main point of the passage?

The information in the passage best supports which one of the following assertions?

PrepTest57 Sec4 Qs 20 & 27

Now, as you glance back over the Roadmapped passage, summarize in your own words the Topic, Scope, Purpose, and Main Idea.

Fractal geometry is a mathematical theory devoted to the study of complex shapes called fractals. Although an exact definition of fractals has not been established, fractals commonly exhibit the property of self-similarity:
(5) the reiteration of irregular details or patterns at progressively smaller scales so that each part, when magnified, looks basically like the object as a whole. The Koch curve is a significant fractal in mathematics and examining it provides some insight into fractal
(10) geometry. To generate the Koch curve, one begins with a straight line. The middle third of the line is removed and replaced with two line segments, each as long as the removed piece, which are positioned so as to meet and form the top of a triangle. At this stage,
(15) the curve consists of four connected segments of equal length that form a pointed protrusion in the middle. This process is repeated on the four segments so that all the protrusions are on the same side of the curve, and then the process is repeated indefinitely on the
(20) segments at each stage of the construction.

Self-similarity is built into the construction process by treating segments at each stage the same way as the original segment was treated. Since the rules for getting from one stage to another are fully
(25) explicit and always the same, images of successive stages of the process can be generated by computer. Theoretically, the Koch curve is the result of infinitely many steps in the construction process, but the finest image approximating the Koch curve will be limited
(30) by the fact that eventually the segments will get too short to be drawn or displayed. However, using computer graphics to produce images of successive stages of the construction process dramatically illustrates a major attraction of fractal geometry:
(35) simple processes can be responsible for incredibly complex patterns.

A worldwide public has become captivated by fractal geometry after viewing astonishing computer-generated images of fractals; enthusiastic practitioners
(40) in the field of fractal geometry consider it a new language for describing complex natural and mathematical forms. They anticipate that fractal geometry's significance will rival that of calculus and expect that proficiency in fractal geometry will allow
(45) mathematicians to describe the form of a cloud as easily and precisely as an architect can describe a house using the language of traditional geometry. Other mathematicians have reservations about the fractal geometers' preoccupation with computer-generated
(50) graphic images and their lack of interest in theory. These mathematicians point out that traditional mathematics consists of proving theorems, and while many theorems about fractals have already been proven using the notions of pre-fractal mathematics,

(55) fractal geometers have proven only a handful of theorems that could not have been proven with pre-fractal mathematics. According to these mathematicians, fractal geometry can attain a lasting role in mathematics only if it becomes a precise
(60) language supporting a system of theorems and proofs.

PrepTest57 Sec4 Qs 20–27

Fractal def.

Koch curve— how generated

Each segment the same

Computer models simple process ≑ complex pattern

Computer images = public interest

Some experts predict huge impact

Others doubt value

Very few new theorems proven w/fractal geo

Needs theorems & proofs

Big Picture Summaries:

Topic:

Scope:

Purpose:

Main Idea:

This chapter continues on the next page ▶ ▶ ▶

Practice

def

Fractal geometry is a mathematical theory devoted
to the study of complex shapes called fractals. Although
an exact definition of fractals has not been established,
fractals commonly exhibit the property of self-similarity:

(5) the reiteration of irregular details or patterns at
progressively smaller scales so that each part, when
magnified, looks basically like the object as a whole.
The Koch curve is a significant fractal in mathematics
and examining it provides some insight into fractal

(10) geometry. To generate the Koch curve, one begins
with a straight line. The middle third of the line is
removed and replaced with two line segments, each as
long as the removed piece, which are positioned so as
to meet and form the top of a triangle. At this stage,

(15) the curve consists of four connected segments of equal
length that form a pointed protrusion in the middle.
This process is repeated on the four segments so that
all the protrusions are on the same side of the curve,
and then the process is repeated indefinitely on the

(20) segments at each stage of the construction.

Self-similarity is built into the construction
process by treating segments at each stage the same
way as the original segment was treated. Since the
rules for getting from one stage to another are fully

(25) explicit and always the same, images of successive
stages of the process can be generated by computer.
Theoretically, the Koch curve is the result of infinitely
many steps in the construction process, but the finest
image approximating the Koch curve will be limited

(30) by the fact that eventually the segments will get too
short to be drawn or displayed. However, using
computer graphics to produce images of successive
stages of the construction process dramatically
illustrates a major attraction of fractal geometry:

(35) simple processes can be responsible for incredibly
complex patterns.

A worldwide public has become captivated by
fractal geometry after viewing astonishing computer-
generated images of fractals; enthusiastic practitioners

(40) in the field of fractal geometry consider it a new
language for describing complex natural and
mathematical forms. They anticipate that fractal
geometry's significance will rival that of calculus and
expect that proficiency in fractal geometry will allow

(45) mathematicians to describe the form of a cloud as easily
and precisely as an architect can describe a house
using the language of traditional geometry. Other
mathematicians have reservations about the fractal
geometers' preoccupation with computer-generated

(50) graphic images and their lack of interest in theory.
These mathematicians point out that traditional
mathematics consists of proving theorems, and while
many theorems about fractals have already been
proven using the notions of pre-fractal mathematics,

(55) fractal geometers have proven only a handful of
theorems that could not have been proven with

complex shapes = fractals

ex. Koch curve

images can be generated by comp

simple processes can cause complex patterns

public captivated

rival calc?

others have reservation

pre-fractal mathematics. According to these
mathematicians, fractal geometry can attain a lasting
role in mathematics only if it becomes a precise

(60) language supporting a system of theorems and proofs.

1. Which one of the following most accurately expresses
   the main point of the passage?

   (A) Because of its unique forms, fractal geometry is
       especially adaptable to computer technology
       and is therefore likely to grow in importance
       and render pre-fractal mathematics obsolete.
   (B) Though its use in the generation of extremely
       complex forms makes fractal geometry an
       intriguing new mathematical theory, it is not
       yet universally regarded as having attained the
       theoretical rigor of traditional mathematics.
   (C) Fractal geometry is significant because of its
       use of self-similarity, a concept that has enabled
       geometers to generate extremely detailed
       computer images of natural forms.
   (D) Using the Koch curve as a model, fractal
       geometers have developed a new mathematical
       language that is especially useful in technological
       contexts because it does not rely on theorems.
   (E) Though fractal geometry has thus far been of
       great value for its capacity to define abstract
       mathematical shapes, it is not expected to be
       useful for the description of ordinary natural
       shapes.

2. Which one of the following is closest to the meaning
   of the phrase "fully explicit" as used in lines 24–25?

   (A) illustrated by an example
   (B) uncomplicated
   (C) expressed unambiguously
   (D) in need of lengthy computation
   (E) agreed on by all

3. According to the description in the passage, each one
   of the following illustrates the concept of self-similarity
   EXCEPT:

   (A) Any branch broken off a tree looks like the
       tree itself.
   (B) Each portion of the intricately patterned frost on
       a window looks like the pattern as a whole.
   (C) The pattern of blood vessels in each part of the
       human body is similar to the pattern of blood
       vessels in the entire body.
   (D) The seeds of several subspecies of maple tree
       resemble one another in shape despite
       differences in size.
   (E) The florets composing a cauliflower head
       resemble the entire cauliflower head.

4. The explanation of how a Koch curve is generated (lines 10–20) serves primarily to

   (A) show how fractal geometry can be reduced to traditional geometry
   (B) give an example of a natural form that can be described by fractal geometry
   (C) anticipate the objection that fractal geometry is not a precise language
   (D) illustrate the concept of self-similarity
   (E) provide an exact definition of fractals

5. Which one of the following does the author present as a characteristic of fractal geometry?

   (A) It is potentially much more important than calculus.
   (B) Its role in traditional mathematics will expand as computers become faster.
   (C) It is the fastest-growing field of mathematics.
   (D) It encourages the use of computer programs to prove mathematical theorems.
   (E) It enables geometers to generate complex forms using simple processes.

6. Each of the following statements about the Koch curve can be properly deduced from the information given in the passage EXCEPT:

   (A) The total number of protrusions in the Koch curve at any stage of the construction depends on the length of the initial line chosen for the construction.
   (B) The line segments at each successive stage of the construction of the Koch curve are shorter than the segments at the previous stage.
   (C) Theoretically, as the Koch curve is constructed its line segments become infinitely small.
   (D) At every stage of constructing the Koch curve, all the line segments composing it are of equal length.
   (E) The length of the line segments in the Koch curve at any stage of its construction depends on the length of the initial line chosen for the construction.

7. The enthusiastic practitioners of fra[ctals] mentioned in lines 39–40 would be [agree] with which one of the following statements:

   (A) The Koch curve is the most easily generated, and therefore the most important, of the forms studied by fractal geometers.
   (B) Fractal geometry will eventually be able to be used in the same applications for which traditional geometry is now used.
   (C) The greatest importance of computer images of fractals is their ability to bring fractal geometry to the attention of a wider public.
   (D) Studying self-similarity was impossible before the development of sophisticated computer technologies.
   (E) Certain complex natural forms exhibit a type of self-similarity like that exhibited by fractals.

8. The information in the passage best supports which one of the following assertions?

   (A) The appeal of a mathematical theory is limited to those individuals who can grasp the theorems and proofs produced in that theory.
   (B) Most of the important recent breakthroughs in mathematical theory would not have been possible without the ability of computers to graphically represent complex shapes.
   (C) Fractal geometry holds the potential to replace traditional geometry in most of its engineering applications.
   (D) A mathematical theory can be developed and find applications even before it establishes a precise definition of its subject matter.
   (E) Only a mathematical theory that supports a system of theorems and proofs will gain enthusiastic support among a significant number of mathematicians.

   PrepTest57 Sec4 Qs 20–27

LSAT Reading Comprehension Passage Types

Experts know that the LSAT generates the same types of passages on test after test. Every LSAT will have one passage from each of these four broad topics: Natural Science, Humanities, Social Science, and Law.

While that's helpful to know, it's not nearly as helpful as knowing that LSAT passages are *structured* in similar—and therefore predictable—ways. The four passage *structure* types are: Theory/Perspective, Event/Phenomenon, Biography, and Debate.

READING COMPREHENSION: PASSAGE TYPES

· **Theory/Perspective**—The passage focuses on a thinker's theory or perspective on some part of the Topic; typically (though not always), the author disagrees and critiques the opponent's perspective or defends his own.
· **Event/Phenomenon**—The passage focuses on an event, a breakthrough development, or a problem that has arisen; when a solution to the problem is proposed, the author most often agrees with the solution (and that represents the passage's Main Idea).
· **Biography**—The passage discusses something about a notable person; the aspect of the person's life emphasized by the author reflects the Scope of the passage.
· **Debate**—The passage outlines two opposing positions (neither of which is the author's) on some aspect of the Topic; the author may side with one of the positions, may remain neutral, or may critique both. (This structure has been rare on recent LSATs.)

The two most common passage types are Theory/Perspective and Event/Phenomenon. When you recognize a passage is one of those prevalent types, there are several things to consider.

· In Theory/Perspective passages, ask yourself the following questions: Does the author advocate for or against a specific theory/perspective/idea? Does the author consider something to be in error and is therefore pushing for a fix? Does the author respond to the viewpoints of critics? What's the author's main point about the newly advocated theory/perspective/idea?
· In Event/Phenomenon passages, ask yourself the following questions: What was the event and its significance, and what did the event change? Is there some breakthrough or change in knowledge/perspective because of the event? If there is a phenomenon, what explanations are discussed?

Perform

Take a look at the following passage. Read the passage strategically and Roadmap it. Then, identify the passage structure. After you're done, compare your work to that of an LSAT expert on the next page.

An effort should be made to dispel the misunderstandings that still prevent the much-needed synthesis and mutual supplementation of science and the humanities. This reconciliation should not be too

(5) difficult once it is recognized that the separation is primarily the result of a basic misunderstanding of the philosophical foundations of both science and the humanities.

Some humanists still identify science with an

(10) absurd mechanistic reductionism. There are many who feel that the scientist is interested in nothing more than "bodies in motion," in the strictly mathematical, physical, and chemical laws that govern the material world. This is the caricature of science drawn by

(15) representatives of the humanities who are ignorant of the nature of modern science and also of the scientific outlook in philosophy. For example, it is claimed that science either ignores or explains away the most essential human values. Those who believe this also

(20) assert that there are aspects of the human mind, manifest especially in the domains of morality, religion, and the arts, that contain an irreducible spiritual element and for that reason can never be adequately explained by science.

(25) Some scientists, on the other hand, claim that the humanist is interested in nothing more than emotion and sentiment, exhibiting the vagrant fancies of an undisciplined mind. To such men and women the humanities are useless because they serve no immediate

(30) and technological function for the practical survival of human society in the material world. Such pragmatists believe that the areas of morality, religion, and the arts should have only a secondary importance in people's lives.

(35) Thus there are misconceptions among humanists and scientists alike that are in need of correction. This correction leads to a much more acceptable position that could be called "scientific humanism," attempting as it does to combine the common elements of both

(40) disciplines. Both science and the humanities attempt to describe and explain. It is true that they begin their descriptions and explanations at widely separated points, but the objectives remain the same: a clearer understanding of people and their world. In achieving

(45) this understanding, science in fact does not depend exclusively on measurable data, and the humanities in fact profit from attempts at controlled evaluation. Scientific humanism can combine the scientific attitude with an active interest in the whole scale of

(50) human values. If uninformed persons insist on viewing science as only materialistic and the humanities as only idealistic, a fruitful collaboration of both fields is unlikely. The combination of science and the humanities is, however, possible, even probable, if we

(55) begin by noting their common objectives, rather than seeing only their different means.

PrepTest57 Sec4 Qs 6–12

Big Picture Summaries:

Topic:

Scope:

Purpose:

Main Idea:

[Handwritten margin notes:]
synthesize two
separation due to misund. of foundtns of science & human.

opinion: scientists only interested in math/physical chem

ignore or explain

aspects of human mind can't be exp. by science

humanist = only emotion

no practical function

combines both

objective the same understanding people & world

note common

Expert Analysis: Roadmapping

Compare your Roadmap to the expert's Roadmap. The LSAT expert sees this as a Theory/Perspective passage. While humanists and scientists disagree, the focus of this passage is not their debate, but rather their mutual misunderstandings. The author's perspective is that each side would benefit from understanding the other and learning to value the other's techniques.

LSAT Passage	Analysis
An effort should be made to dispel the misunderstandings that still prevent the much-needed synthesis and mutual supplementation of science and the humanities. This reconciliation should not be too (5) difficult once it is recognized that the separation is primarily the result of a basic misunderstanding of the philosophical foundations of both science and the humanities. *Auth: reconcile sci/hum* *Basically misunderstood*	**Step 1:** The first sentence begins with the author's clear opinion: We should (strong authorial recommendation) "dispel the misunderstandings" blocking a "much-needed" (strong Emphasis/ Opinion Keyword) synthesis of science and the humanities. In other words: Science and the humanities should be brought together. The author's clear opinion provides the **Topic** (science and the humanities) and **Scope** (the gap that separates them). The next lines (4–8) reveal the author's **Purpose**: to explain that the gap is "primarily the result of" a misunderstanding of each side's underlying philosophy.
Some humanists still identify science with an (10) absurd mechanistic reductionism. There are many who feel that the scientist is interested in nothing more than "bodies in motion," in the strictly mathematical, physical, and chemical laws that govern the material world. This is the caricature of science drawn by (15) representatives of the humanities who are ignorant of the nature of modern science and also of the scientific outlook in philosophy. For example, it is claimed that science either ignores or explains away the most essential human values. Those who believe this also (20) assert that there are aspects of the human mind, manifest especially in the domains of morality, religion, and the arts, that contain an irreducible spiritual element and for that reason can never be adequately explained by science. *Humanists— sci too reductive* *Auth: they don't know real sci* *Ex.*	Paragraph 2 begins with one misunderstanding: *Some humanists claim* scientists reduce everything to the mechanical laws of math, physics, and chemistry. But that's a "caricature" by those "ignorant of" what science really is, and line 17 provides an example: To the ignorant humanists, science is clueless about basic human values because science can't appreciate the "irreducible spiritual element" of the artistic and moral human mind.
(25) Some scientists, on the other hand, claim that the humanist is interested in nothing more than emotion and sentiment, exhibiting the vagrant fancies of an undisciplined mind. To such men and women the humanities are useless because they serve no immediate (30) and technological function for the practical survival of human society in the material world. Such pragmatists believe that the areas of morality, religion, and the arts should have only a secondary importance in people's lives. *Scientists— hum. is just emotion— useless*	Paragraph 3 provides the other misunderstanding: *some scientists claim* that humanists also have a blind spot. The scientists caricature humanists as emotional, sentimental, and undisciplined. Ultimately, the work produced by humanists is "useless because" it can't help our species survive.

LSAT Passage	Analysis
(35) Thus there are misconceptions among humanists and scientists alike that are in need of correction. This correction leads to a much more acceptable position that could be called "scientific humanism," attempting as it does to combine the common elements of both (40) disciplines. Both science and the humanities attempt to describe and explain. It is true that they begin their descriptions and explanations at widely separated points, but the objectives remain the same: a clearer understanding of people and their world. In achieving (45) this understanding, science in fact does not depend exclusively on measurable data, and the humanities in fact profit from attempts at controlled evaluation. Scientific humanism can combine the scientific attitude with an active interest in the whole scale of (50) human values. If uninformed persons insist on viewing science as only materialistic and the humanities as only idealistic, a fruitful collaboration of both fields is unlikely. The combination of science and the humanities is, however, possible, even probable, if we (55) begin by noting their common objectives, rather than seeing only their different means. *Auth: correct the misunder-standing* *Find common ground* *If views stay the same reconcilia-tion unlikely* *If note common obj. combination probable* *PrepTest57 Sec4 Qs 6–12*	The author states that these misconceptions are "in need of correction," and then proposes a "much more acceptable position" called "scientific humanism." This new position accepts that both people of science and people of the arts want to understand the world better. Science doesn't just rely on raw data (lines 45–46), nor are humanists utterly oblivious to "controlled evaluation" (i.e., measurement). The author's **Main Idea** is then clearly stated: Studying the commonalities of both fields will produce a probable "fruitful collaboration."

READING COMPREHENSION QUESTION STRATEGIES

After strategically reading a passage and creating a helpful Roadmap, an LSAT expert is ready to tackle the questions. Step 2 of the Method is vital: Identify the type of question and look for clues that dictate the appropriate strategy.

Prepare

LEARNING OBJECTIVES

In this portion of the chapter, you'll learn to:

· Identify Reading Comprehension question types and answer these questions efficiently

---

Reading Comprehension Question Types

Global questions ask about the passage as a whole:

LSAT Question Stem	Analysis
Which one of the following most accurately expresses the main point of the passage? *PrepTest59 Sec4 Q9*	**Step 2:** "[M]ain point"—this is a Global question. Use the Main Idea summary to predict the correct answer to this question.
Which one of the following most accurately describes the organization of the material presented in the passage? *PrepTest45 Sec2 Q8*	**Step 2:** "[O]rganization of ... the passage"—this question asks about the entire passage, so it's a Global question. Consult the Roadmap to determine the passage's overall structure.
The passages share which one of the following as their primary purpose? *PrepTest59 Sec4 Q6*	**Step 2:** "[P]rimary purpose"—this Global question asks you to identify the purpose "shared" by both passages. Use your Purpose summary to predict.

(handwritten margin note: at least 75% of RC Q's *)*

Must be true even if not explicitly stated

Inference questions ask for a deduction that can be made based on information in the passage.

LSAT Question Stem	Analysis
The author of the passage would be most likely to agree with which one of the following statements? *PrepTest45 Sec2 Q3*	**Step 2:** "[M]ost likely to agree "—this is an Inference question. The stem does not provide any specific research clues, so the correct answer could be supported by any part of the passage.
Which one of the following can most accurately be used to describe the author's attitude toward critics of the Hippocratic oath? *PrepTest45 Sec2 Q13*	**Step 2:** "[A]uthor's attitude"—an Inference question. Refer back to the Keywords in the paragraph where the author discusses the critics.
In calling a population of ants "an intelligence, a kind of live computer" (lines 51-52) the author of passage B most likely means that *PrepTest59 Sec4 Q7*	**Step 2:** "[M]ost likely means"—an Inference question. Reread the line reference in context and look for an answer choice that must be true based upon those statements.
Which one of the following examples best illustrates the type of disaster response recommended by the experts mentioned in the third paragraph? *PrepTest45 Sec2 Q2*	**Step 2:** "[B]est illustrates"—an Inference question. Look for the experts' recommended disaster response, which is found in the third paragraph.

Detail questions ask for a specific fact mentioned in the passage.

LSAT Question Stem	Analysis
According to the passage, the elimination of which one of the following obstacles enabled scientists to identify the evolutionary origins of lichen-forming fungi? *PrepTest45 Sec2 Q18*	**Step 2:** "According to the passage"—this is a Detail question. Check the Roadmap to identify where the author discusses obstacles scientists eliminated.
Which one of the following does the author present as a characteristic of fractal geometry? *PrepTest57 Sec4 Q24*	**Step 2:** "Which of the following does the author present"—a Detail question, because it asks for a specific statement the author makes in the passage. Check the Roadmap to identify where the traits of fractals are discussed, research in the passage, and then make a prediction.

Logic Function questions ask *why* the author chose to include a specific portion of the passage. These questions provide an explicit research clue. Return to the passage and determine the context in which the statements appear.

LSAT Question Stem	Analysis
The author discusses donors in the final paragraph primarily in order to *PrepTest45 Sec2 Q4* ⟶	**Step 2:** "[D]iscusses" and "in order to"—this is a Logic Function question. Return to the final paragraph and read before and after the reference to donors to predict *why* the the author mentioned them.
Which one of the following best describes one of the functions of the last paragraph in the passage? *PrepTest57 Sec4 Q10* ⟶	**Step 2:** "[B]est describes one of the functions"—this is a Logic Function question. Consult the Roadmap to determine the function of the last paragraph in relation to the rest of the passage.

Logic Reasoning questions mirror question types found in the Logical Reasoning section. Use the same approach you would employ for the corresponding question type in the Logical Reasoning section.

LSAT Question Stem	Analysis
The large-scale climate trends discussed in passage A are most analogous to which one of the following elements in passage B? *PrepTest59 Sec4 Q2* ⟶	**Step 2:** "[M]ost analogous"—this is like a Parallel Reasoning question. The research clue here is "large-scale climate trends."
Which of the following would, if true, most weaken the author's argument as expressed in the passage? *PrepTest59 Sec4 Q11* ⟶	**Step 2:** "[M]ost weaken"—this is a Weaken question. Find the answer choice that provides the strongest counter to the author's argument.

Summary of Question Types

Question Type	Identify	Task
Global	"main point"	Think big picture.
	"primary purpose"	Review T/S/P/MI.
	"organization"	Consult your Roadmap.
	"title"	
Detail	"according to"	Research the relevant text.
	"passage states"	Correct answer will be a very close paraphrase of something stated in the passage.
	"author mentions"	
Inference	"author implies"	Research if possible.
	"passage suggests"	Correct answer will follow from the passage but will probably not be a close paraphrase.
	"inferred"	
	"likely to agree with"	
	"author's attitude"	
Logic Function	"function"	Research the relevant text.
	"primarily in order to"	Look at the context to determine why the author included the referenced detail.
	"for the purpose of"	
Logic Reasoning	"supports"	Use the appropriate Logical Reasoning strategy.
	"undermines"	
	"principle"	
	"analogous"	

Practice

Identify the question type indicated by each of the following question stems, and state the most effective way to research the answer.

LSAT Question Stem	My Analysis
Which one of the following would the author be most likely to characterize as an example of a misunderstanding of science by a humanist? *PrepTest57 Sec4 Q7* →	**Step 2:** "[M]ost likely to characterize as an example"—an Inference question. Look for the discussion of humanists' misconceptions, which are found in the second paragraph.
Which one of the following best describes one of the functions of the last paragraph in the passage? *PrepTest57 Sec4 Q10* →	**Step 2:** "[B]est describes one of the functions"—this is a Logic Function question. Consult the Roadmap to determine the function of the last paragraph in relation to the rest of the passage.
9. Which of the following best describes the main idea of the passage? *PrepTest57 Sec4 Q6* →	**Step 2:**
10. It can be inferred from the passage that the author would be most likely to agree with which one of the following statements? *PrepTest57 Sec4 Q8* →	**Step 2:**
11. According to the author, which one of the following is the primary cause of the existing separation between science and humanities? *PrepTest57 Sec4 Q9* →	**Step 2:**
12. The passage suggests that the author would recommend that humanists accept which one of the following modifications of their point of view? *PrepTest57 Sec4 Q11* →	**Step 2:**
13. In using the phrase "vagrant fancies of an undisciplined mind" (lines 27–28), the author suggests that humanists are sometimes considered to be *PrepTest57 Sec4 Q12* →	**Step 2:**

LSAT Question Stem	**My Analysis**
14. Which one of the following most accurately expresses the main point of the passage? *PrepTest45 Sec2 Q1* $\longrightarrow$	**Step 2:**
15. Based on the information in the passage, the author would be most likely to agree with which one of the following statements about the 1984 case in Ontario? *PrepTest45 Sec2 Q26* $\longrightarrow$	**Step 2:**
16. Which one of the following most accurately describes the author's main purpose in lines 11–14 of the passage? *PrepTest45 Sec2 Q21* $\longrightarrow$	**Step 2:**
17. Which one of the following , if true, most weakens the author's criticism of the assumption that parasitic interactions generally evolve toward symbiosis? *PrepTest45 Sec2 Q19* $\longrightarrow$	**Step 2:**
18. Which one of the following inferences about natural disasters and relief efforts is most strongly supported by the passage? *PrepTest45 Sec2 Q6* $\longrightarrow$	**Step 2:**
19. Which one of the following, if true, would lend the most credence to the author's statement in lines 56–58? *PrepTest45 Sec2 Q25* $\longrightarrow$	**Step 2:**

Expert Analysis: Reading Comprehension Question Stems

Compare your characterizations of the question stems to that of an LSAT expert.

LSAT Question Stem	Analysis
9. Which of the following best describes the main idea of the passage? *PrepTest57 Sec4 Q6*	**Step 2:** "[M]ain idea"—a Global question. Consult the Big Picture summary and Main Idea prediction.
10. It can be inferred from the passage that the author would be most likely to agree with which one of the following statements? *PrepTest57 Sec4 Q8*	**Step 2:** "[C]an be inferred"—an Inference question. The right answer will be supported by information presented in the passage.
11. According to the author, which one of the following is the primary cause of the existing separation between science and humanities? *PrepTest57 Sec4 Q9*	**Step 2:** "According to the author"—a Detail question. The correct answer will be a close paraphrase of a statement in the passage.
12. The passage suggests that the author would recommend that humanists accept which one of the following modifications of their point of view? *PrepTest57 Sec4 Q11*	**Step 2:** "The passage suggests"—an Inference question. Research the passage to find the author's opinion on how the humanists' view should change.
13. In using the phrase "vagrant fancies of an undisciplined mind" (lines 27–28), the author suggests that humanists are sometimes considered to be *PrepTest57 Sec4 Q12*	**Step 2:** "[T]he author suggests"—an Inference question. Reread the line reference in context, and look for an answer choice that must be true based on those statements.
14. Which one of the following most accurately expresses the main point of the passage? *PrepTest45 Sec2 Q1*	**Step 2:** "[M]ain point"—a Global question. Consult the Main Idea prediction.
15. Based on the information in the passage, the author would be most likely to agree with which one of the following statements about the 1984 case in Ontario? *PrepTest45 Sec2 Q26*	**Step 2:** "[B]ased on the passage ... most likely to agree"—an Inference question. Look up references to the 1984 case in Ontario and look for opinion Keywords.
16. Which one of the following most accurately describes the author's main purpose in lines 11–14 of the passage? *PrepTest45 Sec2 Q21*	**Step 2:** "[D]escribes the author's main purpose"—a Logic Function question. Refer back to the relevant paragraph and reread those lines in context. Determine why the author included them.
17. Which one of the following, if true, most weakens the author's criticism of the assumption that parasitic interactions generally evolve toward symbiosis? *PrepTest45 Sec2 Q19*	**Step 2:** "[M]ost weakens"—a Logic Reasoning Weaken question. Look up the author's criticism, and find the choice that weakens it.
18. Which one of the following inferences about natural disasters and relief efforts is most strongly supported by the passage? *PrepTest45 Sec2 Q6*	**Step 2:** "[I]nferences ... is most strongly supported"—an Inference question. The correct answer will be supported by information in the passage.
19. Which one of the following, if true, would lend the most credence to the author's statement in lines 56–58? *PrepTest45 Sec2 Q25*	**Step 2:** "[W]ould lend the most credence"—a Logic Reasoning Strengthen question. Find an answer choice that provides the most support for the author's statement.

Researching Reading Comprehension Questions and Predicting the Correct Answer

Once you've identified the question type, it's on to Steps 3 and 4 of the Reading Comprehension Method: Research the appropriate part or parts of the passage and then predict the correct answer.

LSAT STRATEGY

Skills involved in researching the text and predicting the correct answer to Reading Comprehension questions include the ability to do the following:

- Identify and employ five kinds of research clues (line reference, paragraph reference, quoted text, proper nouns, and content clues) in question stems to research the relevant text in a passage.
- Research the relevant text and accurately predict the correct answer to Inference questions featuring referent reading clues.
- Use Topic, Scope, Purpose, and Main Idea summaries to predict the correct answer to Global questions.
- Use Topic, Scope, Purpose, and Main Idea summaries to predict broadly the correct answer to Inference questions lacking referent reading clues.

READING COMPREHENSION: RESEARCH CLUES

- **Line References**—Research around the referenced detail; look for Keywords indicating why the referenced text has been included or how it's used.
- **Paragraph References**—Consult your Roadmap to see the paragraph's scope and function.
- **Quoted Text** (often accompanied by a line reference)—Check the context of the quoted term or phrase; ask what the author meant by it in the passage.
- **Proper Nouns**—Check the context of the person, place, or thing; ask whether the author had a positive, negative, or neutral evaluation of it; ask why it was included in the passage.
- **Content Clues**—Research the passage for terms, concepts, or ideas referenced or alluded to in the question stem; these will almost always refer you to something the author emphasized or stated an opinion on.

Activate Prior Knowledge

To prepare yourself for the following practice, review the LSAT expert's Roadmap and analysis of a passage you saw earlier in the chapter.

LSAT Passage	Analysis
An effort should be made to dispel the misunderstandings that still prevent the much-needed synthesis and mutual supplementation of science and the humanities. This reconciliation should not be too (5) difficult once it is recognized that the separation is primarily the result of a basic misunderstanding of the philosophical foundations of both science and the humanities. *Auth: reconcile sci/hum* *Basically misunderstood*	**Step 1:** The first sentence begins with the author's clear opinion: We should (strong authorial recommendation) "dispel the misunderstandings" blocking a "much-needed" (strong Emphasis/Opinion Keyword) synthesis of science and the humanities. In other words: Science and the humanities should be brought together. Author's clear opinion provides the **Topic** (science and the humanities) and **Scope** (the gap that separates them). The next lines (4–8) reveal the author's **Purpose**: to explain that the gap is "primarily the result of" a misunderstanding of each side's underlying philosophy.
Some humanists still identify science with an (10) absurd mechanistic reductionism. There are many who feel that the scientist is interested in nothing more than "bodies in motion," in the strictly mathematical, physical, and chemical laws that govern the material world. This is the caricature of science drawn by (15) representatives of the humanities who are ignorant of the nature of modern science and also of the scientific outlook in philosophy. For example, it is claimed that science either ignores or explains away the most essential human values. Those who believe this also (20) assert that there are aspects of the human mind, manifest especially in the domains of morality, religion, and the arts, that contain an irreducible spiritual element and for that reason can never be adequately explained by science. *Humanists— sci too reductive* *Auth: they don't know real sci* *Ex.*	Paragraph 2 begins with one misunderstanding: *some humanists claim* scientists reduce everything to the mechanical laws of math, physics, and chemistry. But that's a "caricature" by those "ignorant of" what science really is, and line 17 provides an example: To the ignorant humanists, science is clueless about basic human values because science can't appreciate the "irreducible spiritual element" of the artistic and moral human mind.
(25) Some scientists, on the other hand, claim that the humanist is interested in nothing more than emotion and sentiment, exhibiting the vagrant fancies of an undisciplined mind. To such men and women the humanities are useless because they serve no immediate (30) and technological function for the practical survival of human society in the material world. Such pragmatists believe that the areas of morality, religion, and the arts should have only a secondary importance in people's lives. *Scientists— hum. is just emotion— useless*	Paragraph 3 provides the other misunderstanding: *Some scientists claim* that humanists also have a blind spot. The scientists caricature humanists as emotional, sentimental, and undisciplined. Ultimately, the work produced by humanists is "useless because" it can't help our species survive.

LSAT Passage	Analysis
(35) Thus there are misconceptions among humanists and scientists alike that are in need of correction. This correction leads to a much more acceptable position that could be called "scientific humanism," attempting as it does to combine the common elements of both (40) disciplines. Both science and the humanities attempt to describe and explain. It is true that they begin their descriptions and explanations at widely separated points, but the objectives remain the same: a clearer understanding of people and their world. In achieving (45) this understanding, science in fact does not depend exclusively on measurable data, and the humanities in fact profit from attempts at controlled evaluation. Scientific humanism can combine the scientific attitude with an active interest in the whole scale of (50) human values. If uninformed persons insist on viewing science as only materialistic and the humanities as only idealistic, a fruitful collaboration of both fields is unlikely. The combination of science and the humanities is, however, possible, even probable, if we (55) begin by noting their common objectives, rather than seeing only their different means. *Auth: correct the misunder- standing* *Find common ground* *If views stay the same reconcilia- tion unlikely* *If note common obj. combination probable*	The author states that these misconceptions are "in need of correction," and then proposes a "much more acceptable position" called "scientific humanism." This new position accepts that both people of science and people of the arts want to understand the world better. Science doesn't just rely on raw data (lines 45–46), nor are humanists utterly oblivious to "controlled evaluation" (i.e., measurement). The author's **Main Idea** is then clearly stated: Studying the commonalities of both fields will produce a probable "fruitful collaboration."

PrepTest57 Sec4 Qs 6–12

write prediction then go to 592-593 to answer questions

...4 of the Reading Comprehension Method for each question. Question 21 is filled in as an ...ample.

An effort [should] be made to [dispel] the [misunderstandings] that still [prevent] the [much-needed] synthesis and mutual supplementation of science and the humanities. This reconciliation [should not] be too
(5) difficult once it is recognized that the separation is [primarily] the result of a basic [misunderstanding] of the philosophical foundations of both science and the humanities.

Auth: reconcile sci/hum

Basically misunderstood

Some humanists still identify science with an
(10) [absurd] mechanistic reductionism. There are many who [feel] that the scientist is interested in [nothing more] than "bodies in motion," in the strictly mathematical, physical, and chemical laws that govern the material world. This is the [caricature] of science drawn by
(15) representatives of the humanities who are [ignorant] of the nature of modern science and also of the scientific outlook in philosophy. [For example,] it is [claimed] that science either ignores or explains away the most essential human values. Those who believe this [also]
(20) [assert] that there are aspects of the human mind, manifest [especially] in the domains of morality, religion, and the arts, that contain an irreducible spiritual element and for that reason [can never] be adequately explained by science.

Humanists— sci too reductive

Auth: they don't know real sci

Ex.

(25) Some scientists, [on the other hand,] claim that the humanist is interested in [nothing more] than emotion and sentiment, exhibiting the vagrant fancies of an undisciplined mind. To such men and women the humanities are [useless because] they serve no immediate
(30) and technological function for the practical survival of human society in the material world. Such pragmatists [believe] that the areas of morality, religion, and the arts [should] have [only a secondary] importance in people's lives.

Scientists— hum. is just emotion— useless

(35) [Thus] there are [misconceptions] among humanists and scientists [alike] that are in [need of correction]. This correction leads to a much [more acceptable] position that could be called "scientific humanism," attempting as it does to combine the common elements of both
(40) disciplines. [Both] science and the humanities attempt to describe and explain. It is true that they begin their descriptions and explanations at widely separated points, [but] the objectives remain the same[:] a clearer understanding of people and their world. In achieving
(45) this understanding, science [in fact] [does not depend] [exclusively] on measurable data, and the humanities [in] [fact] profit from attempts at controlled evaluation. Scientific humanism can combine the scientific attitude with an active interest in the whole scale of
(50) human values. If [uninformed] persons [insist] on viewing science as [only] materialistic and the humanities as

Auth: correct the misunder- standing

Find common ground

If views stay the same reconcilia- tion unlikely

[only] idealistic, a [fruitful] collaboration of both fields is [unlikely.] The combination of science and the humanities is, [however,] possible, even probable, [if] we
(55) begin by noting their common objectives, [rather than] seeing [only] their different means.

If note common obj. combination probable

PrepTest57 Sec4 Qs 6–12

20. Which one of the following best describes the main idea of the passage?

Step 2:

Step 3:

Step 4:

Scientic humanism combine 2

21. Which one of the following would the author be most likely to characterize as an example of a misunderstanding of science by a humanist?

Step 2: "[M]ost likely to characterize" indicates an Inference question. "Example of a misunderstanding of science by a humanist" is a research clue. Find the part of the passage that describes how humanists misrepresent the views of scientists.

Step 3: Paragraph 2 discusses humanists' misconceptions of scientists, and lines 10–14 summarize the misconception: Humanists think of scientists as data pushers, soulless, and non-spiritual.

Step 4: Find an answer choice that describes science as embodying an "absurd mechanistic reductionism."

22. It can be inferred from the passage that the author would be most likely to agree with which one of the following statements?

Step 2:

Step 3:

Step 4:

23. According to the author, which one of the following is the primary cause of the existing separation between science and the humanities?

Step 2:

Step 3:

Step 4:

24. Which one of the following best describes one of the functions of the last paragraph in the passage?

Step 2:

Step 3:

Step 4:

25. The passage suggests that the author would recommend that humanists accept which one of the following modifications of their point of view?

Step 2:

Step 3:

Step 4:

26. In using the phrase "vagrant fancies of an undisciplined mind" (lines 27–28), the author suggests that humanists are sometimes considered to be

Step 2:

Step 3:

Step 4:

PrepTest57 Sec4 Qs 6–12

Expert Analysis: Reading Comprehension Steps 2–4

Here's how an LSAT expert completed Steps 2–4 on those question stems. Compare your work.

Analysis	Analysis

20. Which one of the following best describes the main idea of the passage?

Step 2: Identify the Question Type

"[M]ain idea of the passage"—a Global question.

Step 3: Research the Relevant Text

Consult the Roadmap and Main Idea prediction.

Step 4: Make a Prediction

Main idea: Scientists and humanists must correct their misunderstandings and synthesize the approaches of their fields.

22. It can be inferred from the passage that the author would be most likely to agree with which one of the following statements?

Step 2: Identify the Question Type

"[C]an be inferred" and "author would most likely to agree" both indicate this is an Inference question.

Step 3: Research the Relevant Text

No specific research clue. Focus on author's opinion and purpose.

Step 4: Make a Prediction

The question asks what the author would agree with. Paraphrase the author's Purpose and Main Idea: Both scientists and humanists are guilty of misunderstanding the other, and the two groups should resolve their differences.

23. According to the author, which one of the following is the primary cause of the existing separation between science and the humanities?

Step 2: Identify the Question Type

"According to the author"—a Detail question.

Step 3: Research the Relevant Text

The phrase "primary cause of ... separation" leads to paragraph 1, where the author discusses why science and the humanities have yet to synthesize.

Step 4: Make a Prediction

Lines 5–8 directly state that the science-humanities split is "primarily the result of" a basic misunderstanding of each discipline's theoretical underpinnings by the other. Find an answer choice that most closely states that misunderstanding.

24. Which one of the following best describes one of the functions of the last paragraph in the passage?

Step 2: Identify the Question Type

"[B]est describes one of the functions"—a Logic Function question.

Step 3: Research the Relevant Text

The last paragraph is the focus of this question stem. Use the Roadmap to determine what function the last paragraph plays in relation to the entire passage.

Step 4: Make a Prediction

Paragraph 4 offers "a much more acceptable position" that incorporates both disciplines' "common elements." The author's purpose in this paragraph is to offer his case for synthesizing science and humanism.

Analysis	**Analysis**
25. The passage suggests that the author would recommend that humanists accept which one of the following modifications of their point of view?	26. In using the phrase "vagrant fancies of an undisciplined mind" (lines 27–28), the author suggests that humanists are sometimes considered to be

Step 2: Identify the Question Type

"The passage suggests"—an Inference question.

Step 3: Research the Relevant Text

The words "author would recommend" points to paragraph 4, where the author makes recommendations concerning the synthesis of science and humanism.

Step 4: Make a Prediction

The lines that deal directly with humanists' role in bridging the divide are 46–47, in which the author points out that humanists benefit from controlled evaluation, a philosophical approach they hang around the necks of scientists as a shortcoming. So, the author would likely suggest that humanists make room in their viewpoint for more "scientific" approaches to their discipline.

Step 2: Identify the Question Type

"[T]he author suggests"—an Inference question.

Step 3: Research the Relevant Text

Lines 27–28 are clearly relevant, because they're directly referenced in the question stem.

Step 4: Make a Prediction

Having just explained how scientists are wrongly caricatured as soulless stiffs, the author uses lines 27–28 to expose an equally egregious misrepresentation. But it's the following lines (29–31) that convey the widespread misconception that those vagrant, undisciplined fantasies are "useless" for "practical survival." Make a prediction: Humanists are considered to be impractical.

PrepTest57 Sec4 Qs 6, 8–12

Keep those predictions in mind. You'll soon be using them to evaluate the answer choices.

Evaluating Reading Comprehension Answer Choices

Many test takers struggle to get through the Reading Comprehension section in the time allowed. One factor contributing to the time crunch is the tendency to read through answer choices multiple times in the hope that somehow the correct answer will reveal itself. LSAT experts follow a different approach: After having made a prediction in Step 4, they confidently and quickly select the answer choice that is the closest match.

> ## LSAT STRATEGY
>
> Skills involved in evaluating the answer choices in Reading Comprehension questions include the ability to do the following:
>
> · Use a prediction of the correct answer before evaluating the answer choices.
> · Use the Topic, Scope, Purpose, and Main Idea summaries to evaluate the answer choices.
> · Evaluate answer choices by efficiently checking them against the passage text.

Try that now with the same questions you just worked with.

Using the predictions from the previous exercise, evaluate the answer choices from this passage.

An effort should be made to dispel the misunderstandings that still prevent the much-needed synthesis and mutual supplementation of science and the humanities. This reconciliation should not be too
(5) difficult once it is recognized that the separation is primarily the result of a basic misunderstanding of the philosophical foundations of both science and the humanities.

Some humanists still identify science with an
(10) absurd mechanistic reductionism. There are many who feel that the scientist is interested in nothing more than "bodies in motion," in the strictly mathematical, physical, and chemical laws that govern the material world. This is the caricature of science drawn by
(15) representatives of the humanities who are ignorant of the nature of modern science and also of the scientific outlook in philosophy. For example, it is claimed that science either ignores or explains away the most essential human values. Those who believe this also
(20) assert that there are aspects of the human mind, manifest especially in the domains of morality, religion, and the arts, that contain an irreducible spiritual element and for that reason can never be adequately explained by science.

(25) Some scientists, on the other hand, claim that the humanist is interested in nothing more than emotion and sentiment, exhibiting the vagrant fancies of an undisciplined mind. To such men and women the humanities are useless because they serve no immediate
(30) and technological function for the practical survival of human society in the material world. Such pragmatists believe that the areas of morality, religion, and the arts should have only a secondary importance in people's lives.

(35) Thus there are misconceptions among humanists and scientists alike that are in need of correction. This correction leads to a much more acceptable position that could be called "scientific humanism," attempting as it does to combine the common elements of both
(40) disciplines. Both science and the humanities attempt to describe and explain. It is true that they begin their descriptions and explanations at widely separated points, but the objectives remain the same: a clearer understanding of people and their world. In achieving
(45) this understanding, science in fact does not depend exclusively on measurable data, and the humanities in fact profit from attempts at controlled evaluation. Scientific humanism can combine the scientific attitude with an active interest in the whole scale of
(50) human values. If uninformed persons insist on viewing science as only materialistic and the humanities as only idealistic, a fruitful collaboration of both fields is unlikely. The combination of science and the humanities is, however, possible, even probable, if we
(55) begin by noting their common objectives, rather than seeing only their different means.

20. Which one of the following best describes the main idea of the passage?

(A) Scientists' failure to understand humanists hinders collaborations between the two groups.

(B) The materialism of science and the idealism of the humanities have both been beneficial to modern society.

(C) Technological development will cease if science and the humanities remain at odds with each other.

(D) The current relationship between science and the humanities is less cooperative than their relationship once was.

(E) A synthesis of science and the humanities is possible and much-needed.

21. Which one of the following would the author be most likely to characterize as an example of a misunderstanding of science by a humanist?

(A) Science encourages the view that emotions are inexplicable.

(B) Science arises out of practical needs but serves other needs as well.

(C) Science depends exclusively on measurable data to support its claims.

(D) Science recognizes an irreducible spiritual element that makes the arts inexplicable.

(E) Science encourages the use of description in the study of human values.

22. It can be inferred from the passage that the author would be most likely to agree with which one of the following statements?

(A) Scientific humanism is characterized by the extension of description and explanation from science to the humanities.

(B) A clearer understanding of people is an objective of humanists that scientists have not yet come to share.

(C) Controlled measures of aesthetic experience are of little use in the study of the humanities.

(D) Humanists have profited from using methods generally considered useful primarily to scientists.

(E) Fruitful collaboration between scientists and humanists is unlikely to become more common.

23. According to the author, which one of the following is the primary cause of the existing separation between science and the humanities?

(A) inflammatory claims by scientists regarding the pragmatic value of the work of humanists
(B) misunderstandings of the philosophical foundations of each by the other
(C) the excessive influence of reductionism on both
(D) the predominance of a concern with mechanics in science
(E) the failure of humanists to develop rigorous methods

24. Which one of the following best describes one of the functions of the last paragraph in the passage?

(A) to show that a proposal introduced in the first paragraph is implausible because of information presented in the second and third paragraphs
(B) to show that the views presented in the second and third paragraphs are correct but capable of reconciliation
(C) to present information supporting one of two opposing views presented in the second and third paragraphs
(D) to present an alternative to views presented in the second and third paragraphs
(E) to offer specific examples of the distinct views presented in the second and third paragraphs

25. The passage suggests that the author would recommend that humanists accept which one of the following modifications of their point of view?

(A) a realization that the scientist is less interested in describing "bodies in motion" than in constructing mathematical models of the material world
(B) an acknowledgement that there is a spiritual element in the arts that science does not account for
(C) an acceptance of the application of controlled evaluation to the examination of human values
(D) a less strident insistence on the primary importance of the arts in people's lives
(E) an emphasis on developing ways for showing how the humanities support the practical survival of mankind

26. In using the phrase "vagrant fancies of an undisciplined mind" (lines 27–28), the author suggests that humanists are sometimes considered to be

(A) wildly emotional
(B) excessively impractical
(C) unnecessarily intransigent
(D) justifiably optimistic
(E) logically inconsistent

PrepTest57 Sec4 Qs 6–12

COMPARATIVE READING

Since June 2007, every Reading Comprehension section has included three standard passages and exactly one set of Comparative Reading passages. Instead of a single passage of 450 to 500 words, the Comparative Reading set is two shorter passages labeled Passage A and Passage B that together have roughly the same word count. The two passages always share the same Topic and sometimes they'll even share the same Scope. The passages almost always differ, however, in Purpose and Main Idea. That doesn't mean that the two authors categorically disagree. Indeed, many of the questions will reward you for being able to characterize both agreement and disagreement between the two passages.

Prepare

LEARNING OBJECTIVES

In this section of the chapter, you'll learn to:

· Apply the Kaplan Reading Comprehension Method to paired Comparative Reading passages

On Comparative Reading passages, approach strategic reading and Roadmapping just as you would on regular passages with one exception: After you Roadmap the two passages, take a few seconds to catalogue their similarities and differences.

LSAT STRATEGY

To read Comparative Reading passages strategically:

· Roadmap Comparative Reading passages as usual.
· Think about T/S/P/MI for each.
· Consider the relationship between the passages.
· Are the passages different in Scope, Purpose, or Main Idea? The answer will generally be yes; make sure to characterize the differences.
· Do the passages share common details, examples, or evidence? The answer is often yes, but beware, the two authors may reach very different conclusions or make different recommendations based on the same underlying facts.
· If either author makes a contention or recommendation, how would the other author respond to it? The test is fond of Inference questions that ask whether one author would agree or disagree with something the other said.
· Do the two passages share a common principle? If yes, paraphrase the principle. If no, characterize how the authors approach the Topic differently.

Practice

Read and Roadmap the following Comparative Reading selection. Summarize the big picture for each passage independently. Then, compare the passages.

Passage A

[handwritten: comp models able to simulate climate trends]

Recent studies have shown that sophisticated computer models of the oceans and atmosphere are capable of simulating large-scale climate trends with remarkable accuracy. But these models make use of
(5) large numbers of variables, many of which have wide ranges of possible values. Because even small differences in those values can have a significant impact on what the simulations predict, it is important to determine the impact when values differ even
(10) slightly.

[handwritten: variables have impact on predictions]
[handwritten: determine impact]

Since the interactions between the many variables in climate simulations are highly complex, there is no alternative to a "brute force" exploration of all possible combinations of their values if predictions
(15) are to be reliable. This method requires very large numbers of calculations and simulation runs. For example, exhaustive examination of five values for each of only nine variables would require 2 million calculation-intensive simulation runs. Currently
(20) available individual computers are completely inadequate for such a task.

[handwritten: need to explore all combos of values]
[handwritten: ex.]
[handwritten: comps inadequate]

However, the continuing increase in computing capacity of the average desktop computer means that climate simulations can now be run on privately
(25) owned desktop machines connected to one another via the Internet. The calculations are divided among the individual desktop computers, which work simultaneously on their share of the overall problem. Some public resource computing projects of this kind
(30) have already been successful, although only when they captured the public's interest sufficiently to secure widespread participation.

[handwritten: can run on private desktops]
[handwritten: comps work together]
[handwritten: successful only w/ enough participation]

Passage B

[handwritten: problems are parallel]

Researchers are now learning that many problems in nature, human society, science, and engineering are naturally "parallel"; that is, that they can be effectively solved by using methods that work simultaneously in parallel. These problems share the common characteristic of involving a large number of similar elements such as molecules, animals, even people, whose individual actions are governed by simple rules but, taken collectively, function as a highly complex system.

[handwritten: similar elements]

(40) An example is the method used by ants to forage for food. As Lewis Thomas observed, a solitary ant is
(45) little more than a few neurons strung together by fibers. Its behavior follows a few simple rules. But when one sees a dense mass of thousands of ants, crowded together around their anthill retrieving food or repelling an intruder, a more complex picture
(50) emerges; it is as if the whole is thinking, planning, calculating. It is an intelligence, a kind of live computer, with crawling bits for wits.

[handwritten: Ex w/ ants]
[handwritten: ants together more complex]

We are now living through a great paradigm shift in the field of computing, a shift from sequential
(55) computing (performing one calculation at a time) to massive parallel computing, which employs thousands of computers working simultaneously to solve one computation-intensive problem. Since many computation-intensive problems are inherently
(60) parallel, it only makes sense to use a computing model that exploits that parallelism. A computing model that resembles the inherently parallel problem it is trying to solve will perform best. The old paradigm, in contrast, is subject to the speed limits
(65) imposed by purely sequential computing.

[handwritten: shift from sequential to parallel]
[handwritten: def]
[handwritten: makes sense]

PrepTest59 Sec4 Qs 1–8

Topic:	**Topic:**
Scope:	**Scope:**
Purpose:	**Purpose:**
Main Idea: *parallel computing*	**Main Idea:** *parallel computing*

Compare/Contrast the passages: *both solving problem*

Expert Analysis: Roadmapping a Comparative Reading Passage

Here's how an LSAT expert would Roadmap this Comparative Reading selection. Compare your work.

LSAT Passage	Analysis
Passage A Recent studies have shown that sophisticated computer models of the oceans and atmosphere are capable of simulating large-scale climate trends with remarkable accuracy. But these models make use of (5) large numbers of variables, many of which have wide ranges of possible values. Because even small differences in those values can have a significant impact on what the simulations predict, it is important to determine the impact when values differ even (10) slightly. *Comp models can accurately simulate climate but variable concerns*	**Step 1:** This speaks of the promise of computer simulations for modeling climate trends. This provides a general **Topic**, computers, and **Scope**, their use in predictions. The Keyword *but* at the beginning of the second sentence signals a potential complication. Such systems have many variables with large ranges, and even small variability can have a big impact.
Since the interactions between the many variables in climate simulations are highly complex, there is no alternative to a "brute force" exploration of all possible combinations of their values if predictions (15) are to be reliable. This method requires very large numbers of calculations and simulation runs. For example, exhaustive examination of five values for each of only nine variables would require 2 million calculation-intensive simulation runs. Currently (20) available individual computers are completely inadequate for such a task. *To get it right need lots of calculations* *Indiv. computers can't do it*	Paragraph 2 discusses the complications a bit more. The only way to account for these variables is with massive numbers of calculations. The last sentence is the key: Current computers are not able to handle the task.
However, the continuing increase in computing capacity of the average desktop computer means that climate simulations can now be run on privately (25) owned desktop machines connected to one another via the Internet. The calculations are divided among the individual desktop computers, which work simultaneously on their share of the overall problem. Some public resource computing projects of this kind (30) have already been successful, although only when they captured the public's interest sufficiently to secure widespread participation. *Can do it w/ combined indiv. computers on internet* *Public interest impt*	This paragraph provides the **Purpose**: proposing a possible solution to the problem. That solution is the **Main Idea**: By linking networks of individual computers, large problems can be solved much more quickly. The last sentence says that, while this is possible, it will only become widespread when it captures the public's attention. That necessary condition will likely give rise to a question.
Passage B Researchers are now learning that many problems in nature, human society, science, and engineering are (35) naturally "parallel"; that is, that they can be effectively solved by using methods that work simultaneously in parallel. These problems share the common characteristic of involving a large number of similar elements such as molecules, animals, even (40) people, whose individual actions are governed by simple rules but, taken collectively, function as a highly complex system. *"Parallel" problems — many natural probs can be solved at same time b/c function together*	Passage B begins by explaining that many systems in nature are parallel. It then defines parallel systems, the passage's **Topic**, as being made up of many similar items moving simply individually but together moving as a complicated whole. This is a relatively abstract paragraph.

LSAT Passage (cont.)		Analysis (cont.)

An example is the method used by ants to forage for food. As Lewis Thomas observed, a solitary ant is
(45) little more than a few neurons strung together by fibers. Its behavior follows a few simple rules. But when one sees a dense mass of thousands of ants, crowded together around their anthill retrieving food or repelling an intruder, a more complex picture
(50) emerges; it is as if the whole is thinking, planning, calculating. It is an intelligence, a kind of live computer, with crawling bits for wits.

Thomas – Ex. ants akin to a computer

This paragraph makes the abstraction more specific. It starts with an example, ants. Ants are simple creatures that work together to create a complicated system. The paragraph ends with a comparison between ants and computers: An ant colony is a type of living computer. A comparison is a red flag for a potential question later. More importantly, this finally sets up a relationship between both passages—they both talk about computers.

We are now living through a great paradigm shift in the field of computing, a shift from sequential
(55) computing (performing one calculation at a time) to massive parallel computing, which employs thousands of computers working simultaneously to solve one computation-intensive problem. Since many computation-intensive problems are inherently
(60) parallel, it only makes sense to use a computing model that exploits that parallelism. A computing model that resembles the inherently parallel problem it is trying to solve will perform best. The old paradigm, in contrast, is subject to the speed limits
(65) imposed by purely sequential computing.

Big shift from sequential to parallel

Auth – parallel computing is best

Paragraph 3 finally delves into the concept of parallelism in terms of computers, the **Scope**. The **Purpose** is merely to explain what the author calls a "paradigm shift in the field of computing." The **Main Idea** is that there is a shift from using one computer at a time to using many computers at once for computation-intensive problems.

PrepTest59 Sec4 Qs 1–8

Compare/Contrast the Passages: The two passages have a similar Purpose: Both passages consider parallel computing as the solution to problems. Passage B even goes so far as to say that parallel computing mimics natural systems, so its development is a natural progression.

Passage A uses weather models as its primary example, while Passage B speaks abstractly about natural systems. The specific example in Passage B is the ant colony.

Next, you'll see the Parallel Computing passage along with its question set just as it appeared on the test.

...shown that sophisticated
...eans and atmosphere are
...-scale climate trends with
...remarkable accuracy. But these models make use of
(5) large numbers of variables, many of which have wide
ranges of possible values. Because even small
differences in those values can have a significant
impact on what the simulations predict, it is important
to determine the impact when values differ even
(10) slightly.

Since the interactions between the many variables
in climate simulations are highly complex, there is no
alternative to a "brute force" exploration of all
possible combinations of their values if predictions
(15) are to be reliable. This method requires very large
numbers of calculations and simulation runs. For
example, exhaustive examination of five values for
each of only nine variables would require 2 million
calculation-intensive simulation runs. Currently
(20) available individual computers are completely
inadequate for such a task.

However, the continuing increase in computing
capacity of the average desktop computer means that
climate simulations can now be run on privately
(25) owned desktop machines connected to one another
via the Internet. The calculations are divided among
the individual desktop computers, which work
simultaneously on their share of the overall problem.
Some public resource computing projects of this kind
(30) have already been successful, although only when
they captured the public's interest sufficiently to
secure widespread participation.

Passage B

Researchers are now learning that many problems
in nature, human society, science, and engineering are
(35) naturally "parallel"; that is, that they can be
effectively solved by using methods that work
simultaneously in parallel. These problems share the
common characteristic of involving a large number of
similar elements such as molecules, animals, even
(40) people, whose individual actions are governed by
simple rules but, taken collectively, function as a
highly complex system.

An example is the method used by ants to forage
for food. As Lewis Thomas observed, a solitary ant is
(45) little more than a few neurons strung together by
fibers. Its behavior follows a few simple rules. But
when one sees a dense mass of thousands of ants,
crowded together around their anthill retrieving food
or repelling an intruder, a more complex picture
(50) emerges; it is as if the whole is thinking, planning,
calculating. It is an intelligence, a kind of live
computer, with crawling bits for wits.

We are now living through a great paradigm shift
in the field of computing, a shift from sequential
(55) computing (performing one calculation at a time) to
massive parallel computing, which employs
thousands of computers working simultaneously to
solve one computation-intensive problem. Since many
computation-intensive problems are inherently
(60) parallel, it only makes sense to use a computing
model that exploits that parallelism. A computing
model that resembles the inherently parallel problem
it is trying to solve will perform best. The old
paradigm, in contrast, is subject to the speed limits
(65) imposed by purely sequential computing.

27. Which one of the following most accurately expresses
the main point of passage B?

(A) Many difficult problems in computing are
naturally parallel.

(B) Sequential computing is no longer useful
because of the speed limits it imposes.

(C) There is currently a paradigm shift occurring in
the field of computing toward parallel
computing.

(D) Complex biological and social systems are the
next frontier in the field of computer
simulation.

(E) Inherently parallel computing problems are best
solved by means of computers modeled on the
human mind.

28. The large-scale climate trends discussed in passage A
are most analogous to which one of the following
elements in passage B?

(A) the thousands of computers working
simultaneously to solve a calculation-intensive
problem

(B) the simple rules that shape the behavior of a
single ant

(C) the highly complex behavior of a dense mass of
thousands of ants

(D) the paradigm shift from sequential to parallel
computing

(E) the speed limits imposed by computing purely
sequentially

29. It can be inferred that the authors of the two passages would be most likely to agree on which one of the following statements concerning computing systems?

(A) Massive, parallel computing systems are able to solve complex computation-intensive problems without having to resort to "brute force."

(B) Computer models are not capable of simulating the behavior of very large biological populations such as insect colonies.

(C) Parallel computing systems that link privately owned desktop computers via the Internet are not feasible because they rely too heavily on public participation.

(D) Currently available computers are not well-suited to running simulations, even if the simulated problems are relatively simple.

(E) Parallel computing systems employing multiple computers are the best means for simulating large-scale climate trends.

30. The author of passage A mentions public participation (lines 30–32) primarily in order to

(A) encourage public engagement in the sort of computing model discussed in the passage

(B) identify a factor affecting the feasibility of the computing model advocated in the passage

(C) indicate that government support of large-scale computing efforts is needed

(D) demonstrate that adequate support for the type of approach described in the passage already exists

(E) suggest that a computing model like that proposed in the passage is infeasible because of forces beyond the designers' control

31. Passage B relates to passage A in which one of the following ways?

(A) The argument in passage B has little bearing on the issues discussed in passage A.

(B) The explanation offered in passage B shows why the plan proposed in passage A is unlikely to be implemented.

(C) The ideas advanced in passage B provide a rationale for the solution proposed in passage A.

(D) The example given in passage B illustrates the need for the "brute force" exploration mentioned in passage A.

(E) The discussion in passage B conflicts with the assumptions about individual computers made in passage A.

32. The passages share which one of the following as their primary purpose?

(A) to show that the traditional paradigm in computing is ineffective for many common computing tasks

(B) to argue that a new approach to computing is an effective way to solve a difficult type of problem

(C) to convince skeptics of the usefulness of desktop computers for calculation-intensive problems

(D) to demonstrate that a new computing paradigm has supplanted the traditional paradigm for most large-scale computing problems

(E) to describe complex and as yet unsolved problems that have recently arisen in computing

33. In calling a population of ants "an intelligence, a kind of live computer" (lines 51–52) the author of passage B most likely means that

(A) the behavior of the colony of ants functions as a complex, organized whole

(B) the paradigm shift taking place in computing was inspired by observations of living systems

(C) computers are agglomerations of elements that can be viewed as being alive in a metaphorical sense

(D) computer simulations can simulate the behavior of large biological populations with great accuracy

(E) the simple rules that govern the behavior of individual ants have been adapted for use in computer simulations

34. The author of passage B would be most likely to agree with which one of the following statements regarding the computing system proposed in the last paragraph of passage A?

(A) It would be a kind of live computer.

(B) It would be completely inadequate for simulating large-scale climate trends.

(C) It would impose strict limitations on the number of variables that could be used in any simulation it runs.

(D) It would be likely to secure widespread public participation.

(E) It would solve calculation-intensive problems faster than a traditional sequential computer would.

PrepTest59 Sec4 Qs 1–8

Perform

The Universal Declaration of Human Rights (UDHR), approved by the United Nations General Assembly in 1948, was the first international treaty to expressly affirm universal respect for human rights.

(5) Prior to 1948 no truly international standard of humanitarian beliefs existed. Although Article 1 of the 1945 UN Charter had been written with the express purpose of obligating the UN to "encourage respect for human rights and for fundamental

(10) freedoms for all without distinction as to race, sex, language, or religion," there were members of delegations from various small countries and representatives of several nongovernmental organizations who felt that the language of Article 1

(15) was not strong enough, and that the Charter as a whole did not go far enough in its efforts to guarantee basic human rights. This group lobbied vigorously to strengthen the Charter's human rights provisions and proposed that member states be

(20) required "to take separate and joint action and to co-operate with the organization for the promotion of human rights." This would have implied an obligation for member states to act on human rights issues. Ultimately, this proposal and others like it were not

(25) adopted; instead, the UDHR was commissioned and drafted.

The original mandate for producing the document was given to the UN Commission on Human Rights in February 1946. Between that time and the General

(30) Assembly's final approval of the document, the UDHR passed through an elaborate eight-stage drafting process in which it made its way through almost every level of the UN hierarchy. The articles were debated at each stage, and all 30 articles were

(35) argued passionately by delegates representing diverse ideologies, traditions, and cultures. The document as it was finally approved set forth the essential principles of freedom and equality for everyone— regardless of sex, race, color, language, religion,

(40) political or other opinion, national or social origin, property, birth or other status. It also asserted a number of fundamental human rights, including among others the right to work, the right to rest and leisure, and the right to education.

(45) While the UDHR is in many ways a progressive document, it also has weaknesses, the most regrettable of which is its nonbinding legal status. For all its strong language and high ideals, the UDHR remains a resolution of a purely programmatic nature.

(50) Nevertheless, the document has led, even if belatedly, to the creation of legally binding human rights conventions, and it clearly deserves recognition as an international standard-setting piece of work, as a set of aspirations to which UN member states are

(55) intended to strive, and as a call to arms in the name of humanity, justice, and freedom.

[handwritten margin notes: "1st treaty to accept human rights", "language not strong enough for 1945 charter", "proposal not adopted", "Right to work leisure learn", "has weaknesses"]

35. By referring to the Universal Declaration of Human Rights as "purely programmatic" (line 49) in nature, the author most likely intends to emphasize

(A) the likelihood that the document will inspire innovative government programs designed to safeguard human rights

(B) the ability of the document's drafters to translate abstract ideals into concrete standards

(C) the compromises that went into producing a version of the document that would garner the approval of all relevant parties

(D) the fact that the guidelines established by the document are ultimately unenforceable

(E) the frustration experienced by the document's drafters at stubborn resistance from within the UN hierarchy

36. The author most probably quotes directly from both the UN Charter (lines 8–11) and the proposal mentioned in lines 20–22 for which one of the following reasons?

(A) to contrast the different definitions of human rights in the two documents

(B) to compare the strength of the human rights language in the two documents

(C) to identify a bureaucratic vocabulary that is common to the two documents

(D) to highlight what the author believes to be the most important point in each document

(E) to call attention to a significant difference in the prose styles of the two documents

37. The author's stance toward the Universal Declaration of Human Rights can best be described as

(A) unbridled enthusiasm *[handwritten: too strong]*

(B) qualified approval

(C) absolute neutrality

(D) reluctant rejection

(E) strong hostility

38. According to the passage, each of the following is true of the Universal Declaration of Human Rights EXCEPT:

    (A) It asserts a right to rest and leisure.
    (B) It was drafted after the UN Charter was drafted.
    (C) The UN Commission on Human Rights was charged with producing it.
    (D) It has had no practical consequences.
    (E) It was the first international treaty to explicitly affirm universal respect for human rights.

39. The author would be most likely to agree with which one of the following statements?

    (A) The human rights language contained in Article 1 of the UN Charter is so ambiguous as to be almost wholly ineffectual.
    (B) The weaknesses of the Universal Declaration of Human Rights generally outweigh the strengths of the document.
    (C) It was relatively easy for the drafters of the Universal Declaration of Human Rights to reach a consensus concerning the contents of the document.
    (D) The drafters of the Universal Declaration of Human Rights omitted important rights that should be included in a truly comprehensive list of basic human rights.
    (E) The Universal Declaration of Human Rights would be truer to the intentions of its staunchest proponents if UN member countries were required by law to abide by its provisions.

40. Suppose that a group of independent journalists has uncovered evidence of human rights abuses being perpetrated by a security agency of a UN member state upon a group of political dissidents. Which one of the following approaches to the situation would most likely be advocated by present-day delegates who share the views of the delegates and representatives mentioned in lines 11–14?

    (A) The UN General Assembly authenticates the evidence and then insists upon prompt remedial action on the part of the government of the member state.
    (B) The UN General Assembly stipulates that any proposed response must be unanimously accepted by member states before it can be implemented.
    (C) The UN issues a report critical of the actions of the member state in question and calls for a censure vote in the General Assembly.
    (D) The situation is regarded by the UN as an internal matter that is best left to the discretion of the government of the member state.
    (E) The situation is investigated further by nongovernmental humanitarian organizations that promise to disclose their findings to the public via the international media.

PrepTest61 Sec1 Qs 1–6

REFLECTION

Congratulations on your newfound Reading Comprehension abilities. Take a few moments and reflect on how you reached the levels you've demonstrated on those last passages and questions. Ask yourself the following questions.

- How is LSAT Reading Comprehension reading different than reading for school or pleasure? Why is it referred to as strategic reading?
- What does it mean to be an active reader? How do you interrogate the author as you read?
- What role do Keywords play in strategic reading?
- Why is it helpful to jot down brief paraphrases of crucial text?
- Why do you summarize the passage's Topic and Scope and the author's Purpose and Main Idea?
- What are the distinguishing characteristics of the Reading Comprehension question types?
- How do you spot and use research clues in the question stems?
- How can you most appropriately predict the answers to Global and open-ended Inference questions?
- What are the common wrong answer types associated with Reading Comprehension questions?

While these questions will help you reflect on your performance in the Reading Comprehension section, you can actually practice Reading Comprehension skills all the time. Over the coming days and weeks, make a point of reading material that is academic and written at roughly the same level as LSAT Reading Comprehension passages. As you do, interrogate the author. Spot Keywords and summarize the authors' purposes and points of view. Try imagining, or even writing, LSAT questions to accompany the outside reading you do. The more you "think like the testmaker," the closer you are to true LSAT mastery.

ANSWER KEY

Fractal Geometry (pp. 572–573)

1. B
2. C
3. D
4. D
5. E
6. A
7. E
8. D

Science and Humanities (pp. 592–593)

20. E
21. C
22. D
23. B
24. D
25. C
26. B

Parallel Computing (pp. 598–599)

27. C
28. C
29. E
30. B
31. C
32. B
33. A
34. E

Universal Declaration of Human Rights (UDHR) (pp. 600–601)

35. D
36. B
37. B
38. D
39. E
40. A

Complete explanations for these questions can be found in your online resources.

CHAPTER 13

Reading Comprehension Section Management

The bulk of this chapter consists of a complete Reading Comprehension section, followed by an answer key. Complete explanations can be found in your online resources. Taking complete timed practice sections helps you maximize your score by learning to improve section management. Perfecting your timing in LSAT sections involves much more than just "getting faster." Indeed, in many cases, hurrying through the strategic reading and Roadmap step of the Reading Comprehension Method may wind up costing you time by causing you to reread parts of the passage multiple times as you work through the question set. Even worse, failing to summarize the author's Purpose and Main Idea or having a poor grasp of a passage's organization could lead you to wrong answers, costing you points directly.

TIMING AND SECTION MANAGEMENT

Here are a few of the principles of great section management that LSAT experts use to their advantage. Learn them and put them into practice whenever you undertake a timed section or full-test practice.

Reading Comprehension Section Timing: The Basics

The facts: Every Reading Comprehension section has four passages, each with 5–8 questions for a total of 26–28 questions to be completed in 35 minutes.

The strategy: On average, then, you should take 8–9 minutes for each passage. Of that time, you'll usually take 3–4 minutes to read strategically and Roadmap the passage. You'll use the remaining 4½–5½ minutes to answer the questions. Don't rush Step 1 of the Reading Comprehension Method. Approached strategically, the easiest passages may take less than eight minutes—bank that time for the longer and tougher ones. When a passage threatens to drag on much longer than nine minutes, however, be prepared to guess on its toughest questions and move on, saving yourself time to read the next passage and answer its questions.

Efficiency, Not Speed

The facts: You have less time per question in Reading Comprehension than you do in any other section of the LSAT. A good Roadmap will allow you to locate key details quickly to answer several question types. Understanding the passage's Scope and the author's Purpose and Main Idea should help you efficiently answer Global questions and open-ended Inference questions.

The strategy: Follow the Reading Comprehension Method. In the preceding chapters, you've seen how strategic reading and a solid Roadmap reveal the pieces of the passage and the ideas you need to know to answer questions quickly and accurately. Don't let "clock anxiety" tempt you into abandoning the most efficient approach to the Reading Comprehension section. Being methodical does not mean being slow. When you have practiced enough that the Reading Comprehension Method is second nature, you'll find that it provides the shortest and most direct route to correct answers, the single goal of all the work you do on the LSAT.

Triage: Take Control of the Section

The facts: You are under no obligation to do the passages or questions in the order in which they are presented. The first passage in the section is most often (but not always) the easiest for most test takers. Either the third or fourth passage is most often (but not always) the hardest for most test takers.

The strategy: Triage is a term used in the medical profession to refer to the process of determining priorities in an emergency. You can "triage" the Reading Comprehension section by looking for and prioritizing the passages and questions most likely to turn into correct answers for you. Some LSAT experts triage the section by taking a minute or less at the start of the section to look at all four passages and choose an optimal order in which to address them. These experts prioritize passages that, at a glance, have simple prose, clear organization, and/or familiar topics. Other experts follow a predetermined order (1-2-4-3 is a reasonable rule of thumb), but they are willing to skip and come back to a passage or to rearrange their order of attack immediately upon determining that a passage is particularly abstruse or confusing.

Similarly, you can triage the questions within a passage's question set. A passage's Global question is usually the first in the set and should be answered while the Topic/Scope/Purpose/Main Idea summaries are fresh in your mind. By the way, when a passage has two Global questions, the second is usually near the end of the question set; it's worth your while to check for a second Global question because you can answer it with a nearly identical prediction. After that, you may choose to tackle questions with clear research clues in their question stems. These will guide you back to specific details in the passage; these details, as you know from earlier chapters, are usually associated with Keywords that indicate the author's purpose or opinion. Open-ended questions can be time-consuming. Be as strategic as possible with them by eliminating answer choices that conflict with the author's point of view or fall clearly outside the scope of the passage.

Whether you are triaging a section or a set of questions, follow the best practices of a great doctor triaging an emergency: Be decisive and remember that you are in control of the situation.

Skip and Guess Strategically

The facts: You do not need to answer every question to get a great score. Time-consuming questions (e.g., "The passage supports each of the following EXCEPT" questions) are scattered throughout the section. There is no bonus for answering the hardest question(s) in the section.

The strategy: Remember that you are in control of how much time and effort you dedicate to any particular passage or question. Allowing yourself to get into an "ego battle" with particular passages or questions—"I *will* figure this one out no matter what!"—can take time away from other questions you could answer quickly and accurately. Be willing to skip one or two difficult or very time-consuming questions if doing so will allow you to get more questions correct on subsequent passages. Preempt situations in which you are guessing out of frustration—"Okay, I give up. I've already given this two minutes; I'll never get it!"—by learning to guess strategically—"I'll guess on this lengthy Inference question and give myself an extra two minutes for the next two passages." In other words, guess when it is to your benefit to do so. Stay in control of the section and the test.

TAKING THE TIMING SECTION

The Reading Comprehension section that follows was originally Section 2 in PrepTest 45, administered in December 2004.

Proctoring

Complete this section under timed, test-like conditions. Give yourself 35 minutes for the section and finish it in one uninterrupted sitting.

Scoring

After you finish the section, record your answers in the appropriate webgrid (PrepTest 45, Section 2) found in your online resources. This will make your results and percent correct easy to see, and the score report will contain links to the explanations for each question.

Review

For your convenience, complete Answers and Explanations are also available as a PDF file in your online resources. Whether you review the section online or with the PDF, review it completely, even those questions you got right. In addition to reading over the explanations for the right and wrong answers, check to see that you consistently followed the Reading Comprehension Method, read each passage strategically, created a helpful Roadmap, identified each question type, researched and predicted effectively, and answered the questions as efficiently as possible.

PrepTest 45, Section 2

Time—35 minutes
27 Questions

is section is followed by a group of questions to be answered on the basis of what is <u>stated</u> or
ne of the questions, more than one of the choices could conceivably answer the question. However,
wer; that is, the response that most accurately and completely answers the question, and blacken
r answer sheet.

A number of natural disasters in recent years—
such as earthquakes, major storms, and floods—that
have affected large populations of people have forced
relief agencies, communities, and entire nations to
(5) reevaluate the ways in which they respond in the
aftermaths of such disasters. They believe that
traditional ways of dealing with disasters have proved
ineffective on several occasions and, in some cases,
have been destructive rather than helpful to the
(10) communities hit by these sudden and unexpected
crises. Traditionally, relief has been based on the
premise that aid in postdisaster situations is most
effective if given in the immediate aftermath of an
event. A high priority also has been placed on the
(15) quantity of aid materials, programs, and personnel, in
the belief that the negative impact of a disaster can
be counteracted by a large and rapid infusion of aid.

Critics claim that such an approach often creates
a new set of difficulties for already hard-hit
(20) communities. Teams of uninvited experts and
personnel—all of whom need food and shelter—as
well as uncoordinated shipments of goods and the
establishment of programs inappropriate to local
needs can quickly lead to a secondary "disaster" as
(25) already strained local infrastructures break down
under the pressure of this large influx of resources. In
some instances, tons of food have disappeared into
local markets for resale, and, with inadequate
accounting procedures, billions of dollars in aid
(30) money have gone unaccounted for.

To develop a more effective approach, experts
recommend shifting the focus to the long term. A
response that produces lasting benefit, these experts
claim, requires that community members define the
(35) form and method of aid that are most appropriate to
their needs. Grassroots dialogue designed to facilitate
preparedness should be encouraged in disaster-prone
communities long before the onset of a crisis, so that
in a disaster's immediate aftermath, relief agencies
(40) can rely on members of affected communities to take
the lead. The practical effect of this approach is that
aid takes the form of a response to the stated desires
of those affected rather than an immediate, though
less informed, action on their behalf.

(45) Though this proposal appears sound, its success
depends on how an important constituency,
namely donors, will respond. Historically,
donors—individuals, corporations, foundations, and

governmental bodies—have been most likely to
(50) respond only in the immediate aftermath of a crisis.
However, communities affected by disasters typically
have several long-term needs such as the rebuilding
of houses and roads, and thus the months and years
after a disaster are also crucial. Donors that
(55) incorporate dialogue with members of affected
communities into their relief plans could foster
strategies that more efficiently utilize immediate aid
as well as provide for the difficulties facing
communities in the years after a disaster.

1. Which one of the following most accurately expresses
   the main point of the passage?

   (A) The most useful response to a natural disaster
       is one in which relief agencies allow victims to
       dictate the type of aid they receive, which will
       most likely result in the allocation of long-
       term rather than immediate aid.

   (B) The quantity of aid given after a natural
       disaster reflects the desires of donors more
       than the needs of recipients, and in some
       cases great quantities of aid are destructive
       rather than helpful.

   (C) Aid that focuses on long-term needs is difficult
       to organize because, by its very definition, it
       requires that relief agencies focus on
       constructing an adequate dialogue among
       recipients, providers, and donors.

   (D) Disaster relief efforts have been marked by
       inefficiencies that attest to the need for
       donors and relief agencies to communicate
       with affected communities concerning how
       best to meet not only their short-term but
       also their long-term needs.

   (E) Though the years after a disaster are crucial for
       communities affected by disasters, the days
       and weeks immediately after a disaster are
       what capture the attention of donors, thus
       forcing relief agencies into the role of
       mediators between the two extremes.

GO ON TO THE NEXT PAGE.

608

2. Which one of the following examples best illustrates the type of disaster response recommended by the experts mentioned in the third paragraph?

   (A) After a flood, local officials reject three more expensive proposals before finally accepting a contractor's plan to control a local river with a dam.

   (B) Following a plan developed several years ago by a relief agency in consultation with donors and community members, the relief agency provides temporary shelter immediately after a flood and later helps rebuild houses destroyed by the flood.

   (C) Immediately after a flood, several different relief agencies, each acting independently, send large shipments of goods to the affected community along with teams of highly motivated but untrained volunteers to coordinate the distribution of these goods.

   (D) At the request of its donors, a private relief agency delays providing any assistance to victims of a flood until after the agency conducts a thorough study of the types of aid most likely to help the affected community in the long run.

   (E) After a flood, government officials persuade local companies to increase their corporate giving levels and to direct more aid to the surrounding community.

3. The author of the passage would be most likely to agree with which one of the following statements?

   (A) Disaster relief plans are appropriate only for disaster-prone communities.

   (B) When communities affected by disasters have articulated their long-term needs, donors typically have been responsive to those needs.

   (C) Donors would likely provide more disaster relief aid if they had confidence that it would be used more effectively than aid currently is.

   (D) It is not the amount of aid but rather the way this aid is managed that is the source of current problems in disaster relief.

   (E) Few communities affected by disasters experience a crucial need for short-term aid.

4. The author discusses donors in the final paragraph primarily in order to

   (A) point to an influential group of people who have resisted changes to traditional disaster response efforts

   (B) demonstrate that the needs of donors and aid recipients contrast profoundly on the issue of disaster response

   (C) show that implementing an effective disaster relief program requires a new approach on the part of donors as well as relief agencies

   (D) illustrate that relief agencies and donors share similar views on the goals of disaster response but disagree on the proper response methods

   (E) concede that the reformation of disaster relief programs, while necessary, is unlikely to take place because of the disagreements among donors

5. It can be inferred from the passage that the author would be most likely to view a shift toward a more long-term perspective in disaster relief efforts as which one of the following?

   (A) a development that would benefit affected communities as well as aid providers who have a shared interest in relief efforts that are effective and well managed

   (B) a change that would help communities meet their future needs more effectively but would inevitably result in a detrimental reduction of short-term aid like food and medicine

   (C) an approach that would enable aid recipients to meet their long-term needs but which would not address the mismanagement that hampers short-term relief efforts

   (D) a movement that, while well intentioned, will likely be undermined by the unwillingness of donors to accept new methods of delivering aid

   (E) the beginning of a trend in which aid recipients play a major role after a disaster and donors play a minor role, reversing the structure of traditional aid programs

6. Which one of the following inferences about natural disasters and relief efforts is most strongly supported by the passage?

   (A) Although inefficiencies have long been present in international disaster relief programs, they have been aggravated in recent years by increased demands on relief agencies' limited resources.

   (B) Local communities had expressed little interest in taking responsibility for their own preparedness prior to the most recent years, thus leaving donors and relief agencies unaware of potential problems.

   (C) Numerous relief efforts in the years prior to the most recent provided such vast quantities of aid that most needs were met despite evidence of inefficiency and mismanagement, and few recipient communities questioned traditional disaster response methods.

   (D) Members of communities affected by disasters have long argued that they should set the agenda for relief efforts, but relief agencies have only recently come to recognize the validity of their arguments.

   (E) A number of wasteful relief efforts in the most recent years provided dramatic illustrations of aid programs that were implemented by donors and agencies with little accountability to populations affected by disasters.

GO ON TO THE NEXT PAGE.

The moral precepts embodied in the Hippocratic oath, which physicians standardly affirm upon beginning medical practice, have long been considered the immutable bedrock of medical ethics,
(5) binding physicians in a moral community that reaches across temporal, cultural, and national barriers. Until very recently the promises expressed in that oath—for example to act primarily for the benefit and not the harm of patients and to conform to various standards
(10) of professional conduct including the preservation of patients' confidences—even seemed impervious to the powerful scientific and societal forces challenging it. Critics argue that the oath is outdated; its fixed moral rules, they say, are incompatible with more flexible
(15) modern ideas about ethics. It also encourages doctors to adopt an authoritarian stance that depreciates the privacy and autonomy of the patient. Furthermore, its emphasis on the individual patient without regard for the wider social context frustrates the physician's
(20) emerging role as gatekeeper in managed care plans and impedes competitive market forces, which, some critics believe, should determine the quality, price, and distribution of health care as they do those of other commodities. The oath is also faulted for its
(25) omissions: its failure to mention such vital contemporary issues as human experimentation and the relationships of physicians to other health professionals. Some respected opponents even cite historical doubts about the oath's origin and
(30) authorship, presenting evidence that it was formulated by a small group of reformist physicians in ancient Greece and that for centuries it was not uniformly accepted by medical practitioners.

This historical issue may be dismissed at the
(35) outset as irrelevant to the oath's current appropriateness. Regardless of the specific origin of its text—which, admittedly, is at best uncertain—those in each generation who critically appraise its content and judge it to express valid
(40) principles of medical ethics become, in a more meaningful sense, its authors. More importantly, even the more substantive, morally based arguments concerning contemporary values and newly relevant issues cannot negate the patients' need for assurance
(45) that physicians will pursue appropriate goals in treatment in accordance with generally acceptable standards of professionalism. To fulfill that need, the core value of beneficence—which does not actually conflict with most reformers' purposes—should be
(50) retained, with adaptations at the oath's periphery by some combination of revision, supplementation, and modern interpretation. In fact, there is already a tradition of peripheral reinterpretation of traditional wording; for example, the oath's vaguely and
(55) archaically worded proscription against "cutting for the stone" may once have served to forbid surgery, but with today's safer and more effective surgical

techniques it is understood to function as a promise to practice within the confines of one's expertise,
(60) which remains a necessary safeguard for patients' safety and well-being.

Handwritten margin notes: "Oath: benefit not harm conform to standards"; "critics say is outdated"; "oath fails to mention human experiments"

7. Which one of the following most accurately states the main point of the passage?

(A) The Hippocratic oath ought to be reevaluated carefully, with special regard to the role of the physician, to make certain that its fundamental moral rules still apply today.

(B) Despite recent criticisms of the Hippocratic oath, some version of it that will continue to assure patients of physicians' professionalism and beneficent treatment ought to be retained.

(C) Codes of ethics developed for one society at a particular point in history may lose some specific application in later societies but can retain a useful fundamental moral purpose.

(D) Even the criticisms of the Hippocratic oath based on contemporary values and newly relevant medical issues cannot negate patients' need for assurance.

(E) Modern ideas about ethics, especially medical ethics, obviate the need for and appropriateness of a single code of medical ethics like the Hippocratic oath.

8. Which one of the following most accurately describes the organization of the material presented in the passage?

(A) A general principle is described, criticisms of the principle are made, and modifications of the principle are made in light of these criticisms.

(B) A set of criticisms is put forward, and possible replies to those criticisms are considered and dismissed.

(C) The history of a certain code of conduct is discussed, criticisms of the code are mentioned and partially endorsed, and the code is modified as a response.

(D) A general principle is formulated, a partial defense of that principle is presented, and criticisms of the principle are discussed and rejected.

(E) The tradition surrounding a certain code of conduct is discussed, criticisms of that code are mentioned, and a general defense of the code is presented.

GO ON TO THE NEXT PAGE.

9. The passage cites which one of the following as a value at the heart of the Hippocratic oath that should present no difficulty to most reformers?

(A) creation of a community of physicians from all eras, nations, and cultures

(B) constant improvement and advancement of medical science

(C) provision of medical care to all individuals regardless of ability to pay

(D) physician action for the benefit of patients

(E) observance of established moral rules even in the face of challenging societal forces

10. The author's primary purpose in the passage is to

(A) affirm society's continuing need for a code embodying certain principles

(B) chastise critics within the medical community who support reinterpretation of a code embodying certain principles

(C) argue that historical doubts about the origin of a certain code are irrelevant to its interpretation

(D) outline the pros and cons of revising a code embodying certain principles

(E) propose a revision of a code embodying certain principles that will increase the code's applicability to modern times

11. Based on information in the passage, it can be inferred that which one of the following sentences could most logically be added to the passage as a concluding sentence?

(A) The fact that such reinterpretations are so easy, however, suggests that our rejection of the historical issue was perhaps premature.

(B) Yet, where such piecemeal reinterpretation is not possible, revisions to even the core value of the oath may be necessary.

(C) It is thus simply a failure of the imagination, and not any changes in the medical profession or society in general, that has motivated critics of the Hippocratic oath.

(D) Because of this tradition of reinterpretation of the Hippocratic oath, therefore, modern ideas about medical ethics must be much more flexible than they have been in the past.

(E) Despite many new challenges facing the medical profession, therefore, there is no real need for wholesale revision of the Hippocratic oath.

12. Each of the following is mentioned in the passage as a criticism of the Hippocratic oath EXCEPT:

(A) The oath encourages authoritarianism on the part of physicians.

(B) The version of the oath in use today is not identical to the oath formulated in ancient Greece.

(C) The oath fails to address modern medical dilemmas that could not have been foreseen in ancient Greece.

(D) The oath's absolutism is incompatible with contemporary views of morality.

(E) The oath's emphasis on the individual patient is often not compatible with a market-driven medical industry.

13. Which one of the following can most accurately be used to describe the author's attitude toward critics of the Hippocratic oath?

(A) enthusiastic support

(B) bemused dismissal

(C) reasoned disagreement

(D) strict neutrality

(E) guarded agreement

14. Which one of the following would be most suitable as a title for this passage if it were to appear as an editorial piece?

(A) "The Ancients versus the Moderns: Conflicting Ideas About Medical Ethics"

(B) "Hypocritical Oafs: Why 'Managed Care' Proponents are Seeking to Repeal an Ancient Code"

(C) "Genetic Fallacy in the Age of Gene-Splicing: Why the Origins of the Hippocratic Oath Don't Matter"

(D) "The Dead Hand of Hippocrates: Breaking the Hold of Ancient Ideas on Modern Medicine"

(E) "Prescription for the Hippocratic Oath: Facelift or Major Surgery?"

GO ON TO THE NEXT PAGE.

...of a fungus living in symbiosis ...eneficial relationship) with an alga. ...st branches of the complex evolutionary ...ree of fungi have been well established, the ...olutionary origins of lichen-forming fungi have been a mystery. But a new DNA study has revealed the relationship of lichen-forming fungi to several previously known branches of the fungus family tree. The study reveals that, far from being oddities,

(10) lichen-forming fungi are close relatives of such common fungi as brewer's yeast, morel mushrooms, and the fungus that causes Dutch elm disease. This accounts for the visible similarity of certain lichens to more recognizable fungi such as mushrooms.

(15)   In general, fungi present complications for the researcher. Fungi are usually parasitic or symbiotic, and researchers are often unsure whether they are examining fungal DNA or that of the associated organism. But lichen-forming fungi are especially

(20) difficult to study. They have few distinguishing characteristics of shape or structure, and they are unusually difficult to isolate from their partner algae, with which they have a particularly delicate symbiosis. In some cases the alga is wedged between

(25) layers of fungal tissue; in others, the fungus grows through the alga's cell walls in order to take nourishment, and the tissues of the two organisms are entirely enmeshed and inseparable. As a result, lichen-forming fungi have long been difficult to

(30) classify definitively within the fungus family. By default they were thus considered a separate grouping of fungi with an unknown evolutionary origin. But, using new analytical tools that allow them to isolate the DNA of fungi in parasitic or symbiotic

(35) relationships, researchers were able to establish the DNA sequence in a certain gene found in 75 species of fungi, including 10 species of lichen-forming fungi. Based on these analyses, the researchers found 5 branches on the fungus family tree to which

(40) varieties of lichen-forming fungi belong. Furthermore, the researchers stress that it is likely that as more types of lichen-forming fungi are analyzed, they will be found to belong to still more branches of the fungus family tree.

(45)   One implication of the new research is that it provides evidence to help overturn the long-standing evolutionary assumption that parasitic interactions inevitably evolve over time to a greater benignity and eventually to symbiosis so that the parasites will not

(50) destroy their hosts. The addition of lichen-forming fungi to positions along branches of the fungus family tree indicates that this assumption does not hold for fungi. Fungi both harmful and benign can now be found both early and late in fungus

(55) evolutionary history. Given the new layout of the fungus family tree resulting from the lichen study, it appears that fungi can evolve toward mutualism and then just as easily turn back again toward parasitism.

[handwritten annotations: "lichen = fungus in symbiosis"; "lichen close to yeast mushrooms etc"; "complications"; "lichen esp difficult"; "ex"; "difficult to classify"; "DNA sequence in 10 lichen species found to belong to branches of fungus tree"; "evidence against assumption parasite → symb."; "Fungi can be harmful OR AND benign"]

15. Which one of the following most accurately states the main point of the passage?

(A) New research suggests that fungi are not only parasitic but also symbiotic organisms.

(B) New research has revealed that lichen-forming fungi constitute a distinct species of fungus.

(C) New research into the evolutionary origins of lichen-forming fungi reveals them to be closely related to various species of algae.

(D) New research has isolated the DNA of lichen-forming fungi and uncovered their relationship to the fungus family tree.

(E) New research into the fungal component of lichens explains the visible similarities between lichens and fungi by means of their common evolutionary origins.

16. Which one of the following most accurately describes the author's purpose in the last paragraph of the passage?

(A) to suggest that new research overturns the assumption that lichen-forming fungi are primarily symbiotic, rather than parasitic, organisms

(B) to show that findings based on new research regarding fungus classification have implications that affect a long-standing assumption of evolutionary science

(C) to explain the fundamental purposes of fungus classification in order to position this classification within the broader field of evolutionary science

(D) to demonstrate that a fundamental assumption of evolutionary science is verified by new research regarding fungus classification

(E) to explain how symbiotic relationships can evolve into purely parasitic ones

GO ON TO THE NEXT PAGE.

17. Which one of the following most accurately describes the organization of the passage?

(A) explanation of the difficulty of classifying lichens; description of the DNA sequence of lichen-forming fungi; summary of the implications of this description

(B) definition of lichens; discussion of new discoveries concerning lichens' evolutionary history; application of these findings in support of an evolutionary theory

(C) definition of lichens; discussion of the difficulty in classifying their fungal components; resolution of this difficulty and implications of the resulting research

(D) discussion of the symbiotic relationship that constitutes lichens; discussion of how new research can distinguish parasitic from symbiotic fungi; implications of this research

(E) explanation of the symbiotic nature of lichens; discussion of the problems this poses for genetic researchers; delineation of the implications these problems have for evolutionary theory

18. According to the passage, the elimination of which one of the following obstacles enabled scientists to identify the evolutionary origins of lichen-forming fungi?

(A) The DNA of lichen-forming fungi was not easy to separate from that of their associated algae.

(B) Lichen-forming fungi are difficult to distinguish from several common fungi with which they are closely related.

(C) Lichen-forming fungi were grouped separately from other fungi on the fungus family tree.

(D) Lichen-forming fungi are far less common than more recognizable fungi such as mushrooms.

(E) The DNA of lichen-forming fungi is significantly more complex than that of other fungi.

19. Which one of the following, if true, most weakens the author's criticism of the assumption that parasitic interactions generally evolve toward symbiosis?

(A) Evolutionary theorists now postulate that symbiotic interactions generally evolve toward greater parasitism, rather than vice versa.

(B) The evolutionary tree of fungi is somewhat more complex than that of similarly parasitic or symbiotic organisms.

(C) The DNA of fungi involved in symbiotic interactions is far more difficult to isolate than that of fungi involved in parasitic interactions.

(D) The placement of lichen-forming fungi as a separate group on the fungus family tree masked the fact that parasitic fungi sometimes evolved much later than symbiotic ones.

(E) Branches of the fungus family tree that have evolved from symbiosis to parasitism usually die out shortly thereafter.

GO ON TO THE NEXT PAGE.

The following passage was written in the late 1980s.

The struggle to obtain legal recognition of aboriginal rights is a difficult one, and even if a right is written into the law there is no guarantee that the future will not bring changes to the law that
(5) undermine the right. For this reason, the federal government of Canada in 1982 extended constitutional protection to those aboriginal rights already recognized under the law. This protection was extended to the Indian, Inuit, and Métis peoples, the
(10) three groups generally thought to comprise the aboriginal population in Canada. But this decision has placed on provincial courts the enormous burden of interpreting and translating the necessarily general constitutional language into specific rulings. The
(15) result has been inconsistent recognition and establishment of aboriginal rights, despite the continued efforts of aboriginal peoples to raise issues concerning their rights.

Aboriginal rights in Canada are defined by the
(20) constitution as aboriginal peoples' rights to ownership of land and its resources, the inherent right of aboriginal societies to self-government, and the right to legal recognition of indigenous customs. But difficulties arise in applying these broadly conceived
(25) rights. For example, while it might appear straightforward to affirm legal recognition of indigenous customs, the exact legal meaning of "indigenous" is extremely difficult to interpret. The intent of the constitutional protection is to recognize
(30) only long-standing traditional customs, not those of recent origin; provincial courts therefore require aboriginal peoples to provide legal documentation that any customs they seek to protect were practiced sufficiently long ago—a criterion defined in practice
(35) to mean prior to the establishment of British sovereignty over the specific territory. However, this requirement makes it difficult for aboriginal societies, which often relied on oral tradition rather than written records, to support their claims.
(40) Furthermore, even if aboriginal peoples are successful in convincing the courts that specific rights should be recognized, it is frequently difficult to determine exactly what these rights amount to. Consider aboriginal land claims. Even when
(45) aboriginal ownership of specific lands is fully established, there remains the problem of interpreting the meaning of that "ownership." In a 1984 case in Ontario, an aboriginal group claimed that its property rights should be interpreted as full ownership in the
(50) contemporary sense of private property, which allows for the sale of the land or its resources. But the provincial court instead ruled that the law had previously recognized only the aboriginal right to use the land and therefore granted property rights so
(55) minimal as to allow only the bare survival of the

community. Here, the provincial court's ruling was excessively conservative in its assessment of the current law. Regrettably, it appears that this group will not be successful unless it is able to move its
(60) case from the provincial courts into the Supreme Court of Canada, which will be, one hopes, more insistent upon a satisfactory application of the constitutional reforms.

20. Which one of the following most accurately states the main point of the passage?

(A) The overly conservative rulings of Canada's provincial courts have been a barrier to constitutional reforms intended to protect aboriginal rights.

(B) The overwhelming burden placed on provincial courts of interpreting constitutional language in Canada has halted efforts by aboriginal peoples to gain full ownership of land.

(C) Constitutional language aimed at protecting aboriginal rights in Canada has so far left the protection of these rights uncertain due to the difficult task of interpreting this language.

(D) Constitutional reforms meant to protect aboriginal rights in Canada have in fact been used by some provincial courts to limit these rights.

(E) Efforts by aboriginal rights advocates to uphold constitutional reforms in Canada may be more successful if heard by the Supreme Court rather than by the provincial courts.

21. Which one of the following most accurately describes the author's main purpose in lines 11–14 of the passage?

(A) to demonstrate that the decisions of the provincial courts rarely conform to the goals of the constitutional reforms

(B) to locate the source of a systemic problem in protecting aboriginal rights in Canada

(C) to identify the specific source of problems in enacting constitutional reforms in Canada

(D) to describe one aspect of the process by which constitutional reforms are enacted in Canada

(E) to criticize the use of general language in the Canadian constitution

GO ON TO THE NEXT PAGE.

22. The passage explicitly states that which one of the following was intended as a consequence of the constitutional protection of aboriginal rights?

    (A) definition of the type of property rights that apply to aboriginal societies
    (B) establishment of the Supreme Court of Canada as the arbiter of aboriginal rights
    (C) recognition of traditional customs but not those of recent origin
    (D) clarification of which groups comprise the aboriginal population in Canada
    (E) creation of local governments for aboriginal communities

23. The passage provides the most evidence for the claim that the author has a negative attitude toward which one of the following?

    (A) the 1982 constitutional reforms' burdening the provincial courts with the task of interpretation
    (B) the difficulties in interpreting such terms as "indigenous" and "ownership"
    (C) the criterion used to determine which customs are too recent to merit constitutional protection
    (D) the requirement that aboriginal peoples provide documentation for traditional customs
    (E) the definition of ownership imposed by the provincial court in 1984

24. The passage provides evidence to suggest that the author would be most likely to assent to which one of the following proposals?

    (A) Aboriginal peoples in Canada should not be answerable to the federal laws of Canada.
    (B) Oral tradition should sometimes be considered legal documentation of certain indigenous customs.
    (C) Aboriginal communities should be granted full protection of all of their customs.
    (D) Provincial courts should be given no authority to decide cases involving questions of aboriginal rights.
    (E) The language of the Canadian constitution should more carefully delineate the instances to which reforms apply.

25. Which one of the following, if true, would lend the most credence to the author's statement in lines 56–58?

    (A) Other Ontario courts had previously interpreted "use" to include sale of the land or its resources.
    (B) The ruling created thousands of jobs by opening the land in question to logging by a timber corporation.
    (C) Previous court decisions in Ontario have distinguished the right to use land from the right to sell it.
    (D) The ruling prompted aboriginal groups in other provinces to pursue land claims in those courts.
    (E) Prior to the decision in question, the provincial court had not heard a case concerning the constitutional reforms.

26. Based on the information in the passage, the author would be most likely to agree with which one of the following statements about the 1984 case in Ontario?

    (A) The court's ruling directly contravened the language of the constitutional reforms protecting aboriginal land ownership rights in the full modern sense.
    (B) The Supreme Court remains the best hope for the recognition of full aboriginal property rights because provincial courts are not authorized to rule on the definition of property rights.
    (C) If there had been clear documentary evidence that the group had occupied the land before the establishment of British sovereignty, the court would probably have upheld the aboriginal claims.
    (D) The unsatisfactory ruling in the case was the result of pressure from conservative politicians and other conservative interests.
    (E) The court correctly understood the intent of the constitutional reforms, but it failed to apply them correctly because it misconstrued their relation to existing law.

27. The passage as a whole can most accurately be described as

    (A) an argument stressing the need for advocates of certain rights to adopt certain strategies
    (B) a comprehensive study of efforts to guarantee the protection of certain rights
    (C) an examination of problems associated with efforts to protect certain rights
    (D) an argument favoring the need for revising the definition of certain rights
    (E) an attempt to correct misunderstandings regarding the protection of certain rights

S T O P

IF YOU FINISH BEFORE TIME IS CALLED, YOU MAY CHECK YOUR WORK ON THIS SECTION ONLY.
DO NOT WORK ON ANY OTHER SECTION IN THE TEST.

ANSWER KEY

Passage 1—Disaster Relief Policy

1. D
2. B
3. D
4. C
5. A
6. E

Passage 2—Hippocratic Oath

7. B
8. E
9. D
10. A
11. E
12. B
13. C
14. E

Passage 3—Lichen-Forming Fungi

15. D
16. B
17. C
18. A
19. E

Passage 4—Aboriginal Rights in Canada

20. C
21. B
22. C
23. E
24. B
25. A
26. E
27. C

Complete explanations for this section can be found in your online resources.

Acknowledgment is made to the following sources from which material has been adapted for use in this book:

Ronald Dworkin, *Taking Rights Seriously*. ©1977 by Pantheon Books.

James H. March, ed., *The Canadian Encyclopedia*. ©1988 by Hurtig Publishers Ltd.

Christopher B. Ogden, "What Kinds of Help?" ©1993 by Time Inc.

Edmund D. Pellegrino, MD, "Ethics: Rethinking the Hippocratic Oath." ©1996 by the American Medical Association.

Norman Solomon, *Hidden Agenda*. ©1995 by San Francisco Bay Guardian Co., Inc.

Carol Kaesuk Yoon, "Pariahs of the Fungal World, Lichens Finally Get Some Respect." ©June 13, 1995 by *The New York Times*.

Countdown to Test Day

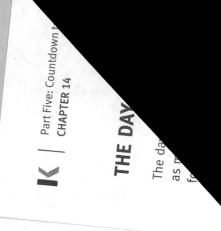

CHAPTER 14

Test Day

Is it starting to feel like your whole life is a buildup to the LSAT? You've known about it for years, worried about it for months, and now spent weeks (at least) in solid preparation for it. As the test gets closer, you may find your anxiety building. Don't worry; after the preparation you've done, you're in good shape for the test. The key to calming any pretest jitters is to be prepared for the road to Test Day and beyond.

THE WEEK BEFORE THE TEST

Your goal during the week before the LSAT is to set yourself up for success on Test Day. Up until this point, you have been working to build your LSAT potential, but Test Day is about achievement.

LSAT STRATEGY

Things to Do Leading Up to Test Day:

- Get your body on schedule for the time of the test, and do LSAT questions at that same time of day.
- Eat, sleep, and exercise.
- Visit your test site; check on public transportation schedule, directions, parking, etc.
- Print out and double-check your admissions ticket.
- Check *www.lsac.org* for the most recent Test Day guidelines.
- Decide whether you want to take the test or withdraw.

Planning Your Remaining Study Time:

- Balance stress management and study.
- Study areas of greatest strength, not only areas of greatest opportunity.
- The majority of your work should be under timed conditions—either Timing or Endurance.
- Still review the Answers and Explanations for every practice problem.
- Remember that you are going to law school.

BEFORE THE TEST

The day before the test is as important as the six days before it. The first instinct of most test takers is to cram as much as possible in hopes of grabbing a few last-second points. But the LSAT isn't a test that can be crammed for. You should think of Test Day as game day. Make sure you can hit your potential when it counts. Relax the day before the test so that you can hit your peak performance when it matters most.

LSAT STRATEGY

The day before the test:

- Relax! Read a book, watch a movie, take a walk, or go shopping.
- Don't take any full-length tests, and preferably don't study at all.
- Get all of your materials together—your admission ticket, plastic bag, snack, watch, and so on.
- Eat a full meal for dinner and get plenty of sleep.

LSAT FACTS

The following items are required for admission on Test Day:

- Admissions ticket that displays the passport photo you uploaded to your LSAC account
- Government-issued ID
- Regular No. 2 pencils (no mechanical pencils)

LSAT STRATEGY

Kaplan recommends you bring the following items with you on Test Day:

- 1-gallon ziplock bag (necessary to store items somewhere other than your desktop)
- A nondigital timing device (i.e., an analog watch)
- A snack for the break (avoid sugary snacks, if possible)
- Bottled beverage
- Eraser (or pencils with quality erasers)
- Pencil sharpener (or just lots of pencils)
- Pain reliever (e.g., aspirin)
- Tissues
- A positive, upbeat attitude!

THE MORNING OF THE TEST

On the morning of the exam, you should obviously get up early to give yourself time to wake up and eat breakfast. Leave early for the test center. A relaxed morning is a much better start than a frantic, stressful one.

LSAT STRATEGY

On the morning of the test:

- Get up early and plan accordingly for commute/traffic/parking.
- Eat an appropriate breakfast.
- Dress in layers (but do not wear a hooded sweatshirt).
- Gather your allowable items into a one-gallon ziplock plastic bag.

When gathering your items into your plastic bag, avoid bringing anything on this list of prohibited items. (This list is not exhaustive, so check the LSAC website for the most up-to-date information.)

LSAT FACTS

The following items are prohibited:

- Cell phones (Leave it at home or in the car.)
- Electronic devices of any kind, including tablets and digital watches
- Ear plugs
- Backpacks or purses
- Mechanical pencils
- Papers or books
- Hats and hooded sweatshirts

AT THE TEST SITE AND DURING THE TEST

Aim to arrive at your testing facility at least 30 minutes before the test is scheduled to begin. Arriving early is not just about being prompt; it's also important to have a game plan for what to do at the testing facility before the exam starts.

LSAT STRATEGY

At the testing facility on Test Day:

- Arrive 30 minutes early.
- Find and use the drinking fountain and bathroom.
- Get into "LSAT mode" by reviewing previous work (discard papers before checking in).
- Enter the testing room a few minutes before the test is set to begin.
- Use the time before the test begins to prepare yourself mentally for the test.

LSAT STRATEGY

What to expect:

- Stress levels will be high.
- It will be cold or hot.
- Students will talk unproductively during the break.
- You will be successful.

LSAT STRATEGY

Three essential takeaways from your Kaplan LSAT training:

- Every question has one right answer and four terrible ones.
- When applicable, strive to predict an answer to all LR and RC questions before evaluating the answer choices.
- Invest the proper time to set up a Logic Game or Roadmap a passage; it will pay dividends in the questions.

LSAT STRATEGY

Taking the test:

- Look forward, not backward—always keep moving through the test and focus on the section you're currently in, not sections you've already done or will do in the future.
- Fill in every bubble.
- Grid appropriately.
- When the proctor says stop, it means stop.
- Relax during the break. Avoid the temptation to try for an unethical advantage by talking about the test to other test takers.
- Don't worry about how you're scoring. Don't try to figure out which section is the experimental one. Focus only on what's in front of you.

LSAT STRATEGY

Staying calm:

- The LSAT is scored on a curve; if something seems challenging, it will likely be challenging for everyone.
- No single question will make or break your score. Keep moving; the questions will be there to return to if you have time later.
- If you lose focus, don't keep rereading the same question; move to a different question and start fresh. Upon return to a question, it may seem more manageable.
- If you panic, stop, put your pencil down, and take a few slow deep breaths. You're prepared for the test, and if today's not your day, you can always take the test again.

PrepTest 54, Section II

Time—35 minutes

26 Questions

...his section are based on the reasoning contained in brief statements or passages. For some ...choices could conceivably answer the question. However, you are to choose the <u>best</u> answer; that ...urately and completely answers the question. You should not make assumptions that are by commonsense standards implausible, superfluous, or incompatible with the passage. After you have chosen the best answer, blacken the corresponding space on your answer sheet.

1. Executive: Our company is proud of its long history of good relations with its employees. In fact, a recent survey of our retirees proves that we treat our employees fairly, since 95 percent of the respondents reported that they had always been treated fairly during the course of their careers with us.

 The executive's argument is flawed in that it

 (A) presents as its sole premise a claim that one would accept as true only if one already accepted the truth of the conclusion
 (B) relies on evidence that cannot be verified
 (C) equivocates on the word "fairly"
 (D) bases a generalization on a sample that may not be representative
 (E) presumes, without providing justification, that older methods of managing employees are superior to newer ones

2. Many of those who are most opposed to cruelty to animals in the laboratory, in the slaughterhouse, or on the farm are people who truly love animals and who keep pets. The vast majority of domestic pets, however, are dogs and cats, and both of these species are usually fed meat. Therefore, many of those who are most opposed to cruelty to animals do, in fact, contribute to such cruelty.

 Which one of the following is an assumption made by the argument?
 (A) Loving pets requires loving all forms of animal life.
 (B) Many of those who are opposed to keeping dogs and cats as pets are also opposed to cruelty to animals.
 (C) Some people who work in laboratories, in slaughterhouses, or on farms are opposed to cruelty to animals.
 (D) Many popular pets are not usually fed meat.
 (E) Feeding meat to pets contributes to cruelty to animals.

3. Statistics from the National Booksellers Association indicate that during the last five years most bookstores have started to experience declining revenues from the sale of fiction, despite national campaigns to encourage people to read more fiction. Therefore, these reading campaigns have been largely unsuccessful.

 Which one of the following statements, if true, most seriously weakens the argument?

 (A) Mail order book clubs have enjoyed substantial growth in fiction sales throughout the last five years.
 (B) During the last five years the most profitable items in bookstores have been newspapers and periodicals rather than novels.
 (C) Fierce competition has forced booksellers to make drastic markdowns on the cover price of best-selling biographies.
 (D) Due to the poor economic conditions that have prevailed during the last five years, most libraries report substantial increases in the number of patrons seeking books on changing careers and starting new businesses.
 (E) The National Booksellers Association statistics do not include profits from selling novels by mail to overseas customers.

4. People who consume a lot of honey tend to have fewer cavities than others have. Yet, honey is high in sugar, and sugar is one of the leading causes of tooth decay.

 Which one of the following, if true, most helps to resolve the apparent paradox described above?

 (A) People who eat a lot of honey tend to consume very little sugar from other sources.
 (B) Many people who consume a lot of honey consume much of it dissolved in drinks.
 (C) People's dental hygiene habits vary greatly.
 (D) Refined sugars have been linked to more health problems than have unrefined sugars.
 (E) Honey contains bacteria that inhibit the growth of the bacteria that cause tooth decay.

GO ON TO THE NEXT PAGE.

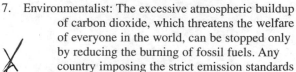

5. Byrne: One of our club's bylaws specifies that any officer who fails to appear on time for any one of the quarterly board meetings, or who misses two of our monthly general meetings, must be suspended. Thibodeaux, an officer, was recently suspended. But Thibodeaux has never missed a monthly general meeting. Therefore, Thibodeaux must have failed to appear on time for a quarterly board meeting.

The reasoning in Byrne's argument is flawed in that the argument

(A) fails to consider the possibility that Thibodeaux has arrived late for two or more monthly general meetings

(B) presumes, without providing justification, that if certain events each produce a particular result, then no other event is sufficient to produce that result

(C) takes for granted that an assumption required to establish the argument's conclusion is sufficient to establish that conclusion

(D) fails to specify at what point someone arriving at a club meeting is officially deemed late

(E) does not specify how long Thibodeaux has been an officer

6. Manufacturers of writing paper need to add mineral "filler" to paper pulp if the paper made from the pulp is to look white. Without such filler, paper products look grayish. To make writing paper that looks white from recycled paper requires more filler than is required to make such paper from other sources. Therefore, barring the more efficient use of fillers in paper manufacturing or the development of paper-whitening technologies that do not require mineral fillers, if writing paper made from recycled paper comes to replace other types of writing paper, paper manufacturers will have to use more filler than they now use.

Which one of the following is an assumption on which the argument depends?

(A) Certain kinds of paper cannot be manufactured from recycled paper.

(B) The fillers that are used to make paper white are harmful to the environment.

(C) Grayish writing paper will not be a universally acceptable alternative to white writing paper.

(D) Beyond a certain limit, increasing the amount of filler added to paper pulp does not increase the whiteness of the paper made from the pulp.

(E) The total amount of writing paper manufactured worldwide will increase significantly in the future.

7. Environmentalist: The excessive atmospheric buildup of carbon dioxide, which threatens the welfare of everyone in the world, can be stopped only by reducing the burning of fossil fuels. Any country imposing the strict emission standards on the industrial burning of such fuels that this reduction requires, however, would thereby reduce its gross national product. No nation will be willing to bear singlehandedly the costs of an action that will benefit everyone. It is obvious, then, that the catastrophic consequences of excessive atmospheric carbon dioxide are unavoidable unless _____.

Which one of the following most logically completes the argument?

(A) all nations become less concerned with pollution than with the economic burdens of preventing it

(B) multinational corporations agree to voluntary strict emission standards

(C) international agreements produce industrial emission standards

(D) distrust among nations is eliminated

(E) a world government is established

8. A clear advantage of digital technology over traditional printing is that digital documents, being patterns of electronic signals rather than patterns of ink on paper, do not generate waste in the course of their production and use. However, because patterns of electronic signals are necessarily ephemeral, a digital document can easily be destroyed and lost forever.

The statements above best illustrate which one of the following generalizations?

(A) A property of a technology may constitute an advantage in one set of circumstances and a disadvantage in others.

(B) What at first appears to be an advantage of a technology may create more problems than it solves.

(C) It is more important to be able to preserve information than it is for information to be easily accessible.

(D) Innovations in document storage technologies sometimes decrease, but never eliminate, the risk of destroying documents.

(E) Advances in technology can lead to increases in both convenience and environmental soundness.

GO ON TO THE NEXT PAGE.

9. Museum visitor: The national government has mandated a 5 percent increase in the minimum wage paid to all workers. This mandate will adversely affect the museum-going public. The museum's revenue does not currently exceed its expenses, and since the mandate will significantly increase the museum's operating expenses, the museum will be forced either to raise admission fees or to decrease services.

Which one of the following is an assumption required by the museum visitor's argument?

(A) Some of the museum's employees are not paid significantly more than the minimum wage.
(B) The museum's revenue from admission fees has remained constant over the past five years.
(C) Some of the museum's employees are paid more than the current minimum wage.
(D) The annual number of visitors to the museum has increased steadily.
(E) Not all visitors to the museum are required to pay an admission fee.

10. Helen: Reading a book is the intellectual equivalent of investing money: you're investing time, thereby foregoing other ways of spending that time, in the hope that what you learn will later afford you more opportunities than you'd get by spending the time doing something other than reading that book.

Randi: But that applies only to vocational books. Reading fiction is like watching a sitcom: it's just wasted time.

Which one of the following most accurately describes the technique Randi uses in responding to Helen's claims?

(A) questioning how the evidence Helen uses for a claim was gathered
(B) disputing the scope of Helen's analogy by presenting another analogy
(C) arguing that Helen's reasoning ultimately leads to an absurd conclusion
(D) drawing an analogy to an example presented by Helen
(E) denying the relevance of an example presented by Helen

11. Contrary to recent speculations, no hardware store will be opening in the shopping plaza. If somebody were going to open a store there, they would already have started publicizing it. But there has been no such publicity.

Which one of the following most accurately expresses the conclusion drawn in the argument?

(A) Some people have surmised that a hardware store will be opening in the shopping plaza.
(B) A hardware store will not be opening in the shopping plaza.
(C) If somebody were going to open a hardware store in the shopping plaza, that person would already have started publicizing it.
(D) It would be unwise to open a hardware store in the shopping plaza.
(E) There has been no publicity concerning the opening of a hardware store in the shopping plaza.

12. Ethicist: Although science is frequently said to be morally neutral, it has a traditional value system of its own. For example, scientists sometimes foresee that a line of theoretical research they are pursuing will yield applications that could seriously harm people, animals, or the environment. Yet, according to science's traditional value system, such consequences do not have to be considered in deciding whether to pursue that research. Ordinary morality, in contrast, requires that we take the foreseeable consequences of our actions into account whenever we are deciding what to do.

The ethicist's statements, if true, most strongly support which one of the following?

(A) Scientists should not be held responsible for the consequences of their research.
(B) According to the dictates of ordinary morality, scientists doing research that ultimately turns out to yield harmful applications are acting immorally.
(C) Science is morally neutral because it assigns no value to the consequences of theoretical research.
(D) It is possible for scientists to both adhere to the traditional values of their field and violate a principle of ordinary morality.
(E) The uses and effects of scientifically acquired knowledge can never be adequately foreseen.

GO ON TO THE NEXT PAGE.

Part Five: Countdown to Test Day
Test Day

13. Consumers seek to purchase the highest quality at the lowest prices. Companies that do not offer products that attract consumers eventually go bankrupt. Therefore, companies that offer neither the best quality nor the lowest price will eventually go bankrupt.

    The conclusion above follows logically if which one of the following is assumed?

    (A) No company succeeds in producing a product that is both highest in quality and lowest in price.

    (B) Products that are neither highest in quality nor lowest in price do not attract consumers.

    (C) Any company that offers either the highest quality or the lowest price will avoid bankruptcy.

    (D) Some consumers will not continue to patronize a company purely out of brand loyalty.

    (E) No company is driven from the market for reasons other than failing to meet consumer demands.

14. The number of serious traffic accidents (accidents resulting in hospitalization or death) that occurred on Park Road from 1986 to 1990 was 35 percent lower than the number of serious accidents from 1981 to 1985. The speed limit on Park Road was lowered in 1986. Hence, the reduction of the speed limit led to the decrease in serious accidents.

    Which one of the following statements, if true, most weakens the argument?

    (A) The number of speeding tickets issued annually on Park Road remained roughly constant from 1981 to 1990.

    (B) Beginning in 1986, police patrolled Park Road much less frequently than in 1985 and previous years.

    (C) The annual number of vehicles using Park Road decreased significantly and steadily from 1981 to 1990.

    (D) The annual number of accidents on Park Road that did not result in hospitalization remained roughly constant from 1981 to 1990.

    (E) Until 1986 accidents were classified as "serious" only if they resulted in an extended hospital stay.

15. Humans are supposedly rational: in other words, they have a capacity for well-considered thinking and behavior. This is supposedly the difference that makes them superior to other animals. But humans knowingly pollute the world's precious air and water and, through bad farming practices, deplete the soil that feeds them. Thus, humans are not rational after all, so it is absurd to regard them as superior to other animals.

    The reasoning above is flawed in that it

    (A) relies crucially on an internally contradictory definition of rationality

    (B) takes for granted that humans are aware that their acts are irrational

    (C) neglects to show that the irrational acts perpetrated by humans are not also perpetrated by other animals

    (D) presumes, without offering justification, that humans are no worse than other animals

    (E) fails to recognize that humans may possess a capacity without displaying it in a given activity

16. "Good hunter" and "bad hunter" are standard terms in the study of cats. Good hunters can kill prey that weigh up to half their body weight. All good hunters have a high muscle-to-fat ratio. Most wild cats are good hunters, but some domestic cats are good hunters as well.

    If the statements above are true, which one of the following must also be true?

    (A) Some cats that have a high muscle-to-fat ratio are not good hunters.

    (B) A smaller number of domestic cats than wild cats have a high muscle-to-fat ratio.

    (C) All cats that are bad hunters have a low muscle-to-fat ratio.

    (D) Some cats that have a high muscle-to-fat ratio are domestic.

    (E) All cats that have a high muscle-to-fat ratio can kill prey that weigh up to half their body weight.

GO ON TO THE NEXT PAGE.

17. Ethicist: The penalties for drunk driving are far more severe when the drunk driver accidentally injures people than when no one is injured. Moral responsibility for an action depends solely on the intentions underlying the action and not on the action's results. Therefore, legal responsibility, depending as it does in at least some cases on factors other than the agent's intentions, is different than moral responsibility.

The claim that the penalties for drunk driving are far more severe when the drunk driver accidentally injures people than when no one is injured plays which one of the following roles in the ethicist's argument?

(A) It is a premise offered in support of the claim that legal responsibility for an action is based solely upon features of the action that are generally unintended by the agent.

(B) It is offered as an illustration of the claim that the criteria of legal responsibility for an action include but are not the same as those for moral responsibility.

(C) It is offered as an illustration of the claim that people may be held morally responsible for an action for which they are not legally responsible.

(D) It is a premise offered in support of the claim that legal responsibility depends in at least some cases on factors other than the agent's intentions.

(E) It is a premise offered in support of the claim that moral responsibility depends solely on the intentions underlying the action and not on the action's result.

18. Columnist: Taking a strong position on an issue makes one likely to misinterpret or ignore additional evidence that conflicts with one's stand. But in order to understand an issue fully, it is essential to consider such evidence impartially. Thus, it is best not to take a strong position on an issue unless one has already considered all important evidence conflicting with that position.

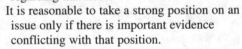

The columnist's reasoning most closely conforms to which one of the following principles?

(A) It is reasonable to take a strong position on an issue if one fully understands the issue and has considered the evidence regarding that issue impartially.

(B) To ensure that one has impartially considered the evidence regarding an issue on which one has taken a strong position, one should avoid misinterpreting or ignoring evidence regarding that issue.

(C) Anyone who does not understand an issue fully should avoid taking a strong position on it.

(D) One should try to understand an issue fully if doing so will help one to avoid misinterpreting or ignoring evidence regarding that issue.

(E) It is reasonable to take a strong position on an issue only if there is important evidence conflicting with that position.

GO ON TO THE NEXT PAGE.

19. The coach of the Eagles used a computer analysis to determine the best combinations of players for games. The analysis revealed that the team has lost only when Jennifer was not playing. Although no computer was needed to discover this information, this sort of information is valuable, and in this case it confirms that Jennifer's presence in the game will ensure that the Eagles will win.

The argument above is most vulnerable to criticism on the grounds that it

(A) infers from the fact that a certain factor is sufficient for a result that the absence of that factor is necessary for the opposite result

(B) presumes, without providing justification, that a player's contribution to a team's win or loss can be reliably quantified and analyzed by computer

(C) draws conclusions about applications of computer analyses to sports from the evidence of a single case

(D) presumes, without providing justification, that occurrences that have coincided in the past must continue to coincide

(E) draws a conclusion about the value of computer analyses from a case in which computer analysis provided no facts beyond what was already known

20. Of the various food containers made of recycled Styrofoam, egg cartons are among the easiest to make. Because egg shells keep the actual food to be consumed from touching the Styrofoam, used Styrofoam need not be as thoroughly cleaned when made into egg cartons as when made into other food containers.

Which one of the following is most strongly supported by the information above?

(A) No food containers other than egg cartons can safely be made of recycled Styrofoam that has not been thoroughly cleaned.

(B) There are some foods that cannot be packaged in recycled Styrofoam no matter how the Styrofoam is recycled.

(C) The main reason Styrofoam must be thoroughly cleaned when recycled is to remove any residual food that has come into contact with the Styrofoam.

(D) Because they are among the easiest food containers to make from recycled Styrofoam, most egg cartons are made from recycled Styrofoam.

(E) Not every type of food container made of recycled Styrofoam is effectively prevented from coming into contact with the food it contains.

GO ON TO THE NEXT PAGE.

21. Most people who become migraine sufferers as adults were prone to bouts of depression as children. Hence it stands to reason that a child who is prone to bouts of depression is likely to suffer migraines during adulthood.

The flawed pattern of reasoning in the argument above is most parallel to that in which one of the following?

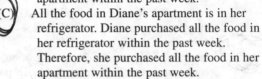

(A) Most good-tempered dogs were vaccinated against rabies as puppies. Therefore, a puppy that is vaccinated against rabies is likely to become a good-tempered dog.

(B) Most vicious dogs were ill-treated when young. Hence it can be concluded that a pet owner whose dog is vicious is likely to have treated the dog badly when it was young.

(C) Most well-behaved dogs have undergone obedience training. Thus, if a dog has not undergone obedience training, it will not be well behaved.

(D) Most of the pets taken to veterinarians are dogs. Therefore, it stands to reason that dogs are more prone to illness or accident than are other pets.

(E) Most puppies are taken from their mothers at the age of eight weeks. Thus, a puppy that is older than eight weeks is likely to have been taken from its mother.

22. Student: The publications of Professor Vallejo on the origins of glassblowing have reopened the debate among historians over whether glassblowing originated in Egypt or elsewhere. If Professor Vallejo is correct, there is insufficient evidence for claiming, as most historians have done for many years, that glassblowing began in Egypt. So, despite the fact that the traditional view is still maintained by the majority of historians, if Professor Vallejo is correct, we must conclude that glassblowing originated elsewhere.

Which one of the following is an error in the student's reasoning?

(A) It draws a conclusion that conflicts with the majority opinion of experts.

(B) It presupposes the truth of Professor Vallejo's claims.

(C) It fails to provide criteria for determining adequate historical evidence.

(D) It mistakes the majority view for the traditional view.

(E) It confuses inadequate evidence for truth with evidence for falsity.

23. At Southgate Mall, mattresses are sold only at Mattress Madness. Every mattress at Mattress Madness is on sale at a 20 percent discount. So every mattress for sale at Southgate Mall is on sale at a 20 percent discount.

Which one of the following arguments is most similar in its reasoning to the argument above?

(A) The only food in Diane's apartment is in her refrigerator. All the food she purchased within the past week is in her refrigerator. Therefore, she purchased all the food in her apartment within the past week.

(B) Diane's refrigerator, and all the food in it, is in her apartment. Diane purchased all the food in her refrigerator within the past week. Therefore, she purchased all the food in her apartment within the past week.

(C) All the food in Diane's apartment is in her refrigerator. Diane purchased all the food in her refrigerator within the past week. Therefore, she purchased all the food in her apartment within the past week.

(D) The only food in Diane's apartment is in her refrigerator. Diane purchased all the food in her refrigerator within the past week. Therefore, all the food she purchased within the past week is in her apartment.

(E) The only food that Diane has purchased within the past week is in her refrigerator. All the food that she has purchased within the past week is in her apartment. Therefore, all the food in her apartment is in her refrigerator.

GO ON TO THE NEXT PAGE.

24. There are 1.3 billion cows worldwide, and this population is growing to keep pace with the demand for meat and milk. These cows produce trillions of liters of methane gas yearly, and this methane contributes to global warming. The majority of the world's cows are given relatively low-quality diets even though cows produce less methane when they receive better-quality diets. Therefore, methane production from cows could be kept in check if cows were given better-quality diets.

Which one of the following, if true, adds the most support for the conclusion of the argument?

(A) Cows given good-quality diets produce much more meat and milk than they would produce otherwise.

(B) Carbon and hydrogen, the elements that make up methane, are found in abundance in the components of all types of cow feed.

(C) Most farmers would be willing to give their cows high-quality feed if the cost of that feed were lower.

(D) Worldwide, more methane is produced by cows raised for meat production than by those raised for milk production.

(E) Per liter, methane contributes more to global warming than does carbon dioxide, a gas that is thought to be the most significant contributor to global warming.

25. To face danger solely because doing so affords one a certain pleasure does not constitute courage. Real courage is manifested only when a person, in acting to attain a goal, perseveres in the face of fear prompted by one or more dangers involved.

Which one of the following statements can be properly inferred from the statements above?

(A) A person who must face danger in order to avoid future pain cannot properly be called courageous for doing so.

(B) A person who experiences fear of some aspects of a dangerous situation cannot be said to act courageously in that situation.

(C) A person who happens to derive pleasure from some dangerous activities is not a courageous person.

(D) A person who faces danger in order to benefit others is acting courageously only if the person is afraid of the danger.

(E) A person who has no fear of the situations that everyone else would fear cannot be said to be courageous in any situation.

26. The government will purchase and install new severe weather sirens for this area next year if replacement parts for the old sirens are difficult to obtain. The newspaper claims that public safety in the event of severe weather would be enhanced if new sirens were to be installed. The local company from which replacement parts were purchased last year has since gone out of business. So, if the newspaper is correct, the public will be safer during severe weather in the future.

The argument's conclusion follows logically from its premises if which one of the following is assumed?

(A) If public safety in the event of severe weather is enhanced next year, it will be because new sirens have been purchased.

(B) The newspaper was correct in claiming that public safety in the event of severe weather would be enhanced if new sirens were purchased.

(C) The local company from which replacement parts for the old sirens were purchased last year was the only company in the area that sold them.

(D) Replacement parts for the old sirens will be difficult to obtain if the government cannot obtain them from the company it purchased them from last year.

(E) Because the local company from which replacement parts had been purchased went out of business, the only available parts are of such inferior quality that use of them would make the sirens less reliable.

S T O P

IF YOU FINISH BEFORE TIME IS CALLED, YOU MAY CHECK YOUR WORK ON THIS SECTION ONLY.
DO NOT WORK ON ANY OTHER SECTION IN THE TEST.

ANSWER KEY

1. D
2. E
3. A
4. E
5. B
6. C
7. C
8. A
9. A
10. B
11. B
12. D
13. B
14. C
15. E
16. D
17. D
18. C
19. D
20. E
21. A
22. E
23. C
24. A
25. D
26. D

Complete explanations for this section can be found in your online resources.

REFLECTION

Argument-Based Questions

· How do you now look at arguments differently?

· When you see an argument, can you zero in on the conclusion directly?

· Is it easier to spot what the author considers to be the direct and relevant evidence for the conclusion?

· Are you able to spot the actual points of disagreement between two speakers?

· Can you separate the author's argumentative strategy from the content of the argument? Do you think you could spot arguments with similar argumentative strategies even if they are on different subjects?

Assumption Family Questions

· When you see an argument, can you determine the author's assumption?

· Are you able to determine the type of assumption the author is making?

· Once you have determined the author's assumption, can you establish the types of facts that would make his reasoning more or less likely to be valid?

· Can you identify and describe the flaws in an author's argument more efficiently and effectively?

Non-Argument Questions

· Are you able to recognize Inference questions and Principle questions calling for an inference?

· What patterns in Inference question stimuli should you be able to recognize?

· Can you remember and use the five tools that help to untangle Inference stimuli?

· Why are Extreme, 180, and Outside the Scope wrong answers so often associated with Inference questions? Can you recognize these wrong answer types when you see them?

· What do Paradox question stimuli always contain?

· Why are Keywords so helpful in untangling Paradox stimuli?

· How can you most effectively predict the correct answer to a Paradox question?

PrepTest 54, Section I, Passages 1 and 2

Time—16 minutes

12 Questions

...ons in this section is based on a single passage or a pair of passages. The questions are to be answered ... or <u>implied</u> in the passage or pair of passages. For some of the questions, more than one of the choices could ... e question. However, you are to choose the <u>best</u> answer; that is, the response that most accurately and completely answers the question, and blacken the corresponding space on your answer sheet.

This passage was adapted from an article published in 1996.

The Internet is a system of computer networks that allows individuals and organizations to communicate freely with other Internet users throughout the world. As a result, an astonishing
(5) variety of information is able to flow unimpeded across national and other political borders, presenting serious difficulties for traditional approaches to legislation and law enforcement, to which such borders are crucial.
(10) Control over physical space and the objects located in it is a defining attribute of sovereignty. Lawmaking presupposes some mechanism for enforcement, i.e., the ability to control violations. But jurisdictions cannot control the information and
(15) transactions flowing across their borders via the Internet. For example, a government might seek to intercept transmissions that propagate the kinds of consumer fraud that it regulates within its jurisdiction. But the volume of electronic communications
(20) crossing its territorial boundaries is too great to allow for effective control over individual transmissions. In order to deny its citizens access to specific materials, a government would thus have to prevent them from using the Internet altogether. Such a draconian
(25) measure would almost certainly be extremely unpopular, since most affected citizens would probably feel that the benefits of using the Internet decidedly outweigh the risks.
One legal domain that is especially sensitive to
(30) geographical considerations is that governing trademarks. There is no global registration of trademarks; international protection requires registration in each country. Moreover, within a country, the same name can sometimes be used
(35) proprietarily by businesses of different kinds in the same locality, or by businesses of the same kind in different localities, on the grounds that use of the trademark by one such business does not affect the others. But with the advent of the Internet, a business
(40) name can be displayed in such a way as to be accessible from any computer connected to the Internet anywhere in the world. Should such a display advertising a restaurant in Norway be deemed to infringe a trademark in Brazil just because it can be
(45) accessed freely from Brazil? It is not clear that any particular country's trademark authorities possess, or should possess, jurisdiction over such displays. Otherwise, any use of a trademark on the Internet

could be subject to the jurisdiction of every country
(50) simultaneously.
The Internet also gives rise to situations in which regulation is needed but cannot be provided within the existing framework. For example, electronic communications, which may pass through many
(55) different territorial jurisdictions, pose perplexing new questions about the nature and adequacy of privacy protections. Should French officials have lawful access to messages traveling via the Internet from Canada to Japan? This is just one among many
(60) questions that collectively challenge the notion that the Internet can be effectively controlled by the existing system of territorial jurisdictions.

1. Which one of the following most accurately expresses the main point of the passage?

(A) The high-volume, global nature of activity on the Internet undermines the feasibility of controlling it through legal frameworks that presuppose geographic boundaries.

(B) The system of Internet communications simultaneously promotes and weakens the power of national governments to control their citizens' speech and financial transactions.

(C) People value the benefits of their participation on the Internet so highly that they would strongly oppose any government efforts to regulate their Internet activity.

(D) Internet communications are responsible for a substantial increase in the volume and severity of global crime.

(E) Current Internet usage and its future expansion pose a clear threat to the internal political stability of many nations.

GO ON TO THE NEXT PAGE.

2. The author mentions French officials in connection with messages traveling between Canada and Japan (lines 57–59) primarily to

   (A) emphasize that the Internet allows data to be made available to users worldwide
   (B) illustrate the range of languages that might be used on the Internet
   (C) provide an example of a regulatory problem arising when an electronic communication intended for a particular destination passes through intermediate jurisdictions
   (D) show why any use of a trademark on the Internet could be subject to the jurisdiction of every country simultaneously
   (E) highlight the kind of international cooperation that made the Internet possible

3. According to the passage, which one of the following is an essential property of political sovereignty?

   (A) control over business enterprises operating across territorial boundaries
   (B) authority over communicative exchanges occurring within a specified jurisdiction
   (C) power to regulate trademarks throughout a circumscribed geographic region
   (D) control over the entities included within a designated physical space
   (E) authority over all commercial transactions involving any of its citizens

4. Which one of the following words employed by the author in the second paragraph is most indicative of the author's attitude toward any hypothetical measure a government might enact to deny its citizens access to the Internet?

   (A) benefits
   (B) decidedly
   (C) unpopular
   (D) draconian
   (E) risks

5. What is the main purpose of the fourth paragraph?

   (A) to call into question the relevance of the argument provided in the second paragraph
   (B) to provide a practical illustration that questions the general claim made in the first paragraph
   (C) to summarize the arguments provided in the second and third paragraphs
   (D) to continue the argument that begins in the third paragraph
   (E) to provide an additional argument in support of the general claim made in the first paragraph

GO ON TO THE NEXT PAGE.

describing muds

Passage A

Drilling fluids, including the various mixtures known as drilling muds, play essential roles in oil-well drilling. As they are circulated down through the drill
(5) pipe and back up the well itself, they lubricate the drill bit, bearings, and drill pipe; clean and cool the drill bit as it cuts into the rock; lift rock chips (cuttings) to the surface; provide information about what is happening downhole, allowing the drillers to monitor the behavior, flow rate, pressure, and
(10) composition of the drilling fluid; and maintain well pressure to control cave-ins.

drill fluids essential

why

Drilling muds are made of bentonite and other clays and polymers, mixed with a fluid to the desired viscosity. By far the largest ingredient of drilling
(15) muds, by weight, is barite, a very heavy mineral of density 4.3 to 4.6. It is also used as an inert filler in some foods and is more familiar in its medical use as the "barium meal" administered before X-raying the digestive tract.

made of

medical

(20) Over the years individual drilling companies and their expert drillers have devised proprietary formulations, or mud "recipes," to deal with specific types of drilling jobs. One problem in studying the effects of drilling waste discharges is that the drilling
(25) fluids are made from a range of over 1,000, sometimes toxic, ingredients—many of them known, confusingly, by different trade names, generic descriptions, chemical formulae, and regional or industry slang words, and many of them kept secret by companies or individual
(30) formulators.

recipes for diff jobs

issue

Passage B

describing environment

Drilling mud, cuttings, and associated chemicals are normally released only during the drilling phase of a well's existence. These discharges are the main environmental concern in offshore oil production, and
(35) their use is tightly regulated. The discharges are closely monitored by the offshore operator, and releases are controlled as a condition of the operating permit.

discharges / environ. concern

One type of mud—water-based mud (WBM)—is a mixture of water, bentonite clay, and chemical
(40) additives, and is used to drill shallow parts of wells. It is not particularly toxic to marine organisms and disperses readily. Under current regulations, it can be dumped directly overboard. Companies typically recycle WBMs until their properties are no longer
(45) suitable and then, over a period of hours, dump the entire batch into the sea.

type of mud

can be dumped

For drilling deeper wells, oil-based mud (OBM) is normally used. The typical difference from WBM is the high content of mineral oil (typically 30 percent).
(50) OBMs also contain greater concentrations of barite, a powdered heavy mineral, and a number of additives. OBMs have a greater potential for negative environmental impact, partly because they do not

another type / difference of 2

disperse as readily. Barite may impact some
(55) organisms, particularly scallops, and the mineral oil may have toxic effects. Currently only the residues of OBMs adhering to cuttings that remain after the cuttings are sieved from the drilling fluids may be discharged overboard, and then only mixtures up to a
(60) specified maximum oil content.

toxic

6. A primary purpose of each of the passages is to

   (A) provide causal explanations for a type of environmental pollution
   (B) describe the general composition and properties of drilling muds
   (C) point out possible environmental impacts associated with oil drilling
   (D) explain why oil-well drilling requires the use of drilling muds
   (E) identify difficulties inherent in the regulation of oil-well drilling operations

7. Which one of the following is a characteristic of barite that is mentioned in both of the passages?

   (A) It does not disperse readily in seawater.
   (B) It is not found in drilling muds containing bentonite.
   (C) Its use in drilling muds is tightly regulated.
   (D) It is the most commonly used ingredient in drilling muds.
   (E) It is a heavy mineral.

8. Each of the following is supported by one or both of the passages EXCEPT:

   (A) Clay is an important constituent of many, if not all, drilling muds.
   (B) At least one type of drilling mud is not significantly toxic to marine life.
   (C) There has been some study of the environmental effects of drilling-mud discharges.
   (D) Government regulations allow drilling muds to contain 30 percent mineral oil.
   (E) During the drilling of an oil well, drilling mud is continuously discharged into the sea.

GO ON TO THE NEXT PAGE

9. Which one of the following can be most reasonably inferred from the two passages taken together, but not from either one individually?

    (A) Barite is the largest ingredient of drilling muds, by weight, and also the most environmentally damaging.
    (B) Although barite can be harmful to marine organisms, it can be consumed safely by humans.
    (C) Offshore drilling is more damaging to the environment than is land-based drilling.
    (D) The use of drilling muds needs to be more tightly controlled by government.
    (E) If offshore drilling did not generate cuttings, it would be less harmful to the environment.

10. Each of the following is supported by one or both of the passages EXCEPT:

    (A) Drillers monitor the suitability of the mud they are using.
    (B) The government requires drilling companies to disclose all ingredients used in their drilling muds.
    (C) In certain quantities, barite is not toxic to humans.
    (D) Oil reserves can be found within or beneath layers of rock.
    (E) Drilling deep oil wells requires the use of different mud recipes than does drilling shallow oil wells.

11. Based on information in the passages, which one of the following, if true, provides the strongest support for a prediction that the proportion of oil-well drilling using OBMs will increase in the future?

    (A) The cost of certain ingredients in WBMs is expected to increase steadily over the next several decades.
    (B) The deeper an offshore oil well, the greater the concentration of barite that must be used in the drilling mud.
    (C) Oil reserves at shallow depths have mostly been tapped, leaving primarily much deeper reserves for future drilling.
    (D) It is unlikely that oil drillers will develop more efficient ways of removing OBM residues from cuttings that remain after being sieved from drilling fluids.
    (E) Barite is a common mineral, the availability of which is virtually limitless.

12. According to passage B, one reason OBMs are potentially more environmentally damaging than WBMs is that OBMs

    (A) are slower to disperse
    (B) contain greater concentrations of bentonite
    (C) contain a greater number of additives
    (D) are used for drilling deeper wells
    (E) cannot be recycled

S T O P

IF YOU FINISH BEFORE TIME IS CALLED, YOU MAY CHECK YOUR WORK ON THIS SECTION ONLY.
DO NOT WORK ON ANY OTHER SECTION IN THE TEST.

ANSWER KEY

Passage 1—Internet Regulation

1. A
2. C
3. D
4. D
5. E

Passage 2—Drilling Muds

6. B
7. E
8. E
9. B
10. B
11. C
12. A

Complete explanations for these passages can be found in your online resources.

Acknowledgment is made to the following source from which material has been adapted for use in this book:

David R. Johnson and David Post, "Law and Borders—The Rise of Law in Cyberspace." ©1996 by the Board of Trustees of the Leland Stanford Jr. University.

REFLECTION

Strategic Reading and the Reading Comprehension Method

· How is LSAT Reading Comprehension reading different than reading for school or pleasure? Why is it referred to as strategic reading?

· What does it mean to be an active reader? How do you interrogate the author as you read?

· What role do Keywords play in strategic reading?

· Why is it helpful to jot down brief paraphrases of crucial text?

· Why do you summarize the passage's Topic and Scope and the author's Purpose and Main Idea?

· What are the distinguishing characteristics of the Reading Comprehension question types?

· How do you spot and use research clues in the question stems?

· How can you most appropriately predict the answers to Global and open-ended Inference questions?

· What are the common wrong answer types associated with Reading Comprehension questions?

PrepTest 54, Section III, Games 1 and 3

Time—16 minutes

10 Questions

Directions: Each group of questions in this section is based on a set of conditions. In answering some of the questions, it may be useful to draw a rough diagram. Choose the response that most accurately and completely answers each question and blacken the corresponding space on your answer sheet.

Questions 1–5

A dance is being choreographed for six dancers: three men— Felipe, Grant, and Hassan—and three women— Jaclyn, Keiko, and Lorena. At no time during the dance will anyone other than the dancers be on stage. Who is on stage and who is off stage at any particular time in the dance is determined by the following constraints:

If Jaclyn is on stage, Lorena is off stage.
If Lorena is off stage, Jaclyn is on stage.
If Felipe is off stage, Jaclyn is also off stage.
If any of the women are on stage, Grant is also on stage.

1. Which one of the following is a list of all of the dancers who could be on stage at a particular time?

(A) Grant
(B) Keiko, Lorena
(C) Grant, Hassan, Lorena
(D) Grant, Hassan, Jaclyn
(E) Felipe, Grant, Jaclyn, Lorena

GO ON TO THE NEXT PAGE.

$$\underset{F\ G\ H}{\overset{M}{\rule{3em}{0.4pt}}} \qquad \underset{J K L}{\overset{W}{\rule{2em}{0.4pt}}}$$

if J → ~L
~L → J
if ~F → ~J
if J K or L → G

2. Which one of the following CANNOT be true at any time during the dance?

- (A) Felipe and Grant are the only men on stage.
- (B) Grant and Hassan are the only men on stage.
- (C) Jaclyn is the only woman on stage.
- (D) Keiko is the only woman on stage.
- (E) Jaclyn and Keiko are the only women on stage.

3. Which one of the following is a complete and accurate list of the dancers any one of whom could be off stage when Jaclyn is on stage?

- (A) Lorena
- (B) Felipe, Lorena
- (C) Hassan, Lorena
- (D) Hassan, Keiko
- (E) Hassan, Keiko, Lorena

4. If there are more women than men on stage, then exactly how many dancers must be on stage?

- (A) five
- (B) four
- (C) three
- (D) two
- (E) one

5. What is the minimum number of dancers that must be on stage at any given time?

- (A) zero
- (B) one
- (C) two
- (D) three
- (E) four

GO ON TO THE NEXT PAGE.

Questions 13–17

A cake has exactly six layers—lemon, marzipan, orange, raspberry, strawberry, and vanilla. There is exactly one bottom layer (the first layer), and each succeeding layer (from second through sixth) completely covers the layer beneath it. The following conditions must apply:

The raspberry layer is neither immediately above nor immediately below the strawberry layer.

The marzipan layer is immediately above the lemon layer.

The orange layer is above the marzipan layer but below the strawberry layer.

13. Which one of the following could be an accurate list of the layers of the cake, from bottom to top?

(A) lemon, marzipan, orange, strawberry, vanilla, raspberry

(B) lemon, marzipan, orange, strawberry, raspberry, vanilla

(C) marzipan, lemon, raspberry, vanilla, orange, strawberry

(D) raspberry, lemon, marzipan, vanilla, strawberry, orange

(E) raspberry, orange, lemon, marzipan, strawberry, vanilla

GO ON TO THE NEXT PAGE.

14. If the strawberry layer is not immediately above the orange layer, then which one of the following could be true?

(A) The raspberry layer is immediately above the vanilla layer.

(B) The raspberry layer is immediately above the orange layer.

(C) The raspberry layer is immediately below the marzipan layer.

(D) The raspberry layer is the second layer.

(E) The raspberry layer is the top layer.

15. If the strawberry layer is not the top layer, then which one of the following is a complete and accurate list of the layers that could be the vanilla layer?

(A) the first, the second, the third, the fourth, the fifth, the sixth

(B) the second, the third, the fourth, the fifth, the sixth

(C) the third, the fourth, the fifth, the sixth

(D) the fourth, the fifth, the sixth

(E) the fifth, the sixth

16. If the lemon layer is third, then which one of the following could be true?

(A) The vanilla layer is fifth.

(B) The vanilla layer is immediately above the raspberry layer.

(C) The orange layer is not immediately above the marzipan layer.

(D) The raspberry layer is above the marzipan layer.

(E) The strawberry layer is not the top layer.

17. Which one of the following could be an accurate list of the two lowest layers of the cake, listed in order from the bottom up?

(A) lemon, raspberry

(B) vanilla, raspberry

(C) marzipan, raspberry

(D) raspberry, marzipan

(E) raspberry, strawberry

S T O P

IF YOU FINISH BEFORE TIME IS CALLED, YOU MAY CHECK YOUR WORK ON THIS SECTION ONLY.
DO NOT WORK ON ANY OTHER SECTION IN THE TEST.

ANSWER KEY

Game 1—Dancers On Stage

1. C
2. D
3. E
4. C
5. C

Game 3—Cake Layers

13. A
14. B
15. E
16. B
17. B

Complete explanations for these games can be found in your online resources.

REFLECTION

Logic Games Method

· What is the purpose of Step 1, and why does an expert always take that step?
· What is the purpose of Step 2, and why does an expert always take that step?
· What is the purpose of Step 3, and why does an expert always take that step?
· What is the purpose of Step 4, and why does an expert always take that step?
· What is the purpose of Step 5, and why does an expert always take that step?

Logic Game Types

· What characteristics help you recognize a Sequencing game?
· How can you tell the difference between a Strict Sequencing game and a Loose Sequencing game?
· What characteristics help you recognize a Selection game?
· What characteristics help you recognize a Matching game?
· What characteristics help you recognize a Distribution game?
· What is the fundamental difference between a Matching game and a Distribution game?
· What characteristics help you recognize a Hybrid game?
· What day to day activities can you think of that mirror Sequencing game actions?
· What day to day activities can you think of that mirror Selection game actions?
· What day to day activities can you think of that mirror Matching game actions?
· What day to day activities can you think of that mirror Distribution game actions?
· What day to day activities can you think of that mirror Hybrid game actions?

Recent Trends

A review of the most recently administered LSATs gives a good indication of what you are likely to see on Test Day.

Logical Reasoning Question Frequency by # of Questions/Test

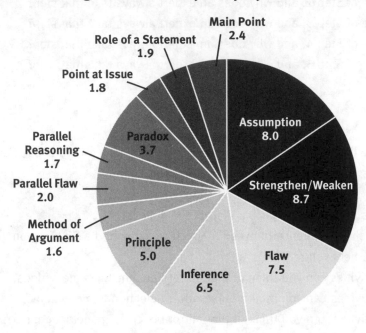

Released LSATs 2012–2016

Reading Comprehension Passage Structure Frequency by Approximate Percentage

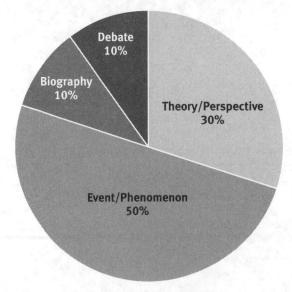

Released LSATs 2012–2016

Reading Comprehension Question Frequency by # of Questions/Test

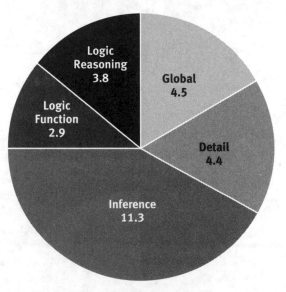

Released LSATs 2012–2016

Part Five: Countdown to Test Day
Test Day

K

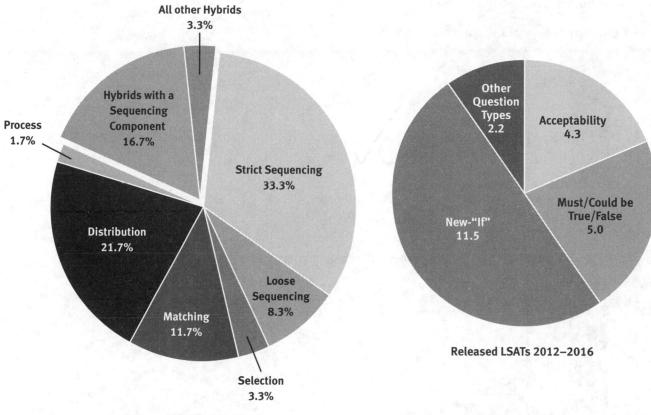

Logic Games Game Type Frequency by Percentage

All other Hybrids
3.3%

Hybrids with a Sequencing Component
16.7%

Process
1.7%

Strict Sequencing
33.3%

Distribution
21.7%

Loose Sequencing
8.3%

Matching
11.7%

Selection
3.3%

Released LSATs 2012–2016

Logic Games Question Type Frequency by # of Questions/Test

Other Question Types
2.2

Acceptability
4.3

Must/Could be True/False
5.0

New-"IF"
11.5

Released LSATs 2012–2016

Most Challenging Section (as reported by students immediately after the test)

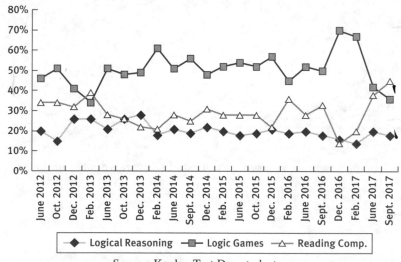

Legend: ◆ Logical Reasoning ■ Logic Games △ Reading Comp.

Source: Kaplan Test Day student surveys

Kaplan Test Day Survey Results

After each test administration, Kaplan surveys our students on various aspects of the Test Day experience. Here are some results from a recent administration:

Did the desk surface give you enough room to work?

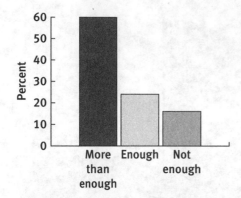

On a scale of 1 to 5, with 5 being the best, how comfortable and quiet was your testing environment?

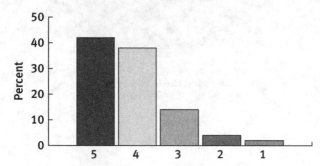

On a scale of 1 to 5, with 5 being the best, how would you rate the effectiveness of proctoring?

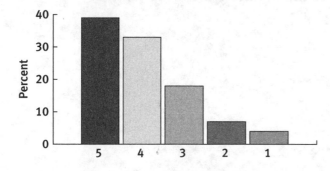

On a scale of 1 to 5, with 5 being the best, how would you rate the overall quality of the experience at your test site?

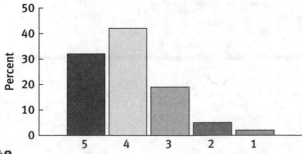

> *"I am so glad you recommended that we to drive to the site one week beforehand. I did it the Saturday prior to the test and figured out the difficult parking situation. I was able to get into the classrooms and make note of the possible types of desks I would be working on—a major plus as I had one of the smaller desk options! I felt more comfortable knowing the environment that I would be working in on that day."*

Takeaway: If you take away the anxiety of the unknowns, then you can just focus on the test.

> *"A girl taking the exam passed out during the first five minutes of the first section. She fell on her face and many people taking the test were very concerned because she was unconscious for a few minutes. The proctors called 911 and spoke on the phone during the test. The whole ordeal lasted about ten minutes but they never stopped timing."*

Takeaway: If there is a problem that can be corrected then and there, do not hesitate to speak up. If something significant occurs, like the situation above, that affects your score, contact the LSAC, and calmly and factually explain the situation. They won't change your score, but they may provide some recourse.

> *"Absolutely loved my test site. The proctors and administration were so great, the rooms were quiet and clean."*

Takeaway: Most LSAT administrations run without any problems. Do not let horror stories of bad proctoring experiences cloud your expectations. Focus on what you can control.

> *"A lot of people took the test today, but I felt confident that I was the most prepared because some people asked really dumb questions like if the writing sample was optional."*

Takeaway: Your experience at Kaplan has prepared you well—all that's left is for you to perform your best!

AFTER THE TEST

If it turns out that Test Day doesn't go *exactly* as planned, that's all right—it rarely, if ever, does, and the LSAT does not require perfection. All of your fellow test takers will likely experience some level of self-doubt as well; that's fairly typical. It is, however, important to know whether a Test Day experience included one of the rare anomalies that actually warrants canceling your score.

Should You Cancel Your Score?

LSAT STRATEGY

Benefits to not canceling your score:

- No matter how you "feel," you don't know for sure how you did. You may have done much better than you think.
- You will have access to the answers you selected during Test Day, which will be an excellent review tool.
- Law schools by and large are not averaging scores, so a single lower score won't be all that detrimental.
- A cancellation still counts against your limit of taking the test three times in two years, so if you end up needing to retake the exam, there's less pressure next time out because at least you have a baseline score on record.

LSAT STRATEGY

Situations that would NOT warrant a score cancellation:

- Minor distractions in the testing facility (pencil tapping, coughing, temperature, etc.)
- Unable to finish or forgot to bubble the last few questions in a section or two
- Small-scale time issues related to the five-minute warning, where clocks were positioned, whether or not the times were written on the board (they aren't required to be, and often aren't)

Situations that *would* warrant a score cancellation:

- Needing to leave the room for an extended time during the test
- A significant gridding mistake affecting a large portion of an entire section
- Large-scale time issues caused by either the proctor or poor personal time management; for example, a shortened section or a complete breakdown in timing, causing a large number of unanswered questions in a section

---

Post-LSAT Festivities

After weeks or months of preparation it's finally over. What do you do now?

- Congratulate yourself!
- Celebrate responsibly!
- Reach out to thank those who made a difference to you during the process.
- After some rest, get started writing your personal statement, requesting letters of recommendation, and gathering your transcripts.

LSAT Strategies, Methods, and Definitions

FORMAL LOGIC

Keywords

Sufficient:
If
All
Any
Every
Each
When
Whenever
Wherever
The only

Necessity:
Then
Requires
Guarantees
Must
Necessary
Bound to lead to
Are destined to
Only (if)
Results in
Produces
Sure to
Always
Unless
Depends on
Without

Mutually Exclusive:
No
Incapable
Impossible
Cannot
None
Neither . . . nor
Never

Translating Conditional Statements into If-Then Format

Formal Logic Statement	Analysis		
If A, then B	If A	→	B
All C are D	If C	→	D
Every E is F	If E	→	F
If G, then not H	If G	→	~H
No I are J	If I	→	~J
Only K are L	If L	→	K
M only if N	If M	→	N
The only O are P	If O	→	P
No Q unless R	If Q	→	R
S unless T	If ~S	→	T
No U without V	If U	→	V
Without W, no X	If X	→	W
Y if, but only if, Z	If Y	→	Z
	If Z	→	Y
AA if, and only if, BB	If AA	→	BB
	If BB	→	AA
If CC, then neither DD nor EE	If CC	→	~DD AND ~EE
FF if GG	If GG	→	FF
HH is always II	If HH	→	II

Contrapositives

FORMING THE CONTRAPOSITIVE

- Reverse the sufficient and necessary terms.
- Negate each term.
- Change *and* to *or* and change *or* to *and* (whenever applicable).

Formal Logic Statement			Contrapositive		
If A	→	B OR C	If ~B AND ~C	→	~A
If D	→	E AND F	If ~E OR ~F	→	~D
If G OR H	→	J	If ~J	→	~G AND ~H
If K AND L	→	M	If ~M	→	~K OR ~L
If N AND O	→	P AND R	If ~P OR ~R	→	~N OR ~O
If S OR T	→	U AND V	If ~U OR ~V	→	~S AND ~T
If W AND X	→	Y OR Z	If ~Y AND ~Z	→	~W OR ~X
If AA OR BB	→	CC OR DD	If ~CC AND ~DD	→	~AA AND ~BB

A Note about Cause-and-Effect Relationships

Cause and effect are important concepts in the law and affect the outcome of many legal cases. Thus, the reasoning underlying cause and effect is tested regularly on the LSAT. The reasoning errors of confusing correlation for causation, or of assuming that some result has only one cause when, in fact, there are multiple factors at work, are often found in the arguments of Logical Reasoning questions.

Some conditional Formal Logic statements reflect a cause-and-effect relationship, but not all. And not all cause-and-effect statements can be expressed in "If ... then" terms. It is important not to confuse the two. Here's a handy way to categorize the relationships between causal statements and conditional statements.

Statements in Which the Cause Is Sufficient, but Not Necessary, for the Result

In this type of statement, the result is guaranteed any and every time that the cause occurs. For example: *If you drop this television from the top of the building, then it will smash.*

But the television could get smashed in other ways, too, right? So while dropping it off of the building is sufficient to smash the TV, it is not necessary. If someone told you their TV got smashed, you wouldn't know for certain that it had been dropped from a great height.

Statements in Which the Cause Is Necessary, but Not Sufficient, for the Result

In this type of statement, the trigger could not happen without the result. You may know, for example, that certain types of ulcers are caused by exposure to the bacteria *Helicobacter pylori*. Thus, we could say: *If a person develops a duodenal ulcer, he has been infected by* H. pylori.

But not everyone who is exposed to the bacteria develops ulcers. Other factors are at work as well. The ulcer is sufficient evidence of exposure to the bacteria, but not the other way around.

Statements in Which the Cause Is Both Necessary and Sufficient for the Result

In this type of statement, the result occurs if, and only if, the cause is present. For example: *Water will freeze into ice if, and only if, it is kept below 32° Fahrenheit.*

Water will always freeze when it is below 32° Fahrenheit, and only under that condition.

Statements That Reflect Causation but Are Not Conditional Statements

Some statements reflect causality but are not strong enough or certain enough to be written in "If ... then" form. For example: *Texting while driving may cause you to get into an accident.*

The word *may* makes this statement too uncertain to translate into conditional Formal Logic terms. In a particular case, we may know that texting while driving was the direct cause of an accident, but we cannot say: *If a person texts while driving, then he will get into an accident.* Nor can we say: *If a person got into an accident, then he was texting while driving.* The best we could say here is: *Texting while driving increases your chances of getting into an accident.*

The LSAT Appendix continues on the next page. ▶ ▶ ▶

LOGIC GAMES

Logic Games Method

STEP 1: OVERVIEW—THE SEAL QUESTIONS

Situation—What is the real-world scenario being described? What is the deliverable information—an ordered list, a calendar, a chart showing what's matched up?

Entities—Who or what are the "moving parts," the people or things I'm distributing, selecting, sequencing, or matching?

Action—What is the specific action—distribution, selection, sequencing, matching, or a combination of those—that I'm performing on the entities?

Limitations—Does the game state parameters (e.g., select four of seven, sequence the entities one per day, or the like) that restrict how I'll set up and sketch the game?

STEP 2: SKETCH

- Create a sketch that depicts the game's action(s) and limitations.
- Aim for a sketch that is easy to read, quick to replicate, and able to account for what is certain and uncertain based on the game's rules.

STEP 3: RULES

- Whenever possible, add information directly to your Master Sketch.
- If you cannot build a rule directly into the Master Sketch, make a shorthand graphical representation of it.
- Write the rules in a way that matches the style and conventions of the Master Sketch.
- Consider both the positive and negative implications of a rule.
- Write similar rules consistently, the same way from game to game.
- When analyzing and drawing rules, always ask the following:
  - What does the rule restrict?
  - What does the rule leave undetermined?
  - Is the rule stated in affirmative or negative terms?
  - If stated affirmatively, can I learn something concrete from its negative implications (or vice versa)?
  - Can I place the rule directly into the sketch framework?
  - If not, how can I best draw the rule to account for what it does and does not restrict?

STEP 4: DEDUCTIONS

Blocks of Entities—two or more players who are always grouped together

Limited Options—rules or restrictions that limit the overall setup to one of two acceptable arrangements

Established Entities—a player locked into a specific space or group

Number Restrictions—rules or limitations that provide guidance about the number of entities assigned to a group or space

Duplications—entities that appear in two or more rules and allow the rules to be combined

STEP 5: QUESTIONS

- Be able to characterize both correct and incorrect answer choices.
- Know the different question types and how to approach each one.
- Don't hesitate to draw a new sketch in "If" questions.
- Use deductions and past work to eliminate wrong answers quickly.

Logic Game Question Types

- **Acceptability:** Use the rules to eliminate violators.
- **Partial Acceptability:** Use the rules to eliminate violators, but some rules may not apply. It may be helpful to deduce the other entities that would be in a full acceptable arrangement.
- **Must Be/Could Be:** Characterize the one right and four wrong choices. Use deductions and previous work to eliminate wrong answers. Be strategic about testing answers.
- **New-"If"s:** Take the "new rule" through Steps 3 and 4, or if the Master Sketch has Limited Options, check to see which option(s) apply.
- **Complete and Accurate List:** The sketches made for other questions in the game may help to narrow the possibilities. Test the remaining possibilities.
- **Completely Determine:** Pick the one answer that establishes every entity. Nailing down a duplicated entity or a Floater can be helpful.
- **Rule Substitution:** Identify what impact the removed rule had. Find another that has the same impact.
- **Rule Change/Suspension:** Repeat Steps 3 and 4 with the new information. Some deductions may have changed.
- **Maximum and Minimum:** Most often in Selection games. Use the Master Sketch, previous work, and number deductions from the Formal Logic rules to find the minimum/maximum known so far, then keep testing one more/less if necessary.
- **Earliest and Latest:** Most often in Sequencing games. Use the Master Sketch, previous work, and deductions to find the earliest/latest known so far, then keep testing one earlier/later if necessary.
- **Supply the If:** Use the Master Sketch to see the possibilities for the entity or slot in question and then use that analysis to determine the kind of additional restriction that would guarantee the desired result.
- **How Many:** Use deductions to count the relevant entities/slots.

Sample Logic Games Sketches

Strict Sequencing

A B C D E F

‾‾ ‾‾ ‾‾ ‾‾ ‾‾ ‾‾
1   2   3   4   5   6

Loose Sequencing

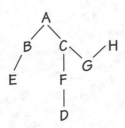

or

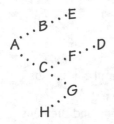

Distribution Games

All entities are used exactly one time.

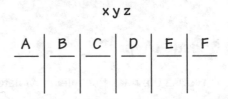

Selection Games

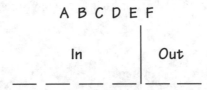

For Selection games defining a specific number of entities, some test takers prefer:

A B C D E F

In	Out
‾‾ ‾‾ ‾‾	‾‾ ‾‾

Matching Games

Entities might be used multiple times.

x y z

A	B	C	D	E	F

or

	A	B	C	D	E	F
x						
y						
z						

Sequencing/Matching Hybrid Games

‾‾ ‾‾ ‾‾ ‾‾ ‾‾ ‾‾ A B C D E F

‾‾ ‾‾ ‾‾ ‾‾ ‾‾ ‾‾ g/h
1   2   3   4   5   6

Typical Rules

Sequencing Rules

A is in a lower numbered position than B.

> A . . . B

A gets out at some time before B.

> A . . . B

A gets out at some time after B.

> B . . . A

A gets out at some time before B but after C.

> C . . . A . . . B

A gets out immediately after B.

> BA

A gets out immediately before B.

> AB

Exactly one person gets out after A but before B.

> A _ B

A is exactly two positions before B.

> A _ B

At least one person gets out after A but before B.

> A _ . . . B

Exactly one person gets out between A and B.

> A/B _ B/A

A is immediately next to B.

> AB or BA

M got out after either V or G but not both.

$$V \ldots M \ldots G \quad or \quad G \ldots M \ldots V$$

or

$$V/G \ldots M \ldots G/V$$

(Exactly one of V or G is before M; the other comes afterward.)

P is ranked after T or before S, but not both.

$$S \diagdown \atop P \diagup_T \quad or \quad P \diagup^S \diagdown_T$$

(Both S and T come before P or both S and T come after P; P can't be in the middle.)

A can come neither immediately before nor immediately after B.

~~AB BA~~

If A is fourth, B is seventh.

$$A_4 \rightarrow B_7$$

$$B_{\sim7} \rightarrow A_{\sim4}$$

If A is not seventh, A is fifth.

$$A_{\sim7} \rightarrow A_5$$

$$A_{\sim5} \rightarrow A_7$$

(Or . . . A is either fifth or seventh. Consider Limited Options if there are further deductions to be made.)

If A is before B, then C is before B. (in a sequence with no ties)

$$A \ldots B \rightarrow C \ldots B$$

$$B \ldots C \rightarrow B \ldots A$$

Selection Rules

If she selects K, she must select M.

$$K \rightarrow M$$

$$\sim M \rightarrow \sim K$$

A is not selected unless B is selected.

$$A \rightarrow B$$

$$\sim B \rightarrow \sim A$$

If George buys A, then he does not buy B.

$$A \rightarrow \sim B$$

$$B \rightarrow \sim A$$

(This rule says we can never have both A and B—so it is often faster/more intuitive to just write "Never AB".)

If George does not buy A, then he buys B.

$$\sim A \rightarrow B$$

$$\sim B \rightarrow A$$

(This rule says we must have A, or B, or both.)

If she selects G, she can select neither H nor Y.

$$G \rightarrow \sim H \text{ and } \sim Y$$

$$H \text{ or } Y \rightarrow \sim G$$

(You can split an "and" result into two pieces—e.g., $G \rightarrow \sim H$; $G \rightarrow \sim Y$)
(You can split an "or" trigger into two pieces—e.g., $H \rightarrow \sim G$; $Y \rightarrow \sim G$)

Either A or B must be selected, but A and B cannot both be selected.

$$A/B$$

(Replace A and B with A/B in the entity list—you'll select exactly one.)

Matching/Distribution Rules

A cannot be in the same group as B.

NEVER AB

(Note that if there are only two groups, this means one of A and B is in the first group and the other is in the second group. This is important to help account for the numbers in each group.)

A is in a group with exactly 2 members.

 A __

A and B are in the same group.

 AB

Abstract rules and considerations

J and K have at least one symptom in common. (What symptom could that be?)

L has a greater number of symptoms than K. (How many could L have? How many could K have?)

Exactly twice as many people are in group 1 as in group 2. (How many people can be in group 1? This will often lead to Limited Options.)

Exactly one entity is in every group. (Which entity could that be? Must it be? Could it not be?)

How does the Testmaker make a game harder?

- Removing the "one entity per position" limitation in Sequencing or other "natural" limitations

- Altering the definition of a week—Monday–Friday? Monday–Sunday? or other common unit

- Incorporating multiple hybrid actions

- Including tough rules—abstract, if/then, undefined group size (Distribution)

- Creating Sequencing games with some repeating elements (4 entities, 7 positions)

- Using scenarios in which not all entities must be used

- Incorporating challenging/time-consuming question types (Rule Substitution, Completely Determine, Partial Acceptability, Rule Change, Supply the If, etc.)

- Writing lengthy answer choices

- Including answer choices that contain conditional statements

Variations on Games

Sequencing

Double/Triple sequencing (either the same entities sequenced multiple times OR multiple different sequences, each with unique entities)

Sequencing over a multiple-week period, but each week has the same schedule (watch for the overlap between the end of one week and the start of the next)

Adding a characteristic to each entity—might sequence children, some of whom are boys and some of whom are girls, and have rules about boys and girls

Circular sequencing—positions might be numbered or unnumbered; could also be along the perimeter of a square

Matching

Matching entities to schedules—looks like a Sequencing game at first glance, but not every entity must be used and some will be repeated

Distribution

Distribute a group of entities that consists of smaller subgroups (e.g., distribute 9 people from 5 children and 4 adults)

The exact number of entities assigned to each group is unknown

Selection

Double selection—entities selected in the first group restrict who can be selected in the second group

Select from a group of entities that consists of smaller subgroups (e.g., select 4 committee members from 5 juniors and 4 seniors)

Hybrid

Sequence a group of entities, then match a second characteristic to each entity

Distribute a group of entities, then within each group create a sequence (Distribution then Sequencing)

Distribute a large group into two smaller groups, which don't account for all the entities (Selection then Distribution)

LOGICAL REASONING

Logical Reasoning Method

THE KAPLAN LOGICAL REASONING METHOD

Step 1: Identify the Question Type

Step 2: Untangle the Stimulus

Step 3: Predict the Correct Answer

Step 4: Evaluate the Answer Choices

Evidence and Conclusion

Keywords

Conclusion:		Evidence:
Therefore	Obviously	Because
Thus	Hence	Since
It is clear	As a result	For
It follows that	This proves that	From the fact that
That is why	Studies suggest	After all
So	This shows	It is clear from
Consequently	Clearly	

Conclusion Types

CONCLUSION TYPES

In an LSAT argument, the conclusion almost always matches one or more of these six types:

- Value Judgment (an evaluative statement; e.g., Action X is unethical or Y's recital was poorly sung)

- If/Then (a conditional prediction, recommendation, or assertion; e.g., If X is true, then so is Y or If you are an M, you should do N)

- Prediction (X *will* or *will not* happen in the future)

- Comparison (X is taller/shorter/more common/less common/etc. *than* Y)

- Assertion of Fact (X is true or X is false)

- Recommendation (we *should* or *should not* do X)

Common Argument Structures

Remember that while the specifics change from question to question, there are certain argument structures that appear repeatedly on the LSAT. When you recognize one of these, you'll have a ready-made prediction as to the assumption, strengtheners, and weakeners. You'll also have insight into the author's flaw: the failure to consider the possible ways of weakening the argument.

C: Conclusion
E: Evidence
A: Assumption
S: Strengthener
W: Weakener

Mismatched Concepts

In arguments with Mismatched Concepts, the conclusion typically contains a new concept or term that was not mentioned in the evidence. When the concept only appears in the conclusion, without the author providing evidence about it, the author must be making an assumption about that term. The assumption will link that unique conclusion term (that doesn't appear in the evidence) to a unique evidence term (that doesn't appear in the conclusion). Just recognizing the Mismatched Concepts can often be enough to get you to the right answer. However, there are four standard relationships that can be applied to the unique terms. Learning these relationships can both help you to learn to recognize the Mismatched Concepts to begin with and add efficiency to your assessment of the answer choices.

MISMATCHED CONCEPTS RELATIONSHIPS

The most commonly assumed relationships between Mismatched Concepts are:

- The terms or concepts are alike/equivalent.
- The terms or concepts are mutually exclusive.
- One term or concept is needed for the other.
- One term or concept represents the other.

I) Equivalent ("similar")—Author shifts topics or terminology in moving from evidence to conclusion so that it is apparent that the author considers the evidence term and the conclusion term to be alike, or at least similar in some way.

C: Solar energy **(X)** is the wave of the future.

E: More and more people will demand cleaner fuels **(Y)**.

A: *Solar energy* **(X)** equates with *cleaner fuels* **(Y)**. **(X is similar to/equated with Y)**

W: A reason solar energy is not clean, e.g., mining the rare metals used in the panels is environmentally damaging or some overlooked alternative, e.g., wind is cleaner and cheaper. **(Attack the connection between X and Y; a potential difference)**

S: Reasons that firm up the connection (that solar energy really is clean) or eliminate a weaken possibility, e.g., doubts about the feasibility of solar energy are unfounded. **(Firm up the connection between X and Y; undermine potential differences)**

II) Mutually Exclusive ("different")—Just like the previous example, except that it is apparent that the author considers the unique evidence term and unique conclusion term to be different. Either the evidence or the conclusion will be phrased negatively ("not") while the other will be phrased positively. So, if the author believes that evidence of X results in a conclusion of Not Y (or vice versa), the author assumes that X and Y are different or incompatible.

C: Solar energy **(X)** is the wave of the future.

E: World governments are restricting sources of "greenhouse gases." **(No Y)**

A: *Solar energy* is **not** a *source of greenhouse gases.* **(X and Y are different/incompatible)**

W: A reason solar energy could be a source of greenhouse gases, e.g., mining, manufacture and shipping of panels currently uses substantial amounts of fossil fuels. **(A way X and Y could be similar/compatible or undermine a purported difference)**

S: A reason supporting that solar energy does not directly or indirectly produce significant greenhouse gases **(Further support for the difference/incompatibility of X and Y)**

III) Requirement ("needs")—Evidence of the absence of one thing being used to support a conclusion that something else is precluded indicates that the author assumes the first thing is a requirement for the other. Evidence of *No X* supporting a conclusion of *No Y* assumes that *Y requires X.*

C: Most people cannot switch to solar energy. **(No X)**

E: Most people cannot make an upfront investment of over $10,000. **(No Y)**

A: Switching to solar energy requires an upfront investment of over $10,000. **(If no Y then no X; X needs Y)**

W: A reason that an upfront investment is not needed, e.g., solar companies will provide leases with no upfront costs. **(A reason to believe that Y is not a requirement for X)**

S: A reason supporting that $10,000 upfront is typically required, e.g., solar companies will only provide leases with no upfront costs to homeowners with top 10% credit scores. **(Support that Y is a requirement for X)**

IV) Representative ("reps")—Evidence of a subset or smaller group used to make a conclusion about a larger group assumes that the subset is representative of the larger.

C: Renewable energy can cost effectively meet the world's energy needs. **(Broad conclusion group/situation)**

E: Studies show that solar power could feasibly meet all power needs in Arizona. **(Specific evidence group/situation)**

A: Solar power in Arizona is representative of the potential of renewable energy worldwide. **(The specific evidence group/situation applies broadly to conclusion group/situation)**

W: A reason that Arizona is not representative of the entire world, e.g., 360 days of intense sunshine with a relatively low population concentrated in two urban areas **(A characteristic or bias inherent in the evidence group/situation that undermines applying it to the broader conclusion group/situation)**

S: A reason that supports applying the Arizona results to the rest of the world, e.g., other studies indicate that political and public support for infrastructure investment is the key factor and levels of support in Arizona are similar or lower than most other areas of the world. **(A reason to believe that the evidence group/situation does represent the conclusion group situation or undermining a potential difference)**

Overlooked Possibilities

> ### OVERLOOKED POSSIBILITIES PATTERNS
>
> Overlooked Possibilities arguments tend to fit one of the following patterns:
>
> - Arrives at a claim of causation based on evidence of correlation
> - Does not consider potential advantages or disadvantages when offering a recommendation
> - Makes a prediction by assuming that circumstances will or will not change
> - Assumes that something will occur simply because it could occur
> - Confuses sufficient and necessary terms
> - Fails to consider other explanations, reasons, or outcomes based on the evidence

I) Causation—

a. Correlation to Causation ("Causal Classic")—if the author jumps from evidence of a correlation to a conclusion claiming causation, the author overlooks the three **ARC** possibilities: an **A**lternative cause; **R**everse causation; or **C**oincidence.

C: The stabilization of the economy has largely been a result of the stabilization of the housing market. **(A claim of causation—recognized by phrases such as "result of"; "produced"; "led to"; "because of"; "due to")**

E: The stabilization of the economy has coincided with the stabilization of the housing market. **(Evidence of a correlation—recognized by phrases such as "coincided with"; "simultaneously"; "subsequent to"; or any suggestion that two things or occurrences are related in time or location)**

A: There's *not* one of the standard alternatives to a claim of causation, e.g., 1) the resurgence in consumer spending was *not* the primary reason for the stabilization of the economy, 2) the stabilization of the economy was *not* itself the cause of the stabilization of the housing market, or 3) it was *not* just a coincidence that both trends occurred at relatively the same time. **(Not one of the ARC alternatives to a claim of causation: Not an Alternative cause; Not Reverse causation; Not Coincidence)**

W: Any of the ARC alternatives to a claim of causation, e.g., 1) a resurgence in consumer spending *was* the primary reason for the stabilization of the economy, 2) rather than a result, the stabilization of the economy *was* the cause of the stabilization of the housing market, or 3) evidence that the housing market and the overall economy do not typically effect each other. **(One of ARC: Alternative cause; Reverse causation; Coincidence/Not connected) Note: you would not weaken such a claim of causation by suggesting that either the housing market or the economy has not actually stabilized; accept the evidence as true.**

S: Elimination of any of the ARC alternatives, e.g., there has *not* been a resurgence in consumer spending, or a broad indication that all else is equal/nothing else could be involved. **(Elimination of any ARC possibilities; in terms of elimination of Alternative causes, the Strengthen answer may undermine a specific alternative cause or more broadly indicate that all else is equal, such as in a two-group study, in which a factor found in one group is claimed to be the cause of a result specific to that group, a strengthen answer choice would indicate that the two groups are otherwise identical in all other respects)**

b. Causal Explanation of Observed Phenomenon ("Funky Phenom")—in these causal arguments, rather than identifying a specific correlation between two phenomenon in the evidence and jumping to a claim that one causes the other, the author's evidence simply consists of an observation of an interesting phenomenon—often somewhat paradoxical—and the conclusion proposes an explanation for its cause. Rather than the 3 ARC alternatives in classic causation, usually only alternative causes (i.e., alternative explanations) are relevant.

C: The sociologist claims that the third graders are displaying an innate sense of egalitarianism. **(A causal explanation of the interesting, often paradoxical, phenomenon noted in the evidence)**

E: A sociologist observes that third grade students wearing mid-tier priced sneakers generally have more friends that those wearing higher priced sneakers. **(Simply the mention of an interesting phenomenon; note in this pattern the evidence does not answer the "why?" of the conclusion; it might seem like background or initially like a conclusion. Recognize this type of evidence by a phrase such as "researchers have observed" that indicates some scientist or academic is pointing out something they noticed that they find interesting; the role of a scientist then becomes to hypothesize some causal explanation, which is the conclusion in this pattern)**

A: There is no other explanation for the popularity of third graders wearing mid-tier sneakers besides an innate egalitarianism. **(No other explanation/alternative cause)**

W: Any alternative explanation, e.g., the most popular mid-tier priced sneaker is endorsed by the latest pop sensation and *all the cool kids wear them*. **(An alternative explanation)**

S: Any support for the author's explanation (often in this pattern there isn't any initial evidence supporting the author's explanation of the phenomenon besides its mere existence), e.g., other studies have noted a trend for greater egalitarianism in people under the age of 10, or any evidence that undermines any alternative explanation, e.g., there did not appear to be anything else special or unique about the mid-tier sneakers besides their moderate price. **(Support for author's explanation or reason undermining any potential alternative explanations)**

II) Recommendations—The author suggests for or against a course of action based on a single benefit or downside, respectively. Any recommendation should be based on a balancing of pros and cons, and assumes that one outweighs the other. LSAT authors will typically only mention what supports their recommendation, without consideration of the other side.

C: "You really should hit up this pizza joint." **(A recommendation for or against a course of action)**

E: "The beer selection is the bomb." **(A positive or negative aspect)**

A: No other factors would undermine the recommendation. **(Pros outweigh the cons, if any; vice versa)**

W: "Yeah, but the pizza itself is dry and chewy." **(A downside; or a positive if recommendation was against)**

S: "But it's a buck a slice and $3 dollar pitchers, and after a few cold ones the pizza tastes pretty . . . alright." **(Another upside or elimination of a downside or the reverse if initially a recommendation against)**

III) Predictions—A conclusion that is future looking/predictive typically relies on evidence of past trends. This assumes that there will not be a change in circumstances.

C: "My team is going to win on Sunday." **(A prediction of a future event)**

E: "The last six times we played your team, we won each by an average of 12 points." **(Past trends; existing circumstances)**

A: No change in circumstances would affect the likelihood of the predicted result. **(The past is predictive of the future; circumstances won't change)**

W: "Sorry, but didn't you hear that your star quarterback somehow managed to break his jaw in practice and is out for six weeks?" **(A change in circumstances)**

S: "Actually, our defense is generally credited with our team's success in those games and all our defensive stars are healthy and ready to play." **(An indication of consistency/no change in circumstances)**

IV) Level of Certainty—(could vs. will; belief vs. fact)—Another Overlooked Possibilities pattern is an author jumping from indefinite evidence (something *could* happen; people *believe* something; etc.) to a very definite conclusion (it *will* happen; it factually *is* the case).

C: Next year will show the strongest economic growth of the last 50 years. **(A definite statement of fact)**

E: According to a survey, a majority of economists believe that there is the potential for a 6% growth in GDP. **(A possibility or belief)**

A: The potential believed in by most economists will come to be. **(The possibility or belief will bear out)**

W: Historically, economist predictions have not accurately foreseen the next year's level of GDP growth. **(An indication that the possibility or belief will not bear out)**

S: A World Bank report extensively detailed factors supporting the potential for such levels of GDP growth. **(A further indication that the possibility or belief will bear out)**

V) Sufficiency/Necessity—The author provides evidence that one thing is sufficient to lead to a result, but then reaches a conclusion that indicates it is necessary for the result to occur. (Less commonly, an author will provide evidence of a necessary condition and then conclude that it is sufficient to guarantee a result).

C: It is almost certain that the soccer field will not be re-sodded. **(No X)**

E: 1) The school board will re-sod the soccer field if the PTA bake sale raises $1000; 2) it is highly unlikely the bake sale will raise that much. **(Y $\rightarrow$ X; No Y)**

A: The only way to re-sod the soccer field is with PTA bake sale money. **(X $\rightarrow$ Y; something that is sufficient to cause a result is the only thing that could cause that result; ignores that there could be other ways for the result to occur)**

W: In past years, in which the PTA bake sale failed to raise the funds, the local car dealership that sponsors the team paid to re-sod the field. **(X does not require Y; even though Y will trigger X, X could occur in the absence of Y)**

S: This year, no other potential sources of funds will be available due to extensive budget cuts. **(X really does require Y)**

VI) "No other . . . ." (factors, reasons, outcomes, explanations)—Somewhat of an Overlooked Possibilities catch-all category, an author of an LSAT argument may simply ignore or fail to consider other factors, options, outcomes, explanations, possibilities, reasons, etc. A handy way to phrase the assumption to an Overlooked Possibilities argument is to start with "No other _____" and fill in the blank as appropriate: "No other factor"; "No other explanation"; "No other option." Generally, recognize an Overlooked Possibilities argument from a conclusion that seems to follow from the evidence but is worded more forcefully or absolutely than such evidence really supports. Some of the previous specific Overlooked Possibilities patterns could fall under this umbrella description, and you've seen the "no other _____" phrasing above already.

C: "I'll bet you anything that Andrew wore his blue Italian designer suit to his Supreme Court argument today." **(An absolutely worded, forceful conclusion that seems to admit of only one possibility)**

E: "He told me that he wore his gray French designer suit to the appellate argument in the case and he never wears the same suit to both." **(Evidence that is not quite as restrictive as the author's conclusion suggests)**

A: Andrew has no other suits. **("No other _____": no other factor; no other option; no other explanation, etc.)**

W: "I'll take that bet; he bought a great pin-striped suit in India just last week." **(Some other _____: option, factor, explanation, reason, etc.)**

S: "Actually, I spilled red wine on that suit when we went to the opera on Saturday." **(Direct support for the initial conclusion or elimination of a weaken possibility)**

Formal Logic in Mismatched Concepts

Many of the arguments containing Mismatched Concepts are, or could easily be, expressed in conditional Formal Logic statements. It might sound awkward to say:

> If a work is a photograph, then it expresses the artist's worldview. Therefore, if a work is a photograph, it is an interpretation of reality. *Paraphrase of PrepTest61 Sec2 Q13*

Nevertheless, the reasoning in the argument, and thus, the author's assumption, is exactly the same.

The advantage of recognizing Formal Logic in Assumption Family questions is that it highlights the Mismatched Concepts very clearly.

	Sample Argument			Analysis		
Evidence	If photograph	→	**express artist's worldview**	If A	→	**B**
Conclusion	If photograph	→	**interpretation of reality**	If A	→	**C**

This provides a neat visual depiction of the argument that makes the author's assumption clear.

	Sample Argument			Analysis		
Evidence	If photograph	→	**express artist's worldview**	If A	→	**B**
Assumption	**If express artist's worldview**	→	**interpretation of reality**	**If B**	→	**C**
Conclusion	If photograph	→	**interpretation of reality**	If A	→	**C**

TEST DAY TIP

LSAT experts differ on how much of the Formal Logic they actually write out on Test Day: Some jot down shorthand nearly every time they encounter Formal Logic while others do it only in the most complex arguments. Practice both approaches to find which works better for you. You may find that being more explicit with Formal Logic initially helps you spot patterns that you'll better analyze in your head later on.

Making It More Difficult: Adding an Extra Concept in the Evidence

Many LSAT arguments with Mismatched Concepts feature two evidentiary statements that can be combined to help you determine the author's assumption. Consider this argument:

> Every member of my research team is an honors student, and every honors student has completed the Great Ideas course. Thus, every member of my research team has read Plato's *Symposium*.

When you combine the two statements in the evidence, this argument takes exactly the same form as the argument about photographs.

	Sample Argument			Analysis
Evidence 1	If research team	→	honors	If A → X
Evidence 2	If honors	→	Great Ideas course	If X → B
Evidence [combined]	If research team	→	**Great Ideas course**	If A → **B**
Assumption	**If Great Ideas course**	→	**read Plato's *Symposium***	**If B → C**
Conclusion	If research team	→	**read Plato's *Symposium***	If A → **C**

Whenever you see two statements in the evidence of an argument containing Mismatched Concepts, consider whether you can combine them into a single, relevant piece of evidence.

Same Necessary Term

So far, the examples you've seen have had the mismatched terms in the necessary (or "then") clause of the Formal Logic statements. Occasionally, you'll see LSAT examples in which the mismatched terms are in the sufficient (or "If") clause. For example:

> Those who are nostalgic for the 1960s love the theater's new musical. So, Ella is going to love the new musical.

	Sample Argument			Analysis		
Evidence	If **nostalgic for the 1960s**	→	love the new musical	If **A**	→	B
Assumption	**If Ella**	→	**nostalgic for the 1960s**	**If C**	→	**A**
Conclusion	If **Ella**	→	love the new musical	If **C**	→	B

Mismatched Concepts in the Evidence—Rare

Very rarely, the LSAT will feature an argument with Mismatched Concepts in which the "gap" is between two pieces of evidence rather than between the evidence and the conclusion. Here's an example:

> On extremely cold days, people are more physically uncomfortable. Moreover, people who are less aware of danger are more likely to jaywalk. From this it can be concluded that on extremely cold days, people are more likely to jaywalk.

	Sample Argument			Analysis
Evidence 1	If extremely cold day	→	**more physically uncomfortable**	If A → **B**
Assumption	**If more physically uncomfortable**	→	**unaware of danger**	**If B → C**
Evidence 2	If **unaware of danger**	→	more likely to jaywalk	If **C** → D
Conclusion	If extremely cold day	→	more likely to jaywalk	If A → D

Negation

Be careful negating terms when using the Denial Test. The negation of "hot" isn't "cold," it's "not hot."

All ↔ not all

None ↔ some

More ↔ less than or equal

Fewer ↔ more than or equal

Must be ↔ need not be

Can be ↔ cannot be

Quantities in Logical Reasoning

Out of a group of 100, here's what each of the following numerical terms means. Be careful; logical meaning on the LSAT is not the same as the way we often use numerical terms in everyday life; notice that most of the terms below just mean "more than zero." In Logical Reasoning questions, it is often helpful to focus on the minimum quantity possible.

None	0
Some	1–100
Few	1–100
Many	1–100
Most	51–100
All	100

Flawed Arguments

- Failure to Consider Alternative Possibilities/ Overlooked Explanations

- Correlation vs. Causation

- Necessity vs. Sufficiency

- Scope Shift—general mismatched concepts between evidence and conclusion

- Representativeness—the study/survey does not involve a large enough quantity or variety of subjects/respondents

- Equivocation—a term is used inconsistently

- Part vs. Whole

- Circular Reasoning—the conclusion relies on the evidence and vice versa

- Evidence Contradicts Conclusion

- Number vs. Percent

- Belief/Opinion vs. Fact

- *Ad Hominem* Attack—the author attacks the argument-maker, rather than the argument

- Absence of Evidence is Evidence of Absence

- Inappropriate Reliance on Authority

- Possibility vs. Certainty

- Group vs. Member

Difficult Questions

How does the Testmaker make a Logical Reasoning question harder?

- Formal Logic in the stimulus

- A long, complex stimulus, or one involving numbers (remember, the LSAT doesn't require you to do math!)

- A convoluted question stem

- Answer choices that are subtly flawed and appear right before the correct answer choice

- Answer choices that are difficult to comprehend (the more confusing it is, the more likely the answer choice is a distracter)

- Answer choices that are extremely similar, and thus harder to differentiate from each other

- General or abstract answer choices (remember to look for one that matches piece by piece with your specific prediction)

- Changing the terminology in the answer choice from what's written verbatim in the stimulus

Logical Reasoning Wrong Answer Types

LOGICAL REASONING: WRONG ANSWER TYPES

- **Outside the Scope**—a choice containing a statement that is too broad, too narrow, or beyond the purview of the stimulus
- **Irrelevant Comparison**—a choice that compares two items or attributes in a way not germane to the author's argument or statements
- **Extreme**—a choice containing language too emphatic to be supported by the stimulus; extreme choices are often (though not always) characterized by words such as *all*, *never*, *every*, or *none*
- **Distortion**—a choice that mentions details from the stimulus but mangles or misstates what the author says or implies about those details
- **180**—a choice that directly contradicts what the correct answer must say (for example, a choice that strengthens the argument in a Weaken question)
- **Faulty Use of Detail**—a choice that accurately states something from the stimulus but in a manner that answers the question incorrectly; this type is rarely used in Logical Reasoning

When Certain Wrong Answer Types Apply:

Extreme

Extreme language is a major problem for most questions throughout LR and RC. The only question types for which extreme language is not a problem are Sufficient Assumption, Strengthen, Weaken, and Principle (Strengthen). Remember that extreme language is usually a very bad thing for a Necessary Assumption question. It is only Sufficient Assumptions for which too extreme is unlikely to be a problem. In fact, for a Sufficient Assumption question you actually must have an absolute forceful answer to prove the conclusion true.

Out of Scope

Out of scope is always a problem, but especially for any Assumption question (both Necessary and Sufficient Assumptions) and Inference questions. For Strengthen, Weaken, and Paradox questions, be hesitant to get rid of something because it sounds new; the new explanation or factor or alternative possibility is often what will weaken an argument or resolve the paradox. Also, if the answer says "not" and is excluding something that the author didn't think about, that answer is not bringing in out of scope information. So, if the argument does not talk at all about rainbows, and answer C that says "rainbows are NOT found in the area" it is not bringing in out of scope information, and it may be correct. If this is a Necessary Assumption question, the easy test is to use the Denial Test by taking out the word "not" and seeing whether the denied answer makes the argument fall apart.

READING COMPREHENSION

Reading Comprehension Method

THE KAPLAN READING COMPREHENSION METHOD

Step 1: Read the Passage Strategically—circle Keywords and jot down margin notes to summarize the portions of the passage relevant to LSAT questions; summarize the author's Topic/Scope/Purpose/Main Idea.

Step 2: Read the Question Stem—identify the question type, characterize the correct and incorrect answers, and look for clues to guide your research.

Step 3: Research the Relevant Text—based on the clues in the question stem, consult your Roadmap; for open-ended questions, refer to your Topic/Scope/Purpose/Main Idea summaries.

Step 4: Predict the Correct Answer—based on research (or, for open-ended questions, your Topic/Scope/Purpose/Main Idea summaries) predict the correct answer.

Step 5: Evaluate the Answer Choices—select the choice that matches your prediction of the correct answer or eliminate the four wrong answer choices.

Reading Comprehension Passage Types

READING COMPREHENSION: PASSAGE TYPES

- **Theory/Perspective**—The passage focuses on a thinker's theory or perspective on some part of the Topic; typically (though not always), the author disagrees and critiques the opponent's perspective or defends his own.
- **Event/Phenomenon**—The passage focuses on an event, a breakthrough development, or a problem that has arisen; when a solution to the problem is proposed, the author most often agrees with the solution (and that represents the passage's Main Idea).
- **Biography**—The passage discusses something about a notable person; the aspect of the person's life emphasized by the author reflects the Scope of the passage.
- **Debate**—The passage outlines two opposing positions (neither of which is the author's) on some aspect of the Topic; the author may side with one of the positions, may remain neutral, or may critique both. (This structure has been rare on recent LSATs.)

The Big Picture

READING COMPREHENSION: THE BIG PICTURE

Topic—the overall subject of the passage

Scope—the particular aspect of the Topic that the author is focusing on

Purpose—the author's reason for writing the passage (express this as a verb—e.g., *to refute, to outline, to evaluate, to critique*)

Main Idea—the author's conclusion or overall takeaway; if you combine the author's Purpose and Scope, you'll usually have a good sense of the Main Idea

Keywords

READING COMPREHENSION: KEYWORD CATEGORIES

Emphasis/Opinion—words that signal that the author finds a detail noteworthy or has a positive or negative opinion about it, or any subjective or evaluative language on the author's part (e.g., *especially, crucial, unfortunately, disappointing, I suggest, it seems likely*)

Contrast—words indicating that the author thinks two details or ideas are incompatible or illustrate conflicting points (e.g., *but, yet, despite, on the other hand*)

Logic—words that indicate an argument, either the author's or someone else's (e.g., *thus, therefore, because*)

Illustration—words indicating an example offered to clarify or support another point (e.g., *for example, this shows, to illustrate*)

Sequence/Chronology—words showing steps in a process or developments over time (e.g., *traditionally, in the past, recently, today, first, second, finally, earlier, since*)

Continuation—words indicating that a subsequent example or detail supports the same point or illustrates the same idea (e.g., *moreover, in addition, and, also, further*)

More Keyword Examples

Emphasis/Opinion

Emphasis

Remarkable

(more/most) Important

Compelling

Substantial

Even more than

Opinion

Believed by

Thought to be

Asserts

Some maintain

Argues that

According to

As X sees it

Remarkably

Surprisingly

Contrast

But

Despite

Yet

Although

However

While

Even so

Nevertheless

Whereas

On the other hand

Conversely

Instead

Logic

Evidence

Because

Since

This is clear from

Conclusion

Thus

Clearly

As a result

And so

Illustration

:

In contrast to

For example

Sequence/Chronology

Timing/Temporal

Since

Until recently

Historically

Traditionally

Sequence/Numerical

Three possible explanations

There are two reasons for this

Continuation

;

In addition

Also

Similarly

Likewise

Words that reveal author's POV:

Negative	Positive	Uncertainty/Qualification
Doubtful	Cogent	Seems
Unconvincing	Compelling	Appears
Unlikely	Promising	Mysterious
Danger		
Harmful		

Research Clues

READING COMPREHENSION: RESEARCH CLUES

- **Line References**—Research around the referenced detail; look for Keywords indicating why the referenced text has been included or how it's used.
- **Paragraph References**—Consult your Roadmap to see the paragraph's scope and function.
- **Quoted Text** (often accompanied by a line reference)—Check the context of the quoted term or phrase; ask what the author meant by it in the passage.
- **Proper Nouns**—Check the context of the person, place, or thing; ask whether the author had a positive, negative, or neutral evaluation of it; ask why it was included in the passage.
- **Content Clues**—Research the passage for terms, concepts, or ideas referenced or alluded to in the question stem; these will almost always refer you to something the author emphasized or stated an opinion on.

Reading Comprehension Wrong Answer Types

READING COMPREHENSION: WRONG ANSWER TYPES

Outside the Scope—a choice containing a statement that is too broad, too narrow, or beyond the purview of the passage

Extreme—a choice containing language too emphatic (*all, never, every, none*) to be supported by the passage

Distortion—a choice that mentions details or ideas from the passage but mangles or misstates what the author says or implies about those details

180—a choice that directly contradicts what the correct answer must say

Faulty Use of Detail—a choice that accurately states something from the passage but in a manner that incorrectly answers the question

Half-Right/Half-Wrong—a choice in which one clause follows from the passage but another clause contradicts or distorts the passage